Oncoplastic and Reconstructive Management of the Breast

Third Edition

Oncoplastic and Reconstructive Management of the Breast

Third Edition

Edited by

Steven J. Kronowitz
Kronowitz Plastic Surgery, PLLC
Houston, Texas

John R. Benson
Cambridge Breast Unit
Addenbrooke's Hospital
and
University of Cambridge
and
School of Medicine
Anglia Ruskin University
Cambridge, United Kingdom

Maurizio B. Nava
Valduce Hospital
Como, Italy
and
University of Milan
Milan, Italy
and
University of Genoa
Genoa, Italy

CRC Press is an imprint of the
Taylor & Francis Group, an **informa** business

CRC Press
Taylor & Francis Group
6000 Broken Sound Parkway NW, Suite 300
Boca Raton, FL 33487-2742

© 2020 by Taylor & Francis Group, LLC
CRC Press is an imprint of Taylor & Francis Group, an Informa business

No claim to original U.S. Government works

Printed on acid-free paper

International Standard Book Number-13: 978-1-8418-4641-5 (Hardback)
978-1-003-00547-6 (eBook)

This book contains information obtained from authentic and highly regarded sources. Reasonable efforts have been made to publish reliable data and information, but the author and publisher cannot assume responsibility for the validity of all materials or the consequences of their use. The authors and publishers have attempted to trace the copyright holders of all material reproduced in this publication and apologize to copyright holders if permission to publish in this form has not been obtained. If any copyright material has not been acknowledged please write and let us know so we may rectify in any future reprint.

Except as permitted under U.S. Copyright Law, no part of this book may be reprinted, reproduced, transmitted, or utilized in any form by any electronic, mechanical, or other means, now known or hereafter invented, including photocopying, microfilming, and recording, or in any information storage or retrieval system, without written permission from the publishers.

For permission to photocopy or use material electronically from this work, please access www.copyright.com (http://www.copyright.com/) or contact the Copyright Clearance Center, Inc. (CCC), 222 Rosewood Drive, Danvers, MA 01923, 978-750-8400. CCC is a not-for-profit organization that provides licenses and registration for a variety of users. For organizations that have been granted a photocopy license by the CCC, a separate system of payment has been arranged.

Trademark Notice: Product or corporate names may be trademarks or registered trademarks, and are used only for identification and explanation without intent to infringe.

Visit the Taylor & Francis Web site at
http://www.taylorandfrancis.com

and the CRC Press Web site at
http://www.crcpress.com

Dr. Kronowitz wishes to dedicate this book to his most magnificent children, Matthew and Lindsay, who despite the tragic loss of their mother Julie at a very age young to breast cancer have become the most amazing people that he knows!

Dr. Benson would like to dedicate this book to his new found blood family (Mark, Emma, Joe, and Dave et al.) whom he has recently been united with after more than 50 years.

Contents

FOREWORDS
  Monica Morrow   xiii
  James C. Grotting   xv
PREFACE   xvii
EDITORS   xix
CONTRIBUTORS   xxi

SECTION I GENERAL TRENDS, PRINCIPLES, AND MATERIALS

1	LATEST TRENDS IN BREAST RECONSTRUCTION	3
	1.1 USA	3
	Jane Y.C. Hui and Todd M. Tuttle	
	1.2 Europe	6
	Ranjeet Jeevan	
2	THE BIOLOGICAL RATIONALE FOR ONCOPLASTIC SURGICAL PROCEDURES	9
	John R. Benson and Maurizio B. Nava	
3	BIOLOGICAL REACTIONS TO RECONSTRUCTIVE MATERIALS	13
	3.1 Biological Reactions to Acellular Dermal Matrices (ADMs)	13
	Steven T. Lanier and John Y.S. Kim	
	3.2 Breast Implant-Associated Anaplastic Large Cell Lymphoma	19
	Mark W. Clemens	
	3.3 Biological Reactions to Autologous Fat Grafting	22
	Animesh Patel and Charles M. Malata	
Editorial Commentary		30

SECTION II PATIENT SELECTION—BREAST-CONSERVING SURGERY OR MASTECTOMY?

4	ONCOLOGIC CONSIDERATIONS	33
	4.1 Diagnostic Imaging	33
	Fiona J. Gilbert	
	4.2 Pathologist	36
	Cansu Karakas and Aysegul A. Sahin	
	4.3 Medical Oncologist	48
	Jessica Taff and Francisco J. Esteva	
	4.4 Radiation Oncologist	50
	Ian Kunkler	
	4.5 Breast Surgeon	53
	Efstathios Karamanos and Lisa A. Newman	
5	RECONSTRUCTIVE PERSPECTIVES	55
	5.1 Breast Surgeon's Perspective	55
	Melissa Anne Mallory and Mehra Golshan	
	5.2 Reconstructive Surgeon's Perspective	58
	Michael Scheflan and Robert Douglas Macmillan	

viii Contents

6	**PATIENTS' PERSPECTIVES**			61
	6.1	The Role of Patient Choice		61
		Claudia R. Albornoz and Andrea L. Pusic		
	6.2	Patients' Expectations		64
		John R. Benson and Guidubaldo Querci della Rovere (posthumous)		

Editorial Commentary — 66

7	**PREOPERATIVE RADIOLOGICAL ASSESSMENT**			69
	Megan Kalambo and Wei Tse Yang			
8	**ONCOPLASTIC PARENCHYMAL RESECTION**			77
	8.1	In Situ Disease		77
		Katrina B. Mitchell and Henry Kuerer		
	8.2	Invasive Carcinoma		80
		Tracy-Ann Moo and Rache M. Simmons		
9	**INTRAOPERATIVE ASSESSMENT**			83
	9.1	Pathological		83
		Sarah E. Pinder and Elena Provenzano		
	9.2	Radiological		86
		Fleur Kilburn-Toppin		
10	**TIMING OF ONCOPLASTIC REPAIR**			89
	Francesco M. Egro and Albert Losken			

Editorial Commentary — 96

SECTION III BREAST-CONSERVING SURGERY AND PARTIAL BREAST RECONSTRUCTION (ONCOPLASTIC REPAIR)

11	**IMMEDIATE REPAIR BEFORE RADIOTHERAPY**			101
	11.1	Local Tissue Rearrangement		101
		11.1.1	Extreme Oncoplasty (USA)	101
			Melvin J. Silverstein	
		11.1.2	My Approach (Europe)	107
			Robert Douglas Macmillan	
	11.2	Dermoglandular Reduction Mammoplasty		109
		11.2.1	My Approach (USA)	109
			Steven J. Kronowitz	
		11.2.2	Our Approach (Europe)	116
			J. Michael Dixon and Cameron Raine	
	11.3	Flap-Based Methods		124
		11.3.1	My Approach (USA)	124
			David Song	
		11.3.2	Our Approach (Europe)	131
			Moustapha Hamdi and Luciano Tracia	
12	**POSTOPERATIVE MARGIN ASSESSMENT (RE-EXCISION OR COMPLETION MASTECTOMY)**			147
	Dorin Dumitru and John R. Benson			
13	**DELAYED ONCOPLASTIC REPAIR—BEFORE RADIOTHERAPY**			153
	Maurice Y. Nahabedian			

Editorial Commentary — 160

14	**DELAYED ONCOPLASTIC REPAIR—AFTER RADIOTHERAPY**			163
	14.1	Considerations		163
		Charles M. Malata, Alexandra Bucknor, and Chidi Ekwobi		
	14.2	Surgical Technique		171
		14.2.1	Our Approach (USA)	171
			Jessica Rose and Aldona Spiegel	
		14.2.2	Our Approach (Europe)	175
			Charles M. Malata, Alexandra Bucknor, and Chidi Ekwobi	

Editorial Commentary — 189

Contents ix

SECTION IV SKIN-SPARING AND NIPPLE-SPARING MASTECTOMY

15 MASTECTOMY AND WHOLE BREAST RECONSTRUCTION: SKIN-SPARING AND NIPPLE-SPARING MASTECTOMY 193

15.1 Oncological Aspects 193
Gerald Gui

15.2 Reconstructive Aspects 198
Gerald Gui

Editorial Commentary 203

16 NIPPLE-SPARING MASTECTOMY 205

16.1 Incisions for Nipple-Sparing Mastectomy 205
Sirwan M. Hadad and Jennifer E. Rusby

16.2 Nipple-Sparing Mastectomy in Breast Ptosis 208
Sirwan M. Hadad and Jennifer E. Rusby

Editorial Commentary 210

SECTION V MASTECTOMY AND WHOLE BREAST RECONSTRUCTION (TIMING AND PATIENT SELECTION)

17 TIMING OF RECONSTRUCTION 213

17.1 Patients Who May Require Postmastectomy Irradiation 213
Sumner Slavin

17.2 Patients Who Will Require Postmastectomy Radiation 221
Margaret S. Roubaud and Patrick B. Garvey

Editorial Commentary 226

18 HOW TO CHOOSE THE OPTIMAL METHOD OF WHOLE BREAST RECONSTRUCTION 227

18.1 My Approach (USA) 227
Steven J. Kronowitz

18.2 Our Approach (South America) 234
Alexandre Mendonça Munhoz, João Carlos Sampaio Goés, and Rolf Gemperli

SECTION VI MASTECTOMY AND WHOLE BREAST RECONSTRUCTION (METHODS AND TECHNIQUES)

19 IMPLANT-BASED WHOLE BREAST RECONSTRUCTION (WITHOUT IRRADIATION) 241

19.1 One-Stage Implant Reconstruction 241

19.1.1 Our Approach (USA) 241
Andrew Salzberg and Jordan Jacobs

19.1.2 My Approach (Europe) 245
Pierluigi Santi

19.2 Two-Stage Implant Reconstruction 252

19.2.1 Our Approach (USA) 252
Patrick Maxwell and Allen Gabriel

19.2.2 Our Approach (South America) 255
Alberto Rancati, Claudio Angrigiani, Marcelo Irigo, and Agustin Rancati

19.3 Acellular Dermal Matrix with Implants 257

19.3.1 My Approach (USA) 257
Hani Sbitany

19.3.2 Our Approach (Europe) 260
Alexandra Molina and Jian Farhadi

19.4 Fat Grafting with Implants 264

19.4.1 Our Approach (Europe) 264
Pietro Berrino and Valeria Berrino

19.4.2 My Approach (Europe) 269
Alessandra Marchi

Editorial Commentary 277

x Contents

20 IMPLANT-BASED WHOLE BREAST RECONSTRUCTION (WITH IRRADIATION) — 279

20.1 Timing of Reconstruction — 279

20.1.1 Our Approach (USA) — 279
Claudia R. Albornoz and Babak Mehrara

20.1.2 My Approach (Europe) — 283
Giuseppe Catanuto

20.2 Technique for Reconstruction — 287

20.2.1 Our Approach (USA) — 287
Sophocles H. Voineskos and Peter G. Cordeiro

20.2.2 Our Approach (Europe) — 290
Andre Spano, Stefano Avvedimento, and Secondo Folli

20.3 Impact of Acellular Dermal Matrices (ADMs) and Fat Grafting on Irradiated Breast Reconstruction — 293

20.3.1 My Approach (USA) — 293
Steven J. Kronowitz

20.3.2 Our Approach (Europe) — 297
Lee Martin and Sonia Bathla

Editorial Commentary — 299

21 FAT GRAFTING EXCLUSIVELY FOR WHOLE BREAST RECONSTRUCTION — 301

21.1 Our Approach (Europe) — 301
Gilles Tousson and Emmanuel Delay

21.2 Stem Cell Expansion and Growth Factor Stimulation — 303
Adam J. Reid

21.3 The Bioengineered Breast — 305
J. Peter Rubin

Editorial Commentary — 307

22 STANDARD AUTOLOGOUS TISSUE FLAPS FOR WHOLE BREAST RECONSTRUCTION — 309

22.1 Latissimus Dorsi Flap (with Implant) — 309
Michel Hector Saint-Cyr

22.2 Totally Autologous Latissimus Dorsi Flap — 312
Eva Weiler-Mithoff and James Mansell

22.3 Pedicled Transverse Rectus Abdominis Myocutaneous (TRAM) Flap — 320
Jean-Yves Petit, Maria Rietjens, and Andrea Manconi

22.4 Free Transverse Rectus Abdominis Myocutaneous (TRAM) Flap — 326
Charles M. Malata and Georgette Oni

22.5 Deep Inferior Epigastric Perforator (DIEP) Flap — 332
Edward Wayne Buchel and Nakul Gamanlal Patel

Editorial Commentary — 338

23 ADVANCED AUTOLOGOUS TISSUE FLAPS FOR WHOLE BREAST RECONSTRUCTION — 339

23.1 Thoracodorsal Perforator (TAP) Flap — 339
Claudio Angrigiani, Alberto Rancati, and Marcelo Irigo

23.2 Robotic Latissimus Dorsi Muscle Harvest — 342
Karim A. Sarhane, Amir E. Ibrahim, and Jesse C. Selber

23.3 Double-DIEP Flap — 345
Phillip Blondeel and Michel Moutran

23.4 Profunda Artery Perforator (PAP) Flap — 349
Joshua L. Levine and Robert J. Allen, Sr.

23.5 Boomerang Gluteal Artery Perforator (GAP) Flap — 351
Edward I. Chang and Steven J. Kronowitz

23.6 Transverse Upper Gracilis (TUG) Flap — 356
Andrei Odobescu, Isak Goodwin, and Rudolf Buntic

23.7 Lumbar Artery Perforator (LAP) Flap — 362
Moustapha Hamdi and Randy De Baerdemaeker

Contents xi

SECTION VII REVISIONAL BREAST RECONSTRUCTION (FOLLOWING BOTH PARTIAL AND WHOLE BREAST RECONSTRUCTION)

24   BREAST REVISION FOLLOWING BREAST CONSERVATION AND ONCOPLASTIC REPAIR   371
Steven J. Kronowitz

25   BREAST REVISION AFTER IMPLANT-BASED BREAST RECONSTRUCTION   379
João Carlos Sampaio Goés, Alexandre Mendonça Munhoz, and Rolf Gemperli

26   BREAST REVISION AFTER MASTECTOMY, WHOLE BREAST RECONSTRUCTION, AND POSTMASTECTOMY RADIATION THERAPY   383
Steven J. Kronowitz

Editorial Commentary   387

SECTION VIII TECHNIQUES FOR DELIVERY OF RADIOTHERAPY

27   PARTIAL OR WHOLE BREAST RADIOTHERAPY AFTER BREAST-CONSERVING SURGERY?   391
Mukesh Bindish Mukesh and Charlotte Coles

28   POSTMASTECTOMY RADIOTHERAPY AFTER WHOLE BREAST RECONSTRUCTION   399
    28.1   Postmastectomy Radiotherapy after Breast Reconstruction Does Not Interfere with Radiation Delivery   399
       Beryl McCormick
    28.2   Postmastectomy Radiotherapy after Whole Breast Reconstruction: Does Breast Reconstruction Interfere
       with Radiation Delivery?   402
       Eric Strom and Wendy Woodward

29   PARTIAL BREAST RADIOTHERAPY AFTER BREAST-CONSERVING SURGERY   405
    29.1   Targeted Radiotherapy as Part of Breast-Conserving Therapy   405
       Jayant S. Vaidya, Michael Douek, Nathan Coombs, Julian Singer, and Jeffrey S. Tobias
    29.2   Postoperative Radiotherapy   411
       29.2.1   Brachytherapy   411
           Nicholas Serrano and Douglas W. Arthur
       29.2.2   Linear Accelerator   414
           Icro Meattini

30   WHOLE BREAST RADIOTHERAPY (BOOST) AFTER PARTIAL MASTECTOMY   417
    30.1   Boost or No Boost to Tumor Bed with Whole Breast Radiotherapy after Partial Mastectomy   417
       Laura Lozza
    30.2   Options for Delivery of Radiotherapy Boost Dose after Partial Mastectomy   421
       Kathryn Huber and David Wazer
    30.3   Intraoperative Brachytherapy plus Postoperative Linear Accelerator for Whole Breast Radiotherapy   423
       Kathryn Huber and David Wazer
    30.4   Intraoperative Linear Accelerator Plus Postoperative Linear Accelerator for Whole Breast Radiotherapy   425
       Laura Lozza

Editorial Commentary   427

SECTION IX TECHNIQUES FOR LYMPH NODE TRANSFER

31   TRANSFER OF VASCULARIZED LYMPH NODE TISSUE   433
    31.1   Our Approach (Taiwan)   433
       Chieh-Han John Tzou and Ming-Huei Cheng
    31.2   Our Approach (Europe)   437
       Jaume Masià, Gemma Pons, and Elena Rodríguez-Bauzà

SECTION X NIPPLE–AREOLA COMPLEX RECONSTRUCTION

32   NIPPLE–AREOLA COMPLEX RECONSTRUCTION   443
    32.1   Nipple–Areola Complex Reconstruction (with and without Biologicals)   443
       Parisa Kamali, Winona Wu, and Samuel J. Lin
    32.2   3-D Tattooing   448
       Vassilis Pitsinis and John R. Benson

Editorial Commentary   451

xii Contents

SECTION XI TRAINING—BREAST SURGERY AS A SPECIALTY

33 THE MODERN SPECIALIST BREAST SURGEON   455
Sue Down, Ismail Jatoi, and John R. Benson

34 BREAST SURGICAL TRAINING   459
   34.1 American Training System   459
      Melissa Anne Mallory and Mehra Golshan
   34.2 European Training System   461
      Fiona MacNeill

Editorial Commentary   463

INDEX   465

Foreword by Monica Morrow

Breast cancer management is becoming increasingly complex. When I began my surgical training, the approach to surgery on the breast—whether diagnosis was lobular carcinoma in situ, ductal carcinoma in situ, or invasive breast carcinoma, was mastectomy. Surgery of the axilla required essentially no thought or discussion; axillary lymph node dissection was the only approach. We have come a long way since that time, thanks in large part to visionaries such as Bernard Fisher and Umberto Veronesi, whose clinical trials led both directly and indirectly to the adoption of breast-conserving surgery, immediate reconstruction, neoadjuvant therapy for operable breast cancer, and sentinel node biopsy. In parallel with the availability of surgical options, which decreased the burden of treatment for patients, improvements in systemic therapy resulted in decreases in breast cancer mortality. More recently, we have recognized that effective systemic therapy also improves local control, allowing decreased use of re-excision in breast-conserving surgery and avoidance of axillary dissection for some node-positive breast cancers. As treatment options with equivalent survival outcomes have multiplied, patient values and preferences have become an essential part of the decision-making process. All of this is good news, and represents progress undreamt of 30 years ago, but has also had the effect of making the treatment selection process increasingly complex.

Faced with a newly diagnosed breast cancer patient, the question is no longer breast conservation versus mastectomy with reconstruction, or mastectomy alone, but rather the following three questions: (1) Is this patient a candidate for breast conservation? (2) If not, will preoperative systemic therapy or an oncoplastic procedure spare her a mastectomy? and (3) Which approach, surgery first or chemotherapy first, will minimize the likelihood of axillary dissection? In attempting to answer these questions, the physician must consider traditional anatomic features that most are quite comfortable with, such as tumor location and tumor size relative to breast size, as well as biologic features not previously used for local-therapy decision-making, such as hormone receptor status and HER2 overexpression, that are predictive of the response to neoadjuvant therapy. The increasing choice of bilateral mastectomy for unilateral,

nongenetic breast cancer, largely driven by patient preference, further complicates these discussions. Indications for postmastectomy radiotherapy continue to evolve, but the need for postmastectomy radiotherapy is often unclear at the time of diagnosis, leading to a discussion of the relative cosmetic merits of breast conservation; unilateral mastectomy and reconstruction with or without radiation; or bilateral mastectomy, reconstruction, and radiation of only one side. Given the level of complexity involved, it is not particularly surprising that the surgical management of breast cancer is considered something to be avoided by many of those who are not specialist breast surgeons.

We have a plethora of level I evidence supporting the majority of the things that we do to treat breast cancer with surgery, radiotherapy, and adjuvant systemic therapy. This allows us to address the most important questions asked by the vast majority of patients: Will this treatment help me to survive or minimize the chance of my cancer recurring? We are on less firm ground, however, when we attempt to compare breast conservation, with and without oncoplastic surgery, or the outcomes of different reconstructive techniques in the patient requiring postmastectomy radiotherapy—questions that are vital to the quality of life of many patients.

In *Oncoplastic and Reconstructive Management of the Breast*, Drs. Kronowitz, Benson, and Nava have recruited an international group of authors to address surgical decision-making from a variety of perspectives, and have packaged this information into bite-size, easily digested chapters. While some general material is provided on patient selection for breast conservation versus mastectomy, radiologic and pathologic assessment, and radiotherapy techniques, this material is covered in multiple textbooks in considerably more depth. The information provided here serves as a refresher course for the experienced surgeon, and a useful summary for trainees and young surgeons trying to synthesize this voluminous dataset. In addition, these chapters serve as a reminder that while striving to employ the latest oncoplastic and reconstructive techniques to improve cosmetic outcome, we must always remember the first and foremost goal of breast cancer surgery: maximizing the likelihood of cure of the patient.

The bulk of the text is devoted to a detailed discussion of the clinical application of a wide variety of oncoplastic and reconstructive surgical techniques, and it is here that the book finds a unique niche. Recognizing that much of what is discussed in these chapters constitutes the "art of surgery" and that level 1 evidence supporting one approach over another is lacking, the editors have wisely recruited more than one expert to discuss their approaches to a variety of common clinical situations, and they have made liberal use of editorial commentaries to address controversies. Thus, the book provides clear evidence that "there is more than one way to skin a cat" and should help trainees and senior surgeons alike avoid the tendency toward rigidity in their practice. This practical, concise approach makes a large amount of material readily accessible to the physician caring for women with breast cancer, and is of value to the surgeon performing a limited amount of breast surgery who will likely never personally perform many of the procedures discussed, as well as to the specialist trainee or breast surgeon.

Overall, this book highlights the enormous progress that has been made in breast cancer management and the number of choices available to patients today. My hope is that by the time the next edition appears, we will have new, high-quality evidence to address many of the management dilemmas discussed here.

Monica Morrow, MD, FACS

Foreword by James C. Grotting

Having been consumed by writing, editing, and rewriting five books, I am always impressed when I see a new book which is really special. *Oncoplastic and Reconstructive Management of the Breast* now in its third edition is a compendium of modern approaches from the broad spectrum of practitioners—surgical oncology, plastic surgeons, radiology, pathology, radiotherapy, and medical oncology. The treatment of breast cancer now requires a multidisciplinary team approach and has evolved to the point where what one specialist does may profoundly affect decision-making by another treating specialist. A perfect example is how radiation is influenced by reconstruction and vice versa. Experts in radiation therapy must communicate with surgical oncologists and plastic surgeons to carefully plan treatment so that the best choices assure that patients are optimally treated. This book brings ideas and people together to the benefit of healthcare professionals and patients. The great appeal of this textbook is the organization of essential up-to-date material in readable concise chapters organized by topic.

One of my favorite aspects of this comprehensive volume is that each topic is discussed in a very "to the point" manner. Most chapters are only three to five pages long even with the beautiful and voluminous illustrations. One can rapidly extract "the meat" of the topic without plowing through pages of history or unrelated material. The very latest studies from the literature are included, which help answer such important questions such as "How should radiation be altered in the presence of a breast prosthesis or autologous reconstruction?" or "What is the role of nipple-preserving mastectomy from the viewpoint of the pathologist, medical oncologist, radiation oncologist, and breast surgeon?" Practical issues such as the best incisions for skin-sparing mastectomy and dealing with the ptotic breast are very helpful for surgeons who are beginning to do these procedures.

A major emphasis is placed on oncoplastic repair and breast-conserving surgery. Oncoplastic surgery has been a concept that has been somewhat slow to take hold in the United States but has been more widely embraced in Europe. Experts from several continents update us on their personal perspective and experience. This is a very valuable learning tool for breast cancer specialists across the globe.

One might ask, how much different could the third edition of a textbook be? The answer is a resounding "completely different!" The key differences between the last edition and this new one is that it is much more visual with text kept to a minimum. The scope of the book has been broadened considerably to include all the new as well as the "gold standard" techniques authored by pioneers of each method in shorter more concise blocks of text which highlight key information rather than too much discursive discussion. Health-related quality of life and healthcare costs are addressed in many of the chapters.

I am very pleased to have been invited to review the finished product and communicate to readers how much I have enjoyed reading and learning from this wonderful book. I predict it will become the most valuable resource of its kind for those who wish to become fully equipped to treat those afflicted with breast cancer.

James C. Grotting, MD, FACS

Preface

As modern specialist breast surgeons and practicing physicians, there is a sense that the pace of clinical work and time pressures can be overwhelming with less time formally allocated to educational activities including background reading (journals and textbooks). Instead, doctors at all levels of seniority are increasingly besieged with demands for chart completion and clinical documentation.

A primary aim in planning this book was to recruit leading specialists in breast cancer care, be they breast surgeons, plastic surgeons, radiation/medical oncologists, radiologists, or pathologists. This collective knowledge and experience has provided an authoritative and definitive text on "cutting-edge" practice and opinion from some of the world's leading experts in the field of breast cancer management. An international perspective is important as physicians practice differently in various parts of the globe based on healthcare resources, training, and social customs. For example, there is a trend for increasing the use of abdominal flap-based reconstruction in the United Kingdom while the reverse trend is apparent in the United States where mesh-assisted implant-based reconstruction has become popular in recent years.

As most physicians no longer have time to peruse lengthy tomes containing a plethora of superfluous material, this book has been uniquely designed around shorter, more concise chapters, which contain essential information that is presented in an applied and pragmatic style. Areas of controversy are emphasized and for surgical topics, which individual and groups of authors have provided an account of "My Approach" or "Our Approach," which enables the reader to rapidly gain an insight into the daily practices of leading experts who have honed down their transfer of knowledge for this purpose and almost draws the reader into their clinical world.

A particular feature of this text is the multidisciplinary nature of the content; it is not exclusively an oncoplastic surgery book. There are several sections devoted to clinical decision-making and selection of patients for optimum type and sequencing of surgery and other modalities of treatment such as radiotherapy. The reader benefits from an appreciation of the different perspectives of multidisciplinary team members and how decision-making must be balanced and take account of patient preference. This inter-disciplinary approach ensures that clinical care is fully integrated and optimized for individual patients. The reader gains an understanding of the key decision points and how clinical algorithms are applied at various stages along a potentially complex breast cancer care pathway.

A novel feature of this book is the introductory "At a Glance" sections and "Editorial Commentaries" written by the editors. The introductory sections "set the scene" and highlight areas where there is lack of clinical consensus, which are further visited in the editorial commentaries that attempt to draw together what may be disparate opinions from invited contributors in a matter of fact style that emphasizes clinical relevance.

The editors have endeavored to produce a text that is both practical and informative without claiming to be comprehensive. The goal was to produce a book that has multidisciplinary appeal and will be useful for established breast cancer specialists, senior trainees, and nurse practitioners. Indeed, it is hoped that this text may inspire other editors to adopt this innovative design for more concise and readable medical books—which accords with contemporary clinical practice.

Steven J. Kronowitz
John R. Benson
Maurizio B. Nava

Editors

Steven J. Kronowitz is a world-renowned expert in the field of breast reconstruction and is best known for his expertise in oncology-related breast reconstruction, radiation-related breast reconstruction, and oncoplastic surgery. He is known internationally for his expertise in multidisciplinary breast cancer care and has developed numerous treatment approaches, techniques, and algorithms that are used worldwide in the care of patients with breast cancer. Besides authoring numerous landmark publications in peer-reviewed journals, Dr. Kronowitz edits his own international textbooks with contributions from the recognized world experts in multidisciplinary breast care. Dr. Kronowitz has published extensively and lectures both nationally and internationally. He is also a basic science researcher focusing on mechanisms of DNA injury and repair after radiation therapy; cell-to-cell interaction and crosstalk; and vascular–stromal and stem cell interaction and transplantation.

Dr. Kronowitz is currently the lead surgeon at Kronowitz Plastic Surgery, an international practice of plastic surgery based in Houston, Texas. He has trained more than 250 residents and fellows in plastic surgery. He has, since 2012, been consistently awarded "Top Doctor" by *U.S. News & World Report; Castle Connelly Top Doctors; Vitals Patients' Choice; American Registry Compassionate Doctor; America's Leading Expert Recognition; and Houston Chronicle's MedCity October 2016 Houston's 200+ Top Doctors: The Best Physicians in 45 Specialties.* He is also a winner of the Cosmetic Surgery Award, *2018 Cosmetic Surgery & Health Magazine*; the 2018 Top Plastic Surgeon in Houston, International Association of Healthcare Professionals; the 2018 Superdoctors, peer-nominated by the Blue Ribbon Panel Review; the 2018 *Leading Physicians of the World*, spotlighted in Renown Publication; and the *New York Times* (National Edition), March 3, 2018, Top Cosmetic Surgeons in America.

Dr. Kronowitz is a member of the American Society of Plastic Surgeons; American Association of Plastic Surgeons; American Society of Reconstructive Microsurgery; American Society of Aesthetic Plastic Surgeons; and is a Fellow of the American College of Surgeons. He serves on the editorial board of both *Plastic and Reconstructive Surgery* and *Plastic and Reconstructive Surgery–Global Open*. He has published more than 100 peer-reviewed publications in the most prestigious surgical journals. Many of these publications were landmark studies in oncology-related breast reconstruction. He travels as an invited lecturer at the most prestigious surgical conferences, medical schools, and hospitals, teaching the techniques he has developed to other plastic surgeons worldwide.

John R. Benson is a consultant breast surgeon at Addenbrooke's Hospital, Cambridge, UK. He qualified from Oxford University Clinical School, Oxford, England, and was awarded doctorates from Oxford and Cambridge Universities (DM [Oxon]; MD [Cantab]). He received specialist training at the Royal Marsden Hospital and Institute of Cancer Research, London, and the New York Hospital–Cornell Medical Center, New York. Professor Benson is a Fellow and Director of Clinical Studies at Selwyn College, Cambridge, an Associate Lecturer, University of Cambridge and Visiting Professor, School of Medicine, Anglia Ruskin University. He is an examiner for the MRCS Intercollegiate Examination, Module Lead for the Masters Programme in Oncoplastic Surgery (University of East Anglia and the Royal College of Surgeons of England), a member of the British Breast Group, and the Executive Board of the Association of Breast Surgery (Ordinary Trustee). His clinical practice is devoted entirely to breast diseases, and current research interests include investigation of a fluorescent navigation system for sentinel lymph node detection. Dr. Benson has more than 120 published articles in leading journals including *The Lancet, Lancet Oncology,* and the *British Journal of Surgery* and has written numerous book chapters and several books in the field of breast diseases (winner of First Prize in the Oncology Section of BMA Medical Book Awards, 2013), a former member of the Planning Committee for the San Antonio Breast Cancer Symposium (2013–2015) and a member of the review panel for ASCO guidelines on breast cancer. Professor Benson is a member of the Oncoplastic Breast Consortium, an international collaboration aimed at developing research strategies for key knowledge gaps in oncoplastic and reconstructive breast surgery.

Maurizio B. Nava qualified from the University of Milan in 1977 and received accreditation in oncology in 1980 and general surgery in 1986. He subsequently specialized in plastic and reconstructive surgery and was Director of the Plastic Surgery Department at the Istituto Nazionale dei Tumori in Milan from 1997 until 2014. He currently holds the post of Adjunct Professor at the Universities of Milan and Genova and is actively involved in national and international studies evaluating implant-based breast reconstruction with a focus on optimizing aesthetic outcomes with use of meshes and fat grafting. Since 2016, Dr. Nava has been Honorary President of G.RE.T.A (Group for Reconstructive and Therapeutic Advancement) which promotes international collaboration in the field of oncoplastic and aesthetic breast surgery and the exchange of ideas with patients. Dr. Nava has published more than 150 articles, is the author of five major textbooks on oncoplastic and reconstructive breast surgery, and coordinates the biennial Milan Oncoplastic Breast meeting. He is a member of several organisations including the European Society of Surgical Oncology (ESSO) and the European Society of Mastology (EUSOMA).

Contributors

Claudia R. Albornoz
University of Chile
Santiago, Chile

Robert J. Allen, Sr.
Louisiana State University Health Sciences Center
New Orleans, Louisiana

Claudio Angrigiani
Henry Moore Institute of Oncology
Universidad de Buenos Aires
Buenos Aires, Argentina

Douglas W. Arthur
Virginia Commonwealth University
Richmond, Virginia

Stefano Avvedimento
Plastic Surgery Department
Istituto Nazionale dei Tumori
Milano, Italy

Sonia Bathla
Aintree University Hospital
Liverpool, United Kingdom

John R. Benson
Cambridge Breast Unit
Addenbrooke's Hospital
and
University of Cambridge
and
School of Medicine
Anglia Ruskin University
Cambridge, United Kingdom

Pietro Berrino
Chirurgia Plastica Genova SRL
Genoa, Italy

Valeria Berrino
Centro Medicina Ceccardi SRL
Genoa, Italy

Phillip Blondeel
Department of Plastic and Reconstructive Surgery
Ghent University Hospital
Ghent, Belgium

Edward Wayne Buchel
Health Science Centre
University of Manitoba
Winnipeg, Canada

Alexandra Bucknor
Charing Cross Hospital
Imperial College NHS Foundation Trust
London, United Kingdom

Rudolf Buntic
Division of Microsurgery
California Pacific Medical Center
and
The Buncke Clinic
San Francisco, California

Giuseppe Catanuto
Department of Surgery
Azienda Ospedaliera Cannizzaro
Catania, Italy

Edward I. Chang
Department of Plastic Surgery
University of Texas MD Anderson Cancer Center
Houston, Texas

Ming-Huei Cheng
Division of Reconstructive Microsurgery
Department of Plastic and Reconstructive Surgery
Chang Gung Memorial Hospital
College of Medicine
Chang Gung University
and
Center for Tissue Engineering
Chang Gung Memorial Hospital
Taoyuan, Taiwan

Mark W. Clemens
Department of Plastic Surgery
The University of Texas MD Anderson Cancer Center
Houston, Texas

Charlotte Coles
Cambridge University Hospital NHS Foundation Trust
Cambridge, United Kingdom

Nathan Coombs
Great Western Hospital
Swindon, United Kingdom

Peter G. Cordeiro
Plastic and Reconstructive Surgical Service
Department of Surgery
Memorial Sloan Kettering Cancer Center
New York, New York

Randy De Baerdemaeker
Department of Plastic, Reconstructive
    and Aesthetic Surgery
University Hospital Brussels (Vrije
    Universiteit Brussel)
Brussels, Belgium

Emmanuel Delay
Plastic Surgery Unit
Surgery Department
Centre Léon Bérard
and
Private Practice
Lyon, France

J. Michael Dixon
Edinburgh Breast Unit
Western General Hospital
Edinburgh, United Kingdom

Michael Douek
Kings College London
London, United Kingdom

Sue Down
James Paget University Hospital
Great Yarmouth, United Kingdom
and
University of East Anglia
Norwich, United Kingdom

Dorin Dumitru
Cambridge Breast Unit
Addenbrooke's Hospital
Cambridge, United Kingdom

Francesco M. Egro
Department of Plastic Surgery
University of Pittsburgh
    Medical Center
Pittsburgh, Pennsylvania

Chidi Ekwobi
The Royal Marsden Hospital
The Royal Marsden NHS Foundation Trust
London, United Kingdom

Francisco J. Esteva
Division of Hematology/Oncology
Laura & Isaac Perlmutter Cancer Center
New York University Langone
    Medical Center
New York, New York

Jian Farhadi
Department of Plastic Surgery
Guy's and St Thomas' NHS Foundation Trust
London, United Kingdom

Secondo Folli
Breast Surgical Oncology Department
Istituto Nazionale dei Tumori
Milano, Italy

Allen Gabriel
Department of Plastic Surgery
Loma Linda University Medical Center
Loma Linda, California

Patrick B. Garvey
Department of Plastic and Reconstructive Surgery
The University of Texas MD Anderson Cancer Center
Houston, Texas

Rolf Gemperli
Plastic Surgery Division
School of Medicine
University of São Paulo
São Paulo, Brazil

Fiona J. Gilbert
Department of Radiology
School of Clinical Medicine
University of Cambridge
Cambridge, United Kingdom

João Carlos Sampaio Goés
Instituto Brasileiro de Combate ao Câncer (IBCC)
and
Hospital Israelita Albert Einstein (HIAE)
São Paulo, Brazil

Mehra Golshan
Department of Surgery Brigham and Women's Hospital
Dana Farber Cancer Institute
Harvard Medical School
Boston, Massachusetts

Isak Goodwin
Division of Plastic and Reconstructive Surgery
University of Utah Health
Salt Lake City, Utah

Gerald Gui
Breast Unit
Royal Marsden NHS Foundation Trust
London, United Kingdom

Sirwan M. Hadad
The Royal Marsden Hospital
The Royal Marsden NHS Foundation Trust
London, United Kingdom

Moustapha Hamdi
Department of Plastic, Reconstructive and Aesthetic Surgery
University Hospital Brussels (Vrije Universiteit Brussel)
Brussels, Belgium

Kathryn Huber
Tufts University School of Medicine
Boston, Massachusetts

Jane Y.C. Hui
Division of Surgical Oncology
Department of Surgery
University of Minnesota
Minneapolis, Minnesota

Amir E. Ibrahim
Division of Plastic Surgery
Department of Surgery
American University of Beirut Medical Center
Beirut, Lebanon

Marcelo Irigo
Henry Moore Institute of Oncology
Universidad de Buenos Aires
Buenos Aires, Argentina

Jordan Jacobs
Mount Sinai Hospital
New York, New York

Ismail Jatoi
Division of Surgical Oncology and Endocrine Surgery
University of Texas Health Center
San Antonio, Texas

Ranjeet Jeevan
Clinical Effectiveness Unit
The Royal College of Surgeons of England
London, United Kingdom

and

The Manchester Centre for Plastic Surgery and Burns
Manchester University NHS Foundation Trust
Manchester, United Kingdom

Megan Kalambo
The University of Texas MD Anderson Cancer Center
Houston, Texas

Parisa Kamali
Amsterdam, The Netherlands

Cansu Karakas
Department of Experimental Radiation Oncology
The University of Texas MD Anderson Cancer Center
Houston, Texas

Efstathios Karamanos
Department of Surgery
Henry Ford Health System
Detroit, Michigan

Fleur Kilburn-Toppin
Addenbrooke's Hospital
Cambridge, United Kingdom

John Y.S. Kim
Department of Plastic Surgery
The University of Texas MD Anderson Cancer Center
Houston, Texas

Steven J. Kronowitz
Kronowitz Plastic Surgery, PLLC
Houston, Texas

Henry Kuerer
Breast Surgical Oncology
The University of Texas
MD Anderson Cancer Center
Houston, Texas

Ian Kunkler
Edinburgh Cancer Centre
University of Edinburgh
Edinburgh, United Kingdom

Steven T. Lanier
Department of Plastic Surgery
The University of Texas MD Anderson Cancer Center
Houston, Texas

Joshua L. Levine
Breast Reconstruction Center of New York City
New York, New York

Samuel J. Lin
BIDMC/HMS Residency Training Program
Harvard Medical School
Boston, Massachusetts

Albert Losken
Emory Division of Plastic and Reconstructive Surgery
Atlanta, Georgia

Laura Lozza
Radiation Oncology 1,
Fondazione IRCCS instituto dei tumori,
Milan, Italy

Robert Douglas Macmillan
Nottingham Breast Institute
Nottingham, United Kingdom

Fiona MacNeill
The Royal Marsden Hospital
The Royal Marsden NHS Foundation Trust
London, United Kingdom

Charles M. Malata
Department of Plastic and Reconstructive Surgery
Cambridge Breast Unit at Addenbrooke's Hospital
Cambridge University Hospitals NHS Foundation Trust

and

Postgraduate Medical Institute
Faculty of Health Sciences of Anglia
    Ruskin University
Cambridge, United Kingdom

Melissa Anne Mallory
Department of Surgery
Brigham and Women's Hospital
Dana Farber Cancer Institute
Harvard Medical School
Boston, Massachusetts

Andrea Manconi
Division of Plastic and Reconstructive Surgery
European Institute of Oncology
Milan, Italy

James Mansell
Hairmyers Hospital
Glasgow, Scotland, United Kingdom

Alessandra Marchi
Unita' Semplice Organizzativa for
    Breast Reconstruction
Main Hospital Borgo Trento
Verona, Italy

Lee Martin
Aintree University Hospital
Liverpool, United Kingdom

Jaume Masià
Plastic Surgery Department
Hospital de la Santa Creu i Sant Pau
Barcelona, Spain

Patrick Maxwell
Department of Plastic Surgery
Loma Linda University Medical Center
Loma Linda, California

Beryl McCormick
Memorial Sloan Kettering Cancer Center
New York, New York

Icro Meattini
Radiation Oncology Unit
Azienda Ospedaliero–Universitaria Careggi
University of Florence
Florence, Italy

Babak Mehrara
Weill Cornell University Medical Center
and
Division of Plastic Surgery
Memorial Sloan Kettering Cancer Center
New York, New York

Katrina B. Mitchell
Breast Surgical Oncology
MD Anderson Cancer Center
Houston, Texas

Alexandra Molina
Department of Plastic Surgery
Queen Victoria Hospital
East Grinstead, United Kingdom

Tracy–Ann Moo
Weill Cornell Medical College
New York, New York

Michel Moutran
Plastic Surgery
Beirut, Lebanon

Katrina B. Mitchell
MD Anderson Cancer Center
Breast Surgical Oncology
Houston, Texas

Mukesh Bindish Mukesh
Colchester Hospital University NHS Foundation Trust
Colchester, United Kingdom

Alexandre Mendonça Munhoz
Breast Reconstruction Group
University of São Paulo School of Medicine
and
Plastic Surgery Division
Hospital Sírio-Libanês
São Paulo, Brazil

Maurice Y. Nahabedian
Department of Plastic Surgery
Georgetown University Hospital
Washington, DC

Maurizio B. Nava
Valduce Hospital
Como, Italy
and
University of Milan
Milan, Italy
and
University of Genoa
Genoa, Italy

Lisa A. Newman
Department of Surgery
Henry Ford Health System
Detroit, Michigan

Andrei Odobescu
Division of Plastic and Reconstructive Surgery
University of Iowa Hospitals and Clinics
Iowa City, Iowa

Georgette Oni
Department of Plastic and Reconstructive Surgery
Addenbrooke's Hospital
Cambridge University Hospitals NHS Foundation Trust
Cambridge, United Kingdom

Animesh Patel
Cambridge Breast Unit
Addenbrooke's Hospital
Cambridge University Hospitals NHS Foundation Trust
Cambridge, United Kingdom

Nakul Gamanlal Patel
Health Science Centre
University of Manitoba
Winnipeg, Canada
and
The Royal Infirmary Hospital
Leicester University Hospitals
Leicester, United Kingdom

Jean-Yves Petit
Division of Plastic and Reconstructive Surgery
European Institute of Oncology
Milan, Italy

Sarah E. Pinder
Division of Cancer Studies
King's College London
London, United Kingdom

Vassilis Pitsinis
University of Dundee, School of Medicine
Ninewells Hospital and Medical School
NHS Tayside
Dundee, Scotland, United Kingdom

Gemma Pons
Plastic Surgery Department
Hospital de la Santa Creu i Sant Pau
Barcelona, Spain

Elena Provenzano
Cambridge Breast Unit
Addenbrooke's Hospital
Cambridge University Hospitals NHS Foundation Trust
Cambridge, United Kingdom

Andrea L. Pusic
Department of Surgery
Weill Cornell University Medical Center
and
Division of Plastic Surgery
Memorial Sloan Kettering Cancer Center
New York, New York

Guidubaldo Querci della Rovere (posthumous)

Cameron Raine
Edinburgh Breast Unit
Western General Hospital
Edinburgh, United Kingdom

Agustin Rancati
Henry Moore Institute of Oncology
Universidad de Buenos Aires
Buenos Aires, Argentina

Alberto Rancati
Henry Moore Institute of Oncology
Universidad de Buenos Aires
Buenos Aires, Argentina

Adam J. Reid
Blond McIndoe Laboratories
University of Manchester
and
Manchester University NHS Foundation Trust
Manchester, United Kingdom

Maria Rietjens
Division of Plastic and Reconstructive Surgery
European Institute of Oncology
Milan, Italy

Elena Rodríguez–Bauzà
Plastic Surgery Department
Hospital de la Santa Creu i Sant Pau
Barcelona, Spain

Jessica Rose
Department of Plastic and Reconstructive Surgery
The University of Texas Health Science
    Center at Houston
Houston, Texas

Margaret S. Roubaud
Department of Plastic and Reconstructive Surgery
The University of Texas MD Anderson Cancer Center
Houston, Texas

J. Peter Rubin
Plastic Surgery
Adipose Stem Cell Center
University of Pittsburgh
Pittsburgh, Pennsylvania

Jennifer E. Rusby
The Royal Marsden Hospital
The Royal Marsden NHS Foundation Trust
London, United Kingdom

Aysegul A. Sahin
Department of Pathology
The University of Texas MD Anderson Cancer Center
Houston, Texas

Michel Hector Saint-Cyr
Baylor Scott & White Clinic
Temple, Texas

Andrew Salzberg
Icahn School of Medicine
Mount Sinai Medical System
New York, New York

Pierluigi Santi
Marianna Pesce
University of Genova
Genova, Italy

Karim A. Sarhane
Department of Surgery
University of Toledo Medical Center
Toledo, Ohio

Hani Sbitany
San Francisco, California

Michael Scheflan
Tel Aviv University
Tel Aviv, Israel

Jesse C. Selber
Department of Plastic Surgery
The University of Texas MD Anderson Cancer Center
Houston, Texas

Nicholas Serrano
Virginia Commonwealth University
Richmond, Virginia

Melvin J. Silverstein
Hoag Breast Program
Hoag Memorial Hospital Presbyterian
Newport Beach, California

and

Keck School of Medicine
University of Southern California
Los Angeles, California

Rache M. Simmons
Weill Cornell Medical College
New York, New York

Julian Singer
Princess Alexandra Hospital
Harlow, United Kingdom

Sumner Slavin
Beth Israel Deaconess Medical Center
Boston, Massachusetts

David Song
Georgetown University School of Medicine
Washington, DC

Andre Spano
Plastic Surgery Department
Istituto Nazionale dei Tumori
Milano, Italy

Aldona Spiegel
Institute for Reconstructive Surgery
Center for Breast Restoration
Houston Methodist Hospital
Houston, Texas

Eric Strom
Department of Radiation Oncology
The University of Texas MD Anderson Cancer Center
Houston, Texas

Jessica Taff
Division of Hematology/Oncology
Laura & Isaac Perlmutter Cancer Center
New York University Langone Medical Center
New York, New York

Jeffrey S. Tobias
University College London Hospitals
London, United Kingdom

Gilles Tousson
Polyclinique du Val de Saône
Mâcon, France

and

Plastic Surgery Unit
Surgery Department
Centre Léon Bérard
Lyon, France

Luciano Tracia
Royal Aesthetic and Medical Clinic
Dubai Healthcare City, Dubai, United Arab Emirates

Todd M. Tuttle
Division of Surgical Oncology
Department of Surgery
University of Minnesota
Minneapolis, Minnesota

Chieh-Han John Tzou
Division of Plastic and Reconstructive Surgery
Department of Surgery
Medical University of Vienna
Vienna, Austria

Jayant S. Vaidya
University College London
London, United Kingdom

Sophocles H. Voineskos
Division of Plastic Surgery
Department of Surgery
McMaster University
and
Surgical Outcomes Research Centre (SOURCE)
McMaster University
Hamilton, Ontario, Canada

David Wazer
Tufts University School of Medicine
Boston, Massachusetts
and
Warren Alpert Medical School of Brown University
Providence, Rhode Island

Eva Weiler-Mithoff
Canniesburn Plastic Surgery Unit
Glasgow Royal Infirmary
Glasgow, Scotland, United Kingdom

Wendy Woodward
Department of Radiation Oncology
The University of Texas MD Anderson Cancer Center
Houston, Texas

Winona Wu
Department of Surgery
Division of Vascular Surgery
Beth Israel Deaconess Medical Center
Boston, Massachusetts

Wei Tse Yang
The University of Texas MD Anderson Cancer Center
Houston, Texas

SECTION I

General trends, principles, and materials

Chapter 1. Latest trends in breast reconstruction 3

Chapter 2. The biological rationale for oncoplastic surgical procedures 9

Chapter 3. Biological reactions to reconstructive materials 13

1

Latest trends in breast reconstruction

AT A GLANCE

The advent of acellular dermal matrix and fat grafting have increased the usage of implant-based reconstruction over the past 4–5 years. Furthermore, increasing numbers of women are choosing to undergo immediate breast reconstruction for a unilateral cancer and requesting simultaneous contralateral prophylactic mastectomy (CPM) with reconstruction. Indeed, a desire for matching breasts may be a driver for increased rates of CPM with women undergoing simultaneous bilateral implant-based reconstruction. The United Kingdom National Mastectomy and Breast Reconstruction Audit revealed a doubling in rates of immediate breast reconstruction from about 10% to 20% over a 4 year period. The availability of breast reconstruction is an important factor and many of these women chose implant-based reconstruction. The emergence of nipple-sparing mastectomy has further improved cosmetic outcomes and the ability to perform one-stage breast reconstruction. Although autologous tissue reconstruction has decreased in recent years, increasing indications for postmastectomy radiotherapy has ensured that type of reconstruction remains relevant due to lower rates of radiation-associated complications with non-allogenic reconstruction.

1.1 USA

Jane Y.C. Hui and Todd M. Tuttle

Introduction

There are two equally effective management strategies in the treatment of early-stage breast cancer: breast-conservation therapy (BCT), consisting of lumpectomy followed by radiotherapy, and mastectomy. Thus, the choice of surgical strategy for most patients is a personal decision, and the option of breast reconstruction plays a role in decision-making. In 1998, the United States (US) Federal Women's Health and Cancer Rights Act mandated insurance coverage for breast reconstruction after mastectomy and contralateral surgery for symmetry to improve access to these services. Following this legislative change, the US saw an increase in rates of immediate breast reconstruction. Nonetheless, despite this increase, only 20%–30% of mastectomy patients receive immediate breast reconstruction.[1–3]

Surgeons and breast reconstruction techniques

The most common type of breast reconstruction performed in the United States is immediate implant-based reconstruction. In a recent survey, 81% of plastic surgeons reported that they predominantly perform immediate breast reconstruction and two-thirds (64%) of surgical oncologists reported that immediate breast reconstruction was most commonly recommended for their patients.[4,5] Moreover, the majority of plastic surgeons nowadays perform implant-based breast reconstruction,[4,6] which contrasts with practice in the late 1990s, when autologous reconstruction was the preferred choice of breast reconstruction.[7] Over the past two decades, the number of implant-based breast reconstruction have steadily increased, while the number of autologous breast reconstruction have progressively declined.

Plastic surgeons in academic practice are more likely to perform autologous breast reconstruction than those in solo practice in a community hospital.[4] This difference may be related to the availability of skilled assistants such as residents and fellows for more labor-intensive procedures and postoperative care. Corroborating this, the only significant predictors of high-volume autologous breast reconstruction are reported to be microvascular fellowship training and involvement with resident training.[6] Kulkarni and colleagues explored reasons why some plastic surgeons do not perform any microvascular breast reconstructive procedures and found that the majority of surgeons surveyed considered reimbursement and time commitment as the primary barriers. Only a minority (17%) reported inadequate training as a barrier.

The decision–making process: surgeons and patients

From the patient's perspective, the medical decision-making process is driven by information gained from discussion with their physician and perhaps online resources. Awareness of breast reconstruction influences the patient's ultimate decision regarding options for oncologic breast surgery. Alderman and colleagues surveyed patients at three months following a breast cancer diagnosis and found that only one-third recalled being told about breast reconstruction during the surgical decision-making process.[8] These patients were significantly younger, had larger tumors, and were more educated. Perhaps not surprisingly, women who were informed of breast reconstruction options were four times more likely to undergo a mastectomy than women who lacked this information.

The level of physician influence also impacts the decision itself and the degree of patient satisfaction with that decision. A recent survey of young breast cancer patients during the first year following diagnosis found that among women who recalled making the surgical decision on their own, 60% underwent contralateral prophylactic mastectomy (CPM), 23% underwent BCT, and 17% underwent unilateral mastectomy.[9] In contrast, among women who recalled that their physician primarily made the decision, only 5.6% underwent CPM, with the remainder of women equally divided between BCT and unilateral mastectomy. Among women who participated in shared decision-making, these three surgical strategies were evenly distributed. Interestingly, among women who were "extremely confident that the decision about surgery for breast cancer was the right one," there were twice as many women with CPM (51%) than BCT (24%) or unilateral mastectomy (25%). Nearly 80% of women who had any mastectomy (unilateral or CPM) had breast reconstruction during the year after diagnosis.

Understanding the motivation behind a patient's choice can help surgeons in guiding any shared decision-making with their patients. A survey undertaken by Duggal and colleagues reported that patients who chose breast reconstruction were motivated by body image, such as "seeking to maintain a balanced appearance," rather than reasons relating to sexuality ("feeling more sexually attractive if I have breast reconstruction") or femininity.[10] In contrast, the most common reason for patients declining breast reconstruction was to avoid additional surgery.[3] For those patients who desired breast reconstruction, but chose a delayed procedure, the need to focus on their cancer treatment prior to breast reconstruction was a major factor influencing their decision. In terms of referral for breast reconstruction, Alderman and colleagues found that surgeons were significantly more likely to refer their patients for breast reconstruction if they were themselves female, had a high breast surgery workload, and were affiliated to cancer centers.[11] The surgeons who were least likely to refer their patients for breast reconstruction tended to perceive issues of access as barriers to breast reconstruction and lower patient priorities for reconstructive procedures. Determining an individual patient's goals and priorities can help frame the discussion of management strategies for breast cancer patients.

Patient satisfaction

Breast reconstruction is an irreversible procedure, and it is important to optimize not only the decision-making process, but also to examine long-term patient satisfaction. Studies have shown that patient satisfaction with cosmetic outcomes is not significantly different between BCT and mastectomy with breast reconstruction, but rates of satisfaction were significantly lower for patients undergoing mastectomy alone.[12,13] Stratification of satisfaction scores according to surgery and breast reconstruction type reveals that abdominal flap breast reconstruction is associated with the highest rates of patient satisfaction and latissimus dorsi flap-based reconstruction is comparable to BCT in terms of patient satisfaction scores.[13] Implant-based breast reconstruction scored lower than BCT on satisfaction criteria, but mastectomy alone had the lowest scores among all types of surgical interventions. Satisfaction scores did not change over time for abdominal or latissimus dorsi flap reconstruction, but values for both implant-based breast reconstruction and BCT declined progressively. Surprisingly, despite having the lowest mean satisfaction scores, patients with mastectomy alone reported increasingly higher satisfaction scores the further they were from the date of surgery (i.e., 20 years versus 1 year), which may reflect gradual adjustment to altered body image and loss of a breast.

CONCLUSION

Despite insurance coverage for breast reconstruction among women with breast cancer in the United States, a substantial proportion of these patients are not receiving immediate breast reconstruction. Although some women wish to avoid more complex surgery or to focus on breast cancer treatment in the immediate setting, overall patient satisfaction may be higher for those who opt for immediate or delayed breast reconstruction. Understanding these different patient perspectives can help surgeons embrace a more comprehensive approach when advising newly diagnosed breast cancer patients of their surgical options, including breast reconstruction. This will allow patients to make a fully informed and patient-driven decision that will retain her satisfaction in the long term.

REFERENCES

1. Yang, Rachel L., Andrew S. Newman, Ines C. Lin, Caroline E. Reinke, Giorgos C. Karakousis, Brian J. Czerniecki, Liza C. Wu, and Rachel R. Kelz. "Trends in immediate breast reconstruction across insurance groups after enactment of breast cancer legislation," *Cancer* 119 (2013):2462–2468.

2. Lang, Julie E., Danielle E. Summers, Haiyan Cui, Joseph N. Carey, Rebecca K. Viscusi, Craig A. Hurst, Amy L. Waer, Michele L. Ley, Stephen F. Sener, and Aparna Vijayasekaran. "Trends in post-mastectomy reconstruction: A SEER database analysis," *Journal of Surgical Oncology* 108 (2013):163–168.

3. Morrow, Monica, Yun Li, Amy K. Alderman, Reshma Jagsi, Ann S. Hamilton, John J. Graff, Sarah T. Hawley, and Steven J. Katz. "Access to breast reconstruction after mastectomy and patient perspectives on reconstruction decision making," *JAMA Surgery* 149 (2014):1015–1021.

4. Gurunluoglu, Raffi, Aslin Gurunluoglu, Susan A. Williams, and Seth Tebockhorst. "Current trends in breast reconstruction: Survey of American society of plastic surgeons 2010," *Annals of Plastic Surgery* 70 (2013):103–110.

5. Lee, Ming, Erik Reinertsen, Evan McClure, Shuling Liu, Laura Kruper, Neil Tanna, J. Brian Boyd, and Jay W. Granzow. "Surgeon motivations behind the timing of breast reconstruction in patients requiring postmastectomy radiation therapy," *Journal of Plastic, Reconstructive & Aesthetic Surgery* (2015). doi:10.1016/j.bjps.2015.06.026.

6. Kulkarni, Anita R., Erika Davis Sears, Dunya M. Atisha, and Amy K. Alderman. "Use of autologous and microsurgical breast reconstruction by U.S. plastic surgeons," *Plastic and Reconstructive Surgery* 132 (2013):534–541.

7. Hernandez-Boussard, Tina, Kamakshi Zeidler, Ario Barzin, Gordon Lee, and Catherine Curtin. "Breast reconstruction national trends and healthcare implications," *The Breast Journal* 19 (2013):463–469.

8. Alderman, Amy K., Sarah Hawley, Jennifer Waljee, Mahasin Mujahid, Monica Morrow, and Steven Katz. "Understanding the impact of breast reconstruction on the surgical decision-making process for breast cancer," *Cancer* 112 (2008):489–494.

9. Rosenberg, Shoshana M., Karen Sepucha, Kathryn J. Ruddy, Rulla M. Tamimi, Shari Gelber, Megan E. Meyer, Lidia Schapira, Steven E. Come, Virginia F. Borges, Mehra Golshan, Eric P. Winer, and Ann H. Partridge. "Local therapy decision-making and contralateral prophylactic mastectomy in young women with early-stage breast cancer," *Annals of Surgical Oncology* 22 (2015):3809–3815.

10. Duggal, Claire S., Drew Metcalfe, Robyn Sackeyfio, Grant W. Carlson, and Albert Losken. "Patient motivations for choosing postmastectomy breast reconstruction," *Annals of Plastic Surgery* 70 (2013):574–580.

11. Alderman, Amy K., Sarah T. Hawley, Jenifer Waljee, Monica Morrow, and Steven J. Katz. "Correlates of referral practices of general surgeons to plastic surgeons for mastectomy reconstruction," *Cancer* 109 (2007):1715–1720.

12. Jagsi, Reshma, Yun Li, Monica Morrow, Nancy Janz, Amy K. Alderman, John Graff, Ann Hamilton, Steven Katz, and Sarah Hawley. "Patient-reported quality of life and satisfaction with cosmetic outcomes after breast conservation and mastectomy with and without reconstruction: Results of a survey of breast cancer survivors," *Annals of Surgery* 261 (2015):1198–1206.

13. Atisha, Dunya M., Christel N. Rushing, Gregory P. Samsa, Tracie D. Locklear, Charlie E. Cox, E. Shelley Hwang, Michael R. Zenn, Andrea L. Pusic, and Amy P. Abernethy. "A national snapshot of satisfaction with breast cancer procedures," *Annals of Surgical Oncology* 22 (2015):361–369.

1.2 EUROPE

Ranjeet Jeevan

Introduction

Any comprehensive evaluation of the latest trends in breast reconstructive practice within Europe must take account of several factors including: (1) underlying differences in the costs involved and the funding available, (2) the perspectives of clinicians and patients with respect to the offer and uptake of reconstruction, respectively, and (3) the scope of any relevant national guidelines. These factors may collectively help explain longitudinal trends and regional variations in current reconstructive practice.

Reconstructive decision-making

There are few European studies examining breast reconstructive decisions made by either clinicians or patients. Two independent qualitative studies of clinician and patient viewpoints undertaken in the United Kingdom (UK) reported similar concerns on a range of issues including: (1) facilitating patient choice, namely, the quantity and quality of information provided, (2) time pressures associated with cancer treatment targets, (3) the degree of patient involvement in decision-making processes, and (4) proximity, accessibility, and range of reconstructive options on offer.[1,2]

A study of ductal carcinoma in situ patients treated at a French cancer center found that surgeon preferences and recommendations were the primary factors influencing the likelihood of immediate reconstruction (IR) being offered to patients, with comorbidities less relevant.[3] In contrast, a national prospective study undertaken in the UK found that surgeons not infrequently considered the offer of immediate reconstruction to be inappropriate due to patient-related clinical, health, or lifestyle problems or an anticipated need for adjuvant radiotherapy.[4] Although many women who chose not to undergo immediate reconstruction prioritized cancer treatment and were relatively unconcerned about the aesthetic outcomes of mastectomy, a sizeable minority highlighted a lack of information and sufficient time for decision-making as a reason for not accepting an offer of immediate reconstruction.[5]

The role of national guidelines

In England, the National Institute for Health and Clinical Excellence (NICE) published early breast cancer guidelines in 2002 and updated these in 2009.[6,7] The latter set of guidelines states that clinicians should, "Discuss immediate breast reconstruction with all patients who are being advised to have a mastectomy, and offer it except where significant comorbidity or (the need for) adjuvant therapy may preclude this option. All appropriate breast reconstruction options should be offered and discussed with patients, irrespective of whether they are all available locally." In 2011, NICE produced a care quality standard requiring healthcare commissioners, providers, and clinicians to ensure that immediate reconstruction is discussed with all patients undergoing a mastectomy for early breast cancer.[8] Although specific national oncoplastic guidelines have been published jointly by breast and plastic surgeons in England,[9,10] similar guidelines have not been forthcoming from other European countries.

Immediate breast reconstruction rates following mastectomy surgery for cancer

Most studies published in Europe provide estimates of longitudinal trends in immediate reconstruction rates using hospital registries and databases (**Table 1.2.1**). The national rate for immediate reconstruction in England increased three-fold between 1997 and 2013 from 7% to 23%.[1,11] Similar changes have been observed in Germany, where the national rate increased from 10% to 13% between 2006 and 2010, but more recent studies indicate current rates of around 30%.[12,13] Similarly, in France, the national immediate reconstruction rate increased from 11% to 13% between 2005 and 2012,[14] while in the Catalonia region of Spain, rates increased from 17% to 23% between 2005 and 2011.[15] In contrast to these national and regional trends, immediate reconstruction rates in Denmark remained unchanged at just 1% between 1999 and 2006.[16]

These increases in immediate reconstruction rates observed in several European countries are likely due to a number of concomitant factors, including: (1) improved breast cancer treatments, (2) availability of a wider range of reconstructive options, (3) a greater attention to aesthetic outcomes, (4) more appropriately trained and specialized surgeons, and (5) funding specifically allocated for immediate reconstruction.

Table 1.2.1 Longitudinal trends in national and regional rates of immediate breast reconstruction across Europe

Country	Study time period	Immediate reconstruction rate (%)
England	1997 to 2013	7 to 23
Germany	2006 to 2010	10 to 13
Germany	2015	30
France	2005 to 2012	11 to 13
Spain (Catalonia)	2005 to 2011	17 to 23
Denmark	1999 to 2006	1

Regional and institutional variation in immediate breast reconstruction rates

Studies have consistently demonstrated variation in immediate reconstruction rates within European countries. In the UK, three separate studies have shown variation in rates of immediate reconstruction across healthcare regions (cancer networks) based on analyses of both administrative and prospectively collected audit data.[11,17,18] A preliminary retrospective analysis (2006–2009) revealed variations in immediate reconstruction rates at network level from 8% to 32%, while a subsequent national audit (2008–2009) found a range of 9% to 43%, and the most recent time period examined (2013–2014) showed variation from 16% to 56%.

In France, immediate reconstruction rates were found to be significantly higher in specialist cancer centers (19%) and regional teaching hospitals (14%) compared with an overall figure of 8%, while increased hospital case volume was also associated with a higher immediate reconstruction (IR) rate.[14] Similar conclusions were apparent from the Catalonia region of Spain where hospital type was also found to determine the likelihood of IR being undertaken.[15]

Types of reconstructive procedures performed

A national prospective study conducted in 2008–2009 reported that 41% of immediate and 58% of delayed reconstructions (DR) undertaken in England used autologous tissue alone. About one-quarter of immediate reconstruction (22%) and delayed reconstruction (26%) utilized a flap together with an implant, while 37% of immediate reconstruction and 16% of delayed reconstruction used an implant alone (**Table 1.2.2**).[18] Recent analyses suggest that the proportion of autologous procedures has increased even further, indicating that reconstructive trends in the UK differ from those of the United States where there has been a reduction in use of autologous tissue and corresponding increase in implant-based reconstruction in recent years (especially with the advent of acellular dermal matrices).

This may partly be due to the differing influence of costs, tariffs and incentives for procedures undertaken within a managed national health service system. This could also reflect directives from national guidelines that require all appropriate reconstructive options to be offered to patients.[7] Comparable data on IR and DR procedure types are not currently available for other European countries.

Breast reconstruction following prophylactic or risk-reducing mastectomy surgery

Minimal data are available on prophylactic and risk-reducing mastectomy with or without concurrent reconstruction in European countries. Analyses undertaken in England reported that the number of bilateral mastectomy cases undertaken annually tripled for the period 2002–2011 in women without breast cancer from 71 to 255 and almost doubled from 529 to 931 in women with breast cancer over the same period.[19] Furthermore, immediate reconstruction rates doubled across both groups during the study period, reaching 90% for the non-breast cancer group by 2011.

CONCLUSION

Rates of immediate reconstruction in Europe have increased in parallel with those in the United States, but with key differences in terms of both the types of procedures undertaken and the degree of variation between hospitals and different regions. More national and international comparative data are required to fully evaluate these trends and address possible sources of variation in practice.

REFERENCES

1. Jeevan R, Browne JP, van der Meulen J, Pereira J, Caddy CM, Sheppard C et al. First annual report of the national mastectomy and breast reconstruction audit 2008. Leeds, UK: The NHS Information Centre; 2008.

2. Potter S, Mills N, Cawthorn S, Wilson S, Blazeby J. Exploring inequalities in access to care and the provision of choice to women seeking breast reconstruction surgery: A qualitative study. *Br J Cancer*. 2013; 109(5):1181–1191.

3. Naoura I, Mazouni C, Ghanimeh J, Leymarie N, Garbay JR, Karsenti G, Sarfati B, Leduey A, Kolb F, Delaloge S, Rimareix F. Factors influencing the decision to offer immediate breast reconstruction after mastectomy for ductal carcinoma in situ (DCIS): The institut gustave roussy breast cancer study group experience. *Breast*. 2013; 22(5):673–675.

4. Jeevan R, Cromwell D, Browne JP, van der Meulen J, Pereira J, Caddy CM et al. Second annual report of the national mastectomy and breast reconstruction audit 2008. Leeds, UK: The NHS Information Centre; 2009.

5. Jeevan R, Cromwell D, Browne JP, van der Meulen J, Pereira J, Caddy CM et al. Third annual report of the national mastectomy and breast reconstruction audit 2008. Leeds, UK: The NHS Information Centre; 2010.

6. National Institute for Clinical Excellence. *Guidance on Cancer Services. Improving Outcomes in Breast Cancer–Manual Update.* London, UK: NICE; 2002.

Table 1.2.2 Reconstructive procedure type in England, 2008–2009

Procedure type	Immediate reconstruction	Delayed reconstruction
	/n (%)	/n (%)
Flap only (autologous)	1408 (41)	1012 (58)
Flap with implant	735 (22)	438 (26)
Implant only	1246 (37)	281 (16)

7. National Institute for Health and Clinical Excellence. *Early and Locally Advanced Breast Cancer: Diagnosis and Treatment* (Clinical Guideline 80). London, UK: NICE; 2009.

8. National Institute for Health and Clinical Excellence. *Breast Cancer* (Quality Standard 12). London, UK: NICE; 2011.

9. Association of Breast Surgery at BASO; Association of Breast Surgery at BAPRAS; Training Interface Group in Breast Surgery, Baildam A, Bishop H, Boland G, Dalglish M et al., Oncoplastic breast surgery—A guide to good practice. *Eur J Surg Oncol.* 2007; 33(Suppl 1):S1–23.

10. Cutress RI, Summerhayes C, Rainsbury R. Guidelines for oncoplastic breast reconstruction. *Ann R Coll Surg Engl.* 2013; 95(3):161–162.

11. Jeevan R, Mennie JC, Mohanna P-N, O'Donoghue JM, Rainsbury RM, Cromwell DA. National trends and regional variation in immediate breast reconstruction rates between April 2000 and March 2014. *BJS.* 2016; 103(9):1147–1156.

12. Heil J, Rauch G, Szabo AZ, Garcia-Etienne CA, Golatta M, Domschke C, Badiian M et al. Breast cancer mastectomy trends between 2006 and 2010: Association with magnetic resonance imaging, immediate breast reconstruction, and hospital volume. *Ann Surg Oncol.* 2013; 20(12):3839–3846.

13. Gerber B, Marx M, Untch M, Faridi A. Breast reconstruction following cancer treatment. *Dtsch Arztebl Int.* 2015 31; 112(35–36):593–600.

14. Rococo E, Mazouni C, Or Z, Mobillion V, Koon Sun Pat M, Bonastre J. Variation in rates of breast cancer surgery: A national analysis based on French hospital episode statistics. *Eur J Surg Oncol.* 2016; 42(1):51–58.

15. Escribà JM, Pareja L, Esteban L, Gálvez J, Melià A, Roca L et al. Trends in the surgical procedures of women with incident breast cancer in Catalonia, Spain, over a 7-year period (2005–2011). *BMC Research Notes.* 2014; 7(1):587.

16. Hvilsom GB, Hölmich LR, Frederiksen K, Steding-Jessen M, Friis S, Dalton SO. Socioeconomic position and breast reconstruction in Danish women. *Acta Oncol.* 2011; 50(2):265–273.

17. Jeevan R, Cromwell DA, Browne JP, Trivella M, Pereira J, Caddy CM et al. Regional variation in use of immediate breast reconstruction after mastectomy for breast cancer in England. *Eur J Surg Oncol.* 2010; 36:750–755.

18. Jeevan R, Cromwell DA, Browne JP, Pereira J, Caddy CM, Sheppard C et al. Findings of a national comparative audit of mastectomy and breast reconstruction surgery in England. *J Plast Reconstr Aes.* 2014; 67(10):1333–1344.

19. Neuburger J, Macneill F, Jeevan R, van der Meulen JH, Cromwell DA. Trends in the use of bilateral mastectomy in England from 2002 to 2011: retrospective analysis of hospital episode statistics. *BMJ Open.* 2013; 3(8):e003179. doi:10.1136/bmjopen-2013-003179.

2

The biological rationale for oncoplastic surgical procedures

JOHN R. BENSON AND MAURIZIO B. NAVA

AT A GLANCE

Oncoplastic surgical procedures combine the principles and techniques of oncological and plastic surgery to optimize outcomes in terms of both disease-free survival and cosmesis. The extent of local treatments to the breast and status of surgical margins influence the chance of distant metastases and impact on longer-term survival. Oncoplastic surgery permits excision of tumors with wide margins of clearance and minimizes the need for re-excision. Nonetheless, rates of in-breast recurrence are not directly related to the width of margin clearance and definition of a negative margin as "no tumor at ink" imply that smaller volumes of excision without any oncoplastic correction may be sufficient for some patients in receipt of adjuvant therapies.

INTRODUCTION

The term oncoplastic surgery generally refers to wide excision of a breast tumor followed by immediate partial breast reconstruction. This restoration of a partial breast deformity as a single stage procedure draws upon techniques developed by plastic surgeons for cosmetic reshaping of the breast and has been subsequently adopted by oncological surgeons for management of breast cancer cases involving breast conservation. Oncoplastic surgery has generated much enthusiasm among both patients and surgeons, which is predicated on high levels of patient satisfaction coupled with excellent cosmetic outcomes and oncological safety.

There are three fundamental questions to ask when deciding on the optimum type of surgery for breast cancer patients, and these will guide clinical decision-making:

1. Can the cancer be removed with a standard wide local excision only with or without minor glandular readjustment?
2. If not, would an oncoplastic procedure either as a component of primary surgery or following neoadjuvant

chemotherapy permit excision of the tumor with negative margins and a good aesthetic outcome after radiotherapy?
3. Are the chances of achieving clear resection margins and restoration of breast volume and shape with partial breast reconstruction so small that breast-conserving surgery is inadvisable?

These questions can be challenging and demand joint decision-making both within the context of a multidisciplinary team and direct discussion with patients. Careful radiological evaluation is mandatory with integration of information from clinical examination, mammography, ultrasound, and MRI assessment. The extent of disease, its proximity to the nipple-areola complex, and the distribution of cancer either radially or circumferentially are crucial factors which are collectively important for definitive planning of any oncoplastic procedure. It is now acknowledged that perhaps up to one-quarter of cases of ipsilateral breast tumor recurrence (IBTR) following wide local excision are a determinant of distant metastases and directly impact upon overall survival.[1] Rates of IBTR must be minimized, although evidence suggests that rates of recurrence are not inversely related to the width of a "negative margin."[2] Oncoplastic surgery should not be undertaken with the aim of obtaining wide surgical margins of clearance per se, but rather to achieve "negative" margins and an optimum cosmetic result.[3] Oncoplastic procedures often permit wide resection of tissue, which increases the chance of tumor-free margins with evidence that positive margins under these circumstances usually reflects extensive disease for which mastectomy (rather than re-excision) is indicated. It has been suggested that rates of local relapse could be reduced by more aggressive approaches to breast-conserving surgery and margin width, but currently there are no data on longer-term follow-up of oncoplastic cases to support this contention.[4]

HISTORICAL

The operation of radical mastectomy is attributed to William Stewart Halsted and was rapidly implemented as routine surgical practice for breast cancer patients in the first half of the twentieth century.[5] This procedure is now outmoded in an era of induction chemotherapy, but was presaged on the assumption that breast cancer arose from a single focus and spread contiguously and centrifugally over time with progressive involvement of adjacent tissue and the lymphatic system of the breast. The Halstedian paradigm prevailed for much of the first half of the twentieth century. Halsted observed that many patients developed local recurrence before any manifestation of distant disease or death from breast cancer. A fundamental principle of the so-called Halstedian hypothesis was that maximal efforts at local control would prolong survival; Halsted firmly believed that breast cancer originated as a localized disease and that cure rates could be improved by a more meticulous and comprehensive surgical approach to the disease with en bloc resection of the breast, pectoral muscles, and axillary lymph nodes. Local recurrence was considered to be the cause of distant metastases and the aim was to minimize rates of local relapse.[6] An alternative hypothesis was proposed by Bernard Fisher contending that breast cancer is a local manifestation of a systemic disease with complex interactions between the host, the primary tumor, and distant micrometastases.[7] The corollary of this opposing viewpoint was that surgery could only achieve local control of disease and some form of systemic treatment was necessary to improve overall survival. This hypothesis of "biological predeterminism" was supported by results of randomized controlled clinical trials conducted during the 1970s and 1980s. These demonstrated breast cancer-specific and overall survival benefits of adjuvant systemic treatments which targeted occult micrometastatic disease.[8] Nonetheless, recent meta-analyses have reinforced the link between local control and long-term survival and emphasized the importance of locoregional therapies.[9]

BREAST-CONSERVING SURGERY

Breast-conservation surgery has been established over the past 30 years as the preferred standard of surgical management for women with early-stage breast cancer.[10] Longer-term follow-up data from several prospective randomized controlled trials have demonstrated survival equivalence for breast-conservation therapy compared with *radical* or *modified radical* mastectomy.[11–13] An update of the National Surgical Adjuvant Breast and Bowel Project (NSABP) B-06 trial with 20-year follow-up confirms that postoperative irradiation improves local recurrence-free survival with similar distant disease-free and overall survival for modified radical mastectomy, wide local excision and radiotherapy, or wide local excision alone.[14] These findings suggest that residual cancer cells are a determinant of local failure, but not distant disease. There is a finite rate of ipsilateral breast tumor recurrence (IBTR) for patients undergoing breast-conservation therapy with recent estimates of between 3.5% and 6.5% at 10 years.[15] Moreover, systemic therapies reduce rates of IBTR by approximately one-third and are halved with anti-HER2 directed therapies. Breast-conservation surgery represents a balance between oncological mandates and cosmetic outcomes and aims to excise a tumor with "*negative*" margins and acceptable cosmesis. Rates of in-breast recurrence are determined by negative margin status, but *no direct* relationship exists between margin width and IBTR.[2] A consensus statement has decreed that an adequate margin exists when tumor is not touching ink and recommends this as the standard definition for invasive cancer.[16] A negative margin does *not* imply absence of residual disease within remaining breast tissue, but implies a residual burden of tumor sufficiently low to be controlled with adjuvant treatments (radiotherapy and chemo/hormonal therapies). Local surgery does *not* completely eliminate residual disease burden with local recurrence determined by a combination of surgery, tumor biology, radiation, and systemic therapies.[15] Although histological examination of mastectomy specimens reveals that many tumors are multifocal with additional tumor foci beyond the index lesion, contemporary rates of IBTR after breast-conserving therapy are very low.

SELECTION OF PATIENTS FOR ONCOPLASTIC SURGERY

Most patients deemed eligible for breast-conserving surgery will have a favorable tumor to breast size ratio and be suitable for conventional forms of wide local excision in which the tumor is excised with a 1–2 cm margin of surrounding breast tissue without any need to formally remodel the breast. Though a re-excision may be required in up to one-quarter of cases to achieve microscopically clear radial resection margins, an optimal cosmetic outcome should be attainable in the long term after radiotherapy to the breast.

Conversely, completion mastectomy is clearly indicated in some patients on the basis of tumor size and/or location, multifocality, or patient choice.

Between these two extremes is a "gray area" in which the limits of breast-conserving surgery are being approached, and the patient may be better served with a skin- or nipple-sparing mastectomy and immediate breast reconstruction at the outset.[4] For these patients, there is a risk that the tumor cannot be adequately excised without cosmetic detriment. It becomes progressively more difficult to achieve a good cosmetic outcome as the proportion of breast tissue removed increases. Studies have shown that cosmetic results relate to both breast size and weight of the resected specimen. Though the absolute volume of tissue excised is surgeon dependent, a greater percentage excision is associated with larger tumors. When more than 10%–20% of breast tissue is removed, there is a risk of an unsatisfactory cosmetic result, but relatively modest losses of 5%–10% of breast volume from tumors in cosmetically sensitive areas (medial and inferior quadrants) can adversely affect cosmesis.[17] Validated methods can be used for estimating the percentage of breast volume excised (EPBVE) from mammographic measurements together with the weight of the resected specimen. The EPBVE was a key determinant of cosmetic outcome and patient satisfaction following breast-conserving surgery.[17] Psychological adjustment following breast-conserving surgery correlates with cosmesis, and results of breast-conserving surgery have hitherto failed to meet patient expectations in up to 30% of cases.[18,19] Oncoplastic techniques provide the opportunity for enhancing quality of life by improving cosmetic outcome and psychological well-being.

Though margin status and the presence or absence of an extensive in situ component are the principle determinants of local recurrence, consistent associations have been found for tumors >2 cm in size.[20] For node-positive patients, tumor size exceeding 5 cm was the only risk factor for local recurrence on multivariate analysis.[21] Therefore, it is likely that the risk of relapse would remain high for larger tumors despite adequate surgical clearance. Nonetheless, it may be possible to excise large areas of non-high-grade ductal carcinoma in situ (>4 cm) with clear margins and partially reconstruct the breast with autologous tissue replacement. Age less than 35 years and family history of breast cancer are additional factors which must be considered when selecting patients for either oncoplastic surgery with a high EPBVE or skin-sparing mastectomy with whole breast reconstruction (higher risk of local recurrence or de novo cancer risk). Though it may not be feasible in routine clinical practice to formally estimate the EPBVE from radiological measurements of tumor and breast size, MRI assessment of all patients is advisable. This can confirm unifocality or exclude multifocal disease involving different quadrants. Where imaging is equivocal and tumor parameters are borderline for breast-conserving surgery, it may be preferable to undertake a two-stage procedure. Initial "wide" local excision of tumor permits full histopathological evaluation with assessment of margins. A definitive oncoplastic procedure can subsequently be carried out either 2–3 weeks later or following radiotherapy to the breast. A one-stage procedure is optimal and avoids any technical difficulties relating to the sequelae of previous surgery and radiotherapy (scarring, fibrosis). There are less likely to be problems with skin viability when completion mastectomy is undertaken after simple excision of tumor compared with a more complex oncoplastic procedure with parenchymal undermining and transposition.

TECHNIQUES OF ONCOPLASTIC SURGERY

Oncoplastic surgery in the context of partial breast reconstruction encompasses both volume replacement and volume displacement techniques.[4] The former imports additional tissue in the form of a flap and attempts to compensate for loss of volume from surgical ablation. By contrast, the latter rearranges the remaining breast tissue using methods of glandular advancement which serve to redistribute the parenchyma and minimize the impact of wide local excision. In effect, the volume loss is absorbed over a wider area without concomitant reshaping of the breast. Volume displacement surgery is less extensive than for autologous tissue transfer and there is no donor site morbidity. However, the reconstructed breast is of smaller overall volume and a symmetrization procedure on the contralateral side is often required. This applies particularly to therapeutic mammoplasty where tumor excision is incorporated into a standard or modified reduction procedure.

Volume displacement represents the simplest option for partial breast reconstruction and is usually preferred over techniques for volume replacement which involve more extensive surgery with harvesting of a myocutaneous (e.g., latissimus dorsi) or subcutaneous (e.g., thoracodorsal/intercostal artery perforator) flap. These flaps cannot subsequently be used for whole breast reconstruction should the patient develop local recurrence and require mastectomy. Volume displacement techniques are only possible in patients with medium to large breasts, whereas replacement techniques are suited to small breasted women. The choice of method is determined by both the breast volume and the size of the surgical cavity for infill.

CONCLUSION

The development of oncoplastic surgery and partial breast reconstruction is a natural evolution in the application of breast-conserving surgery to management of breast cancer. Nonetheless, these techniques remain contentious and careful selection of patients is crucial. Partial breast reconstruction should not be attempted in patients who are not amenable to breast-conserving surgery from an oncological perspective and for whom mastectomy is warranted. Oncoplastic intervention can facilitate wide surgical clearance of a tumor and genuinely improve a patient's cosmetic outcome where larger resections are required. The techniques should be integrated with ablative breast surgery to avoid emergence of a "breast cripple." However, they can be employed to correct deformities resulting from previous breast-conserving surgery combined with radiotherapy. Alternatively, partial breast reconstruction can be done as a planned delayed procedure (before or after radiotherapy). Cross-specialty training opportunities are fostering increasing numbers of oncoplastic breast surgeons and those surgeons without oncoplastic competencies should work cooperatively with plastic surgeons to provide a comprehensive service. Notwithstanding surgical expertise, these techniques are relevant to a limited proportion of patients and should only be offered in units managing large numbers of breast cancer patients.[22]

The indications for formal volume replacement and displacement surgery in the context of breast-conserving surgery need clarification. Ongoing audit and evaluation will in time provide information on cosmetic results together with psychological and oncological outcomes which will guide patient selection and management.

REFERENCES

1. Benson JR, Teo K. Breast cancer local therapy: What is its effect on mortality? *World J Surg* 2012; 1432–2323.
2. Singletary SE. Surgical margins in patients with early-stage breast cancer treated with breast conservation therapy. *Am J Surg* 2002; 184: 383–393.
3. Down SK, Jha PK, Burger A, Hussein MI. Oncological advantages of oncoplastic breast conserving surgery in treatment of early breast cancer. *Breast J* 2013; 19(1): 56–63.
4. Benson JR, Shamim AM. Volume replacement and displacement techniques in oncoplastic surgery. *Adv Breast Cancer* 2008; 1–8.
5. Halsted WS. The results of radical operations for the cure of cancer of the breast performed at the Johns Hopkins hospital from June 1889 to January 1894. *Ann Surg* 1898; 20: 497–455.
6. Halsted CP, Benson JR, Jatoi I. A historical account of breast cancer surgery: Beware of local recurrence but be not radical. *Future Oncol* 2014; 10(9): 1649–1657.
7. Fisher B, Anderson, S, Fisher, ER et al. Significance of ipsilateral breast tumour recurrence after lumpectomy. *Lancet* 1991; 338: 327–331.
8. Benson JR, Querci della Rovere G. The biological significance of ipsilateral local recurrence of breast cancer: Determinant or indicator of poor prognosis. *Lancet Oncol* 2002; 3: 45–49.

9. Early Breast Cancer Trialists Collaborative Group (EBCTCG). Effects of radiotherapy and of differences in the extent of surgery for early breast cancer on local recurrence and 15 year survival: An overview of the randomized trials. *Lancet* 2005; 366: 2087–2106.
10. NIH Consensus Statement. Breast cancer screening for women ages 40–49. *NIH Consens State* 1997; 15(1): 1–35.
11. Veronesi U, Cascinelli N, Mariani L et al. Twenty year follow up of a randomized study comparing breast conserving surgery with radical mastectomy for early breast cancer. *N Engl J Med* 2002; 347: 1227–1231.
12. Litiere S, Werutsky G, Fentiman IS et al. Breast-conserving therapy versus mastectomy for stage I–II breast cancer: 20 year follow up of the EORTC 10801 phase 3 randomised trial. *Lancet* 2012; 13(14).
13. Benson JR. Long-term outcome of breast conserving surgery. *Lancet Oncol* 2012; 13(14): 331–333.
14. Fisher B, Joeng J-H, Anderson S et al. Twenty-five year follow up of a randomized trial comparing radical mastectomy, total mastectomy and total mastectomy followed by irradiation. *N Engl J Med* 2002; 347: 567–575.
15. Morrow M, Harris JR, Schnitt SJ. Surgical margins in lumpectomy for breast cancer, bigger is not better. *N Engl J Med* 2012; 367: 79–82.
16. Moran MS, Schnitt SJ, Giuliano AE et al. Society of surgical oncology–American society for radiation oncology consensus guideline on margins for breast-conserving surgery with whole-breast irradiation in stage I and II invasive breast cancer. *J Clin Oncol* 2014; 32(14): 1507–1515.
17. Cochrane R, Valasiadou P, Wilson A et al. Cosmesis and satisfaction after breast conserving surgery correlates with percentage of breast volume excised. *Br J Surg* 2003; 90: 1505–1509.
18. Olivotto IA, Rose MA, Osteen RT et al. Late cosmetic outcome after conservative surgery and radiotherapy: Analysis of causes of cosmetic failure. *In J Rad Oncol Biol Phys* 1989; 17: 747–775.
19. Taylor ME, Perez CA, Halverson KJ et al. Factors influencing cosmetic results after conservation therapy for breast cancer. *In J Rad Oncol Biol Phys* 1995; 31: 753–764.
20. Van Dongen JA, Bartelink H, Fentimen I et al. Factors influencing local relapse and survival and results of salvage treatment after breast conserving treatment in operable breast cancer. EORTC trial 10801 *Eur J Cancer* 1992; 28A: 808–815.
21. Fisher BJ, Perera FE, Cooke AL et al. Long term follow up of axillary node positive breast cancer patients receiving adjuvant systemic therapy alone: Patterns of recurrence. *In J Radiat Oncol Biol Phys* 1997; 38: 541–550.
22. Down SK, Peirera J, Leinster S, Simpson A. Training the oncoplastic surgeon—Current and future perspectives. *Gland Surg* 2013; 2(3): 126–127.

3

Biological reactions to reconstructive materials

AT A GLANCE

Breast reconstructive techniques have been highly reliant on use of non-autologous materials for augmentation purposes. Although these avoid the problems of donor site morbidity, there are potential issues of durability due to innate biological reactions of the host to foreign materials. There is a relatively high incidence of infection and failure leading to extrusion of material. The advent of "medical grade silicone" permitted development of silicone breast implants more than 50 years ago. These have revolutionized breast reconstruction and seem to be making a comeback after earlier concerns about carcinogenic potential together with perceived complexities of autologous tissue reconstruction. Nonetheless, a rare association between breast implant and development of anaplastic large cell lymphoma (ALCL) adjacent to the implant capsule is increasingly being recognized as with testing for specific cell surface markers that are not routinely evaluated when capsules are excised. Presentation with a delayed seroma is now considered a potential form of ALCL. The natural history of ALCL resembles skin lymphoma with a relatively benign course, and capsule resection alone may be sufficient treatment without the need for either chemotherapy or radiotherapy. Use of acellular dermal matrix (ADM) has become the method for augmenting the subpectoral pocket in more than 50% of implant-based breast reconstruction in the United States. Longer-term follow-up is essential to confirm both safety and suitability of these materials, which are relatively expensive and should be used selectively. This section will explore the histological findings in both animal and human studies of biopsy taken from skin, ADM, and implant capsule in both non-irradiated and irradiated patients. Implant-based reconstruction is increasing and technical developments such as cohesive gel implants and ADMs have permitted "direct-to-implant" techniques and expanded the range of options available over the past 5 years. Moreover, preliminary results suggest that ADM may suppress the inflammatory process in the irradiated breast and reduce pseudocapsule formation.

3.1 BIOLOGICAL REACTIONS TO ACELLULAR DERMAL MATRICES (ADMs)

Steven T. Lanier and John Y.S. Kim

What is acellular dermal matrix?

An acellular dermal matrix (ADM) is derived from dermis (usually of human cadaveric or porcine origin) which has been treated by one of various methods to remove antigenic, cellular components while leaving behind the extracellular matrix (ECM). The ECM component of dermis is a three-dimensional construct of secreted products from dermal fibroblasts, including collagen, elastin, laminin, fibronectin, glycosaminoglycans (GAGs), and a host of growth factors. These residual ECM components in ADMs are intended to serve as a regenerative template for functional tissue replacement. These provide the structural framework and chemical stimulus to promote tissue-specific host cell migration, differentiation, and proliferation in a process referred to as "constructive remodeling."[1] Preservation of the ECM ultrastructure, GAG, and growth factor content is an important determinant of ADM integration into the host tissue bed (i.e., the overlying mastectomy skin flap) in the context of breast reconstruction.

Why use acellular dermal matrix?

ADM is a commonly used adjunct in prosthetic-based breast reconstruction with purported benefits that include better anatomic control of implant position, superior inframammary fold definition, faster and fewer expansions to achieve desired breast volume, decreased capsular contracture, and improved aesthetic outcomes. Indications for use of ADM in breast reconstruction have been reviewed in depth elsewhere.[2,3] Proposed indications include: (1) nipple-sparing mastectomy with direct-to-implant reconstruction, (2) large breasts with a significant discordance between the outer mastectomy skin-flap lamella and the inner pectoralis major lamella, (3) anticipated postoperative radiation, (4) non-ptotic breasts, (5) insufficient pectoralis major coverage of the expander/implant, or (6) significant breast skin excess.[3,4] Proposed contraindications include obesity, large breasts, preoperative radiation therapy, current smoking, and thin or poorly vascularized mastectomy skin flaps.[3] While the importance placed on each of these factors in decision-making for ADM varies between surgeons, algorithms to help guide rational patient selection for optimal outcomes have been proposed.[5]

Matrix effects on biologic reactions to acellular dermal matrices

Biologic scaffolds such as ADMs have the potential to undergo "constructive remodeling," whereby cellular migration into the matrix, recruitment and differentiation of stem cells, along with blood vessel and nerve ingrowth can create new functional tissue for reconstructive purposes.[6] The desired functional profile of the biologic scaffold varies by the tissue type it is intended to replace. ADMs are primarily used for structural support and are intended to serve as a regenerative framework to allow ingrowth of fibroblasts and blood vessels to support new collagen deposition.[7] This process is driven by both the ultrastructure of the ECM itself as well as residual growth factors and chemokines retained within the matrix. In addition to these intrinsic properties of ADMs, methods used to decellularize the matrix as well as patient-specific factors have significant effects on the inflammatory response to an implanted ADM and its ultimate degree of integration. We refer broadly to these host/ADM interactions as the "biologic reaction to acellular dermal matrices."

The decellularization process involves a balance between the competing aims of complete removal of antigenic cellular material (nucleic acids, lipids, and certain cellular proteins) and preserving the structure of ECM (collagen, elastin, GAGs, and growth factors), such that it provides an optimal substrate for regeneration of functional host tissues. In contrast to thinner tissues such as intestinal submucosa, the thickness and complexity of dermis requires more intensive mechanical and chemical methods to achieve adequate decellularization.[8] These harsher processing methods have

been shown to result in variable degradation of extracellular matrix structure as well as reduction in GAG and growth factor content. However, failure of a decellularization method to remove major histocompatibility complex (MHC) antigens to below a critical level will result in a failure of matrix remodeling and incorporation.[7] A variety of decellularization methods have been described, including mechanical, chemical, enzymatic, and detergent-based protocols, and often a combination of these.[1] The optimal decellularization protocol depends on tissue type, thickness, shape, cell density, and matrix density and thus will vary by tissue of origin and reconstructive purposes.[1] While decellarization protocols of particular commercially available ADMs are proprietary, they presumably involve some combination of the above-reported methods.

Each method of decellarization has advantages and limitations with respect to these two competing aims. Purely physical methods such as the use of multiple freeze-thaw cycles have the advantage of avoiding chemical agents that can be retained in the matrix, though may not result in sufficient decellularization for thicker tissues such as dermis.[7] Agitation is commonly employed in combination with a chemical agent or detergent to achieve superior decellularization. A drawback of detergent use is that it may weaken the collagen network of the matrix and denature growth factors, and residual detergent left in the ADM can be cytotoxic, inhibiting cell migration and proliferation.[9] Addition of an enzymatic nuclease (DNAse or RNAase) to the above protocols is common in order to remove residual nucleic acids.

While the immune response to allogenic organ transplantation has been well delineated, less is known about the immune response to decellularized matrices.[10] Because many of the components of the ECM are highly conserved across species, they do not result in host immune system activation in the way that residual species-specific cellular components do.[11] Furthermore, the decellularization process itself may alter residual antigenic epitopes such that they do not illicit a host immune response or there may be a threshold concentration that must be met in order to illicit an inflammatory response in host tissue.[11]

As with any implanted material, the biologic reaction to ADM follows what is known as the tissue response continuum, which involves a sequence of host reactions that include tissue injury, blood-material interactions, provisional matrix formation, acute inflammation, chronic inflammation, and a foreign body reaction.[12,13] The tissue response to implanted decellularized ECM is characterized by a similar inflammatory progression that accompanies normal wound healing, with an early neutrophil infiltrate that shifts to a mononucleocyte/macrophage predominance by 72 hours.[14] Acute inflammation is an essential component of all wound healing. However, various factors affect the duration of the acute inflammatory process and subsequently determine whether acute inflammation results in healing and incorporation of a biomaterial (i.e., ingrowth of native parenchymal cells) or encapsulation and failure of integration. Properties of the ADM such as size, shape, and chemical and physical properties are key determinants of the intensity and duration of this acute inflammatory process and whether it resolves through incorporation of the ADM or continues as a chronic, fibrotic inflammatory response.[15]

Histologic studies of implanted porcine small intestinal submucosa derived ECM have shown that it is entirely degraded and replaced by functional host tissue during a process of constructive remodeling.[14] However, the extent to which thicker acellular dermis is similarly degraded and replaced varies. Furthermore, what constitutes complete ADM remodeling in breast reconstruction is not yet well-defined.[16] Histologic evaluation of both human and porcine dermal matrices in a rat abdominal wall model showed incomplete cellular penetration of the full thickness of the material, more than 1-year post-implantation,[17] whereas other studies have reported significant cellular infiltration of ADM at earlier time points.[18]

Important differences in biologic responses to implanted ECM have been demonstrated based on the extent of decellularization. Brown et al.[19] showed in an experimental murine abdominal wall defect model that implantation of a porcine bladder derived ECM with residual cellular components results in a shift of host monocytes to a pro-inflammatory M1 phenotype characterized by IL-1B, IL-6, and tumor necrosis factor alpha (TNFa). In contrast, implantation of decellularized ECM resulted in an M2 phenotype macrophage predominance, which is known to play an important role in tissue repair and regeneration.[19,20] A correlation has been shown between integration and switch to an M2 monocyte phenotype.[21] Thus, a failure of adequate decellularization can result in a pro-inflammatory host state that impairs ADM remodeling and incorporation. Furthermore, inadequately decellularized matrices have been associated with seroma formation in a murine abdominal wall implant model.[10]

While decellularization protocols for commercial matrices remain proprietary, characteristics of certain ADMs have been studied by independent investigators with varied methodology and results. Gilbert and colleagues tested a number of commercial matrices for residual DNA content, only one of which, AlloDerm, was an acellular dermal matrix which had no detectable residual DNA. The same group has recently published a comparison of AlloDerm and AlloMax in a porcine breast tissue expander model, comprehensively evaluating multiple batches of these matrices for thickness, permeability, residual nucleic acid content, a number of growth factors, and cytocompatibility.[18] AlloDerm was found to be thicker and less porous than AlloMax, though AlloDerm contained more basic fibroblast growth factor (bFGF) and vascular endothelial growth factor (VEGF). Neither AlloDerm nor AlloMax was found to be completely decellularized, with both containing cellular components and residual large fragments of dsDNA. AlloDerm retained significantly more dsDNA and was found to contain intact donor cells. With respect to cytocompatibility, fibroblasts showed higher in vitro growth on AlloDerm when compared to AlloMax, whereas the opposite was true for microvascular endothelial cells. Histology of the implanted

ADMs harvested at the 12-week time point showed that AlloMax had greater cellularity than AlloDerm at various anatomic locations, though the type of cells infiltrating the matrices was not delineated. AlloDerm resulted in greater multinuclear giant cell formation. A similar degree of time dependent neovascularization was observed for both matrices. At 12 weeks, AlloDerm was 50% remodeled, whereas AlloMax was 80% remodeled, a difference that was strongly correlated with residual DNA in the matrices. However, the investigators do not correlate these in vivo changes with any metrics of mechanical performance.

Multiple other groups have compared integration of various human cadaveric and procine dermal matrices based on degree of cellular infiltration and neovascularization.[23–27] A review of all of these studies is beyond the scope of this chapter, but no dermal matrix has been established as superior based on this work in both animal models and human biopsy material.

Collagen cross-linking in ADMs has been shown to be another determinant of biologic response. The purpose of cross-linking is to mechanically strengthen the ADM and prevent its degradation.[7,28] Intentional cross-linking occurs through the use of chemical agents such as gluteraldhyde, whereas unintentional cross-linking of collagen can result from processes such as gamma irradiation used to sterilize the ADM.[7] Cross-linked porcine ADM has been shown to undergo less cellular infiltration and neovascularization when compared to non-cross-linked porcine ADM.[29] However, newer cross-linking technologies may offer benefits of improved strength paired with improved biointegration.[30]

Patient and technical factors that influence the biologic reaction to ADM

Incorporation of the biologic is a key determinant of reconstructive success, as failure to do so is the root cause of a number of reconstructive complications. A continuum between poor and good integration of the ADM can be conceptualized (**Figure 3.1**). With poor integration, the resolution of the acute inflammatory process initiated by implantation is with a chronic, smoldering inflammation characterized by a foreign body reaction against the material (**Figure 3.2**).[31] This, in turn, predisposes to seroma formation, which itself can lead to additional complications.[32] In contrast, facile integration leads to resolution of the acute inflammatory phase with tissue remodeling characterized by revascularization of the matrix and a decreased foreign body response.

A number of factors, including both the structure and functionality of the ECM itself and residual effects of the decellularization method employed have been discussed. While these intrinsic qualities of the ADM are of great importance, patient-specific factors represent an additional variable. Importantly, surgeon judgment through judicious patient selection can minimize adverse effects related to this aspect of the biological reaction.

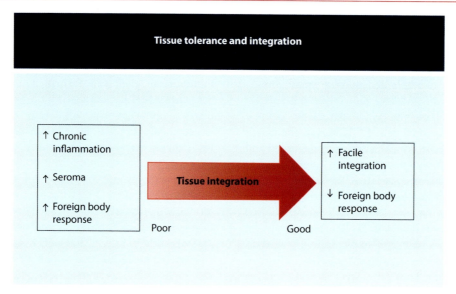

3.1 Continuum of ADM integration: poor integration of the ADM results in chronic inflammation and foreign body response, which predisposes to seroma formation and other resultant complications.

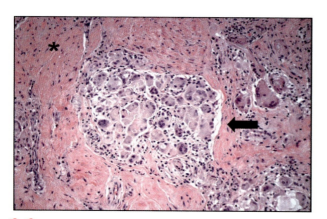

3.2 Histology showing chronic inflammation surrounding unincorporated ADM at second stage breast reconstruction. Arrow indicates encapsulation of the ADM material in a foreign body response. Multinucleated foreign body giant cells are seen immediately adjacent to the arrow. (From Buck, D.W. et al., *Plast. Reconstr. Surg.*, 124, 174e–176e, 2009.)

Recent work by Cavallo and colleagues utilized a semi-quantitative scoring system for matrix remodeling to analyze biopsy ADM samples from 62 patients at a second stage breast reconstruction and attempted to correlate integration of ADM with various patient factors. In a multivariate model, the authors found that pack-year history of smoking, corticosteroid use, and timing of radiation therapy were all associated with statistically significant lower remodeling scores.[33] The BREASTrial, a prospective randomized controlled trial (RCT) comparing AlloDerm to DermaMatrix identified a BMI >30, greater breast mass, larger tissue expander size, and greater intraoperative fill volume as a predictor of poor ADM integration, which was associated with a longer need for drains.[34] All of these measures reflect a larger breast size, which may translate to a mismatch between the outer mastectomy skin envelope lamella and the inner pectoralis/ADM lamella. This mismatch hinders apposition of ADM to the overlying mastectomy skin flap and, in turn, leads to poor integration.

A key theme linking together these risk factors is mastectomy skin-flap vascularity. Flap vascularity is of paramount importance for expedient wound healing and incorporation of a biologic. Compromised flap vascularity has been linked to smoking, peripheral vascular disease, and hypertension, and thus these factors may predispose to poor ADM integration and complications.[35–36] A further challenge to achieving ADM incorporation in breast reconstruction is that both surfaces of the ADM are not in apposition with a vascularized tissue bed.[16] Rather, the deep surface abuts a prosthesis, while the superficial surface is opposed to the mastectomy skin flap, which can be of variable vascular quality.

Excessive fibroblast infiltration as part of the fibrotic response to preoperative radiation could potentially disrupt incorporation of ADM into the surrounding tissue.[3] A combination of chemotherapy and radiation following first stage tissue expander (TE) reconstruction with AlloDerm has been shown to result in a significantly higher percentage of specimens showing gross lack of incorporation at the time of second stage reconstruction.[16] Histologic analysis confirmed that ADM from patients who received chemotherapy had less type I collagen, less cellular infiltration, and less extracellular matrix deposition and neovascularization. Failure of integration can result in a host of complications including infection, seroma, need for explantation, and poor aesthetic outcome. However, in the context of postoperative radiation, ADM can enable an accelerated expansion of the prosthetic pocket to final volume and guard against skin-flap necrosis and reduce rates of explantation.[37]

CONCLUSION

Clinicians and scientists are beginning to understand the individual effects that a host of important ADM characteristics have on ultimate performance in patients and clinical outcomes. An awareness of the basic methodologies of decellularization and the competing needs to fully remove cellular material while preserving ECM structure and growth factor function is essential for practicing surgeons. Moreover, an understanding of the effects of insufficient decellularization on host inflammatory response will enable the surgeon to ask educated questions about properties of these matrices as they become integrated into clinical practice. Data from basic science studies examining matrix composition and integration need to be correlated with clinical outcomes, such as mechanical performance and complication rates. This will yield valuable information that can potentially not only guide clinical decision-making and selection of matrices, but also improvements in matrix production.

REFERENCES

1. Crapo, P. M., et al. (2011). An overview of tissue and whole organ decellularization processes. *Biomaterials* 32(12): 3233–3243.
2. Nahabedian, M. Y. and S. L. Spear (2011). Acellular dermal matrix for secondary procedures following prosthetic breast reconstruction. *Aesthet Surg J* 31(7 Suppl): 38S–50S.
3. Vu, M. M. and J. Y. Kim (2015). Current opinions on indications and algorithms for acellular dermal matrix use in primary prosthetic breast reconstruction. *Gland Surg* 4(3): 195–203.
4. Zhong, T. et al. (2013). The multi centre Canadian acellular dermal matrix trial (MCCAT): Study protocol for a randomized controlled trial in implant-based breast reconstruction. *Trials* 14: 356.
5. Jordan, S. W. et al. (2014). An algorithmic approach for selective acellular dermal matrix use in immediate two-stage breast reconstruction: Indications and outcomes. *Plast Reconstr Surg* 134(2): 178–188.
6. Keane, T. J. et al. (2015). Methods of tissue decellularization used for preparation of biologic scaffolds and in vivo relevance. *Methods* 84: 25–34.
7. Novitsky, Y. W. and M. J. Rosen (2012). The biology of biologics: Basic science and clinical concepts. *Plast Reconstr Surg* 130(5 Suppl 2): 9S–17S.
8. Reing, J. E. et al. (2010). The effects of processing methods upon mechanical and biologic properties of porcine dermal extracellular matrix scaffolds. *Biomaterials* 31(33): 8626–8633.
9. Boone, M. A. et al. (2015). Recellularizing of human acellular dermal matrices imaged by high-definition optical coherence tomography. *Exp Dermatol* 24(5): 349–354.
10. Keane, T. J. et al. (2012). Consequences of ineffective decellularization of biologic scaffolds on the host response. *Biomaterials* 33(6): 1771–1781.
11. Keane, T. J. and S. F. Badylak (2015). The host response to allogeneic and xenogeneic biological scaffold materials. *J Tissue Eng Regen Med* 9(5): 504–511.
12. Anderson, J. M. (2001). Biological responses to materials. *Annu Rev Mater Res* 31: 81–110.
13. Wells, A. et al. (2015). Skin tissue repair: Matrix microenvironmental influences. *Matrix Biol* 49: 25–36.
14. Badylak, S. et al. (2002). Morphologic study of small intestinal submucosa as a body wall repair device. *J Surg Res* 103(2): 190–202.
15. Anderson, J. M. et al. (2008). Foreign body reaction to biomaterials. *Semin Immunol* 20(2): 86–100.
16. Myckatyn, T. M. et al. (2015). The impact of chemotherapy and radiation therapy on the remodeling of acellular dermal matrices in staged, prosthetic breast reconstruction. *Plast Reconstr Surg* 135(1): 43e–57e.
17. Bryan, N. et al. (2014). The in vivo evaluation of tissue-based biomaterials in a rat full-thickness abdominal wall defect model. *J Biomed Mater Res B Appl Biomater* 102(4): 709–720.
18. Carruthers, C. A. et al. (2015). Histologic characterization of acellular dermal matrices in a porcine model of tissue expander breast reconstruction. *Tissue Eng Part A* 21(1–2): 35–44.
19. Brown, B. N. et al. (2012). Macrophage phenotype as a predictor of constructive remodeling following the implantation of biologically derived surgical mesh materials. *Acta Biomater* 8(3): 978–987.
20. Orenstein, S. B. et al. (2010). Activation of human mononuclear cells by porcine biologic meshes in vitro. *Hernia* 14(4): 401–407.
21. Lucke, S. et al. (2015). Acute and chronic local inflammatory reaction after implantation of different extracellular porcine dermis collagen matrices in rats. *Biomed Res Int* 2015: 938059.
22. Gilbert, T. W. et al. (2009). Quantification of DNA in biologic scaffold materials. *J Surg Res* 152(1): 135–139.
23. Glasberg, S. B. and D. Light (2012). AlloDerm and Strattice in breast reconstruction: A comparison and techniques for optimizing outcomes. *Plast Reconstr Surg* 129(6): 1223–1233.
24. Chauviere, M. V. et al. (2014). Comparison of AlloDerm and AlloMax tissue incorporation in rats. *Ann Plast Surg* 73(3): 282–285.
25. Richter, G. T. et al. (2007). Histological comparison of implanted cadaveric and porcine dermal matrix grafts. *Otolaryngol Head Neck Surg* 137(2): 239–242.
26. De Silva, G. S. et al. (2014). Lack of identifiable biologic behavior in a series of porcine mesh explants. *Surgery* 156(1): 183–189.
27. Sandor, M. et al. (2014). Comparative host response of 2 human acellular dermal matrices in a primate implant model. *Eplasty* 14: e7.
28. Carlson, T. L. et al. (2013). Effect of cross-linked and non-cross-linked acellular dermal matrices on the expression of mediators involved in wound healing and matrix remodeling. *Plast Reconstr Surg* 131(4): 697–705.
29. Mestak, O. et al. (2014). Comparison of cross-linked and non-cross-linked acellular porcine dermal scaffolds for long-term full-thickness hernia repair in a small animal model. *Eplasty* 14: e22.
30. Lee, J. H. et al. (2015). Characterization and tissue incorporation of cross-linked human acellular dermal matrix. *Biomaterials* 44: 195–205.
31. Buck, D. W. et al. (2009). Diagnostic dilemma: Acellular dermis mimicking a breast mass after immediate tissue expander breast reconstruction. *Plast Reconstr Surg* 124(1): 174e–176e.
32. Kim. J. Y. S. and C. M. Connor. (2012). Focus on technique: Two stage implant-based breast reconstruction. *Plast Reconstr Surg* 130(5S-2S): 104S–115S.

33. Cavallo, J. A. et al. (2015). Remodeling characteristics and collagen distributions of biologic scaffold materials biopsied from postmastectomy breast reconstruction sites. *Ann Plast Surg* 75(1): 74–83.
34. Mendenhall, S. D. et al. (2015). The BREASTrial Stage II: ADM breast reconstruction outcomes from the time of implant exchange to 3 months post-op. *Plast Reconstr Surg* 136(4 Suppl): 111–112.
35. Seth, A. K. et al. (2011). Additive risk of tumescent technique in patients undergoing mastectomy with immediate reconstruction. *Ann Surg Oncol* 18(11): 3041–3046.
36. McCarthy, C. M. et al. (2008). Predicting complications following expander/implant breast reconstruction: An outcomes analysis based on preoperative clinical risk. *Plast Reconstr Surg* 121(6): 1886–1892.
37. Spear, S. L. et al. (2012). Two-stage prosthetic breast reconstruction using AlloDerm including outcomes of different timings of radiotherapy. *Plast Reconstr Surg* 130(1): 1–9.

3.2 BREAST IMPLANT–ASSOCIATED ANAPLASTIC LARGE CELL LYMPHOMA

Mark W. Clemens

Approximately 1.5 million prostheses are implanted annually worldwide for breast augmentation and reconstructive indications.[1] In 2011, and updated in 2016, the United States Food and Drug Administration (FDA) released a safety communication stating, "Women with breast implants may have a very small but increased risk of developing anaplastic large cell lymphoma (ALCL) in the scar capsule adjacent to an implant."[2] This warning was based upon case reports dating back to a seminal case described by Keech and Creech in 1997.[3] Breast implant-associated anaplastic large cell lymphoma (BI-ALCL) is a rare malignancy arising in an effusion or scar capsule surrounding a breast prosthesis.[4] There are 118 individual case reports and nearly 200 pathologically confirmed cases to date, although the incidence, etiology, and predisposing risk factors have not been fully established.[5]

Lymphoma is a cancer of the immune system developing from lymphocytes and is the most common malignancy of the blood and broadly includes Hodgkin's lymphoma, non-Hodgkin's lymphoma (NHL), and a variety of lymphoproliferative disorders.[6] In the United States, among approximately 68,000 cases of NHL, which include an estimated incidence of purely T-cell NHL diagnoses of 17,000, there have been almost 2000 cases of ALCL.[7,8] Systemic ALCL is further classified by either the expression or absence of the anaplastic lymphoma kinase (ALK) tyrosine kinase receptor gene translocation and carries a 5-year median overall survival between 30% and 50%. Standard first-line chemotherapy is cyclophosphamide, hydroxydaunorubicin, vincristine, and prednisone. When treated with chemotherapy, ALK positive ALCL has a higher overall 5-year survival rate than systemic ALK-ALCL (58% vs 34%, respectively).[9]

Recognition of BI-AlCl

Since the FDA safety communication in 2011, a number of major government agencies around the world have developed BI-ALCL statements which include: the National Comprehensive Cancer Network in 2012,[10] World Health Organization and the International Agency for Research on Cancer in 2014,[11] together with the United States National Cancer Institute,[12] and the French National Cancer Institute (Agence Nationale de Sécurité du Médicament) in 2015.[13] A Dutch study found a positive association for the development of ALCL in women with breast implants compared to those without an implant with an odds ratio of 18.2 (95% confidence interval, 2.1–156.8). Based upon these data, the authors estimated an incidence for BI-ALCL cases of 0.1–0.3 per 100,000 per annum among women with prostheses.

All reported cases of BI-ALCL are purely T-cell, ALK negative, and express the CD30 cell surface protein.[14] Most cases are diagnosed during implant revision surgery performed for late onset (>12 months), persistent seroma and may be associated with symptoms of pain, breast lumps, swelling, or breast asymmetry. The number of BI-ALCL cases reported in primary augmentation and reconstruction for breast cancer or prophylaxis are nearly equivalent. All major implant manufacturers have been involved with BI-ALCL cases. Nonetheless, no risk factors have been clearly identified for ALCL, although many theories have been presented which are predicated on the predominance of textured implant cases. These include a subclinical biofilm leading to T-cell hyperplasia, response to particulate from textured implants with repeated capsular abrasion, genetic predisposition, or an autoimmune etiology. However, none of these observations have been confirmed in formal epidemiological studies.[15,16] Further research is required to identify modifiable risk factors, susceptible populations, and optimal screening and surveillance modalities.

Management of suspicious and confirmed cases

The mean age for BI-ALCL is 52 years old (range 28–87 years) with a median period of 9 years (range 1–32 years) between implantation and lymphoma diagnosis.[17] Any seroma occurring more than 1 year after implantation which is not readily explainable by infection or trauma should be considered suspicious for disease. One-third of patients present with a mass, which may indicate a more aggressive clinical course. Ultrasound has a sensitivity and specificity of 84% and 75%, respectively, for BI-ALCL and can be used as a screening tool for suspected cases. Moreover, in combination with positron emission–computed tomography (PET-CT) for confirmed cases, ultrasound can be used to determine local extent and for surveillance of disease.[18] For any suspected case of BI-ALCL, periprosthetic fluid aspirate should be sent to pathology for cytologic evaluation and CD30 immunohistochemistry, with clear details of clinical history and a stated intent to "rule out BI-ALCL" (**Figure 3.2.1**).

Patients with biopsy proven BI-ALCL must be referred to a lymphoma oncologist. Surgical treatment of BI-ALCL requires complete tumor ablation, which includes removal of the implant, complete removal of any disease mass with negative margins, and total capsulectomy.[19] Because an implant capsule may drain to multiple regional lymph node basins, there does not appear to be a role for targeted sentinel lymph node biopsy in the treatment of BI-ALCL. Fine-needle aspiration of enlarged lymph nodes can yield a false-negative and therefore excisional biopsies should be performed of any suspicious lymph nodes. Involvement of a multidisciplinary oncological team is strongly recommended for optimal surgical control and overall management. An incomplete resection or inadequate local surgical control may subsequently be compensated for by adjuvant treatments such as chemotherapy and radiation therapy,

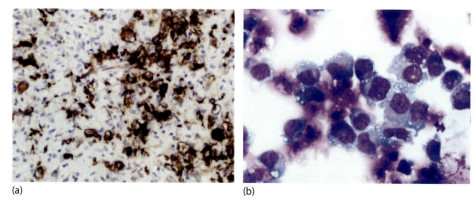

3.2.1 Wright Giemsa staining from a malignant effusion of BI-ALCL demonstrating pleomorphic cells with horseshoe-shaped nuclei, nuclear folding, and abundant vacuolated cytoplasm (a). CD30 Immunohistochemistry in tissue section of BI-ALCL (b).

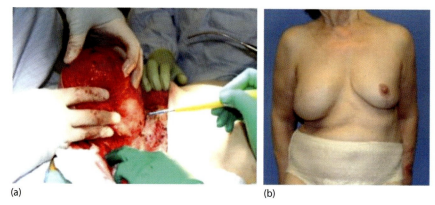

3.2.2 Clinical image of a 77-year-old woman who received a right breast reconstruction for breast cancer with a textured silicone implant. Eleven years after implantation, she developed swelling of the right breast of recent onset which was aspirated and diagnosed as BI-ALCL. (a) Patient received a total capsulectomy and implant removal. (b) Patient received no further adjunctive treatments and is currently disease free.

whereas complete surgical resection may be definitive treatment in the majority of cases (**Figure 3.2.2**). Surgery should be performed with strict oncologic techniques including use of specimen orientation sutures, placement of surgical clips within the tumor bed, and use of fresh instruments if performing a contralateral explantation. At this time, the FDA does not recommend screening or prophylactic implant removal for asymptomatic patients or patients with familial susceptibility cancer. Radiation therapy has also been used for local control of disease, and further research is required to determine specific indications for adjunctive treatments. Patients with a breast mass have a worse overall and progression-free survival (P = 0.052 and P = 0.03, respectively). At this time, it is unclear whether the association of a mass and an adverse prognosis reflects a more aggressive variant, more progressive disease, or even a consequence of inadequate surgical ablation. Advances in the treatment of T-cell lymphomas provide an opportunity for treatment of BI-ALCL refractory to surgical therapy alone. Brentuximab vedotin is a novel anti-CD30 monoclonal antibody that has changed the management of systemic ALCL with a reported objective response rate of 86% and complete remission rate of 59% in relapsed or refractory systemic ALCL.[20] The median overall survival for BI-ALCL is 12 years (median follow-up, 2 years; range, 0–14 years).[19]

The informed consent process for breast implant surgery should include the risk of BI-ALCL.[21] The United States FDA recommends that all confirmed cases of BI-ALCL be reported to the PROFILE registry (Patient Registry and Outcomes For breast Implants and anaplastic large cell Lymphoma etiology and Epidemiology) developed by the American Society of Plastic Surgeons (www.thepsf.org/PROFILE).

Timely diagnosis of BI-ALCL will depend on the millions of women with breast implants having access to heightened surveillance, knowledgeable physicians, together with appropriate investigation and medical care. BI-ALCL is a rare lymphoma associated with breast implants although the exact etiology and pathogenesis remain unclear. Accurate diagnosis and complete surgical treatment is important for definitive treatment of patients.

REFERENCES

1. International Society of Aesthetic Plastic Surgery 2015 Global Statistics Retrieved from http://www.isaps.org accessed January 1, 2016.
2. U.S. Food and Drug Administration. (2011). Anaplastic large cell lymphoma (ALCL) In *Women with Breast Implants: Preliminary FDA Findings and Analyses*. Retrieved from www.fda.gov accessed January 15, 2016.
3. Keech JA. and Creech BJ. Anaplastic T-cell lymphoma in proximity to a saline-filled breast implant. *Plas Reconstr Surg* 1997; 100(2):554–555.
4. Kim B, Roth C, Chung KC et al. Anaplastic large cell lymphoma and breast implants: A systematic review. *Plas Reconstr Surg* 2011; 127:2141–2150.
5. Brody GS, Deapen D, Taylor CR. Anaplastic large cell lymphoma occurring in women with breast implants: Analysis of 173 cases. *Plast Reconstr Surg* 2015; 135(3):695–705.
6. General Information About Adult Non-Hodgkin Lymphoma. *Nat Cancer Inst* website accessed November 20, 2014.
7. SEER Data Fact Sheets: Non-Hodgkin Lymphoma website, http://seer.cancer.gov/statfacts/html/nhl.html accessed November 10, 2014.
8. Altekruse SF, Kosary CL, Krapcho M et al. (Eds.). *SEER Cancer Statistics Review, 1975–2007*. Bethesda, MD: National Cancer Institute, 2010.
9. Savage KJ, Harris NL, Vose JM et al. ALK- anaplastic large-cell lymphoma is clinically and immunophenotypically different from both ALK+ ALCL and peripheral T-cell lymphoma, not otherwise specified: Report from the international peripheral T-cell lymphoma project. *Blood* 2008; 111:5496–5504.
10. NCCN Clinical Practice Guidelines in Oncology (NCCN Guidelines®) for Non-Hodgkin's Lymphomas. January 25, 2012. www.nccn.org, accessed August 1, 2015.
11. IARC Monographs on the Evaluation of Carcinogenic Risks to Humans. Report of the Advisory Group to Recommend Priorities for IARC Monographs during 2015–2019, April 18, 2014. http://monographs.iarc.fr, accessed August 1, 2015.
12. US National Cancer Institute, Treatment for health professionals. http://www.cancer.gov/, accessed August 1, 2015.
13. Institut National du Cancer. *Agence Nationale de Sécurité du Médicament. Breast Implant Associated Anaplastic Large Cell Lymphoma: Expert Opinion*, February 1, 2015.
14. Clemens MW, Miranda RN. Commentary on: Lymphomas associated with breast implants: A review of the literature: Table 1. *Aesthet Surg J.* 2015; 35(5):545–547.
15. Hu H, Aljohani K, Almatroudi A et al. Bacterial biofilm infection detected in breast implant associated anaplastic large cell lymphoma. *Plast Reconstr Surg* 2016; 137(6):1659–1669.
16. Yoshida SH, Swan S, Teuber SS, Gershwin ME. Silicone breast implants: Immunotoxic and epidemiologic issues. *Life Sci* 1995; 56(16):1299–1310.
17. Miranda RN, Aladily TN, Prince HM et al. Breast implant-associated anaplastic large-cell lymphoma: Long-term follow-up of 60 patients. *J Clin Oncol* 2014; 32:114–120.
18. Beatriz EA, Miranda RN, Rauch GM et al. Breast implant-associated anaplastic large cell lymphoma: Sensitivity, specificity and findings of imaging studies in 44 patients. *Breast Cancer Res Treat* 2014; 147(1):1–14.
19. Clemens MW, Medeiros LJ, Butler CE et al. Complete surgical excision is essential for the management of patients with breast implant-associated anaplastic large-cell lymphoma. *J Clin Onc* 2015; 34(2):160–168.
20. Younes A, Bartlett NL, Leonard JP et al. Brentuximab vedotin for relapsed CD30positive lymphomas. *N Engl J Med* 2010; 363:1812–1821.
21. Clemens MW, Butler CE, Miranda R. Breast implant informed consent should include the risk of ALCL. *Plast Reconstr Surg* 2016; 137(4):1117–1122.

3.3 BIOLOGICAL REACTIONS TO AUTOLOGOUS FAT GRAFTING

Animesh Patel and Charles M. Malata

Introduction

Autologous transplantation of fat is a surgical technique that has been used for over a century. Following early reports, concerns emerged regarding the survival and longevity of fat grafts, which led to a decrease in popularity. The advent of liposuction in the 1980s provided a novel method for harvesting of fat grafts and there has been a resurgence of interest in the potential of fat transplantation. Further refinements in techniques for harvesting, processing, and injecting fat grafts have subsequently led to improvements in rates of graft survival, and autologous fat grafting now constitutes a significant component of the reconstructive surgeon's armamentarium. However, there is no universally accepted method for harvesting and processing these grafts and many areas of controversy remain. Recent advances in understanding the physiology of adipose tissue and appreciation of fat as a source of stem cells have stimulated continued interest and generated further controversy in this field.

To date, autologous fat grafting has been utilized in many cosmetic and reconstructive procedures of the breast, some of which are listed in **Table 3.3.1**. However, there is lingering controversy relating to the specific applications of fat grafting following either surgery to the native breast or after breast cancer surgery (mastectomy or wide local excision).

Overview of fat biology

EMBRYOLOGY

In humans, fat development begins in utero with adipose tissue becoming detectable between the 14th and 16th weeks of gestation. From the 2nd trimester onward, mesenchymal cell aggregation occurs, and the intricate link between adipogenesis and angiogenesis becomes established.

At this stage, primitive blood vessels and capillary networks develop around which mesenchymal cells, which are derived from pluripotent embryonic stem cells, differentiate into preadipocytes. As development continues, the preadipocyte differentiates into an immature adipose cell, which subsequently differentiates into the mature adipocyte. Macroscopic fat lobules are made up of aggregations of these adipocytes. During the 3rd trimester, lobules are deposited in anatomical locations typical of a newborn, and these increase in size throughout fetal life.

FUNCTION

There are two subtypes of adipose tissue—composed of either brown or white fat. Brown fat is abundant in the newborn and

---

Table 3.3.1 Potential uses of autologous fat grafting in cosmetic and reconstructive breast surgery

- Breast augmentation for micromastia or breast atrophy
- Deformity post-breast augmentation
  - To cover palpable or visible implants
- Correction of tuberous breast deformity
- Correction of Poland's deformities
- Correction of post-lumpectomy deformities
- Postmastectomy reconstruction
- As an adjunct to other forms of breast reconstruction
  - To fill dents/improve contour following implant or flap-based reconstruction
  - To provide extra volume following previous reconstruction
  - To minimize capsular contracture following implant-based reconstruction
  - To improve radiotherapy-induced skin and soft tissue changes
- Nipple reconstruction

---

its main function is heat insulation and thermoregulation. Brown fat is gradually replaced by white fat with maturation.

The functions of fat include:

- Triglyceride storage
- Free fatty acid release
- Oestrogen synthesis
- Steroid hormone storage
- Secretion of leptin
- Exocrine secretion of peptides involved in adipocyte metabolism
- Source of adipose-derived stem cells (ASCs)

MORPHOLOGY OF ADIPOSE TISSUE AND THE ADIPOCYTE

Adipocyte differentiation begins with the pluripotent stem cell, which gives rise to a mesenchymal precursor cell, a cell that has the potential to differentiate into one of a variety of cell lines, such as bone, muscle, cartilage, or fat. Given the correct molecular and cellular events, the precursor differentiates into a preadipocyte, which will then terminally differentiate into the mature adipocyte. Individual adipocytes are tightly packed together by the colloid osmotic pressure of the interstitium.

The preadipocyte is a flat cell with a central nucleus and as it differentiates, small lipid droplets start to accumulate within it. As the cell matures further, the lipid droplets become larger and coalesce, resulting in the appearance of the terminally differentiated adipocyte. The mature adipocyte is 95% triglyceride by weight and is made up of a large, central lipid droplet, surrounded by a very thin layer of cytoplasm enclosed in a cell membrane.

With increased dietary fat intake, the adipocyte converts circulating glucose into fatty acids and stores them as triglyceride in the lipid droplet. When dietary intake is low, the converse occurs, and stored triglyceride is broken down by hormone-sensitive lipases and released as fatty acids and glycerol.

Adipose tissue is found throughout the adult body, and there is significant inter-individual variation in its anatomical distribution. It is present in abundance in the subcutis and bowel mesenteries. Indeed it is the former's prevalence at specific sites, such as the abdomen, buttocks, and thighs, that provides the source for the autologous fat graft. Adipose tissue blood flow and metabolism also vary according to anatomical location, through processes that are regulated by hormones involved in lipid metabolism-some of which are secreted by the adipocyte itself. These include adenosine, angiotensin II, and prostacyclin.

In addition to the adipocyte, the stromal vascular fraction of adipose tissue contains a number of cell lineages including fibroblasts, smooth muscle cells, endothelial cells, ASCs, and immune modulators such as monocytes and lymphocytes. Fat lobules are comprised of all these cells held together by a framework of extracellular matrix. The lobules that make up adipose tissue are separated by fibrous septae, and each lobule constitutes an independent morphological and angiological unit, containing thousands of individual adipocytes. Larger branches of blood vessels course within the septae, and an axial artery divides into a fine network of capillaries which encircle individual adipocytes.

An appreciation of this intricate vascular arrangement is important for understanding the pathophysiological principles of autologous fat grafting.

What is a fat graft and how does it "take?"

A graft is defined as a block of tissue that is completely separated from its native blood supply and transferred to a new site where it is reliant upon its recipient bed for nutrition and revascularization. If these processes are successful and the graft survives, it is said to have "taken."

The process by which a fat graft takes can be summarized as follows:

- *Ischemia and plasma imbibition*
  Immediately after the fat graft is harvested, it is subject to a period of ischemia, during which blood vessels within the graft collapse and metabolism temporarily slows (it may even cease depending on ischemia time). Adipocytes have high rates of metabolic activity, approaching those of skeletal muscle, and therefore ischemia is poorly tolerated. In the first few days after graft transfer, cells at the recipient site infiltrate the surgical site during a phase of acute inflammation. Subsequently, the graft undergoes a process of plasma imbibition—the fat graft "drinks" or imbibes plasma from the recipient bed with direct diffusion of nutrients from the recipient plasma into the graft.

- *Revascularization*
  After about 4 days, blood flow resumes within the smaller vessels of the graft, as a likely consequence of spontaneous anastomosis between recipient and graft blood vessels (a process which commences after 48 hours). Formation of new blood vessels (neovascularization) from the recipient bed into the graft occurs concurrently. In vivo, it is likely that both of these processes contribute to initial graft revascularization, although the process of neovascularization may take longer to establish. Irrespective of pathophysiological mechanisms, adipocytes and preadipocytes are very sensitive to the period of ischemia prior to vascularization becoming re-established and any intervention promoting vascularization will enhance graft survival.

- *Proliferation*
  Once small vessel revascularization has occurred, the fat graft undergoes a proliferative phase, characterized by larger vessel vascularization and subsequent proliferation of existing adipocytes and preadipocytes with re-differentiation of de-differentiated adipocytes and ASCs.

GRAFT SURVIVAL

Lyndon Peer proposed the "cell survival theory" which suggests that after a period of ischemia following graft harvest, some adipocytes will die, others will survive as adipocytes, while the remaining will undergo de-differentiation.[1,2] If the fat graft survives, the tissue will revascularize and cells will either continue to survive as adipocytes or those that have de-differentiated will re-differentiate into adipocytes. Although not appreciated at the time this theory was proposed, the presence of ASCs in the graft will further enhance graft viability by improving revascularization and healing. Moreover, ASCs themselves can differentiate into new adipocytes.

Technical aspects

When harvested appropriately, intact parcels of fat will generally contain intact viable fat lobules. Bearing in mind each fat lobule can be regarded as a single angio-biological unit of tissue, it follows that fat grafts are more likely to survive when "...their vessels and septi intact...." To minimize damage, gentle atraumatic handling of fat grafts at each stage from the time of harvest to placement at the recipient site is crucial. Although a variety of techniques have been used over the years, the most common method of autologous fat transfer is that described by Sydney Coleman, and the technical aspects of this technique are discussed below.[3,4]

- *Donor site selection*
  There is no consensus as to what constitutes an ideal donor site and most anatomical sites can potentially be used depending on the quantity of fat required, the patient's body habitus, and ease of accessibility.
  Adipose tissue has biochemical and morphological characteristics that are anatomically site-specific. In particular,

adipose tissue from the thigh area (referred to as the riding breeches area by Illouz[5]) has a greater capability to acquire lipid and is more resistant to biochemical breakdown due to increased expression of anti-lipolytic α-2 receptors which block triglyceride catabolism. In addition to having the highest lipogenic activity, thigh and buttock adipocytes tend to be of larger cell size on average. The existence of fewer connective tissue septae renders the adipose tissue relatively less vascular and grafts harvested therefrom will contain less extravasated blood. Fat harvested from the anterior abdominal wall (especially the paraumbilical area) is more vascular and may have significantly more blood contamination by comparison with other sites.

Patient positioning during the procedure will also influence the choice of donor site, and many surgeons will opt to harvest fat from the abdomen and thighs, as this does not involve turning the patient mid-procedure.

It is well recognized that fat retains *donor site memory*. When an abdominal (deep inferior epigastric perforator [DIEP] or transverse rectus abdominis myocutaneous [TRAM]) flap is used to reconstruct a breast, the reconstructed breast will respond to nutritional changes in a similar way to abdominal tissue. Thus, weight gain or loss will be reflected in the reconstructed breast as if the tissue had remained on the abdominal wall. Likewise, when transferred to a recipient site, a fat graft will retain the metabolic and storage properties of the donor site. Hence, choice of donor site can have a significant impact on the subsequent behavior of any successfully transplanted fat graft.

Surgeons should be mindful that areas of the body that are known by the patient to be stable in response to dietary changes of fat intake should be resistant to change if the patient gains or loses weight subsequently. Fat grafts from these particular areas may have better longevity.

- *Harvest by lipoaspiration*
Lipoaspiration is the favored technique for harvesting fat grafts. Large volumes of fat cells can be harvested and, in most patients, there is an abundance of donor sites to choose from. Furthermore, the procedure can be carried out under local anesthetic with minimal risk to the patient. As harvesting is done by liposuction, donor site skin incisions are small (<1 cm) and larger incisions (with associated scarring) required for open excision of fat are unnecessary. A significant advantage of liposuction is the simultaneous contouring of the donor area, which can result in cosmetic improvement at this site.
- *Effect of infiltration solution on lipoaspirate*
Tumescent infiltration of the donor areas with a mixture of local anesthetic and adrenaline prior to harvest is common practice.

1. Lidocaine
Lidocaine and other amide local anesthetics have been shown to improve wound healing by reducing leukocyte migration and activation and also reducing release of toxic metabolites such as oxygen free

radicals. On the other hand, lidocaine has a negative effect on glucose transport, lipolysis, and growth of adipocytes in culture. Although some authors choose not to use lidocaine, the effects of infiltration are reversed by washing of cells, and adipocytes can rapidly recover function and growth irrespective of the duration of lidocaine exposure. The main advantage of local anesthetic is provision of analgesia to the donor area.

2. Adrenaline
The presence of blood (and serum) in the lipoaspirate is thought to have a negative impact on adipocyte viability. These factors evoke a recipient site inflammatory response and are known to be associated with an increased risk of infection and ultimately graft failure. The vasoconstrictive action of adrenaline will help in this regard, although it might be argued that adrenaline will further constrict the vasculature of the adipocyte during transfer and reduce graft take (although this has not been shown in practice).

- *Effect of suction on lipoaspirate*
Liposuction employs a negative pressure mechanical suction, which contrasts with Coleman's technique of manual aspiration with a blunt-tip cannula connected to a syringe. At low suction pressures, there is little difference in adipocyte viability between fat harvested by manual or mechanical suction. However, at the levels of negative pressure that are conventionally used for liposuction, adipocyte viability and survival rates fall significantly following transfer. Therefore, techniques of manual aspiration or mechanical suction at low pressures are preferred.

Coleman's technique involves using a 10 mL syringe connected to an aspiration cannula. The plunger on the syringe is withdrawn 2–3 mL and suction pressure maintained while the surgeon harvests the graft. If the plunger is withdrawn maximally, pressures can reach those associated with mechanical suction, and this maneuver is best avoided. Gentle syringe aspiration minimizes trauma to the harvested fat, and this is a crucial aspect in maximizing graft survival.

- *Choice of lipoaspiration cannula and syringe*
Pierre Fournier[6] pioneered the use of needle and syringe for fat grafting in the early 1990s. Although various designs of cannula have been described since, the crucial factors are the diameter of the shaft lumen and design of the tip.

Larger liposuction cannula or needles are associated with increased graft viability, whereas narrower gauge instruments are associated with increased adipocyte damage. Although a sharp tip will pass through donor tissues more easily, there is an increased risk of damage to adipocytes, and the surgeon must also be aware of potential accidental injury to neurovascular structures. These problems can be avoided by routine use of blunt-tip cannula.

Coleman describes placing a blunt-tip cannula (2 mm internal diameter) into the donor site via 3 mm skin incisions. The cannula is attached to a 10 mL syringe with a Luer-Lock. Steady withdrawal of the plunger generates negative pressure and a gentle to-and-fro or a curetting motion harvests fat into the holes of the cannula, with subsequent passage into the syringe barrel. This is then disconnected and processed according to the surgeon's preference.

- *Processing of harvested fat*

Whether manual or mechanical suction is used, the lipoaspirate is a heterogeneous mixture of viable adipocytes, non-viable cells, infiltration fluid, oil, blood, and debris. To maximize the chance of graft survival, elements other than viable adipocytes need to be removed in order to minimize any inflammatory reaction at the recipient site.

The sedimentation technique involves allowing the lipoaspirate to stand whereby the fat separates from blood and debris under the force of gravity (different densities). Fournier describes placing syringes of harvested fat vertically in a test tube holder and allowing the fat to separate into two distinct layers of adipose tissue above and a "hydrohematic fraction" below. The latter is discarded after decanting off the adipose tissue in the upper fraction and the lipoaspirate is washed further with saline. This is repeated until the fat is bloodless, and then it is ready for use.

Some surgeons choose to wash the lipoaspirate in physiological solutions. However, this is not practiced widely as irrigating the harvested fat may cause mechanical and osmotic trauma.

The current method adopted as choice for purifying the lipoaspirate is centrifugation. It is important that the surgeon is familiar with the basic principles before using this technique. If high centrifugal forces are generated, the viability of fat grafts can be compromised and it is suggested that a force of 1200 g is sufficient to separate viable adipocytes while at the same time minimizing cellular damage. Coleman's technique involves centrifugation at 3000 rpm for 3 minutes, using a small centrifuge that generates a force of 1286 g. It must be remembered that centrifuges with larger diameters may be associated with higher centrifugal forces, reaching levels that could potentially damage adipocytes. As explained by Newtonian mechanics, when using larger centrifuges, the frequency of revolutions will need to be decreased to reduce the centrifugal force generated. Many centrifuges only have adjustable settings for speed and, hence, to make the necessary calculations of appropriate force, it is important to know the relationship between revolutions per minute and relative centrifugal force. This is given by the formula

$$F = (1.118 \times 10^{-5})RS^2$$

where R is the radius (from the center of rotor to the sample, in centimeters), S is the speed (in revolutions per minute), and F is the centrifugal force, in g. Care must be taken in ensuring appropriate settings, as excessive forces are associated with decreased adipocyte (>4000 g), and ASC (>3000 g) viability.

Typically, centrifugation separates the lipoaspirate into three distinct fractions, according to density. The least dense component of the lipoaspirate comprises oil, which consists of triglyceride derived from disrupted adipocytes. The lowest layer is made up of blood, water, and aqueous elements such as the infiltration fluid. The central layer is made up of viable adipocytes, and it is this layer that must be isolated prior to transfer. The oily layer is removed by decanting and any remnants of oil are removed by wicking, for example, with the end of a sterile gauze. The stopper from the Luer-Lock end of the syringe is carefully removed and the lowermost layer is siphoned off, while being careful not to disturb any of the middle layer.

This is crucial as the lower portion of this fatty layer is actually more dense and, as well as containing more concentrated fat, it contains a significantly higher number of ASCs. It is these important progenitor cells that may have importance in both the short- and long-term survival of the graft.

Although centrifugation is commonly used, other techniques including washing, decanting, and filtration are also described, but there is no evidence to suggest the superiority of any one method.

Chemically enhancing the lipoaspirate prior to transfer has been attempted in order to "prime" the adipocytes. Insulin and insulin-like growth factor are required for adipocyte differentiation, and insulin can be added to harvested fat to promote this. Similarly, autologous platelet-rich plasma has been combined with lipoaspirate prior to injection as a means of stabilizing the fat grafts as well as promoting healing, through platelet-derived growth factors. Experimental studies suggest that enhancing the lipoaspirate with pro-angiogenic factors, such as vascular endothelial growth factor, may further improve graft survival and the quality of the grafted fat. However, these growth factors are rarely used in practice.

In addition to enhancing graft take, there are other reasons for purification of the fat prior to transfer: if contaminants remain, then the true volume of the injection will not reflect the actual amount of viable fat graft being transferred. Thus, both surgeon and patient will have a false impression of true volume of adipose tissue that is being "grafted." Non-viable components of the lipoaspirate may indeed lead to adverse sequelae. Furthermore, by purifying the lipoaspirate into adipocytes only, the surgeon has a reproducible technique that can be measured, allowing results to be more objectively evaluated and compared.

- *Fat injection techniques*

To minimize trauma to the fat graft and maximize adipocyte viability, selection of injection cannula and correct placement of the fat graft are important. Prior to injection, the processed fat must be transferred from the aspiration syringe to the injection syringe, and this is carried out using a special connector.

● *Injection cannula*

The choice of whether to use a sharp or blunt injection cannula will depend on the condition of the recipient site and aims of surgery. A sharp tip will pass through tissues easier, which may be useful if fat is being placed in the subdermal plane or in fibrous/scar tissue. On the other hand, there may be a higher risk of bleeding (which may compromise graft take) and accidental injury to adjacent structures. There is also a rare, but potentially fatal risk of intravascular injection and fat embolism. Using a blunt cannula for injection reduces these risks, but these can be more difficult to pass through tissues that are scarred from previous surgery.

● *Graft dimension*

In 1994, Carpaneda[7] and Ribeiro showed that fat grafts larger than 3 mm in diameter were less likely to survive than smaller ones, with an inverse relationship between graft size and viability for grafts over 3 mm. The fat graft must be within 1.5 mm of the vascularized recipient bed for effective plasma imbibition to occur. To avoid fat grafts larger than 3 mm, the cannula gauge must be size-restricted. It is perhaps not surprising that leading proponents of fat grafting advocate placement of small droplets rather than large boluses of fat.

● *Graft placement*

The most commonly used method of graft placement is using the blunt-tip cannula connected to either a 1, 2, or 3 mL syringe, as described by Coleman.

Through 2 mm skin incisions, the cannula is passed into the recipient site, thus creating a tunnel. The plunger is depressed and small parcels of fat are deposited along the tract of the tunnel as the cannula is withdrawn (i.e., retrograde placement). This procedure is done manually and steady maintenance of a low injection pressure will place grafts evenly along the tract avoiding deposition of larger boluses. Once fat is seen extruding from the incision sites, it is reasonable to assume the tunnel is saturated and no more fat should be injected at the site. Retrograde placement also minimizes the risk of accidental intravascular injection. The recipient tissue through which the tunnels are made anchors the graft as well as providing nutrition.

Even when relatively large quantities of fat graft are required, Coleman reiterates the importance of minimizing the amount of fat deposited with each withdrawal (0.2 mL) so as to maximize contact between graft and the vascularized recipient bed. In these circumstances, each small aliquot of graft should be placed in a separate tunnel, thus avoiding isolated clumps, which encourage uneven contours and formation of liponecrotic cysts from graft

failure. Tunnels should be made in multiple directions and at varying depths to separate individual aliquots of graft and maximize graft-bed contact area. Thus, a 3-D lattice-like construct is created within the recipient site and placement of the grafts requires a meticulous technique.

The anatomical layer into which fat is injected depends on the aim of the surgery and tissues available as potential recipient sites. Experimental studies suggest that grafting into the supra-muscular plane is associated with a greater chance of graft success compared to the submuscular or subcutaneous spaces. As perforating blood vessels arise from the superficial surface of the muscle, grafts placed within this layer may revascularize better. Injection directly into muscle may result in even better fat graft survival, as exemplified by the technique of "lipomodeling" used to complement autologous latissimus dorsi flap breast reconstructions.

● *Overcorrection*

Because of the high incidence of graft resorption, many surgeons advocate overcorrecting defects when grafting fat. However if not performed correctly, placement of too much graft at a single recipient site will compromise graft survival with undesirable consequences. With appropriate technique, significant volumes of fat can be transferred, but basic principles described above must be adhered to. Hence, smaller volumes in multiple procedures are preferable to a single large volume transfer.

Adipose-derived stem cells

Adipose tissue is an important source of stem cells. The stromal vascular fraction of adipose tissue contains a special subgroup of multipotent stem cells, similar in characteristics to bone marrow-derived mesenchymal stem cells and possessing the ability to differentiate into a number of mesenchymal cell lines. Adult adipose tissue contains up to 5000 ASCs per gram of fat (some 500 times more than an equivalent volume of adult bone marrow).

In autologous fat grafting, the impact of ASCs is likely to be many-fold. Firstly, ASCs are known to secrete a number of pro-angiogenic growth factors that will improve vascularity at the surgical site and may even themselves differentiate into vascular endothelial cells, further enhancing graft take by encouraging graft revascularization. Secondly, these ASCs are precursors of the preadipocyte and differentiation into "new" adipocytes will add to the volume of graft. Thirdly, many ASCs will remain and function as ASCs. The exact role of these stem cells in modifying local cellular events is not clear at present, but they may facilitate interaction between graft and recipient bed together with surrounding tissues in the long term.

ASCs are more prevalent in excised fat specimens than aspirated fat. This relative deficiency may partially explain the high rates of fat resorption following grafting with lipoaspirate. In native adipose tissue, ASCs are found between adipocytes and the extracellular matrix and are known to influence adipocyte cell turnover, a process which occurs slowly. If aspirated fat is transferred to a recipient site where there is relative lack of ASCs, it is conceivable that the fat will not behave in the way that it did at its original (donor) site. However, if ASCs are transferred with the fat, there should be a theoretical advantage in terms of graft survival. Hence, the ability to concentrate ASCs as well as viable adipocytes is another reason in favor of centrifugation. The technique of preparing a separate fraction of isolated ASCs to supplement a standard fat graft (so-called cell-assisted lipotransfer) has been proposed. Early results are encouraging and suggest improved graft survival compared to conventional fat injection.

ASCs are thought to have specific beneficial effects on radiotherapy-induced skin and soft tissue changes in breast cancer patients. Significant improvements in subcutaneous fibrosis, skin atrophy, and even radiation-induced ulceration following injections with purified lipoaspirate have been reported. Interestingly, autologous fat grafting has also been shown to minimize the risk of severe capsular contracture that is often seen with implant-based breast reconstruction following radiotherapy. Similarly, reduction in the severity of capsular contracture in patients who have previously undergone implant-based reconstruction has also been demonstrated. Although the underlying mechanisms for these clinical observations remain poorly understood, ASCs have been implicated.

However, injection of adipose tissue and in particular ASCs remains controversial because of the unknown effects on recipient tissue and in particular the oncological risk in cancer-prone organs such as the breast. In addition to promoting healing of tissues, experimental studies have shown that adipose tissue and ASCs have the potential to be pro-carcinogenic through several established pathobiological mechanisms:

- Secretion of pro-angiogenic factors
- Secretion of anti-apoptotic factors
- Suppression of T-cell function
- Aromatase activity promoting conversion of androgens to estrogens
- Growth-promoting effect on estrogen receptor (ER)-positive and ER-negative cancer cells.

Therefore, many surgeons are wary of autologous fat grafting of native breast tissue in patients with a genetic predisposition or significant family history of breast cancer. Similarly, in patients who have undergone breast-conservation therapy, it remains unknown whether subsequent ipsilateral breast cancer recurrence may somehow be induced or accelerated by the process of fat grafting.

It should be remembered that with every fat cell that is transferred, there are accompanying stem cells. Although studies have shown this co-transfer to be beneficial in certain patient groups, further research is necessary to clarify the precise effects on native breast tissue after augmentation and especially residual breast tissue following breast-conservation surgery. To date, despite the theoretical concerns, current evidence does not suggest an increased risk of cancer recurrence in actual patients undergoing fat grafting as part of their reconstruction.

Complications and controversies

With the significant number of variables that can potentially affect outcome, a strict protocol and meticulous technique is necessary to minimize the risk of complications. Reported complications include infection, hematoma, and seroma formation, which can occur either at recipient or donor sites. More serious complications such as fat embolism have been reported following fat injections to the head and neck region, but rarely involving the breast. The more unpredictable outcomes of fat injections are rates of resorption and graft longevity.

GRAFT FAILURE AND RESORPTION

Graft resorption is seen in varying degrees, but with improved techniques, better graft retention rates are attainable.

Early revascularization is essential for graft survival and any factor that interferes with this process may contribute to graft failure. These potentially include the following:

- *Shearing*
  If not correctly immobilized, grafts may become dislodged from the recipient bed, thus preventing the initial phases of graft healing being established. Appropriate dressings in the early postoperative period will minimize any shearing forces, although these should not be too compressive.
- *Infection*
  There is a higher risk of infection in the presence of contamination (with blood or oil), which highlights the importance of purifying the graft material. Sterile technique is essential. The use of prophylactic antibiotics may help in reducing infection risk.
- *Excessive graft volume*
  Use of too large a graft compared to the ability of the recipient site to revascularize it prevents efficient plasma imbibition throughout the entire graft. Although the periphery of the graft may receive adequate nutrition from the recipient bed, the central core will die, resulting in areas of fat necrosis.

LIPONECROTIC CYSTS

In the event of graft failure, small areas of non-viable fat graft can be phagocytosed by recipient site macrophages, but larger volumes will undergo necrosis and lead to formation of liponecrotic cysts. Histological analyses have revealed three types of cysts:

- A thin-walled cyst made up of a thin collagen capsule containing liquefied fat
- A thick-walled cyst made up of a thick collagen capsule, containing degenerate fat and multinuclear cells
- An atypical cyst made up of irregular collagen in the capsule

Although the exact pathogenesis of cyst formation is not clear, it appears that as the transplanted adipocyte dies, lipid droplets are released into recipient tissues, and fat combines with circulating calcium to form calcifications. The accompanying recipient site inflammatory reaction creates an inflammatory mass, which eventually develops into the mature cyst containing varying degrees of calcification within its wall. Consequently, areas of microcalcification and cyst formation will potentially develop where grafts have failed.

INTERFERENCE WITH BREAST CANCER DETECTION

Calcifications and signs of cyst formation can be detected radiologically as early as 3 months–6 months after grafting, and liponecrotic cysts tend to become noticeable many months afterward (sometimes presenting as palpable lumps). It is precisely these sequelae of fat necrosis that led to serious reservations about the safety of fat grafting to the breast in the late 1980s. The eminent surgeon Carl Hartrampf Jr.,[8] commented that trying to examine a patient who had developed such lumps after fat grafting would be,

> "...a nightmare for the physician. A curable early cancer could easily be missed if these nodules are ignored..."

Other surgeons expressed similar objections. As a counterargument, Mel Bircoll[9] pointed out that many "routine" plastic and reconstructive surgical interventions to the breast, including breast reduction and augmentation, can also result in calcifications.

Nonetheless, in 1987, the American Society of Plastic Surgeons declared that breast augmentation using autologous fat grafting should not be performed because of these concerns. Subsequently, the idea of injecting fat into the breast became a taboo subject and fell out of favor with most practitioners. A handful of surgeons persisted with refinement of the technique in an attempt to minimize risks and achieve more predictable outcomes.

Twenty years later, an American Society of Plastic Surgeons[10] task force undertook a review of the existing literature and recommended that,

> "...Fat grafting may be considered for breast augmentation and correction of defects associated with medical conditions and previous breast surgeries... Because longevity of the graft is unknown, additional treatments may be necessary to obtain the desired effect. Additionally, fluctuations in body weight can affect graft volume over time...
>
> Patients should be made aware of the potential complications and should provide written informed consent acknowledging their understanding of these risks."

Of note, this task force highlighted concerns that had previously been raised regarding the use of autologous fat grafting in breast cancer patients.

> "When determining whether or not a patient is an appropriate candidate for autologous fat grafting to the breast, physicians should exercise caution when considering high-risk patients (i.e., those with risk factors for breast cancer: BRCA-1, BRCA-2, and/or personal or familial history of breast cancer). Baseline mammography (within American College of Surgeons or American Cancer Society guidelines) is recommended."

Despite perceived difficulties, recent advances in imaging techniques have increased the confidence of radiologists in distinguishing the calcifications of fat necrosis from those associated with malignancy.

These radiological characteristics may help to differentiate benign liponecrotic cysts from malignant lesions, but it should be remembered that any degree of radiological suspicion should prompt further investigation to establish a diagnosis, and this may require surgical biopsy. Baseline imaging prior to fat grafting should be undertaken and subsequent clinical and radiological follow-up carried out by practitioners with specialist expertise in diagnosis and assessment of breast diseases.

To date, there have been no confirmed cases of delay in the diagnosis of breast cancer among patients who have undergone autologous fat grafting, but all patients must be appropriately counselled and give fully informed consent prior to undergoing this form of surgery. Recent evidence suggests that fat grafting into the breast as part of the patient's reconstructive journey is safe and effective.

CONCLUSION

Autologous fat has many characteristics that make it an ideal "filler." These include being:

- Cheap
- Readily available
- Biocompatible
- Hypoallergenic
- Customizable to the individual
- Of a consistency and feel similar to normal tissues

Despite fulfilling the above criteria, a persistent concern over the years has been failure to predict graft survival and ensure longevity. The risk of complications is relatively low, but cost-effectiveness is unproven and many patients require multiple procedures to achieve the desired result. The potential applications of autologous fat grafting in cosmetic and reconstructive breast surgery are numerous, although long-term clinical follow-up data are limited.

REFERENCES

1. Billings E Jr., May JW Jr. Historical review and present status of free fat graft autotransplantation in plastic and reconstructive surgery. *Plast Reconstr Surg.* 1989; 83(2):368–381.
2. Peer LA. Loss of weight and volume in human fat grafts: With postulation of a "cell survival theory." *Plast Reconstr Surg.* 1950; 5(3):217–230.
3. Coleman SR. Facial recontouring with lipostructure. *Clin Plast Surg.* 1997; 24(2):347–367.
4. Coleman SR, Saboeiro AP. Fat grafting to the breast revisited: safety and efficacy. *Plast Reconstr Surg.* 2007;119(3):775–785.
5. Illouz YG. Present results of fat injection. *Aesthetic Plast Surg.* 1988;12(3):175–181.
6. Fournier PF. Fat grafting: My technique. *Dermatol Surg.* 2000;26(12):1117–1128.
7. Carpaneda CA, Ribeiro MT. Percentage of graft viability versus injected volume in adipose autotransplants. *Aesthetic Plast Surg.* 1994;18(1):17–19.
8. Hartrampf CR Jr., Bennett GK. Autologous fat from liposuction for breast augmentation. *Plast Reconstr Surg.* 1987;80(4):646.
9. Bircoll M. Reply (letter). *Plast Reconstr Surg.* 1987;80(4):647.
10. Gutowski KA, ASPS Fat Graft Task Force. Current applications and safety of autologous fat grafts: A report of the ASPS fat graft task force. *Plast Reconstr Surg.* 2009;124(1):272–280.

EDITORIAL COMMENTARY

Over the past two decades, there has been a steady increase in rates of immediate breast reconstruction that has been witnessed in both the United States and Europe with contemporary rates of between 20% and 30%. There are different systems for healthcare funding around the world with insurance coverage dominant in countries such as the United States while public funded healthcare is increasingly subject to restrictions, especially in areas such as breast reconstruction. For whatever reason, it is evident that large numbers of women in developed countries undergoing mastectomy are not in receipt of immediate breast reconstruction. Surgical practice for types of reconstruction has notably changed in recent years; in the later years of the millennium, autologous tissue-based reconstruction was the most common in the United States, but now there is a progressive move away from autologous to implant-based reconstruction. Furthermore, in the United Kingdom, there has been a dramatic decline in use of implant-assisted latissimus dorsi flap reconstruction with the advent of acellular dermal matrices (ADM), and currently, there is a vogue for prepectoral implant-based reconstruction which avoids any disruption of the chest wall musculature and improves symptoms of postoperative pain and possibly functional outcomes. Reconstruction with an implant and ADM alone represents a technically simpler operation than raising a latissimus dorsi or abdominal flap but it remains unclear whether these flaps are tolerant of postmastectomy radiotherapy. Across the United States, reconstructive practices differ greatly between academic and community hospitals. This may reflect availability of junior residents to assist with more complex flap-based procedures while methods of reimbursement will influence patterns of reconstructive practice across the world; in the United Kingdom, individual healthcare trusts are tightening eligibility criteria for certain types of reconstruction. There is evidence that if patients are well-informed about breast reconstruction, they are more likely to opt for mastectomy rather than breast-conserving surgery as a surgical option. Moreover, both clinical decision-making and patient satisfaction are greatly influenced by surgeons, and true surgical equipoise may not exist when the surgeon is biased in favor of a particular treatment pathway. Research has confirmed that randomization of patients to types of reconstruction is difficult and often patients wish to retain a genuine choice with respect to this aspect of their treatment. Perhaps not surprisingly, if women are driving the decision-making process, they are more likely to request contralateral prophylactic mastectomy. However, it is essential that women are accurately informed with decisions guided by evidence rather than emotion or intuition.

Outcomes for shared decision-making are much better and surgeons must strive to understand the reasons behind a patient's choice. Interestingly, patient satisfaction scores for global health-related quality of life are higher for mastectomy-only patients several years after surgery.

Issuance of national guidelines can influence rates of immediate breast reconstruction; it has been decreed in the United Kingdom that immediate breast reconstruction should be offered to all women undergoing mastectomy (unless contraindicated) with accompanying information of appropriate quantity and quality. Cancer treatment targets place both patients and healthcare workers under some pressure in terms of timing and organization of immediate breast reconstruction and may ultimately result in delayed reconstruction for some patients. Careful patient selection is of paramount importance for breast reconstruction and patients themselves cannot have "surgery on demand." Comorbidities may preclude certain types of reconstruction and patients can lose weight and optimize body mass index when a delayed procedure is planned.

Increased rates of immediate breast reconstruction in Europe have generally paralleled those in the United States and reflect general improvements in cancer treatment, technical options available, training of surgeons, and funding. Although the advent of acellular dermal matrices has revolutionized reconstructive practice in the past few years, it currently remains unclear what the net benefits will be and whether acellular dermal matrices offer protection from the effects of radiotherapy with a lower rate of capsular contracture from the need for fewer expansions. Incorporation of a biologic is the key to success and will minimize complications in the long term. Poor integration of materials such as acellular dermal matrices with native tissues will lead to chronic inflammatory states and problems such as seroma and "red breast" syndrome. It will be essential in the forthcoming years to assess a range of new devices used in breast reconstruction and ascertain how the characteristics and properties of each determine performance and clinical outcomes. Concerns have arisen about anaplastic large cell lymphoma (ALCL) in the context of breast implants following issue of a safety communication in 2011 warning about the development of ALCL in the scar capsule. A limited number of case reports exist in the literature but the exact aetiology and pathogenesis of ALCL remain unknown. Details about ALCL should be included in patient information leaflets and a registry established in all countries for reporting cases. Patients should have access to enhanced surveillance and a high index of suspicion maintained by clinicians.

SECTION II

Patient selection—breast-conserving surgery or mastectomy?

Chapter 4.	Oncologic considerations	33
Chapter 5.	Reconstructive perspectives	55
Chapter 6.	Patients' perspectives	61
Chapter 7.	Preoperative radiological assessment	69
Chapter 8.	Oncoplastic parenchymal resection	77
Chapter 9.	Intraoperative assessment	83
Chapter 10.	Timing of oncoplastic repair	89

4

Oncologic considerations

AT A GLANCE

Longer-term follow-up of breast-conservation therapy (BCT) trials have established oncological equivalence with mastectomy in terms of overall survival. Oncoplastic techniques offer the potential for resection of tumors exceeding 4–5 cm with clear surgical margins in women with larger breasts, although induction chemotherapy can often reduce initial tumor size. Where there is genuine surgical equipoise and no definite indication for mastectomy such as multicentricity, several factors will influence the recommendation for either breast-conserving surgery or skin-sparing mastectomy (SSM) with reconstruction. Factors such as young age (<35 years) and family history of breast cancer may prompt mastectomy to minimize risk of local recurrence or a de novo cancer. Likewise, mastectomy may avoid the detrimental and unpredictable effects of radiotherapy on native breast/flap tissues and potential restriction of future reconstructive options. SSM with reconstruction can produce an excellent match in terms of size and shape, whereas BCT with partial breast reconstruction usually necessitates a contralateral adjustment. Nipple-sparing mastectomy negates one advantage of BCT and will influence patient perspective on the relative merits of each approach, and the clinical decision-making process must integrate disease, treatment, and patient related factors.

4.1 DIAGNOSTIC IMAGING

Fiona J. Gilbert

Oncologic considerations: diagnostic imaging

Mammography and ultrasound are the diagnostic tools used for initial assessment of the breast when cancer is suspected. Both methods provide an indication of the likelihood of malignancy, size of the index lesion, and whether or not there is additional disease in the breast. Mammography tends to give a more accurate assessment of tumor size, whereas ultrasound is more operator dependent and may underestimate size. Reporting guidelines now encourage not only measurement of the tumor size in two dimensions, but also the specific distance of the tumor from the nipple and the chest wall. Mammography also gives an approximation of breast size in relation to tumor extent, which will aid surgical planning.

In younger women and those with dense breasts, the sensitivity of mammography is much lower than in older post-menopausal women due to the presence of fibroglandular tissue masking tumors. If there is insufficient surrounding fat, then cancers cannot be seen against the similar attenuation values of fibroglandular tissue. Some studies have indicated that mammographic sensitivity can be less than 50% in women with very dense breasts or who are under 40 years of age.[1] Ultrasound can be associated with even lower sensitivity for small cancers with some high-risk screening studies reporting sensitivity values less than 50%.[2] Ultrasound is therefore recommended as an adjunct to mammography rather than as a primary diagnostic tool. However, in those women with dense breast tissue where the visibility of tumors is restricted for mammography, ultrasound is a useful complementary examination permitting an increase in cancer detection rates. Breast density can be measured in several ways, but methods of automated measurement appear promising and can yield robust and reproducible results.[3]

The ability to accurately measure tumor size can be more problematic for both mammography and ultrasound with tumor margins being particularly difficult to define when a tumor is located in a zone of fibrocystic change. Furthermore, the precise size of lobular cancers is notorious for underestimation with these conventional imaging techniques.

Patient selection for breast-conserving surgery can be refined by magnetic resonance imaging (MRI) in certain circumstances including: (1) women with dense breast tissue, (2) where there is lobular cancer, (3) where there is a discrepancy in tumor size of more than 10 mm, or (4) where there is an increased risk of contralateral breast cancer.[4] The increased sensitivity of MRI compared to mammography and ultrasound will allow detection of additional disease and more accurate tumor delineation. However, the specificity of MRI can be problematic, necessitating pathological confirmation of additional disease by image-guided biopsy, particularly where this will potentially lead to a change of management plan. Up to 60% of additional disease found on MRI will be identified by a "second look" ultrasound, which can then be used to guide core biopsy. However, if the suspicious area is not found on ultrasound, then an MRI-guided biopsy is indicated. This should be performed after careful review of all images in a multidisciplinary setting; the surgical team should confirm that any additional foci of disease will change management from breast conservation to involve either a wider local excision or mastectomy.[5] By contrast, if no management change is proposed consequent to a positive biopsy, then further tissue acquisition would be deemed unnecessary and can be avoided.

The arguments for and against preoperative MRI have been well documented in the literature. The protagonists believe that preoperative MRI will reduce re-excision rates due to better delineation of tumor extent, reduce local recurrence rates, and improve diagnosis of synchronous contralateral disease. The arguments against preoperative MRI are centered around an increase in preoperative biopsies, which can delay surgery, result in unnecessary additional expense, and increase mastectomy rates (which can be for benign disease if additional biopsies are not undertaken). There is indirect evidence that radiotherapy and other adjuvant treatment can successfully treat any additional foci of disease not seen on mammography and ultrasound. In a meta-analysis of 3112 patients randomized to MRI or no MRI, re-excision rates were identical (11.4%), but the MRI group had an increased number of mastectomies (25% compared to 18.2%).[6] Analysis of individual patient data revealed no differences in eight-year local recurrence-free survival between the MRI (97%) and no-MRI (95%) groups.[7] The detection of additional disease requires a high resolution technique in conjunction with a high relaxivity contrast agent.[8] Ductal carcinoma in situ (DCIS) can be particularly difficult to detect on MRI, as it tends to enhance to a lesser extent than invasive disease and later on than invasive disease. DCIS has a type 1 enhancement curve with a steadily increasing signal over

time rather than a type 3 malignant curve (rapid enhancement and wash out). Nonetheless, high-grade DCIS is generally detected more reliably than low-grade DCIS.[9]

Assessment of residual disease following surgery is difficult, but MRI has a sensitivity of 80% and may be worthwhile when there are involved margins and there is a possibility that ultimately mastectomy may be required (rather than re-excision) to clear all residual disease.[10] In neoadjuvant chemotherapy patients, especially those with regimens containing doxorubicin or taxanes, there are dramatic reductions in contrast enhancement secondary to decreased vascularity, and this can make the detection of residual disease more challenging.[11] A pre-chemotherapy MRI examination is helpful and allows mapping out of tumor extent, which renders subsequent MRI interpretation more straightforward. In those cases where there is in excess of a 90% response to treatment, individual viable cells cannot be detected with MRI.

Contrast-enhanced spectral mammography (CESM) is a recognized technique which is gaining popularity. Following intravenous bolus injection of iodinated contrast, a high and low energy mammogram is taken. The low energy image is similar to a normal mammogram with the peak kilovolts set below 33 kV. The high energy image uses a peak kilovolt of 45 kV–49 kV and extra x-ray filtration to ensure that the x-ray beam spectrum is almost entirely above the k-edge of iodine and gives only 20% additional radiation dose. This subtraction x-ray technique maximizes the conspicuity of the contrast and highlights enhancing areas with a resolution 10-fold greater than MRI.[12] This technique has comparably high sensitivity to MRI, but with increased specificity. When assessing lesion size, CESM was superior to mammography and closely correlates with pathological size and is within 10 mm of MRI size estimates.[13,14] For determining lesion extent, CESM was of equal sensitivity to MRI in terms of assessing the index tumor, but slightly inferior when assessing additional foci (sensitivity for CESM compared to MRI 83%–100% and 93%–98%, respectively).[13,15,16]

A fundamental challenge lies in understanding which radiologically detected cancers need to be treated and which can be left alone. The recognition by national screening programs that cancers are being over diagnosed (the finding of cancers which would not have become apparent in a woman's lifetime without a screening test) means that care must be taken not to overtreat. The LORIS trial is tackling this problem by randomizing women with low-risk DCIS to watchful active imaging or standard of care.[17] The ability to identify forms of DCIS which require more active intervention will come from a combination of histopathological and molecular parameters, which are discussed in other sections of this book. This will also inform the most appropriate treatment for additional disease. However, consideration of functional information from MRI in the form of pharmacokinetic parameters from dynamic contrast enhancement, apparent diffusion weighted MRI to assess the stroma adjacent to the tumor may become relevant in treatment planning. Positron emission tomography can deliver metabolic information about cell turnover, vascularity, and hypoxia, which may influence subsequent management. However, large studies are required before these potential predictive biomarkers can be introduced into routine treatment planning.

REFERENCES

1. Kolb TM, Lichy J and Newhouse JH. Comparison of the performance of screening mammography, physical examination, and breast US and evaluation of factors that influence them: An analysis of 27,825 patient evaluations. *Radiology* 225 (2002): 165–175.
2. Leach MO, Boggis CR, Dixon AK, Easton DF, Eeles RA, Evans DG, Gilbert FJ et al., Screening with magnetic resonance imaging and mammography of a UK population at high familial risk of breast cancer: A prospective multicentre cohort study (MARIBS). *Lancet* 365 (2005): 1769–1678.
3. Morrish OW, Tucker L, Black R, Willsher P, Duffy SW and Gilbert FJ. Mammographic breast density: Comparison of methods for quantitative evaluation. *Radiology* 275 (2015): 356–365.
4. Sardanelli F, Boetes C, Borisch B, Decker T, Federico M, Gilbert FJ, Helbich T, et al. Magnetic resonance imaging of the breast: Recommendations from the EUSOMA working group. *Eur J Cancer* 46 (2010): 1296–1316.
5. Dall BJ, Vinnicombe S, Gilbert FJ. Reporting and management of breast lesions detected using MRI. *Clin Radiol.* 66 (2011): 1120–1128.
6. Houssami N, Turner R and Morrow M. Preoperative magnetic resonance imaging in breast cancer: Meta-analysis of surgical outcomes. *Ann Surg.* 257 (2013): 249–255.
7. Houssami N, Turner R, Macaskill P, Turnbull LW, McCready DR, Tuttle TM, Vapiwala N and Solin LJ. An individual person data meta-analysis of preoperative magnetic resonance imaging and breast cancer recurrence. *J Clin Oncol.* 32 (2014): 392–401.
8. Gilbert FJ, van den Bosch HCM, Petrillo A, Siegmann K, Heverhagen JT, Panizza P, Gehl H-B et al., Comparison of gadobenate dimeglumine-enhanced breast MRI and gadopentetate dimeglumine-enhanced breast MRI with mammography and ultrasound for the detection of breast cancer. *J Magn Reson Imaging* 39 (2014): 1272–1286.
9. Kuhl CK, Schrading S, Bieling HB, Wardelmann E, Leutner CC, Koenig R, Kuhn W and Schild HH. MRI for diagnosis of pure ductal carcinoma in situ: A prospective observational study. *Lancet* 370 (2007): 485–492.
10. Chae EY, Cha JH, Kim HH, Shin HJ, Kim H, Lee J and Cheung JY. Evaluation of residual disease using breast MRI after excisional biopsy for breast cancer. *AJR* 200 (2013): 1167–1173.
11. Denis F, Desbiez-Bourcier AV, Chapiron C, Arbion F, Body G and Brunereau L. Contrast enhanced magnetic resonance imaging underestimates residual disease following neoadjuvant docetaxel based chemotherapy for breast cancer. *EJSO* 30 (2004): 1069–1076.
12. Lobbes MB, Smidt ML, Houwers J, Tjan-Heijnen VC, Wildberger JE. Contrast enhanced mammography: Techniques, current results, and potential indications. *Clin Radiol.* 68 (2013): 935–944.
13. Jochelson MS, Dershaw DD, Sung JS, Heerdt AS, Thornton C, Moskowitz CS, Ferrara J and Morris EA. Bilateral contrast-enhanced dual-energy digital mammography: Feasibility and comparison with conventional digital mammography and MR imaging in women with known breast carcinoma. *Radiology* 266 (2013): 743–751.
14. Lobbes MBI, Lalji UC, Nelemans PJ, Houben I, Smidt ML, Heuts E, de Vries B, Wildberger JE and Beets-Tan RG. The quality of tumor size assessment by contrast-enhanced spectral mammography and the benefit of additional breast. *MRI J Cancer* 6 (2015): 144–150.
15. Fallenberg EM, Dromain C, Diekmann F, Engelken F, Krohn M, Singh JM, Ingold-Heppner B, Winzer KJ, Bick U and Renz DM. Contrast-enhanced spectral mammography versus MRI: Initial results in the detection of breast cancer and assessment of tumour size. *Eur Radiol.* 24 (2014): 256–264.
16. Łuczyńska E, Heinze-Paluchowska S, Hendrick E, Dyczek S, Ryś J, Herman K, Blecharz P and Jakubowicz J. Comparison between breast MRI and contrast-enhanced spectral mammography. *Med Sci Monit.* 21 (2015): 1358–1367.
17. Francis A, Fallowfield L and Rea D. The LORIS trial: Addressing overtreatment of ductal carcinoma in situ. *Clin Oncol (R Coll Rdiol)* 27 (2015): 6–8.

4.2 PATHOLOGIST

Cansu Karakas and Aysegul A. Sahin

Introduction

The standard treatment for early breast cancer over the last few decades has increasingly been breast-conserving therapy, consisting of local removal of the tumor, followed by radiation therapy. The goals of breast-conserving therapy are to surgically excise the tumor and to preserve breast contour and body image. Careful selection of patients is essential to minimize the likelihood of local recurrence. Although breast-conserving surgery is the preferred surgical treatment option wherever possible, total mastectomy is required for tumor control in some patients and may provide more satisfactory outcomes than would be obtained with breast-conserving therapy.

Accurate histopathologic assessment of the primary tumor, including histologic subtype, grade, surgical margin status, and molecular markers is a crucial factor for selection of patients who are eligible for breast-conserving therapy (**Figure 4.2.1**) or mastectomy (**Figure 4.2.2**). A multidisciplinary team of experts in medical oncology, surgery, radiation oncology, and pathology will collectively take account of biological and clinical features to determine appropriate treatment. In this chapter, we discuss the specific biological and histopathological features associated with local recurrence as they relate to decision-making for clinical management.

In situ carcinoma

DUCTAL CARCINOMA IN SITU

Since mammographic screening was established, the incidence of ductal carcinoma in situ (DCIS) has dramatically increased. DCIS encompasses a heterogeneous group of lesions in terms of morphology, underlying genetic

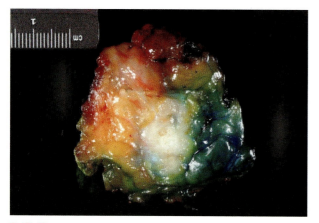

4.2.1 Gross picture of breast-conserving therapy specimen inked for margin evaluation. Cut surface reveals a white, firm tumor which has relatively ill-defined margins.

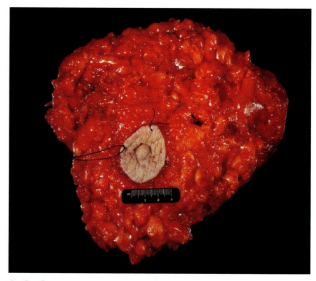

4.2.2 Skin-sparing total mastectomy specimen. Skin edges contain sutures for specimen orientation.

alterations, and biomarker expression. Because of this biological and clinical heterogeneity, there are multiple treatment options based on differences in risk of recurrence. Currently, treatment options for DCIS include breast-conserving surgery alone, breast-conserving surgery plus radiotherapy, and total mastectomy. However, there is no clear consensus on which of these is optimal. Hence, the assessment of clinical and pathologic factors related to risk of recurrence is important for identification of subgroups of patients who should undergo mastectomy rather than breast-conserving surgery.

Although breast-conserving approaches have high rates of success, total mastectomy is recommended in some circumstances. These include extensive or multicentric DCIS, inability to attain negative surgical margins, patient preference, large invasive tumor size, and diffuse microcalcifications visible on imaging studies. Clinical algorithms can aid in decision-making about optimal treatment. For example, the Van Nuys Prognostic Index quantifies and gives a combined score for five known risk factors (margin status, histologic subtype, extent of necrosis, tumor size, and patient age), which are important in predicting local recurrence.[1] This algorithm continues to be used by some clinicians in making their therapeutic decisions. An alternative pathologic classification system for grading DCIS has been published which identifies a subgroup of patients with particularly poor outcome. Women who have high-grade tumors with more than 50% solid architecture and associated comedo-type necrosis have significantly greater risk of recurrent DCIS or invasive carcinoma than patients whose tumors only demonstrated features of high nuclear grade.[2] In univariate analysis, high cytonuclear grade, larger lesion size, solid architectural growth pattern, presence of necrosis or chronic inflammation, incompleteness of the excision, and smaller margin width were associated with ipsilateral recurrence.

Studies evaluating the risk of recurrence in DCIS patients have revealed that patients with comedo-type DCIS, high-grade lesions, cribriform and solid growth patterns, positive surgical margins, and younger patients carry a higher local recurrence rate after breast-conserving therapy compared with patients without these characteristics.[3–8] In addition, the extent of the lesion and obtaining an adequate margin of excision that is tumor free ("safe" margin) are important for minimizing the risk of recurrence after breast-conserving therapy in patients with DCIS.[6,9] A recent study compared all types of treatment for DCIS patients treated with local excision, local excision with radiotherapy, and mastectomy. This study specifically evaluated different criteria for selecting low-risk DCIS lesions. With a 6.7-year median follow-up, conservative treatment was associated with a higher local recurrence rate ($p = 0.025$). In a selected population of patients with tumor size <10 mm, low or intermediate grade, and margins >2 mm, women treated by local excision and radiotherapy versus excision alone showed no significant differences in local relapse ($p = 0.91$).[10] The 10-year overall survival rate was 99.7%, with no difference between treatment groups.

Recent studies have also focused on biomarkers and genomic scores to identify low- and high-risk DCIS lesions. p16, Ki-67, and COX-2 overexpression have been identified as predictive markers for high-risk lesions and can be used as biomarkers for treatment.[11,12] The importance of tumor biology in locoregional recurrence has been studied using the Oncotype DX breast cancer assay for DCIS patients. The Oncotype DX assay is a unique genomic test that uses clinicopathologic features to provide an individualized risk score based on 21 specific genes, enabling prediction of the risk of locoregional recurrence in DCIS patients treated with breast-conserving therapy. This important advance allows deeper understanding of the tumor biology for each patient to help guide treatment decisions.[13,14] Initial validation of Oncotype DX has been studied in a prospective trial of 327 patients. The primary objective was to determine whether the assay's DCIS score was associated with the risk of an ipsilateral breast event. The study results met the objective; DCIS score was significantly associated with the risk of developing an ipsilateral breast event ($p = 0.02$). The second validation study included DCIS patients who were treated with breast-conserving therapy alone with clear margins. Their results confirmed those of the previous study; two-thirds (62.2%) of the study patients had a low-risk score. The remaining patients had an intermediate or high score, and 10-year local recurrence rates were significantly higher in the intermediate- and high-risk group than in the low-risk group ($p = 0.002$).[14]

In summary, breast-conserving therapy with or without radiotherapy and mastectomy are both valid treatment choices for DCIS. Optimum treatment is determined by characteristics of the tumor, clinical features, and patient preference. The role of the pathologist is to sample the lesion adequately, to establish the correct diagnosis, and to clearly report clinically important pathologic information, such as the size of the lesion, nuclear grade, presence of necrosis, and distance to margins, to guide the treatment. Genomic studies or biomarkers could further help to select candidates for the appropriate treatment strategy.

DUCTAL CARCINOMA IN SITU WITH MICROINVASION

A subset of DCIS patients have a small amount of invasive disease upon final pathologic analysis. DCIS with microinvasion, also referred to as "microinvasive carcinoma," is a pre-invasive stage of breast carcinoma and is pathologically defined by the presence of minimal invasion of the basement membrane by a very small amount of cancer cells into the surrounding stroma as seen by conventional light microscopic evaluation[15] (**Figure 4.2.3a, b**). DCIS with microinvasion constitutes less than 1% of all breast carcinomas and 5%–10% of all DCIS cases.[16] Because of its relative rarity, understanding of the biologic behavior of this disease remains unclear; there are no comprehensive studies and well-established criteria for definition of this entity.

There is little information regarding treatment outcome for microinvasive carcinoma of the breast as a separate entity. Several studies have evaluated the clinicopathologic features of DCIS with microinvasion compared with pure DCIS in patients treated with breast-conserving therapy or mastectomy and showed that microinvasion was associated with a higher frequency of microcalcifications,

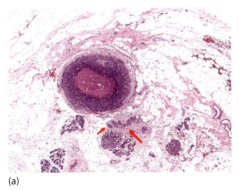
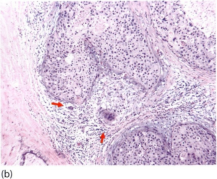

(a) (b)

4.2.3 (a) High-grade DCIS with microinvasion (microinvasive carcinoma). Arrow indicates areas of stromal invasion. (b) DCIS with microinvasion of periductal stroma by tumor cell groups.

higher nuclear grade, larger DCIS tumor size, and comedonecrosis.[17,18] However, DCIS with microinvasion and DCIS did not significantly differ in terms of disease recurrence and overall survival.[17] Although most existing data on DCIS with microinvasion are retrospective with small numbers of patients,[18–20] a relatively large study recently assessed long-term outcomes for 321 patients with DCIS and 72 patients with DCIS with microinvasion treated with breast-conserving surgery and radiotherapy.[15] Microinvasion did not significantly predict for worse local-regional-free survival, distant metastasis-free survival, or overall survival in comparison to those patients with DCIS alone.[15] Although the prognosis of DCIS with microinvasion is thought to be similar to pure DCIS and early-stage breast cancer, several studies have reported a 2%–29% likelihood of lymph node metastasis in patients with DCIS with microinvasion.[15,21–30] Lyons and colleagues[31] studied 112 patients with DCIS with microinvasion who underwent sentinel lymph node biopsy. In these patients, 12% had positive sentinel lymph node biopsy findings and, among these, 2.7% had macrometastasis and 10% had micrometastasis or isolated tumor cells. Axillary lymph node dissection was performed in all patients with macrometastasis and revealed additional positive nodes in 67% of the patients. With a 6-year median follow-up time, among 98 patients with negative sentinel lymph node findings, there were five cases of locoregional recurrence and four contralateral primary breast cancers. Among the 14 patients with positive sentinel lymph node biopsy findings (82% of whom received systemic adjuvant therapy), there were no cases of locoregional recurrence or metastasis.[31]

In conclusion, these findings suggest that the clinicopathologic features and outcomes of patients with DCIS with microinvasion seem to be equivalent to those of patients with DCIS without microinvasion. DCIS with microinvasion has an excellent prognosis and the risk of recurrence after breast-conserving therapy or mastectomy seems to be small. However, patients with DCIS with microinvasion have about a 2%–29% chance of having lymph node metastasis and thus should undergo axillary lymph node sampling. For deciding an appropriate treatment, extensive sampling, careful pathologic evaluation of high-grade DCIS for the presence of microinvasion, and assessment of margin status are very important.

LOBULAR CARCINOMA IN SITU

Contemporary studies have confirmed that lobular carcinoma in situ (LCIS) (**Figure 4.2.4**) is a risk factor for the development of ipsilateral and/or contralateral invasive breast cancer or nonobligatory premalignant lesion.[32–34] Appropriate treatment options for LCIS described in the literature include simple excision with regular follow-up and unilateral or bilateral total mastectomy.

LCIS is frequently multicentric and bilateral and has been linked to an increased risk of invasive breast carcinoma, either ductal or lobular.[33,35,36] Chuba and colleagues[35] studied subsequent invasive breast cancer risk in a series of

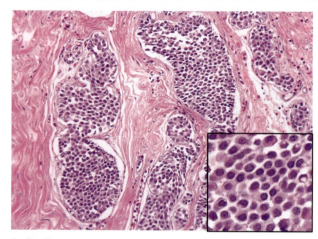

4.2.4 A classic lobular carcinoma in situ showing monotonous tumor cells with minimal atypia in expanded lobules. Inset shows high magnification. Tumor cells have round hyperchromatic nuclei with focal intracytoplasmic mucin.

4853 patients with LCIS. The risk of developing cancer after LCIS was higher, and the risk was equal for both breasts.[35] Several groups have evaluated whether LCIS as a component of invasive cancer is associated with higher local recurrence rates compared with invasive cancer without LCIS. Sasson and colleagues[36] investigated the impact of LCIS on the risk of ipsilateral local recurrence after breast-conserving therapy in more than 1000 women with stage I and II breast cancer. LCIS was present in 65 of 1274 patients.[36] The 10-year cumulative rate of ipsilateral local recurrence was significantly higher in women with associated LCIS (29% vs 6% of women without LCIS; p = 0.0003).[36] The majority of these recurrences were invasive. However, other studies support the view that the presence of LCIS, even at the resection margin, is not a risk factor for local recurrence of either DCIS or invasive carcinoma.[37]

The results of studies assessing the risk of locoregional recurrence in patients with and without LCIS at the surgical margins have been controversial. Several studies have evaluated the impact of LCIS at the lumpectomy margin in patients who were treated with breast-conserving therapy. LCIS was associated with a higher likelihood of breast tumor recurrence when present at the margin than for negative margins.[38,39] However, in a retrospective study of more than 2000 stage T1 and T2 breast cancer patients treated with lumpectomy and radiotherapy, the presence of LCIS at the margin did not increase the risk of locoregional recurrence, which was consistent with previous studies.[40] In current practice, re-excision for LCIS-positive margins is not required in breast-conserving therapy unless there is a concomitant invasive carcinoma or DCIS.

Pleomorphic lobular carcinoma in situ (PLCIS) is a variant of LCIS with distinct clinical, histologic, and imaging findings. PLCIS lesions tend to have central comedonecrosis and higher nuclear grade, which may lead to incorrect classification as DCIS (**Figure 4.2.5**).[41] However, lack of E-cadherin expression is a characteristic feature that

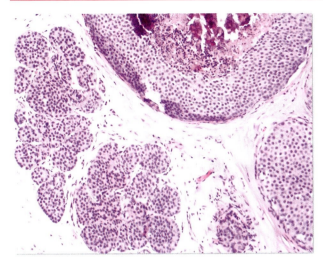

4.2.5 Pleomorphic lobular carcinoma in situ. Tumor cells involve lobular units and are associated with comedo-type necrosis.

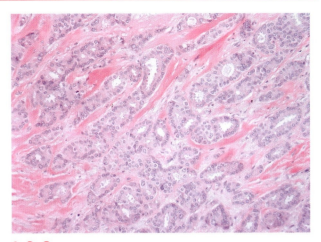

4.2.6 H&E stained section of a well-differentiated invasive ductal carcinoma. The tumor cells are arranged in the fibrotic stroma as well-formed glands.

is helpful in distinguishing PLCIS from classic DCIS. PLCIS shows different marker expression than classic LCIS, such as high Ki-67 proliferation index and more p53 protein accumulation, which are indicative of more aggressive behavior. Hence, diagnosis of PLCIS warrants careful evaluation of the entire lesion, adequate sampling, and more intensive treatment.[42–44] Several studies have revealed that PLCIS found at the surgical margin is associated with an increased recurrence rate when compared to classic LCIS. For this reason, re-excision is recommended when surgical margins are positive for PLCIS in breast-conserving therapy.[42,45,46]

In conclusion, if LCIS is seen in association with the primary tumor and is present at the surgical resection margin, it should be noted in the pathology report. No further excision is required to obtain negative margins for LCIS, but an additional margin excision is recommended for PLCIS. It is important to involve the clinicians to understand implications of these cases and to avoid overinterpretation of findings. Further re-excision is not indicated in the majority of cases. LCIS should not be considered a contraindication to breast-conserving surgery.

Invasive carcinoma

HISTOLOGIC SUBTYPES OF BREAST CARCINOMA

Breast cancer encompasses a wide variety of morphological features, immunohistochemical profiles, and histologic subtypes with different biological behaviors. Verifying histologic type and correlating these findings to clinical presentation are essential in treatment of patients with breast cancer. There are more than 20 histologic subtypes of invasive breast carcinoma. When an invasive carcinoma does not show a specific histologic feature, the tumor is classified as "invasive carcinoma, not otherwise specified, or invasive ductal carcinoma." Invasive ductal carcinoma is the most common subtype of breast cancer,[47] accounting for about 60%–70% of all breast cancers (**Figures 4.2.6 and 4.2.7**). Among the special histologic subtypes, invasive lobular carcinoma is the most common and is characterized by small, uniform, round cells with minimal pleomorphism and scant cytoplasm that infiltrate the stroma in single files (**Figure 4.2.8a, b**).[48] Because of its diffusely infiltrative growth pattern and lack of surrounding desmoplastic (fibrous) reaction, this type of cancer tends not to form distinct masses, making them difficult to palpate on physical examination or detect on mammography. These challenges in defining the tumor by various imaging modalities may render assessment of disease extent more difficult and may lead to increased re-excision rates after breast-conserving therapy.[49,50]

The underlying biology in invasive lobular cancer is distinct from that of invasive ductal carcinoma. Several studies have shown that the rate of pathological complete response to neoadjuvant chemotherapy is significantly lower in invasive

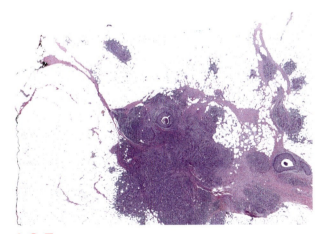

4.2.7 H&E stained section of a poorly differentiated invasive ductal carcinoma. The tumor shows predominantly solid growth pattern with focal DCIS component. The tumor is away from the inked margin.

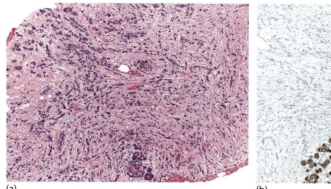
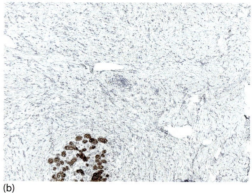

4.2.8 (a) Classic invasive lobular carcinoma with typical streaming pattern of the tumor cells. Tumor cells are usually small, round with minimal pleomorphism, and loosely dispersed throughout the fibrotic stroma. (b) Corresponding E-Cadherin staining of the tumor shows absence of immunoreactivity, whereas normal breast ducts show strong membranous staining and serve as internal control.

lobular carcinoma than in invasive ductal carcinoma.[51,52] In addition, lobular subtypes are associated with increased incidence of multifocality and contralateral disease.[53]

During the last decade, several studies have focused on comparison of surgical treatment approaches for types of invasive carcinomas. However, results from both large randomized trials and retrospective studies have been conflicting in terms of estimating recurrence risk for different histologic subtypes after breast-conserving therapy. Despite differences in tumor biology, several retrospective studies have shown that the long-term outcomes are equivalent for patients with lobular and ductal carcinomas undergoing breast-conserving therapy.[52,54–56] Braunstein and colleagues[57] evaluated local recurrence rates for invasive lobular carcinoma following breast-conserving therapy, in a cohort of 998 breast-conserving therapy patients (74% with invasive ductal carcinoma, 8% with invasive lobular carcinoma, and 18% with mixed pathology). This analysis took account of biologic subtype and margin status. The 10-year local recurrence rates were 5.5% with invasive ductal carcinoma, 4.4% for invasive lobular carcinoma, and 1.2% for mixed histology (p = 0.08). Of note, patients with invasive lobular carcinoma had a higher likelihood of initially positive surgical margins after breast-conserving therapy compared to those with invasive ductal carcinoma or mixed histology (45.0% vs 17.5% and 18.5%, respectively; p<0.001). Patients with invasive lobular carcinoma had increased re-excision rates due to positive margins (57.1% vs 40.4% and 36.9%, respectively; p = 0.02); however, final margin status was not significantly different between groups of patients with invasive lobular and ductal carcinomas (p = 0.88). Moreover, on multivariate analysis using invasive ductal carcinoma as the reference, histologic subtype was not a predictor for local recurrence (p = 0.52).[57]

Another retrospective study evaluated local recurrence according to surgical treatment option in 736 patients diagnosed with stage I–III invasive lobular carcinoma. Women were treated with breast-conserving surgery (52%) or mastectomy (48%) and after a follow-up of 72 months, local recurrence rates following breast-conserving surgery and mastectomy did not significantly differ (4.5% vs 3.4%; p = 0.58). Pathologic tumor size, high histologic grade, and positive margin status (tumor cells at the inked margin) were associated with increased local recurrence rate, whereas age younger than 40 years and positive margin status were associated with ipsilateral breast tumor recurrence.[58]

These studies concluded that diagnosis of invasive lobular carcinoma is not a contraindication for breast-conserving therapy. Treatment options for both lobular and ductal breast cancers should be similar and histologic subtype is not a significant independent predictor of recurrence or survival.[53–56] Rates of re-excision to achieve negative margins appear to be higher for the lobular subtype; nonetheless, these patients are considered candidates for breast-conserving therapy if the tumor is not diffusely present throughout the breast and the lesion can be excised with tumor-free margins.

Molecular subtypes of breast carcinoma

Advanced molecular techniques such as gene expression profiling have revealed details about the heterogeneity of breast cancer. Thus distinct subgroups of breast cancer, with different biologic and clinical behavior, have been identified. In clinical practice, surrogate markers have been used to identify these molecular subtypes.[59,60] Since microarray technology is not available for treatment planning in routine clinical practice, breast cancers are classified according to expression of three common markers—estrogen receptor (ER), progesterone receptor (PR), and human epidermal growth factor receptor 2 (HER2), which are tested for using standard immunohistochemistry on routinely processed tissue sections (**Figure 4.2.9**). In addition to standard patient and pathologic characteristics, molecular subtypes may provide further information on recurrence risk in breast cancer patients from new prognostic, predictive, and therapeutic targets.[59–61] Several studies have evaluated the association of a particular molecular subtype with increased local or distant recurrence after breast-conserving therapy or mastectomy. In a retrospective study of 793 patients, Nguyen and colleagues[61]

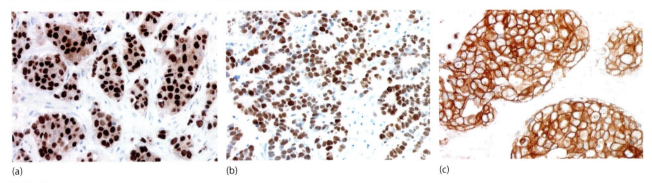

4.2.9 Immunohistochemistry analysis of invasive breast carcinoma. (a) ER+ strong intensity. (b) PR+ moderate intensity. (c) HER2 overexpression, score 3+.

found that triple-negative breast cancers (lacking ER, PR, and HER2 expression by immunohistochemistry), were associated with higher risk of local recurrence among women who received BCT.[61] Similarly, other studies found that after either breast-conserving therapy or mastectomy, rates of locoregional recurrence are higher for the triple-negative subtype than ER-positive disease in patients undergoing either breast-conserving surgery or mastectomy.[62–64]

Studies have also compared longer-term outcomes for triple negative breast cancer patients treated with BCT or mastectomy. A recent MD Anderson study evaluated the impact of treatment type on rates of locoregional recurrence among 1325 triple negative breast cancer patients treated with either breast-conserving therapy or total mastectomy.[65] With a median follow-up of 62 months, patients in the breast-conserving therapy group had a higher locoregional recurrence-free survival rate than patients in the mastectomy group (76% vs 71%; p = 0.032). Furthermore, distant metastasis-free survival (68% vs 54%, respectively; p<0.0001) and overall survival (74% vs 63%; p<0.0001) were also significantly higher in patients who received breast-conserving therapy versus total mastectomy. On multivariate analysis, clinicopathologic factors such as high nuclear grade, lymphovascular invasion, T classification, and close or positive margins were significantly associated with increased locoregional recurrence. However, the difference in likelihood of locoregional recurrence by surgical approach lost significance (mastectomy versus BCT; p = 0.55), showing the effect of underlying tumor biology.[65] In another study, outcomes for 202 triple negative breast cancer patients who were undergoing breast-conserving therapy (61 patients) or mastectomy (141 patients) were reviewed. Five-year disease-free survival rates were not significantly different between the two groups (p = 0.14). Five-year overall survival estimates were significantly better for the breast-conserving therapy group (89% vs 69%; p = 0.018) most likely due to larger tumor size and higher disease stage in the mastectomy group. However, surgical treatment approach had no effect on disease-free survival or overall survival on multivariate analysis.[66]

Increased knowledge of tumor biology and developments in systemic targeted treatment options, such as anti-HER2 therapy, have contributed to decreasing rates of local recurrence. A recent study evaluated locoregional recurrence rates in relation to tumor biology among 1000 patients with early-stage invasive breast cancer. The risk of recurrence varied with biomarker subtype, with HER2-overexpressing and triple-negative subtypes having the highest rates. However, when recurrence rates were analyzed as a function of time (i.e., before versus after introduction of anti-HER2 therapy), HER2-positive patients no longer had elevated recurrence rates compared to ER-positive, HER2-negative patients. Importantly, the type of surgery did not influence the risk of local recurrence in patients given optimal systemic treatment; the overall local recurrence rates were 3.2% after breast-conserving surgery compared with 3.8% after mastectomy (p = 0.617).[67] These results were consistent with a previous meta-analysis evaluating the impact of breast cancer subtype on locoregional recurrence in patients undergoing either mastectomy (5148 patients) or breast-conserving therapy (7174 patients). For all patients regardless of surgery type, the risk of recurrence for luminal-subtype tumors was lower than for HER2-overexpressing (RR 0.34; 95% CI 0.26–0.45) or triple-negative (RR 0.38; 95% CI 0.23–0.61) tumors. Furthermore, patients with HER2-overexpressing tumors had a greater risk of locoregional recurrence than did those with triple-negative tumors (RR 1.44; 95% CI 1.06–1.95) following breast-conservation therapy. By contrast, there was no difference between the two tumor subtypes after mastectomy (RR 0.91; 95% CI 0.68–1.22).[68]

Another biological difference between molecular subtypes is the timing of recurrence, which occurs predominantly within the first 5 years after diagnosis for triple-negative and HER2-expressing patients, whereas for cancers with ER expression, locoregional recurrence takes a longer time to develop.[62] Pilewskie and colleagues[69] investigated the effect of negative margin width on local recurrence in 535 triple-negative breast cancer patients who underwent breast-conservation therapy: In those with a wider margin obtained on mastectomy, there was no reduction in local recurrence. The authors concluded that locoregional recurrence is more closely correlated with tumor biology, and aggressive tumor biology cannot be overcome with more extensive surgery.[62,69] Improvements in adjuvant systemic therapy are needed to reduce recurrence rates further in these patients with high-risk disease. Taken together, evidence suggests that despite the aggressive nature of triple negative breast cancer, breast-conserving therapy rather than total mastectomy can be a surgical option for appropriately selected patients. Thus, currently, no molecular subtype should be considered a contraindication for breast-conserving therapy.

New staging criteria are necessary for accurate delineation of a patient's prognosis in the current era of widespread use of neoadjuvant systemic therapy. Mittendorf and colleagues demonstrated that intrinsic tumor biology is a critical prognostic indicator for women who undergo neoadjuvant therapy for breast cancer.[70] They proposed a scoring system which was developed and validated using information from 2377 patients with invasive non-metastatic breast cancer treated with neoadjuvant chemotherapy and HER2-targeted therapy (if appropriate). Previously applied staging systems incorporate pretreatment clinical stage, ER status, grade, and post-treatment pathologic stage. However, they do not include HER2 status or response to neoadjuvant treatment. Compared with either clinical stage or pathologic stage alone, this new scoring system facilitates a more refined stratification of disease-specific survival, especially among HER2-positive patients. The latter now receive HER2-targeted therapy along with chemotherapy, which has improved clinical outcomes considerably among patients with this subtype of breast cancer. Use of this model may have clinical implications, as 75% of patients have a refined prognostic classification using this new system; these data again support the notion that tumor biology is a strong driver of long-term outcomes.[70]

In summary, understanding individual patient tumor biology has significant implications for therapeutic management. Complete pathologic description of the tumor biopsy material is critical for optimal decision-making regarding the sequence of local and systemic therapies. In selection of the surgical approach, patients should be assessed individually based on risk factors such as histologic tumor type and tumor biology, which can more accurately determine the tumor burden that can be safely removed by breast-conserving therapy.

PRESENCE OF AN EXTENSIVE INTRADUCTAL COMPONENT

An extensive intraductal component is defined as intraductal cancer occupying at least 25% of the invasive tumor or lesions composed primarily of DCIS with one or more foci of invasive carcinoma.[71]

Although an extensive intraductal component had previously been considered a contraindication to breast-conserving therapy, it is now considered a risk factor for local recurrence when the status of excision margins has not been evaluated or is unknown.[72-74] Park and colleagues investigated factors affecting positive margins and the impact of a positive margin on outcomes after breast-conserving therapy in 705 breast cancer patients. Ninety-five (13.5%) patients had positive margins at initial resection. A positive margin at initial resection was significantly associated with the presence of an extensive intraductal component (p<0.001). However, an extensive

intraductal component was not a risk factor for local failure if negative margins were achieved. Other factors related to positive margins were lobular histology (p = 0.001) and four or more involved lymph nodes (p = 0.015). Patients with positive margins showed an advanced nodal stage, which was a significant factor for locoregional failure.[75]

Studies have reported a higher incidence rate of residual disease in patients with an extensive intraductal component than in patients without an extensive intraductal component.[76-78] As an example, in one study, 535 women who underwent breast-conserving therapy were examined for significant factors related to rates of re-excision and recurrence. Among patients who underwent re-excision, younger age and an extensive intraductal component were predictors for residual disease.[77] A recent study of 720 breast cancer patients investigated the predictors for residual disease after breast-conserving therapy and found that an extensive intraductal component, lymphovascular invasion, tumor at an inked margin, and more than a single affected margin were more often associated with residual disease.[79] However, local failure rates were not any greater provided negative margins of resection were achieved. This suggests that an extensive intraductal component is not a contraindication to breast-conserving therapy per se.

Therefore, routine assessment of margins of resection is an important component of histologic evaluation in women undergoing breast-conserving therapy, particularly those with an extensive intraduct component. In order to achieve negative surgical margins in breast-conserving therapy, combined clinical, radiologic, and pathologic evaluation is essential. The pathology report should specify whether extensive DCIS is present. The presence of an extensive intraductal component is a sign that disease in the breast may be more extensive than clinically suspected, but is not in itself a contraindication of breast-conserving therapy. Patients with an extensive intraductal component and negative margins are still acceptable candidates for breast-conserving therapy.

MARGINS AND INTRAOPERATIVE MARGIN ASSESSMENT

To minimize the risk of local recurrence after breast-conserving therapy, evaluation of surgical margins during and after the surgical procedure is important for achieving pathologically confirmed clear margins. After a careful gross examination, the surgical specimen must be appropriately inked, thinly sliced, and adequately sampled to enable reporting of the presence or absence of gross or microscopic carcinoma in the excision margins. Several studies have revealed that women with negative excision margins have low local recurrence rates following breast-conserving therapy, while positive resection margins are associated with a higher local recurrence rate.[80-84] Patients may require re-excision if initial excision results in close or positive resection margins.

The definition of an optimal margin width remains controversial. Recently, a definitive guideline was developed by a multidisciplinary group with the objective of reducing high re-excision rates in women with stage I or II breast cancer undergoing breast-conserving therapy.[85] The guideline authors reviewed 33 studies covering 28,162 patients and concluded that more widely clear margins do not decrease ipsilateral breast tumor recurrence risk compared to margins containing no tumor at ink. Among patients who had unfavorable tumor biology, a wider clear margin did not reduce the risk of ipsilateral recurrence.[85] Similar guidelines have also been published recently for DCIS.[86]

Currently, there are several intraoperative margin assessment techniques, including frozen section,[87,88] touch imprint cytology,[89] and shaved margin analysis.[90] It has been suggested obtaining extra shaved margins can decrease the rate of positive margins by almost 50% and thus decreasing the need for additional breast surgery.[91] Careful intraoperative evaluation with incorporation of a specimen x-ray is another method of evaluating margins. Patients with larger tumor size, multifocality, or an extensive intraductal component should be assessed more carefully to reduce the need for re-excision and avoid re-operation.[87]

MULTIFOCAL CARCINOMA

Multifocal breast cancer is defined as the occurrence of two or more carcinomas within different quadrants of the breast or the presence of multiple foci of the same tumor arising from the same quadrant. The presence of multifocal carcinomas has varied widely in the literature depending on definition and the methods used for pathologic sampling.[92]

The presence of an extensive multifocal breast cancer, with or without associated diffuse calcification and an associated extensive intraduct component, is considered a contraindication for breast-conserving surgery. Such cases may have a substantial tumor burden after breast-conserving surgery and a higher risk of local recurrence.[93] However, some studies have shown that patients with early-stage multicentric disease can safely undergo breast-conserving therapy with low recurrence risk if negative margins are obtained.[92,94] Indeed, the clinical significance of multicentric/multifocal breast cancer remains controversial. Contradictory results have been found in a few studies that investigated the prognostic significance of multicentric/multifocal tumors.[95,96] Despite the paucity of data from long-term studies, patients with multifocal disease may be candidates for breast-conserving therapy based on clinicopathologic and radiologic findings.

LYMPHOVASCULAR INVASION

Lymphovascular invasion describes what occurs when tumor cells enter the lymphatic spaces and/or blood vessels or both surrounding the tumor and represents a critical step in metastasis.[97] Routine histologic assessment of lymphovascular invasion is a crucial part of pathology reporting in breast cancer patients (**Figure 4.2.10**). Studies of the prognostic value of lymphovascular invasion in breast cancer have demonstrated a clear relationship between its presence and worse outcome in lymph node-negative patients. The presence of lymphovascular invasion as a predictor of outcome in patients with positive lymph nodes is less certain and use of lymphovascular invasion in clinical management decisions is debatable. Rakha and colleagues[97] studied the prognostic value of lymphovascular invasion in a large series of patients with operable breast cancers (pathologic T1 [pT1]-pT2 tumors). Across their entire cohort of patients, they found a strong association between lymphovascular invasion and both breast cancer-specific and distant metastasis-free survival; on multivariate analyses, lymphovascular invasion emerged as an independent predictor of both survival measures in patients with operable breast cancer. The authors concluded that in patients with invasive breast cancer and negative lymph nodes, lymphovascular invasion can be used as a strong predictor of outcome.[97] Another study evaluated patients with lymph node-positive breast cancer who had been treated with either mastectomy or wide local tumor resection and found lymphovascular invasion to be significantly associated with poor disease-free survival ($p<0.001$) and overall survival ($p = 0.006$).[98] A recent

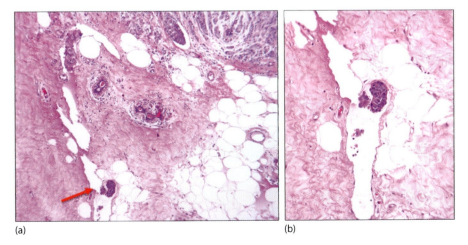

(a) (b)

4.2.10 (a) H&E section of invasive carcinoma with lymphovascular invasion. Arrow indicates tumor cells within lymphatic space. (b) Higher magnification of the lymphovascular invasion.

study investigated the predictive role of lymphovascular invasion in women younger than 40 years old diagnosed with locally advanced breast cancer (T3-4N0, T1-4N1). Within this patient population, treated with multiple modalities, triple-negative status, lymphovascular invasion, and number of positive lymph nodes were significantly associated with poorer overall survival. Moreover, in all treatment groups, lymphovascular invasion was associated with distant metastasis, locoregional recurrence, and poorer recurrence-free survival.[99]

CONCLUSION

In summary, despite the high degree of heterogeneity in breast cancer at the molecular and histologic levels, clinicopathologic factors alone do not influence the choice of surgery when tumor biology is managed appropriately. Innate tumor biology has a major impact on patient outcomes regardless of tumor subtype.

REFERENCES

1. Silverstein, M.J. and M.D. Lagios, Choosing treatment for patients with ductal carcinoma in situ: Fine tuning the university of Southern California/Van Nuys Prognostic Index. *J Natl Cancer Inst Monogr*, 2010. 2010(41): pp. 193–196.
2. Pinder, S.E. et al., A new pathological system for grading DCIS with improved prediction of local recurrence: Results from the UKCCCR/ANZ DCIS trial. *Br J Cancer*, 2010. 103(1): pp. 94–100.
3. Fisher, E.R. et al., Pathologic findings from the national surgical adjuvant breast project (NSABP) Protocol B-17. Intraductal carcinoma (ductal carcinoma in situ). The national surgical adjuvant breast and bowel project collaborating investigators. *Cancer*, 1995. 75(6): pp. 1310–1319.
4. Fisher, E.R. et al., Pathologic findings from the national surgical adjuvant breast Project (NSABP) eight-year update of Protocol B-17: Intraductal carcinoma. *Cancer*, 1999. 86(3): pp. 429–438.
5. Boyages, J., G. Delaney, and R. Taylor, Predictors of local recurrence after treatment of ductal carcinoma in situ: A meta-analysis. *Cancer*, 1999. 85(3): pp. 616–628.
6. Bijker, N. et al., Breast-conserving treatment with or without radiotherapy in ductal carcinoma-in-situ: Ten-year results of european organisation for research and treatment of cancer randomized phase III trial 10853–A study by the EORTC breast cancer cooperative group and EORTC radiotherapy group. *J Clin Oncol*, 2006. 24(21): pp. 3381–3387.
7. Kong, I. et al., Age at diagnosis predicts local recurrence in women treated with breast-conserving surgery and postoperative radiation therapy for ductal carcinoma in situ: A population-based outcomes analysis. *Curr Oncol*, 2014. 21(1): pp. e96–e104.
8. Donker, M. et al., Breast-conserving treatment with or without radiotherapy in ductal carcinoma In Situ: 15-year recurrence rates and outcome after a recurrence, from the EORTC 10853 randomized phase III trial. *J Clin Oncol*, 2013. 31(32): pp. 4054–4059.

9. Sanders, M.E. et al., The natural history of low-grade ductal carcinoma in situ of the breast in women treated by biopsy only revealed over 30 years of long-term follow-up. *Cancer*, 2005. 103(12): pp. 2481–2484.
10. Frank, S. et al., Ductal carcinoma in situ (DCIS) treated by mastectomy, or local excision with or without radiotherapy: A monocentric, retrospective study of 608 women. *Breast*, 2016. 25: pp. 51–56.
11. Generali, D. et al., COX-2 expression is predictive for early relapse and aromatase inhibitor resistance in patients with ductal carcinoma in situ of the breast, and is a target for treatment. *Br J Cancer*, 2014. 111(1): pp. 46–54.
12. Kerlikowske, K. et al., Biomarker expression and risk of subsequent tumors after initial ductal carcinoma in situ diagnosis. *J Natl Cancer Inst*, 2010. 102(9): pp. 627–637.
13. Solin, L.J. et al., A multigene expression assay to predict local recurrence risk for ductal carcinoma in situ of the breast. *J Natl Cancer Inst*, 2013. 105(10): pp. 701–710.
14. Rakovitch, E. et al., A population-based validation study of the DCIS Score predicting recurrence risk in individuals treated by breast-conserving surgery alone. *Breast Cancer Res Treat*, 2015. 152(2): pp. 389–398.
15. Parikh, R.R. et al., Ductal carcinoma in situ with microinvasion: Prognostic implications, long-term outcomes, and role of axillary evaluation. *Int J Radiat Oncol Biol Phys*, 2012. 82(1): pp. 7–13.
16. Adamovich, T.L. and R.M. Simmons, Ductal carcinoma in situ with microinvasion. *Am J Surg*, 2003. 186(2): pp. 112–116.
17. Sue, G.R. et al., Predictors of microinvasion and its prognostic role in ductal carcinoma in situ. *Am J Surg*, 2013. 206(4): pp. 478–481.
18. Vieira, C.C. et al., Microinvasive ductal carcinoma in situ: Clinical presentation, imaging features, pathologic findings, and outcome. *Eur J Radiol*, 2010. 73(1): pp. 102–107.
19. Solin, L.J. et al., Microinvasive ductal carcinoma of the breast treated with breast-conserving surgery and definitive irradiation. *Int J Radiat Oncol Biol Phys*, 1992. 23(5): pp. 961–968.
20. Margalit, D.N. et al., Microinvasive breast cancer: ER, PR, and HER-2/neu status and clinical outcomes after breast-conserving therapy or mastectomy. *Ann Surg Oncol*, 2013. 20(3): pp. 811–818.
21. Klauber-DeMore, N. et al., Sentinel lymph node biopsy: Is it indicated in patients with high-risk ductal carcinoma-in-situ and ductal carcinoma-in-situ with microinvasion? *Ann Surg Oncol*, 2000. 7(9): pp. 636–642.
22. Intra, M. et al., Sentinel lymph node metastasis in microinvasive breast cancer. *Ann Surg Oncol*, 2003. 10(10): pp. 1160–1165.
23. Camp, R. et al., Sentinel lymph node biopsy for ductal carcinoma in situ: An evolving approach at the university of Florida. *Breast J*, 2005. 11(6): pp. 394–397.
24. Zavagno, G. et al., Sentinel lymph node metastasis from mammary ductal carcinoma in situ with microinvasion. *Breast*, 2007. 16(2): pp. 146–151.
25. Sakr, R. et al., Ductal carcinoma in situ: Value of sentinel lymph node biopsy. *J Surg Oncol*, 2006. 94(5): pp. 426–430.

26. Katz, A. et al., Sentinel lymph node positivity of patients with ductal carcinoma in situ or microinvasive breast cancer. *Am J Surg*, 2006. 191(6): pp. 761–766.
27. Gray, R.J. et al., The optimal management of the axillae of patients with microinvasive breast cancer in the sentinel lymph node era. *Am J Surg*, 2007. 194(6): pp. 845–848; discussion 848–849.
28. Guth, A.A. et al., Microinvasive breast cancer and the role of sentinel node biopsy: An institutional experience and review of the literature. *Breast J*, 2008. 14(4): pp. 335–339.
29. Pimiento, J.M. et al., Role of axillary staging in women diagnosed with ductal carcinoma in situ with microinvasion. *J Oncol Pract*, 2011. 7(5): pp. 309–313.
30. Ko, B.S. et al., Risk factor for axillary lymph node metastases in microinvasive breast cancer. *Ann Surg Oncol*, 2012. 19(1): pp. 212–216.
31. Lyons III, J.M. et al., Axillary node staging for microinvasive breast cancer: Is it justified? *Ann Surg Oncol*, 2012. 19(11): pp. 3416–3421.
32. Haagensen, C.D. et al., Lobular neoplasia (so-called lobular carcinoma in situ) of the breast. *Cancer*, 1978. 42(2): pp. 737–69.
33. Page, D.L. et al., Lobular neoplasia of the breast: Higher risk for subsequent invasive cancer predicted by more extensive disease. *Hum Pathol*, 1991. 22(12): pp. 1232–1239.
34. Rosen, P.P. et al., Lobular carcinoma in situ of the breast. Detailed analysis of 99 patients with average follow-up of 24 years. *Am J Surg Pathol*, 1978. 2(3): pp. 225–251.
35. Chuba, P.J. et al., Bilateral risk for subsequent breast cancer after lobular carcinoma-in-situ: Analysis of surveillance, epidemiology, and end results data. *J Clin Oncol*, 2005. 23(24): pp. 5534–5541.
36. Sasson, A.R. et al., Lobular carcinoma in situ increases the risk of local recurrence in selected patients with stages I and II breast carcinoma treated with conservative surgery and radiation. *Cancer*, 2001. 91(10): pp. 1862–1869.
37. Ciocca, R.M. et al., Presence of lobular carcinoma in situ does not increase local recurrence in patients treated with breast-conserving therapy. *Ann Surg Oncol*, 2008. 15(8): pp. 2263–2271.
38. Apple, S.K. et al., Significance of lobular intraepithelial neoplasia at margins of breast conservation specimens: A report of 38 cases and literature review. *Diagn Pathol*, 2010. 5: pp. 54.
39. Jolly, S. et al., The impact of lobular carcinoma in situ in association with invasive breast cancer on the rate of local recurrence in patients with early-stage breast cancer treated with breast-conserving therapy. *Int J Radiat Oncol Biol Phys*, 2006. 66(2): pp. 365–371.
40. Sadek, B.T. et al., Risk of local failure in breast cancer patients with lobular carcinoma in situ at the final surgical margins: Is re-excision necessary? *Int J Radiat Oncol Biol Phys*, 2013. 87(4): pp. 726–730.
41. Downs-Kelly, E. et al., Clinical implications of margin involvement by pleomorphic lobular carcinoma in situ. *Arch Pathol Lab Med*, 2011. 135(6): pp. 737–743.
42. Chivukula, M. et al., Pleomorphic lobular carcinoma in situ (PLCIS) on breast core needle biopsies: Clinical significance and immunoprofile. *Am J Surg Pathol*, 2008. 32(11): pp. 1721–1726.
43. Chen, Y.Y. et al., Genetic and phenotypic characteristics of pleomorphic lobular carcinoma in situ of the breast. *Am J Surg Pathol*, 2009. 33(11): pp. 1683–1694.
44. Masannat, Y.A. et al., Challenges in the management of pleomorphic lobular carcinoma in situ of the breast. *Breast*, 2013. 22(2): pp. 194–196.
45. Pieri, A., J. Harvey, and N. Bundred, Pleomorphic lobular carcinoma in situ of the breast: Can the evidence guide practice? *World J Clin Oncol*, 2014. 5(3): pp. 546–553.
46. Flanagan, M.R. et al., Pleomorphic lobular carcinoma in situ: Radiologic-Pathologic features and clinical management. *Ann Surg Oncol*, 2015. 22(13): pp. 4263–4269.
47. Dillon, D., A.J. Guidi, and S.J. Schnitt, Pathology of Invasive Breast Cancer, in *Diseases of the Breast*, Harris J.R., Morrow M., Osborne C.K., Editor. 2014, Lippincott Williams & Wilkins.
48. Tavassoli, F.A., Lobular Neoplasia, in *Pathology of the Breast*, Tavassoli F.A., Editor. 1992, Stamford (CT): Appleton and Lange. pp. 263–291.
49. Delpech, Y. et al., Clinical benefit from neoadjuvant chemotherapy in oestrogen receptor-positive invasive ductal and lobular carcinomas. *Br J Cancer*, 2013. 108(2): pp. 285–291.
50. Katz, A. et al., Primary systemic chemotherapy of invasive lobular carcinoma of the breast. *Lancet Oncol*, 2007. 8(1): pp. 55–62.
51. Loibl, S. et al., Response and prognosis after neoadjuvant chemotherapy in 1,051 patients with infiltrating lobular breast carcinoma. *Breast Cancer Res Treat*, 2014. 144(1): pp. 153–162.
52. Cristofanilli, M. et al., Invasive lobular carcinoma classic type: Response to primary chemotherapy and survival outcomes. *J Clin Oncol*, 2005. 23(1): pp. 41–48.
53. Arpino, G. et al., Infiltrating lobular carcinoma of the breast: Tumor characteristics and clinical outcome. *Breast Cancer Res*, 2004. 6(3): pp. R149–R156.
54. Vo, T.N. et al., Outcomes of breast-conservation therapy for invasive lobular carcinoma are equivalent to those for invasive ductal carcinoma. *Am J Surg*, 2006. 192(4): pp. 552–555.
55. Moran, M.S., Q. Yang, and B.G. Haffty, The Yale University experience of early-stage invasive lobular carcinoma (ILC) and invasive ductal carcinoma (IDC) treated with breast conservation treatment (BCT): Analysis of clinical-pathologic features, long-term outcomes, and molecular expression of COX-2, Bcl-2, and p53 as a function of histology. *Breast J*, 2009. 15(6): pp. 571–578.
56. Santiago, R.J. et al., Similar long-term results of breast-conservation treatment for stage I and II invasive lobular carcinoma compared with invasive ductal carcinoma of the breast: The University of Pennsylvania experience. *Cancer*, 2005. 103(12): pp. 2447–2454.
57. Braunstein, L.Z. et al., Invasive lobular carcinoma of the breast: Local recurrence after breast-conserving therapy by subtype approximation and surgical margin. *Breast Cancer Res Treat*, 2015. 149(2): pp. 555–564.
58. Sagara, Y. et al., Surgical options and locoregional recurrence in patients diagnosed with invasive lobular carcinoma of the breast. *Ann Surg Oncol*, 2015. 22(13): pp. 4280–4286.
59. Perou, C.M. et al., Molecular portraits of human breast tumours. *Nature*, 2000. 406(6797): pp. 747–752.

60. Sorlie, T. et al., Gene expression patterns of breast carcinomas distinguish tumor subclasses with clinical implications. *Proc Natl Acad Sci U S A*, 2001. 98(19): pp. 10869-10874.

61. Nguyen, P.L. et al., Breast cancer subtype approximated by estrogen receptor, progesterone receptor, and HER-2 is associated with local and distant recurrence after breast-conserving therapy. *J Clin Oncol*, 2008. 26(14): pp. 2373-2378.

62. Millar, E.K. et al., Prediction of local recurrence, distant metastases, and death after breast-conserving therapy in early-stage invasive breast cancer using a five-biomarker panel. *J Clin Oncol*, 2009. 27(28): pp. 4701-4708.

63. Voduc, K.D. et al., Breast cancer subtypes and the risk of local and regional relapse. *J Clin Oncol*, 2010. 28(10): pp. 1684-16891.

64. Demirci, S. et al., Breast conservation therapy: The influence of molecular subtype and margins. *Int J Radiat Oncol Biol Phys*, 2012. 83(3): pp. 814-820.

65. Adkins, F.C. et al., Triple-negative breast cancer is not a contraindication for breast conservation. *Ann Surg Oncol*, 2011. 18(11): pp. 3164-3173.

66. Parker, C.C. et al., Is breast conservation therapy a viable option for patients with triple-receptor negative breast cancer? *Surgery*, 2010. 148(2): pp. 386-391.

67. Aalders, K.C. et al., Contemporary locoregional recurrence rates in young patients with early-stage breast cancer. *J Clin Oncol*, 2016. 34(18): pp. 2107-2114.

68. Lowery, A.J. et al., Locoregional recurrence after breast cancer surgery: A systematic review by receptor phenotype. *Breast Cancer Res Treat*, 2012. 133(3): pp. 831-841.

69. Pilewskie, M. et al., Effect of margin width on local recurrence in triple-negative breast cancer patients treated with breast-conserving therapy. *Ann Surg Oncol*, 2014. 21(4): pp. 1209-1214.

70. Mittendorf, E.A. et al., The neo-bioscore update for staging breast cancer treated with neoadjuvant chemotherapy: Incorporation of prognostic biologic factors into staging after treatment. *JAMA Oncol*, 2016. 2(7): pp. 929-936.

71. Schnitt, S.J. and J.R. Harris, Evolution of breast-conserving therapy for localized breast cancer. *J Clin Oncol*, 2008. 26(9): pp. 1395-1396.

72. Smitt, M.C. et al., Predictors of reexcision findings and recurrence after breast conservation. *Int J Radiat Oncol Biol Phys*, 2003. 57(4): pp. 979-985.

73. Swanson, G.P., K. Rynearson, and R. Symmonds, Significance of margins of excision on breast cancer recurrence. *Am J Clin Oncol*, 2002. 25(5): pp. 438-441.

74. Holland, R. et al., The presence of an extensive intraductal component following a limited excision correlates with prominent residual disease in the remainder of the breast. *J Clin Oncol*, 1990. 8(1): pp. 113-118.

75. Park, S. et al., The impact of a focally positive resection margin on the local control in patients treated with breast-conserving therapy. *Jpn J Clin Oncol*, 2011. 41(5): pp. 600-608.

76. Atalay, C. and C. Irkkan, Predictive factors for residual disease in re-excision specimens after breast-conserving surgery. *Breast J*, 2012. 18(4): pp. 339-344.

77. Smitt, M.C. and K. Horst, Association of clinical and pathologic variables with lumpectomy surgical margin status after preoperative diagnosis or excisional biopsy of invasive breast cancer. *Ann Surg Oncol*, 2007. 14(3): pp. 1040-1044.

78. Rodriguez, N., L.K. Diaz, and E.L. Wiley, Predictors of residual disease in repeat excisions for lumpectomies with margins less than 0.1 cm. *Clin Breast Cancer*, 2005. 6(2): pp. 169-172.

79. Alrahbi, S. et al., Extent of margin involvement, lymphovascular invasion, and extensive intraductal component predict for residual disease after wide local excision for breast cancer. *Clin Breast Cancer*, 2015. 15(3): pp. 219-226.

80. Dunne, C. et al., Effect of margin status on local recurrence after breast conservation and radiation therapy for ductal carcinoma in situ. *J Clin Oncol*, 2009. 27(10): pp. 1615-1620.

81. Meric, F. et al., Positive surgical margins and ipsilateral breast tumor recurrence predict disease-specific survival after breast-conserving therapy. *Cancer*, 2003. 97(4): pp. 926-933.

82. Cowen, D. et al., Local and distant failures after limited surgery with positive margins and radiotherapy for node-negative breast cancer. *Int J Radiat Oncol Biol Phys*, 2000. 47(2): pp. 305-312.

83. Park, C.C. et al., Outcome at 8 years after breast-conserving surgery and radiation therapy for invasive breast cancer: Influence of margin status and systemic therapy on local recurrence. *J Clin Oncol*, 2000. 18(8): pp. 1668-1675.

84. Leong, C. et al., Effect of margins on ipsilateral breast tumor recurrence after breast conservation therapy for lymph node-negative breast carcinoma. *Cancer*, 2004. 100(9): pp. 1823-1832.

85. Moran, M.S. et al., Society of surgical oncology-American society for radiation oncology consensus guideline on margins for breast-conserving surgery with whole-breast irradiation in stages I and II invasive breast cancer. *J Clin Oncol*, 2014. 32(14): pp. 1507-1515.

86. Morrow, M. et al., Society of surgical oncology-American society for radiation oncology-American society of clinical oncology consensus guideline on margins for breast-conserving surgery with whole-breast irradiation in ductal carcinoma in situ. *J Clin Oncol*, 2016.

87. Cabioglu, N. et al., Role for intraoperative margin assessment in patients undergoing breast-conserving surgery. *Ann Surg Oncol*, 2007. 14(4): pp. 1458-1471.

88. Riedl, O. et al., Intraoperative frozen section analysis for breast-conserving therapy in 1016 patients with breast cancer. *Eur J Surg Oncol*, 2009. 35(3): pp. 264-270.

89. Creager, A.J. et al., Intraoperative evaluation of lumpectomy margins by imprint cytology with histologic correlation: A community hospital experience. *Arch Pathol Lab Med*, 2002. 126(7): pp. 846-848.

90. Camp, E.R. et al., Minimizing local recurrence after breast conserving therapy using intraoperative shaved margins to determine pathologic tumor clearance. *J Am Coll Surg*, 2005. 201(6): pp. 855-861.

91. Chagpar, A.B. et al., A randomized, controlled trial of cavity shave margins in breast cancer. *N Engl J Med*, 2015. 373(6): pp. 503-510.

92. Yerushalmi, R. et al., Is breast-conserving therapy a safe option for patients with tumor multicentricity and multifocality? *Ann Oncol*, 2012. 23(4): pp. 876-881.

93. Kurtz, J.M. et al., Breast-conserving therapy for macroscopically multiple cancers. *Ann Surg*, 1990. 212(1): pp. 38–44.

94. Carpenter, S. et al., Optimal treatment of multiple ipsilateral primary breast cancers. *Am J Surg*, 2008. 196(4): pp. 530–536.

95. Joergensen, L.E. et al., Multifocality as a prognostic factor in breast cancer patients registered in Danish breast cancer cooperative group (DBCG) 1996-2001. *Breast*, 2008. 17(6): pp. 587–591.

96. Litton, J.K. et al., Multifocal breast cancer in women < or =35 years old. *Cancer*, 2007. 110(7): pp. 1445–1450.

97. Rakha, E.A. et al., The prognostic significance of lymphovascular invasion in invasive breast carcinoma. *Cancer*, 2012. 118(15): pp. 3670–3680.

98. Song, Y.J. et al., The role of lymphovascular invasion as a prognostic factor in patients with lymph node-positive operable invasive breast cancer. *J Breast Cancer*, 2011. 14(3): pp. 198–203.

99. Khwaja, S.S. et al., Lymphovascular space invasion and lack of downstaging after neoadjuvant chemotherapy are strong predictors of adverse outcome in young women with locally advanced breast cancer. *Cancer Med*, 2016. 5(2): pp. 230–238.

4.3 MEDICAL ONCOLOGIST

Jessica Taff and Francisco J. Esteva

Randomized clinical trials have shown no difference in overall survival for breast-conserving surgery compared with mastectomy for patients with early-stage breast cancer.[1] It is well established that adjuvant chemotherapy, endocrine, and HER2-targeted therapies decrease the risk of both locoregional and systemic recurrence in at-risk breast cancer patients.[2] In the 1970s, it was hypothesized that administration of chemotherapy prior to surgery would improve clinical outcome by eradicating microscopic metastases without delay. However, the National Surgical Adjuvant Breast and Bowel protocol B-18 showed no statistical difference in disease-free survival and overall survival when doxorubicin and cyclophosphamide were given either pre- or postoperatively. Although the initial hypothesis was refuted, the B-18 trial established the safety of neoadjuvant chemotherapy in patients with operable breast cancer.[3] Furthermore, this study showed that patients achieving pathologic complete response (pCR) had improved disease-free and overall survival compared to patients with residual disease at the time of definitive surgery. A meta-analysis of 11 clinical trials involving 11,955 patients confirmed the strong prognostic value of pCR irrespective of the initial stage and molecular subtype of breast cancer.[4] The pCR rate is higher in patients with triple negative and HER2 overexpressing breast cancers. Trastuzumab monoclonal antibody therapy has been shown to improve the efficacy of chemotherapy in HER2-positive breast cancer, resulting in higher pCR rates compared to chemotherapy alone.[5] Pertuzumab is a monoclonal antibody that inhibits dimerization of the HER2 protein to other HER family members.[6] When this agent is added to docetaxel and trastuzumab, not only are there changes in tumor characteristics which influence surgical options, but also prolongation of progression-free survival (12.4 months in the control group versus 18.5 months in the pertuzumab group [Hazard Ratio (HR) 0.62, 95% CI 0.5–0.75; p < 0.001]).[7] Neoadjuvant chemotherapy is associated with lower pCR rates in patients with hormone receptor-positive breast cancer compared to HER2-positive or TNBC. Nonetheless, these hormone receptor sensitive patients can still benefit from neoadjuvant chemotherapy or endocrine therapy to improve their options for breast-conserving surgery. Overall, those patients with a pCR have excellent clinical outcomes and one of the main challenges therapeutically is how to select the most appropriate systemic therapy upfront. In 2014, the United States Food and Drug Administration approved pertuzumab in combination with trastuzumab and taxane chemotherapy in the neoadjuvant setting, and this represents the first approval for any new therapy based on pCR as the primary endpoint for tumor response.

Preoperative chemotherapy can provide patients the option of oncoplastic breast surgery when it would otherwise not be feasible due to tumor characteristics such as size and location. Its use can render inoperable tumors operable and can downstage cancers to allow breast-conserving therapy. Patients with tumors >5 cm often derive the greatest benefit from neoadjuvant chemotherapy (independent of nodal involvement), as successful breast conservation is more difficult to achieve with larger tumors. Patients with tumors initially larger than 5 cm may witness the greatest incremental change in tumor size in response to neoadjuvant chemotherapy.[8]

In patients with locally advanced breast cancer, neoadjuvant chemotherapy (with or without targeted biological agents) may facilitate cytoreduction such that the patient achieves pCR at the time of excision. Absence of pathological evidence of disease in the breast and axillary lymph nodes at the time of surgery is the strongest predictor of disease-free and overall survival for all breast cancer subtypes. Furthermore, in a cohort of 259 patients treated with either breast-conserving surgery or oncoplastic breast surgery after primary chemotherapy, larger volumes of tissue were excised from the patients receiving oncoplastic breast surgery. At median follow-up of 46 months, rates of both local and distant recurrence were similar for both groups.[9]

In discussion of new surgical techniques for improved cosmetic outcomes, timing in relation to chemotherapy is an important consideration. Risk of breast cancer recurrence is highest in the first 2–3 years after surgery and surgical trauma is known to increase the number of circulating tumor cells. This might provide a rationale for starting chemotherapy as soon as possible. A study of 285 breast cancer patients showed that oncoplastic breast surgery does not contribute to delays in starting chemotherapy more than is in the case for patients undergoing modified radical mastectomy or lumpectomy.[10] As for any surgical technique, complications linked to wound healing provide the greatest potential threat to initiation of chemotherapy, but these were not significantly increased in the group undergoing oncoplastic breast surgery.

Any effect of increased time to chemotherapy is controversial, even when surgical delays do occur. A study from the United Kingdom of 686 patients failed to identify a significant survival benefit when patients with early-stage breast cancer started chemotherapy soon after surgery,[11] but others have argued that adjuvant chemotherapy started more than 12 weeks from surgery is associated with statistically inferior survival.[12] When patients are stratified by tumor characteristics and stage, delays in chemotherapy greater than 8 weeks are thought to contribute to worse outcomes in those with at least stage III breast cancer, triple negative, and trastuzumab-treated HER-2-positive breast cancers.[13]

Despite evidence that breast-conservation surgery has outcomes equivalent to mastectomy, an increasing number of women are choosing more radical surgical options including contralateral prophylactic mastectomy. A 14-year report from the University of Louisville noted a decrease in mastectomy rates from 1995–2004, with an increase in mastectomy and contralateral mastectomy thereafter.[14] This was confirmed by a more recent study of more than 1.2 million adult women showing that one-third (35.5%)

of patients deemed eligible for breast-conserving surgery underwent mastectomy for the period 1998 to 2011, with the greatest increase in mastectomy rates among women with node-negative and in situ disease.[15] This trend toward radical surgery is thought to be driven by patient preference with no evidence for any survival benefit from mastectomy and contralateral prophylactic mastectomy compared with unilateral breast-conserving surgery.[16]

In summary, oncoplastic breast surgery, particularly following neoadjuvant chemotherapy, can offer patients the opportunity for excellent cosmetic results without compromising risk of breast cancer recurrence. Opportunities for breast conservation using oncoplastic breast surgery techniques are particularly suited to tumors which respond to neoadjuvant chemotherapy, and additional systemic therapies are under investigation for patients with residual disease at the time of definitive surgery.

REFERENCES

1. Simone NL, Dan T, Shih J et al. Twenty-five year results of the national cancer institute randomized breast conservation trial. *Breast Cancer Research and Treatment* 2012;132:197–203.
2. Early Breast Cancer Trialists' Collaborative G, Peto R, Davies C et al. Comparisons between different polychemotherapy regimens for early breast cancer: meta-analyses of long-term outcome among 100,000 women in 123 randomised trials. *Lancet* 2012;379:432–444.
3. Rastogi P, Anderson SJ, Bear HD et al. Preoperative chemotherapy: Updates of national surgical adjuvant breast and bowel project protocols B-18 and B-27. *Journal of Clinical Oncology: Official Journal of the American Society of Clinical Oncology* 2008;26:778–785.
4. Cortazar P, Zhang L, Untch M et al. Pathological complete response and long-term clinical benefit in breast cancer: The CTNeoBC pooled analysis. *Lancet* (London, England) 2014;384:164–172.
5. Buzdar AU, Valero V, Ibrahim NK et al. Neoadjuvant therapy with paclitaxel followed by 5-fluorouracil, epirubicin, and cyclophosphamide chemotherapy and concurrent trastuzumab in human epidermal growth factor receptor 2-positive operable breast cancer: An update of the initial randomized study population and data of additional patients treated with the same regimen. *Clinical Cancer Research* 2007;13:228–233.
6. Nahta R, Hung MC, Esteva FJ. The HER-2-targeting antibodies trastuzumab and pertuzumab synergistically inhibit the survival of breast cancer cells. *Cancer Research* 2004;64:2343–2346.
7. Baselga J, Cortes J, Kim SB et al. Pertuzumab plus trastuzumab plus docetaxel for metastatic breast cancer. *New England Journal of Medicine* 2012;366:109–119.
8. Fisher B, Brown A, Mamounas E et al. Effect of preoperative chemotherapy on local-regional disease in women with operable breast cancer: Findings from national surgical adjuvant breast and bowel project B-18. *Journal of Clinical Oncology: Official Journal of the American Society of Clinical Oncology* 1997;15:2483–2493.
9. Mazouni C, Naveau A, Kane A et al. The role of oncoplastic breast surgery in the management of breast cancer treated with primary chemotherapy. *Breast* (Edinburgh, Scotland) 2013;22:1189–1193.
10. Dogan L, Gulcelik MA, Karaman N, Ozaslan C, Reis E. Oncoplastic surgery in surgical treatment of breast cancer: Is the timing of adjuvant treatment affected? *Clinical Breast Cancer* 2013;13:202–205.
11. Shannon C, Ashley S, Smith IE. Does timing of adjuvant chemotherapy for early breast cancer influence survival? *Journal of Clinical Oncology: Official Journal of the American Society of Clinical Oncology* 2003;21:3792–3797.
12. Lohrisch C, Paltiel C, Gelmon K et al. Impact on survival of time from definitive surgery to initiation of adjuvant chemotherapy for early-stage breast cancer. *Journal of Clinical Oncology: Official Journal of the American Society of Clinical Oncology* 2006;24:4888–4894.
13. Gagliato Dde M, Gonzalez-Angulo AM, Lei X et al. Clinical impact of delaying initiation of adjuvant chemotherapy in patients with breast cancer. *Journal of Clinical Oncology: Official Journal of the American Society of Clinical Oncology* 2014;32:735–744.
14. Dragun AE, Pan J, Riley EC et al. Increasing use of elective mastectomy and contralateral prophylactic surgery among breast conservation candidates: A 14-year report from a comprehensive cancer center. *American Journal of Clinical Oncology* 2013;36:375–380.
15. Kummerow KL, Du L, Penson DF, Shyr Y, Hooks MA. Nationwide trends in mastectomy for early-stage breast cancer. *Journal of the American Medical Association surgery* 2015;150:9–16.
16. Benson JR, Winters ZE. Contralateral prophylactic mastectomy. *British Journal of Surgery* 2016;103:10:1249–1250.

4.4 RADIATION ONCOLOGIST

Ian Kunkler

Introduction

Postoperative radiotherapy remains the standard of care after breast-conserving surgery for most patients[1] and for those at higher risk following mastectomy.[2] There is level 1 evidence from the Oxford Overview of over 10,000 women included in trials of breast-conserving surgery with or without whole breast radiotherapy that radiotherapy halves the risk of local recurrence.[3] In addition, there is long-term evidence for the value of delivering a boost of irradiation to the area of the tumor bed after breast-conserving surgery and whole breast radiotherapy,[4] particularly in women under the age of 50. Several issues related to irradiation postmastectomy and breast reconstruction and post breast-conserving surgery will be discussed and include: (a) radiation toxicity, (b) target coverage, (c) timing of radiotherapy and specific to breast-conserving surgery, and (d) localization of the site of surgical excision for targeting a radiation boost. Close liaison is needed between surgeon and radiation oncologist to plan management for patients who are potential candidates for reconstruction and postoperative radiotherapy.

The evidence base for radiotherapy practice in the context of oncoplastic surgery is weak for both groups of patients. There are no randomized trials evaluating the effects of adjuvant irradiation on the reconstructed breast. Most studies are based on retrospective data from single institutions, often heterogeneous in make-up, with small sample sizes and inconsistent methods of evaluation.[5] Standardized methods for evaluation of clinical outcomes of reconstruction with and without irradiation are needed. However, type of reconstruction is being collected in the BIG 2-04 MRC SUPREMO trial[6] of postmastectomy radiotherapy for intermediate risk breast cancer (currently in follow-up phase) and may provide useful data on impact of reconstruction on quality of life.

The rapid rise in use of oncoplastic surgical techniques for breast conservation (such as remodeling with a breast reduction technique [mammoplasty]) presents new challenges for the radiation oncologist, particularly in relation to localization of the tumor bed for radiotherapy "boost planning" after mammoplasty. It is important that overall rates of locoregional control are not compromised by cosmetic considerations, which may prompt either omission of radiation when indicated or use of suboptimal dose and fractionation or radiotherapy technique.

Toxicity of radiation

Radiation may have adverse consequences on the cosmetic outcome of breast reconstruction due to fibrosis, edema, and changes in the microvasculature.

Radiation is considered to induce fibrosis in the stroma of fat tissue, causing cell death and fat necrosis, although the exact mechanism is not well understood.[7,8] Deep inferior epigastric perforator flaps and muscle-sparing free transverse rectus abdominis myocutaneous flaps are particularly prone to radiation induced fat necrosis.[8] The incidence of fat necrosis in a systematic review of over 5000 patients showed that for patients who had a reconstruction and no radiotherapy, the incidence of fat necrosis was 8.7% compared to 22.3% for patients receiving post reconstruction radiotherapy (p < 0.001).[9] Whether radiation has deleterious effects on free flap reconstruction is controversial and conflicting data have been published. Increased risks of capsular contracture, implant deflation or rupture, wound dehiscence, and infection have been reported after postmastectomy radiotherapy.[10,11] In a systematic review of pooled data from the literature, the incidence of complications for immediate autologous breast reconstructions was similar with or without adjuvant irradiation.[12] In a large prospective study of two-stage implant reconstruction with or without radiation, 1415 patients treated by a single surgeon had a mean follow-up of 56.8 months. Rates of both implant loss (9.1% vs 0.5%, p < 0.001) and capsular contracture (6.9% vs 0.5%, p < 0.01) were found to be higher in irradiated patients.[13] Moreover, there was no difference in rates of implant replacement between irradiated and non-irradiated patients and more than 90% of patients had good to excellent cosmesis. Of note, there is no evidence that the metallic component of the implant ports contributes to higher complication rates and no excess of dose in the metal part of the implant was found in a study using a phantom.[14]

Timing of radiotherapy and reconstruction

The optimal timing and technique of breast reconstruction in patients for whom postmastectomy radiotherapy is indicated remains controversial and in particular there is no robust evidence that immediate breast reconstruction delays radiotherapy.[1] In patients who have received or are due to receive postmastectomy radiotherapy, delayed autologous tissue reconstruction is generally recommended after irradiation.[15] In a more recent systematic review of the literature, a total of 37 studies were categorized as follows in relation to timing of radiotherapy in the context of breast reconstruction[16]:

1. Autologous reconstruction after radiotherapy
2. Definitive implant reconstruction after radiotherapy
3. Autologous reconstruction before radiotherapy
4. Definitive implant reconstruction before radiotherapy

The authors found a very wide range for both rates of complications (8.7%–70.0%) and acceptable cosmetic outcomes (41.4%–93.3%). A higher complication and revision rate was found when implant-based reconstruction was performed after radiotherapy. For autologous reconstruction, fibrosis was more common when reconstruction was undertaken first. In a second analysis comparing category 1 versus 3 and 2 versus 4 studies, no significant differences in complication rates were found.

Is radiation overage of the reconstructed breast adequate and doses to critical structures acceptable?

There have been conflicting reports on the quality of radiation planning in terms of adequacy of coverage for the reconstructed breast.[17,18] In the study of Motwani and colleagues, there was reduced coverage of the target volume and increased dose to normal structures for patients undergoing chest wall radiotherapy after immediate reconstruction.[18] By contrast, Koutcher and colleagues examined outcomes among 42 patients treated by the modern technique of intensity-modulated radiotherapy in which the intensity of the radiation beam can be adapted to maximize coverage of the target volume, while minimizing dosage to normal structures. This study showed that in 73% of cases all chest wall borders were covered, local control was excellent, and there were acceptable doses to lung and heart, even when the internal mammary nodes were treated.[17] However, there was no comparison available of patients receiving postmastectomy radiotherapy without reconstruction and the sample size was small. Nonetheless, immediate breast reconstruction followed by chest wall irradiation may be considered a safe and effective option with modern radiotherapy techniques.

Mammoplasty and postoperative radiotherapy

The main challenge for the radiation oncologist is correct identification of the original tumor bearing tissue to determine which area has to be boosted. The tumor bed needs to be accurately defined to minimize both risk of local recurrence and local complications of radiotherapy. Transposition, excision, and rotation of breast tissue may make it difficult or impossible to define the original site of tumor excision. Boost irradiation is known to be associated with poor cosmesis.[19] The only published study that has investigated the correlation between tumor bed after oncoplastic surgery or standard lumpectomy involved 31 consecutive patients (13 simple lumpectomy and 18 oncoplastic surgery[20]). A contrast-enhanced CT scan in the radiotherapy treatment position was carried out 1 week before surgery. One or more clips had been placed in the tumor cavity at the time of lumpectomy or oncoplastic surgery. Four oncoplastic techniques were employed and included:

1. V-mammoplasty outer for outer quadrant lesions
2. V-mammoplasty inner for lower pole inner quadrant lesions
3. Superior pedicle mammoplasty inverted-T for upper pole lesion
4. Round block mammoplasty for upper pole lesions (required larger tissue resection)

A postoperative contrasted-enhanced CT scan in the treatment position was carried out 4–5 weeks after surgery. The pre- and postoperative CT scans were fused. A radiation oncologist outlined the gross tumor volume which involved all the clips, the clinical target volume which involved all the clips plus an additional 0.5 cm margin, and the planning target volume. The latter included clinical target volume clips and gross tumor volume plus an overall margin of 5 mm in lateral and 10 mm in craniocaudal directions for setup uncertainties. The tumor bed was treated by either an electron or photon boost. There was a significantly larger volume of excision with oncoplastic surgery than lumpectomy, although average tumor size was also significantly greater for the oncoplastic group (18.6 vs 11.7 mm, p = 0.03). A significantly larger margin of normal tissue was excised with oncoplastic procedures than lumpectomy (9.06 vs 5.42 mm, p = 0.027). Provided that at least three clips are used to define the tumor bed, it can be equally satisfactorily delineated for patients undergoing either oncoplastic surgery or standard lumpectomy.

REFERENCES

1. "Early and locally advanced breast cancer: Diagnosis and treatment." *National Institute for Clinical Excellence* (2008).
2. Coates AS, Winer EP, Goldhirsch A, Gelber RD et al. "Tailoring therapies-improving the management of early breast cancer: St Gallen international expert consensus on the primary therapy of early breast cancer 2015." *Panel Members. Ann Oncol* (2015): 26(8): 1533–1546.
3. Early Breast Cancer Trialists' Collaborative Group (EBCTCG), "Effect of radiotherapy after breast-conserving surgery on 10-year recurrence and 15-year breast cancer death: Meta-analysis of individual patient data for 10 801 women in 17 randomised trials." *Lancet*, 378: (2011): 1707–1716.
4. Bartelink H, Maingon P, Poortmans P, Weltens C et al. "Whole-breast irradiation with or without a boost for patients treated with breast-conserving surgery for early breast cancer: 20-year follow-up of a randomised phase 3 trial European organisation for research and treatment of cancer radiation oncology and breast cancer groups," *Lancet Oncol* (2015) 16:47–56.
5. Potter S, Brigic A, Whiting PF, Cawthorn SJ et al. "Reporting outcomes of breast reconstruction; a systematic review." *J Natl Cancer Inst* (2011): 103:31–46.
6. Kunkler IH, Canney P, van Tienhoven G, Russell NS; MRC/EORTC (BIG 2-04) SUPREMO Trial Management Group. "Elucidating the role of chest wall irradiation in 'intermediate-risk' breast cancer: The MRC/EORTC SUPREMO trial." *Clin Oncol (R Coll Radiol)* (2008): 20(1):31–34.
7. Rogers NE and Allen RJ. "Radiation effects on breast reconstruction with deep inferior epigastric perforator flap." *Plast Reconstr Surg* (2002): 109:1919–1924.
8. Garvey PB, Clemens MW, Hoy AE, Smith B et al. "Muscle-sparing TRAM flap does not protect breast reconstruction from postmastectomy radiation damage compared to DIEP flap." *Plast Reconstr Surg* (2014): 155:223–233.
9. Clarke-Pearson EM, Chadha M, Dayan E, Dayan JH et al. "Comparison of irradiated versus non irradiated DIEP flaps in patients undergoing immediate bilateral DIEP reconstruction with unilateral postmastectomy radiation therapy (PMRT)." *Ann Plast Surg* (2013): 71:250–254.

10. Chawla AK, Kachnik LA, Taghian AG, Niemierko A et al. "Radiotherapy and breast reconstruction: Complications and cosmesis with TRAM versus tissue expander/implant." *Int J Rad Oncol Biol* (2002): 54:520–526.

11. Krueger EA, Wilkins EG, Strawderman M, Cederna P et al. "Complications and patient satisfaction following expander/implant breast reconstruction: Outcomes, complications, aesthetic results and satisfaction among 156 patients." *Plast Reconst Surg* (2004): 113:877081.

12. Schaverien MV, Macmillan DR, McCulley SJ et al. "Is immediate autologous breast reconstruction with postoperative radiotherapy good practice? A systematic review of the literature." *J Plast Reconstr Aesth Surg* (2013): 66:1637–1651.

13. Cordeiro PG, Albornoz CR, McCormick B, Hugh Q et al. "The impact of postmastectomy radiotherapy on two-stage implant breast reconstruction: An analysis of long-term surgical outcomes, aesthetic result and satisfaction over 13 years." *Plast Reconstr Surg* (2014): 134:588–595.

14. Moni J, Graves-Ditman M, Cederna P, Griffith K et al. "Dosimetry around metallic ports in tissue expanders in patients receiving postmastectomy radiation therapy, an ex-vivo evaluation." *Med Dosim* (2003): 29:49–54.

15. Kronowitz SJ, Robb GL. "Radiation therapy and breast reconstruction: A critical review of the literature." *Plast Reconstr Surg* (2009): 124:395–408.

16. Berbers J, van Baardwij A, Houben R, Heuts E et al. "Reconstruction: Before or after mastectomy radiotherapy? A systematic review of the literature." *Eur J Cancer* (2014): 50:2752–2762.

17. Koutcher L, Ballungrud A, Cordeiro PG, McCormick B et al. "Postmastectomy intensity modulated radiation therapy following immediate expander-implant reconstruction." *Radiother Oncol* (2010): 94:319–323.

18. Motwani SB, Strom EA, Schecter NR, Butler CE et al. "The impact of immediate breast reconstruction on the technical delivery of postmastectomy radiotherapy." *Int J Rad Oncol Biol Phys* (2006) 76–82.

19. Vrieling C, Collette L, Fourquet A, Hoogenraad WJ et al. "The influence of patient, tumor and treatment factors on the cosmetic results after breast-conserving therapy in the EORTC 'boost vs. no boost' trial." EORTC radiotherapy and breast cancer cooperative groups. *Radiother Oncol* (2000): 55:219–232.

20. Furet E, Peurien D, Fournier-Bidoz NV, Servoir V et al. "Plastic surgery for breast conservation therapy: How to define the volume of the tumor bed for the boost?" *Eur J Surg Oncol* (2014): 40:830–834.

4.5 BREAST SURGEON

Efstathios Karamanos and Lisa A. Newman

Women receiving a new diagnosis of breast cancer are simultaneously traumatized by fears related to mortality risks as well as potentially disfiguring surgery and the morbidity of systemic therapies. One of the first decisions that many of these patients face is the choice of pursuing breast-conserving surgery (lumpectomy plus breast radiation) versus mastectomy. Multiple prospective randomized control trials conducted internationally have confirmed the survival equivalence for these two surgical approaches, as mortality risk from breast cancer is generally defined by the underlying tumor biology and its distant organ metastatic potential.[1-4] The multidisciplinary breast oncology team assesses the metastatic risk by evaluating the cancer stage, which is determined by tumor size and regional/axillary nodal status as well as by tumor biomarker expression (estrogen receptor, progesterone receptor, and HER2/neu). This assessment is then utilized to determine the systemic therapy needs of individual patients.

Since mastectomy does not confer any survival advantage over breast-conservation approaches, it is reasonable to encourage lumpectomy in the majority of women presenting with clinically early-stage disease. Breast preservation requires that the patient commit to adjuvant radiation therapy (usually given as whole-breast treatment in daily fractions over 3 or 5 weeks) and to long-term surveillance to check for evidence of either local recurrence (which usually occurs within the first 5 years of treatment and at the lumpectomy bed) or the development of a new primary breast cancer (which is a cumulative risk over time and can occur in either breast).

Despite the survival equivalence of breast-conserving surgery and mastectomy, several criteria are accepted as identifying patients who are better-served from an oncological perspective by mastectomy:

1. Inflammatory breast cancer is associated with high risk of both local and distant recurrence and this group of patients are generally managed with more aggressive treatments involving neoadjuvant chemotherapy followed by modified radical mastectomy and postmastectomy radiation (as well as adjuvant endocrine therapy in the setting of hormone receptor-positive disease).
2. Lack of access to a radiation facility.
3. Inability to obtain a margin-negative lumpectomy despite re-excision(s).
4. Diffuse malignant microcalcifications on mammography.
5. Multiple breast tumors that cannot be resected within a single margin-negative lumpectomy.

6. Contraindication to radiation therapy:

   a. Prior breast irradiation (e.g., breast-conserving surgery for cancer or Mantle irradiation for Hodgkin's lymphoma)
   b. Pregnancy (selected pregnant breast cancer patients can be offered breast conservation if radiotherapy can be deferred until after delivery, late third trimester, or in patients receiving chemotherapy during their second and third trimesters)
   c. Connective tissue disorders such as Sjogren's syndrome or scleroderma with significant dermatologic involvement, which is intolerant of radiation toxicity to the skin

Over the past few decades, several advances have occurred that have expanded eligibility for breast-conservation approaches:

1. Ability to offer lumpectomy to relatively larger/bulky tumors in women with a breast size that can accommodate resection with a cosmetically acceptable outcome. Although all patients should be informed of the risk of an asymmetric breast appearance following large-volume lumpectomy and whole breast radiation-related shrinkage, individual patients must define their personal threshold for an unacceptable aesthetic result. Improvements in reconstructive options for lumpectomy defects have addressed many of these cosmetic issues, such as fat grafting; use of reduction mammoplasty-style lumpectomies; and/or contralateral breast reduction mammoplasty.
2. Use of neoadjuvant chemotherapy to downstage primary breast tumors and improve eligibility for a smaller-volume lumpectomy.
3. Widespread adoption of the recently published consensus statement on lumpectomy margins which defines a negative margin as being no cancer cells present at the inked lumpectomy surface ("no tumor at ink").[5,6]

While many patients require mastectomy on oncological grounds, some patients are motivated to pursue mastectomy as a personal preference because of a desire to reduce their likelihood of developing a new primary breast cancer (which would then mandate repeating the breast cancer treatment experience). Advances in breast reconstruction techniques have resulted in significant improvements in quality of life and psychosocial satisfaction for patients undergoing mastectomy.

A personal history of breast cancer is a well-documented risk factor for development of a new primary breast cancer. The latter occurs at a rate of 0.25%–1% per year, but can be reduced by 50%–70% by taking advantage of the chemopreventive effects of endocrine therapy in patients with hormone receptor-positive disease. In women with hereditary susceptibility for breast cancer (such as BRCA1 or BRCA2 mutation-carriers), this risk can be up to 4%–5% per year. It is therefore not uncommon for young breast cancer patients and BRCA1/2 mutation carriers to request bilateral mastectomy surgery when diagnosed with unilateral disease. It is essential that any patient contemplating contralateral prophylactic mastectomy (CPM) be clearly informed that: (i) CPM does not guarantee prevention of a new breast cancer and microscopic foci of breast tissue can reside in the mastectomy skin flaps or in the axilla and be a source of subsequent malignancy and (ii) CPM does not confer any survival advantage and mortality risk tends to be determined by the innate aggressiveness and stage of the first breast cancer.[7,8]

Oncologic issues related to anticipated axillary nodal surgery may also influence a patient's choice for lumpectomy versus mastectomy. The American College of Surgeons Oncology Group Z0011 prospective randomized clinical trial[9,10] established the safety of avoiding a completion axillary lymph node dissection (ALND) in patients undergoing breast-conserving surgery managed by lumpectomy and whole breast radiation when either micro- or macrometastatic disease is identified in one or two sentinel lymph nodes. This trial randomized lumpectomy patients with T1/T2 invasive breast cancer and limited axillary nodal burden of metastases to undergo either completion axillary lymph node dissection (ALND) or axillary observation. The equivalence of results are at least partly explained by the fact that whole breast radiation will also cover the low axilla, and therefore can sterilize residual metastatic disease in the preserved non-sentinel nodes. Furthermore, in the setting of mastectomy as primary surgical treatment, completion ALND following resection of metastatic sentinel lymph nodes is generally recommended and can guide further treatment as the total count of axillary nodes containing metastases may determine whether a patient receives postmastectomy radiation.[11] It can therefore often be advantageous for patients to undergo an upfront sentinel lymph node biopsy prior to the definitive mastectomy, as detection of sentinel node metastatic disease might encourage a patient to reconsider breast conservation as a strategy of avoiding the need for completion ALND. An upfront sentinel lymph node biopsy will also provide important information regarding the possible need for postmastectomy radiation therapy and therefore also influence plans for type of immediate reconstruction.

As described above, newly diagnosed breast cancer patients are faced with a variety of treatment options and sequences and oncologically appropriate counseling requires a proactive, coordinated effort by the multidisciplinary team. This should include a surgical breast oncologist, a plastic/reconstruction surgeon, a radiation oncologist, and a medical oncologist for optimal management and a fully informed patient.

REFERENCES

1. Newman LA, Washington TA. New trends in breast conservation therapy. *Surg Clin North Am.* 2003;83: 841–883.
2. Agarwal S, Pappas L, Neumayer L, Kokeny K, Agarwal J. Effect of breast conservation therapy vs mastectomy on disease-specific survival for early-stage breast cancer. *JAMA Surg.* 2014;149: 267–274.
3. Simone NL, Dan T, Shih J et al. Twenty-five year results of the national cancer institute randomized breast conservation trial. *Breast Cancer Res Treat.* 2012;132: 197–203.
4. Fisher B, Anderson S, Bryant J et al. Twenty-year follow-up of a randomized trial comparing total mastectomy, lumpectomy, and lumpectomy plus irradiation for the treatment of invasive breast cancer. *N Engl J Med.* 2002;347: 1233–1241.
5. Moran MS, Schnitt SJ, Giuliano AE et al. Society of surgical oncology-american society for radiation oncology consensus guideline on margins for breast-conserving surgery with whole-breast irradiation in stages I and II invasive breast cancer. *J Clin Oncol.* 2014;32: 1507–1515.
6. Buchholz TA, Somerfield MR, Griggs JJ et al. Margins for breast-conserving surgery with whole-breast irradiation in stage I and II invasive breast cancer: American society of clinical oncology endorsement of the society of surgical oncology/American society for radiation oncology consensus guideline. *J Clin Oncol.* 2014;32: 1502–1506.
7. Newman LA, Kuerer HM, Hung KK et al. Prophylactic mastectomy. *J Am Coll Surg.* 2000;191: 322–330.
8. Newman LA. Contralateral prophylactic mastectomy: Is it a reasonable option? *JAMA.* 2014;312: 895–897.
9. Giuliano AE, McCall L, Beitsch P et al. Locoregional recurrence after sentinel lymph node dissection with or without axillary dissection in patients with sentinel lymph node metastases: The American college of surgeons oncology group Z0011 randomized trial. *Ann Surg.* 2010;252: 426–432; discussion 432–423.
10. Giuliano AE, Hunt KK, Ballman KV et al. Axillary dissection vs no axillary dissection in women with invasive breast cancer and sentinel node metastasis: A randomized clinical trial. *JAMA.* 2011;305: 569–575.
11. Lyman GH, Temin S, Edge SB et al. Sentinel lymph node biopsy for patients with early-stage breast cancer: American society of clinical oncology clinical practice guideline update. *J Clin Oncol.* 2014;32: 1365–1383.

5

Reconstructive perspectives

AT A GLANCE

Breast-conservation surgery (BCS) represents a balance between oncological mandates and cosmetic outcomes and aims to excise tumor with "negative" margins and acceptable cosmesis. Many tumors are multifocal with additional tumor foci beyond the index lesion, yet contemporary rates of ipsilateral breast tumor recurrence after breast-conserving therapy are very low. Local surgery does not completely eliminate residual disease burden and local recurrence is determined by a combination of surgery, tumor biology, radiation, and systemic therapies. Oncoplastic techniques have advanced the limits of BCS and permit resection of relatively large tumors with negative margins and low rates of ipsilateral breast tumor recurrence (IBTR). The ratio of resected to remaining volume of breast tissue is particularly important together with tumor location and will determine the need for partial breast reconstruction—or even mastectomy. Decision-making demands careful judgment when selecting patients for standard BCS, BCS with local tissue rearrangement, or BCS with a regional flap. Moreover, some patients may be better served by skin-sparing mastectomy at the outset and whole breast reconstruction.

5.1 BREAST SURGEON'S PERSPECTIVE

Melissa Anne Mallory and Mehra Golshan

Introduction

Nearly 100,000 breast reconstructions are performed annually in the United States, making it the most common reconstructive procedure performed by American plastic surgeons in 2014.[1,2] Designed to restore breast size, shape, and appearance, breast reconstruction can improve psychological, social, emotional, and functional outcomes following mastectomy procedures and can significantly enhance aesthetic results compared to mastectomy alone.[3,4] The option for reconstruction may influence a patient's preference between breast-conserving therapy and mastectomy, highlighting the importance of early reconstruction discussions with patients requiring breast cancer surgery. Ultimately, decisions regarding reconstruction should be predicated on thorough discussions between patients and their multidisciplinary breast team. Breast surgical oncologists are fundamental in ensuring that all eligible patients are offered reconstruction, as they are often the gatekeepers for referral to plastic surgeons.

Mastectomy and reconstruction

Mastectomy is an option for the oncologic management of patients with breast cancer and for patients at extremely high risk of developing breast cancer. Currently, 38% of all mastectomies performed annually in America involve reconstruction, with rates at some centers approaching 60%.[5–9] Simultaneous contralateral prophylactic or therapeutic mastectomy with or without reconstruction is often performed and bilateral mastectomy has nearly tripled in the United States in recent decades.[5–7,10,11] Modified radical mastectomy (consisting of removal of the breast and level I–II axillary nodes) and total or simple mastectomy (equivalent to modified radical mastectomy, but sparing the axillary contents) are preferred in patients not undergoing immediate reconstruction (IR). Skin-sparing mastectomy, which maintains the majority of the natural breast skin envelope and the inframammary fold (while removing all glandular breast tissue), is associated with superior cosmetic outcomes as it provides a more natural shape and contour and is ideal for most patients undergoing IR.[12,13] Skin-sparing mastectomies are oncologically safe for stage 0–III breast tumors and in high-risk women.[14–16] In select patients undergoing

IR, the nipple-areola sparing mastectomy (NSM) may be considered. However, patient selection is a key to avoid compromising the oncologic integrity of the operation. Ideal NSM candidates have small-to-moderate breast sizes, minimal ptoss, and early-stage tumors with tumor to nipple-areola complex distances of more than 2 cm. NSM is contraindicated for Paget's disease, nipple involvement/nipple retraction, bloody nipple discharge, and multicentricity and should be approached with caution in patients requiring postoperative radiation and those with large breast volumes because the risk of skin/nipple necrosis following NSM is increased in these groups.[17,18]

Selecting among reconstruction options

Patient and tumor-related factors should be considered when making reconstruction decisions. Oncologic therapy takes precedence and reconstruction choices should balance this principle with the wishes of the patient. Patient preferences, comorbidities, and the need for postmastectomy radiation (PMRT) and/or chemotherapy should be considered by the careteam before the definitive reconstructive plan is offered to the patient. Obesity, insulin-dependent diabetes mellitus, chronic obstructive pulmonary disease, smoking, and connective tissue disorders can increase the risk of postoperative complications and, when poorly controlled, may be relative contraindications to IR.[19,20] IR offers substantial psychosocial benefits and often achieves improved aesthetic outcomes compared to delayed reconstruction; however, IR procedures have prolonged operating times (which can become significant with multiple comorbidities) and can have increased complication rates.[20-22] Older age should not in itself prohibit reconstruction. Although autologous approaches can minimize breast-related complications, success with implant-based repair has also been reported.[23,24] Delayed operations minimize the risk of poorly perfused skin flaps on reconstruction outcomes and allows for adjuvant therapy completion prior to definitive reconstruction. However, they require additional surgery and are associated with diminished aesthetic results compared to IR techniques.[25]

The main advantages of implant/expander-based operations are reduced operating time and procedure invasiveness, decreased healing time, and less scarring. However, multiple expansion visits and an implant-exchange surgery are required with two-stage methods. While PMRT can be delivered with implant reconstruction, both aesthetic outcomes and radiation delivery can be negatively impacted. Autologous procedures provide a more durable and natural reconstruction, but are more lengthy and invasive and can result in both donor and reconstruction site complications. Radiation impact on autologous flaps is variable, and the placement of larger flaps does not always lead to optimal results. Ideally, PMRT patients are identified preoperatively, although, postoperative pathologic evaluation can sometimes be required to make this determination. PMRT presents a challenge for reconstruction, as radiation-related fibrosis can compromise the quality of skin and underlying tissues, which can decrease aesthetic results and increase implant loss rates.[26,27] In general, when PMRT is necessary, our group prefers either no reconstruction or two-stage implant/expander reconstruction, placing an expander with acellular dermal matrix at the time of mastectomy. Acellular dermal matrix allows for better expander coverage and has been shown to improve aesthetic outcomes and minimize contracture rates in patients requiring PMRT.[26,28,29] Appropriate deflation of the expander, depending on dosimetry requirements, may be necessary to minimize complications and ensure optimal quality of radiation delivery. Definitive reconstruction with either implant- or flap-based techniques is performed at least 6 months after PMRT is completed.[26]

CONCLUSION

Breast reconstruction is an option for all patients undergoing mastectomy. Nonetheless the best technique varies based on individual patient preferences, comorbidities, and cancer biology. Treatment delays are best avoided by ensuring early discussion of breast reconstruction risks and benefits. This should involve multidisciplinary input from surgical, medical, and radiation oncologists, as well as reconstruction surgeons. Through coordinated multidisciplinary care, breast and plastic surgeons can work together to improve cosmetic outcomes without sacrificing the quality of cancer treatment provided.

REFERENCES

1. ASPS ASoPS. 2014 Plastic surgery statistics. Accessed October 23, 2015. http://www.plasticsurgery.org/news/plastic-surgery-statistics/2014-statistics.html. 2015.
2. Alderman A, Gutowski K, Ahuja A, Gray D. ASPS clinical practice guideline summary on breast reconstruction with expanders and implants. *Plast Reconstr Surg.* 2014;134(4):648e–655e.
3. Alderman AK, Wilkins EG, Lowery JC, Kim M, Davis JA. Determinants of patient satisfaction in postmastectomy breast reconstruction. *Plast Reconstr Surg.* 2000;106(4):769–776.
4. Jagsi R, Li Y, Morrow M, Janz N, Alderman A, Graff J et al. Patient-reported quality of life and satisfaction with cosmetic outcomes after breast conservation and mastectomy with and without reconstruction: Results of a survey of breast cancer survivors. *Ann Surg.* 2015.
5. Albornoz CR, Matros E, Lee CN, Hudis CA, Pusic AL, Elkin E et al. Bilateral mastectomy versus breast-conserving surgery for early-stage breast cancer: The role of breast reconstruction. *Plast Reconstr Surg.* 2015;135(6):1518–1526.
6. Kurian AW, Lichtensztajn DY, Keegan TH, Nelson DO, Clarke CA, Gomez SL. Use of and mortality after bilateral mastectomy compared with other surgical treatments for breast cancer in California, 1998–2011. *JAMA.* 2014;312(9):902–914.

7. Kwok AC, Goodwin IA, Ying J, Agarwal JP. National trends and complication rates after bilateral mastectomy and immediate breast reconstruction from 2005 to 2012. *Am J Surg.* 2015;210(3):512–516.

8. National Accreditation Program for Breast Centers. Chicago, IL: American College of Surgeons; 2014. Available from: https://www.facs.org/~/media/files/quality%20programs/napbc/2014%20napbc%20standards%20manual.ashx.

9. Golshan M, Losk K, Kadish S, Lin NU, Hirshfield-Bartek J, Cutone L et al. Understanding process-of-care delays in surgical treatment of breast cancer at a comprehensive cancer center. *Breast Cancer Res Treat.* 2014;148(1):125–133.

10. Cemal Y, Albornoz CR, Disa JJ, McCarthy CM, Mehrara BJ, Pusic AL et al. A paradigm shift in U.S. breast reconstruction: Part 2. The influence of changing mastectomy patterns on reconstructive rate and method. *Plast Reconstr Surg.* 2013;131(3):320e–326e.

11. Kummerow KL, Du L, Penson DF, Shyr Y, Hooks MA. Nationwide trends in mastectomy for early-stage breast cancer. *JAMA Surg.* 2015;150(1):9–16.

12. Simmons RM, Adamovich TL. Skin-sparing mastectomy. *Surg Clin North Am.* 2003;83(4):885–899.

13. Cocquyt VF, Blondeel PN, Depypere HT, Van De Sijpe KA, Daems KK, Monstrey SJ et al. Better cosmetic results and comparable quality of life after skin-sparing mastectomy and immediate autologous breast reconstruction compared to breast conservative treatment. *Br J Plast Surg.* 2003;56(5):462–470.

14. Downes KJ, Glatt BS, Kanchwala SK, Mick R, Fraker DL, Fox KR et al. Skin-sparing mastectomy and immediate reconstruction is an acceptable treatment option for patients with high-risk breast carcinoma. *Cancer.* 2005;103(5):906–913.

15. Rivadeneira DE, Simmons RM, Fish SK, Gayle L, La Trenta GS, Swistel A et al. Skin-sparing mastectomy with immediate breast reconstruction: A critical analysis of local recurrence. *Cancer J.* 2000;6(5):331–335.

16. Dawood S, Merajver SD, Viens P, Vermeulen PB, Swain SM, Buchholz TA et al. International expert panel on inflammatory breast cancer: Consensus statement for standardized diagnosis and treatment. *Ann Oncol.* 2011;22(3):515–523.

17. Munhoz AM, Montag E, Filassi JR, Gemperli R. Immediate nipple-areola-sparing mastectomy reconstruction: An update on oncological and reconstruction techniques. *World J Clin Oncol.* 2014;5(3):478–494.

18. Nahabedian M. "Breast reconstruction following mastectomy: Indications, techniques, and results." In *Current Surgical Therpay.* 10th ed, edited by Cameron JL, Cameron AM, 559–563. Philadelphia, PA: Elsevier/Saunders. 2011.

19. Lin KY, Johns FR, Gibson J, Long M, Drake DB, Moore MM. An outcome study of breast reconstruction: Presurgical identification of risk factors for complications. *Ann Surg Oncol.* 2001;8(7):586–591.

20. Nahabedian M. Overview of breast reconstruction. In: UpToDate, Chagpar AB, Butler CE(Ed), UpToDate, Waltham, MA. Accessed on October 23, 2015. 2015.

21. Nano MT, Gill PG, Kollias J, Bochner MA, Malycha P, Winefield HR. Psychological impact and cosmetic outcome of surgical breast cancer strategies. *ANZ J Surg.* 2005;75(11):940–947.

22. Wilkins EG, Cederna PS, Lowery JC, Davis JA, Kim HM, Roth RS et al. Prospective analysis of psychosocial outcomes in breast reconstruction: One-year postoperative results from the Michigan Breast Reconstruction Outcome Study. *Plast Reconstr Surg.* 2000;106(5):1014–1025; discussion 26–27.

23. De Lorenzi F, Rietjens M, Soresina M, Rossetto F, Bosco R, Vento AR et al. Immediate breast reconstruction in the elderly: Can it be considered an integral step of breast cancer treatment? The experience of the European institute of oncology, Milan. *J Plast Reconstr Aesthet Surg.* 2010;63(3):511–515.

24. Walton L, Ommen K, Audisio RA. Breast reconstruction in elderly women breast cancer: A review. *Cancer Treat Rev.* 2011;37(5):353–357.

25. Kronowitz SJ, Kuerer HM. Advances and surgical decision-making for breast reconstruction. *Cancer.* 2006;107(5):893–907.

26. Clemens MW, Kronowitz SJ. Current perspectives on radiation therapy in autologous and prosthetic breast reconstruction. *Gland Surg.* 2015;4(3):222–231.

27. Barry M, Kell MR. Radiotherapy and breast reconstruction: A meta-analysis. *Breast Cancer Research and Treatment.* 2011;127(1):15–22.

28. Ibrahim AM, Koolen PG, Ganor O, Markarian MK, Tobias AM, Lee BT et al. Does acellular dermal matrix really improve aesthetic outcome in tissue expander/implant-based breast reconstruction? *Aesthetic Plast Surg.* 2015;39(3):359–368.

29. Moyer HR, Pinell-White X, Losken A. The effect of radiation on acellular dermal matrix and capsule formation in breast reconstruction: Clinical outcomes and histologic analysis. *Plast Reconstr Surg.* 2014;133(2):214–221.

5.2 RECONSTRUCTIVE SURGEON'S PERSPECTIVE

Michael Scheflan and Robert Douglas Macmillan

In this chapter, the oncological reasons for recommending one of these procedures (oncoplastic lumpectomy versus mastectomy and reconstruction), over the other are discussed. Although some of these are debatable, most are recognized as being relevant and indeed critical to surgical planning. The relative merits of both these surgical options will be considered and the reasons why one option might be preferred over the other.

There are very few contraindications to mastectomy and breast reconstruction and relatively few absolute contraindications to breast-conserving surgery. The principle objection to breast-conserving surgery is the maximum limit to the volume that can be excised while maintaining an acceptable appearance. Breast-conserving surgery is the most efficient surgical procedure for treating breast cancer in most women. It can be undertaken as an ambulatory procedure, is the best option for leaving a sensate breast, and when performed as an appropriate option in selected patients will be associated with the best aesthetic outcomes for breast cancer surgery in most cases. However, there are potential disadvantages to this procedure that include: (1) the possibility of incomplete margins requiring further surgery, (2) the need for radiotherapy with concomitant side effects of breast tenderness, fibrosis, skin changes, and potentially varying degrees of long-term atrophy, and (3) long-term radiological surveillance with the need for further investigation or surgical intervention in up to 50% of patients over a 10-year period. In addition, there is a possibility of developing a second breast cancer in the remaining ipsilateral breast tissue.[1–3]

Aesthetic outcomes which are comparable to breast conservation can be achieved with mastectomy and breast reconstruction, although this is usually more difficult and may be associated with a higher incidence of complications. The benefits of mastectomy and reconstruction include avoidance of radiotherapy for the majority of patients and the need for further breast screening and risk of a further cancer arising in the conserved breast. The "trade-offs" are several and include: (1) bigger surgery, (2) longer recovery, (3) higher risk of complications, (4) additional surgical procedures due to complications, (5) revisions or two-stage tissue expander reconstruction, (6) loss of or decreased sensation, and (7) a donor site with its potential morbidity for autologous reconstruction.

In modern practice, a satisfactory outcome for the surgical treatment of breast cancer can be defined as one that not only achieves local control of disease, but also results in an acceptable aesthetic outcome with minimal morbidity.

Given the favorable long-term survival of most women with breast cancer, the longevity of the aesthetic outcomes is also important. From the viewpoint of a reconstructive surgeon, breast cancer diagnosis and its treatment has a negative impact in terms of effects on physical and psychological aspects of quality of life. Therefore, if something positive can be offered to minimize this trauma, then it should be offered to all women without prohibitive comorbidities, who desire breast reconstruction. Rebuilding breast contour, balance, and symmetry with adjustment of overall breast aesthetics to more closely match a woman's preferred shape and size may go some way to redressing the balance and a sense of well-being—it is the authors' opinion that surgeons treating women with breast cancer have a particular obligation in this regard.

Most studies of breast-conserving surgery judge aesthetic outcome by the degree to which the appearance of the breast has been adversely affected by treatment, with the ultimate aim being maintenance of form. If a full range of options is available, including volume displacement by breast reduction and therapeutic mammoplasty, as well as volume replacement techniques, then breast-conserving surgery can preserve form in almost all cases and can even be associated with aesthetic improvement.[4] Acceptance of a result that is significantly worse than the patient's natural breast is no longer necessary. Similarly, it is unacceptable for surgeons to create a defect in the expectation that this can be corrected at a later date or filling it with saline and hoping this will suffice. There is a pervading concept that bad cosmesis is the price to pay for effective oncological surgery, when the reality is that it is not. However, optimal cosmetic outcomes are dependent on availability of expertise to offer a range of appropriate options and recognize the indications for each of these. Depending on average tumor size within a particular practice, at least 50% of women undergoing breast-conserving surgery are suitable for an oncoplastic procedure, which also extend the limits for breast-conserving surgery and allow more women to avoid mastectomy. In those patients for whom the need for postmastectomy radiotherapy can be identified preoperatively, breast conservation with immediate oncoplastic reconstruction might represent a good option. Radiotherapy generally has more profound effects on chest wall tissues and the postmastectomy reconstructed breast than for breast conservation. Similar considerations apply to obese patients and smokers who are at a high risk for "full" breast reconstruction and developing complications from skin-sparing or nipple-sparing mastectomy. Women with macromastia are usually excellent candidates for breast conservation and this should be offered even for larger tumor sizes.

Whole breast reconstruction can achieve improved overall breast aesthetics in selected patients who desire changes in native breast shape and form. If enhanced breast size is desired by the patient, this can often be satisfactorily achieved with implant-based breast reconstruction.

It is important to identify preoperatively the end goals of oncoplastic and reconstructive surgery in terms of aesthetics. This is often difficult when early priorities are cancer treatment and in circumstances when a definitive surgical pathway cannot be agreed. It is then important that the first surgery is performed in a manner which is sympathetic to the options a woman may subsequently chose as a long-term solution. This should therefore take account of incision placement and skin preservation. To reiterate, it is no longer acceptable to create a "hole" that can be "filled" at some future stage with no coherent plan to optimize cosmetic outcomes and quality of life.

It can be argued that the greatest advances in patient selection for mastectomy or breast conservation have been in those countries where oncoplastic surgery is widely practiced. Women benefit most when managed by a surgical team who can provide a comprehensive cancer and reconstructive service and delivery of care is not hampered by territorial difficulties. They do not see the territorial difficulties. Patients would not understand the latter or find acceptable the reasons why they persist.

There has been a trend over recent years in the United States for a decrease in rates of breast conservation with an increase in rates of bilateral mastectomy which may reflect American reimbursement policies.[5] Interestingly, these trends have not been observed in most other developed countries to the same extent and may partly be related to differences in availability of oncoplastic breast-conserving surgery. The "drives" for one type of surgery or the other are likely to be culturally dependent and also be influenced by availability of expertise, and the perceived strengths of a team will always be a determinant of patient choice. A well-coordinated breast cancer patient care between the breast oncologist, breast surgeon, reconstructive surgeon, and radiation oncologist is the key for success. An expertly performed mastectomy and reconstruction is likely to be a much better outcome than a badly performed breast-conservation for instance.

There is potential for improvements in optimizing outcomes for both these surgical options and recognition of appropriate indications. However, perhaps the greatest need is for an increase in the availability of oncoplastic expertise to maximize options for breast conservation. Most women will choose conservation rather mastectomy (with or without reconstruction) when given the choice. As a profession and within our multidisciplinary teams we should constantly be striving to raise the bar and set higher standards for aesthetic outcomes.

REFERENCES

1. Lee G. Wilke, Tomasz Czechura, Chih Wang, Brittany Lapin, Erik Liederbach, David P. Winchester, Katharine Yao. Repeat surgery after breast conservation for the treatment of stage 0 to II breast carcinoma: A report from the national cancer data base, 2004–2010. *JAMA Surg.* 2014;149(12):1296–1305

2. Larissa Nekhlyudov, Laurel A. Habel, Ninah Achacoso, Inkyung Jung, Reina Haque, Laura C. Collins, Stuart J. Schnitt, Charles P. Quesenberry Jr, Suzanne W. Fletcher. Ten-year risk of diagnostic mammograms and invasive breast procedures after breast-conserving surgery for DCIS. *J Natl Cancer Inst* 2012;104:614–621

3. Nehmat Houssami, Linn A. Abraham, Diana L. Miglioretti, Edward A. Sickles, Karla Kerlikowske, Diana S. M. Buist, Berta M. Geller, Hyman B. Muss, Les Irwig. Accuracy and outcomes of screening mammography in women with a personal history of early-stage breast cancer. *JAMA.* 2011;305(8):790–799

4. Macmillan RD, James R, Gale KL, McCulley SJ. Therapeutic mammaplasty. *J Surg Oncol.* 2014;110(1):90–95

5. Albornoz CR, Matros E, Lee CN, Hudis CA, Pusic AL, Elkin E, Bach PB, Cordeiro PG, Morrow M. Bilateral mastectomy versus breast-conserving surgery for early-stage breast cancer: The role of breast reconstruction. *Plast Reconstr Surg.* 2015;135(6):1518–1526

6

Patients' perspectives

AT A GLANCE

Patient choice and expectation are of paramount importance in the context of breast reconstruction, which is usually requested for practical and emotional reasons. The former includes avoidance of use of an external prosthesis and changes in sexual relations, while the latter to issues such as maintenance of femininity, regaining confidence, and "feeling oneself again." Reconstruction is trying to re-establish gender identity which is threatened by the mutilating nature of mastectomy. However, even the best reconstruction can only mimic the natural breast, but can help restore altered body image and sexuality, and emphasizes the importance of patient-reported outcome measures (PROMs) for global health-related quality-of-life assessment. PROMs are not physician measured, but reflect what a patient feels and her level of satisfaction. Measurement tools such as BREAST-Q incorporate various domains including physical, psychological, and sexual. PROMs may improve preoperative education, shared decision-making, and outcomes in breast reconstruction with enhanced quality of life.

6.1 THE ROLE OF PATIENT CHOICE

Claudia R. Albornoz and Andrea L. Pusic

Introduction

Traditionally, the success of a surgical procedure was evaluated in terms of clinician-reported outcomes such as morbidity and/or mortality. Increasingly, however, we now appreciate the importance of the patient perspective, particularly with regards to outcomes such as quality of life and patient choice. For procedures such as reconstructive breast surgery, the goal of surgery is to improve body image. While clinician-reported outcomes remain important, information about the quality-of-life consequences of the different procedures and comparative effectiveness of various techniques from the patient's perspective complements our understanding of surgical outcomes.[1] In the same manner that surgical techniques have evolved, the way we evaluate outcomes is changing with increasing importance placed on the patient perspective.

Patient-reported outcomes are any report of the status of a patient's health condition that comes directly from the patient, without interpretation by a clinician or anyone else. The outcome can be measured in absolute terms (e.g., severity of symptoms) or as a change from a previous measure (e.g., change in physical well-being/back/shoulder pain preoperative and postoperative breast reduction).[2] Patient-reported outcome measures are specially designed questionnaires that can be used to evaluate aspects of outcomes that were once considered too subjective and difficult to measure. Patient-reported outcome measures provide a way to quantify how patients perceive their health and the impact symptoms/treatments have on their health-related quality of life. Information provided by patients may enable clinicians to implement interventions (e.g. improve pain control, provide physical therapy), compare the effectiveness of different treatments modalities, or improve surgical techniques. The development of the BREAST-Q, a patient-reported outcome measure designed specifically for breast surgery patients, has provided a way to reliably evaluate patient satisfaction with their breasts and breast-related quality of life.[3] The BREAST-Q has been translated and linguistically validated into 28 languages and has now been used in studies involving over 20,000 patients internationally.[6] Such studies increasingly allow benchmarking and comparison across surgical techniques and patient populations.

Breast cancer is one of the most common malignancies in females, affecting 1 out of 8 women. While the majority of women will survive their cancer, surgical and adjuvant treatments may lead to important body image and quality-of-life sequelae. Breast reconstruction can minimize deformity and alleviate much of the distress associated with mastectomy. When a woman faces a diagnosis of breast cancer, she is presented with several alternatives of treatment that may be overwhelming. For example, patients requiring mastectomy must decide if they wish to proceed with reconstruction and, if so, the preferred type and timing. There are no right or wrong answers to such decisions, as breast reconstruction is very much a "preference-sensitive" decision that should be made together by the patient and her reconstructive surgeon considering clinical factors in conjunction with the patient's own values and preferences. In breast cancer surgery, the quality of the decisions can be estimated by the extent to which patients are informed about expected outcomes, involved in decision-making, and undergo treatments that reflect their values.[4] Provision of high-quality patient-reported outcome measures data to prospective patients can help them better understand expected outcomes from a patient perspective.

With the objective of decreasing the gap in knowledge about expected outcomes in breast reconstruction, the National Cancer Institute funded the Mastectomy Reconstruction Outcomes Consortium study. The study, now in its fifth year, is a prospective multicenter study from 11 centers in the United States and Canada, which aims to address complications, patient satisfaction, and quality of life comparing the main options for breast reconstruction. Information from this study will be important to help new breast cancer patients understand expected results of and make informed decisions about their preferred method of reconstruction.[5]

What do we know so far?

Patients with unilateral breast cancer who choose to undergo contralateral prophylactic mastectomy with bilateral reconstruction report higher satisfaction with breasts than do patients who undergo unilateral mastectomy with reconstruction alone.[6,7,8] Quality-of-life outcomes, such as psychosocial and sexual well-being, however, do not differ and physical well-being of the chest area may be compromised.

In terms of timing of reconstruction, several studies show that patients who choose immediate breast reconstruction had higher levels of satisfaction with breasts and psychosocial, sexual, and physical well-being than patients with mastectomy alone.[9-12] A study by Zhong et al., prospectively compared 106 patients who underwent immediate and delayed autologous breast reconstruction. Patients with delayed reconstruction had impaired pre-reconstruction body image, sexual, and psychosocial well-being. Immediate reconstruction restores the look and feel of a woman's breast, as patients report

satisfaction similar to their preoperative status as measured by the BREAST-Q.[13]

Patients choose their method of reconstruction based on a number of factors, including recovery time, simplicity of the surgery, and aesthetic results, among others.[14] Reconstruction with implants is increasing in the United States, even though it is known that long-term quality of life and satisfaction are higher with autologous tissue than prosthetic devices.[10,15] A large study by Atisha and colleagues, surveying 7,619 volunteers from the Army of Woman, found that patients with autologous reconstruction had higher breast satisfaction scores than patients with implant reconstruction, breast-conserving therapy, or mastectomy only. Women who underwent autologous reconstruction had higher physical well-being scores and decreased chronic physical morbidity compared to patients who underwent prosthetic-based reconstruction.[16]

When choosing implant reconstruction, another major decision a woman must make is which type of implant to use: saline or silicone implants. Silicone implants compared with saline implants in breast reconstruction are associated with higher satisfaction with outcome, psychosocial, and sexual well-being.[17,18] The use of shaped versus round silicone-based implants in breast reconstruction has not been associated with differences is satisfaction or quality of life.[19]

For patients who undergo abdominally based autologous breast reconstruction, breast satisfaction does differ based on the approach to tissue transfer,[20] but physical well-being of the abdomen is higher for deep inferior epigastric perforator flaps compared with pedicled transverse rectus abdominis myocutaneous flaps controlling for confounders.[21]

CONCLUSION

Women diagnosed with breast cancer and requiring mastectomy face several difficult decisions, such as whether or not to proceed with reconstruction and, if so, the timing and type of reconstructive surgery. Patient-reported outcome data can help inform patients about expected outcomes by providing insight from other patients that have already experienced these various options.

REFERENCES

1. Karanicolas PJ, Bickenbach K, Jayaraman S et al. Measurement and interpretation of patient-reported outcomes in surgery: An opportunity for improvement. *J Gastrointest Surg.* 2011;15(4):682–689.

2. Food and Drug Administration. Patient-reported outcome measures: Use in medical product development to support labeling claims. http://www.fda.gov/downloads/Drugs/Guidances/UCM193282.pdf. 2009;Consulted October 1, 2015.

3. Pusic AL, Klassen AF, Scott AM, Klok JA, Cordeiro PG, Cano SJ. Development of a new patient-reported outcome measure for breast surgery: The BREAST-Q. *Plast Reconstr Surg.* 2009;124(2):345–353.

4. Lee CN, Chang Y, Adimorah N et al. Decision making about surgery for early-stage breast cancer. *J Am Coll Surg.* 2012;214(1):1–10.

5. U.S. National Institutes of Health. Mastectomy reconstruction outcomes consortium (MROC) Study (MROC). https://clinicaltrials.gov/ct2/show/NCT01723423. Consulted October 1, 2016.

6. Cohen WA, Mundy LR, Ballard TN et al. The BREAST-Q in surgical research: A review of the literature 2009–2015. *J Plast Reconstr Aesthet Surg.* 2016;69(2):149–162.

7. Koslow S, Pharmer LA, Scott AM et al. Long-term patient-reported satisfaction after contralateral prophylactic mastectomy and implant reconstruction. *Ann Surg Oncol.* 2013;20(11):3422–3429. doi: 10.1245/s10434-013-3026-2. [Online May 13, 2013].

8. Hwang ES, Locklear TD, Rushing CN et al. Patient-reported outcomes after choice for contralateral prophylactic mastectomy. *J Clin Oncol.* 2016;34(13):1518–1527.

9. Dean NR, Yip JM, Birrell S. Rotation flap approach mastectomy. *ANZ J Surg.* 2013;83(3):139–145.

10. Eltahir Y, Werners LL, Dreise MM et al. Quality-of-life outcomes between mastectomy alone and breast reconstruction: Comparison of patient-reported BREAST-Q and other health-related quality-of-life measures. *Plast Reconstr Surg.* 2013;132(2):201e–209e.

11. Jeevan R, Cromwell DA, Browne JP et al. Findings of a national comparative audit of mastectomy and breast reconstruction surgery in England. *J Plast Reconstr Aesthet Surg.* 2014;67(10):1333–1344.

12. Atisha DM, Rushing CN, Samsa GP et al. A national snapshot of satisfaction with breast cancer procedures. *Ann Surg Oncol.* 2015;22(2):361–369.

13. Zhong T, Hu J, Bagher S et al. A comparison of psychological response, body image, sexuality, and quality of life between immediate and delayed autologous tissue breast reconstruction: A prospective long-term outcome study. *Plast Reconstr Surg.* 2016;138(4):772–780.

14. Gopie JP, Hilhorst MT, Kleijne A et al. Women's motives to opt for either implant or DIEP-flap breast reconstruction. *J Plast Reconstr Aesthet Surg.* 2011;64(8):1062–1067.

15. Hu ES, Pusic AL, Waljee JF et al. Patient-reported aesthetic satisfaction with breast reconstruction during the long-term survivorship period. *Plast Reconstr Surg.* 2009;124(1):1–8.

16. McCarthy CM, Mehrara BJ, Long T et al. Chest and upper body morbidity following immediate postmastectomy breast reconstruction. *Ann Surg Oncol.* 2014;21(1):107–112.

17. Macadam SA, Ho AL, Cook EF, Jr., Lennox PA, Pusic AL. Patient satisfaction and health-related quality of life following breast reconstruction: Patient-reported outcomes among saline and silicone implant recipients. *Plast Reconstr Surg.* 2010;125(3):761–771.

18. McCarthy CM, Klassen AF, Cano SJ et al. Patient satisfaction with postmastectomy breast reconstruction: A comparison of saline and silicone implants. *Cancer.* 2010;116(24):5584–5591.

19. Macadam SA, Ho AL, Lennox PA, Pusic AL. Patient-reported satisfaction and health-related quality of life following breast reconstruction: A comparison of shaped cohesive gel and round cohesive gel implant recipients. *Plast Reconstr Surg.* 2013;131(3):431–441.

20. Schwitzer JA, Miller HC, Pusic AL et al. Satisfaction following unilateral breast reconstruction: A comparison of pedicled TRAM and free abdominal Flaps. *Plast Reconstr Surg Glob Open.* 2015;3(8):e482.

21. Macadam SA, Zhong T, Weichman K, Papsdorf M, Lennox PA, Hazen A, Matros E, Disa J, Mehrara B, Pusic AL. Quality of life and patient-reported outcomes in breast cancer survivors multicenter comparison of four abdominally based autologous reconstruction methods. *Plast Reconstr Surg.* 2016;137(3):758–771.

6.2 PATIENTS' EXPECTATIONS

John R. Benson and Guidubaldo Querci della Rovere (posthumous)

The expectations of patients undergoing immediate breast reconstruction may differ from those contemplating a delayed procedure. Although both groups desire an acceptable cosmetic result, the former may have greater emotional and psychological issues due to the need for simultaneously coping with loss of a breast and a new cancer diagnosis. By contrast, patients seeking delayed breast reconstruction have overcome the initial fears of a potential life-threatening condition, completed a treatment program, and resumed a more normal lifestyle. Nonetheless, these women have complex psychology and constitute a selected group who are prepared to endure further surgery for the benefits of improved cosmesis without which life would be unbearable for many. Delayed breast reconstruction is technically more challenging than an immediate breast reconstruction where much of the skin envelope (and indeed even the nipple-areolar complex) may be preserved which greatly enhances the final cosmetic results. However, women undergoing a delayed procedure may compare the reconstructed breast with a mastectomy wound while the comparator for immediate breast reconstruction patients will be their normal breast. Expectations vary among patients whatever the timing of breast reconstruction, and surgeons must understand this fact and adapt their clinical and technical expertise to the needs of patients and not vice-versa—surgeons should not inappropriately recommend a particular type of reconstruction based on some preferred surgical technique. In general, women who seek breast reconstruction to avoid wearing an external prosthesis and wish to undergo a relatively simple procedure with minimal complications are best suited to an implant-based reconstruction (with or without acellular dermal matrix), provided reasonable symmetry can be achieved. On the other hand, those women who seek a nearly perfect result with a soft and natural feeling breast and wish to avoid an implant and minimize donor site morbidity should be recommended a muscle-sparing abdominal flap-based breast reconstruction.

Expectations

REASONS FOR CHOOSING BREAST RECONSTRUCTION

The expectations of women undergoing breast reconstruction are closely related to the reasons for choosing this procedure in the first instance, which are broadly grouped as practical and emotional:

Practical—The use of an external prosthesis is very inconvenient for many women, especially those who lead an active life and participate in sporting activities. These devices feel less secure and restrict the choice of clothing that can be worn (especially beach and evening wear). Reconstruction may help ameliorate any impact of breast cancer surgery on sexual relationships, although resumption of normal sexual activity depends not only on the cosmetic outcome of BR, but also on the emotional status of the patient and the attitude of her partner.

Emotional—Women will seek BR in order to preserve their sense of femininity and to remain sexually attractive and more confident. This relates to "feeling oneself" again and is part of the deeply rooted biological, emotional, and cultural needs of gender identity which is threatened by the mutilation of extirpative breast surgery. BR can re-establish these characteristics to varying degrees in the majority of patients and while BR can help restore body image and sexuality, it is still at best only a facsimile of a natural breast. Even the finest surgical outcomes will be associated with scarring, altered sensation, and functional limitations from donor site morbidity.

Expectations

COSMETIC RESULTS OF RECONSTRUCTION

A patient's expectations of the final cosmetic result will be determined by any relevant prior knowledge and influenced by information derived from friends, the media, and, increasingly, the Internet. Any misperceptions must be corrected and fully informed consent obtained before proceeding with any form of breast reconstruction. Sufficient time must be allowed for this consent process, and specialist breast care nurses exercise a valuable role in clarifying and processing information for patients. Access to postoperative photographs showing a *spectrum* of outcomes and talking to other breast reconstruction patients who have undergone a similar procedure can be helpful. Patients should be informed about length of recovery, side effects of surgery, and possible complications, and be made aware that further corrective surgery may be indicated (even in the absence of complications). A patient's quest for "perfection" can end in extreme disappointment, and unrealistic expectations must be tempered.

Meeting patients' expectations

It is imperative to be honest and realistic with patients in terms of the outcomes of breast reconstruction and to constantly emphasize that a reconstructed breast can never be the same as a normal breast. Some goals of breast reconstruction are readily achievable while others require more complex surgical interventions which may involve contralateral breast surgery.

Breast symmetry—This is the single most important aim of breast reconstruction which will conceal the disfigurement of mastectomy and help patients return to a normal social and emotional life. There are two components to symmetry—equality of volume and equality of shape, with the former more easily attainable nowadays with expandable implants and surgical adjustment of the contralateral breast. Matching of breast shape is more challenging, but many women are content with symmetry of shape when wearing a bra than when unclothed and can wear low necklines with a balanced cleavage. Temporary alterations in breast shape occur with submuscular placement of implants, which often settles with time as muscles adjust and become less prone to "squashing" of implants during physical activities.

Skin sensation—Creation of a sensate breast after breast reconstruction is difficult with current techniques, although methods for reinnervation are being explored. The skin islands associated with myocutaneous flaps will inevitably lack sensation, but areas of numbness over native mastectomy flaps can spontaneously improve. Patients should be warned in advance about loss of sensation in the reconstructed breast.

The nipple—Loss of the nipple is perhaps the most significant aspect of mastectomy, as this represents an erogenous zone and its sensory function cannot be reliably restored with any surgical technique at the present time. In cases of prophylactic mastectomy and selected cases of skin-sparing mastectomy for cancer, the nipple can be preserved although sensation is likely to be severely compromised. Moreover, nipple preservation in larger, ptotic breasts might require some form of mastopexy, which can jeopardize both the sensation and viability of the nipple. The surgeon can surgically recreate a nipple from a cosmetic perspective, but these are often not durable and become paler with loss of projection over time. Prosthetic silicone nipples can be fashioned from a mold of the contralateral nipple and are a satisfactory alternative.

Scarring—Some women falsely believe that the term "oncoplastic" implies scar-free surgery, but this is never the case. Scars can be placed discretely to ensure they are concealed as far as possible, but many reconstructive and reductive procedures on the breast involve extensive scarring and patients should be forewarned about this.

Complications—The incidence of complications is related to the magnitude of the surgical procedure as well as the experience of the surgeon. Patients must be informed of potential complications, and when these occur, they must be recorded adequately in the notes and made available for future audits. Even minor complications can delay recovery or necessitate further surgical intervention and cause anxiety and frustration for a patient and her family. Complete failure of breast reconstruction with flap necrosis or explanation can be psychologically devastating for patients, who then require much time to regain confidence in their surgeon and re-establish expectations from breast reconstruction.

Informed consent

Both volume displacement and replacement techniques represent more complex and challenging surgery than standard wide local excision where a variable amount of breast tissue is removed, but no formal attempt made to reconstruct the breast. Patients must be aware of the pattern of scarring, which may be more extensive than anticipated for a reductional procedure. Moreover, patients must be informed of any need for surgery to the contralateral breast to achieve symmetrization and the possibility of completion mastectomy in the event of incomplete tumor excision. The latter may be particularly traumatic after bilateral oncoplastic surgery, and the patient will be faced with the prospect of whole breast reconstruction. A woman may choose to have a normal sized breast with a localized defect rather than a nicely shaped, but smaller breast with concomitant scarring and a contralateral breast reduction. Conversely, she may opt for a mastectomy with immediate breast reconstruction rather than an attempt at breast conservation with oncoplastic techniques in order to minimize any chances of recurrence or to avoid radiotherapy. Patients should be warned of possible delays to adjuvant treatment in the event of any complications and be made aware of fat necrosis, which can give rise to a worrisome lump in the breast. Where volume replacement techniques are employed, significant donor site morbidity can occur with seroma formation and even wound dehiscence.

CONCLUSION

Patients' needs and expectations vary greatly and surgeons must take account of this and adjust surgical techniques accordingly. Knowledge and adequate information giving are the foundations of informed consent. Healthcare workers must employ an honest and realistic approach when dealing with breast reconstruction patients whose level of satisfaction is often more dependent on adequate information and counseling than by an impressive technical result.

FURTHER READING

1. Rowland JH, Dioso J, Holland JC et al. Breast reconstruction and mastectomy: Who seeks it, who refuses? *Plast Reconstr Surg* 1995; 95: 812–822
2. Brandberg Y, Sandelin K, Erikson S et al. Psychological reactions, quality of life and body image after bilateral prophylactic mastectomy in women at high risk for breast cancer: A prospective 1-year follow up study. *J Clin Oncol* 2008; 26: 3918–3919
3. Reaby LL. Reasons why women who have mastectomy decide to have or not to have breast reconstruction. *Plast Reconstr Surg* 1998; 101: 1810–1818
4. Anderson SG, Rodin J, Ariyan S. Treatment considerations in postmastectomy reconstruction: Their relative importance and relationship to patient satisfaction. *Ann Plast Surg* 1994; 33: 263–270
5. Neill KM, Armstrong, Burnett CB. Choosing reconstruction after mastectomy: A qualitative analysis. *Oncol Nurs Forum* 1998; 25: 743–750
6. Harcourt D, Rumsey N. Mastectomy patients' decision-making for or against immediate breast reconstruction. *Psychooncology* 2004; 13: 106–115

EDITORIAL COMMENTARY

Initial breast imaging assessment aims to establish the size, number, and distance of lesions from the nipple and their proportional relation to overall breast size. Mammography with adjunctive ultrasound examination is the mainstay of diagnostic imaging but mammography is less sensitive in younger women and those with dense breast tissue. A background of florid fibrocystic changes or a lobular phenotype can preclude accurate delineation of tumor extent, and magnetic resonance imaging (MRI) examination is valuable in these circumstances as an additional modality for investigation. MRI imaging not only aids planning of more complex oncoplastic procedures but can change the surgical strategy from conservation to mastectomy (with or without whole breast reconstruction). It is important to biopsy any additional tumor foci detected in other quadrants where confirmation of malignancy would usually mandate mastectomy. When these additional foci are not visualized on second-look ultrasound, then MRI-guided biopsy may be indicated where the index of suspicion remains high. Indications for preoperative MRI remain controversial in the context of conventional breast-conservation procedures, but this investigation should routinely be undertaken for all patients undergoing a therapeutic mammoplasty or other level II oncoplastic procedures to reduce the chance of completion mastectomy. MRI can be performed postoperatively to assess residual disease when positive margins are obtained after standard lumpectomy/wide local excision. Contrast-enhanced spectral mammography may have comparable sensitivity but greater specificity and radio-pathological correlation compared to MRI—but be much cheaper. Functional MRI with information derived from pharmacokinetic parameters can evaluate stromal elements and inform preoperative planning. Positron emission tomography (PET) is not yet ready for incorporation into routine diagnostic pathways and results of ongoing studies are awaited. Accurate histopathological evaluation of a tumor is crucial in selection of patients for breast-conserving surgery. There is now better clarity on definition of a negative surgical margin after breast-conserving surgery and improved understanding of how innate tumor biology influences risk of local recurrence. Essential pathological information includes tumor size, grade, type, presence of necrosis, margin width, and marker profile (ER, PR, and HER2). Genomic information may further aid selection of patients for optimum treatment in the future and predict which cases of ductal carcinoma in situ are likely to progress to invasive malignancy. In turn, this will permit reduction of adjuvant therapies and ultimately avoid surgical excision in a selected group of low-risk patients.

It is now well-established that adjuvant systemic therapies reduce risk of locoregional as well as distant recurrence with particular impact from anti-HER2-directed therapies. Patients with a complete pathological response following neoadjuvant chemotherapy have improved disease-free and overall survival compared to those with residual disease. Cancer stem cells in residual tissue can be targeted with adjuvant chemotherapy after surgery as part of a "sandwich" approach, but this could lead to increased rates of surgical complications, particularly for reconstruction patients. Neoadjuvant chemotherapy downstages disease and permits oncoplastic breast surgery when mastectomy would otherwise be necessary. Although patients with tumors exceeding 5 cm tend to show better responses to chemotherapy, breast-conserving surgery can be more difficult to achieve when the initial tumor is relatively large. There is no evidence that performance of more complex oncoplastic breast surgery delays the start of chemotherapy nor is associated with increased rates of complications. Delays in chemotherapy of more than 8 weeks might lead to worse outcomes for certain types of tumors, such as triple negative, HER2 positive, and locally advanced disease (stage III).

Radiotherapy is indicated for most cases of breast-conserving surgery and up to one-third of mastectomy patients. Radiation toxicity impacts on cosmesis, healing, and capsule formation, although no randomized data exists on the effects of radiotherapy on surgical outcomes. Oncoplastic techniques involve rearrangement of glandular tissue and this can interfere with the subsequent localization of the tumor bed for administration of any radiotherapy boost. Oncological outcomes must not be compromised by omission or reduction in dosage of radiotherapy for cosmetic purposes. There is currently no evidence that the use of acellular dermal matrices offers protection against capsule formation/contracture and prepectoral placement of implants should not be used when postmastectomy radiotherapy is anticipated. Deep inferior epigastric perforator flaps and muscle-sparing free flaps are prone to fat necrosis secondary to irradiation. For implant-based reconstruction, there are well-documented risks from radiotherapy including capsular contracture, implant deflation/rupture, wound dehiscence, and infection. Therefore postmastectomy radiotherapy is associated with both increased rates of complications and revision. Interestingly, a systematic review using pooled data suggests that complication rates for autologous breast reconstruction are independent of postmastectomy radiotherapy. Delayed breast reconstruction may be recommended for patients who have already received radiotherapy and for whom irradiation is scheduled. There is some evidence for increased rates of fibrosis (and possibly fat necrosis) when radiotherapy follows abdominal flap-based reconstruction. It remains unclear to what extent breast reconstruction leads to reduced coverage of the target volume and increases radiotherapy dosage to normal tissues. Newer techniques of partial breast irradiation such as intensity-modulated radiotherapy can maximize relevant tissue coverage and minimize exposure of normal tissues to radiation in breast reconstruction patients. Mammoplasty techniques create challenges for the radiation oncologist in terms of which areas of the partially reconstructed breast should receive a boost dose. The placement of clips immediately after tumor excision but before rearrangement of tissues and disruption of the original surgical cavity can help plan subsequent radiotherapy. At least three clips should be applied to the tumor bed, but ideally six clips will adequately delineate the tumor bed after both oncoplastic and routine breast-conserving surgery. Contrast-enhanced CT can assist treatment planning and outline both gross tumor and clinical target volumes.

Randomized trials have confirmed equivalence of outcomes for patients undergoing either breast-conserving surgery or mastectomy. The former is appropriate for the majority of patients who can be satisfactorily managed with conventional breast-conserving surgery with or without level I oncoplastic adjustment. Probably fewer than 15% of patients require more complex oncoplastic surgery (level II) to achieve adequate resection and maintain local control with optimal cosmesis. Conversely, mastectomy is mandated for reasons including (i) failure to obtain negative resection margins despite re-excision(s), (ii) multifocal cancers involving more than one breast quadrant, (iii) inflammatory cancers, (iv) lack of access or contraindications to radiotherapy, (v) prior irradiation, (vi) pregnancy, and (vii) connective tissue disorders.

Oncoplastic breast surgery has advanced the limits of conventional breast conservation and permitted excision of larger tumors with correction of lumpectomy defects using oncoplasty and other techniques such as fat grafting. Downstaging of tumors with neoadjuvant chemotherapy and formal definition of a negative margin as "no tumor at ink" have facilitated attempts at breast-conserving surgery by reduction of absolute tumor size and less stringent requirements for surgical re-excision. Contralateral prophylactic mastectomy as part of "maximal surgery" (bilateral mastectomy and reconstruction) is justified in patients with hereditary susceptibility such as BRCA1/2 mutations in whom the risk of contralateral breast cancer is about 2%–5% per year (once a unilateral breast cancer has been diagnosed). Otherwise, patients without genetic-based risk factors should appreciate that contralateral prophylactic mastectomy does not confer any survival advantage and mortality is determined by characteristics of the initial ipsilateral cancer. Contemporary decision-making for breast-conserving surgery versus mastectomy might influence management of the axilla. Hence those patients with one or two positive sentinel nodes could potentially avoid further axillary treatment if managed according to a Z0011 pathway with breast irradiation (high tangent fields) and systemic therapy. Those patients undergoing mastectomy with macrometastatic disease in sentinel nodes cannot safely avoid completion axillary lymph node dissection, especially in the absence of postmastectomy radiotherapy (where an axillary field could be added). Surgical options for breast cancer patients are complex and any definitive treatment plan must encompass multidisciplinary team working, shared decision-making, and a fully informed consent process.

Breast reconstruction aims to restore physical breast form after mastectomy, but also improves psychosocial, emotional and functional outcomes. The primary extirpative procedure may be influenced by discussions on reconstruction; breast oncologists must refer patients appropriately to plastic surgeons yet at the same time act as responsible "gatekeepers." It is essential that eligible patients be offered reconstruction with a full repertoire of techniques available. Skin-sparing forms of mastectomy are now widely practised and confirmed to be oncologically safe for stage 0–III disease. High-risk women without breast cancer (prophylactic surgery) and carefully selected patients with smaller localized cancers in small–moderate-sized breasts can be offered nipple-sparing mastectomy without compromise of outcomes in terms of local recurrence or overall survival.

The type of reconstruction chosen must balance oncological mandates with patient and surgeon preference. Comorbidities and need for postmastectomy radiotherapy are major factors to take account of together with body mass index and age. Delayed breast reconstruction should be considered when mastectomy flap perfusion is potentially threatened and completion of adjuvant treatments before reconstruction is preferred. A delayed procedure can be undertaken 6–12 months later using either implant or flap-based techniques.

The type and timing of breast reconstruction must be carefully judged for each patient and will depend on a balance of factors. Implant/expander-based operations are a technically simpler, less invasive, and shorter surgical procedure with less scarring but can adversely affect the delivery of postmastectomy radiotherapy and cosmetic outcomes post-irradiation. Autologous tissue flaps have long been considered the "Rolls Royce" of breast reconstruction from an aesthetic perspective. However, these are time-consuming operations with a higher risk of complications as well as donor site morbidity. As discussed earlier, reports are variable on the incidence of fat necrosis/fibrosis following irradiation, but these flaps are generally durable in the setting of adjuvant treatments. When genuine surgical equipoise exists, a patient's decision for mastectomy (rather than breast conservation) can be influenced not only by available reconstructive options but also by issues such as avoidance of radiotherapy, the need for future surveillance, and risk of de novo cancer in the conserved breast. Nonetheless, any decisions for "bigger surgery" must consider recovery time, complications, further operations, and potential donor site morbidity. It should also be noted that a reconstructed breast is insensate whereas breast-conservation surgery preserves nipple innervation. A variety of volume displacement and replacement techniques permit breast-conservation surgery to preserve an aesthetically pleasing breast form in most cases. It is no longer appropriate to claim that a bad cosmetic result is "the price to pay" for a robust cancer operation. In the event of poor cosmesis, adjuvant techniques such as fat grafting permit a degree of amelioration for adverse sequelae of surgery and radiotherapy. Whenever a definitive surgical plan cannot be agreed upon preoperatively, then ablative surgery alone should be undertaken which is sympathetic to a patient's likely longer-term reconstructive aspirations.

The evolution of oncoplastic surgery has allowed many women to benefit from a multidisciplinary team offering a comprehensive cancer and reconstructive service. All "breast surgeons" are in a sense "oncoplastic" and whatever their precise breed must work cooperatively with plastic surgeons to ensure that the mix of surgical skills can be optimally applied to maximize oncological, aesthetic, and patient-reported outcomes. There is now a greater appreciation of a patient's perspective and issues such as quality of life and patient choice. These complement traditional outcomes based on objective surgical criteria. Patient-reported outcome measures are increasingly being employed to evaluate more subjective quality-of-life outcomes relating to psychosocial, emotional, and functional domains. Several validated questionnaires now exist including BREAST-Q that can be used in separate components or as a whole (available in 28 languages). Incorporation of patient-reported outcome measures with more objective clinical parameters will inform future patient choice and lead to improvements in clinical care.

The benefits of immediate breast reconstruction in terms of psychological, sexual, and physical well-being have been documented, although breast reconstruction is a "preference sensitive" decision which must be individualized and made jointly between a patient and her surgeon(s). Outcomes of breast cancer surgery are best when clinical decision-making integrates information-giving, shared decision-making, and patients' personal values. This in turn will improve understanding of expected outcomes and inform the decision-making process.

Notwithstanding clinician reservations about contralateral prophylactic mastectomy, patients with unilateral breast cancer who opt for contralateral prophylactic mastectomy with bilateral reconstruction have higher levels of "breast" satisfaction that may partly reflect improved symmetry. Interestingly, the rise in implant-based immediate breast reconstruction in the United States has paralleled higher rates of patient satisfaction and better long-term quality of life for autologous tissue reconstruction. Moreover, anatomical shaped implants are neither associated with improved patient satisfaction nor quality of life.

Surgeons and other healthcare workers must be honest and realistic with patients when discussing outcomes of breast reconstruction and emphasize that a reconstructed breast is a facsimile of a normal breast. Levels of patient satisfaction are often more related to adequate information and a robust shared decision-making process than an aesthetically pleasing cosmetic result.

7

Preoperative radiological assessment

MEGAN KALAMBO AND WEI TSE YANG

AT A GLANCE

Accurate radiological assessment of a breast tumor is essential prior to definitive surgical intervention. Impalpable lesions require localization with ultrasound or stereotactic techniques and more extensive areas of calcification may demand multiple wires. Clip placement at the start of neoadjuvant chemotherapy provides valuable guidance in the event of a complete clinical and radiological response. Breast-conserving surgery aims to remove the tumor with a minimal amount of surrounding normal breast tissue to achieve "negative" margins. The tumor will be centered within a conventional wide local excision specimen, but may be eccentrically positioned when more complex oncoplastic resections are planned. Careful review of breast imaging will minimize the need for re-excision, which can be technically challenging in these circumstances.

INTRODUCTION

Breast cancer is now the second most frequently diagnosed cancer in women, and this is largely attributable to well-developed screening programs and advances in diagnostic technology. Despite its ranking as the number one cause of newly diagnosed cancer in women in the United States, overall survival rates have steadily improved over the past six decades.[1] These improved outcomes are collectively related to early detection and diagnosis, introduction of systemic therapies, and improved local control with both surgery and radiation therapy.

Imaging of the patient with newly diagnosed breast cancer aids clinical staging by firstly mapping disease extent in preparation for surgical planning and secondly screening of the contralateral breast for synchronous disease. The American Joint Committee on Cancer staging system for breast cancer (7th edition) provides a tumor-node-metastasis classification scheme used by clinicians to determine both prognosis and treatment.[2] The role of biologic tumor markers has emerged as an additional tool beyond grade and stage to assist in the prognostic assessment and treatment strategy.[3,4] Staging information helps determine surgical planning, the role and timing of chemotherapy

or hormonal therapy, and the scope of radiation therapy. Under this classification scheme, as the size of the tumor and regional lymph node metastases increase, there is a general increase in cancer stage, conferring a poorer prognosis and diminished survival rate.

At the authors' institution, patients with breast cancer are evaluated with multimodality imaging for local and regional staging. In this chapter, we will discuss the primary modalities used in the preoperative assessment of breast cancer, emerging imaging technologies, and the pertinent radiologic information that can alter not only stage, prognosis, and treatment, but also potentially impact upon oncoplastic strategies.

ROLE OF FULL-FIELD MAMMOGRAPHY AND DIGITAL BREAST TOMOSYNTHESIS

Full-field digital mammography continues to be the initial modality of choice in the detection of breast cancer and helps to define the extent and three dimensional location of abnormalities that require additional imaging evaluation. In general, those cancers detected at mammographic screening tend to be earlier in stage, with 75% of screen-detected cancers being stage 0 or 1, whereas more than half of clinically detected cancers are stage II or higher.[5]

With high contrast resolution and sophisticated processing algorithms improving the conspicuity of calcifications, digital mammography has steadily replaced film-screen mammography over the past decade. This has resulted in earlier detection of breast cancers, particularly high-grade ductal carcinoma in situ which often manifests as microcalcifications.[6,7]

Digital breast tomosynthesis is a new technique which produces a three dimensional derivative of full-field digital mammography using reconstructions of the breast from multiple low-dose digital images, acquired along a 15–50 degree arc. This process reduces the effect of tissue superimposition and results in enhanced visibility, detection, and evaluation of non-calcified mammographic lesions.[8,9] Digital breast tomosynthesis also assists in lesion localization and determining mammographic extent of non-calcified disease in women with suspected or known breast cancer.

Several studies have also shown improved visibility of invasive breast cancers with digital breast tomosynthesis that are subtle or occult on conventional mammography (**Figure 7.1**).[8-11] Mariscotti and colleagues compared the accuracy of multimodality staging of breast cancer and showed that digital breast synthesis had a higher sensitivity than digital mammography alone for the detection of malignant lesions.[8] Similarly, others have reported that up to 16% of invasive breast cancers are occult on conventional mammography compared with only 3% for digital breast tomosynthesis.[9]

Tumor visualization on mammography varies across histologic subtypes of breast cancer. In the setting of invasive lobular carcinoma which displays the classic single file tumor growth pattern, lesions are routinely difficult to detect on full-field digital mammography.[12] Comparative studies of digital mammography versus digital tomosynthesis for the detection of invasive lobular cancer have demonstrated both increased sensitivity and diagnostic accuracy with use of combined full-field digital mammography with digital breast tomosynthesis versus full-field digital mammography alone.[12]

In an effort to reduce overall dose, cost, and scan time associated with the combination of full-field digital mammography and digital breast tomosynthesis (DBT), novel approaches using integrated two-dimensional synthetic techniques reconstructed from the DBT acquisition are being developed and introduced into clinical practice (C-View 2D; Hologic, Bedford, Mass). This software is used to create a synthesized two-dimensional image from the digital breast tomosynthesis acquisition, which results in a lower patient radiation dose.[12] Preliminary data suggest that the combination of current reconstructed two-dimensional images and digital breast tomosynthesis performed comparably to full-field digital mammography plus digital breast tomosynthesis in terms of cancer detection rates and false-positive scores, while reducing average glandular dose by nearly 50%.[12,13]

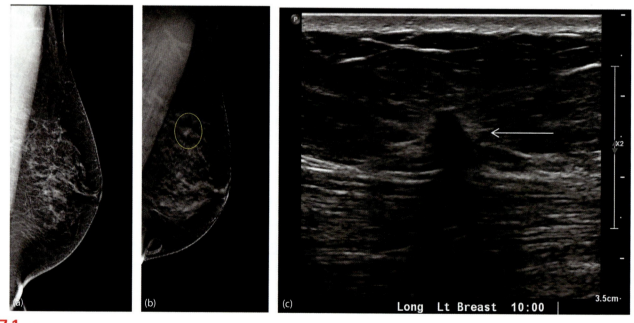

7.1 Mammographic (a) and tomosynthetic (b) images demonstrate an asymmetry in the superior left breast, only seen on tomosynthesis imaging (yellow circle). (c) Subsequent ultrasound shows a correlative irregular hypoechoic mass in the left breast in the 10 o'clock position (white arrow). Subsequent ultrasound-guided biopsy demonstrated invasive ductal carcinoma.

BREAST CANCER STAGING WITH MAMMOGRAPHY

Holland and colleagues evaluated mastectomy specimens of patients with invasive breast cancer and discovered that over 60% of cases had additional foci of malignancy within the ipsilateral breast.[14] These rates of multifocality are substantially higher for invasive lobular than for invasive ductal cancer.[15–17]

Mammography can detect additional malignant foci which render disease either multifocal (more than one foci of cancer within the same quadrant <5 cm apart) or multicentric (two or more foci of cancer in different quadrants >5 cm apart). This constitutes valuable information that may alter the patient's treatment pathway and change the surgical plan from breast conservation to mastectomy when multicentric disease is confirmed.

Once a lesion is identified as a known or suspected breast cancer, continued meticulous examination of the whole breast is required. Each lesion should be documented with its respective clock position, distance from the nipple, and relationship to other significant findings. A complete mammographic evaluation should include the following: (1) the total span of disease, (2) the presence of any contralateral disease, (3) associated skin thickening, (4) axillary and supraclavicular lymphadenopathy, and (5) skin, nipple, or chest wall extension.

When additional foci of disease have been detected, those that would render the cancer multifocal or multicentric must be confirmed with tissue biopsy. These additional foci may be evaluated with stereotactic biopsy in the setting of microcalcification or with ultrasound and possible guided tissue biopsy in the setting of non-calcified lesions. Any biopsy-proven additional foci of disease should also be documented with clip marker placement to aid in pre-surgical localization and guarantee excision at the time of surgery (**Figure 7.2**).

HIGH RESOLUTION WHOLE BREAST SONOGRAPHY

Sonography is widely accepted as the best adjunct to mammography in the diagnostic workup of discrete breast masses. At the University of Texas MD Anderson Cancer Center, ultrasound has been used as the modality of choice in the local and regional staging of invasive breast cancer for over two decades.

Whole breast ultrasound can also be performed to determine the presence of multifocal or multicentric disease. The ipsilateral regional nodal basins, including axillary, infraclavicular, supraclavicular, and internal mammary regions are evaluated for regional metastatic adenopathy, all of which influence disease stage and prognosis.

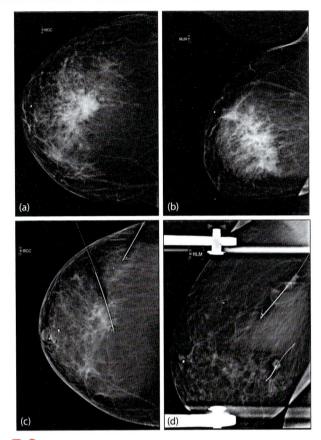

7.2 Mammogram images (a) and (b) demonstrate a patient with extensive multicentric right breast malignancy. Images (c) and (d) demonstrate favorable response to chemotherapy, rendering this patient eligible for needle localized segmental mastectomy with oncoplastic reconstruction.

It is important to note that ultrasound is not a standard method for evaluation of suspicious microcalcifcations detected mammographically which usually undergo stereotactic biopsy for histologic assessment. Ultrasound has a very high detection for masses, but consistently fails to reproduce microcalcifications which are associated with neither a mass lesion nor distortion on mammography (which is common in the setting of ductal carcinoma in situ). Several studies have reported that detection of sonographically visible pure ductal carcinoma in situ occurs in less than 50% of patients.[18–20]

The local staging of invasive breast cancer includes documentation of the maximum diameter of the largest invasive tumor to determine the T in the tumor-node-metastasis classification scheme. In the absence of limiting technical factors, high resolution ultrasound can accurately assess T stage, particularly in the setting of masses measuring approximately 2 cm (the cutoff for T1 tumors).[21]

SONOGRAPHIC ASSESSMENT OF UNIFOCAL, MULTIFOCAL, AND MULTICENTRIC DISEASE

Ultrasound may detect otherwise clinically and mammographically occult tumor foci, and this often occurs in patients with dense breast tissue on mammography.[22] A study evaluating whole breast ultrasound after mammography in patients with known or suspected breast cancer reported invasive tumor foci to be visible on ultrasound in 94% of cases compared with 81% for mammography.[22] In the absence of technical limitations, ultrasound has the ability to detect additional malignant foci rendering the disease multifocal or multicentric. As with mammography, meticulous examination of the whole breast is required together with precise documentation of each lesion including clock position, distance from the nipple, and distance from the primary tumor. When additional foci of disease have been detected, those that would define the cancer as multifocal or multicentric must be confirmed with tissue biopsy. Following core biopsy of the index lesion, these additional foci can be sampled with ultrasound-guided fine-needle aspiration. Any biopsy-proven additional foci of disease should also be documented with clip marker placement to aid in localization and ensure excision at the time of surgery.

REGIONAL NODAL STAGING WITH SONOGRAPHY

Ultrasound is more sensitive than physical examination for detection of axillary nodal metastases and can visualize high axillary, infraclavicular, and internal mammary nodes that cannot be assessed with palpation or mammography.[23,24]

In the absence of distant metastatic disease, the presence or absence of axillary metastases is the strongest individual prognostic indicator for breast cancer, and nodal status has a major influence on management.[24–26] The ACOSOG Z0011 trial determined that axillary lymph node dissection was not necessary in clinically node-negative patients undergoing breast-conservation therapy with 1–2 positive sentinel lymph nodes. At 6-year follow-up, there were no significant differences in loco regional recurrence and 5-year disease-free survival rates between sentinel lymph node dissection only versus axillary lymph node dissection groups.[24]

The ACOSOG Z1071 trial evaluating sentinel lymph node biopsy in patients with clinically node-positive disease receiving neoadjuvant chemotherapy has demonstrated the feasibility of sentinel lymph node biopsy alone in appropriately selected patients with clinically involved (cN1) disease undergoing neoadjuvant chemotherapy. This data confirm the utility of placing clips at the time of needle-guided lymph node biopsy in patients with cN1 disease to facilitate excision of any biopsy-proven metastatic node at the time of definitive surgery.[27–29]

The sonographic appearance of metastatic nodes vary across a wide spectrum, with cortical morphology shown to be more accurate than size when assessing the presence or absence of metastatic disease.[30,31] Due to the occasional overlap in sonographic features between benign and indeterminate lymph nodes, fine-needle aspiration cytology or core biopsy of sonographically indeterminate/suspicious lymph nodes can provide a more definitive diagnosis than ultrasound evaluation alone. Reported sensitivities of ultrasound-guided fine-needle aspiration cytology range from 73% to 88%.[30,31] Due to a finite false-negative rate, negative findings on axillary sonography or tissue biopsy do not preclude the need for sentinel lymph node biopsy.

The identification of metastatic disease in higher nodal categories may alter the disease stage and treatment recommendations (**Figure 7.3**). Therefore, in patients with

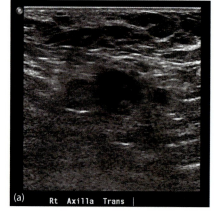 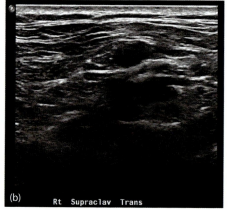

7.3 Ultrasound images demonstrate metastatic disease to the axillary level I (a) and supraclavicular nodal basin (b), consistent with N3 disease. Documented disease extent and nodal involvement at diagnosis is used for adjuvant radiation port planning.

multiple levels of suspicious lymphadenopathy, the largest abnormal lymph node in the highest nodal category is selected for biopsy.

CONTRAST-ENHANCED MRI

The role of preoperative magnetic resonance imaging (MRI) in the locoregional staging of newly diagnosed breast cancer continues to be an evolving field. Given the high sensitivity of MRI, clinical outcomes that are potentially improved by use of preoperative MRI include reduction in rates of re-excision, in-breast local recurrence, and subsequent development of a new contralateral cancer or distant metastasis. However, the routine use of preoperative MRI remains controversial because of conflicting reports on how MRI imaging influences these surgical and long-term outcomes.

In the setting of newly diagnosed breast cancer, MRI has been shown to be more accurate in determining true tumor size and disease extent when compared to conventional mammography and ultrasound (**Figure 7.4**).[32] In a meta-analysis of 19 studies that included 2610 patients, preoperative MRI depicted additional sites of disease which were occult using other imaging techniques in 16% of patients.[33] In addition, staging-oriented bilateral breast MRI has demonstrated the presence of a synchronous tumor site in the contralateral breast in 3%–5%.[34] Despite the detection of additional disease, several retrospective studies have concluded that preoperative breast MRI does not lead to reductions in: (1) risk of local or distant recurrence, (2) re-operation rates, or (3) rates of conversion from conservation therapy to mastectomy.[35,36] Furthermore, Yi and colleagues compared rates of breast cancer disease-free survival in patients with newly diagnosed breast cancer with and without preoperative MRI imaging and found no reduction in risk of local-regional nor distant recurrence in the two patient populations. Nonetheless, a reduced risk of contralateral breast cancer recurrence was observed in patients receiving preoperative MRI.[37]

Advocates of MRI cite several advantages including: (1) improved selection of patients for breast-conserving surgery, (2) a decrease in the number of surgical procedures needed to obtain clear margins, and (3) the synchronous detection of contralateral cancers (**Figure 7.5**). However, there are no data from prospective randomized trials that demonstrate improved outcomes from the addition of breast MRI to the diagnostic workup of newly diagnosed breast cancer. Furthermore, any suspicious lesions seen on MRI must be biopsied to confirm diagnosis before planning definitive surgery. The low specificity of MRI (68%) coupled with high false-positive rates (30%–45%) can lead to additional testing and biopsies, increased patient anxiety, and medical costs with potential delays in definitive treatment. As a result, breast cancer staging with MRI should be judiciously used in defined groups of patients for whom a potential benefit in terms of local staging can be expected. These populations include the following groups:

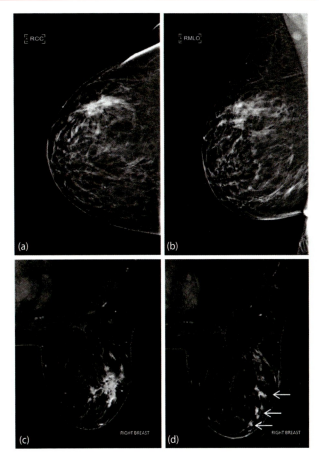

7.4 Mammogram images (a and b) demonstrate a large palpable malignancy presenting as an area of architectural distortion in the upper outer quadrant of the right breast. Subsequent MRI imaging (c and d) demonstrates the malignancy appearing as an irregular mass with associated clumped non-mass enhancement. Additional areas of similar appearing clumped non-mass enhancement were documented inferior, lateral, and anterior to the known malignancy (arrows), further delineating disease extent.

a. Women diagnosed with axillary nodal metastases and a clinically ocular primary tumor
b. Patients presenting with clinical disease extent larger than is apparent on mammography or ultrasound
c. Assessment of possible extension of tumor into the pectoralis fascia/muscle (**Figure 7.6**)
d. Women with locally advanced breast cancer being considered for neoadjuvant chemotherapy
e. Women at high risk for contralateral disease
f. Patients undergoing elective contralateral mastectomy

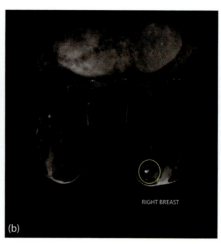
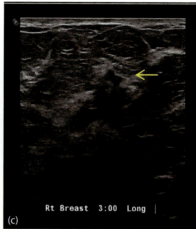

7.5 MRI images in a patient with known left breast malignancy demonstrate the known malignancy (a) as an irregular mass with associated clumped non-mass enhancement in the left lateral breast (white arrow). (b) A small enhancing irregular mass (yellow circle) is noted in the right breast. (c) MRI-directed right breast ultrasound shows the right breast mass (yellow arrow), which was subsequently targeted for ultrasound-guided biopsy revealing invasive ductal carcinoma.

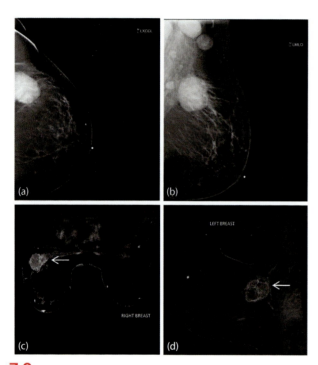

7.6 Mammogram (a and b) and MRI (c and d) images demonstrate a large posterior unifocal left breast malignancy with chest wall invasion confirmed on contrast-enhanced MRI imaging (c and d). The presence of adjacent pectoralis muscle enhancement (arrows) confirms invasion of the mass into the pectoralis musculature, rendering the patient stage T4.

PET-CT AND MOLECULAR BREAST IMAGING

Advanced functional imaging techniques are also available in specific patient populations to aid in the detection and staging of breast cancer. Positron emission–computed tomography (PET)/computed tomography (CT) imaging is considered in patients with inflammatory or locally advanced breast cancer for the detection of distant metastatic disease.[38] Molecular breast imaging remains largely investigative in the context of breast cancer staging, but shows promise for improved sensitivity and specificity when further evaluating mammographically suspicious lesions, particularly in patients with dense breast tissue.

REFERENCES

1. Budzar, A. U., T. A. Buchholz, S. H. Taylor, G. N. Hortobagyi, and K. K. Hunt. 2013. Chapter 4: Breast cancer. In *60 Years of Survival Outcomes at the University of Texas MD Anderson Cancer Center*, (Ed.) M.A. Rodriguez, R.S. Walters, and T.W. Burke, pp. 19–34. New York: Springer.
2. Edge, S. B., D. R. Byrd, C. C. Comptom et al. 2010. *AJCC Cancer Staging Manual*. 7th ed. pp. 347–376. New York: Springer.
3. Dawood, S., R. Hu, M. D. Homes et al. 2011. Defining breast cancer prognosis based on molecular phenotypes: Results from a large cohort study. *Breast Cancer Res Treat* 126(1):185–192.
4. Yi, M., E. A. Mittendorf, J. N. Cormier et al. 2011. Novel staging system for predicting disease-specific survival in patients with breast cancer treated with surgery as the first intervention: Time to modify the current American Joint Committee on Cancer staging system. *J Clin Oncol* 29:4654–4661.
5. Tabar, L., S. W. Duffy, B. Vitak et al. 1999. The natural history of breast carcinoma: What have we learned from screening? *Cancer* 86:449–462.
6. Weigel, S., T. Decker, E. Korsching et al. 2010. Calcifications in digital mammographic screening: Improvement of early detection of invasive breast cancers? *Radiology* 255:738–745.
7. Del Turco, M. R., P. Mantellini, S. Ciatto et al. 2007. Full-field digital versus screen-film mammography: Comparative accuracy in concurrent screening cohorts. *AJR* 189:860–866.

8. Mariscotti, G., N. Houssami, M. Durando et al. 2014. Accuracy of mammography, digital breast tomosynthesis, ultrasound and MR imaging in preoperative assessment of breast cancer. *Anticancer Res* 34(3):1219–1225.

9. Dang, P. A., K. L. Humphrey, P. E. Freer et al. 2013. Comparison of lesion detection and characterization in invasive cancers using breast tomosynthesis versus conventional mammography [abstr]. In *Radiological Society of North America Scientific Assembly and Annual Meeting Program*, p. 156. Oak Brook, IL: Radiological Society of North America.

10. Skaane, P., A. I. Bandos, R. Gullien et al. 2013. Comparison of digital mammography alone and digital mammography plus tomosynthesis in a population-based screening program. *Radiology* 267(1):47–56.

11. Ciatto, S., N. Houssami, D. Bernardi et al. 2013. Integration of 3D digital mammography with tomosynthesis for population breast-cancer screening (STORM): A prospective comparison study. *Lancet Oncol* 14:583–589.

12. Hilleren, D. J., I. T. Andersson, K. Lindholm et al. 1991. Invasive lobular carcinoma: Mammographic findings in a 10-year experience. *Radiology* 178(1):149–154.

13. Zuley, M. L., B. Guo, V. J. Catullo et al. 2014. Comparison of two dimensional synthesized mammograms versus original digital mammograms alone and in combination with tomosynthesis images. *Radiology* 271(3):664–671.

14. Holland, R., S. H. Veling, M. Mravunac et al. 1985. Histologic multifocality of Tis, T1-2 breast carcinomas: Implications for clinical trials of breast conserving surgery. *Cancer* 56:979–990.

15. Lesser, M. L., P. P. Rosen, and D. W. Kinne. 1982. Multicentricity and bilaterality in invasive breast carcinoma. *Surgery* 91:234–240.

16. Mann, R. M., J. Veltman, J. O. Barentsz et al. 2008. The value of MRI compared to mammography in the assessment of tumour extent in invasive lobular carcinoma of the breast. *Eur J Surg Oncol* 34:135–142.

17. Lopez, J. K., and L. W. Bassett. 2009. Invasive lobular carcinoma of the breast: Spectrum of mammographic, US, and MR imaging findings. *RadioGraphics* 29:165–176.

18. Scoggins, M. E., P. S. Fox, H. M. Kuerer et al. 2015. Correlation between sonographic findings and clinicopathologic and biologic features of pure ductal carcinoma in situ in 691 patients. *AJR Am J Roentgenol* 204(4):878–888.

19. Moon, W. K., J. S. Myung, Y. J. Lee et al. 2002. US of ductal carcinoma in situ. *RadioGraphics* 22:269–280; discussion, 280–281.

20. Park, J. S., Y. M. Park, E. K. Kim et al. 2010. Sonographic findings of high-grade and non-high-grade ductal carcinoma in situ of the breast. *J Ultrasound Med* 29:1687–1697.

21. Fornage, B. D., O. Toubas, and M. Morel. 1987. Clinical, mammographic, and sonographic determination of preoperative breast cancer size. *Cancer* 60:765–771.

22. Berg, W. A., and P. L. Gilbreath. 2000. Multicentric and multifocal cancer: Whole-breast US in preoperative evaluation. *Radiology* 214:59–66.

23. Sacre, R. A. 1986. Clinical evaluation of axillary lymph nodes compared to surgical and pathological findings. *Eur J Surg Oncol* 12:169–173.

24. Pamilo, M., M. Soiva, and E. M. Lavast. 1989. Real time ultrasound, axillary mammography and clinical examination in the detection of axillary lymph node metastases in breast cancer patients. *J Ultrasound Med* 8:115–120.

25. Ecanow, J. S., H. Abe, G. M. Newstead, D. B. Ecanow, and J. M. Jeske. 2013. Axillary staging of breast cancer: What the radiologist should know. *RadioGraphics* 33:1589–1612.

26. Carter, C., C. Allen, and D. Henson. 1989. Relation of tumor size, lymph node status, and survival in 24,740 breast cancer cases. *Cancer* 63:181–187.

27. Beenken, S., M. Urist, Y. Zhang et al. 2003. Axillary lymph node status, but not tumor size, predicts locoregional recurrence and overall survival after mastectomy for breast cancer. *Ann Surg* 237:732–738.

28. Boughey, J. C., V. J. Suman, E. A. Mittendorf et al. 2015. Factors affecting sentinel lymph node identification rate after neoadjuvant chemotherapy for breast cancer patients enrolled in ACOSOG Z1071 (Alliance). *Ann Surg* 261(3):547–552.

29. Caudle, A., W. Yang, E. Mittendorf et al. 2015. Selective surgical localization of axillary lymph nodes containing metastases in patients with breast cancer: A prospective feasibility trial. *JAMA Surg* 150:137–143.

30. Mainiero, M. B., C. M. Cinelli, S. L. Koelliker et al. 2010. Axillary ultrasound and fine needle aspiration in the preoperative evaluation of the breast cancer patient: An algorithm based on tumor size and lymph node appearance. *AJR* 33:1589–1612.

31. Bedi, D. G., R. Krishnamurthy, S. Krisnamurthy et al. 2008. Cortical morphologic features of axillary lymph nodes as a predictor of metastasis in breast cancer: In vitro sonographic study. *AJR* 191:646–652.

32. Berg, W. A., L. Gutierrez, M. S. NessAiver et al. 2004. Diagnostic accuracy of mammography, clinical examination, US, and MR imaging in preoperative assessment of breast cancer. *Radiology* 233:830–849.

33. Houssami, N., S. Ciatto, M. Petra et al. 2008. Accuracy and surgical impact of magnetic resonance imaging in breast cancer staging: Systematic review and meta-analysis in detection of multifocal and multicentric cancer. *J Clin Oncol* 26:3248–3258.

34. Liberman, L., E. A. Morris, C. M. Kim et al. 2003. MR imaging findings in the contralateral breast of women with recently diagnosed breast cancer. *AJR* 180:333–341.

35. Hwang, N., D. E. Schiller, P. Crystal et al. 2009. Magnetic resonance imaging in the planning of initial lumpectomy for invasive breast carcinoma: Its effect on ipsilateral breast tumor recurrence after breast-conservation therapy. *Ann Surg Oncol* 16:3000–3009.

36. Solin, L. J., S. G. Orel, W. T. Hwang et al. 2008. Relationship of breast magnetic resonance imaging to outcome after breast-conservation treatment with radiation for women with early stage invasive breast carcinoma or ductal carcinoma in situ. *J Clin Oncol* 26:386–391.

37. Yi, A., N. Cho, K. S. Yang et al. 2015. Breast cancer recurrence in patients with newly diagnosed breast cancer without and with preoperative MR imaging: A matched cohort study. *Radiology* 276(3):695–705.

38. Le-Petross, C. H., L. Bidaut, and W. T. Yang. 2008. Evolving role of imaging modalities in inflammatory breast cancer. *Semin Oncol* 35(1):51–63.

8

Oncoplastic parenchymal resection

AT A GLANCE

Oncoplastic techniques continue to advance the limits of breast-conservation surgery by permitting larger volumes of tissue to be excised while yielding an acceptable cosmetic result. Though significant breast deformity can accompany more extensive resections, it is the percentage rather than absolute volume of breast tissue excised that is critical. When more than 10%–20% of breast tissue is removed from an average (or 30% from a large) sized breast, there is a risk of an unsatisfactory cosmetic result. Moreover, relatively modest losses of 5%–10% breast volume in smaller breasts or in sensitive zones (medial/inferior quadrants) can adversely affect cosmesis. Options for partial breast reconstruction include local glandular rearrangement or composite tissue flaps with a non-axial blood supply, reduction mammoplasty, and regional or distant flaps. The optimum choice will be determined by breast size and percentage breast excision together with tumor location, need for re-excision, degree of ptosis, and timing of radiotherapy. Exciting prospects exist for preserving a cosmetically acceptable breast while satisfying oncological mandates.

8.1 IN SITU DISEASE

Katrina B. Mitchell and Henry Kuerer

The diagnosis of ductal carcinoma in situ (DCIS) has risen in the era of modern mammography,[1–2] necessitating a coordinated approach between the oncologic resection and possible subsequent oncoplastic reconstruction. The key issues from an oncologic perspective include the following: (1) the decision to undergo breast-conserving therapy versus total mastectomy with or without contralateral prophylactic mastectomy (CPM), (2) whether to perform sentinel lymph node biopsy (SLNB), and (3) the status of surgical margins. All of these factors influence oncoplastic reconstruction and will be reviewed in this chapter.

The oncologic surgical approach to DCIS has traditionally been determined by factors such as tumor size and pathologic classification, age, and patient or provider choice or concern for risk of recurrence and desire to avoid repeat intervention.[3–4] More recent advances in genetic testing have also been shown to influence surgical decision-making.[5] Breast-conserving therapy remains the most common approach to resection of screen-detected DCIS and currently relates to potential overtreatment and the possibility of eliminating surgery in selected cases.

Nevertheless, total mastectomy rates for DCIS remain significant and often will prompt requests for immediate breast reconstruction.

A recent study demonstrated that mastectomy rates for DCIS initially declined for the period 1998–2004 from 36 to 28%, but subsequently increased through 2011 to reach about 33%, this correlated with a concomitant increase in rates of CPM. Younger women compared with older women were more likely to undergo total mastectomy and mastectomy was also predicted by medical comorbidities, higher tumor grade, treatment at an academic facility, and residence at a greater distance from a medical facility.[6] A separate study found that younger women were more likely to undergo CPM, as were those women with an identified BRCA mutation or family history of ovarian cancer.[5] Additionally, it has been suggested that the current availability of high-quality immediate breast reconstructive options may be influencing patients and providers to proceed with total mastectomy rather than breast-conservation therapy in DCIS.[7–8]

Traditionally, SLNB dissection has been recommended for DCIS patients undergoing total mastectomy and those with microinvasive disease on histopathology and is used on a discretionary basis for large and/or high-grade tumors.[9] However, a recent study from MD Anderson concluded that routine SLNB should not be performed unless a patient is at high risk for invasive disease.[10] This recommendation represents clinical progress in refining the surgical management of DCIS, a disease for which up to one-third of patients underwent full axillary dissection for treatment of their disease in the early 1990s.[11]

Since development of the Van Nuys Prognostic Index in the 1980s to predict recurrence risk for DCIS, there has been general agreement that a 2 to 3 mm surgical margin is acceptable if postoperative radiotherapy is administered.[12-15] However, given the current concern for overtreatment of low-risk DCIS lesions, the issue of margin status as an independent predictor of recurrence has been re-examined. Some multidisciplinary groups are comfortable with no tumor on ink for DCIS (if all microcalcifications are removed and patients receive radiotherapy), whereas the University of Southern California recently argued that margins of >10 mm alone provide recurrence risks similar to that of breast-conserving therapy with radiotherapy.[16] The MD Anderson Cancer Center has concluded that post-mastectomy radiation is only indicated for patients with *multiple* close or positive margins.[17] In addition, work from this institution has shown that 28% of patients with DCIS undergo directed cavity re-excision based on intraoperative assessment through radiology and gross tissue inspection.[18]

Despite high-quality reconstructive options being increasingly available coupled with decreased risk of recurrence and need for future interventions with total mastectomy, individualized prognostic indicators for DCIS should be developed in order to more safely offer breast-conserving therapy.[19-21] This includes incorporation of molecular assessment of tumor biology to better predict behavior and using advanced imaging techniques to guide surgical approaches more accurately.[21] The Eastern Cooperative Oncology Group E5194 study addressed the utility of the Oncotype DX® (Genentech, Houston, TX) breast cancer multi-gene assay to predict DCIS recurrence risk. Results suggest that a continuous DCIS score (calculated from seven cancer-related genes and five reference genes in the Oncotype DX assay) can aid decision-making regarding adjuvant radiotherapy and identify cases in which it safely can be omitted.[22] In addition, the ongoing UK LORIS (Low-Risk DCIS) trial is investigating whether surgery and/or radiotherapy may be omitted from the treatment algorithm in low-risk DCIS in favor of active surveillance. It is believed that this trial will not only provide critical insight into the natural history of low-risk DCIS, but also define the way in which patients are monitored for progression of disease while under active surveillance. In addition, this groundbreaking trial will provide information about patient quality of life and health economics.[19,23]

Oncoplastic planning will be influenced by a variety of factors including the type of oncologic surgical resection performed, the utilization or elimination of radiotherapy from the treatment algorithm, and methods for assessing DCIS margin status. At a time when mastectomy rates are increasing and favorable reconstructive options are becoming more widely available to patients, breast surgical oncologists are nevertheless questioning overtreatment of DCIS and developing strategies to better predict behavior of individual DCIS lesions. Oncologic approaches to DCIS will likely undergo radical changes in the next decade, and this will impact on the role of oncoplastic interventions for management of this disease. It will be more crucial than ever that oncologic resection and oncoplastic reconstruction be carefully coordinated both among surgical as well as colleagues in radiation and medical oncology.

REFERENCES

1. Kuerer HM, Albarracin CT, Yang WT, Cardiff RD, Brewster AM, Symmans WF et al. Ductal carcinoma in situ: State of the science and roadmap to advance the field. *J Clin Oncol* 2009; 27: 279–288.
2. Siegel R, Naishadham D, and Jemal A. Cancer statistics, 2013. *CA Cancer J Clin* 2013; 63: 11–30.
3. Silverstein MJ. The university of Southern California/Van Nuys Prognostic index for ductal carcinoma in situ of the breast. *Am J Surg* 2003; 186: 337–343.
4. Sue GR, Lannin DR, Au AF, Narayan D, and Chagpar AB. Factors associated with decision to pursue mastectomy and breast reconstruction in the treatment of ductal carcinoma of the breast. *Am J Surg* 2013; 206: 682–685.
5. Elsayegh N, Kuerer HM, Lin H, Guiterrez Barrera AM, Jackson M, Muse KL et al. Predictors that influence contralateral prophylactic mastectomy election among women with ductal carcinoma in situ who were evaluated for BRCA gene testing. *Ann Surg Oncol* 2014; 11: 3466–3472.
6. Rutter CE, Park HS, Killelea BK, and Evans SB. Growing use of mastectomy for ductal carcinoma in situ of the breast among young women in the United States. *Ann Surg Oncol* 2015; 7: 2378–2386.
7. Ashfaq A, McGhan LJ, Pockaj BA, Gray RJ, Bagaria SP, McLaughlin SA et al. Impact of breast reconstruction on the decision to undergo contralateral prophylactic mastectomy. *Ann Surg Oncol* 2014; 21: 2934–2940.
8. Habermann EB, Thomsen KM, Hieken TJ, and Boughey JC. Impact of availability of immediate breast reconstruction on bilateral mastectomy rates for breast cancer across the United States: Data from the nationwide inpatient sample. *Ann Surg Oncol* 2014; 10: 3290–3296.
9. Julian TB, Land SR, Fourchotte V, Haile SR, Fisher ER, Mamounas EP et al. Is sentinel node biopsy necessary in conservatively treated DCIS? *Ann Surg Oncol* 2007; 8: 2202–2208.
10. Francis AM, Haugen CE, Grimes LM, Crow JR, Yi M, Mittendorf EA et al. Is sentinel lymph node dissection warranted for patients with a diagnosis of ductal carcinoma in situ? *Ann Surg Oncol* 2015; 22(13): 4270–4279.
11. Baxter NN, Virnig BA, and Durham SB. Trends in the treatment of ductal carcinoma in situ of the breast. *J Natl Cancer Inst* 2004; 96: 443–448.

12. Silverstein MJ, Poller DN, Waisman JR, Colburn WJ, Barth A, Gierson ED et al. Prognostic classification of breast duct carcinoma in situ. *Lancet* 1995; 345: 1154–1157.

13. Silverstein M, Lagios M, Craig P, Waisman JR, Lewinsky BS, Colburn WJ et al. The Van Nuys Prognostic index for ductal carcinoma in situ. *Breast J* 1996; 2: 38–40.

14. Silverstein MJ and Buchanan C. Ductal carcinoma in situ: USC/Van Nuys Prognostic index and the impact of margin status. *Breast* 2003; 12: 457–471.

15. Boughey JC, Gonzalez RJ, Bonner E, and Kuerer HM. Current treatment and clinical trial developments for ductal carcinoma in situ of the breast. *Oncologist* 2007; 11: 1276–1287.

16. Macdonald HR, Silverstein MJ, Lee LA, Ye W, Sanghavi P, Holmes DR et al. Margin width as the sole determinant of local recurrence after breast conservation in patients with ductal carcinoma in situ. *Am J Surg* 2006; 192: 420–422.

17. Fitzsullivan E, Lari SA, Smith B, Caudle AS, Krishnamurthy S, Lucci A et al. Incidence and consequence of close margins in patients with ductal carcinoma-in situ treated with mastectomy: Is further therapy warranted? *Ann Surg Oncol* 2013; 13: 4103–4112.

18. Cablioglu N, Hunt KK, Sahin AA, Kuerer HM, Babiera GV, Singletary SE et al. Role for intraoperative margin assessment in patients undergoing breast-conserving therapy. *Ann Surg Oncol* 2007; 14: 1458–1471.

19. Kuerer HM. Ductal carcinoma in situ: Treatment or active surveillance? *Expert Rev Anticancer Ther* 2015; 7: 777–785.

20. Rakovitch E, Nofech-Mozes S, Hanna W, Baehner FL, Saskin R, Butler SM et al. A population-based validation study of the DCIS Score predicting recurrence risk in individuals treated by breast-conserving therapy alone. *Breast Cancer Res Treat* 2015; 152: 389–398.

21. Wells CJ, O'Donoghue C, Ojeda-Fournier H, Retallack HE, and Esserman LJ. Evolving paradigm for the management of DCIS. *J Am Coll Radiol* 2013; 10: 918–923.

22. Solin LJ, Gray R, Baehner FL, Butler SM, Hughes LL, Yoshizawa C et al. A multigene expression assay to predict local recurrence risk for ductal carcinoma in situ of the breast. *J Natl Cancer Inst* 2013; 105: 701–710.

23. Francis A, Fallowfield L, and Rea D. The LORIS Trial: Addressing overtreatment of ductal carcinoma in situ. *Clin Oncol (R Coll Radiol)* 2015; 27: 6–8.

8.2 INVASIVE CARCINOMA

Tracy-Ann Moo and Rache M. Simmons

Breast-conserving surgery for invasive breast cancer has been shown to have outcomes equivalent to mastectomy in terms of overall and breast cancer-specific survival in multiple randomized controlled trials.[1,2] The Early Breast Cancer Trialists' Collaborative Group analyzed data from randomized controlled trials which included 42,000 women over 78 trials. In a comparison of mastectomy versus lumpectomy and radiation, at 15 years, there was no difference in overall survival or breast cancer-specific survival among both groups.[3] With regards to local recurrence, improvements in methods of margin assessment and administration of systemic therapy have led to a decrease in rates of local recurrence since these randomized trials were performed. In a longitudinal analysis done by Cabioglu and colleagues, investigators looked at ipsilateral breast tumor recurrence in patients with invasive breast cancer treated between 1970 and 1996. Patients treated prior to 1994 had a significantly higher local recurrence rate compared to those treated after 1994, 5.7% versus 1.3% (p = 0.001). Those patients treated after 1994 were also less likely to have positive or unknown margins and more likely to receive systemic therapy.[4] Accordingly, the option of breast-conservation therapy has become a standard of care for patients being treated with invasive breast cancer.

Selection criteria for breast conservation prior to the introduction of oncoplastic techniques were primarily based on size. This essentially restricted breast conservation to women with small tumors or a high breast to tumor volume ratio. The advent of oncoplastic techniques for breast-conserving surgery and an increase in the use of pre-operative systemic chemotherapy has led to an expansion of these criteria such that women with larger tumors are now candidates for breast conservation. Mammoplasty-based oncoplastic techniques allow resection of greater than 20% of the breast volume with preservation of aesthetic results. The central tenets of breast-conserving surgery, however, remain the same: first, the tumor should be resected with negative margins and, secondly, acceptable aesthetic outcomes must be achieved.

Incision orientation and placement for tumor resection varies based on planned oncoplastic technique. Non-palpable lesions require preoperative placement of a radiologic marker either by wire or radioactive seed localization. The tumor should be resected with wide margins and a contemporary method of margin assessment employed. It is important that negative margins are achieved when performing oncoplastic breast conservation, as the management of positive margins can pose a significant challenge. If margins return positive, tissue rearrangement will make identification of the cavity for re-excision very difficult, if not impossible in some cases. In those cases for which it can be anticipated that wide resection may not ensure negative margins, a staged procedure should be planned or methods of intraoperative margin assessment considered. Retrospective studies have identified various clinicopathologic features that decrease the likelihood of successfully obtaining negative margins. These include invasive lobular subtype, extensive microcalcifications on mammogram, multifocal disease, and DCIS. Clough and colleagues analyzed 272 patients undergoing mammoplasty-based oncoplastic breast conservation and reported an 11.9% rate of positive margins with an average tumor size of 2.6 cm and resection weight of 175 g. In 33 (12%) of these cases, a second operation was required to clear the margins and 91% of patients were ultimately able to achieve breast conservation with an oncoplastic technique. Examination of clinicopathologic features that influenced positive margins revealed histologic subgroup, tumor size and grade to be associated with positive margins. However, multivariate analysis identified only patients with invasive lobular cancer to be at significantly higher risk of positive margins.[5] Amabile and colleagues examined factors contributing to the risk of re-excision after oncoplastic breast-conserving surgery in 129 patients, all of whom were treated with oncoplastic surgery between 2009 and 2013, included patients who had been treated with neoadjuvant chemotherapy. A re-excision rate of 30.3% was reported and factors which predicted re-excision were multiple and included being overweight (p = 0.0.2), the presence of microcalcifications on mammography (p = 0.003), and tumor multifocality (p = 0.03).[6] Similarly, in an analysis of oncologic outcomes in 1035 patients undergoing oncoplastic breast-conserving surgery, the presence of multifocal or multicentric disease and DCIS were found to be associated with positive margins (p < 0.001).[7]

Utilization of neoadjuvant chemotherapy in the treatment of advanced breast cancer has also led to a broadening of indications for breast conservation. In many cases despite evident shrinkage of tumors in response to neoadjuvant chemotherapy, a significant defect may remain after resection. In these instances, an oncoplastic repair is necessary to achieve adequate aesthetic results. Mazouni and colleagues examined 259 patients treated with breast conservation following neoadjuvant chemotherapy from January 2002 to November 2010. Forty-five patients had some form of oncoplastic breast-conserving surgery, while the majority (214) underwent standard breast conservation. Median tumor size for both groups was 4 cm and the median operative specimen volume in the oncoplastic breast surgery group was 180 versus 98 cm^2 in the standard breast-conservation group (p = 0.0001). Both re-excision and mastectomy rates were comparable for the standard and oncoplastic breast surgery groups (re-excision rate of 9% versus 2% [p = 0.22] and mastectomy rate of 24% versus 18%, respectively [p = 0.03]). Moreover, at a median follow-up of 46 months, both local and distant relapse rates were similar. Oncoplastic breast-conserving surgery thus allowed for greater excision volumes after neoadjuvant chemotherapy while achieving comparable oncological outcomes to standard breast-conserving surgery.[8]

Contemporary techniques of oncoplastic breast surgery adhere to fundamental principles of breast conservation with the primary goal of parenchymal resection being to maintain oncologic safety by achieving clear surgical margins. The oncologic surgeon should bear in mind those clinicopathologic features, which may increase the risk of positive margins in order to plan an appropriate primary resection and any subsequent re-excision which may be necessary.

REFERENCES

1. Simone, N. L. *et al.* Twenty-five year results of the national cancer institute randomized breast conservation trial. *Breast Cancer Res. Treat.* 132, 197–203 (2012).
2. Fisher, B. *et al.* Twenty-year follow-up of a randomized trial comparing total mastectomy, lumpectomy, and lumpectomy plus irradiation for the treatment of invasive breast cancer. *N. Engl. J. Med.* 347, 1233–1241 (2002).
3. Clarke, M. *et al.* Effects of radiotherapy and of differences in the extent of surgery for early breast cancer on local recurrence and 15-year survival: An overview of the randomised trials. *Lancet* 366, 2087–2106 (2005).
4. Cabioglu, N. *et al.* Improving local control with breast-conserving therapy: A 27-year single-institution experience. *Cancer* 104, 20–29 (2005).
5. Clough, K. B. *et al.* Positive margins after oncoplastic surgery for breast cancer. *Ann. Surg. Oncol.* (2015). doi:10.1245/s10434-015-4514-3.
6. Amabile, M.-I. *et al.* Factors predictive of re-excision after oncoplastic breast-conserving surgery. *Anticancer Res.* 35, 4229–4234 (2015).
7. Rezai, M., Kraemer, S., Kimmig, R., and Kern, P. Breast conservative surgery and local recurrence. *Breast* (2015). doi:10.1016/j.breast.2015.07.024.
8. Mazouni, C. *et al.* The role of oncoplastic breast surgery in the management of breast cancer treated with primary chemotherapy. *Breast* 22, 1189–1193 (2013).

9

Intraoperative assessment

AT A GLANCE

Thorough intraoperative margin assessment is valuable when partial breast reconstruction is undertaken as an immediate procedure. Glandular rearrangement or local/distant flap-based reconstruction hinders individual margin re-excision and positive margins may necessitate completion mastectomy with sacrifice of any flap. Surgeons must work cooperatively with pathology colleagues to ensure that local procedures for inking, specimen imaging, and serial sectioning permit complete (one-piece) tumor excision, accurate histological assessment, and declaration of margin negativity.

9.1 PATHOLOGICAL

Sarah E. Pinder and Elena Provenzano

The intraoperative evaluation of margins following wide local excision (WLE) for either ductal carcinoma in situ (DCIS) or invasive breast cancer may involve a variety of approaches that includes radiological, pathological (macroscopic and microscopic), or the utilization or novel techniques such as: (1) intraoperative ultrasound, (2) near-infrared fluorescence optical imaging, amongst others. (3) x-ray diffraction technology, (4) radiofrequency spectroscopy, and (5) terahertz and Cerenkov luminescence imaging, amongst others. However, pathological methodologies that are more commonly practiced include macroscopic assessment, with and/or without cytological or frozen section examination. There is evidence that a combination of radiological and pathological assessment (macroscopic and/or microscopic examination) are particularly effective and associated with lower re-excision and, more importantly, local recurrence rates.[1] Indeed, relatively simple gross specimen examination can reduce the need for a second operation to obtain complete surgical excision.[2] This can be effectively combined with specimen slice x-ray examination to reduce re-excision rates for patients with DCIS.[3]

Others advocate microscopic examination of the margins using either touch imprint cytology (TIC) or frozen section examination. The former incorporates selection of areas of concern and a process of "pressing" these onto glass microscope slides, immediately fixing the sample and staining with subsequent light microscopic assessment of the cytological preparations produced. Alternatively, a small fragment of tissue (1–2 mm) can be "squashed" between two slides or a scrape from a scalpel blade over the surface is smeared onto the slide. These techniques will only detect tumor cells that are present at the surface of the specimen, that is, *at* the margin and not some distance therefrom.

Frozen section examination of margins requires initial naked eye identification of the most worrisome area(s) at the edge of the specimen. A small portion(s) is then sampled and subjected to rapid freezing, section cutting with a cryostat, staining with hematoxylin and eosin, and then microscopic examination. This must be performed after the specimen has been weighed, measured, and inked (ideally with different colors) according to local protocols. There are two approaches to frozen section in this context: A portion from the edge of the specimen can be taken and examined *face up*, which will permit detection of tumor present *at the* surface of the specimen, or a section can be taken at right angles to the edge of the specimen, which can detect tumor at some short distance from the margin and allow measurement of the margin distance.

All intraoperative techniques require experience and expertise on the part of the pathologist and recognition of artifacts that inevitably occur. However, errors in frozen section assessment occasionally happen with 57% resulting from misinterpretation, 24% from microscopic sampling, 9.5% from gross sampling with 9.5% reported to arise from lack of communication between the pathologist and surgeon.[4] Moreover, although frozen section can be employed for rapid diagnosis, including assessment of margins, it cannot be as accurate, nor replace, formalin fixed, paraffin wax-embedded tissue assessment. Apart from the inherent issues of sampling error, frozen section examination requires technical expertise, particularly in the processes of rapid freezing and section cutting, which greatly influence the interpretation of slides. Of note, another potential problem with pathological intraoperative assessment of margins relates to use of diathermy/cautery by surgeons. This causes thermal damage which is predominantly seen on the outside of the specimen, that is, the area to be examined when assessing margin status. Diathermy is damaging to epithelial cells and may cause potential problems especially with assessment of intraductal epithelial proliferations (such as distinguishing hyperplasia from DCIS).

Despite these technical difficulties, individual groups have obtained excellent results with either TIC or frozen section assessment. For example, D'Halluin and colleagues reported an average response time of 10 minutes with TIC, with values for sensitivity of 88.6%, specificity of 92.2%, positive predictive value of 73.6%, and a negative predictive value of 97%. Moreover, 12% of secondary re-excision procedures for positive margins were avoided.[5] Similarly, frozen section for identification of positive margins has been reported to have a sensitivity of 0.83, a specificity of 0.93, predictive positive value of 0.62, and a negative predictive value of 0.97.[6] However, not all groups report such high negative predictive values, leading some to conclude that: "intraoperative exam of surgical margins by frozen section is not superior to a macroscopy and/or cytology exam."[7]

One reason for this variation in published results is the practicality of assessment in terms of time and resources required. The pathologist cannot assess the entire surface of a WLE specimen with frozen section examination; correlation with intraoperative radiological examination allows targeting of the area(s) of greatest concern in order to provide a sufficiently rapid result which is of value to the surgeon. However, it is also evident that involved or close margins may not necessarily be those that were anticipated macroscopically, even in the fixed specimen.[8] For this reason, despite optimizing surgical-radiological-pathological correlation with thorough examination of formalin-fixed specimens, the false-negative rate for intraoperative margin assessment using either TIC or frozen section is unlikely to approach 0%.

Narrow margins between the breast tumor and edges of the surgical specimen are increasingly being accepted by multidisciplinary teams as sufficiently adequate for margin clearance (including "no tumor at ink"). While this potentially reduces the total volume of breast tissue excised with consequent cosmetic benefits, it does not simplify intraoperative pathological assessment. If all edges of the tumor are closer to the periphery of the specimen, selection of those most appropriate for frozen section examination becomes more problematic and the pathologist has greater difficulty in identifying which aspects of the margins to assess. Examination of all margins of a relatively small wide local excision specimen would create difficulties in subsequent sampling and examination of the fixed specimen. This would adversely affect careful diagnostic and prognostic evaluation and should not be encouraged.

TIC has the advantage of retaining overall architecture of the specimen and allowing multiple cytological preparations to be taken, but this requires much expertise and time. It is estimated that frozen section or TIC assessment adds an average of 20–30 minutes to the overall surgical procedure time.[9] In essence, the higher the proportion of the specimen to be examined, the longer the pathological examination will take. At some point this becomes an issue in terms of both anesthesia time and for overall service organization and planning of operating lists.

Thus, the value of intraoperative pathological assessment must be balanced against overall service provision, and be adequately resourced. It must be performed by experienced pathologists supported by expert technicians. It should be recognized that even with these caveats, both false-negative as well as false-positive results can occur. Close cooperation and communication between the surgeon and the pathologist is essential with prior planning of individual cases. This will ensure that the pathologist has all relevant information from any prior biopsy (including histological grade and subtype of the cancer). Correlation between pathology and radiological features of the WLE specimen x-ray will help optimize outcomes and minimize re-excision.

REFERENCES

1. Pinotti JA, Carvalho FM. Intraoperative pathological monitorization of surgical margins: A method to reduce recurrences after conservative treatment for breast cancer. *Eur J Gynaecol Oncol.* 2002;23(1):11–16.

2. Fleming FJ, Hill AD, Mc Dermott EW, O'Doherty A, O'Higgins NJ, Quinn CM. Intraoperative margin assessment and re-excision rate in breast conserving surgery. *Eur J Surg Oncol.* 2004;30(3):233–237.

3. Chagpar A, Yen T, Sahin A, Hunt KK, Whitman GJ, Ames FC, Ross MI et al. Intraoperative margin assessment reduces reexcision rates in patients with ductal carcinoma in situ treated with breast-conserving surgery. *Am J Surg.* 2003;186(4):371–377.

4. Rogers C, Klatt EC, Chandrasoma P. Accuracy of frozen-section diagnosis in a teaching hospital. *Arch Pathol Lab Med.* 1987;111:514–517.

5. D'Halluin F, Tas P, Rouquette S, Bendavid C, Foucher F, Meshba H, Blanchot J, Coué O, Levêque J. Intra-operative touch preparation cytology following lumpectomy for breast cancer: A series of 400 procedures. *Breast.* 2009;18(4):248–253. doi:10.1016/j.breast.2009.05.002.

6. Caruso F, Ferrara M, Castiglione G, Cannata I, Marziani A, Polino C, Caruso M, Girlando A, Nuciforo G, Catanuto G. Therapeutic mammaplasties: Full local control of breast cancer in one surgical stage with frozen section. *Eur J Surg Oncol.* 2011;37(10):871–875. doi:10.1016/j.ejso.2011.07.002.

7. Novita G, Filassi JR, Ruiz CA, Ricci MD, Pincerato KM, de Oliveira Filho HR, Soares JM, Baracat EC. Evaluation of frozen-section analysis of surgical margins in the treatment of breast cancer. *Eur J Gynaecol Oncol.* 2012;33(5):498–501.

8. Hodi Z, Ellis IO, Elston CW, Pinder SE, Donovan G, Macmillan RD, Lee AH. Comparison of margin assessment by radial and shave sections in wide local excision specimens for invasive carcinoma of the breast. *Histopathology.* 2010;56(5):573–580. doi:10.1111/j.1365-2559.2010.03518.x.

9. Butler-Henderson K, Lee AH, Price RI, Waring K. Intraoperative assessment of margins in breast conserving therapy: A systematic review. *Breast.* 2014;23(2):112–119. doi:10.1016/j.breast.2014.01.00.

9.2 RADIOLOGICAL

Fleur Kilburn-Toppin

The value of obtaining adequate surgical margins to decrease local recurrence rates in patients undergoing breast conservation is well established.[1] Although recurrence risk does not decrease proportionally with margin width, sufficient tissue must be excised to achieve "negative" margins and this must be balanced against obtaining a good cosmetic appearance. The ideal scenario is to have a single operative procedure, but close or positive margins are found in up to 40% of cases and require subsequent re-excision or mastectomy. This results in the patient having to undergo additional surgical procedures with concomitant increased medical costs and patient anxiety. Furthermore, larger total volumes of breast tissue are generally removed when re-excision is necessary, which may result in a worse cosmetic outcome.

Therefore, adequate assessment of surgical margins at initial operation is essential from both oncological and cosmetic perspectives. Radiological evaluation has an important role in assessing adequacy of tumor excision for non-palpable lesions.

Specimen radiography is a commonly used radiological tool for assessment and management of non-palpable lesions. Utilization of specimen radiography is well-established and is the gold standard in many centers. The main aim is to determine whether the targeted lesion has been successfully removed and to assess margins around the tumor to determine if further tissue must be excised. For non-palpable lesions, wire-guided wide local excision is often performed and involves insertion of a thin guide wire under ultrasound or mammographic control into the tumor. After surgical excision, the specimen is orientated and carefully marked, according to local protocols prior to imaging (**Figure 9.2.1**).

There is no definite consensus as to what constitutes "close" or near margins on specimen radiology, but tumors extending to the specimen edge have been shown to have a high positive predictive value for pathological involvement. False-positives can occur, for example, in tumors where the spicules may represent desmoplastic reaction rather than true tumor involvement or in cases of DCIS where adjacent benign microcalcifications may be misinterpreted as involvement. Conversely, margins which are deemed radiologically "negative" on specimen radiography have been shown to have poor predictive value for negative histopathological margins.[2] Graham and colleagues examined the efficacy of specimen radiography in evaluating surgical margins for impalpable breast carcinomas and demonstrated that the positive predictive value for margins involved by tumor was 98%, but the negative predictive value for tumor-free margins was only 32%. This is most likely because the histological extent of the tumor is underestimated on mammography and specimen

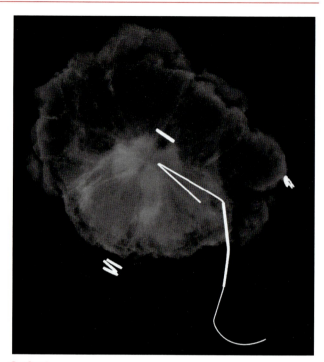

9.2.1 Specimen radiograph of a 15 mm Grade 1 invasive ductal carcinoma, No Special Type (NST) following wire-guided wide local excision. Localization wire is seen in situ. Despite the tumor spicules appearing close to the medial margin (3 clips) on histology the tumor lay more than 2 mm from all radial excision margins and no further surgery was required. False-positives such as this may occur due to tumor desmoplastic reaction rather than true tumor involvement.

radiography is only a single view.[3] Britton and colleagues showed that in fewer than half of specimen radiographs, the closest margins corresponded to the closest pathological margin. Various factors have been proposed to account for this, including errors in orientation or interpretation of clip markers, errors of surgical clip placement, or mammographically occult cancer extending beyond the specimen margin. Two-view specimen mammography as opposed to single view, which is routinely obtained, has been shown to halve the operation rate in one study from 12% to 5%.[4]

Various factors have been shown to increase the chance of positive margins including multifocality, large tumors, and extensive DCIS.[5] The incidence of DCIS has increased over recent years alongside use of breast-conserving surgery as treatment. Close or positive margins after breast-conserving surgery for DCIS have been reported in up to 60% of cases, but intraoperative margin assessment by gross pathological examination as well as sliced specimen radiography may aid intraoperative decision-making and decrease the need for additional surgical procedures for margin control.[6]

The limitations of the specimen radiography in predicting margin status has attracted some criticism in its use as a tool for assessing adequacy of tumor excision[7]

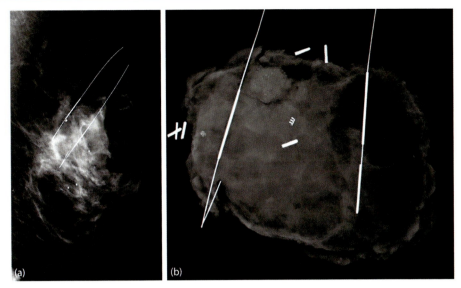

9.2.2 (a) Two localization wires inserted under mammographic control to mark the superior and inferior extent of the visualized 28 mm cluster of microcalcification within the upper outer aspect of the left breast, biopsy proven as high-grade DCIS. (b) Subsequent specimen radiograph demonstrated calcification extending to the superior margin (2 clips), deemed positive on subsequent histopathology for malignancy at the superior margin and requiring subsequent re-excision.

and has prompted the development of newer techniques to improve margin assessment. Intraoperative ultrasound has been used in studies of both palpable and non-palpable lesions, either solely or as an adjunct to standard assessment. Some studies have shown improved negative margin rates, but this only applies to tumors seen clearly on ultrasound. Some investigating intraoperative ultrasound have shown positive margin rates ranging from 3% to 11%,[8] with consequently fewer additional treatment interventions. Intraoperative ultrasound is not currently in routine use which may partly be attributable to lack of surgical experience and radiological availability.[9]

Portable radiography systems (e.g., Faxitron) are increasingly being employed to provide immediate radiographic assessment of margins. This allows the operating surgeon to assess the specimen radiograph in the operating theater, thereby reducing logistical problems associated with sending specimens to the radiology department. Portable radiography systems can reduce operating time by up to 20 minutes.[10] A study by Bathla and colleagues[11] using 2D Faxitron showed that sensitivity and specificity of intraoperative assessment of margins was 58.5% and 91.8%, respectively. There was an improved rate of margin clearance and lower re-operative rate than has been previously described despite slightly larger initial specimen volumes. Other studies have shown that with adequate training, surgical evaluation of specimen radiographs is comparable to evaluation by radiologists.[12]

Newer techniques at the experimental stage include micro CT,[13] near-infrared optical imaging, high frequency ultrasound, and x-ray diffraction.[14] Each of these shows promising results for radiological margin assessment, but require further analysis before introduction into clinical practice.

Intraoperative margin assessment is a multidisciplinary process requiring close cooperation between radiologists, surgeons, and pathologists. The gold standard imaging technique is specimen radiography, but this has shortcomings due to inaccurate prediction of negative margins and should be used carefully with other tools. Rates of re-excision can potentially be improved by careful review of preoperative imaging, an awareness of which tumors are more likely to have positive margins, and accurate preoperative localization (**Figure 9.2.2**). The latter may be improved by incorporation of newer techniques such as intraoperative ultrasound, CT, and portable radiography systems.

REFERENCES

1. Cabioglu N, Hunt KK, Sahin AA et al. Role for intraoperative margin assessment in patients undergoing breast-conserving surgery. *Ann Surg Oncol.* 2007;14(4):1458–1471.
2. Graham RA, Homer MJ, Sigler CJ et al. The efficacy of specimen radiography in evaluating the surgical margins of impalpable breast carcinoma. *Am J Roentgenol.* 1994;162:33–36.
3. Britton PD, Sonoda LI, Yamamoto AK, Koo B, Soh E, Goud A. Breast surgical specimen radiographs: How reliable are they? *Eur J Radiol.* 2011;79(2):245–249.
4. McCormick JT, Keleher AJ, Tikhomirov VB, Budway RJ, Caushaj PF. Analysis of the use of specimen mammography in breast conservation therapy. *Am J Surg.* 2004;188(4):433–436.

5. Saadai P1, Moezzi M, Menes T. Preoperative and intraoperative predictors of positive margins after breast-conserving surgery: A retrospective review. *Breast Cancer.* 2011;18(3):221–225.

6. Chagpar A, Yen T, Sahin A et al. Intraoperative margin assessment reduces re-excision rates in patients with ductal carcinoma in situ treated with breast-conserving surgery. *Am J Surg.* 2003;186(4):371–347.

7. Bimston DN, Bebb GG, Wagman LD. Is specimen mammography beneficial? *Arch Surg.* 2000;135(9):1083–1086.

8. Olsha O, Shemesh D, Carmon M, Sibirsky O, Abu Dalo R, Rivkin L, Ashkenazi I. Resection margins in ultrasound-guided breast-conserving surgery. *Ann Surg Oncol.* 2011;18(2):447–452.

9. Krekel NM, Haloua MH, Lopes Cardozo AM et al. Intraoperative ultrasound guidance for palpable breast cancer excision (COBALT trial): A multicentre, randomised controlled trial. *Lancet Oncol.* 2013;14(1):48–54.

10. Kaufman CS, Jacobson L, Bachman BS et al. Intraoperative digital specimen mammography: Rapid, accurate results expedite surgery. *Ann Surg Oncol.* 2007;14:1478–1485.

11. Bathla L, Harris A, Davey M, Sharma P, Silva E. High resolution intra-operative two-dimensional specimen mammography and its impact on second operation for re-excision of positive margins at final pathology after breast conservation surgery. *Am J Surg.* 2011;202(4):387–394.

12. Coombs NJ, Vassallo PP, Parker AJ, Yiangou C. Radiological review of specimen radiographs after breast localisation biopsy is not always necessary. *Eur J Surg Oncol.* 2006;32(5):516–519.

13. Tang R, Buckley JM, Fernandez L et al. Micro-computed tomography (Micro-CT): A novel approach for intraoperative breast cancer specimen imaging. *Breast Cancer Res Treat.* 2013;139(2):311–316.

14. Thill M, Baumann K, Barinoff J. Intraoperative assessment of margins in breast conservative surgery—Still in use? *J Surg Oncol.* 2014;110(1):15–20.

10

Timing of oncoplastic repair

FRANCESCO M. EGRO AND ALBERT LOSKEN

AT A GLANCE

Although the incidence of a positive postoperative tumor margin after partial mastectomy has been shown to be lower with repair than without repair, the optimal timing of repair has been controversial. The availability of intraoperative tumor margin assessment can assist in this process. However, many surgeons do not have access, but instead rely on preoperative mammography and ultrasonography to determine the optimal timing for repair. In addition, whether a patient will undergo local tissue repair or a flap can also be an important component of this decision.

INTRODUCTION

Breast-conservation therapy (BCT) represents the culmination of surgical and oncological efforts to seek alternatives to standard treatments, involving smaller resection sizes and the addition of new modalities (chemotherapy and radiotherapy). BCT involves excision of a breast tumor and its surrounding margins (breast-conservation surgery or lumpectomy) followed by adjuvant radiotherapy. It is now an established option for the management of early-stage breast cancer and, when compared to mastectomy, allows preservation of the native breast while maintaining similar survival rates.[1-6] Local recurrence rates have been found to be either comparable[3,6] or higher[1,4,5] for BCT compared with mastectomy. The reason appears to be the lack of negative margins, which is imperative to avert recurrence. However, local failures can be salvaged with a completion mastectomy and no detriment to survival.[7]

Radiotherapy is a key component in breast-conservation therapy and significantly reduces recurrence rates by 16%–25%[8,9] and 15-year risk of breast cancer death by 4%.[8] Radiation exacerbates lumpectomy deformities by increasing breast parenchymal density, skin thickness and tightening, breast distortion, pigmentation changes, breast shrinkage, and fibrosis, with an average reduction in breast volume of 10%–20%.[10-13] Factors that affect aesthetic outcomes following radiotherapy include:

- *Breast size*: Studies have consistently found greater degrees of asymmetry, retraction, and late radiation changes in larger breasts.[11,14]
- *Breast tissue*: Worse outcomes have been noted in patients with a lower proportion of breast tissue and a degree of fat replacement.[14]
- *Irradiation technique*: Worse outcomes are associated with a boost dose of radiotherapy and therapy incorporating iridium rather than electrons.[15]
- *Surgical techniques*: Worst outcomes occur with significant undermining of the breast and/or devascularization leading to poor healing, compromise of skin flaps, or fat necrosis.

The search for optimal oncological control and the desire to minimize the risk of breast deformity has led to the concept of "oncoplastic" repair, which can be broadly classified as: (1) volume replacement where tissue is transposed from one location to another (e.g., local or distant flaps) and (2) volume displacement where breast parenchyma is rearranged to reconstruct the defect (e.g., reduction mammoplasty). The indications for each method depend on breast size, defect size, and location. The most commonly used volume displacement technique (especially in patients with

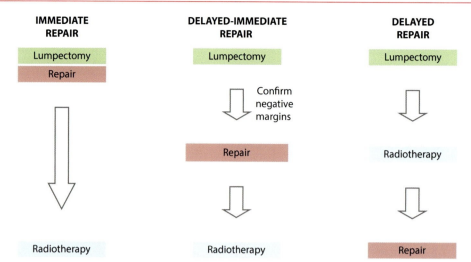

10.1 *Timing of oncoplastic repair.* Immediate: Reconstruction performed at the time of lumpectomy prior to radiation. Delayed-immediate: Reconstruction performed after lumpectomy but prior to radiation. Delayed: Reconstruction performed after lumpectomy and radiation.

macromastia) is reduction mammoplasty.[16,17] Oncoplastic repair in breast cancer patients who require lumpectomy can be performed at different times (**Figure 10.1**): immediate, delayed-immediate, and delayed. This chapter discusses these various aspects and the implications of timing of oncoplastic repair.

IMMEDIATE REPAIR

Immediate repair involves performing a breast oncoplastic procedure at the time of lumpectomy and thus prior to the use of radiotherapy (**Figure 10.2**)[18].

Indications

The decision for undertaking immediate repair is multifactorial and is essentially based on oncologic safety issues. When reconstruction of a partial mastectomy defect is planned, immediate repair is the preferred approach in over 90% of cases.[18] The indications for immediate repair are similar to those for any oncoplastic procedure including large breasts, tumors in cosmetically sensitive locations (i.e., medial, central, and inferior), a large tumor-to-breast ratio, and the need for a generous resection.

Advantages

NUMBER OF OPERATIONS

When the oncoplastic repair is performed at the time of tumor resection, this is often one-stage surgery, leading to a reduction in total number of operations,[19] and the psychological impact from any deformity consequent to BCT.[20] In a recent study, we demonstrated that immediate reduction mammoplasty resulted in the least number

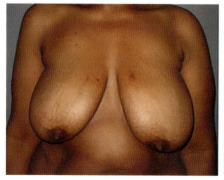 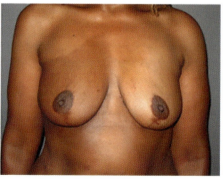

10.2 *Immediate repair.* A 45-year-old woman presented with macromastia and a history of right breast cancer. She underwent a lumpectomy, which weighed 85 g, and an immediate oncoplastic reduction mammoplasty on that side, for a total weight of 397 g. She had a contralateral oncoplastic reduction mammoplasty weighing 595 g. Preoperative (left) and 2 years postradiation (right) photographs are shown. (From Egro, F.M. et al., *Plast. Reconstr. Surg.*, 135, 963e–971e, 2015[18] and reprinted with permission by Wolters Kluwer Health, Philadelphia, PA.)

of operations (mean $= 1.2$, maximum $= 3$) compared to a delayed-immediate (mean $= 2$, maximum $= 4$) or a delayed approach (mean $= 2.2$, maximum $= 3$; $p < 0.001$).[18]

WIDER RESECTION MARGINS

An immediate approach allows the oncological surgeon to widely resect a tumor and thereby reduce the chance of margin involvement.[21,22] The volume of the excised specimen and nearest radial margin widths using an immediate oncoplastic approach are higher than for conventional breast-conservation surgery alone. Free surgical margins equal or greater than either 5 mm or 10 mm were obtained more frequently using oncoplastic surgery than standard breast-conservation surgery.[23]

OCCULT MALIGNANCY DETECTION

Breast cancer within the opposite breast is occasionally found incidentally (1.2%–4.3%) in those patients who undergo immediate contralateral reduction mammoplasty for purposes of symmetry in breast reconstruction.[24,25] This discovery will usually mandate additional therapy including axillary staging (sentinel lymph node biopsy) and breast irradiation.

LOWEST COMPLICATION RATE

It is always preferable to operate on a non-irradiated breast if possible, and patients in our study undergoing immediate oncoplastic reduction mammoplasty had fewer complications than for the other two approaches (immediate, 20.5%; delayed-immediate, 33.3%; delayed, 60.0%; $p < 0.001$). Significantly lower rates of hematoma formation (immediate, 1.7%; delayed-immediate, 11.1%; delayed, 0.0%; $p = 0.040$), fat necrosis (immediate, 0.9%; delayed-immediate, 0.0%; delayed, 8.0%; $p = 0.047$), and asymmetry or deformity were observed (immediate, 8.5%; delayed-immediate, 44.4%; delayed, 24.0; $p < 0.001$). Furthermore, reducing breast size by means of reduction mammoplasty facilitates a more homogenous delivery of radiation at lower mean dose levels. Therefore, reduction before radiotherapy reduces late radiation complications in patients with large breasts,[14,18,26] and surgery is technically easier to perform on a breast that is neither acutely inflamed as in delayed-immediate reconstruction or scarred and irradiated as in delayed reconstruction.

IMPROVED AESTHETIC OUTCOMES

Radiotherapy has a major impact on aesthetic aspects of the breast following BCT and can lead to both breast parenchyma and skin changes.[11,14] These aesthetic complications can be minimized by reducing the breast size or reshaping the parenchymal defect at the time of lumpectomy, while the tissues remain soft and reliably perfused. Moreover, an understanding of breast contraction and volume loss that occurs following radiation permits anticipation of volume changes and making appropriate allowances when reducing the contralateral side. This was confirmed by a series of studies that reported a trend for improved aesthetic outcomes in patients undergoing immediate oncoplastic repair, although did not reach statistical significance when compared to other groups.[18,21,27]

IMPROVED PATIENT SATISFACTION

Levels of patient satisfaction following oncoplastic repair are high,[17,18,28,29] with several studies examining patient satisfaction before and after radiotherapy; women with immediate reconstruction had better outcomes when compared with the other two approaches, but no studies have demonstrated any statistically significant differences between approaches.[18,27,28] This positive trend for patient satisfaction is likely attributable to multiple factors including: (1) higher aesthetic outcomes, (2) lower complication rates, and (3) lower number of operations needed.[18]

Disadvantages

RE-EXPLORATION IN PATIENTS WITH CLOSE OR POSITIVE MARGINS

Rearrangement of glandular tissue makes re-excision challenging, as it may be difficult to locate the residual tumor and may jeopardize oncological outcomes.[25] Munhoz et al. showed that immediate re-excision was needed in fewer than 10% (9.4%) of cases, and positive margins were identified in 5.7% of patients who were previously found to have negative margins.[25,30] Studies have identified several risk factors that increase the chance of positive margins and include age less than 35–40 years old, extensive in situ carcinoma, and large tumor size.[29,31] In order to minimize the risk of re-exploration, a delayed-immediate approach might be beneficial in these patients. However, should re-exploration be necessary, this should be carried out jointly by both breast and plastic surgeon in order to maximize the chance of successfully identifying the tumor bed. When the latter is not identified, the patient might need to undergo a mastectomy associated with appropriate reconstruction.

POSTOPERATIVE SURVEILLANCE

Breast scarring from immediate repair and radiotherapy may obscure or mimic malignancy on mammography and lead to diagnostic uncertainty[25] with tissue sampling being required in one-quarter (26%) of patients undergoing routine radiological surveillance following reduction mammoplasty, which is higher than BCT alone.[29] Nonetheless, mammographic screening following immediate repair has been shown to have comparable levels of sensitivity as for imaging of breast in patients with standard BCT.

LOGISTICS

Ensuring that both oncological and plastic surgeons are available at the same time can produce logistical problems which impact on service delivery and organization of operating lists.

DELAYED–IMMEDIATE REPAIR

Delayed-immediate repair refers to performing breast oncoplastic repair within 1–3 weeks after the lumpectomy, but before radiotherapy. The timing of repair depends on definitive histopathology report as well as scheduling issues. Confirmation of final margin status allows any re-excision to be performed before the repair if required.[18] This approach is often preferable when local tissue transfer techniques are used.

Indications

The decision for undertaking delayed-immediate repair is based on issues of oncologic safety and the availability of an experienced surgeon with knowledge of oncoplastic techniques, be this a plastic surgeon or breast surgeon with oncoplastic competency. Unlike immediate repair, there is no requirement for a facility which offers intraoperative evaluation of surgical margins. A delayed-immediate repair may be favored in patients when the risk of margins involved by cancer is higher (namely age younger than 35–40, extensive ductal carcinoma in situ, and large tumor size).[18,29,31] It is also a reasonable approach to adopt when the breast surgeon has concerns about achieving clear margins or when coordinating schedules between the two services is not possible. Another indication is in those patients who have had a lumpectomy and are already aware of a defect which can be corrected prior to administration of radiotherapy.

Advantages

DEFINITIVE SURGICAL MARGINS

The main advantage of delayed-immediate repair is confirmation of negative surgical margins before committing to partial reconstruction of the breast and patients undergoing radiotherapy. This approach therefore offers the benefits of immediate reconstruction particularly with respect to oncological safety, especially in those patients at higher risk of positive surgical margins.[29]

EASIER RE-EXPLORATION IN PATIENTS WITH CLOSE OR POSITIVE MARGINS

Rearrangement of glandular tissue at the time of lumpectomy can make re-excision challenging because of the difficulty to locate the residual tumor. Delayed-immediate repair offers the benefits of an easier re-excision of the tumor cavity if positive margins are confirmed. This can often safely be performed at the time of reconstruction

LOWER COMPLICATION RATE

As discussed above, reshaping of the breast is technically easier without radiation-induced fibrosis, leading to better aesthetic results and lower complications.[18,21] The complication profile is similar to the immediate group in the sense that reconstruction precedes radiotherapy and radiation is being delivered to a smaller breast.[14,18,26] Patients undergoing delayed-immediate repair were shown to have significantly lower complication rates than for patients with delayed repair, with the lowest rates for infection (immediate, 3.4%; delayed-immediate, 0.0%; delayed, 16.0%; $p = 0.019$) and fat necrosis (immediate, 0.9%; delayed-immediate, 0.0%; delayed, 8.0%; $p = 0.047$) among all three approaches.

IMPROVED PATIENT SATISFACTION

Two studies have shown that women undergoing delayed-immediate repair were more satisfied than patients undergoing repair after radiotherapy, but worse than for immediate repair (non-significant differences).[18,27] This positive trend might be linked to improved aesthetic outcomes, lower complication rates, and better visual appreciation of the defect left by lumpectomy.[18]

LOGISTICS

Since the oncological and reconstruction components are performed on separate days, the breast and plastic surgeons can schedule their respective procedures independently. Furthermore, delayed-immediate repair is advantageous for institutions that lack intraoperative surgical margin assessment.

Disadvantages

NUMBER OF OPERATIONS

Although confirmation of negative margins prior to reconstruction would eliminate concerns about margin status, a delayed immediate approach would involve an unnecessary second procedure in around 90% of patients who do not require re-excision.[29] In a recent study, we showed that patients undergoing delayed-immediate repair required a mean number of two operations (maximum of four operations) compared to immediate (mean = 1.2; maximum of 3) and delayed approaches (mean = 2.2; maximum of 3; $p < 0.001$).[18]

DISTORTION OF LANDMARKS

Although re-exploration might be easier than for the immediate approach, technical difficulties might be encountered such as inflammation, edema, scar tissue, and distortion of landmarks.

HIGHER HEMATOMA AND ASYMMETRY RATES

Reconstruction of a defect in the setting of postoperative inflammation within a healing lumpectomy cavity can potentially create challenges not seen in the immediate group despite being performed prior to radiotherapy. Hematoma rates were higher (immediate, 1.7%; delayed-immediate, 11.1%; delayed, 0.0%; $p = 0.040$) and patients were 8.7 times ($p = 0.027$) more likely to develop asymmetry or deformity[18] when a delayed-immediate approach was utilized.

REDUCED AESTHETIC RESULTS

Delaying repair provides the opportunity for patients to assess the extent of the lumpectomy deformity and allows them to be involved in the decision-making process and decide whether to continue with reconstruction or not. Nonetheless, delayed-immediate repair appears to be associated with worse aesthetic outcomes when compared with the other two approaches, but no studies have demonstrated a statistical significance.[18,27]

DELAYED REPAIR

Delayed repair involves performing an oncoplastic intervention at an unspecified time interval following lumpectomy and radiotherapy (**Figure 10.3**),[18] although typically is not performed within a year of completing radiation therapy. Delayed repair more often involves a local flap; however, reduction techniques can be performed in selected patients with larger breasts.

Indications

The decision to perform delayed repair is based on cases where the extent of the deformity is unexpected, access to a plastic surgeon is unavailable at the time of resection, or the patient decides to delay the reconstructive surgery for personal reasons.

Advantages

DEFINITIVE ONCOLOGICAL TREATMENT

The main advantage of delayed repair is ensuring negative surgical margins and completion of adjuvant therapies (radiotherapy and/or chemotherapy) before undergoing reconstruction of the breast. It is reassuring for patients to know that the oncological aspects of treatment are completed before embarking on the reconstructive journey.

Disadvantages

HIGH COMPLICATION RATE

Radiation induces a range of skin changes including thickening, tightening, and abnormal pigmentation. Furthermore, it exacerbates lumpectomy deformities by increasing breast parenchymal density, distortion, and shrinkage with an average of 10%–20% reduction in breast volume.[10–13] The reshaping of the breast is easier without radiation-induced fibrosis and leads to better aesthetic results and lower complication rates.[18,21] Performing oncoplastic reconstruction on an irradiated breast is controversial given the increased potential for complications, poor outcomes, and unpredictable risks.[18,21,27,28] Our study found that a delayed approach has the highest complication rates (immediate, 20.5%; delayed-immediate, 33.3%; delayed, 60.0%; $p < 0.001$), together with the highest incidence of infection (immediate, 3.4%; delayed-immediate, 0.0%; delayed, 16.0%; $p = 0.019$) and rates of fat necrosis (immediate, 0.9%; delayed-immediate, 0.0%; delayed, 8.0%; $p = 0.047$). Multivariate analysis also confirmed that patients undergoing delayed repair were 7.7 times more likely to have any complication ($p = 0.015$), and 86 times more likely to be complicated by infection ($p = 0.032$). The higher incidence of fat necrosis in delayed repair is not surprising because radiation is known to cause a slower re-establishment of the local blood supply from the underlying irradiated chest wall to the rearranged breast tissue.[18] Many patients are not candidates for this approach after radiotherapy and more conservative nipple repositioning and limited undermining will improve outcomes.

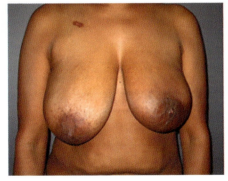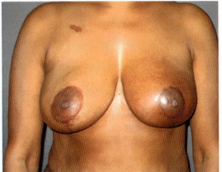

10.3 *Delayed repair.* A 49-year-old woman presented with macromastia and breast asymmetry, who completed breast-conservation therapy 5 years previously for a left breast cancer. She underwent a delayed bilateral oncoplastic reduction mammoplasty removing 460 g on the right side and 150 g on the left side leading to improvement in shape and symmetry. Preoperative (left) and 3 years postoperative (right) photographs are shown. Note that the non-irradiated breast is more likely to settle with time compared with the irradiated breast. (Figure taken from Egro, F.M. et al., *Plast. Reconstr. Surg.*, 135, 963e–971e, 2015[18], and reprinted with permission by Wolters Kluwer Health, Philadelphia, PA.)

NUMBER OF OPERATIONS

In a recent study, we demonstrated that patients undergoing delayed oncoplastic reduction mammoplasty required the most number of operations, with a mean of 2.2 operations (maximum 3) compared to oncoplastic reduction mammoplasty before radiotherapy (immediate, mean = 1.2; maximum of 3; and delayed-immediate, mean = 2; maximum of 4; $p < 0.001$).[18] With the additional challenges associated with an irradiated breast, it often requires more procedures to get the appropriate shape and symmetry.

REDUCED AESTHETIC RESULTS

Delayed repair appears to produce worse aesthetic outcomes when compared with an immediate approach, but no studies have demonstrated any statistically significant differences.[18,21,27] Furthermore, delayed repair is 9 times ($p = 0.027$) more likely to lead to asymmetry or deformity.[18] When patients are well selected and the most appropriate technique is undertaken, the majority of patients can end up with good cosmesis.[18]

REDUCED PATIENT SATISFACTION

Delayed repair appears to produce less patient satisfaction when compared with the other two approaches, but no studies have demonstrated a statistically significant difference.[18,27,28] Despite the added morbidity and lower aesthetic results, the majority of patients end up feeling satisfied with the final outcome. The likely reason is that women seeking delayed repair live with a breast deformity for many years, so any improvement in their breast appearance is considered a bonus. Furthermore, women scheduled for repair after radiotherapy are probably exposed to more counseling and therefore are better informed regarding increased surgical risks.[18]

CONCLUSION

Patient education and selection are essential to maximizing patient satisfaction and aesthetic outcomes, while at the same time ensuring surgical and oncological safety. This is of particular importance in patients undergoing delayed partial breast repair because the potential for greater complication rates exists. The delayed-immediate approach carries similar risks to the immediate approach, which may relate to repair being performed before radiotherapy and is usually performed only in patients for whom there is concern about surgical margin clearance. Despite the advantage of margin status certainty, an additional operation is necessary and can result in higher complication rates than for an immediate approach. Most patients who present after radiotherapy with a lumpectomy deformity might not have had the option of oncoplastic repair. However, although complication rates are higher in patients undergoing delayed repair, appropriate patient selection allows improved aesthetic outcomes and patient satisfaction.

REFERENCES

1. Jacobson, J.A. et al., Ten-year results of a comparison of conservation with mastectomy in the treatment of stage I and II breast cancer. *N Engl J Med*, 1995. **332**(14): 907–911.
2. Fisher, B. et al., Reanalysis and results after 12 years of follow-up in a randomized clinical trial comparing total mastectomy with lumpectomy with or without irradiation in the treatment of breast cancer. *N Engl J Med*, 1995. **333**(22): 1456–1461.
3. Arriagada, R. et al., Conservative treatment versus mastectomy in early breast cancer: Patterns of failure with 15 years of follow-up data. Institut Gustave-Roussy Breast Cancer Group. *J Clin Oncol*, 1996. **14**(5): 1558–1564.
4. van Dongen, J.A. et al., Long-term results of a randomized trial comparing breast-conserving therapy with mastectomy: European Organization for Research and Treatment of Cancer 10801 trial. *J Natl Cancer Inst*, 2000. **92**(14): 1143–1150.
5. Veronesi, U. et al., Twenty-year follow-up of a randomized study comparing breast-conserving surgery with radical mastectomy for early breast cancer. *N Engl J Med*, 2002. **347**(16): 1227–1232.
6. Blichert-Toft, M. et al., Long-term results of breast conserving surgery vs. mastectomy for early stage invasive breast cancer: 20-year follow-up of the Danish randomized DBCG-82TM protocol. *Acta Oncol*, 2008. **47**(4): 672–681.
7. Losken, A. and M. Hamdi, Partial breast reconstruction: Techniques in oncoplastic surgery. 2009, St. Louis, MO: Quality Medical Pub. xxiii, 589 p.
8. Darby, S. et al., Effect of radiotherapy after breast-conserving surgery on 10-year recurrence and 15-year breast cancer death: Meta-analysis of individual patient data for 10,801 women in 17 randomised trials. *Lancet*, 2011. **378**(9804): 1707–1716.
9. Fisher, B. et al., Twenty-year follow-up of a randomized trial comparing total mastectomy, lumpectomy, and lumpectomy plus irradiation for the treatment of invasive breast cancer. *N Engl J Med*, 2002. **347**(16): 1233–1241.
10. Olivotto, I.A. et al., Late cosmetic outcome after conservative surgery and radiotherapy: Analysis of causes of cosmetic failure. *Int J Radiat Oncol Biol Phys*, 1989. **17**(4): 747–753.
11. Moody, A.M. et al., The influence of breast size on late radiation effects and association with radiotherapy dose inhomogeneity. *Radiother Oncol*, 1994. **33**(2): 106–112.
12. Braw, M. et al., Mammographic follow-up after breast conserving surgery and postoperative radiotherapy without boost irradiation for mammary carcinoma. *Acta Radiol*, 1991. **32**(5): 398–402.
13. Waljee, J.F. et al., Predictors of breast asymmetry after breast-conserving operation for breast cancer. *J Am Coll Surg*, 2008. **206**(2): 274–280.
14. Gray, J.R. et al., Primary breast irradiation in large-breasted or heavy women: Analysis of cosmetic outcome. *Int J Radiat Oncol Biol Phys*, 1991. **21**(2): 347–354.
15. Hill-Kayser, C.E. et al., Long-term clinical and cosmetic outcomes after breast conservation treatment for women with early-stage breast carcinoma according to the type of breast boost. *Int J Radiat Oncol Biol Phys*, 2011. **79**(4): 1048–1054.
16. Clough, K.B. et al., Mammoplasty combined with irradiation: Conservative treatment of breast cancer localized in the lower quadrant. *Ann Chir Plast Esthet*, 1990. **35**(2): 117–122.

17. Spear, S.L. et al., Experience with reduction mammoplasty combined with breast conservation therapy in the treatment of breast cancer. *Plast Reconstr Surg*, 2003. **111**(3): 1102–1109.
18. Egro, F.M. et al., The use of reduction mammoplasty with breast conservation therapy: An analysis of timing and outcomes. *Plast Reconstr Surg*, 2015. **135**(6): 963e–971e.
19. Losken, A., X.A. Pinell, and B. Eskenazi, The benefits of partial versus total breast reconstruction for women with macromastia. *Plast Reconstr Surg*, 2010. **125**(4): 1051–1056.
20. Clough, K.B., S.S. Kroll, and W. Audretsch, An approach to the repair of partial mastectomy defects. *Plast Reconstr Surg*, 1999. **104**(2): 409–420.
21. Kronowitz, S.J. et al., Determining the optimal approach to breast reconstruction after partial mastectomy. *Plast Reconstr Surg*, 2006. **117**(1): 1–11; discussion 12–14.
22. Kaur, N. et al., Comparative study of surgical margins in oncoplastic surgery and quadrantectomy in breast cancer. *Ann Surg Oncol*, 2005. **12**(7): 539–545.
23. Giacalone, P.L. et al., Comparative study of the accuracy of breast resection in oncoplastic surgery and quadrantectomy in breast cancer. *Ann Surg Oncol*, 2007. **14**(2): 605–614.
24. Colwell, A.S. et al., Occult breast carcinoma in reduction mammoplasty specimens: 14-year experience. *Plast Reconstr Surg*, 2004. **113**(7): 1984–1988.
25. Munhoz, A.M. et al., Critical analysis of reduction mammoplasty techniques in combination with conservative breast surgery for early breast cancer treatment. *Plast Reconstr Surg*, 2006. **117**(4): 1091–1103; discussion 1104–1107.
26. Brierley, J.D. et al., The influence of breast size on late radiation reaction following excision and radiotherapy for early breast cancer. *Clin Oncol (R Coll Radiol)*, 1991. **3**(1): 6–9.
27. Patel, K.M. et al., A head-to-head comparison of quality of life and aesthetic outcomes following immediate, staged-immediate, and delayed oncoplastic reduction mammoplasty. *Plast Reconstr Surg*, 2011. **127**(6): 2167–2175.
28. Munhoz, A.M. et al. Outcome analysis of immediate and delayed conservative breast surgery reconstruction with mastopexy and reduction mammoplasty techniques. *Ann Plast Surg*, 2011. **67**(3): 220–225.
29. Losken, A. et al., Management algorithm and outcome evaluation of partial mastectomy defects treated using reduction or mastopexy techniques. *Ann Plast Surg*, 2007. **59**(3): 235–242.
30. Munhoz, A.M. et al., Superior-medial dermoglandular pedicle reduction mammoplasty for immediate conservative breast surgery reconstruction: Technical aspects and outcome. *Ann Plast Surg*, 2006. **57**(5): 502–508.
31. Tartter, P.I. et al., Lumpectomy margins, reexcision, and local recurrence of breast cancer. *Am J Surg*, 2000. **179**(2): 81–85.

EDITORIAL COMMENTARY

Patients with newly diagnosed early-stage breast cancer undergo multimodality imaging to assess the extent of disease and stage patients locoregionally (tumor size, nodal status). Mammography is the primary radiological investigation both for screen-detected and symptomatic cancers except for very young patients. Full-field digital mammography (FFDM) has now replaced traditional film-screen mammography and has greater sensitivity for the detection of microcalcification (and therefore diagnosis of high nuclear grade DCIS). A further advance has been digital breast tomosynthesis that reduces the effects of tissue superimposition and permits noncalcified cancers within dense breast tissue to be more readily detected. Several studies are reporting promising results from comparison of conventional mammography and digital breast tomosynthesis with FFDM. In particular, lobular cancers are more easily detected with a combination of FFDM and digital breast tomosynthesis; this may offer an advantage over MRI, which has poor radiopathological correlation for this histological subtype.

Breast ultrasound is routinely employed as a radiological adjunct in the evaluation of a discrete breast mass. Once a suspicious lesion is detected by mammography, ultrasound can be used to confirm likely malignancy and accurately measure tumor dimensions. Assessment of ipsilateral axillary nodes with needle biopsy of abnormal nodes is now routinely performed at the time of needle biopsy of the primary breast lesion. Some units in the United States have abandoned routine preoperative ultrasound as this may commit patients with biopsy-proven nodal metastases to an axillary dissection when sentinel lymph node biopsy might otherwise be undertaken. If only one to two nodes with macrometastases are found on sentinel node biopsy, then further axillary treatment could be omitted (based on the American College of Surgeon Oncology Group Z0011 trial). In Europe, axillary ultrasound is routinely performed and numbers of abnormal nodes recorded.

The routine use of preoperative breast MRI remains controversial due to uncertainties about reduction in rates of re-excision, ipsilateral breast tumor recurrence, and impact on incidence of contralateral disease or distant metastases. Nonetheless, MRI is more accurate than either mammography or ultrasound for local tumor staging and is indicated for clarification of tumor extent, to exclude or confirm any suspicion of multifocal disease and for lobular cancers. Any suspicious lesions found on MRI must be evaluated with second-look ultrasound in the first instance and MRI-guided biopsy where appropriate. It should be noted that no randomized data supports routine use of preoperative MRI in terms of local recurrence and disease-free survival while a finite false-positive rate generates patient anxiety and extra costs from additional biopsies that can delay timing of definitive surgical treatment.

PET-CT and molecular breast imaging can potentially improve overall sensitivity and specificity of breast imaging but very small additional tumor foci may be adequately treated by adjuvant treatment including breast irradiation and systemic therapies.

Accurate assessment of tumor extent is particularly important for patients undergoing breast-conserving surgery with immediate partial breast reconstruction involving more complex level II oncoplastic procedures such as therapeutic mammoplasty or chest wall flaps (TDAP; LICAP). When margins of surgical clearance for either invasive or non-invasive disease are in doubt, then a two-stage volume replacement method is sensible (definitive histology results may necessitate mastectomy).

The diagnosis of pure DCIS lesions has increased dramatically in the screening era and now constitutes 20% of all new breast cancer diagnoses. Most cases of screen-detected DCIS are small, localized lesions which can be managed with standard wire-guided/radioactive seed localized wide local excision. Larger lesions up to 6–7 cm might be suitable for a therapeutic mammoplasty in a large breasted patient but otherwise mastectomy with whole breast reconstruction is warranted. Radiotherapy is indicated for all cases of DCIS treated with breast-conserving surgery, except for smaller (<15 mm) cases of low/intermediate nuclear grade lesions. Moreover, there is a balance between overtreatment of DCIS and minimizing rates of local recurrence—half of which will be invasive disease. Various molecular predictors of in-breast recurrence are now being incorporated into clinical decision-making such as estrogen receptor, progesterone receptor, HER2, and molecular subtype. A recurrence risk score based on a restricted (12 gene) Oncotype-DX assay can stratify DCIS patients into low, high, and very high-risk groups. Younger patients are more likely to undergo mastectomy based on either surgeon recommendation or patient preference, and in recent years, contralateral prophylactic mastectomy rates have increased for pure DCIS as for invasive breast cancer—once again this is more evident in younger women and those with a strong family history of breast or ovarian cancer (or carriage of a BRCA1/2 gene mutation).

Axillary lymph node dissection is no longer performed for DCIS, and sentinel lymph node biopsy is indicated only for cases of high and intermediate grade DCIS requiring mastectomy and for microinvasion on core needle biopsy. Very few cases of conservatively treated DCIS require sentinel lymph node biopsy. There is an international consensus that "no tumor at ink" is an adequate margin of clearance for invasive carcinoma or the same admixed with DCIS. However, this margin mandate does not apply to pure DCIS for which radial margins should be at least 1 mm (Association of Breast Surgery, United Kingdom) and preferably 2 mm. The issue of margins is important for those lesions not treated with radiotherapy, but wider margins of up to 10 mm cannot be advocated as a means of avoiding radiotherapy in selected patients. Three trials around the world have recently been initiated which aim to explore the feasibility and safety of active surveillance compared with standard treatment for low-risk forms of DCIS. These are the LORIS trial (United Kingdom), LORD (Netherlands), and COMET (United States).

Planning of oncoplastic surgery for DCIS requires close cooperation between surgeons, radiologists, and pathologists. The need for radiotherapy in the majority of cases of breast conservation will influence the timing of partial breast reconstruction with techniques involving chest wall flaps. However, development of molecular predictors for local recurrence may allow safe omission of radiotherapy in selected cases of DCIS which may be relatively extensive and high grade (with or without necrosis), yet have a favorable molecular profile.

Rates of re-excision following standard breast-conserving surgery are approximately 20% for invasive disease and up to 30% for DCIS. Reduced stringency for definition of a pathologically negative margin has already led to a reduction in rates of re-excision in many units. Nonetheless, rates of 15%–20% remain relatively high and are inconvenient to patients, compromise cosmetic results, and incur additional healthcare costs. Despite emergence of several novel technologies for direct assessment of margins during surgery, microscopic examination of margins with either touch imprint cytology or frozen section represents the most accurate method available. Specimen radiology with directed cavity shaves combined with pathological assessment reduces both re-excision rates and local recurrence. However, there are logistical problems for both frozen section and touch imprint cytology; the latter requires an experienced cytopathologist for the interpretation of specimens. These intraoperative methods for pathological examination cannot sample the entire specimen and with adoption of a narrower margin mandate ("no tumor at ink" or 1 mm) surgical specimens are likely to become smaller. Excessive sampling of a smaller specimen could jeopardize definitive examination of the fixed formalin paraffin-embedded specimens. Moreover, if the tumor lies relatively close to all surfaces, it is more challenging for the pathologist to select the most appropriate area for frozen section analysis and discussion with surgical and radiological colleagues is essential.

Surgeons must liaise closely with their radiological colleagues to ensure accurate preoperative localization of impalpable lesions and adequacy of tumor excision. Sometimes a post-biopsy clip will have migrated and lie away from the site of core needle biopsy. This can be problematic when the only abnormality is microcalcification and much of this has been removed. The entry point of the wire may be distant to the lesion and an ultrasound skin marker can be used to indicate the direct skin projection of the lesion and help plan the surgical incision. Wire localization remains the standard method but radioactive seed localization and paramagnetic seeds (magseed) are being evaluated and compares favorably with conventional wire-guided methods. Intraoperative ultrasound can be a valuable adjunct to specimen radiography and reduce rates of positive margins for both palpable and impalpable lesions visible on ultrasound. Portable radiography systems such as the faxitron are convenient and shorten overall operating time. Moreover, there is evidence that evaluation by surgeons is of comparable accuracy to radiologists and could be advantageous for more complex cases requiring multiple or bracketing wires. Cavity shaves taken at the time of surgery should be guided by specimen radiography although some surgeons perform routine cavity shaves from all radial surfaces without cosmetic detriment.

In contrast to mastectomy patients, all breast-conserving surgery patients require radiotherapy which adversely impacts on cosmesis by inducing a spectrum of changes including increased breast density and tightening, thickening, and pigmentation of the skin together with breast shrinkage and fibrosis. These changes collectively result in a 10%–20% reduction of breast volume. Therefore partial breast reconstruction is often necessary as any surgical defect will be compounded by the effects of radiotherapy. The sequencing and timing of partial breast reconstruction in relation to radiotherapy are critical as the latter will affect both native residual breast tissue and any imported tissue as part of a volume replacement technique involving some form of mammoplasty. Irrespective of whether volume replacement or displacement is employed, oncoplastic repair can be undertaken as an immediate, delayed-immediate, or delayed procedure. Radiotherapy is administered at different times in relation to the extirpative and reconstructive stages of surgery. Immediate repair of a partial mastectomy defect is ideal from a surgical perspective and avoids operating on either scarred or irradiated tissue that otherwise remains soft with good perfusion. Furthermore, this approach is associated with the least number of operations and confers psychological benefits for patients. Oncoplastic breast surgery involves wide resection of tumors with low risk of positive margins (<10%), and mastectomy rather than re-excision is usually indicated in the event of involved margins. For those patients with large breasts, reduction of breast size from a therapeutic mammoplasty can reduce the chance of dose inhomogeneity and late radiation effects. Immediate repair is contraindicated when there is a higher chance of positive resection margins (young age, extensive DCIS, large tumor size) when a delayed repair is preferable and can precede radiotherapy (but follow any re-excision prompted by definitive histology which could be done at the time of reconstruction). This delayed-immediate approach is particularly suited to repair using local flaps and allows time for coordination of surgical schedules.

Delayed repair is usually a consequence of an unexpected defect or deformity resulting from a previous lumpectomy with radiotherapy. Volume replacement with local flaps is preferred but reduction mammoplasty techniques may be appropriate for larger breasts.

Despite importation of fresh vascularized tissue, delayed partial breast reconstruction is associated with higher rates of complications (8 fold) than immediate or delayed-immediate approaches. Fat necrosis is more likely when glandular tissue is mobilized from the chest wall due to radiotherapy-induced endarteritis obliterans that can impair viability of not only glandular tissue but also skin flaps and the nipple-areola complex. Notwithstanding additional morbidity and poorer cosmetic outcomes, overall levels of patient satisfaction are high and not significantly different from more immediate oncoplastic repair. However, studies have confirmed a trend toward better outcome measures for patient satisfaction among women undergoing immediate compared with delayed-immediate/ delayed approaches.

Immediate, delayed-immediate, and delayed partial breast reconstruction each have clinical application, but aesthetic outcomes, patient satisfaction, and potential complications must be evaluated for each approach and a balance reached based on patient-related factors and available surgical expertise.

Breast-conserving surgery and partial breast reconstruction (oncoplastic repair)

Chapter 11. Immediate repair before radiotherapy — 101

Chapter 12. Postoperative margin assessment (re-excision or completion mastectomy) — 147

Chapter 13. Delayed oncoplastic repair—before radiotherapy — 153

Chapter 14. Delayed oncoplastic repair—after radiotherapy — 163

11

Immediate repair before radiotherapy

11.1 LOCAL TISSUE REARRANGEMENT

AT A GLANCE

There is tremendous variation in terms of the definition and techniques of local tissue rearrangement. Extirpative breast surgeons will often perform a simple plication of the tumor defect, and reconstructive surgeons will perform more advanced displacement techniques, like concentric mastopexy for upper pole defects. The indications for local tissue rearrangement is also controversial with many reconstructive surgeons preferring nipple-sparing mastectomy as compared to breast-conserving surgery in patients with A- or B-cup breasts with early-stage breast cancer. In contrast to some extirpative breast surgeons and radiation oncologists, many reconstructive surgeons consider this technique only ideal for C-cup breasts with small tumors and none to minimal breast ptosis and need for breast skin resection.

11.1.1 Extreme oncoplasty (USA)

Melvin J. Silverstein

Breast conservation has traditionally been limited to stage I and II breast cancer spanning 50 mm or less in overall extent. Extreme oncoplasty or radical conservation is a form of breast-conserving surgery which employs oncoplastic techniques to avoid mastectomy in a patient who does not fulfill the traditional criteria for breast conservation in the opinion of most physicians and would otherwise require mastectomy.[1,2] Due to the extent and more advanced stage of these cancers, many of these extreme oncoplasty patients will need postmastectomy radiation therapy.[3] Extreme oncoplasty can

be considered for: (a) patients with tumors larger than 50 mm, if the breast is of suitably large size, (b) some multifocal or multicentric lesions, (c) extensive ductal carcinoma in situ (DCIS) or extensive intraductal component greater than 50 mm, (d) patients with a previously irradiated breast with a new or recurrent cancer within that breast, and (e) patients with large locally advanced breast cancer with a partial imaging response to neoadjuvant chemotherapy. Patients within these categories have generally not been considered acceptable candidates for breast conservation based upon results of prospective trials demonstrating equality of outcomes for breast-conserving surgery compared with mastectomy for stages I and II breast cancer[4-6] together with the NIH Consensus Development Conference recommendations for breast conservation.[7]

Why, then, should anyone want to treat these patients with breast conservation? Firstly, some patients simply want and insist upon breast conservation even when poor candidates and advised against this surgical recommendation. The prospective randomized trials upon which breast conservation is based included tumors up to 5 cm in maximum diameter. There are no prospective randomized data for larger lesions nor are there ever likely to be. But it might be asked what is the difference between a 49 mm cancer that qualifies for conventional breast-conserving surgery and a 53 mm cancer that does not? When breast conservation is performed for a patient initially considered to be a good candidate, but who turns out to have a cancer greater than 50 mm in extent on final pathology, most surgeons will recommend irradiation of that breast, if excision margins are "negative." Most would not convert to a mastectomy based solely on tumor size larger than 50 mm. When such a patient is treated conservatively, this is done without support from any level I (randomized) evidence.

The most important reason for considering extreme oncoplasty is that breast-conservation therapy yields a better quality of life when compared with a combination of mastectomy, reconstruction, and radiation therapy. Moreover, rates of overall survival are likely to be similar.[8]

Global quality-of-life measures must be considered for patients undergoing mastectomy, reconstruction, and radiation therapy. Thus, for most patients, a submuscular expander will be placed deep to the pectoralis major muscle at the time of mastectomy which can be associated with postoperative pain. Furthermore, there are drains, a foreign body, the potential for infection, and period of time is required for expansion. The final reconstruction requires another operation whether this be expander to implant exchange or perhaps an autologous flap. Use of an autologous flap involves a longer procedure, with additional operative risks and donor site morbidity. Additional operations may be required to adjust the breast and nipple as well as tattooing of the areola. There is also the opposite breast to consider with prophylactic mastectomy and reconstruction or a reduction mammoplasty as options for symmetry. The mastectomy (either unilateral or bilateral) will leave an insensate breast, and the final cosmetic result will range from poor to excellent. In the author's experience based on observation of more than 1000 reconstructed patients, fewer than a quarter would be rated as excellent. There is a further issue of residual breast tissue which is needed to maintain viability of the skin and nipple (when the latter is preserved). The amount of residual tissue varies, depending on how the mastectomy was technically performed and the thickness of the flaps. Following mastectomy with reconstruction, most high-risk patients will require radiation therapy.[3] Currently, patients with tumors greater than 5 cm receive radiation therapy together with those patients with four or more positive nodes on final histology. Many radiation oncologists also treat patients with one to three positive nodes with postmastectomy irradiation, but this does not include the supraclavicular nodes.[8] Patients with extensive lymphovascular invasion will be recommended for radiation therapy, as will patients with close or involved margins following mastectomy. In other words, radiation therapy will be recommended for many patients following mastectomy and certainly for the majority of patients who qualify for extreme oncoplasty. If the patient is going to receive radiation therapy following a mastectomy with reconstruction, the author would generally prefer to save the patient's breast if it is technically possible and oncologically sound.

Radiation therapy is generally not "friendly" toward reconstruction.[9] In particular, there is a risk of capsular contracture when an implant-based reconstruction is used or breast shrinkage from irradiation of autologous tissue. Radiation therapy is often inconvenient from the patient's perspective, causes some morbidity, and may interfere with the timing of chemotherapy—as well as being expensive.

Following mastectomy with reconstruction, if radiation therapy is not administered, then up to 5%–10% of breast tissue (depending on the thickness of the flaps) is not treated and this includes the dermal lymphatics. Compare and contrast this with breast conservation using a Wise-pattern reduction or split reduction excision[10] and a simultaneous contralateral reduction for symmetry. This can be performed with a single operation and no drains and the breast looks better immediately and later on. There is less pain, less expense, shorter hospital stay, no foreign body, and no donor site morbidity. Furthermore, the breasts are more functional and sensate, and, collectively, these factors result in a better body image and a happier patient.[11] Most importantly, breast conservation with reduction allows a patient to forget that she had breast cancer, not right away, but at some point in the future. In six months or a year, the patient will be getting dressed and she has two normal looking albeit reduced breasts. The appearance of the latter is good, the breasts are sensate, and more importantly, the patient feels like a normal woman. She will be reminded of breast cancer only when she sees it featured on television or it is time for the next appointment with her doctor. If she had a mastectomy, even with an excellent reconstruction, she will nonetheless be reminded that she had breast cancer on a daily basis for the rest of her life.

Oncoplastic breast conservation is a tool that should be added to our armamentarium in the fight against breast cancer. These techniques should be taught to all surgeons who aspire to treat patients with breast cancer. General surgeons who have not been trained in oncoplastic surgery should work closely with a plastic surgeon in order to offer their patients the best possible state-of-the-art care. Breast surgical fellowship programs should be expanded to include comprehensive experience in breast oncoplastic surgery. Extreme oncoplasty is an evolutionary leap in the progression of breast-conserving surgery—some may even consider it revolutionary.

CASE EXAMPLES

Case 1: A 51-year-old woman presented with a 6 cm–7 cm palpable mass in the upper outer quadrant of her left breast (**Figure 11.1.1.1a**). Imaging revealed a multifocal left breast lesion measuring up to 69 mm (**Figure 11.1.1.1b**). Core biopsy confirmed a grade II invasive ductal carcinoma that was estrogen and progesterone receptor positive, HER2 negative, and with a value of 30% for Ki-67. Core biopsy of an axillary node showed metastatic breast cancer. The patient was treated with neoadjuvant chemotherapy with a moderate imaging response. She underwent wide segmental resection using a split reduction approach[2,10] (**Figure 11.1.1.1c–h**). The final tumor spanned 61 mm with treatment effect. Five out of 21 nodes contained tumor with evidence of treatment effect. The patient received whole breast and nodal radiation therapy and is alive and well 2 years after surgery. Breast magnetic resonance imaging (MRI) and Positron emission tomography–computed tomography (PET-CT) scans are negative for both locoregional and distant disease.

Case 2: A 65-year-old woman underwent screening mammography (**Figure 11.1.1.2a**). Multiple nodules were seen in the left breast, spanning 9 cm (**Figure 11.1.1.2b**).

11.1 Local tissue rearrangement 103

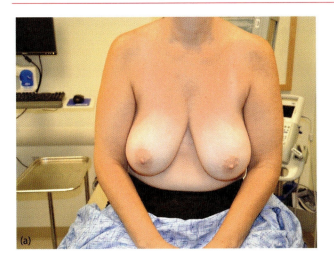

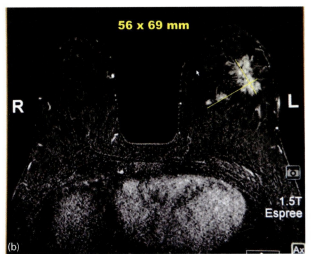

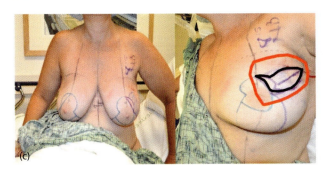

11.1.1.1 (a) 51-year-old patient with 6–7 cm left breast mass. She is preneoadjuvant chemotherapy; (b) MRI showed a multifocal left breast carcinoma spanning 69 mm by 56 mm; (c) (Left) the patient is preoperative and marked for a left split reduction and a right standard reduction for symmetry and risk reduction. (Right) The black line shows the overlying skin that will be removed as part of the split reduction. The red line shows the amount of tissue that will be removed.

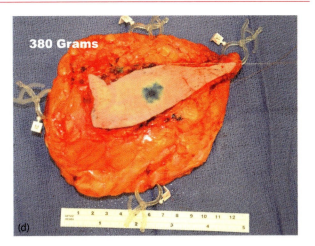

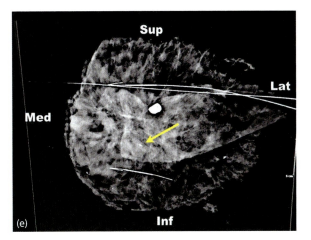

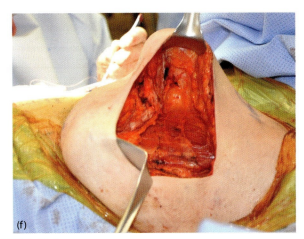

11.1.1.1 (d) A 380 g specimen has been removed; (e) specimen radiograph revealed the microclip marking the original lesion (yellow arrow). It has been widely excised. Overlying skin can be seen; (f) the left breast segment has been excised to the chest wall.

(*Continued*)

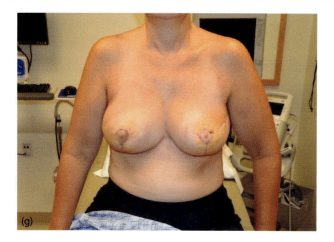

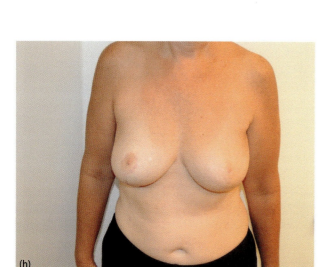

11.1.1.1 (Continued) (g) The patient is 6 days postoperative; and (h) the patient received whole breast and nodal radiation therapy. She is 2 years postoperative without local or distant recurrence.

Core biopsy of two of the nodules revealed low-grade invasive ductal carcinoma with associated DCIS. The invasive cancer was estrogen and progesterone receptor positive and HER2 negative with a low Ki-67 count (<14). The patient underwent wide excision using a reduction approach (**Figure 11.1.1.2c–h**). Final pathology revealed nine separate foci of invasion, the largest of which measured 13 mm. Low-grade DCIS extended over an area of 90 mm. All surgical margins were greater than 10 mm and lymph nodes were all negative. She received postoperative whole breast radiation therapy and chemotherapy. At 7 years postoperative follow-up, the patient is alive and well without local or distant recurrence (**Figure 11.1.1.2h**).

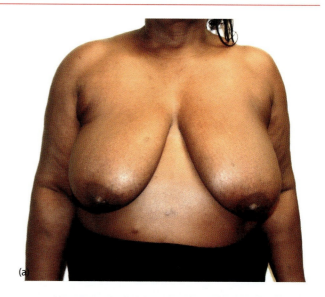

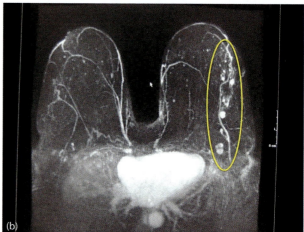

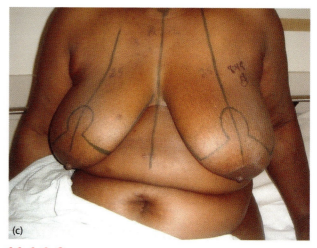

11.1.1.2 (a) A 65-year-old patient with multiple left breast masses spanning 9 cm discovered during screening mammography. (b) MRI shows multiple left breast lesions spanning 90 mm; (c) the patient has been marked for a standard reduction after the placement of four left breast bracketing guide wires. *(Continued)*

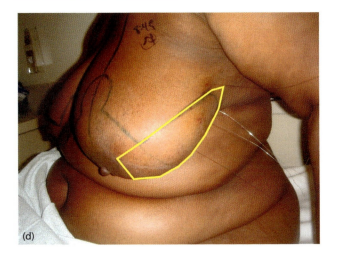
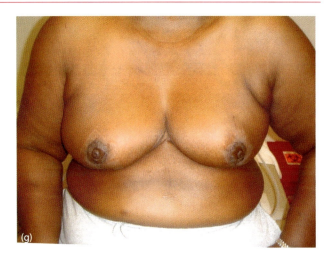
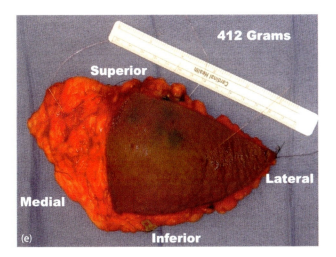
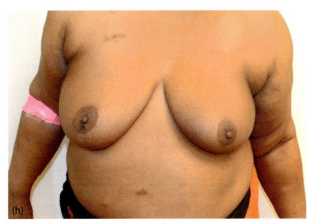
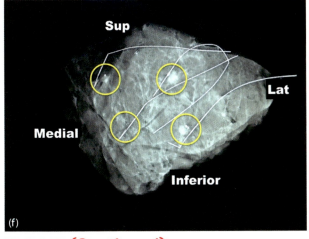

11.1.1.2 (Continued) (d) The yellow line marks the skin resection. A wider segment of tissue was removed; (e) a 412 g specimen was removed. The tissue toward the left of the specimen without overlying skin was behind the nipple; (f) the specimen radiograph shows four suspicious areas marked in yellow and four guide wires. *(Continued)*

11.1.1.2 (Continued) (g) The patient is 6 days postoperative; and (h) the patient received whole breast radiation therapy and chemotherapy. She is 7 years postoperative without local or distant recurrence.

REFERENCES

1. Silverstein M. Radical mastectomy to radical conservation (Extreme Oncoplasty): A revolutionary change. *J Am Coll Surg.* 2016;222:1–9.
2. Silverstein M, Savalia N, Khan S, Ryan J. Extreme oncoplasty: Breast conservation for patients who need mastectomy. *Breast J.* 2015;21:52–59.
3. Vilarino-Varela M, Chin Y, Makris A. Current indications for post-mastectomy radiation. *Int Semin Surg Oncol.* 2009;6:5–6.
4. Fisher B, Bauer M, Margolese R et al. Five-year results of a randomized clinical trial comparing total mastectomy and lumpectomy with or without radiation therapy in the treatment of breast cancer. *N Eng J Med.* 1985;312:665–673.
5. Van Dongen J, Bartelink H, Fentiman I et al. Randomized clinical trial to assess the value of breast-conserving therapy in stage I and II breast cancer, EORTC 10801 trial. *Monogr Natl Cancer Inst.* 1992; 11:15–18.

6. Veronesi U, Saccozzi R, Del Vecchio M et al. Comparing radical mastectomy with quadrantectomy, axillary dissection and radiotherapy in patients with small cancers of the breast. *N Engl J Med.* 1981;305:6–10.
7. NIH Consensus Group. NIH consensus conference. Treatment of early breast cancer. *J Am Med Assoc.* 1991;265:391–395.
8. Early Breast Cancer Trialists' Collaborative Group (EBCTCG). Effects of radiotherapy and differences in the extent of surgery for early breast cancer on local recurrence and 15-year survival: An overview of the randomized trials. *Lancet.* 2005;366:2087–2106.
9. Moulds JEC, Berg CD. Radiation therapy and breast reconstruction. *Radiat Oncol Invest.* 1998;6(2):81–89.
10. Silverstein MJ, Savalia N, Khan S et al. Oncoplastic split reduction with intraoperative radiation therapy. *Ann Surg Oncol.* 2015;22(10):3405–3406.
11. Crown A, Wechter D, Grumley J. Oncoplastic breast-conserving surgery reduces mastectomy and postoperative re-excision rates. *Ann Surg Oncol.* 2015;22:3363–3368.

11.1.2 My approach (Europe)

Robert Douglas Macmillan

There are many algorithms describing approaches to breast-conserving surgery that utilize various techniques for partial defect reconstruction to achieve an acceptable aesthetic outcome.[1] In experienced hands, a range of approaches can give consistently good results. But for the inexperienced, a wide array of options can be quite bewildering, making it difficult to select the right option for the right situation, with an unsatisfactory result often being the consequence of not getting this right.

It is important therefore to appreciate the concepts of planning breast-conserving surgery. Broadly speaking, techniques fall into four main categories.

The chart shown in **Figure 11.1.2.1** illustrates the categories of surgical technique. The chart plots breast size (estimated volume or bra size) on the x-axis against percentage of breast excision on the y-axis, which is the proportion of the tissue removed by the wide local excision relative to breast size. For the purposes of this chart, it is estimated that, for any given tumor size, a wide local excision removes the cancer and a 1 cm macroscopic circumferential margin of surrounding tissue. There may of course be reasons to consider a wider margin, and there are limitations to accurate calculation of breast size preoperatively. Therefore, this chart should not be taken as prescriptive, but rather a guide to broad principles of partial breast reconstruction.

The chart shows the percentage excision relative to any given tumor size. Our group has previously correlated this with patient satisfaction in a study performed on women who did not have oncoplastic breast-conserving surgery. This showed that depending on tumor location, percentage excisions of more than 5%–15% are generally associated with an unsatisfactory outcome if oncoplastic surgery is not used.[2] Nowadays, many would consider that all breast surgery is oncoplastic, but in reality there are simple and more complex forms of oncoplastic surgery.

Simple wide local excision: For those whose practice includes screen-detected disease with smaller tumor size on average, it may be more appropriate to keep surgery very simple, with minimum undermining of surrounding tissue and closure of the surgical defect. The main oncoplastic requirement in these circumstances is careful incision planning and tissue handling. The use of skin undermining with simple wide local excision can allow greater parenchymal mobility when the tumor defect does not easily collapse. However, extensive local undermining of skin or parenchyma is often more disruptive and potentially unpredictable compared to a formal oncoplastic procedure. Patients suitable for these "simple" categories of procedure are most commonly found in the group of breast and tumor size illustrated in the chart shown.

THERAPEUTIC REDUCTION MAMMAPLASTY

For women with large breasts, and in particular those with any morbidity associated with breast size, bilateral breast reduction should always be offered. This is a good option for any woman seeking or accepting a breast reduction procedure,

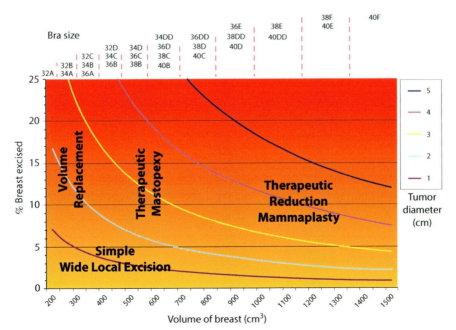

11.1.2.1 Four categories of oncoplastic breast-conserving surgery according to breast volume and percentage of breast tissue removed.

with most sizes of cancer deemed suitable for breast conservation including those with very small cancers. Breast reduction can minimize additional morbidity from radiotherapy due to dose inhomogeneity, as well as conferring quality-of-life benefits. For those with larger cancers, a significant volume reduction can enable breast conservation and constitute an attractive option when compared to mastectomy and reconstruction. Within this category of procedure therefore, women are undergoing a significant reduction in overall breast size with a large volume of normal breast tissue being removed in addition to the wide local excision. Breast shape is maintained by creation of secondary pedicles in addition to the basic nipple pedicle. Nonetheless, there are many ways for achieving an acceptable breast shape and most large-breasted women with breast cancer are not candidates for standard techniques of breast reduction. For high-risk cases, simplified forms of breast reduction can safely achieve similar aims if a woman is prepared to accept the associated scarring. Moreover, breast reduction becomes a much simpler procedure if a woman accepts having her nipples removed as part of the resection.

THERAPEUTIC MASTOPEXY

For women with ptotic breasts who do not necessarily desire breast reduction, but are otherwise accepting of an alteration in breast shape, therapeutic mastopexy is often the procedure of choice. The key principle here is that breast volume reduction is attributable to the wide local excision itself. Hence, there is usually only a small overall reduction in breast volume with the procedure being more akin to a mastopexy than a reduction with the additional benefit of improved breast aesthetic. This category of procedure has a wide range of possibilities and many are described that involve some form of skin reduction and nipple re-positioning combined with wide local excision. The author's preference is to use whole or hemi-breast rotations. Therapeutic mastopexy is most commonly indicated for women with well-proportioned breasts who have some degree of ptosis as illustrated in the chart.

VOLUME REPLACEMENT

For women with small or non-ptotic breasts, breast form is optimally maintained by combining the wide local excision with some form of volume replacement. Once again, many different methods have been described. However, there are very few cases and no tumor locations that are not suitable for a local perforator flap. The lateral-, medial-, and anterior intercostal artery perforator flaps along with the lateral thoracic artery perforator flap provide versatile local means of volume replacement with acceptable donor site scarring. In those requiring a larger volume flap with greater reach, a thoracodorsal artery perforator flap may occasionally be used.

The author's approach is therefore to keep things simple wherever possible and especially in those women with very small cancers. Breast reduction is offered to all women with very large breasts. Volume replacement with a local perforator flap and therapeutic mastopexy both give the option of maintaining a good breast shape and symmetry in the range of breast size that is most commonly encountered. With minor modification as necessary, the four main categories of procedure described can be employed to manage a wide local excision defect in any part of the breast and as such it would be rare to encounter a situation where one of these categories of procedure was not the best option. Surgery is almost always performed at one surgical sitting with simultaneous symmetrizing reduction/mastopexy or volume replacement as appropriate to the category of technique being used. Overall, our approach aims to offer women with breast cancer the benefit of established principles of cosmetic and reconstructive surgery and although these have evolved over many years, the principles illustrated in our chart remain constant. However, as stated at the outset, there are many different ways of performing oncoplastic breast-conserving surgery, and in general, the simplest technique in each of the four categories described is likely to be the best one. Many women are prepared to accept small indentations and asymmetries that surgeons would not be "proud of" and the primary focus should always be a successful oncological outcome. However, oncoplastic surgery allows this aim to be combined with an acceptable aesthetic outcome.

REFERENCES

1. www.orbsweb.com.
2. Cochrane RA, Valassiadou P, Wilson ARM, Al-Ghazal SK, Macmillan RD. Cosmesis and satisfaction after breast-conserving surgery correlates with the percentage of breast volume excised. *Br J Surg* 2003;90:1505–1509.

11.2 DERMOGLANDULAR REDUCTION MAMMOPLASTY

AT A GLANCE

Reduction mammoplasty techniques are most often used for patients with large-sized (D-cup or larger) breasts. Both vertical and Wise skin pattern techniques are used for these repairs. The blood supply to the dermoglandular pedicles can be based either superiorly or inferiorly with many variations depending on the location of the tumor defect. The increasing use of neoadjuvant chemotherapy, which tends to reduce tumor size, is often used to increase the eligibility of large-breasted patients for this technique. Oncoplastic reduction mammoplasty can also be ideal for large-breasted patients with locally advanced breast cancer (stage III breast cancer), who are known preoperatively to require radiotherapy and who are at increased risk for complications with implanted-based reconstruction in the setting of radiotherapy.

11.2.1 My approach (USA)

Steven J. Kronowitz

Oncoplastic surgery is state-of-the-art for repair of partial mastectomy defects.[1] Oncoplastic surgery is optimally employed before delivery of radiotherapy.[2] Depending on factors such as pathology, access to intraoperative tumor margin assessment, and surgeon preference, oncoplastic procedures can be performed immediately at the time of partial mastectomy or delayed before radiation therapy— the latter allows for review of final pathology prior to repair. However, delayed repair before radiation delivery requires two separate surgical procedures and the aesthetic outcome is not always as favorable as for immediate oncoplasty. Immediate oncoplastic dermoglandular repair before radiotherapy can involve a range of creative designs which are aimed at rearranging the remaining breast tissue after partial mastectomy. Patients with large-sized breasts, including those women with C-cup and D-cup breasts or larger benefit from use of any remaining breast tissue to repair the breast.[1]

In those patients with C-cup breasts with upper quadrant tumors and some degree of breast ptosis, displacement concentric mastopexy can be an ideal choice for repair (**Figure 11.2.1.1**). The advantage of this approach is that repair elevates the position of the nipple-areola complex and displaces the lower pole breast tissue to fill upper pole defects. After radiotherapy, the region of the defect is fat grafted and the contralateral breast may be made smaller with direct liposuction. Nonetheless, because the defect is repaired prior to radiotherapy, there is usually absence of any localized deformity, with only a diffuse loss of breast volume from radiotherapy. In consequence, the second stage of repair often involves fat grafting to the entire involved breast after radiotherapy to replace the diffuse volume loss with minor adjustment to the contralateral breast for symmetry.

Mammoplasty is the optimal approach to repair partial breast deformities before radiotherapy in patients with D-cup-sized breasts or larger.[3] Standardization of technique has become an important initiative in the United States as a means of encouraging reconstructive breast surgeons to routinely perform oncoplasty.[4] Vertical incisions are used in large, ptotic-shaped breasts with narrow-base widths. Kronowitz described a systematic approach to using vertical oncoplasty for repair of partial mastectomy defects located anywhere within the breast (**Figure 11.2.1.2**). In patients with upper pole defects, a superomedial or superolateral dermoglandular pedicle is used for repair, whereby the lower central breast tissue is rotated into the upper pole defect either clockwise or counter clockwise, respectively (**Figure 11.2.1.3**). With lower pole defects, the use of dual dermoglandular pedicles allows for both elevation of the nipple-areola complex and filling of the defect. For defects located within the lower inner quadrant, both a superior and inferolateral dermoglandular pedicle is utilized for repair (**Figure 11.2.1.4**). Similarly, defects in the lower outer quadrant are repaired with a superior pedicle and inferomedial pedicle. The superior dermoglandular pedicle elevates the position of the nipple-areola complex and the inferiorly based dermoglandular pedicle advances either medially or laterally to fill the defect.

A Kronowitz-Wise oncoplasty is preferred for patients with large, D-cup breasts with wide-base widths in which the lateral breast extends into the axilla (**Figure 11.2.1.5**). The designation of seven zones within the breast that correspond to straightforward dermoglandular designs has simplified and organized approaches to repair of partial mastectomy defects in patients with wide, D-cup-sized breasts (**Figure 11.2.1.6**).[5,6] The utilization of inferiorly based dermoglandular pedicles, most commonly, the inferomedial dermoglandular pedicle, provides an opportunity to debulk the lateral breast and axillary region in order to redefine and narrow the breast, while providing additional blood supply to the nipple-areola complex and cleavage to the breasts.

Resection of tumors is performed using an access incision along the Wise skin pattern. After creation of the dermoglandular pedicle, the Wise skin flap is redraped overlying the inferiorly based dermoglandular pedicle. With lower inner and lower outer quadrant defects, the Wise skin flap serves as the reconstructive component by retaining the thickness of the breast tissue on the undersurface of the medial or lateral aspect of the Wise skin flap, respectively. Upon closure of the Wise skin flap, the thick region of the Wise skin flap fills the lower pole defect.

For tumors located within zone 1, the dermoglandular design preserves the medial wedge of breast tissue, usually

110 Immediate repair before radiotherapy

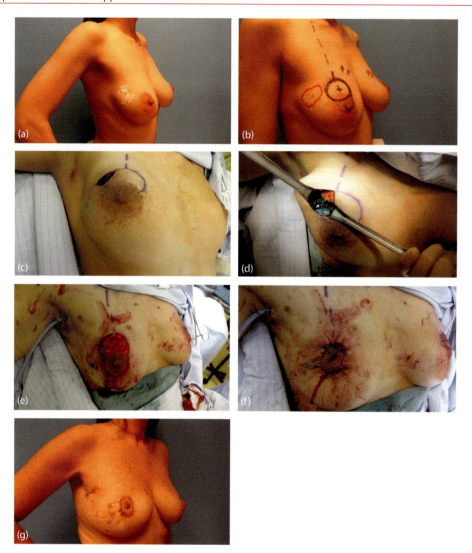

11.2.1.1 Concentric mastopexy technique to repair partial mastectomy defects. (a) Preoperative views of a 37-year-old with C-cup-size, non-ptotic breasts, who has a 2 cm invasive breast cancer in the 10:00 position in the right breast. (b) Preoperative markings for bilateral concentric mastopexy. (c) Intraoperative view of access incision the breast surgeon used to perform the partial mastectomy. (d) Defect after partial mastectomy. (e) After direct repair of the defect and de-epithelialization of concentric region. (f) After purse-string closure of the concentric region using permanent suture. (g) Postoperative views: 6 weeks after an immediate repair of the right breast using the concentric mastopexy technique and left concentric mastopexy for symmetry.

discarded with a standard breast reduction using an inferior dermoglandular pedicle. This not only fills the upper inner quadrant defect when the Wise skin pattern is closed, but also provides additional blood supply to the nipple-areola complex through the intercostal and internal mammary blood vessels (**Figure 11.2.1.7**).[6] The medial wedge is preserved for all tumor locations, except for the lower inner quadrant in which it is excised with the tumor, because breast tumor excisions tend to follow the mammary ductal system that extend under the nipple-areola complex and denude the blood supply. Another region of the breast that is common for breast tumors is located in zone 6, the upper outer quadrant of the breast. In zone 6, an inferomediolateral dermoglandular pedicle is used for the repair. The lateral wedge of the inferior dermoglandular pedicle, that is usually resected with an inferior dermoglandular pedicle, is retained and used to fill the upper outer defect upon closure of the Wise skin flap. With this tumor location, the medial wedge is also retained to maintain the cleavage of the breast and to enhance the blood supply to the nipple-areola complex.

Typically, the contralateral non-cancer mammoplasty is performed simultaneously with the oncoplastic repair for displacement mastopexy and for vertical oncoplasty. For Wise oncoplasty, the patient can choose whether the contralateral non-cancer mammoplasty is performed immediately or 6 months after radiotherapy.[1] The contralateral mammoplasty for symmetry is performed using the same dermoglandular design that was used for the oncoplastic repair. In contrast to concentric and vertical oncoplasty, postponement

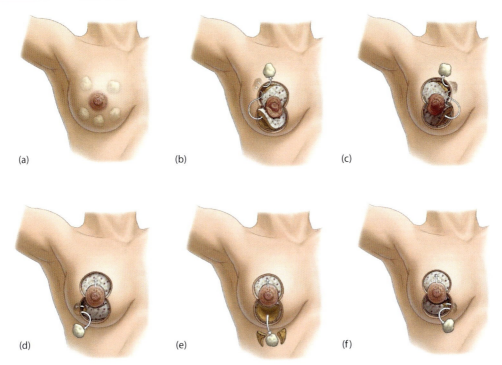

11.2.1.2 Kronowitz vertical oncoplasty. (a) Designation of vertical oncoplasty design is based on five tumor locations within the breast. (b) For tumors located within the upper outer aspect of the breast, a superomedial dermoglandular pedicle is used with clockwise rotation. (c) For tumors located within the upper inner aspect of the breast, a superolateral dermoglandular pedicle with counterclockwise rotation into the defect. (d) Lower outer defects are repaired using a two-dermoglandular technique. A superior dermoglandular pedicle to reposition the nipple higher on the breast mound and an inferomedial dermoglandular pedicle that is advanced laterally into the defect. (e) For lower central defects, the standard superior dermoglandular pedicle is utilized. (f) Similar to defects located in the lower outer aspect of the breast, defects located in the lower inner quadrant are repaired using two deromglandular pedicles. A superior dermoglandular pedicle is used to elevate the nipple and areola complex, and an inferolateral dermoglandular pedicle is used to fill the defect by medial advancement.

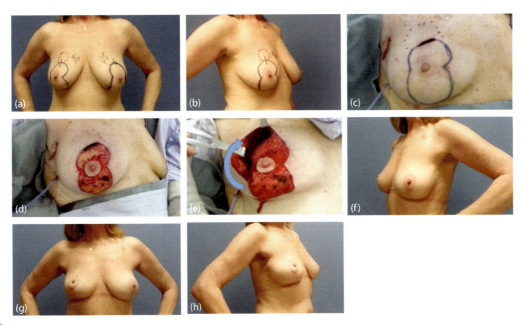

11.2.1.3 38-year-old female with right breast cancer. (a and b) Preoperative views: Vertical skin resection pattern and location of cancer (red dashed line). (c) Intraoperative view: Access incision along vertical skin pattern used for resection of tumor. (d) Intraoperative view: De-epithelialized vertical dermoglandular pedicle. (e) Intraoperative view after creation of superomedial dermoglandular pedicle prior to clockwise rotation (blue arrow) into superior defect. (f–h) Views after radiation therapy prior to planned revision breast reconstruction.

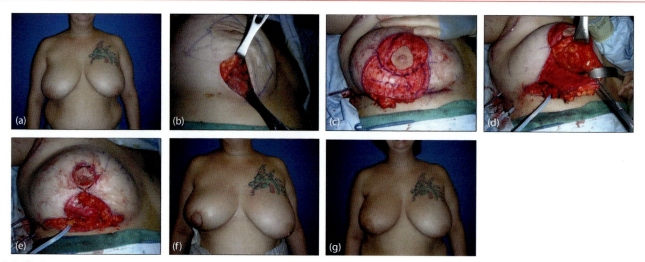

11.2.1.4 Dual-dermoglandular pedicle technique for lower pole defects. (a) Preoperative view of 35-year-old female with right breast cancer. (b) Intraoperative view of the defect in the lower inner quadrant of the breast. (c) Intraoperative view of design of dual-dermoglandular pedicles used for repair. (d) Intraoperative view of the inferolateral dermoglandular pedicle being advanced medially into the defect. (e) Intraoperative view after superior advancement of the superior dermoglandular pedicle and inset of the inferolateral pedicle. (f) Postoperative view 2 weeks after surgery. (g) Postoperative view: 2 months after radiation therapy. The patient is planned for fat grafting the right breast and symmetry procedure to left breast.

of any contralateral mammoplasty for symmetry with Wise oncoplasty is because inferiorly based dermoglandular pedicles allow for significant reduction in breast volume resection if required after radiotherapy. With concentric and vertical mammoplasty, any potential reduction in volume of tissue resected is limited. Moreover, if additional volume reduction is required after radiotherapy in order to maintain symmetry with a concentric or vertical oncoplastic breast, direct liposuction is usually the best option. Therefore, delaying the contralateral non-cancer mammoplasty with concentric or vertical oncoplasty offers no benefit to the patient.

Timing is an important consideration for oncoplastic surgery—either immediate or delayed procedures before radiotherapy are preferred with whole breast radiotherapy.[5] Delayed oncoplasty after whole breast radiotherapy is unsafe and the authors discourage this approach. Unexpected deformities occurring after partial mastectomy should be repaired prior to radiotherapy (**Figure 11.2.1.8**).[6] The method of radiotherapy delivery can significantly impact the timing and technique for repair of partial mastectomy defects. When whole breast irradiation is employed, a flap is usually required for delayed repair because dermoglandular oncoplasty is associated with high rates of complications. Partial breast irradiation allows for delayed repair after radiotherapy using dermoglandular oncoplasty which can utilize the surrounding non-irradiated breast tissue.

Although oncoplastic procedures vary widely within the United States, it is generally recommended that whenever feasible, oncoplasty preceding whole breast radiotherapy is preferable. This is associated with the lowest complication rates and involves the simplicity of using the remaining breast tissue, which maintains the color and texture match of the repaired breast.[6] An important question is whether the oncoplastic repair should be performed immediately at the time of the partial mastectomy or delayed until after the partial mastectomy, but before the radiotherapy. Unfortunately, not all surgeons have access to reliable intraoperative tumor margin assessment, but most patients do undergo preoperative mammography and ultrasonography that can assist the breast reconstructive surgeon in determining the most appropriate timing for repair. Patients without or only localized microcalcifications on mammography and those with unifocal tumors may be suitable candidates for immediate repair at the time of partial mastectomy. However, those patients with diffuse microcalcifications on mammography or those with multifocal tumors on ultrasound will likely benefit from waiting (delayed before radiotherapy) until final pathology margin assessment is available, and thereafter proceed with dermoglandular oncoplasty. In summary, immediate repair before radiotherapy in patients with D-cup-sized breasts or larger can best be accomplished using dermoglandular oncoplasty. Concentric displacement, vertical oncoplasty, or Wise oncoplasty are extremely versatile techniques and can be routinely used in most patients who undergo breast-conserving surgery.

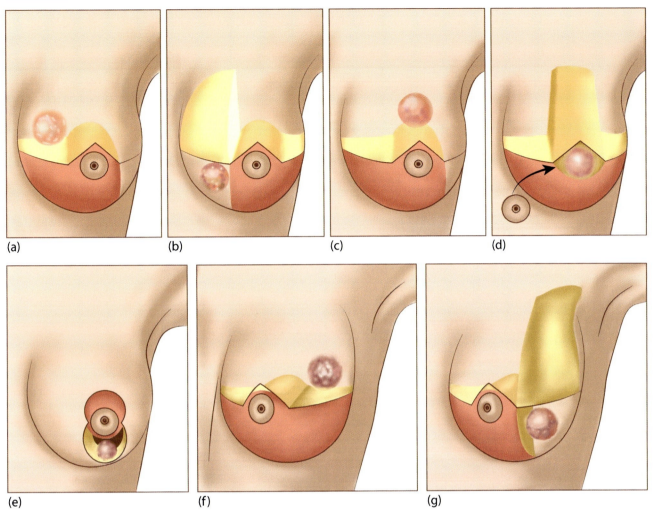

11.2.1.5 Straightforward dermoglandular pedicle designs to repair partial mastectomy defects using the breast reduction technique that corresponds with the zone designations (tumor location). (a) Upper-inner quadrant (zone 1). Inferomedial dermoglandular pedicle. The retained medial component fills the defect upon closure of the Wise skin pattern and maintains the cleavage of the breast. (b) Lower-inner quadrant (zone 2). Inferolateral dermoglandular pedicle. The retained lateral component provides additional blood supply to the nipple-areola complex if tumor resection encroaches on the inferior pedicle. A thick layer of subcutaneous tissue is maintained on the medial aspect of the Wise skin pattern flap to fill the defect upon closure of the Wise skin pattern and maintain cleavage of the breast. (c) Upper-central quadrant (zone 3). Inferomedial dermoglandular pedicle. Retained medial component provides a cosmetic advantage and additional blood supply to the nipple-areola complex in patients with very large ptotic breasts, possibly obviating the need for a free nipple graft. (d) Middle-central quadrant (zone 4). Amputative design with free nipple graft and maintenance of a thick layer of subcutaneous tissue on the central aspect of the Wise skin pattern flap to fill the defect and improve contour. (e) Lower-central quadrant (zone 5). Vertical skin pattern with superiorly based dermoglandular mammoplasty. The vertical mammoplasty can also be used to repair defects in zones 1 and 7 by retaining the inferior aspect of the dermoglandular pedicle and basing the blood supply to this region either medially with lateral advancement (zone 7 repair) or laterally with medial advancement (zone 1 repair). (f) Upper-outer quadrant (zone 6). Inferomediolateral dermoglandular pedicle. The retained lateral component fills the defect upon closure of the Wise skin pattern, and the retained medial component provides cosmetic advantage. (g) Lower-outer quadrant (zone 7). Inferomedial dermoglandular pedicle. The retained medial component provides a cosmetic advantage and additional blood supply to the nipple-areola complex if lateral resection encroaches on the blood supply to the nipple-areola complex. A thick layer of subcutaneous tissue is maintained on the lateral aspect of the Wise skin pattern flap to fill the defect.

114 Immediate repair before radiotherapy

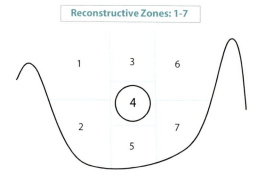

11.2.1.6 Zone designations of the breast based on tumor location used to determine the design for the dermoglandular pedicle to repair a partial mastectomy defect.

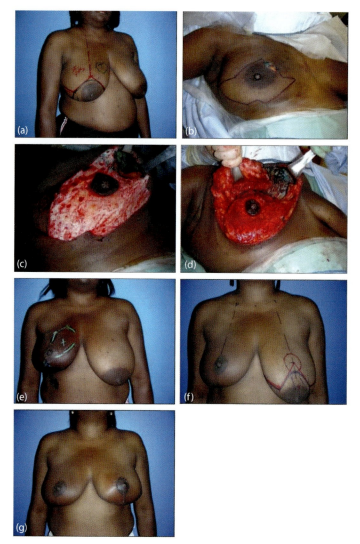

11.2.1.7 Breast repair after a partial mastectomy in a 41-year-old woman with a 36DD bra size who presented with a T2N0 (stage IIA) invasive ductal carcinoma in the upper-inner quadrant of the right breast (zone 1). (a) Preoperative views: Wise skin pattern markings and the inferomedial dermoglandular pedicle in preparation for repair with the breast reduction technique. (b) Intraoperative views showing the tumor resection, which was performed through an access incision along the superior limb of the Wise pattern. (c and d) Intraoperative views showing the de-epithelialized inferomedial dermoglandular pedicle and after creation of both the dermoglandular pedicle and the Wise skin flap, which in certain zones (zones 2 and 7) can serve as separate reconstructive components. (e) During radiation therapy, showing the boost to the tumor bed and whole breast treatment. (f) Postoperative view: 10 months after repair showing how the retained medial wedge of breast tissue filled the defect in zone 1. The surgeon can plan for contralateral breast reduction using the same inferomedial dermoglandular design. (g) Postoperative view: 1 month after contralateral breast reduction for symmetry.

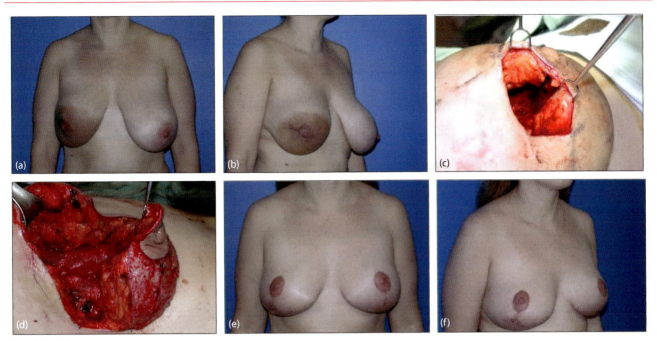

11.2.1.8 Unexpected deformity after partial mastectomy. (a and b) 34-year-old woman who presented 2 weeks after a right partial mastectomy with significant concerns regarding cosmetic outcome. (c) Intraoperative view of exploration of blood supply to dermoglandular pedicle prior to performing Kronowitz-Wise mammoplasty. (d) Intraoperative view showing the blood supply was adequate to perform a delayed repair before radiation therapy using an infeomedial dermoglandular pedicle. (e and f) Postoperative views.

REFERENCES

1. Kronowitz SJ. State of the art and science in postmastectomy breast reconstruction. *Plast Reconstr Surg.* 2015;135(4):755e-771e.
2. Kronowitz SJ, Kuerer HM, Buchholz TA, Valero V, Hunt KK. A management algorithm and practical oncoplastic surgical techniques for repairing partial mastectomy defects. *Plast Reconstr Surg.* 2008;122(6):1631-1647.
3. Losken A, Hamdi M. Partial breast reconstruction: Current perspectives. *Plast Reconstr Surg.* 2009;124(3):722-736.
4. Losken A, Styblo TM, Carlson GW, Jones GE, Amerson BJ. Management algorithm and outcome evaluation of partial mastectomy defects treated using reduction or mastopexy techniques. *Ann Plast Surg.* 2007;59(3):235-242.
5. Kronowitz SJ, Robb GL. Breast reconstruction and adjuvant therapies. *Semin Plast Surg.* 2004;18(2):105-115.
6. Kronowitz SJ, Feledy JA, Hunt KK, Kuerer HM, Youssef A, Koutz CA, Robb GL. Determining the optimal approach to breast reconstruction after partial mastectomy. *Plast Reconstr Surg.* 2006;117(1):1-11; discussion 12-14.

11.2.2 Our approach (Europe)

J. Michael Dixon and Cameron Raine

INTRODUCTION

Studies have shown a continued fall in local recurrence rates following breast-conserving surgery and data now suggest that not only are survival and local recurrence rates as good with breast-conserving surgery as with mastectomy, they may even be better.[1] There is no subgroup who benefit from mastectomy and with modern oncoplastic techniques there are few contra-indications to breast-conserving surgery. Therapeutic mammoplasty permits increasing numbers of women to have breast-conserving surgery.

IMPORTANT GUIDING PRINCIPLES

Outcomes including local recurrence and survival may be better for breast-conserving surgery and radiation compared with mastectomy alone. Body image and short- and long-term pain are better for breast-conserving surgery compared with mastectomy. There is a lower rate of lymphedema associated with breast-conserving surgery and axillary lymph node dissection compared with mastectomy and axillary lymph node dissection.

Therapeutic mammoplasty extends the option of breast-conserving surgery to more women, and our results show that it increases the completeness of excision. To ensure a high rate of complete excision, neoadjuvant chemotherapy and neoadjuvant endocrine therapy can reduce tumor size and be combined with therapeutic mammoplasty, and the authors use this approach in large numbers of women before surgery. Neoadjuvant therapy allows better planning and scheduling of surgery and allows patients time to make an informed choice when considering the option of mastectomy or therapeutic mammoplasty.

When performing therapeutic mammoplasty for impalpable disease and particularly for ductal carcinoma in situ (DCIS), it is imperative to have adequate preoperative assessment of the extent of disease. In most patients with DCIS, this requires magnification mammography *and* in many MRI. The extent of any non-invasive disease should be marked with clips prior to any treatment. In invasive disease, all tumor foci should be clipped. On the day of surgery, if the disease is impalpable then accurate localization should be performed. The authors' current preference for accurate localization is to use multiple wires.

OPERATION

Therapeutic mammoplasty is used in the authors' unit for a wide range of situations including multisite disease and for extensive DCIS measuring up to 15 cm.

Therapeutic mammoplasty should be performed through the same range of incision patterns used in plastic surgery for breast reduction. This essentially means that most patients should have either a Wise pattern or vertical scar mammoplasty. Although round block breast reductions are in widespread use by oncoplastic breast surgeons, the authors rarely use them because they permit limited resection only and lead to a flattening of the central part of the breast. Excision of skin over the cancer using racquet incisions is rarely indicated unless the cancer is close to or involves the skin. If the nipple is to be excised, then this can be included in the vertical scar. The blood supply to the nipple may be compromised by the resection or the nipple may have to be moved so far that its viability is adversely affected. Under these circumstances a free nipple grafting approach may allow nipple preservation.

On the day of the surgery, skin incisions and nipple position are carefully marked preoperatively by an experienced surgeon. There are some guiding principles for marking up patients. It is imperative that the nipple is not placed too high, and the authors' approach is to mark the new breast meridian and place the new nipple location 8–10 cm below the upper breast margin. This typically correlates with a position either at, or just above, the inframammary fold when projected onto the anterior breast in the standing position (**Figures 11.2.2.1 and 11.2.2.2**).

The authors favor a simultaneous bilateral procedure, which is considered to make financial sense, and in their practice few patients have needed any additional procedures to achieve symmetry. Ideally, the operation is performed by two surgeons which is more cost-effective in terms of theater time and has the advantage for the patient that they have a shorter anesthetic. Both surgeons should have oncoplastic expertise and an optimal combination is an oncoplastic breast surgeon and a plastic surgeon. However, an

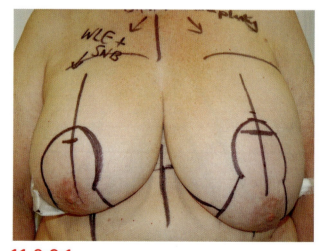

11.2.2.1 Patient 1 carcinoma right breast. This breast was the smaller breast prior to surgery. Marking for a Wise pattern breast reduction and excision of cancer.

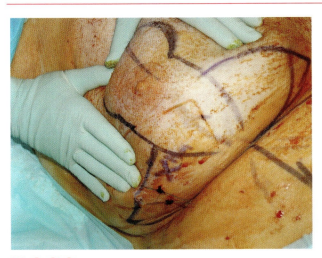

11.2.2.2 Wires in place with a 45 mm nipple marker being used to mark the incision around the nipple.

experienced trainee working with a single oncoplastic surgeon is another option.

The surgeon operating on the normal breast reduces it to the optimal size. On the opposite breast the surgeon makes an incision along part of the breast reduction markings and removes the cancer with a generous margin (**Figures 11.2.2.3, 11.2.2.4, and 11.2.2.5**). The role of the oncoplastic surgeon who performs the excision is to excise the disease to clear margins. For this reason, the initial excision should be a wide excision of the cancer without concern about cutting across any pedicles or removing any breast tissue that can be resected later as part of the breast reduction. In patients with impalpable cancers, the disease is often not at the anatomical site in the breast that was estimated based on mammograms. Excising a single specimen to include the wide excision and breast reduction in one piece is not advised as this can limit reconstructive options.

The wide excision specimen should be orientated with metal clips that can be seen on a specimen radiograph and is x-rayed preferably in the operating room with a device such as the Faxitron (**Figure 11.2.2.6**). If disease appears close to any radial margin, then further tissue from that margin is excised. All specimens are weighed. Once the weight of excision from the normal, non-cancer breast is known, this can be used to guide further resection of breast tissue from the cancer side in an attempt to optimize final symmetry (**Figures 11.2.2.7 and 11.2.2.8**). It is the authors' usual practice to leave the cancer side slightly larger than the contralateral normal breast to allow for post radiotherapy volume loss. Given the key surgical objective is a complete resection of the cancer to clear margins, as much tissue as possible should be excised at the wide local excision site and only then should resection of breast tissue elsewhere be considered to optimize final shape and volume symmetry. The authors' practice is to place ligaclips at the margins of the wide excision cavity prior to performing the mammoplasty so that if re-excision is needed, the margins have been marked. A flexible approach is adopted to the nipple pedicle and a variety of primary and secondary pedicles used to close the defect. It is important to ensure that any pedicle used is well vascularized. Although widely used, the authors have experienced more problems with long inferior pedicles in large breasts than with any of the other pedicles. It is crucial that there is adequate nipple projection at the end of the procedure. With the approach described, the rate of margin involvement is less than 5%.

In these figures (**Figures 11.2.2.9–11.2.2.33**), three patients undergoing wide excision and mammoplasty are shown to demonstrate our approach. The final two illustrations show characteristic long-term results (**Figures 11.2.2.34 and 11.2.2.35**).

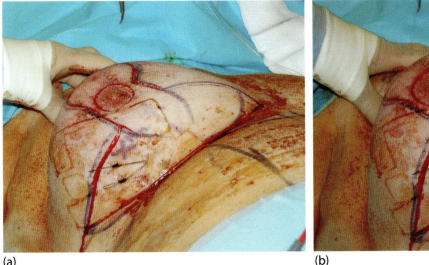
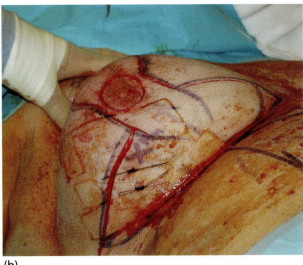

(a)   (b)

11.2.2.3 (a) Skin incision take to level of dermis; (b) skin incision deepened to level of dermis.

118 Immediate repair before radiotherapy

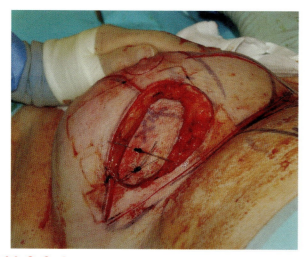

11.2.2.4 Performing the wide excision skin. The lesion was superficial so skin over the lesion was removed.

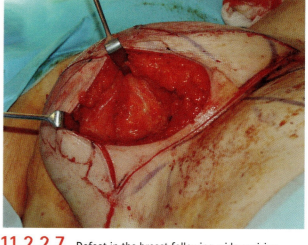

11.2.2.7 Defect in the breast following wide excision.

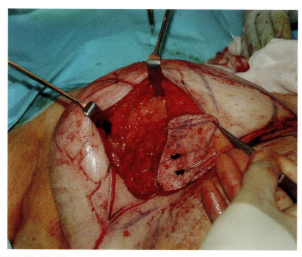

11.2.2.5 The incision is deepened and portion of tissue containing the cancer and calcification is dissected free from the surrounding normal breast.

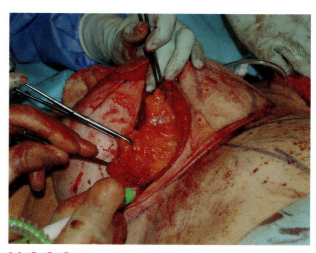

11.2.2.8 Excision of further tissue from around the inferior cavity of the wide excision to increase the likelihood of clear margins.

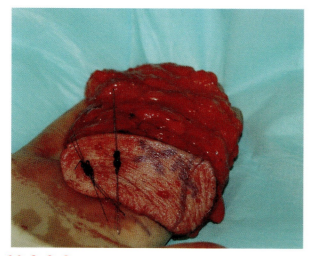

11.2.2.6 The cancer and surrounding tissue have been removed and will now be x-rayed.

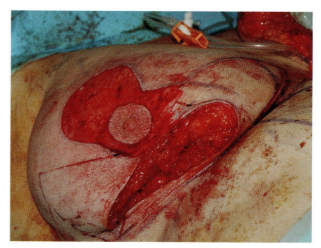

11.2.2.9 The skin around the nipple has been de-epithelialized.

11.2 Dermoglandular reduction mammoplasty 119

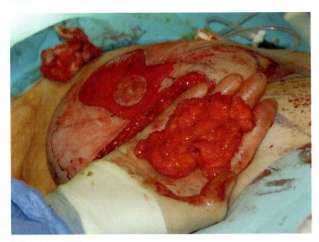

11.2.2.10 Inferior cavity shave specimen.

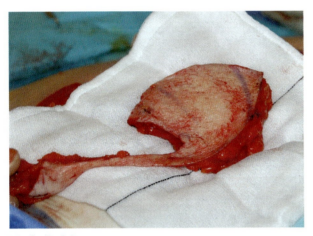

11.2.2.11 Further breast reduction tissue has been excised incorporating skin and more breast tissue from around the wide excision. Amount excised based on weight of the tissue removed from the contralateral breast.

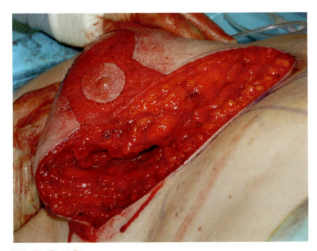

11.2.2.12 Breast after cancer and surrounding tissue has been removed. Note the defect laterally in the right breast and the limited amount of tissue that has been removed from the breast medially.

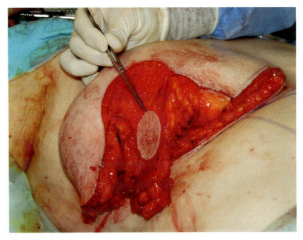

11.2.2.13 The breast tissue on either side of the nipple has been incised and the nipple is kept alive on a superior pedicle.

11.2.2.14 The skin is tacked with a series of subcuticular sutures to ensure the nipple is not under tension. Note the scar for the sentinel node biopsy in the axilla.

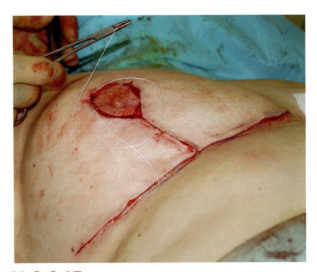

11.2.2.15 Gore-Tex suture is placed to stop the nipple areola area stretching later.

120 Immediate repair before radiotherapy

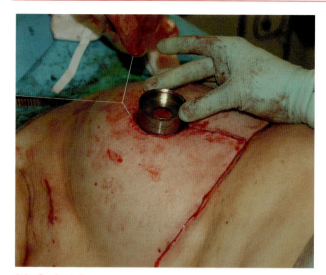

11.2.2.16 The Gore-Tex suture is tied around the nipple marker.

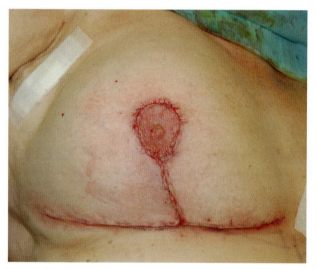

11.2.2.17 The wounds are closed with absorbable subcuticular sutures. Glue and steristrips are applied later as for the axillary wound that can be seen.

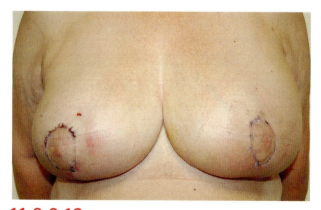

11.2.2.18 Patient 3 weeks after surgery showing reasonable symmetry and all wounds have healed well. Some glue can still be seen adherent to the wounds.

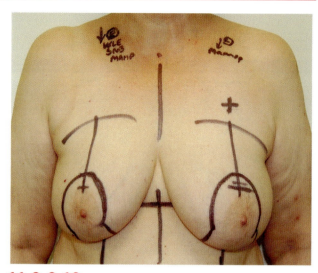

11.2.2.19 Patient 2 preoperation. She has a cancer in the medial aspect of the right breast. Shows preoperative Wise pattern markings. The cancer is medial in the breast.

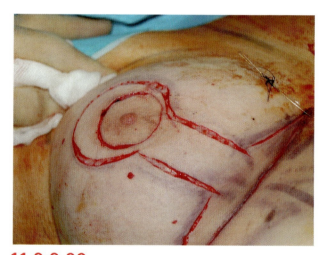

11.2.2.20 Incision scored to dermis. Note the wire to mark the cancer medially.

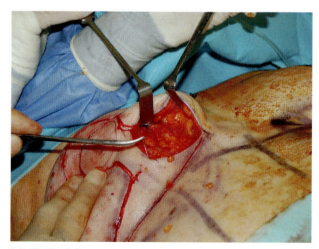

11.2.2.21 Skin over the medial cancer has been elevated and the wire delivered through the skin, and it can be seen passing into the breast parenchyma.

11.2 Dermoglandular reduction mammoplasty 121

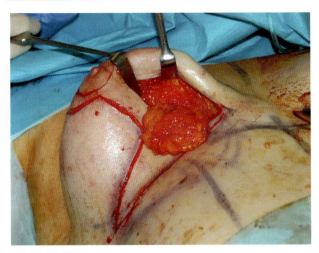

11.2.2.22 The excision is almost complete. Note the small volume excision in this patient.

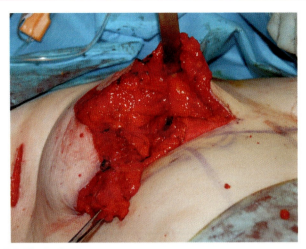

11.2.2.25 The remaining tissue is used to reconstruct the defect, and in this patient a portion of the de-epithelized skin has been left partially attached to the lateral breast.

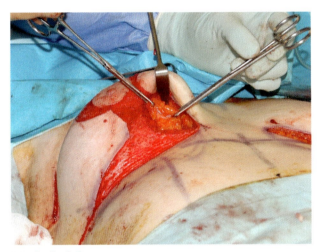

11.2.2.23 The remaining skin has been de-epithelialized and further tissue is now removed from around the margins of the wide excision.

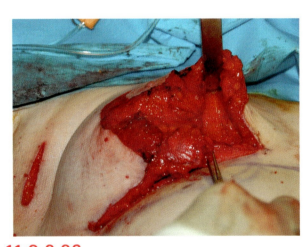

11.2.2.26 The de-epithelized tissue left attached to the lateral breast is moved medially to fill the defect. Tissue left medially attached to the lower dermis is also used as a secondary pedicle to close the medial defect.

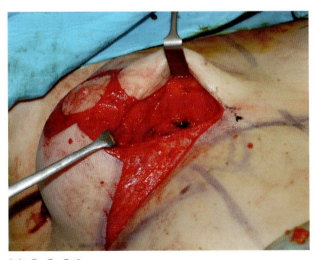

11.2.2.24 All tissue to be excised has been removed.

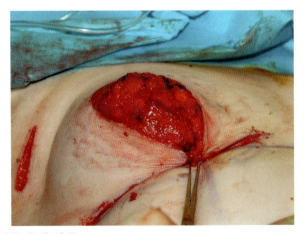

11.2.2.27 The skin is brought together before closure to ensure that the defect in the breast is filled and there is no tension on any of the pedicles.

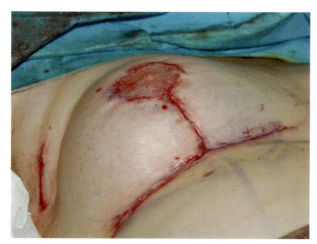

11.2.2.28 The wound is closed in layers with absorbable sutures.

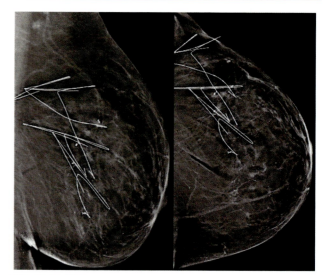

11.2.2.31 Mammogram of four wires in breast pre-therapeutic mammoplasty.

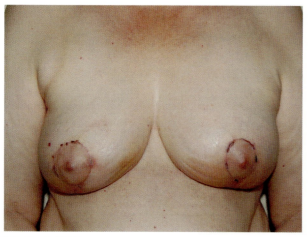

11.2.2.29 Patient 3 weeks after surgery. Right breast is slightly larger than the left, but usually shrinks with radiotherapy.

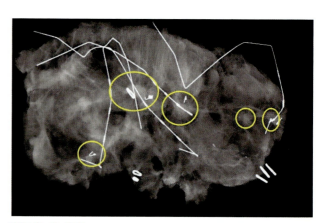

11.2.2.32 Specimen x-ray of four-wire five cancer excision.

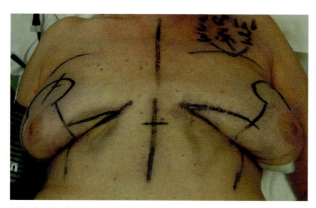

11.2.2.30 Preoperative view of breasts of patient with five cancers left breast.

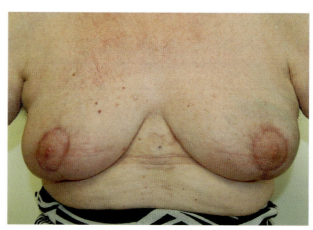

11.2.2.33 Result after excision of five cancers and bilateral mammoplasty.

REFERENCE

1. Hwang ES, Lichtensztajn DY, Gomez SL, Fowble B, Clarke CA. Survival after lumpectomy and mastectomy for early stage invasive breast cancer: The effect of age and hormone receptor status. *Cancer* 2013;119(7):1402–1411.

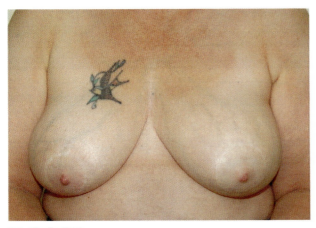

11.2.2.34 Result at 2 years after excision of two cancers left breast therapeutic mammoplasty and radiotherapy.

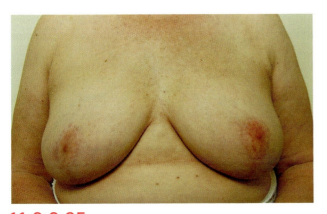

11.2.2.35 Wide excision mammoplasty and radiotherapy showing good symmetry at 2 years.

11.3 FLAP-BASED METHODS

AT A GLANCE

In the past, flaps were only used for repair of partial mastectomy defects after radiotherapy, but are increasingly being used for immediate repair before radiotherapy. However, many surgeons who perform the flap repair before radiotherapy prefer to wait until after the results of the permanent pathology, so-called, delayed, before radiotherapy. The advantage of performing flap repair before radiotherapy is that they do not require skin replacement and the skin island can either not be used or de-epithelialized and positioned under the native breast skin. In this scenario, the flaps tend to tolerate the radiotherapy. This approach can be ideal for patients with small-sized breasts with locally advanced breast cancer (known preoperatively to require radiotherapy) who do not have autologous tissue options for impact-based reconstruction after radiotherapy.

11.3.1 My approach (USA)

David Song

Oncoplastic surgery is an emerging field aimed at optimal aesthetic breast preservation in the face of breast cancer treatment. The importance of a multidisciplinary approach for optimal patient care and appropriate patient selection cannot be overemphasized. For maximum success, this discipline requires cooperation between various specialists including oncologic breast surgeons, breast radiographers, radiation oncologists, pathologists, and reconstructive plastic surgeons. In addition to patient selection, other issues such as timing of oncoplastic intervention, timely analysis of pathologic margin status, appropriate marking of the tumor bed for later radiation boost, and appropriate breast imaging studies are all crucial to the success of oncoplastic breast reconstruction.[1]

INTRINSIC BREAST FLAP ONCOPLASTIC RECONSTRUCTION: PREOPERATIVE ASSESSMENT
Patient selection

A multidisciplinary approach is taken to determine patient candidacy for breast-conserving therapy with oncoplastic reconstruction. Patients are identified as candidates for breast-conserving surgery with oncoplastic reconstruction when deemed at high-risk for a suboptimal aesthetic outcome with breast-conservation surgery alone. This particularly applies to patients with tumors located in the central or inferior poles of the breast and/or their tumor is relatively large compared to breast size. If more than one-third of the breast tissue needs to be removed during oncologic excision, then one option for volume replacement is a pedicled thoracodorsal artery perforator flap. This can be used for reconstruction instead of volume displacement involving intrinsic parenchymal flap rearrangement.

Oncoplastic reconstruction timing

In terms of timing of reconstruction, patients may undergo: (1) immediate (at the same time as partial mastectomy), (2) early (after partial mastectomy and pathological confirmation of negative margins, but before radiation therapy), or (3) delayed (after partial mastectomy and radiation therapy) oncoplastic reconstruction. Currently, the author's preferred technique for timing of oncoplastic reconstruction is an early procedure. Patients are thus given two surgical dates: the first for oncologic resection and sentinel lymph node biopsy, and the second after knowledge of final margin pathology. During the second surgical procedure, if pathologic margins are negative, then the patient may proceed with oncoplastic reconstruction; if pathologic margins are positive, then margin re-excision is completed followed by oncoplastic surgery. Immediate reconstruction is usually reserved for patients who lack adequate breast volume for re-resection should they have positive surgical margins.

INTRINSIC BREAST FLAP ONCOPLASTIC RECONSTRUCTION: SURGICAL TECHNIQUES
Surgical planning

In planning for oncoplastic reconstruction using intrinsic breast flaps, preoperative markings are jointly agreed by oncologic and plastic surgeons. These markings depend upon the location of the tumor and, thus, the resultant defect. In general, defects are grouped into the following categories: superior, medial, lateral, central, or inferior pole.

Surgical principles

The following principles are applied when approaching oncoplastic reconstruction, irrespective of breast quadrant. Firstly, dermoglandular flap selection for preservation of blood supply and repositioning of the nipple-areola complex. Secondly, parenchymal flap rearrangement to fill the lumpectomy defect and, finally, re-draping of skin over the rearranged parenchyma. Surgical resections that necessitate removal of the nipple-areola complex are reconstructed using a vertical reduction skin pattern approach, medial breast dermoglandular pedicle for neo-nipple-areola complex replacement, and parenchymal breast flap rearrangement with re-draping of skin.

Intrinsic breast flap reconstruction techniques based on defect location

Inferior pole defect

Midline inferior pole parenchymal defects are approached via a vertical breast reduction incision (**Figure 11.3.1.1**). Medial and lateral parenchymal pillars on either side of the inferior midline defect are elevated and brought to the midline to fill the defect. The skin is re-draped inferiorly over the parenchymal rearrangement, and the vertical inferior incision is closed in the midline. The nipple relies on its superior pedicle for its blood supply and can be repositioned in the setting of breast ptosis.

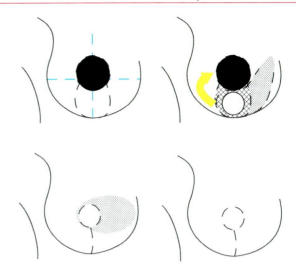

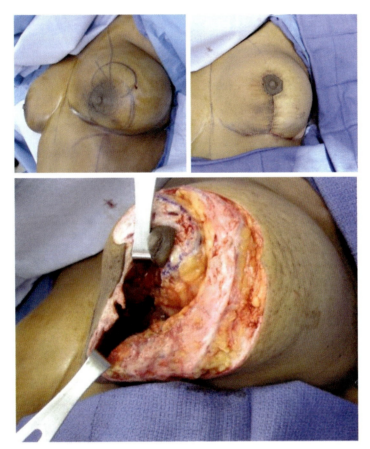

11.3.1.1 53-year-old female with large inferior and medial pole defect after lumpectomy, corrected with a lateral based breast flap and a vertical skin closure.

126 Immediate repair before radiotherapy

Central defect

Centrally located parenchymal defects involving removal of the nipple-areola complex are approached via a vertical breast reduction incision (**Figures 11.3.1.2 through 11.3.1.4**). A neo-nipple-areola complex is created from inferior-pole skin, based on either a medial or lateral dermoglandular pedicle which is rotated superiorly into the central defect. The vertical inferior incision is closed in the midline in the usual reduction fashion.

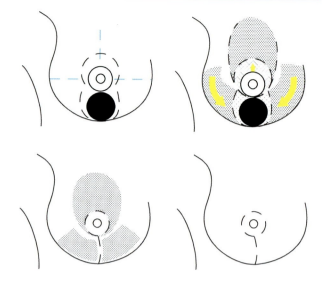

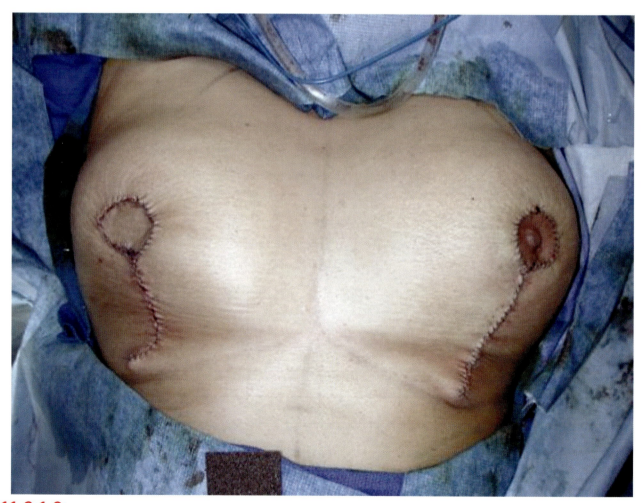

11.3.1.2 47-year-old female with a central pole, nipple-areola defect after lumpectomy corrected with a medial based dermal-glandular pedicle with skin to replace the nipple-areola defect.

11.3 Flap-based methods   127

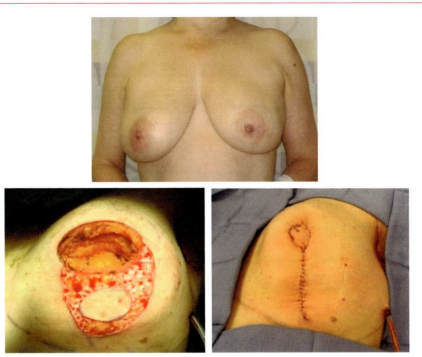

11.3.1.3 52-year-old female with central left lumpectomy reconstructed with a medial-based dermal-glandular pedicle with immediate on-table result.

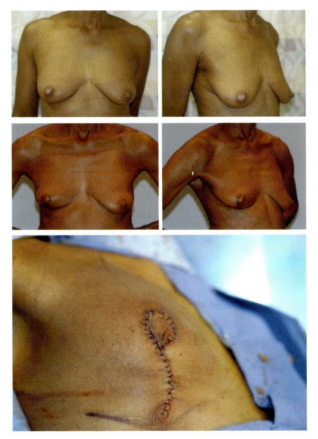

11.3.1.4 71-year-old female with Paget's disease of the right nipple showing the sequence of reconstruction with an immediate on-table and a 6-month follow-up result.

128　Immediate repair before radiotherapy

Superior pole defect

Superiorly located parenchymal defects are best approached using a z-plasty technique. A lateral parenchymal flap that extends inferiorly is elevated. Blood supply to the nipple-areola complex relies on a medial pedicle included within a parenchymal flap. A "parenchymal z-plasty" is performed, transposing the medial and lateral parenchymal flaps toward one another to fill the superior defect. The parenchyma is secured and skin closed in the standard fashion.

Lateral pole defect

Lateral parenchymal defects are approached via either a periareolar incision or a lateral breast incision (**Figures 11.3.1.5 and 11.3.1.6**). An inferior parenchymal flap is elevated and transposed into the lateral defect. The nipple-areola complex relies on a superomedial pedicle for its blood supply. The lateral skin is re-draped over the parenchymal rearrangement and closed primarily.

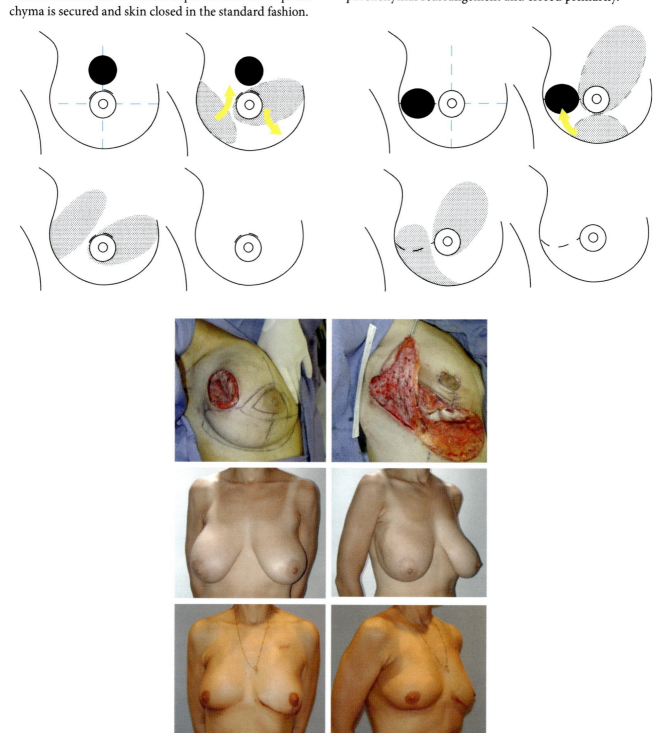

11.3.1.5　37-year-old female with re-excision lumpectomy for positive margins of the right breast. She was reconstructed with an inferiorly based parenchymal flap and a contralateral reduction for symmetry. The follow-up pictures after 2 years.

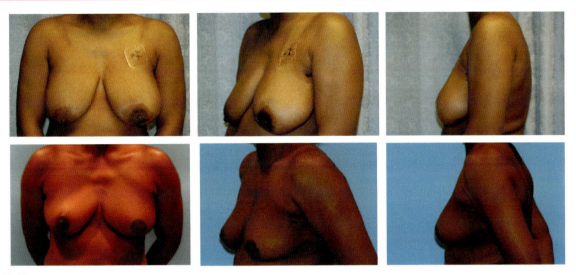

11.3.1.6 55-year-old female with left sub-areolar lumpectomy reconstructed with a superior and laterally based parenchymal flap. Results after 1 year.

Medial pole defect

Medial parenchymal defects are rare, but are approached using a periareolar incision. The medial parenchymal defect is shaped into a pie wedge (**Figures 11.3.1.7 and 11.3.1.8**). The skin is elevated from the superior and inferomedial parenchymal pillars adjacent to the wedge. These pillars are approximated into the defect for closure, and the skin is re-draped over the parenchymal rearrangement. The nipple-areola complex relies on a lateral pedicle and can be repositioned on this pedicle in the setting of ptosis. The skin incisions are closed primarily.

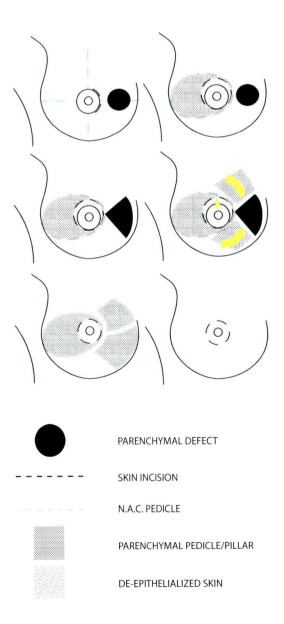

PARENCHYMAL DEFECT

SKIN INCISION

N.A.C. PEDICLE

PARENCHYMAL PEDICLE/PILLAR

DE-EPITHELIALIZED SKIN

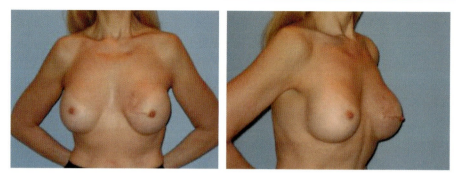

11.3.1.7 62-year-old female with a medial lumpectomy defect. She has a prior augmentation mammoplasty and was reconstructed with a "pie-wedge" closure technique.

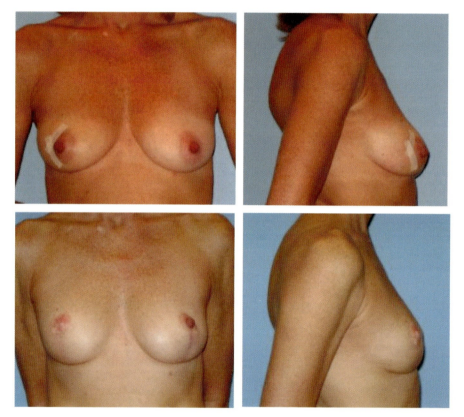

11.3.1.8 40-year-old female with a right breast lumpectomy removing the nipple and areola reconstructed with an inferiorly based dermal-glandular flap. Follow-up pictures at 8 months are shown after nipple reconstruction and areola tattooing.

INTRINSIC BREAST FLAP ONCOPLASTIC RECONSTRUCTION: POSTOPERATIVE CARE

Oncoplastic procedures are completed on an outpatient basis. Drains are typically not used postoperatively. Radiation therapy is typically initiated at least 4 to 6 weeks postoperatively. If a neo-nipple-areola complex creation is required as part of the oncoplasty procedure, the final nipple reconstruction is completed at 12 weeks postoperatively.

REFERENCE

1. Roughton MC, Shenaq D, Jaskowiak N, Park JE, Song DH. Optimizing delivery of breast conservation therapy. *Ann Plas Surg.* 2012;69(3):250–255. doi:10.1097/SAP.0b013e31822afa99.

11.3.2 Our approach (Europe)

Moustapha Hamdi and Luciano Tracia

DEFINITION

The advantages of pedicled perforator flaps have been widely described and are of proven benefit.[1] They are based on the principle of sparing the underlying muscle with its motor innervation when harvesting the flap which allows breast surgeons to resect a tumor with as wide margins as is oncologically necessary without fear of a poor cosmetic result. Moreover, these flaps act as a vascularized tissue scaffold that can support the survival of free fat grafts. This is especially important given that adjuvant breast irradiation is mandatory for breast-conserving therapy,[2] and fat transfer techniques may be used to overcome late sequelae of radiation therapy and achieve a larger breast volume. Pedicled perforator flaps that are useful for breast reconstruction can be classified according to the source vessel from which the perforator arises[3]:

- Thoracodorsal artery perforator (TDAP)
- The intercostal artery perforator (ICAP) originating from the lateral region (LICAP) or from the anterior region upon the rectus muscle (AICAP)
- The branch to the serratus anterior perforator (SAAP)
- The superior epigastric artery perforator (SEAP)
- The internal mammary artery perforator (IMAP)

ANATOMY

The thoracodorsal artery perforator flap

The major vascular axis supplying the TDAP flap is the same as that for the latissimus dorsi muscle, namely, the thoracodorsal vessels. The thoracodorsal vessels most commonly divide into two primary muscular branches: the transverse branch and the lateral or vertical branch[4] (**Figure 11.3.2.1**). The first perforator is located approximately 6–8 cm below the posterior axillary fold and may be either a branch of the distal part of the main thoracodorsal trunk or arise from its lateral branch. Subsequent perforators, up to a total of three, arise at intervals of 1.5–4 cm inferiorly off the lateral branch. The first and second perforators are found in a constant position in the majority of patients (**Figure 11.3.2.2a**). Each perforator follows an oblique course for 3–5 cm through the substance of the muscle giving off numerous muscular branches before penetrating through the dorsal thoracic fascia to supply the overlying skin and subcutaneous fat layers. Each perforating artery is 0.3–0.6 mm in diameter and accompanied by two venae comitantes.[5] The lateral row does not pierce the muscle and provides the "direct" TDAP perforators. The medial row of perforators enter and course through the muscle before reaching the skin and subcutaneous tissues.

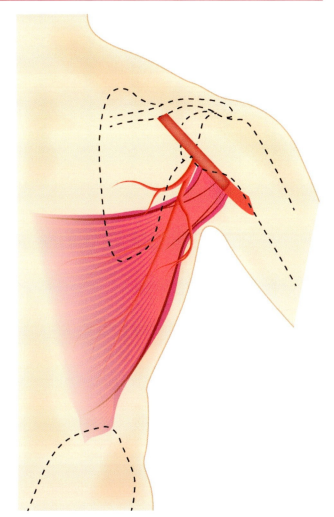

11.3.2.1 The anatomy of the thoracodorsal vessels. The main pedicle provides five branches; however, the vertical and the horizontal branches are the most developed. Perforators rise from both branches. Direct (septal) perforator is found in 55% of the cases (arrow).

The intercostal artery perforator flap

The intercostal vessels form an arcade between the aorta and the internal mammary vessels and divide into four segments designated vertebral, intercostal, intermuscular, and rectus (**Figure 11.3.2.3**). *Intercostal artery perforator* flaps are classified as follows:

1. The dorsal intercostal artery perforator flap which is based on perforators originating from the vertebral segment of the intercostal vessels.
2. The lateral intercostal artery perforator flap which is based on perforators arising from the intercostal segment.[6] The largest perforator is most frequently found in the 6th intercostal space and located approximately 1.0–3.5 cm from the anterior border of the latissimus dorsi muscle.
3. The anterior intercostal artery perforator flap. The nutrient perforators for this flap arise from the muscular or rectus segment (**Figure 11.3.1.3**).

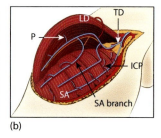

11.3.2.2 The illustrations show the relationship between the latissimus dorsi muscle, the thoracodorsal vessels and their perforators (muscular and septal), intercostal perforators and intercostal nerves, and the serratus branch.

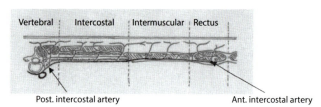

11.3.2.3 The intercostal vessels with its four segments: vertebral, intercostal, intermuscular, and rectal.

The serratus anterior perforator flap

The serratus anterior artery perforator flap is based on a connection between the thoracodorsal artery branch to the serratus anterior muscle and the intercostal perforators (**Figure 11.3.2.2b**). A vascular connection between the intercostal perforators and this serratus anterior branch is found in about 20% of cases, which allows harvesting of the intercostal perforator flaps with the serratus anterior branch as a main pedicle.

The superior epigastric artery perforator flap

The superior epigastric artery is the inferior continuation of the internal mammary artery and enters the rectus abdominis muscle on its deep surface, approximately 7 cm below the costal margin (**Figure 11.3.2.4**). Several perforators arise from branches of this vessel, between the costal margin and the first tendinous intersection.[7] The SEAP flaps are based on perforators arising from either the superficial or the deep branch of the superior epigastric artery, and the corresponding perforator flaps are named SSEAP and DSEAP, respectively. There are four dominant perforators which are evaluated within four zones along the Y-axis at distances of 0–5, 5–10, 10–15, and 15–20 cm.[8] Emerging perforators with a caliber of more than 0.5 mm are most frequently encountered within an area 2–6 cm from the midline and 0–10 cm below the xiphoid process.

The internal mammary artery perforator flap

The internal mammary (or thoracic) artery arises from the first part of the subclavian artery. It is accompanied in its distal part by two venae comitantes, which usually merge

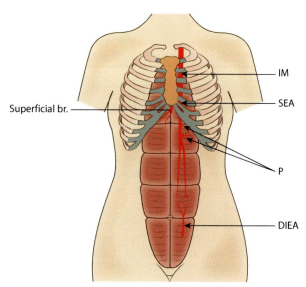

11.3.2.4 The anatomy of the SEA vessels. SEA = Superior epigastric artery, P = perforator, and DIEA = deep inferior epigastric artery.

between the third and fourth intercostal spaces to form one internal mammary vein.[9] The perforators arise from the first to the fifth intercostal spaces (**Figure 11.3.2.5**). The dominant perforator is located in the second intercostal space in two-thirds of patients, and the average pedicle

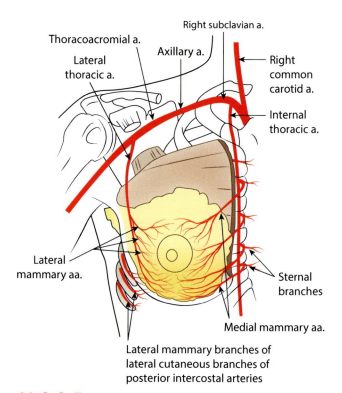

11.3.2.5 The anatomy of the internal mammary perforators.

length solely based on the dominant perforator is 47 mm (range: 30–66 mm).[10]

HISTORY

In 1995, Angrigiani and colleagues[11] first described the thoracodorsal artery perforator flap as a free flap transferred for management of a cervical burn contracture. It was subsequently employed as a pedicled flap for breast reconstruction by the senior author's group. As long ago as 1984, Badran and El-Helaly[12] harvested fasciocutaneous intercostal flaps without including the underlying muscles as a lateral intercostal free flap. Similar to its counterpart, the deep inferior epigastric artery perforator flap, the superior epigastric artery gives off a series of perforators that pass through the rectus muscle to supply the skin of the upper abdomen. Taylor and Palmer demonstrated these vascular patterns with injection studies.[13] The internal mammary artery perforator flap was first described by Kalender and colleagues in 2000 for reconstruction of the breast in patients with post burn skin contracture.[14]

PATIENT HISTORY AND PHYSICAL FINDINGS

Preoperative evaluation for these perforator flaps should include standard work-up as for any other flaps used for autologous breast reconstruction. Physical examination should focus on several aspects. Firstly, the skin of the lateral chest wall region is inspected for scarring or previous incision sites when assessing suitability for TDAP/LiCAP/SAAP flaps. Secondly, the skin of the abdomen is inspected for SEAP/AICAP flaps and that of the chest wall inspected for an IMAP flap. Finally, tissue bulk is examined with a pinch test.

IMAGING

Careful mapping of vessels is a decisive step in the choice of perforator and reduces both the operative time and complication rate significantly. Potential perforators are identified using a unidirectional Doppler (8 Hz), and the flap is subsequently designed to incorporate the chosen perforator.[15] For the TDAP, LICAP/SAAP flaps, Doppler examination is performed with patients in a lateral decubitus position with 90° shoulder abduction and 90° elbow flexion while for IMAP, SEAP, and AICAP flaps, this is done in a supine position. Preoperative localization of various perforators can also be determined with other modalities such as MRI and CT angiography.[16]

SURGICAL MANAGEMENT

The principal indications for pedicled perforator flaps are partial or total breast reconstruction (with or without implants), as a salvage procedure for partial free flap necrosis and for autologous breast augmentation.[17] It should be emphasized that if there is sufficient tissue, then reshaping the ipsilateral breast, together with reduction of the opposite breast for symmetrization might be the best option for some patients. The major indications for pedicled perforator flaps are defects of more than 30% of the breast volume, deformity involving two or more quadrants of the breast, or in cases where tumor resection leads to an unacceptable aesthetic result. In the majority of cases, contralateral breast remodeling is necessary to achieve breast symmetry, and further surgical correction with or without fat grafting might be needed if the initial deformity was severe.

Postmastectomy reconstruction with or without implant

The combination of an expander or implant with the latissimus dorsi musculocutaneous flap is well established as a safe and reliable method for postmastectomy reconstruction. Replacing the classical latissimus dorsi musculocutaneous flap with a TDAP flap is appealing for postmastectomy reconstruction as this spares one of the largest muscles in the body. Nonetheless, the TDAP provides less volume than the classical latissimus dorsi musculocutaneous flap, which may necessitate placement of an expander or an implant.[18,19] When the axillary-back fat fold is sufficiently thick, total breast reconstruction solely with a pedicled TDAP flap is feasible. With the resurgence of fat grafting during the last decade, use of pedicled perforator flaps as a vascularized tissue scaffold for subsequent fat grafting is a useful alternative to the free perforator flap for total autologous breast reconstruction.

Salvage procedure after partial necrosis of flap in breast reconstruction

The TDAP flap is preferred when necrosis involves more than 40% of the breast, but other options are the LICAP and AICAP flaps that can provide cover for necrotic areas at the lateral and medial extremities of the breast, respectively.

Autologous breast augmentation

Pedicled perforator flaps can be used for breast augmentation in situations such as breast asymmetry, bilateral breast augmentation without the use of implants, and as a combined augmentation-mastopexy procedure in massive weight loss patients. The TDAP and LICAP flaps are valuable techniques for redistribution of redundant tissue to reshape the breast according to the auto-augmentation principle.

Contraindications

1. *Inadequate surgical experience*: Harvesting of a local perforator flap demands considerable expertise and familiarity with the technique as well as sufficient knowledge of the local anatomy.
2. *Location of the deformity*: The area of the defect may be awkward to access, especially when localized in the inferomedial quadrant which is difficult to reach by a pedicled perforator flap based on the axillary vessels. However, the AICAP or SEAP flaps are ideal for defects in this location.
3. *Previous surgeries that could damage the vessels*
   - Previous axillary or thoracic surgery with damage to the thoracodorsal pedicle is a typical contraindication for using a TDAP flap, but not for a LICAP flap
4. *General diseases*
   - Clinical examination should consider general condition of the patient and the risk factors, such as obesity, smoking history, or any other disease (diabetes mellitus, arterial hypertension, etc.)

Positioning

- The choice of flap depends on the location of the tissue defect, the available donor sites, and the volume and type of tissue to be replaced (**Figure 11.3.2.6**).[20]
  - The **TDAP** is performed with patients in a lateral decubitus position with 90° of shoulder abduction and 90° of elbow flexion.
- The TDAP flap is ideally used for lateral and anterolateral defects of the thorax and has an important place in the reconstruction of the two lateral quadrants of the breast in partial breast reconstruction both in a primary and in a secondary setting. The flap is also useful in implant breast reconstruction for extra coverage of the device without sacrifice of the muscle or as an auto-augmentation flap in post bariatric patients.
- Due to its anatomical position, the same indications could be used for the **SAAP** flap when the TDAP is not available.
- The **LICAP** flap is performed in the same position of the TDAP. This flap has its main use as a pedicled flap for lateral thoracic defects, supero-lateral abdominal defects, axillary defects, and for (supero- or infero-) lateral breast defects, for which it is most commonly used. A previous damage to the thoracodorsal vessels becomes an indication for this kind of flap. The LICAP flap can also be used for post massive weight-loss patients. In these cases, patients desire to get rid of excessive tissue over the lateral thorax.[21] When performing a mastopexy in these patients, this excess tissue can be used as a pedicled flap in order to augment the breast (pedicled flap auto-augmentation). Obviously LICAP flaps have to be harvested bilaterally in these cases.
- The **SEAP** and the **AICAP** flaps are suitable in selected cases with defects of the medial/inferior breast quadrants with the patient placed in a supine position. Due to insufficient reach of the laterally based pedicled flaps, these flaps become the first option.
- Also for the **IMAP**, the patient is placed in a supine position. The indications of this flap are limited by the status of the contralateral breast.[22] In the literature, it

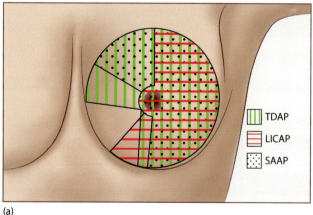 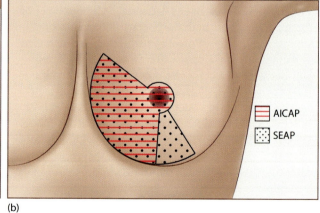

(a) (b)

11.3.2.6 Indications for pedicled perforator flaps depending on the defect location: (a) defects located on the superior, supero-lateral, and latero-inferior quadrants; and (b) defects located on the medial or infero-medial quadrants.

was used for the reconstruction of the contralateral small- to medium-sized chest wall defect localized in the medial area.

Approach

- **TDAP**
  - Before starting the surgery, the patient is preoperative marked. The borders of the LD muscle are marked with the patient standing with both hands pressed on the hips. The flap is designed like the classic LD myocutaneous flap, but to include any possible septo-cutaneous perforators.
  - The anterior aspect of the flap should always overlie the anterior border of the LD, reaching the lateral border of the inframammary fold.
  - The flap measurements are determined by the size of the defect and the ability for primary closure of the donor site estimated by a pinch test.
  - The skin paddle can be designed in every possible direction on a perforator. The flap should be done in a horizontal fashion (in the line of the bra) in order to better hide the scar in the bra, with the scar following the skin lines.
  - Flaps as big as 14×25 cm have been raised on a single perforator without any significant complications.
- **SAAP/LICAP**
  - Similar to the TDAP flap, the patient is marked pre-operatively with localization of the perforators and positioned on the lateral side. The flap dimensions can reach a length of 20–25 cm and a width of up to 12 cm can be closed primarily.
- **AICAP/SEAP**
  - The skin paddle is marked over the upper abdomen and incorporates the identified perforator. The flap is usually designed over the midline and extends later-ally under the inframammary fold along the rib.
  - The flap width is determined by pinch test and varies between 4 and 8 cm. The donor site is closed primar-ily, but refixation of the inframammary fold may be necessary in the case of a high-tension closure.
- **IMAP**
  - The flap is marked upon the main perforators includ-ing as much as possible of them. In this kind of flap, it is very important to choose carefully the design of the flap in order to respect the donor site and project an aesthetic reconstruction of the contralateral breast.[23]

SURGICAL TECNIQUE
TDAP (Figures 11.3.2.7 and 11.3.2.8)

- The flap is outlined above the mapped perforator as described above (**Figure 11.3.2.7a**).
- The skin incision is done at the lower and anterior border of the flap. The first step in dissecting a TDAP flap is to look for the anterior border of the LD mus-cle as this is the reference line for localization of the perforators.[24]
- The dissection is then pursued in the loose areolar plane just superficial to the muscular fascia, from lat-eral to medial and from distal to proximal. A nice per-forator bundle, including one artery and two veins, is looked for and is visually evaluated for its size and pulse (**Figure 11.3.2.7b**).
- In case the perforators are inadequate in size, the flap harvesting is continued as muscle sparing LD, preserv-ing a small piece of muscle attached to the posterior wall of the perforators, sacrificing only minimum fibers and, most important, salvaging the muscle innervation.
- If there is a doubt about the quality of the perforator, it is left in place and the dissection pursued until a final decision can be taken. If two (or more) perforators lie on the same line during intramuscular dissection, it is advisable to harvest them together in order to improve flap perfusion.
- Once the perforator is chosen, it is further freed into the muscle after opening of the fascia. Dissection is done by splitting of the muscle fibers longitudinally (thus not cutting them) with micro scissors, while clipping or coagulating side branches with a bipolar (**Figure 11.3.2.7c**).
- Dissection is pursued until the deep surface of the mus-cle is reached and dissection is then done by elevating the anterior border of the muscle, further freeing the pedicle 360°. Further dissection proceeds proximally as for a classical thoracodorsal pedicle such as in a latissi-mus dorsi flap elevation with sparing of the motor nerve branches (**Figure 11.3.2.7d**).
- The flap is passed under the lateral part of the LD mus-cle, which makes the pedicle even longer and finally to the breast defect through the axilla (**Figure 11.3.2.7e**).
- The flap is then paased into the axillary area (**Figure 11.3.2.7f**).
- The flap positioned into the breast defect (**Figure 11.3.2.7g**).

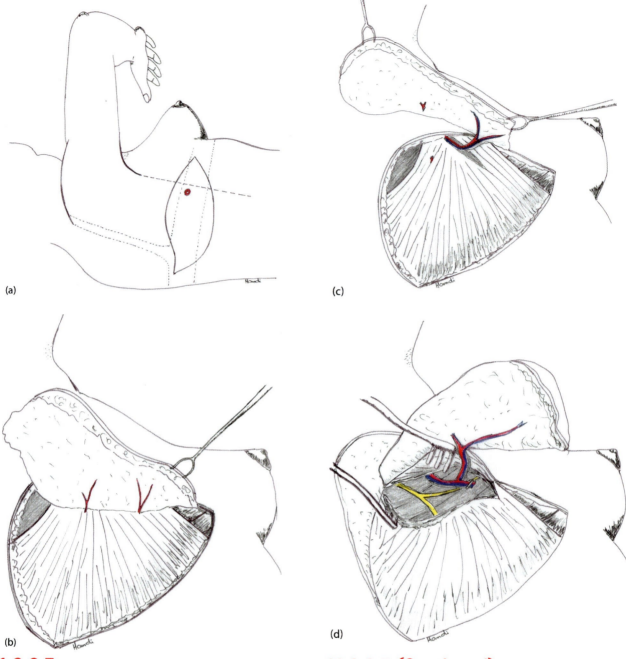

11.3.2.7 Surgical technique of TDAP flap harvesting. (a) Flap design. The perforator is located using unidirectional Doppler and is usually found 6–8 cm from the posterior axillary fold. The flap is designed within the bra region (dotted line) and crosses the anterior border of the LD muscle (dashed line). (b) The flap is dissected from the LD muscle until the perforators are encountered. *(Continued)*

11.3.2.7 (Continued) Surgical technique of TDAP flap harvesting. (c) The LD muscle is split and the perforator dissected back to the main pedicle. (d) The thoracodorsal pedicle dissected proximally to obtain adequate length. The TD nerve is preserved. *(Continued)*

11.3 Flap-based methods 137

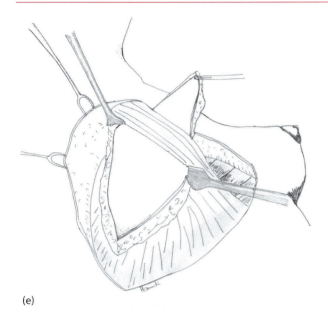

(e)

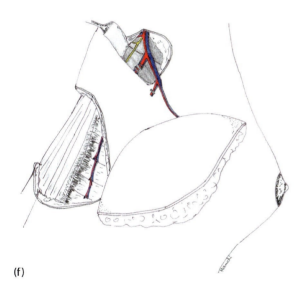

(f)

11.3.2.7 (Continued) Surgical technique of TDAP flap harvesting. (e) The flap is passed through the split LD muscle. (f) The flap is pulled through the axillary incision and into the breast defect.   (*Continued*)

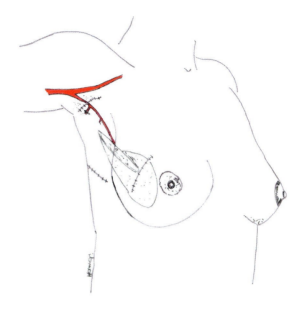

(g)

11.3.2.7 (Continued) Surgical technique of TDAP flap harvesting. (g) The TDAP flap folded to fit the breast defect.

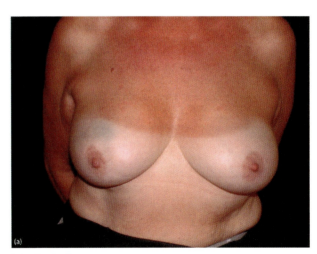

11.3.2.8 A 61-year-old patient with a ductal carcinoma in the superolateral quadrant of the right breast. The patient was a good candidate for quadrantectomy with axillary dissection and immediate partial breast reconstruction with a TDAP flap. (a–c) Preoperative views and TDAP flap design.   (*Continued*)

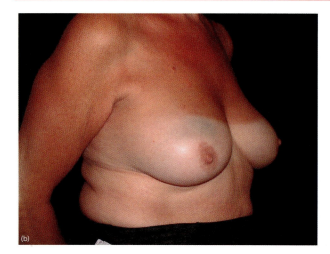

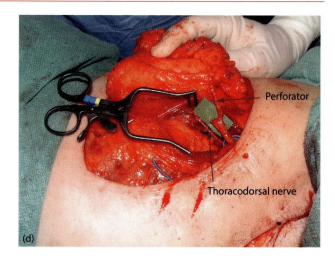

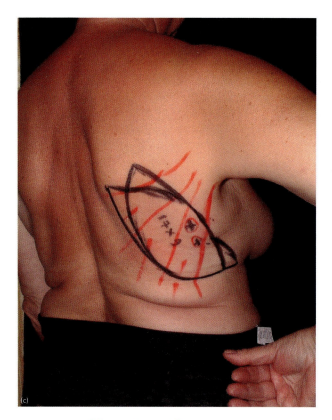

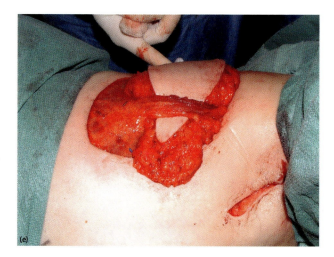

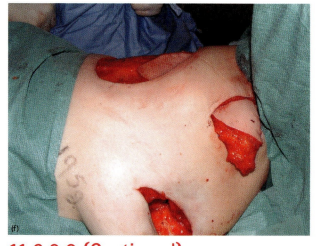

11.3.2.8 (Continued) A 61-year-old patient with a ductal carcinoma in the superolateral quadrant of the right breast. The patient was a good candidate for quadrantectomy with axillary dissection and immediate partial breast reconstruction with a TDAP flap. (a–c) Preoperative views and TDAP flap design.
(*Continued*)

11.3.2.8 (Continued) A 61-year-old patient with a ductal carcinoma in the superolateral quadrant of the right breast. The patient was a good candidate for quadrantectomy with axillary dissection and immediate partial breast reconstruction with a TDAP flap. (d) The flap was based on one perforator (arrow) and the thoracodorsal nerve was spared. (e) The flap was dissected and passed through the anterior border of the latissimus dorsi muscle. (f) The flap was then passed through the axilla and into the breast defect.
(*Continued*)

11.3 Flap-based methods 139

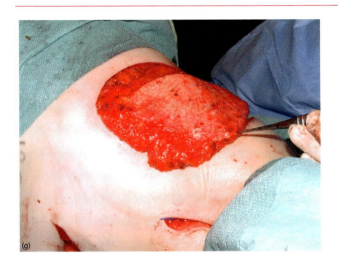

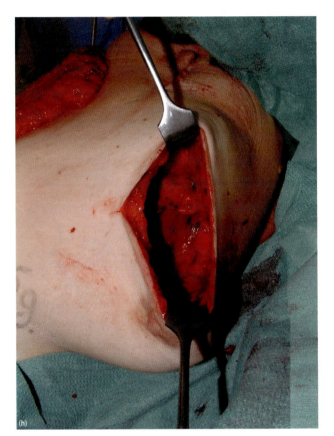

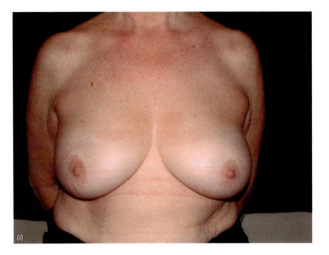

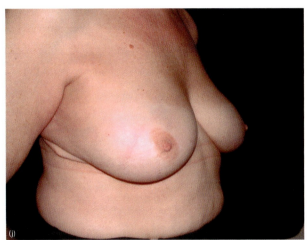

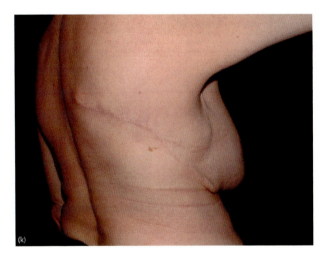

11.3.2.8 (Continued) A 61-year-old patient with a ductal carcinoma in the superolateral quadrant of the right breast. The patient was a good candidate for quadrantectomy with axillary dissection and immediate partial breast reconstruction with a TDAP flap. (g) The flap skin was de-epithelialized. (h) The defect in the superolateral quadrant of the right breast after resection of 195 g. *(Continued)*

11.3.2.8 (Continued) A 61-year-old patient with a ductal carcinoma in the superolateral quadrant of the right breast. The patient was a good candidate for quadrantectomy with axillary dissection and immediate partial breast reconstruction with a TDAP flap. (i–k) The results with the donor site 18 months postoperatively.

LICAP/SAAP

- The LICAP flap is raised from posterior to anterior to allow easy elevation of the flap. The thoracodorsal perforators are preserved until the intercostal perforator is found. Once the small cutaneous branch is identified, it is followed in order to encounter the bigger anterior branch.[25] The surgical technique is showed in **Figure 11.3.2.9**.
- If the size of the intercostal perforator is adequate, the further dissection is performed within the serratus muscle.
- The thoracodorsal perforator is then clipped and the flap raised on the intercostal perforator.
- A pedicle length of up to 5 cm can be obtained without dissection in the costal groove. With this length, defects of the superior and lateral parts of the breast can be reached.
- If a longer pedicle is required (for use as a pedicled or free flap) dissection of the pedicle should be carried out in the costal groove. This dissection can be performed by retracting both serratus anterior and latissimus dorsi muscle and by splitting their fibers in their length thus reducing donor site morbidity. The intercostal muscles should then be resected in order to expose the main pedicle after identifying its junction with the lateral cutaneous branch. When a sensate flap is harvested, the cutaneous nerve can be stripped from the intercostal nerve over the desired length.
- A longer pedicle length can alternatively be obtained when a connection of the intercostal perforator and the serratus anterior vessels are found. When such a connection is found (only 21% of cases) a serratus anterior

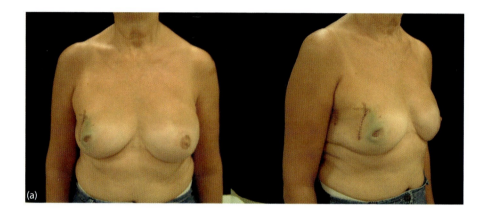

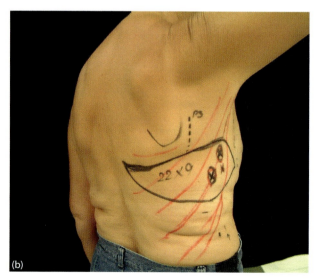

11.3.2.9 A 59-year-old patient was admitted for quadrantectomy with immediate partial breast reconstruction for a right-sided breast cancer located in the superolateral quadrant. (a) Preoperative views. (b) Flap design with the mapped perforators. *(Continued)*

11.3 Flap-based methods 141

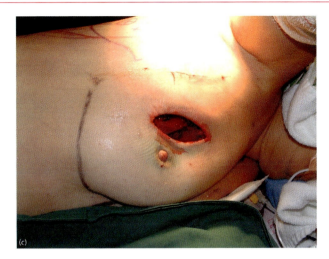

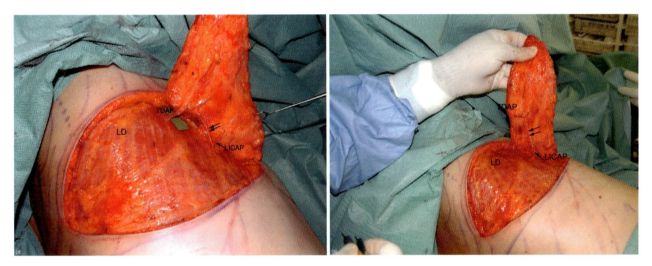

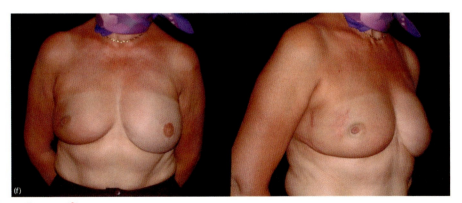

11.3.2.9 (Continued) A 59-year-old patient was admitted for quadrantectomy with immediate-partial breast reconstruction for a right-sided breast cancer located in the superolateral quadrant. (c) The defect after the quadrantectomy. (d) Perioperative view showing two perforators, one TDAP and one LICAP (one arrow). The IC nerve (two arrows) was included in the flap. (e) The TDAP was clipped and the flap was based on the LICAP (one arrow) and the IC nerve (two arrows). (f) Postoperative views.

artery perforator flap (**SAAP** flap) can be harvested. With a pedicle of 6–9 cm, this flap can reach well into the retro-areolar region.

AICAP

- The dissection is lateral to medial and in a caudal to cranial direction. The vessels are harvested by splitting the muscle (pectoral major or rectus abdominis based on the perforator location). Dissection through the rib might be necessary in lower intercostal spaces seven through nine.[26]
- **Figure 11.3.2.10** illustrates a clinical case of AICAP flap.

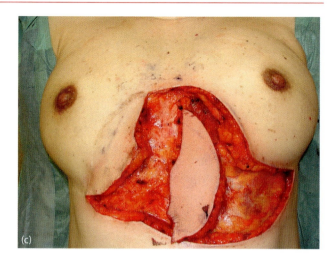

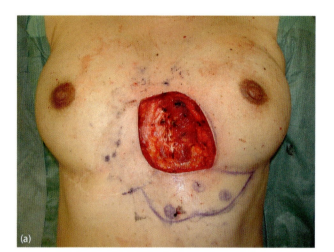

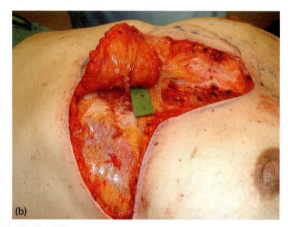

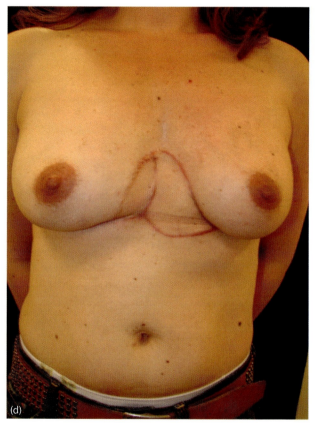

11.3.2.10 A patient with dermato-fibrosarcoma over the pre-sternal area treated with wide excision and coverage with an AICAP flap harvested on the right side. Two years later, she developed a local recurrence extending to the medial quadrant of the left breast. (a) Wide resection was done and an AICAP flap was designed over the upper left abdomen. Perforators were localized preoperatively using a handheld Doppler. (b) The anterior intercostal perforator was dissected within the left rectus abdominis muscle. *(Continued)*

11.3.2.10 (Continued) A patient with dermato-fibrosarcoma over the pre-sternal area treated with wide excision and coverage with an AICAP flap harvested on the right side. Two years later, she developed a local recurrence extending to the medial quadrant of the left breast. (c) The flap was completely islanded and rotated 90° anticlockwise to cover the defect. The donor site was primarily closed with abdominal advancement. (d) The final result with complete wound healing.

SEAP

- The SEAP flap, a transversely oriented skin island based on the superior epigastric artery perforators, can be designed to cross the midline. The flap's arc of rotation easily reaches the lower half of the anterior chest wall and the upper half of the abdominal wall.[27]
- Depending on the skin laxity and indication, the flaps are designed vertically on the paramedian region, or transversely under the inframammary fold or from the midline at the lower edge of the defect.
- The flap is approached from lateral to medial, suprafascial until the perforator is encountered. The SEA perforators usually have a suprafascial course above the deep fascia for 1–3 cm.[28]
- It's recommended to open the deep fascia only where the perforator pierces it. Rectus abdominis muscle fibers are then split and the perforator dissection is performed.

IMAP

- The dissection is done from the lateral to the medial aspect of the chest, in order to approach the vessels perforating the great pectoralis muscle and entering the flap medially on its deep surface within 3–4 cm from the midsternal line.[29]
- The perforators are isolated through the muscle, separating the fibers, until the mammary artery and veins are encountered. After the dissection of a single or multiple perforators, it's possible to choose to remove also a rib in order to gain more length of the pedicle.

PEARLS AND PITFALLS

Flap orientation	• Longitudinally oriented is indicated for upper arm, elbow, shoulder, neck, and upper back reconstruction • Transversally oriented is mostly indicated in reconstructive breast surgery. Closure takes advantage of the natural skin folds of the back and the scar can be hidden in the brassiere in women, but can still provoke a contour deformity especially if unilaterally harvested, though the defect is far less conspicuous than in the traditional musculocutaneous latissimus dorsi flap
Perforator mapping	• Use every available radiological method in your institute to map the perforator before surgery • Although, the anatomy of the LD muscle is constant, however, the location of the thoracodorsal and the intercostal perforators are quite variable • The CT scan and the use of the Doppler in the planning of the operation reduce the risk of mistakes

(Continued)

Flap harvesting	• Searching the mapped perforator started from lateral to medial. When no thoracodorsal perforators are found or they are very small, alternative options should be available for reconstruction (LICAP or SAAP)
	  • However, in specific situations, converting the TDAP flap to muscle sparing TD flap is imperative
	  • When tiny, but pulsating, perforators are found, a muscle-sparing thoracodorsal (MS-TD I) flap is used including a 4–2 cm LD muscle piece
	  • If the perforators are very tiny and non-pulsating, then the flap should be converted to (MS-TD II) flap, including up to 5 cm in order to incorporate a maximum number of perforators within the flap
	  • If most of the LD muscle is harvested, the flap is dissected as a MS-TD III

OUTCOMES

- Our experience has shown stable results in the long term.
- However, one may expect breast asymmetry due to different aging processes between the two breasts. The non-irradiated side may become more ptotic as compared to the irradiated one. On the other hand, the irradiated side may show sign of total breast atrophy. When the breast asymmetry becomes obvious, fat grafting alone or with contralateral breast remodeling is indicated.
- Lipofilling of the breast is proven to be a safe, reliable method for the transposition of autologous fatty tissue in contour deformed areas of the breast.[30,31]
- The fat grafting can be done in order to make refinements in volume, projection, or contour irregularities due to fat necrosis or flap contractures. Fat grafting is also used for the treatment of skin atrophy of the breast after irradiation.[32,33]

POSTOPERATIVE CARE

- Patients required an average of 1.3 procedures (range, 1–3), at an average follow-up of 2.5 years. Eighty percent of patients had only one reconstructive operation, 14% required a second operation, and 6% a third.
- Patient surveillance proceeds on a regular basis, in the same manner as before the surgical correction. Good communication between the plastic surgeon, oncologist, and radiologist is essential for proper follow-up of these patients.[34]

COMPLICATIONS

- Donor site morbidity after harvesting locoregional pedicle perforator flaps for partial breast reconstruction is reduced to a minimum.
- Partial or total flap losses are very rare incidents.
- Only a very limited rate of seroma formation has been observed and treated mainly conservatively.
- Wound dehiscence of the donor site usually when closed under tension is another infrequent event managed with local treatment.
- Unpleasing scars, flap contractures, and volume loss are less rare sequelae and may need secondary surgical treatment (lipofilling or liposuction).
- It is hard to predict the long-term outcomes of partial breast reconstruction with pedicled perforator flaps due to the indefinite impact of irradiation to the final result.
- Finally, some patients who undergo partial breast reconstruction with a TDAP flap document an initial decrease in forward arm elevation and passive abduction which recovers over time.

REFERENCES

1. Hamdi M, Rasheed, MZ. Advances in autologous breast reconstruction with pedicled perforator flaps. *Clin Plast Surg.* 2012;39(4):477–490. doi:10.1016/j.cps.2012.07.016.
2. Coopey SB, Tang R, Lei L, Freer PE, Kansal K, Colwell AS, Gadd MA, Specht MC, Austen WG Jr, Smith BL. Increasing eligibility for nipple-sparing mastectomy. *Ann Surg Oncol.* 2013;20(10):3218–3222. doi:10.1245/s10434-013-3152-x.
3. Hamdi M, Van Landuyt K, Monstrey S, Blondeel P. Pedicled perforator flaps in breast reconstruction: A new concept. *Br J Plast Surg.* 2004;57(6):531–539.
4. Angrigiani C, Rancati A, Escudero E, Artero G. Extended thoracodorsal artery perforator flap for breast reconstruction. *Gland Surg.* 2015;4(6):519–527. doi:10.3978/j.issn.2227-684X.2015.04.20.
5. Heitmann C, Guerra A, Metzinger SW et al. The thoracodorsal artery perforator flap: anatomical basis and clinical application. *Ann Plast Surg.* 2003;30:343–346.
6. Hamdi M, Spano A, Van Landuyt K et al. The lateral intercostal artery perforators: Anatomical study and clinical applications in breast surgery. *Plast Reconstr Surg.* 2008;121(2):389–396.
7. Hamdi M, Craggs B, Stoel AM, Hendrickx B, Zeltzer A. Superior epigastric artery perforator (SEAP) flap: Anatomy, clinical applications and review of literature. *J Reconstr Microsurg.* 2014;30(7):475–482. doi:10.1055/s-0034-1376399.
8. Schmidt M, Tinhofer I, Duscher D, Huemer GM. Perforasomes of the upper abdomen: An anatomical study. *J Plast Reconstr Aesthet Surg.* 2014;67(1):42–47. doi:10.1016/j.bjps.2013.08.017.
9. Schellekens PP, Paes EC, Hage JJ, van der Wal MB, Bleys RL, Kon M. Anatomy of the vascular pedicle of the internal mammary artery perforator (IMAP) flap as applied for head and neck reconstruction. *J Plast Reconstr Aesthet Surg.* 2011;64(1):53–57. doi:10.1016/j.bjps.2010.03.054.
10. Murray AC, Rozen WM, Alonso-Burgos A, Ashton MW, Garcia-Tutor E, Whitaker IS. The anatomy and variations of the internal thoracic (internal mammary) artery and implications in autologous breast reconstruction: Clinical anatomical study and literature review. *Surg Radiol Anat.* 2012;34(2):159–165. doi:10.1007/s00276-011-0886-7.
11. Angrigiani C, Grilli D, Siebert J. Latissimus dorsi musculocutaneous flap without muscle. *Plast Reconstr Surg.* 1995;96(7):1608–1614.
12. Badran HA, El-Helaly MS, Safe I. The lateral intercostal neurovascular free flap. *Plast Reconstr Surg.* 1984;73:17–26.
13. Taylor GI, Palmer JH. The vascular territories (angiosomes) of the body: Experimental study and clinical applications. *Br J Plast Surg.* 1987;40(2):113–141.
14. Kalender V, Aydm H, Karabulut AB, Ozcan M, Amiraslanov A. Breast reconstruction with the internal mammary artery pedicled fasciocutaneous island flap: description of a new flap. *Plast Reconstr Surg.* 2000;106(7):1494–1498; discussion 1499–1500.
15. Hamdi M, Van Landuyt K, Van Hedent E, Duyck P. Advances in autogenous breast reconstruction: The role of preoperative perforator mapping. *Ann Plast Surg.* 2007;58(1):18–26.
16. Hamdi M, Van Landuyt K, Ulens Sara et al. The role of the multi-detector CT scan images in preoperative perforator mapping and clinical applications of the superior epigastric artery perforators flaps. *J Plast Reconstr Asthet Surg.* 2009;62(9):1127–1134.
17. Hamdi M, Rasheed MZ. Advances in autologous breast reconstruction with pedicled perforator flaps. *Clin Plast Surg.* 2012;39(4):477–490. doi:10.1016/j.cps.2012.07.016.
18. Hamdi M, Salgarello M, Barone-Adesi L, Van Landuyt K. Use of the thoracodorsal artery perforator (TDAP) flap with implant in breast reconstruction. *Ann Plast Surg.* 2008;61:143–146.
19. Santanelli F, Longo B, Germano S, Rubino C, Laporta R, Hamdi M. Total breast reconstruction using the thoracodorsal artery perforator flap without implant. *Plast Reconstr Surg.* 2014;133(2):251–254.
20. Spear SL, Davison SP. Aesthetic subunits of the breast. *Plast Reconstr Surg.* 2003;112:440–447.
21. Hamdi M, Van Landuyt K, Blondeel P, Hijjawi JB, Roche N, Monstrey S. Autologous breast augmentation with the lateral intercostal artery perforator flap in massive weight loss patients. *J Plast Reconstr Aesthet Surg.* 2009;62(1):65–70.
22. Schwabegger AH, Piza-Katzer H, Pauzenberger R, Del Frari B. The internal mammary artery perforator (IMAP) breast-flap harvested from an asymmetric hyperplastic breast for correction of a mild funnel chest deformity. *Aesthetic Plast Surg.* 2011;35(5):928–932. doi:10.1007/s00266-011-9697-9.
23. Vesely MJ, Murray DJ, Novak CB, Gullane PJ, Neligan PC. The internal mammary artery perforator flap: An anatomical study and a case report. *Ann Plast Surg.* 2007;58(2):156–161.

24. Angrigiani C, Rancati A, Artero G, Escudero E, Khouri RK. TDAP: Island versus propeller. *J Plast Reconstr Aesthet Surg.* 2015;25:S1748–S6815(15)00555-0. doi:10.1016/j.bjps.2015.11.009.

25. Hakakian CS, Lockhart RA, Kulber DA, Aronowitz JA. Lateral intercostal artery perforator flap in breast reconstruction: A simplified pedicle permits an expanded role. *Ann Plast Surg.* 2016;24. [Epub ahead of print].

26. Carstensen L, Bigaard J. Management of central breast tumors with immediate reconstruction of the nipple-areola complex: A suggested guide. *Breast* 2015;24(1):38–45. doi:10.1016/j.breast.2014.11.002.

27. Kundu N, Chopra K, Morales R, Djohan R, Chung T, Gastman BR. Superior epigastric artery perforator (SEAP) flap: A novel approach to autologous breast reconstruction. *J Plast Reconstr Aesthet Surg.* 2015;68(4):519–524. doi:10.1016/j.bjps.2014.12.006.

28. Hamdi M, Craggs B, Stoel AM, Hendrickx B, Zeltzer A. Superior epigastric artery perforator (SEAP) flap: Anatomy, clinical applications and review of literatur. *J Reconstr Microsurg.* 2014;30(7):475–482. doi:10.1055/s-0034-1376399.

29. Rüegg EM, Lantieri L, Marchac A. Dual perforator propeller internal mammary artery perforator (IMAP) flap for soft-tissue defect of the contralateral clavicular area. *J Plast Reconstr Aesthet Surg.* 2012;65(10):1414–1417. doi:10.1016/j.bjps.2012.03.009.

30. Masia J, Bordoni D, Pons G, Liuzza C, Castagnetti F, Falco G. Oncological safety of breast cancer patients undergoing free-flap reconstruction and lipofilling. *Eur J Surg Oncol.* 2015;41(5):612–616. doi:10.1016/j.ejso.2015.02.008.

31. Rigotti G, Marchi A, Micciolo PR et al. On the safety of autologous fat grafting for breast reconstruction. *Plast Reconstr Surg.* 2012;130(1):206e–207e.

32. Khouri RK, Smit JM, Cardoso E et al. Percutaneous aponeurotomy and lipofilling: A regenerative alternative to flap reconstruction? *Plast Reconstr Surg.* 2013;132(5):1280–1290.

33. Rigotti G, Marchi A, Micciolo R et al. Autologous fat grafting in breast cancer patients. *Breast* 2012;21(5):690.

34. Veronesi U, Cascinelli N, Mariani L et al. Twenty-year follow-up of a randomized study comparing breast-conserving surgery with radical mastectomy for early breast cancer. *N Engl J Med.* 2002;347:1227–1232.

12

Postoperative margin assessment (re-excision or completion mastectomy)

DORIN DUMITRU AND JOHN R. BENSON

INTRODUCTION

Breast-conservation surgery is the preferred standard of care for surgical management of women with early-stage breast cancer over the past 30 years (NIH Consensus Conference 1991). Successful breast-conserving surgery entails excision of the tumor with an adequate amount of surrounding normal breast parenchyma such that negative resection margins are obtained. Longer-term follow-up data from several prospective randomized controlled trials have shown equivalent survival for breast-conserving surgery combined with breast radiotherapy when compared with *radical* or *modified radical* mastectomy.[1–5] Introduction of breast-conservation therapy has coincided with instigation of mammography screening programs and smaller tumor size at presentation. Moreover, improvements in adjuvant therapies including radiotherapy, chemotherapy, and hormonal/biological therapies have collectively reduced rates of ipsilateral breast tumor recurrence. There is a finite rate of ipsilateral breast tumor recurrence for breast-conserving surgery patients with current estimates supporting an annual rate of less than 1% for specialist breast practices and corresponding rates of between 3.5% and 6.5% at 10 years.[6] Systemic chemo-hormonal therapies reduce rates of ipsilateral breast tumor recurrence by approximately one-third, and targeted anti-HER2 therapies can lead to halving of local in-breast recurrence.

DEFINITION OF A NEGATIVE MARGIN

Despite these dramatic improvements in rates of local control following breast-conserving therapy, between 20% and 30% of patients with either invasive or non-invasive disease typically require re-operation following initial breast-conserving surgery (be this cavity re-excision or mastectomy). These high rates of re-excision are often prompted by a component of ductal carcinoma in situ (DCIS) that usually has no clinical correlate and may be under estimated in radiological extent. Until recently, there has been much variation in opinion among surgeons and radiation oncologists as to what constitutes an adequate or "negative" surgical margin after breast-conserving surgery. Surgical margin status is considered a major predictor of ipsilateral breast tumor recurrence, but no consensus on what constitutes an "*adequate*" width of surgical margin existed until publication of an international consensus statement in 2014.[7] Breast-conservation surgery represents a balance between oncological mandates and cosmetic outcomes with surgeons aiming to excise tumor with "*negative*" margins and acceptable cosmesis; the closer ink is to tumor, then the narrower are margins, and a positive margin is associated with ink on cancer cells (**Figure 12.1**). It is unacceptable to have tumor at the margin, as positive margins are associated with a doubling of rates of ipsilateral

12.1 Macroscopic assessment and inking breast wide local excision specimen.

Table 12.1

	Consensus mandate policies	
	Invasive cancer	Pure ductal carcinoma in situ (DCIS)
ABS UK[a]	1 mm	1 mm
SSO-ASTRO[b]	No tumor at ink	2 mm

[a] Association of Breast Surgery United Kingdom
[b] Society of Surgical Oncology and American Society of Radiation Oncology

breast tumor recurrence compared with non-positive margins. However, there is no correlation between the width of surgical margin and rates of ipsilateral breast tumor recurrence.[8] A large meta-analysis of 21 studies involving 14,571 patients with invasive breast cancer confirmed that the odds ratio for local recurrence was 2.42 (p<0.001) for positive margins (i.e., tumor at ink). Of note, there was no statistically significant difference in rates of local recurrence between individual margin widths of >1 mm, >2 mm, or >5 mm. In particular, a margin width of 2 mm or 5 mm was not necessarily better than a narrower margin of 1 mm when results were adjusted for follow-up time and receipt of a radiation therapy boost and endocrine therapy. A 1 mm margin was therefore deemed to be adequate, provided patients received optimal adjuvant therapy.[9] An update of this meta-analysis involving 28,162 patients with invasive breast cancer and 1506 ipsilateral breast tumor recurrence events employed random-effects logistic meta-regression and defined a relative category of "close" with cancer cells between a defined distance (negative margin) and the surgical resection margins (no tumor at ink).[10] The odds ratio for ipsilateral breast tumor recurrence was 1.98 (p < 0.001) for positive or close margins compared with negative margins and 2.44 (p < 0.0001) for positive versus negative margins. There was no statistical evidence that increase in margin width from "no tumor at ink" to 1, 2, or 5 mm influenced odds of local recurrence with adjustment for follow-up time. Nonetheless, it should be noted that this meta-analysis contained few cases permitting direct comparison of a 1 mm margin versus "no tumor at ink" and, for this reason, some have adopted 1 mm as the minimum margin mandate for invasive disease (with or without admixed DCIS) and also for pure forms of DCIS. Nonetheless, "no tumor at ink" has been widely adopted by more than two-thirds of surgeons in the United States, and this minimization of margin mandate has led to a reduction in rates of re-excision at Memorial Sloan Kettering Cancer Centre from 21% to 15%.[11] In the authors' own unit, a change in margin mandate from 2 mm to "no tumor at ink" led to a decrease in re-excision from 21% to 13%, and adoption of guidelines from the Association of Surgeons (United Kingdom) (Table 12.1) has stabilized re-excision rates between 16% and 17% (most cases of re-excision were for margins of 1–2 mm).[12]

INTRAOPERATIVE ASSESSMENT

Nonetheless, rates of re-excision and re-operation following routine breast-conserving surgery for both palpable and impalpable lesions remains high, and this has spurred efforts to develop reliable intraoperative assessment tools which can provide a timely indication of whether re-excision of a cavity margin is indicated at the time of primary surgery. More conventional imaging methods of specimen radiography and intraoperative ultrasound share the limitation of detecting DCIS and microscopic margin involvement, while pathological assessment with frozen section and touch imprint cytology is labor intensive. Many surgeons perform intraoperative radiological assessment of impalpable (and sometime palpable) lesions using portable x-ray devices such as the Faxitron (Figure 12.2). Use of intraoperative specimen radiography is reported to more than halve rates of positive margins (from 12% to 5%)[13] and the correspondingly high negative margin rates can potentially lead to savings of time and costs. Another intraoperative imaging modality for reducing rates of margin positivity at initial surgery is intraoperative ultrasound examination that can be performed by surgeons who are increasingly ultrasound competent. The COBALT study is a prospective multicenter trial that addressed the hypothesis that use of intraoperative ultrasound for wide local excision of palpable breast cancers could potentially spare healthy tissue and improve both surgical margin status and cosmesis. The trial was conducted in the Netherlands, but accrued

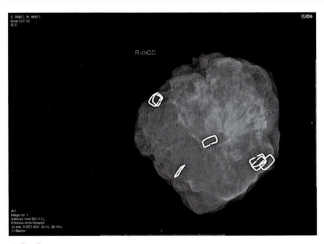

12.2 Faxitron: Intraoperative assessment of margins in breast-conserving surgery.

a relatively small number of patients in relation to number of centers and participating surgeons. Notwithstanding this comment, the trial had 80% power to detect an 18% reduction in re-excision rates. A total of 120 patients with palpable early-stage primary invasive breast cancer (T1–2, N0-1) were randomized to either ultrasound-guided surgery or palpation-guided surgery. Some patients had invasive tumor associated with DCIS that influenced rates of margin positivity. Nonetheless, use of ultrasound significantly increased the negative margin rate from 83% for palpation-guided surgery to 94% for ultrasound-guided surgery (p = 0.03). Moreover, specimen volumes at first excision were significantly lower for the ultrasound-guided surgery group compared with the palpation-guided surgery group (p = 0.048). The trial contained a quality of life sub-study and also examined cosmetic outcomes.[14]

Routine cavity shaves—Several observational studies have shown a significant reduction in rates of re-excision when additional tissue is routinely removed from all margins of the surgical cavity (× 6).[15,16] Some of these studies report adverse effects on cosmesis, but a trial involving 235 patients with stage 0–III breast cancer undergoing breast-conserving surgery randomized patients to routine cavity shaves or not. A statistically significant reduction in margin positivity rate (19% versus 34%; p = 0.01) was observed compared with rates prior to randomization (36% shave group; 34% non-shave group). This was associated with a commensurate reduction in rates of re-operation to achieve negative margins for the shave compared with non-shave groups (10% versus 21%, respectively; p = 0.02), although there was no statistically significant difference in total specimen weight between the two groups. A comparison of different intraoperative margin management techniques examined three approaches—routine cavity shave margins, macroscopic assessment of margins, and no formal margin assessment. Routine cavity shaves with a minimum thickness of 1 cm were taken from four surfaces and macroscopic assessment of margins involved the pathologist examining the specimen for assessment of margin status. The distance of tumor from each radial margin (medial, lateral, superior, and inferior) was measured and if less than 5 mm, this prompted re-excision of that margin. The remaining group underwent re-excision at the discretion of the operating surgeon. Comparison of the two groups with formal assessment of margins revealed a re-excision rate of 25% compared with 34% for the group without formal evaluation of margins and a statistically significant reduction in the chance of residual disease following the initial surgical procedure (p = 0.02).[17]

Intraoperative pathological assessment—Both frozen section and touch imprint cytology are time consuming and require input from a pathologist; in terms of diagnostic accuracy, frozen section was found on meta-analysis to have a pooled sensitivity of 0.86 (95% CI 0.78–0.91) and specificity of 0.96 (95% CI 0.92–0.98), but with significant heterogeneity between studies. By comparison, cytology had a pooled sensitivity of 0.91 (95% CI 0.71–0.97) and specificity of 0.95 (95% CI 0.90–0.98).[18] In terms of comparative performance, these tissue-based techniques are most accurate for intraoperative margin assessment, but have very poor uptake in routine clinical practice. This most likely relates to the logistical issues of slow turnaround times, disruption of operating lists, and availability of pathology staff.[18] Use of frozen section in American practice is reported to reduce rates of re-operation from 13.2% to 3.6%,[19] although it remains unclear what proportion of practices in the United States employ methods for intraoperative assessment of margins.[18]

Novel technologies—In recent years several novel technologies have been explored for assessment of margin status in light of limitations of the above methods, especially for impalpable lesions and DCIS. It is essential that these newer technologies have similar diagnostic accuracy to conventional methods involving pathological examination of tissue. However, they must also offer advantages in terms of turnover times, practicality, and cost before introduction into routine clinical practice (especially in a managed healthcare system). Some of these can detect microscopic malignancy at the edges of the surgical specimen and therefore have potential to reduce margin positivity and rates of re-excision to a much greater degree than conventional methods for intraoperative specimen radiography. These newer methods for assessment of surgical margins generally involve some form of electromagnetic waves that can penetrate the surface of the specimen to a variable depth and can distinguish between benign and

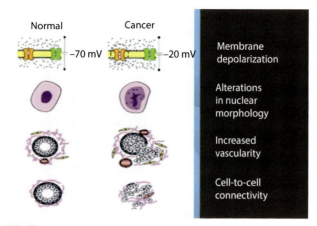

12.3 Probe: Tissue assessment.

malignant tissue in real time. Interestingly, recent reduction in margin mandate for both invasive and non-invasive cancer favor these emergent technologies which have limited tissue penetrance and are ideally suited for detection of cancer cells within 1 mm of the inked specimen margin.[17] These emergent technologies include devices such as MarginProbe, ClearEdge, and the intriguing intelligent knife which analyzes the electrosurgical plume of diathermy smoke to determine the structural lipid profile of tissue (**Figure 12.3**).[20–23] These can potentially improve intraoperative margin assessment and reduce rates of re-excision, but further technological developments are required to augment image processing and facilitate clinical usage. Moreover, these novel techniques must compare favorably with direct tissue-based methods such as frozen section and cytology that are notably more sensitive and specific than most other methods of margin assessment. Nonetheless, issues such as time, cost, and reliability must be factored into any final evaluation and devices such as MarginProbe and ClearEdge may find clinical utility in routine daily practice where surgical workloads are substantial.

ONCOPLASTIC SURGERY

The advent of oncoplastic surgery has permitted wide resection of breast tissue with tumor-free margins such that more than 20% of breast volume can be removed in non-cosmetically sensitive zones of the breast. Oncoplastic breast-conserving surgery for partial breast reconstruction involves either simple tissue mobilization (level 1) or local flap/therapeutic mammoplasty (level II). Volume displacement involves rearrangement of the remaining breast tissue with glandular advancement and redistribution of the parenchyma. By contrast, volume replacement techniques import additional tissue in the form of a flap and compensate for loss of volume from surgical ablation. Volume replacement maintains the original breast size without the need for contralateral adjustment. Oncoplastic breast surgery allows generous resection of tissue with several reports confirming mean tumor size to be twice that for conventional breast-conservation surgery (2.7 cm versus 1.2 cm). Furthermore, there is a reduction in rates of positive margins (12% versus 21%; $p < 0.0001$) with lower rates of re-excision (14.6% versus 4%),[24,25] but no convincing evidence to date of reduction in rates of in breast recurrence. Perhaps ironically, there is now a minimum margin mandate that may be achieved with conventional breast-conserving surgery without the need for more complex level II procedures that are typically associated with much wider margins of resection. Krishna Clough has applied these so-called adaptive oncoplastic techniques to a group of 175 consecutive patients with both unifocal (n=148) and multifocal breast cancers (n=27) and reports low re-operation rates, good cosmetic results, and minimal delays to adjuvant treatments. Of note, rates of margin positivity were comparable for unifocal (10.6%) and multifocal breast cancers (17.2%).[26]

It is essential to be confident about margins of resection when undertaking more complex oncoplastic surgery for partial breast reconstruction. When margin clearance is in doubt, it is preferable to undertake a two-stage procedure with initial wide tumor excision and then delayed partial breast reconstruction with a chest wall perforator flap or therapeutic mammoplasty. It is important to identify relevant cavity surfaces in the event of positive margins and re-excision can be undertaken at the time of the second surgical procedure (prior to any major glandular rearrangement or flap mobilization). Breast irradiation is administered between 4 weeks and 6 weeks after completion of surgery and should not be intermitted with first- and second-stage surgery.

The EORTC trial demonstrated the benefit of a single boost dose (16 Gy) for local control of unifocal invasive cancers treated with breast-conservation therapy.[27] Despite improved local control, a boost dose is associated with potential adverse effects with increased acute toxicity and long-term fibrosis. Moreover, there is a paucity of data pertaining to the impact of an additional radiation dose to breast tissue in the case of multiple ipsilateral breast cancers. The latter could involve either an extended boost or two separate fields for multicentric cancers in a large breast treated with double lumpectomy.

CONCLUSION

There is now clarity on the definition of a negative margin following breast-conserving surgery with a minimal mandate of either "no tumor at ink" or 1 mm for invasive cancer and

1 mm or 2 mm for DCIS (**Table 12.1**). These narrow margin widths have promoted lower rates of re-excision with attendant cost savings and reduced anxiety and inconvenience to patients. Several emergent technologies exist which can potentially improve intraoperative margin assessment and thereby reduce rates of re-excision. Nonetheless, further technological developments are required to augment image processing and facilitate routine clinical usage. These must compare favorably with direct tissue-based methods such as frozen section and cytology that are notably more sensitive and specific than most other methods of margin assessment. Oncoplastic surgery permits excision of tumors with wide surgical margins and therefore is associated with lower rates of re-excision and appears oncologically equivalent to standard breast conservation in terms of ipsilateral breast tumor recurrence. Moreover, there is evidence from observational studies testifying to the safety of oncoplastic surgical procedures for multiple ipsilateral cancers in carefully selected patients.

REFERENCES

1. Sarrazin D, Dewar JA, Arriagada, R et al. Conservative management of breast cancer. *Br J Surg* 1986; 73: 604–606.
2. van Dongen JA, Voogd AC, Fentiman IS et al. Long-term results of a randomized trial comparing breast-conserving therapy with mastectomy: European organization for research and treatment of cancer 10801 trial. *J Natl Cancer Inst* 2000; 92 (14): 1143–1150.
3. Veronesi U, Cascinelli N, Mariani L et al. Twenty-Year follow-up of a randomized study comparing breast-conserving surgery with radical mastectomy for early breast cancer. *New Engl J Med* 2002; 347: 1227–1232.
4. Litiere S, Werustsky G, Fentiman I et al. Breast conserving surgery versus mastectomy for stage I–II breast cancer: 20 year follow up of the EORTC 10801 phase 3 randomised trial. *Lancet Oncol* 2012; 13(4): 412–419.
5. Benson JR. Longer term outcomes of breast conservation therapy. Lancet Oncol 2012; 13(4):331–333.
6. Morrow M, Harris JR, Schnitt SJ. Surgical margins in lumpectomy for breast cancer—Bigger is not better. *N Engl J Med* 2012; 367: 79–82.
7. Moran MS, Schnitt SJ, Giuliano AE et al. Society of surgical oncology–American society for radiation oncology consensus guideline on margins for breast-conserving surgery with whole-breast irradiation in stages I and II invasive breast cancer. *Ann Surg Oncol* 2014; 21: 704.
8. Singletary SE. Surgical margins in patients with early-stage breast cancer treated with breast conservation therapy. *Am J Surg* 2002; 184(5): 383–393.
9. Houssami N, Macaskill P, Marinovich ML et al. Meta-analysis of the impact of surgical margins on local recurrence in women with early-stage invasive breast cancer treated with breast-conserving therapy. *Eur J Cancer* 2010; 46: 3219–3232.

10. Houssami N, Macaskill P, Marinovich ML, Morrow M. The association of surgical margins and local recurrence in women with early-stage invasive breast cancer treated with breast-conserving therapy: A meta-analysis. *Ann Surg Oncol* 2014; 21(3): 717–730.
11. Rosenberger LH, Mamtani A, Fuzesi S et al. Early adoption of the SSO-ASTRO consensus guidelines on margins for breast conserving with whole breast irradiation in stage I and II invasive breast cancer: Initial experience form Memorial Sloan Kettering Cancer Center. *Ann Surgical Oncol* 2010; 23(10): 3239–3246.
12. Jiwa N, Ayyar S, Provenzano E et al. The impact of a change in margin width on rates of re-excision following breast conserving surgery. *Eur J Surg Oncol* 2016; 42(5): S33.
13. McCornick JT, Keleher AJ, Tikhomirov VB et al. Analysis of the use of specimen mammography in breast conservation therapy. *Am J Surg* 2004; 188(4): 433–436.
14. Krekel NM, Haloua MH, Lopes Cardozo AM et al. Intraoperative ultrasound guidance for palpable breast cancer excision (COBALT trial): A multicentre, randomised controlled trial. *Lancet Oncol* 2013; 14(1): 48–54.
15. Jacobson AF, Asad J, Boolbol SK et al. Do additional shaved margins at the time of lumpectomy eliminate the need for re-excision? *Am J Surg* 2008; 196(4): 556–558.
16. Mook J, Klein R, Kobbermann A et al. Volume of excision and cosmesis with routine cavity shave margins technique. *Ann Surg Oncol* 2012; 19(3): 886–889.
17. Bolger JC, Solon JG, Khan SA et al. A comparison of intra-operative margin management techniques in breast conserving surgery: A standardized approach reduces the likelihood of residual disease without increasing operative time. *Breast Cancer* 2015; 22(3): 262–268.
18. St John ER, Al-Khudairi R, Ashrafian H et al. (2017) Diagnostic accuracy of intraoperative techniques for margin assessment in breast cancer surgery: A meta-analysis. *Ann Surg* 2017; 265(2): 300–310.
19. Boughey JC, Hieken TJ, Jakus JW et al. Impact of analysis of frozen section margin on re-operation rates in women undergoing lumpectomy for breast cancer: Evaluation of the national surgical quality improvement program data. *Surgery* 2014; 156(1): 190–197.
20. Thill M. MarginProbe: Intraoperative margin assessment during breast conserving surgery by using radiofrequency spectroscopy. *Expert Rev Med Devices* 2013; 10(3): 301–315.
21. JM Dixon, Renshaw L, Young O et al. Intra-operative assessment of excised breast tumour margins using ClearEdge imaging device. *Eur J Surg Oncol* 2016; 42: 1834–1840.
22. St John E, Rossi M, Balog J et al. Real time intraoperative classification of breast tissue with the intelligent knife. *Eur J Surg Oncol* 2016; 42(5): S25.
23. St John E, Balog J, McKenzie JS et al. Rapid evaporative ionisation mass spectrometry of electrosurgical vapours for the identification of breast pathology: Towards an intelligent knife for breast cancer surgery. *Breast Cancer Res* 2017; 19(1): 59.
24. Losken A, Dugal CS, Styblo TM, Carlson GW. A meta-analysis comparing breast conservation therapy alone to the oncoplastic technique. *Ann Plast Surg* 2014; 72(2): 145–149.

25. Chakravorty A, Shrestha AK, Sanmugalingam N et al. How safe is oncoplastic breast conservation? A comparative analysis with standard breast conserving surgery. *Eur J Surg Oncol* 2012; 38(5): 395–398.

26. Clough KB, Ganveia PF, Benyahi D et al. Positive margins after oncoplastic surgery for breast cancer. *Ann Surg Oncol* 2015; 22(13): 4247–4253.

27. Bartelink H, Maingon P, Poortmanns P et al. Whole breast irradiation with or without a boost for patients treated with breast conserving surgery for early breast cancer: 20 year follow up of a randomized phase 3 trial. *Lancet Oncol* 2015; 16(1): 47–56.

13

Delayed oncoplastic repair—before radiotherapy

MAURICE Y. NAHABEDIAN

AT A GLANCE

Unfortunately, not all surgeons have access to reliable intraoperative tumor margin assessment, but most patients do undergo preoperative mammography and ultrasonography that can assist in determining the most appropriate timing for repair. Certainly, obtaining a negative postoperative tumor margin is appropriate in the circumstance that a flap is selected as the method of repair. Regardless of the scenario, delayed repair before radiotherapy is a reasonable option. However, it is imperative that the repair be performed within a few weeks of partial mastectomy so that radiotherapy is not delayed.

Oncoplastic surgery of the breast has gained universal acceptance from both breast and plastic surgeons. Reconstructive outcomes have been shown to be associated with fewer contour abnormalities and improved symmetry compared to lumpectomy or partial mastectomy without reconstruction.[1-3] In addition, oncoplastic surgery prior to irradiation has fewer complications than mastectomy and radiation therapy.[4] Moreover, reconstructive procedures tend to have improved surgical and aesthetic outcomes when performed prior to radiation therapy when compared to procedures which follow radiation therapy.[1]

The purpose of oncoplastic surgery is to perform the ablative component of surgery together with the reconstruction prior to radiation therapy to minimize abnormalities of breast contour and surgical complications as well as improving clinical outcomes. Whether radiation therapy is performed immediately following partial mastectomy or on a delayed-immediate basis, but prior to radiation therapy is a matter of debate, but it is acknowledged that both options are preferred to delayed reconstructive procedures following radiation therapy. This chapter will address four important questions that include whether there is a difference between immediate and delayed-immediate repair prior to radiation therapy; the role of pathologic margin assessment; reconstructive differences in surgical approach, and optimal timing of oncoplastic repair.

COMPARISON WITH IMMEDIATE REPAIR BEFORE RADIOTHERAPY

Options for repair of partial mastectomy defects include volume displacement (reduction mammoplasty, tissue rearrangement, mastopexy) and volume replacement (local flaps) techniques.[5-7] Whether these are performed immediately and before radiation therapy or on a delayed-immediate basis prior to irradiation is dependent upon the reliability of tumor margin assessment intraoperatively. The advantage of immediate repair is a single operation with a small risk of positive margins on permanent pathology which may in some cases require salvage mastectomy. The advantage of a delayed-immediate repair before radiation is absence of any concerns about final pathologic margins. Once there is pathologic clarity of margins, the second operation is performed using a volume displacement or replacement technique—with avoidance of mastectomy. The second operation is ideally performed within 2 weeks of the ablative procedure, although, this may vary based on circumstances. A crucial question is whether surgical outcomes are different in terms of oncologic or aesthetic outcomes when comparing immediate or delayed-immediate cohorts.

There have been two studies evaluating and comparing outcomes after immediate and delayed-immediate oncoplastic surgery. Patel and colleagues studied 16 patients

Table 13.1 Patient satisfaction using BreastQ following immediate, delayed-immediate, and delayed oncoplastic reduction mammaplasty

	Overall score	Immediate	Staged-immediate	Delayed	p-value
Satisfaction with breast	3.67	3.83	3.72	3.49	0.26
Satisfaction with outcome	2.67	2.83	2.68	2.52	0.55
Psychosocial well-being	4.23	4.41	4.29	4.03	0.73
Sexual well-being	3.58	3.67	3.6	3.5	0.67
Physical well-being	4.29	4.31	4.5	4.04	0.42

Source: Patel, K. et al., *Plast. Reconstr. Surg.*, 127, 2167–2175, 2011.

Table 13.2 Complications and patient satisfaction following immediate, delayed-immediate, and delayed oncoplastic surgery

	Overall	Immediate	Delayed-immediate	Delayed	p
Patients	160	117	18	25	
Overall complications	28.10%	20.50%	33.30%	60%	0.001
Infection	5%	3.40%	0	16%	0.019
Fat necrosis	1.90%	0.90%	0	8%	0.047
Mean satisfaction	69.80%	72.80%	68%	61.80%	NS
Mean aesthetic outcome	62.50%	63.90%	54.60%	58.80%	NS

Source: Ergo, F.M. et al. *Plast Reconstr Surg.*, 135, 963–971, 2015.

statistical differences between the three cohorts. However, overall scores were highest for the immediate group followed by the delayed-immediate group for all quality-of-life domains except physical well-being (Table 13.1).

In a more recent study evaluating a larger cohort of patients, Losken reviewed 160 patients following immediate (n = 117), delayed-immediate (n = 28), and delayed (n = 25) oncoplastic reduction mammoplasty[9] (Table 13.2). The mean number of procedures for the immediate cohort was 1.2 and for the delayed-immediate cohort 2.4 (p < 0.001). The mean time interval from tumor excision to reduction for the delayed-immediate cohort was 0.7 days. Overall complication rates for the immediate and delayed-immediate cohorts were 20.5% and 33.3%, respectively. The most common complication for both cohorts was related to delayed healing and asymmetry or distortion.

ISSUES RELATING TO PATHOLOGICAL MARGINS

It is clear that oncoplastic surgery is a valuable tool in the setting of breast-conservation therapy, although the question of equivocal or positive pathologic margins following ablation remains. Fueling this controversy is lack of any clear definition of what constitutes a negative margin. A positive margin is usually defined as tumor cells present at the cut edge of the specimen or within 1 mm of the edge. A negative margin is generally accepted as >1 mm of normal cells between the tumor, although margins are often considered close when between 1–2 mm in width.

Various studies have evaluated the issue of positive margins and re-excision or mastectomy following oncoplastic surgery. Kaur and colleagues prospectively compared 30 women undergoing quadrantectomy with 30 women having an oncoplastic resection and found greater resection volumes (200 g vs 118 g; p = .16) and fewer close or positive margins (16.7% vs 43.3%; p = 0.5) in the oncoplastic group.[10] Giacalone compared 43 women undergoing quadrantectomy alone with 30 women having oncoplastic reconstruction and demonstrated surgical margins exceeding 5 mm in 67% of the oncoplastic group versus 42% of the quadrantectomy-alone group (p = 0.3).[11] In a review of 540 consecutive oncoplastic procedures, Fitoussi and colleagues showed incomplete excision in 19% of cases with half of these requiring completion mastectomy equating to 10% of all patients.[12] In a review of 20 women undergoing oncoplastic reduction, Losken and colleagues reported a re-excision rate of 15%,[13] while Kronowitz and colleagues found positive margins in 7% of women following oncoplastic breast surgery, all of whom had completion mastectomy.[14] Although the likelihood of a positive margin following partial mastectomy is low, studies have consistently shown that 5%–20% of patients will have close or involved margins.[12,15]

In a definitive attempt to resolve the issue of margins, Losken and colleagues evaluated margin status in two cohorts of ablative breast surgery patients. The first cohort had tumor resection with immediate oncoplastic

of whom 5 had immediate (pre-radiation), 6 had delayed-immediate (pre-radiation), and 5 patients had delayed reduction mammoplasty (postradiation).[8] The average time interval between ablative surgery and reduction mammoplasty was 0 days, 49 days, and 734 days, respectively. Of the 5 women with immediate oncoplastic reduction, 2 had positive margins on final pathology which necessitated salvage mastectomy (40%). Of the 6 women having delayed-immediate oncoplastic reduction mammoplasty, 1 developed local recurrence and underwent mastectomy (16.7%). Quality-of-life analysis was performed on three-quarters of patients post operatively and demonstrated no

Table 13.3 Tumor margin considerations following oncoplastic surgery versus breast-conservation surgery

Outcome	Oncoplastic	Lumpectomy	p
Number	83	139	
Lumpectomy weight	161 grams	57.3 grams	< 0.001
Mean margin invasive cancer	5.3 mm	3.3 mm	0.01
Closest margin to cancer	4.3 mm	2.8 mm	0.01
Positive margins (<1 mm)	24.10%	41.00%	0.01
Re-excision	12%	25.90%	0.01
Mastectomy	2.40%	9.40%	0.05

Source: Losken, A. et al., Aesthet Surg J., 34, 1185–1191, 2014.

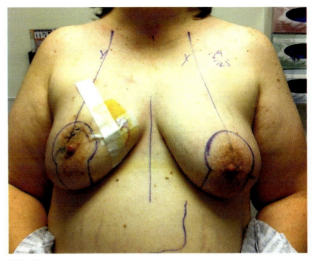

13.1 Preoperative image demonstrating wire localization of tumor.

reduction, while the second cohort had tumor resection alone.[13] Margin positivity was arbitrarily defined as the presence of cancer cells within 1 mm from the edge of the specimen (Table 13.3). The mean specimen weights for cohorts 1 and 2 were 161 and 57.3 grams respectively (p < .001) and the incidence of positive margins (<1 mm) was significantly lower for cohort 1 compared to cohort 2 (24.1% vs 41.0%; p = .01). Furthermore, the width of the closest margin to tumor (invasive or non-invasive) was significantly greater for cohort 1 compared to cohort 2 (4.3 vs 2.8 mm; p = .01). Re-excision was performed less frequently for cohort 1 compared to cohort 2 (12.0% vs 25.9%; p = .01) and completion mastectomy was performed less frequently for cohort 1 (2.4% vs 9.4%; p = .05). Odds ratio (OR) analysis confirmed that odds of a positive margin (defined as <1 mm) were almost 50% less for cohort 1 (OR: 0.47; 95% CI: 0.26–0.87; p = .02), and the odds ratio for re-excision were reduced by 60% (OR: 0.41; 95% CI: 0.19–0.88; p = .02). Thus, wider margins of excision obtained with oncoplastic surgery are associated with fewer positive margins and additional surgery (re-excisions and completion mastectomy) compared to lumpectomy alone.

There are several methods by which margins can be assessed intraoperatively for impalpable lesions. Most surgeons use wire localization under mammographic guidance (Figure 13.1), with the tip of the wire corresponding to location of the tumor (Figure 13.2). Following partial mastectomy, the specimen is color coded with ink (Figures 13.3 and 13.4). Additional margins from the superior, inferior, medial, and lateral aspects of the cavity may be taken and sent to pathology. Specimens are imaged to assess location of the tumor and wire (Figure 13.5). Once radiologic and pathologic confirmation of clear margins have been obtained, small clips or beads are placed along the perimeter of the cavity (Figure 13.6).

The delayed-immediate approach to patients with diffuse or extensive disease can effectively reduce the incidence of

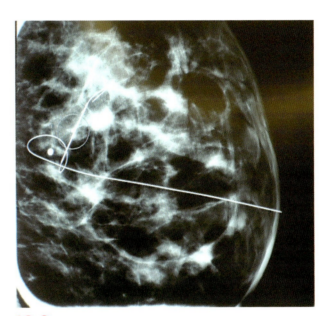

13.2 Preoperative radiographic image demonstrating the tip of the wire at the tumor.

positive margins.[14,16] There are circumstances when results of frozen section analysis are equivocal or there may be concerns regarding the multifocality or large size of a tumor. Patel and colleagues reported that the delayed-immediate approach was associated with lower rates of positive margins compared with the immediate group (0% vs 40%). It should be emphasized, however, that this was an early outcome study with a small number of patients. Furthermore, others have shown positive margins (<1 mm) in 24% in this setting.[13] As an aside, it is important to differentiate a positive margin from local recurrence. There was one patient in this series who developed local recurrence after a delayed-immediate oncoplastic reduction mammoplasty, and this led to completion mastectomy.

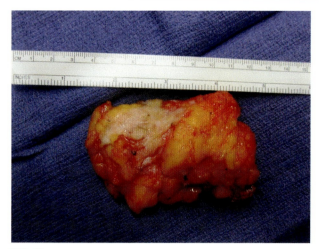

13.3 Intraoperative image of the excised breast specimen.

13.4 Intraoperative image of the color-coated breast specimen.

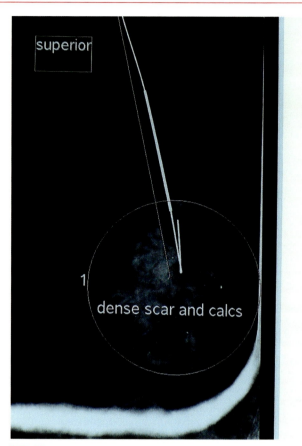

13.5 Postoperative radiographic image of the excised specimen and wire demonstrating complete excision.

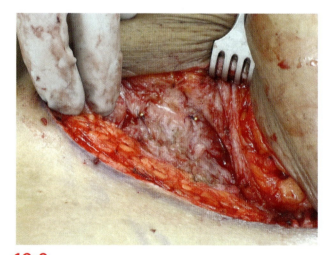

13.6 The ablative cavity is lined with implantable beads to assist the radiation oncologist in targeting the area.

RECONSTRUCTIVE DIFFERENCES IN SURGICAL APPROACH

Surgical approaches for immediate and delayed-immediate oncoplastic reconstruction are reviewed in this section. In the immediate setting, wire localization of the tumor is necessary and there is usually no scar tissue to excise. Moreover, the breast contour is likely to be natural and the parenchyma unaltered. In the delayed-immediate setting, the cancer has already been excised and there may be some early breast distortion with mild to moderate amounts of scar tissue. A seroma is often present at the excision site. In either scenario, radiation therapy has not yet been administered.

When a delayed-immediate reduction mammoplasty is scheduled, skin markings are delineated using an inverted-T or a short scar pattern. The orientation of the pedicle will be based on the site of the partial mastectomy defect. The pathological weight of the original specimen is ascertained.

Reconstructive differences in surgical approach 157

The partial mastectomy scar is excised when it lies within the proposed incision pattern and sometimes excised when outwith. The areola is delineated using a cookie-cutter with a diameter ranging from 38–45 mm, and the pedicle is oriented to optimize vascularity of the nipple-areola complex. The pedicle is usually opposite the side of the cavity. The partial mastectomy site is identified and any seroma is drained and the fluid discarded. The cavity is re-excised and sent for pathological examination. A pedicle is designed that can be readily rotated to fill the residual defect. The ipsilateral reduction mammoplasty is completed based on standard principles and the contralateral breast reduced in size using conventional techniques of reduction mammoplasty. **Figures 13.7 through 13.11** illustrate a patient who has undergone delayed-immediate reduction mammoplasty.

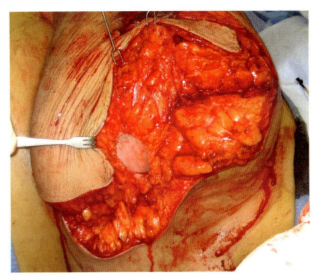

13.9 Intraoperative image of the old partial mastectomy cavity.

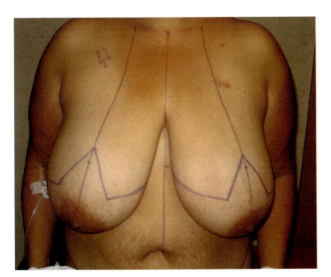

13.7 Preoperative image of a woman with mammary hypertrophy and left partial mastectomy scheduled for delayed-immediate reduction mammoplasty. The inverted-T pattern is delineated.

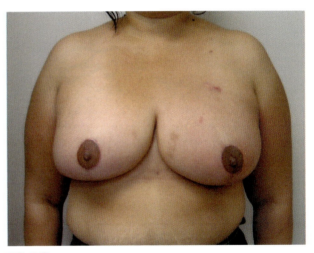

13.10 Postoperative image following bilateral reduction mammoplasty before radiation therapy.

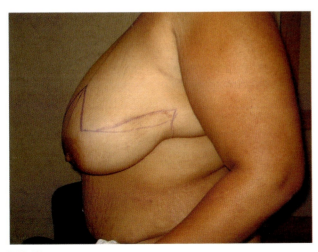

13.8 Preoperative lateral view demonstrating the excisional site.

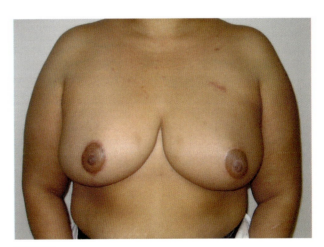

13.11 Postoperative image following bilateral reduction mammoplasty following radiation therapy.

When a delayed-immediate latissimus dorsi flap or TDAP flap is scheduled, the skin markings are once again delineated. The previous incision is opened, the partial mastectomy site is identified, and any seroma drained (the surface can be excised). An assessment of volume is made and the weight of the original specimen obtained. Once scar tissue is released, the patient is sat upright to assess the breast contour. The patient is then placed in the lateral decubitus position to facilitate harvesting of the flap which is based on standard principles and technique. The entire latissimus dorsi muscle or just a small portion can be harvested with the flap. A high subcutaneous tunnel is created and the flap is tunneled into the breast defect. A portion of the epidermal skin of the flap is sometimes exteriorized for monitoring purposes, while the remainder of the flap is de-epithelized and then inset.

OPTIMAL TIMING FOR ONCOPLASTIC REPAIR

The timing of oncoplastic repair is ultimately based upon whether or not clear margins are obtained at the initial excision. Final endpoints include aesthetic outcome, patient satisfaction, and the need for surgical re-excision or mastectomy. The untoward effects of reduction mammoplasty following breast conservation have been examined; Spear and colleagues have reported complications in 5/18 women (32%) ranging from minor delayed healing, superficial infection, and mild skin necrosis to major events (extensive fat necrosis requiring flap reconstruction).[17] Specific studies comparing oncoplastic reduction mammoplasty or latissimus dorsi flap reconstruction prior to radiation have revealed superior outcomes when compared to delayed reduction mammoplasty or latissimus dorsi flaps after radiation. Kronowitz and colleagues reported complication rates of 26% and 42% in immediate and delayed cohorts, respectively.[6] Within the immediate cohort, flaps were associated with higher complication rates than reduction mammoplasty or mastopexy. A good to excellent outcome was achieved in 57% of patients that had a reduction mammoplasty and in 33% of patients having a flap-based reconstruction in the immediate setting. Munhoz and colleagues performed a similar comparison and showed a complication rate of 22.6% and 31.5% in the immediate and delayed cohorts, respectively.[2] Skin necrosis was the most common complication in both cohorts and occurred in 7.5% and 18.4% of patients, respectively.

From an oncologic perspective, immediate or delayed-immediate oncoplastic surgery is feasible. Losken studied 86 consecutive women with either ductal carcinoma in situ (DCIS) or invasive breast cancer and assessed ipsilateral breast cancer recurrence following reduction mommoplasty.[18] After a median followup of 4.5 years, six women developed ipsilateral breast tumor recurrence within the tumor bed and outside the tumor bed in one patient. The 5-year rates of local control were 91% and 93% for women with in situ and invasive breast cancer, respectively. Interestingly, all women that required salvage mastectomy in this series had surgical

margins that were persistently positive. This underlines the benefits of delayed-immediate reconstruction following partial mastectomy especially in those women with DCIS, intraductal disease, or calcifications which are extensive. These characteristics are associated with the highest incidence of positive margins.

When evaluating patient satisfaction and aesthetic outcomes between immediate and delayed-immediate cohorts, there are no statistically significant differences.[9] A survey of 61 immediate and 15 delayed-immediate oncoplastic reduction mammoplasties revealed a mean patient satisfaction rating of 72.8% and 68%, respectively (**Table 13.2**). The mean aesthetic outcomes for immediate and delayed-immediate cohorts were 63.4% and 56.5% (non-significant difference). Thus, from an aesthetic and patient satisfaction perspective, it does not appear to matter whether the reconstructive procedures are performed immediately or delayed. However, what does matter is that these procedures be performed prior to radiation therapy.

CONCLUSION

In summary, both immediate and delayed-immediate are acceptable algorithms for oncoplastic surgery. The delayed-immediate approach allows for absolute confirmation of margins and is recommended for women with extensive DCIS, extensive intraductal disease/calcifications, and when there is intraoperative uncertainty about pathological tumor margin status. The ideal time interval between ablative and reconstructive surgery is generally considered to be about 2 weeks.

REFERENCES

1. Losken A, Pinell-White X, Hodges M, Ergo FM. Evaluating outcomes after correction of the breast conservation therapy deformity. *Ann Plast Surg* 2015; 74: S209–S213.
2. Munhoz AM, Aldrighi CM, Montag E. Outcome analysis of immediate and delayed conservative breast surgery reconstruction with mastopexy and reduction mammaplasty techniques. *Ann Plast Surg.* 2011; 67(3): 220–225.
3. Losken A, Dugal CS, Styblo TM, Carlson GW. A meta-analysis comparing breast conservation therapy alone to the oncoplastic technique. *Ann Plast Surg* 2014; 72: 145–149.
4. Peled AW, Sbitany H, Foster R, Esserman LJ. Oncoplastic mammoplasty as a strategy for reducing reconstructive complications associated with postmastectomy radiation therapy. *Breast Journal,* 2014; 20(3): 302–307.
5. Kronowitz SJ, Hunt KK, Kuerer HM et al. Practical guidelines for repair of partial mastectomy defects using the breast reduction technique in patients undergoing breast conservation therapy. *Plast Reconstr Surg.* 2007; 120:1755–1768.
6. Kronowitz SJ, Feledy JA, Hunt KK et al. Determining the optimal approach to breast reconstruction after partial mastectomy. *Plast Reconstr Surg.* 2006; 117(1): 1–11.

7. Losken A, Styblo TM, Carlson GW et al. Management algorithm and outcome evaluation of partial mastectomy defects treated using reduction or mastopexy techniques. *Ann Plast Surg.* 2007; 59:235–242.

8. Patel KM, Hannan C, Gatti M, Nahabedian MY. A head to head comparison of quality of life and aesthetic outcomes following immediate, staged-immediate, and delayed oncoplastic reduction mammaplasty. *Plast Reconstr Surg.* 2011; 127(6): 2167–2175.

9. Egro FM, Pinell-White X, Hart AM, Losken A. The use of reduction mammaplasty with breast conservation therapy: An analysis of timing and outcomes. *Plast Reconstr Surg.* 2015; 135(6): 963–971.

10. Kaur N, Petit JY, Rietjens M et al. Comparative study of surgical margins in oncoplastic surgery and quadrantectomy in breast cancer. *Ann Surg Oncol.* 2005; 12(7): 539–545.

11. Giacalone PL, Roger P, Dubon O et al. Comparative study of the accuracy of breast resection in oncoplastic surgery and quadrantectomy in breast cancer. *Ann Surg Oncol.* 2007; 14(2): 605–614.

12. Fitoussi AD, Berry MG, Fama F et al. Oncoplastic breast surgery for cancer: Analysis of 540 consecutive cases. *Plast Reconstr Surg.* 2010; 125:454–462.

13. Losken A, Pinell-White X, Hart AM, Freitas AM, Carlson GW, Styblo TM. The oncoplastic reduction approach to breast conservation therapy: Benefits for margin control. *Aesthet Surg J.* 2014; 34(8) 1185–1191.

14. Kronowitz SJ. Practical guidelines for repair of partial mastectomy defects using the breast reduction technique in patients undergoing breast conservation therapy: Reply. *Plast Reconstr Surg.* 2008; 122:676–677.

15. Rietjens M, Urban CA, Rey PC et al. Long-term oncological results of breast conservative treatment with oncoplastic surgery. *Breast* 2007; 16:387–395.

16. Song HM, Styblo TM, Carlson GW et al. The use of oncoplastic reduction techniques to reconstruct partial mastectomy defects in women with ductal carcinoma in situ. *Breast J.* 2010; 16:141–146.

17. Spear SL, Rao SS, Patel KM, Nahabedian MY. Reduction mammaplasty and mastopexy in previously irradiated breasts. *Aesthet Surg J.* 2014; 34(1): 74–78.

18. Eaton BR, Losken A, Okwan-Duodu D et al. Local recurrence patterns in breast cancer patients treated with oncoplastic reduction mammaplasty and radiotherapy. *Ann Surg Oncol.* 2014; 21:93–99.

EDITORIAL COMMENTARY

Over the past 15 years, there has been an explosion in use of oncoplastic repair after lumpectomy for early breast cancer. As a junior attending, I vividly recall seeing patients with gross radiation-induced deformities which they should not be forced to endure. These patients presented for consultation in search of a simple, non-complicated fix, but instead would be offered surgical remediation with a flap to optimize healing within the irradiated environment. However, this was not what these patients wanted, which is why they chose breast-conserving surgery at the outset as opposed to mastectomy Moreover, most of these patients would not be seen again for routine review. Thanks to the efforts and pioneering work of many breast and plastic surgeons in educating other colleagues and patients, these more extreme deformities are now seen less often. Chapters 11, 12, and 13 provide authoritative and up-to-date information from the world's leading experts. Readers are encouraged to embrace these principles and techniques and disseminate to others.

Dr. Silverstein is a pre-eminent leader in this field along with other individuals such as Krishna Clough and the late Steven Kroll. Silverstein explains the approach of "extreme oncoplasty" for patients who would not fulfill the usual conventional criteria for breast-conserving surgery and adamantly believes that this provides a better quality of life than mastectomy. In some aspects, I am in agreement with him, although nipple-sparing mastectomy with immediate reconstruction avoids radiation in the majority of patients, and can produce outstanding outcomes with contemporary levels of surgical expertise and materials. Furthermore, as for other contributing authors to this oncoplasty section, Silverstein prefers breast-conserving surgery in large-breasted patients who will subsequently require postmastectomy radiation. He maintains that this will lead to superior cosmetic outcomes and fewer complications.

Mr. Robert Douglas Macmillan presents the European perspective and provides a useful graphically categorized plot of breast size versus percentage volume of breast tissue excised. This can help determine the optimal technique for repair of partial mastectomy defects and in particular correlates with levels of patient satisfaction. By contrast, in my opposing chapter from the American perspective, I chose to focus on differentiating between use of Wise versus Vertical Pattern dermatoglandular repair. Like Silverstein, I would recommend that those patients with large breasts and advanced breast cancer undergo partial instead of total mastectomy, provided that this is feasible oncologically. This conservation approach is more likely to optimize outcomes and minimize complications. In general, large breasted patients who undergo mastectomy and whole breast reconstruction (even with a simple tissue expander inserted at the time of mastectomy) tend to fare less well both in the immediate postoperative period and longer term.

Dr. Dixon emphasizes the important point that patients who undergo oncoplastic surgery along with partial mastectomy have lower rates of positive tumor margins postoperatively (approximately 5%) compared with up to 20% for conventional breast-conserving surgery (lumpectomy). He also advocates increased usage of neoadjuvant chemotherapy in eligible patients, not only to increase suitability for partial mastectomy but also to reduce morbidity associated with mastectomy. Dixon favors any contralateral symmetrizing reduction at the same time as oncoplastic dermoglandular repair. In contrast, for patients undergoing Wise pattern dermoglandular repair, I prefer to perform any contralateral symmetrizing surgery approximately 6 months after completion of radiation therapy to obtain a better match with the repaired breast. In terms of other techniques discussed (including vertical oncoplasty), I am in agreement with Dixon and also perform contralateral symmetry surgery at the time of oncoplastic repair because the amount of parenchymal tissue that can be removed is limited (as opposed to a Wise pattern with an inferiorly-based dermoglandular pedicle technique). The contralateral breast can usually be revised with lipoaspiration alone and combined with de-epithelized nipple repositioning. Fat grafting of a repaired, irradiated breast volume can also seed stems cells into the breast parenchyma and this may subsequently reduce contractile forces (fat grafting can be undertaken for this purpose even when volume is not required).

Dr. Song is an expert in pedicled thoracodorsal artery perforator (TDAP) flaps for breast reconstruction and provides a brilliant and comprehensive chapter on his approach to flap-based repair. Nonetheless, I would challenge his decision to perform an immediate pedicled flap at the time of partial mastectomy due to the potential consequences of positive tumor margins postoperatively and the possibility of conversion to completion mastectomy. If a flap is raised at the time of partial mastectomy and a positive margin is found, then re-resection can be carried out and any additional loss of volume compensated for. However, in my personal experience, it is imperative to return to the operating room as soon as possible before the flap becomes integrated with surrounding breast parenchymal tissues.

The author has one such a scenario of extensively positive margins after performing an immediate TDAP flap repair which necessitated a completion mastectomy. The patient returned to the operating room soon after learning of the histology result and I was able to unfold the TAP flap and perform an immediate reconstruction with a breast implant after mastectomy. Moreover, post-mastectomy radiation was not required in this particular case. However, I would emphasize that in patients in whom I perform immediate dermoglandular oncoplastic repair and are found to have positive tumor margins on definitive pathology, re-operation occurs as soon as possible. I reopen the repair and expose the initial defect which allows the breast surgeon to perform additional resection of tissue in the region of the positive margin.

Dr. Hamdi is an innovator of local perforator pedicled skin flaps for repair of partial mastectomy defects and provides a detailed account of anatomy, patient positioning, indications, techniques, and pitfalls. Maurice Nahabedian is a leading advocate for delayed repair of partial mastectomy defects with a pause of approximately 2 weeks, after which time pathological margin status will be known. He provides an excellent overview of those studies that have compared quality-of-life outcomes and complications for patients undergoing either immediate or delayed repair before radiation. These studies conclude that immediate repair offers net benefits in this context. However, waiting for the permanent pathological margins before performing an oncoplastic repair is always a safe option, especially if intraoperative assessment of tumor margins is not available or there is evidence of extensive micro-calcifications or multicentric disease on preoperative imaging.

14

Delayed oncoplastic repair—after radiotherapy

AT A GLANCE

Many patients unfortunately continue to present for repair after radiotherapy. Besides relatively small defects that can be repaired using percutaneous needle release and serial fat grafting, patients presenting for repair after radiotherapy often require an extensive flap. Most of these patients are not interested in a flap repair, which is the reason they selected breast-conserving surgery. In addition, when flaps are used for delayed repair after radiotherapy the skin island must be used to replace breast skin because of a contracted irradiated deformity. Many of these patients did not even have skin resected as part of the tumor resection. Furthermore, the texture and color match of these flaps (intercostal or thoracodorsal artery perforator flap) do not match the breast. Advances in oncoplastic repair should prevent deformities requiring repair after radiotherapy.

14.1 CONSIDERATIONS

Charles M. Malata, Alexandra Bucknor,
and Chidi Ekwobi

Comparison of delayed repair after radiotherapy to immediate–before or delayed–before radiotherapy

INTRODUCTION

Oncoplastic breast-conserving surgery may be carried out as either a one- or two-stage procedure, and it is crucial to consider the effect of the timing of radiotherapy on any subsequent repair. The latter may be performed at different time intervals in relation to radiotherapy, namely, as follows:

1. Immediate reconstruction at the time of breast-conserving surgery and before radiotherapy: *"Immediate-before."*
2. Delayed reconstruction after breast-conserving surgery, but before radiotherapy. This is usually within the first 2–3 weeks after initial extirpative surgery when results of definitive histology are available: *"Delayed-before."*[1]

3. Delayed reconstruction after radiotherapy, usually months or years after radiotherapy: *"Delayed-after."*

"IMMEDIATE-BEFORE"

Whenever possible, partial breast reconstruction should be performed at the time of breast-conserving surgery and prior to radiotherapy. This *"Immediate-before"* radiotherapy reconstruction is indicated if a poor cosmetic result is anticipated after conventional breast-conserving surgery. For example, tumors that are located in high-risk anatomical sites, such as the infero-medial quadrant of the breast, where resection causes maximal distortion and any residual defects are likely to be conspicuous. This is a one-stage procedure which is often preferable to patients, but requires intraoperative confirmation of complete tumor excision with frozen-section analysis of the specimen. Where this is not possible, it is sensible to undertake surgery as a two-stage *procedure*. This tends to be associated with better cosmetic results as the color and texture of the breast is similar and does not involve manipulation of irradiated tissue.

Where possible, partial breast reconstruction should be performed at the time of breast-conserving surgery and prior to any radiotherapy. There are several advantages stemming from operating on radiation-naïve tissues. These include improved viability of any parenchymal rearrangement, greater pliability of local tissues, and increased ease of local or perforator flap reconstruction with a reduction in complications. Egro and colleagues reported that immediate oncoplastic reconstruction with reduction mammoplasty compared with delayed reconstruction is associated with fewer complications (20.5% vs 60.0%), fewer issues of asymmetry (8.5% vs 24%), and less frequent need for surgical revision (1.2% vs 2.2%).[2] Another important advantage relates to the psychological benefits of waking up with a reconstructed breast (still having two breasts).[3]

The need for coordination of a joint plastic, oncoplastic, breast and plastic surgery operating list may introduce delays in the timing of the surgery. Disruption to the reconstructive schedule may occur in the event of positive resection margins on the frozen section. Finally, there is a risk of compromise to the radiotherapy regimen: Thus, Motwani and colleagues found in a study of more than 100 patients ($n = 112$) that half (52%) of radiotherapy plans were compromised in patients undergoing immediate reconstruction followed by radiotherapy, compared with just 7% of those who did not undergo reconstruction ($p < 0.0001$). These compromised radiotherapy plans included reduced chest wall coverage and increased lung and cardiac exposure.[4,5]

"DELAYED-BEFORE"

"Delayed-before" radiotherapy reconstruction is performed after breast-conserving surgery, following disclosure of definitive histology, but before commencement of radiotherapy. This approach is indicated in those situations where there is uncertainty about whether clear margins will be obtained or not. This knowledge of resection margin histology is the main advantage over the immediate-before technique and avoids sacrifice of any immediate partial breast reconstruction in the event of positive margins. "Delayed-before" is also preferable to "delayed-after" radiotherapy from the point of view of surgical impact of radiotherapy on tissues, thus making volume displacement techniques involving parenchymal rearrangements feasible (**Figure 14.1.1**).

This category might also include those patients where immediate reconstruction was thought not to be appropriate or was perhaps declined by the patient, but who unexpectedly required reconstruction due to an unfavorable cosmetic result.

"DELAYED-AFTER"

This topic has been covered in Chapter 13.4.2 "Delayed Oncoplastic Repair—Before Radiotherapy."

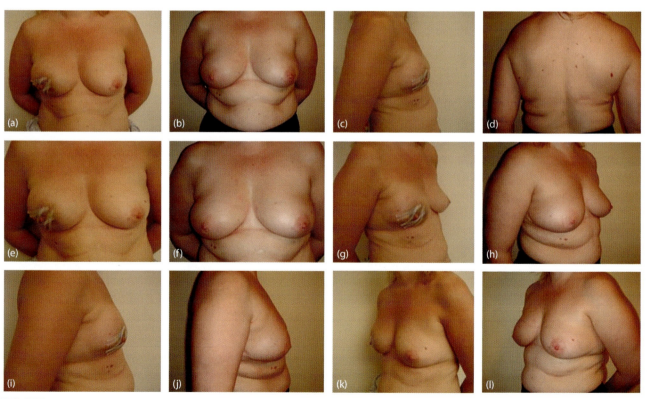

14.1.1 Delayed-immediate (*delayed-before*) partial breast reconstruction with a latissimus dorsi flap: This 47-year-old nulliparous patient required two lumpectomies to achieve clear margins of a laterally placed tumor of the right breast. The wide local excision was performed via a lateral periareolar incision with a lateral racquet extension without sacrificing the nipple areolar complex. A totally buried LD flap was used to reconstruct the breast-conserving surgical defect—the bulk was provided by the de-epithelialised skin, subcutaneous and subfascial fat combined with the muscle. Note the excellent correction of the contour deformity 18 months postoperatively and postradiation. The patient remains disease-free 9 years later.

Reconstructive implications: partial or whole breast irradiation

INDICATIONS

Whole breast external beam radiotherapy is used after breast-conserving surgery to reduce the risk of local recurrence in patients with early invasive breast cancer. The entire breast parenchyma is irradiated with a boost to the tumor site in selected cases.[6,7]

An alternative to whole breast irradiation is partial breast irradiation where the tissue around the tumor bed is targeted. Moreover, the overall duration of treatment can be shortened with these regimens for accelerated hypofractionated partial breast irradiation.[8] The European Society for Medical Oncology recommends that the use of accelerated partial breast irradiation might be considered in patients at low risk for local recurrence, including those with "unicentric, unifocal, node-negative, non-lobular breast cancer, up to 3 cm." Nonetheless, results of long-term randomized trials are still awaited.[7]

METHODS OF ADMINISTERING RADIOTHERAPY

1. *External radiotherapy*

   Conventional, external beam radiotherapy is distributed over a wide area of the breast. The use of multiple fractions reduces the incidence of acute side effects and increases therapeutic efficacy. External beam radiotherapy can be administered to the whole or part of the breast. Common radiotherapy regimens for whole breast irradiation typically involve 40–50 Gy delivered in fraction sizes of 2–2.67 Gy over a period of 3 or 5 weeks.[9]

2. *Internal breast radiotherapy*

   Intraoperative radiotherapy permits administration of a single radiotherapy dose.[10] Targeted intraoperative radiotherapy based on the TARGIT trial is performed immediately after removal of the cancer, when an applicator housing a radioactive source is placed in the tumor bed for up to 30 minutes. 20 Gy of radiation is delivered to the tumor bed, which attenuates to 5–7 Gy 1 cm beyond the surgical cavity, thus sparing the remaining breast tissue.[10] A randomized trial involving 3451 women with early-stage invasive ductal carcinoma (up to 2.5 cm in size) found that rates of ipsilateral breast cancer recurrence were significantly higher for TARGIT compared with external beam radiotherapy at a median follow-up of 5 years. However, these rates for the intraoperative group fell within a pre-defined non-inferiority margin and significantly fewer non-breast cancer deaths occurred in the TARGIT group. In addition, the study showed that there were "significantly fewer grade 3 or 4 radiotherapy-related complications with TARGIT than external beam radiotherapy."[10]

   Internal breast radiotherapy using brachytherapy is another method of delivering radiation directly to the tumor bed. Under anesthetic, an applicator with an external component is placed into the tumor bed. Patients are subsequently connected to a machine that delivers radioactive, metal beads through the applicator into the breast, patients receive this treatment over several days as an in-patient.

3. *Combined approach*

   In selected cases (namely, patients under the age of 50 years with extensive lymphovascular invasion on definitive histology), standard external beam radiotherapy is combined with a boost dose—"three randomized controlled trials evaluating a tumor bed boost after whole breast radiotherapy have shown a small, but statistically significant benefit to the delivery of a boost dose in patients with invasive tumors" (*Radiotherapy dose fractionation guidelines*).

EFFECTS OF RADIOTHERAPY ON THE BREAST AND RELATION TO RECONSTRUCTION AND CONTRALATERAL SURGERY

Radiotherapy has profound effects on tissues of the breast, initially causing generalized edema (**Figure 14.1.2**), skin erythema, and later hypo- or hyperpigmentation, telangiectasia, and atrophy. Subsequently, the breast parenchyma undergoes fibrosis and retraction.

The breast may increase in size after radiotherapy as it becomes chronically edematous from impaired lymphatic drainage or become smaller as a result of radiotherapy-induced fat necrosis, fibrosis, and consequent atrophy[11] with both contributing to postoperative asymmetry.[11] Radiotherapy tends to make the breast firmer, more indurated, and difficult to reshape at a later date (**Figure 14.1.3**).[12,13]

Reconstructive options depend on three key factors: (a) the ratio of the volume of the defect to that of the remaining breast tissue, (b) the location of the defect, and (c) the available local tissues.[14–17] It should be noted the irradiated breast may need further surgical manipulation in the future. Furthermore, the contralateral breast is frequently reduced or uplifted as a balancing procedure, but this should be deferred until the ipsilateral breast has settled to its final size and contours.

Notwithstanding such comments, in the authors' unit, the preference is to undertake simultaneous, contralateral breast reduction or mastopexy (**Figure 14.1.4**). Steps are taken to reduce the asymmetry by routinely leaving the contralateral breast at least 10% smaller than the ipsilateral breast which will be irradiated. This practice accords with the recommendations of the Emory University group;[18] the authors have not found radiation-induced shrinkage or fibrosis of the breast to be a major problem. However, others, such as the MD Anderson Cancer Center group, prefer any contralateral balancing reduction to be performed sequentially after radiotherapy to the index breast has been completed.[19]

166 Delayed oncoplastic repair—after radiotherapy

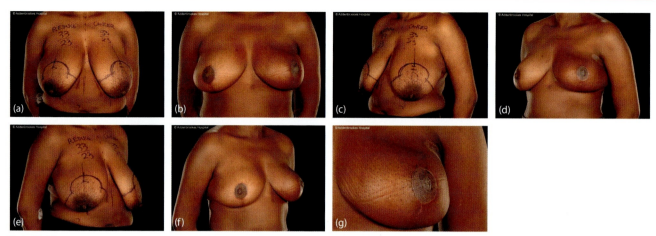

14.1.2 44-year-old patient with oedema and hyperpigmentation after whole breast irradiation following a left therapeutic mammoplasty for a superiorly located tumor and a balancing breast reduction—pre- and 6-month postoperative appearances. A closeup image of the left irradiated breast clearly demonstrates the swelling, peau d'orange appearance and the hyperpigmentation.

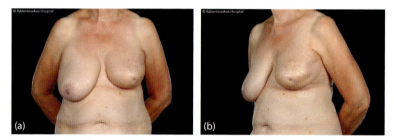

14.1.3 69-year-old with significantly unequal breasts (post-lumpectomy and radiotherapy 27 years earlier) presented with a 7 mm focus of high-grade DCIS. Despite this being amenable to another wide local excision (based on its size and location) a mastectomy was recommended instead because of the tight skin with prominent radiation changes combined with postradiation fibrosis of the breast tissue.

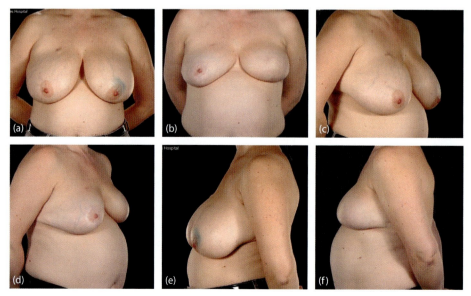

14.1.4 Balancing contralateral breast reduction at the same time as a Grisotti flap partial reconstruction of the left breast following wide local excision and sentinel lymph node biopsy. Corresponding right-sided images taken 4 years postoperatively.

Percutaneous needle scar release and autologous fat grafting

Autologous fat grafting to treat post-radiotherapy defects after breast-conserving surgery (BCS) has gained widespread popularity in recent years.[20,21] In addition to filling the breast contour defect, ameliorating the radiation-induced skin changes, and improving scarring, other advantages include reduced donor site morbidity and performing surgery that is technically less complex than flap harvest and transfer. Autologous fat grafting is indicated in volume restoration for patients who decline or are not suitable for the above two techniques, implant-based or flap reconstruction. Fat grafting is now being routinely employed to increase the range of reconstructive options available to surgeons in the delayed setting. Implant-based reconstruction after first-stage fat grafting is considered as a viable option for some women.[22,23] Fat grafting is particularly useful in small breasts (A/B/C cups) after conventional breast-conservation therapy to release scars.[16]

Reported concerns about use of autologous fat grafting for cases of breast-conserving surgery include fat necrosis, indeterminate calcifications, and whether secondary breast tissue changes might mask or even lead to cancer recurrence. The RESTORE-2 trial, a prospective clinical trial using autologous adipose-derived regenerative cell-enriched fat grafting for reconstruction of partial breast defects, has demonstrated no increase in local cancer recurrence.[21] Other recent reviews have likewise found no increased risk of cancer recurrence in this setting.[24,25] However, there remain concerns about this particular application of autologous fat grafting, notably among surgeons in continental Europe,[26] who highlight the potential for stem cell-induced changes in dormant cancer cells. Caution should be exercised, and the cancer recurrence risk should be determined before any surgery.[27]

Fat grafting is combined with percutaneous needle scar release or "subcision" of scars resulting from breast-conserving surgery that have been exposed to radiotherapy. In certain circumstances, subcision can be utilized on its own, as a minimally invasive procedure that can be performed under local anesthetic. In combination with fat grafting, it facilitates the injection of fat and attainment of a more aesthetic breast contour. Moreover, scar release helps prevent subsequent retraction and is best used for localized scars (**Figure 14.1.5**).

FAT TRANSFER

The technique used for fat transfer is largely based on the original techniques described by Coleman.[28,29] In the authors' institution, the entire procedure is almost always performed under general anesthesia, during which a single dose of prophylactic antibiotic is administered.

1. Preparation of the recipient site
   Scarring after lumpectomy may restrict the "filling" of the soft tissue defect, which needs to be addressed from the outset with pre-tunneling and, occasionally,

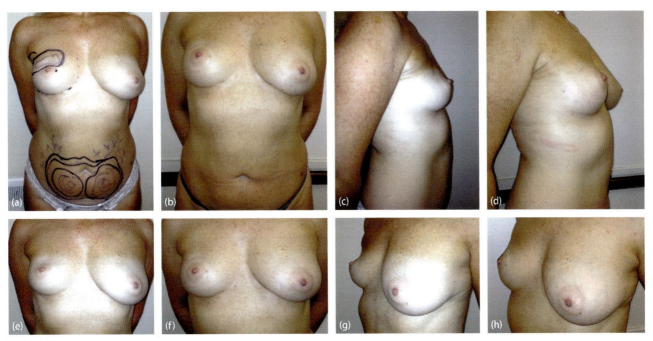

14.1.5 This patient had had a wide local excision followed by radiotherapy. She developed a deep contour defect with the skin tethered to the muscle. There was distortion of the nipple (pulled up), breast shrinkage, and significant asymmetry. The initial operation involved intraoperative scar release with a sharp v-shaped cannula + fat grafting from the abdomen. There was significant improvement after transferring 120 mL of fat (50 mL into the lumpectomy defect and 70 mL into the breast parenchyma). The patient subsequently underwent differential implant augmentation and contralateral symmetrising surgery (augmentation-mastopexy of the non-irradiated breast).

subcision of the overlying scar to release tethered skin. Subcision is performed with a 16 or 18 French gauge hypodermic needle or v-shaped dissector. The needle or v-dissector is introduced via a small stab incision in the skin in the vicinity of the scar. This site should allow easy reach of the "micro-injection" cannula to the recipient site, and the resulting scar should preferably be hidden. The entry point is then dilated with the use of a small hemostat to ensure easy passage of the cannula through the dermis. Pre-tunneling is then performed in a multi-planar and multi-directional manner, starting in the deeper tissues and then moving in a superficial direction. The efficiency of this process can be enhanced by using looping sutures into the scar and applying vertical traction to it which allows easier subcision.[30,31]

2. Fat harvest

Potential donor sites include the anterior abdominal wall, inner and outer thighs, and flanks. In terms of abdominal wall fat, it should be kept in mind that the lower abdominal pannus may later be required for autologous reconstruction and is therefore best avoided.

Areas are infiltrated with a mixture of 1 liter Hartmann's solution, 1 mL of 1:1000 adrenaline and 30 mL of 1% lignocaine.[32] After local infiltration and creation of tumescence, fat aspiration is performed, and the adrenaline effect helps minimize any bleeding. Use of a micro-aspiration needle with 10 cc Luer-Lock syringes is advantageous as these can be directly loaded into a centrifuge. For practical purposes, a larger liposuction cannula can be used to expedite fat harvest. Comparable volumes are harvested from mirror-image sites on both sides of the body.

A recent review suggested that use of larger harvesting cannulae may improve the viability of fat cells.[33] However, use of smaller cannulae incurs less donor site morbidity and enables selection of smaller fat globules, which may improve the ease of re-injection.[33]

3. Fat preparation

The fat is centrifuged at 3000 rpm for 3 minutes. The aqueous portion is decanted, and the fat oils at the top of the syringe are soaked off, leaving "pure fat." This separated fat is then transferred/loaded into 1 mL syringes for injection.

4. Injection technique

Pre-tunneling as described above facilitates the infiltration of fat with a micro-injection cannula. The technique personally used by the author involves advancing the cannula through the tissue, then injecting on partial withdrawal of the cannula. The process is repeated continuously in a multi-directional and multi-planar manner to promote dispersion of fat cells and increase surface-to-volume contact within the breast[34] which enhances graft take. Several layers of injection are preferable which effectively introduce tunnels of fat micro-beads. This, in turn, prevents accumulation of larger fat droplets which are themselves prone to fat necrosis, cyst formation, or calcification. Overcorrection of fat cells is necessary in order to mitigate the inevitable resorption and volume loss that occurs.[33] It is important to overcorrect because of the estimated (30%–50%) resorption of the fat grafted or transferred[35]; the authors recommend injecting twice as much as the resected volume.

There is growing confidence in the use of large-volume grafts to increase overall breast volume in addition to correcting any local defect resulting from breast-conserving therapy (**Figure 14.1.6**). These are usually harvested with 3 mm liposuction cannulae and processed similarly.

The main advantage of lipofilling or autologous fat grafting is that it enables reconstruction of defects in cosmetically sensitive areas that are otherwise difficult to manage such as the upper inner quadrants. Furthermore, it does not hinder mammographic interpretation and can potentially reduce the need for major glandular, myocutaneous, or perforator flap mobilization.

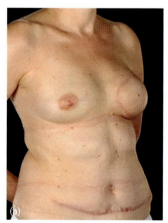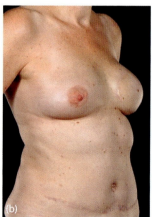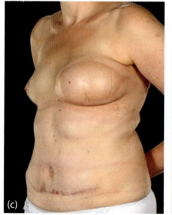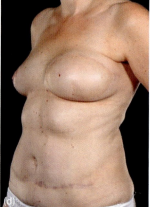

14.1.6 Volume augmentation of the contralateral breast by autologous fat grafting. 14 months after autologous flap grafting (AFG) to right breast to match the DIEP reconstructed left breast. This was performed under local anaesthetic in two sessions.

REFERENCES

1. Kronowitz, SJ. (2010) Delayed-immediate breast reconstruction: Technical and timing considerations. *PRS*. 125(2) 463–474.
2. Egro, FM., Pinell-White, X., Marie Hart, A., Losken, A. (2015) The use of reduction mammoplasty with breast conservation therapy: An analysis of timing and outcomes. *PRS*. 135(6) 963–971.
3. Kronowitz, SJ. (2007) Immediate versus delayed reconstruction. *Clin Plast Surg*. 34: 39–50.
4. Motwani, SB., Strom, EA., Schechter, NR., Butler, CE., Lee GK., Langstein, HN., Kronowitz., SJ., Meric-Bernstam, F., Ibrahim, NK., Buchholz, TA. (2006) The impact of immediate breast reconstruction on the technical delivery of postmastectomy radiotherapy. *Int J Radiat Oncol Biol Phys*. 66(1) 76–82.
5. Schechter, NR., Strom, EA., Perkins, GH., Arzu, I., McNeese, MD., Langstein, HN., Kronowitz, SJ. et al. (2005) Immediate breast reconstruction can impact postmastectomy irradiation. *Am J Clin Onc*. 28(5) 485–494.
6. National Institute for Clinical Excellence. (2009). *Early and Locally Advanced Breast Cancer: Diagnosis and Treatment*. NICE Clinical Guidelinesnice: Cardiff, WA. pp. 16–17 org.uk/guidance/cg80.
7. Senkus, E., Kyriakides, S., Ohnom, S., Penault-Llorca, F., Poortmans, P., Rutgers, E., Zackrisson, S., Cardoso, F., on behalf of the ESMO Guidelines Committee. (2015) Primary breast cancer: ESMO clinical practice guidelines for diagnosis, treatment and follow-up. *Ann Oncol*. 26(sup 5): v8–v30.
8. Lehman, M., Hickey, BE., Francis, DP., See AM. (2014) Partial breast irradiation for early breast cancer. *Cochrane Database Syst Rev*. 6:CD007077.
9. Vaidya, J., Wenz, F., Bulsara, M. (2006) Board of the Faculty of Clinical Oncology, The Royal College of Radiologists. *Radiotherapy Dose-Fractionation*. p26.
10. Vaidya, JS., Wenz, F., Bulsara, M., Tobias, JS., Joseph, DJ., Keshtgar, M., Flyger, HL. et al. (2014). Risk-adapted targeted intraoperative radiotherapy versus whole-breast radiotherapy for breast cancer: 5-year results for local control and overall survival from the TARGIT-A randomised trial. *Lancet*. 15;383(9917):603–613.
11. . Kronowitz et al. (2007).
12. Classen, J., Nitzsche, S., Wallwiener, D. et al. (2010) Fibrotic changes after postmastectomy radiotherapy and reconstructive surgery in breast cancer. A retrospective analysis in 109 patients. *Strahlenther Onkol*. 186:630.
13. Lam, TC., Hsieh, F., Salinas, J., Boyages, J. (2015) Can an immediate 2-stage breast reconstruction be performed after previous conservative surgery and radiotherapy? *Plast Reconstr Surg Glob Open*. 3(7):e473.
14. Clough KB, Kroll SS, Audretsch W. (1999) An approach to the repair of partial mastectomy defects. *PRS*. 104:409–420.
15. Clough, K., Lewis, J., Couturaud, B., Fitoussi, A., Nos, C., Falcou, M. (2001). Oncoplastic techniques allow extensive resection for breast conserving therapy of breast carcinomas. *Annals of Surg*. 237(1):26–34.
16. Kronowitz, S., Kuerer, H., Buchholz, T., Valero, V., Hunt, K. (2008). A management algorithm and practical oncoplastic surgical techniques for repairing partial mastectomy defects. *Plast Reconstr Surg*. 122(6):1631–1647.

17. Lee, J., Kim, M., Park, H., Yang, J. (2014). Oncoplastic volume replacement techniques according to the excised volume and tumour location in small- to moderate-sized breasts. *Gland Surg*. 3(1):14–21.
18. Losken, A., Hamdi, M. *Partial Breast Reconstruction: Techniques in Oncoplastic Surgery*. CRC Press: Boca Raton, FL. 2009. – CMM has the book at home – chapter.
19. Kronowitz. (2009)
20. Patel, AJ., Benson, JR., Malata, CM. The science of autologous fat grafting. In: Querci della Rovere G, Benson JR & Nava M (Eds.), *Oncoplastic & Reconstructive Surgery of the Breast*. 2nd Ed, Informa Healthcare Publishers. London, UK 2010, Chapter 29. 223–233.
21. Pérez-Cano, R., Vranckx JJ., Lasso JM., Calabrese C., Merck, B., Milstein, AM., Sassoon, E., Delay, E., Weiler-Mithoff, EM. (2012) Prospective trial of adipose-derived regenerative cell (ADRC)-enriched fat grafting for partial mastectomy defects: The RESTORE-2 trial. *Eur J Surg Oncol*. 38(5):382–389.
22. Sarfati, I., Ihrai, T., Kaufman, G., Nos, C., Clough, KB. (2011) Adipose-tissue grafting to the post-mastectomy irradiated chest wall: Preparing the ground for implant reconstruction. *JPRAS* 64(9):1161–1166.
23. Ribuffo, D. and Atzeni, M. (2012) Outcome of different timings of radiotherapy in implant-based breast reconstruction: Clinical evidence of benefit to using adipose-derived stem cells. *PRS*. 130(3) Viewpoints pp 498–499.
24. Gale, K., Rakha, E., Ball, G., Tan, V., McCulley, S., Macmillan, R. (2015). A case controlled study of the oncological safety of fat grafting. *Plast Reconstruc Surg*. 135(5), 1263–1275.
25. Brenelli, F., Rietjens, M., De Lorenzi, F., Pinto-Neto, A., Rossetto, F., Martella, S., Rodrigues, JR., Barbalho, D. Epub 2014 Oncological safety of autologous fat grafting after breast conservative treatment: A prospective evaluation. *Breast J*. 20(2):159–165. doi:10.1111/tbj.12225. Jan 23.
26. Mestak, O., Hromadkova, V., Fajfrova, M., Molitor, M., & Mestak, J. (2015). Evaluation of oncological safety of fat grafting after breast-conserving therapy: A prospective study. *Ann Surg Oncol* (PMID 26467459), epub ahead of print.
27. Ihrai, T., Charalambos, G., Machiavello, JC., Chignon-Sicard, B., Figi, A., Raoust, I., Yveline, B., Fouche, Y., Flipo, B. (2013) Autologous fat grafting and breast cancer recurrences: Retrospective analysis of a series of 100 procedures in 64 patients. *J Plast Surg Hand Su*. 47(4):273–275.
28. Coleman, S. (2001). Structural fat grafts—The ideal filler? *Clin Plas Surg*. 28(1), 111–119.
29. Pu, L., Coleman, S., Cui, X., Ferguson, R., Vasconez, H. (2008). Autologous fat grafts harvested and refined by the Coleman technique: A comparative study. *PRS*. 122(3), 932–937.
30. Pereira et al. (2015)
31. PRS Glob Open (2015)
32. Patel, A., Benson, J., Malata, C. (2010). The science of autologous fat grafting. In *Oncoplastic and Reconstructive Surgery of the Breast* (pp. 223–233). London, UK: Informa Healthcare Publishers.
33. Gabriel, A., Champaneria, MC., Maxwell, GP. (2015) Fat grafting and breast reconstruction: Tips for ensuring predictability. *Gland Surg*. 4(3):232–243.

34. Coleman, S. (1997). Facial recontouring with lipostructure. *Clin Plas Surg.* 24(2), 347–367.

35. Fehlauer, F., Tribius, S., Holler, U., Rades, D., Kuhlmey, A., Bajrovic, A. et al. (2003). Long-term radiation sequelae after breast-conserving therapy in women with early-stage breast cancer: An observational study using the LENT-SOMA scoring system. *Int J Radiat Oncol Biol Phys.* 1(55), 651–658.

36. Hoppe, D. et al. (2013). Breast reconstruction de novo by water-jet assisted autologous fat grafting–A retrospective study. *Ger Med Sci.* 11.

37. Nahabedian, MY., Momen, B. (2008) The impact of breast reconstruction on the oncologic efficacy of radiation therapy. *Ann Plast Surg.* 60: 244–250.

38. Bajaj, A., Kon, P., Oberg, K., Miles, D. (2004). Aesthetic outcomes in patients undergoing breast conservation therapy for the treatment of localised breast cancer. *Plas Reconstr Surg.* 114(6), 1442–1449.

39. Slavin, S., Love, S., Sadowsky, N. (1992). Reconstruction of the radiated partial mastectomy defect with autogenous tissues. *Plast Reconstr Surg.* 90(5), 854–865.

14.2 SURGICAL TECHNIQUE

14.2.1 Our approach (USA)

Jessica Rose and Aldona Spiegel

Increasing numbers of patients are seeking partial breast reconstruction after lumpectomy. Widespread screening mammography has resulted in earlier diagnosis, and neoadjuvant chemotherapy can downstage large tumors.[1,2] This had led to more patients to become candidates for breast conservation. Factors such as improved body image and comparable overall survival rates for stage I–II tumors in patients who undergo breast conservation versus mastectomy, influence a woman's decision to choose this option.[1-3] However, breast-conservation therapy may lead to aesthetic deformities which include skin damage and loss, distortion, retraction, and volume asymmetry. Furthermore, changes may occur in the nipple position and all these effects can be worsened by fibrosis and retraction from irradiation of the breast.[1,3] Since the majority of patients are treated with breast conservation, it follows that there are many women who desire treatment to reconstruct these defects which often present in a delayed fashion some time after completion of surgery and radiotherapy.[2] Ideally, partial breast reconstruction should be performed immediately, as operating within an irradiated field is more technically challenging, with less predictable results and higher rates of complications.[1,4]

Presuming the patient presents with a defect as a delayed effect of treatment and is free of recurrent disease, the precise nature of the defect must be assessed with careful examination of skin quality. The defect in breast skin and volume must be evaluated, in order to plan an appropriate form of reconstruction.[1,2] It cannot be overemphasized that radiation-induced skin damage and shrinkage is of particular concern for reconstructive surgeons. Partial breast reconstruction can be performed by utilizing either volume rearrangement (displacement) or volume replacement techniques. A key point of discussion with the patient is long-term radiological follow-up of both ipsilateral and contralateral breasts, as some women experience anxiety with surveillance mammography. They should therefore be informed that they do have the option of undergoing a completion mastectomy and total reconstruction.

VOLUME REARRANGEMENT

The breast lumpectomy defect is evaluated by estimating the missing breast volume and assessing the skin deficit or any nipple malposition, as well as the size and shape of the contralateral breast. If the deficits of breast volume and skin are minimal with good nipple position and an appropriately sized contralateral breast, then simple local tissue rearrangement can be performed involving advancement, rotation, or transposition of the breast parenchyma.[4,5] For more significant defects with nipple malposition and a larger contralateral breast with marked asymmetry, volume rearrangement techniques can be performed and range from local tissue repositioning to oncoplastic techniques using breast reduction or mastopexy methods. When more than 20% of breast tissue is removed, significant asymmetry results, and oncoplastic reduction techniques are warranted for reconstruction.[3,6] Patients need to have larger breasts (about D-cup size) and tumors or lumpectomy defects amenable to a reduction pattern. Breast tissue rearrangement is oncologically safe, and a contralateral reduction for symmetry can reduce the risk of a metachronous contralateral malignancy by up to one-third.[3] The options for the incision pattern are outside the scope of this chapter, but a variety of nipple pedicles and skin patterns can accommodate individual defects.[6] It is preferable to perform oncoplastic reconstruction in the immediate setting, as scarring and fibrosis from radiation cause a lack of tissue compliance, making it difficult to move tissue and fill the defect.[7] Delayed procedures have high rates of complications, reported in up to 50% of patients in some series, and include wound dehiscence, nipple necrosis, fat necrosis, and a poor aesthetic result.[1,2,4,7-9] Nonetheless, performing these partial breast reconstructions as a delayed procedure ensures negative resection margins.[2] When performing delayed oncoplastic reconstruction, it is important to compensate for radiation changes. It is preferable to create a wider nipple pedicle to undermine the skin as little as possible, fashion thick skin flaps (greater than 1.5 cm), and position the nipple appropriately. It is important to note that the irradiated side will remain mostly unchanged, whereas the contralateral side will stretch and have more ptosis over time.[1,10]

VOLUME REPLACEMENT

For those patients with larger defects and/or smaller breasts, volume replacement techniques are needed.[2,11] Patients with an unfavorable tumor-to-breast ratio have better aesthetic outcomes when flaps are used instead of local tissue or reduction techniques.[4] Although flaps supply healthy and well-vascularized tissue for the reconstruction, there are disadvantages to use of flaps: (1) the skin paddle may be of a poor color match, (2) the donor site may take away future reconstructive options in the event the patient suffers a recurrence, and (3) there are risks of donor site complications.[2] These options are better discussed according to location of the reconstruction.

SUPEROLATERAL/INFEROLATERAL DEFECTS

A number of reconstructive options exist for patients with lateral defects, since this location has the advantage of facilitating use of adjacent excess axillary tissue which can be mobilized and transferred into the defect. The thoracodorsal artery perforator flap[1,2,12]. which can be based on either the medial or lateral perforating branches permits a relatively large skin paddle.[12] The scar can be concealed under the arm, it provides a good skin color match, and this flap can help reduce unwanted axillary tissue.[4,5,12] Less commonly utilized fasciocutaneous perforator flap options include the lateral intercostal artery perforator flap[11,12] and the superior epigastric artery perforator flap.[1,11] The latissimus dorsi flap is also a common choice to fill in lateral defects and can usually be transferred with sufficient bulk of tissue to obviate the need for symmetrization procedure. Moreover, the muscle can be mobilized and used without a skin paddle if additional volume only is required.[1,5] However, a latissimus dorsi flap reconstruction necessitates a relatively large incision on the back, sacrifices a major muscle, and can be prone to donor site complications, particularly pain and seroma formation which can lead to wound dehiscence.[5]

Distal flaps are also a possibility in this context, including the mini-DIEP (deep inferior epigastric perforator) and mini-SIEA (superficial inferior epigastric artery) flaps that can be anastomosed to the serratus branch or the internal mammary vessels for purposes of preserving the thoracodorsal artery in case of possible need for a latissimus option as a salvage procedure for recurrence.[1,13]

MEDIAL DEFECTS

Medial defects are more difficult to reconstruct due to a general paucity of local tissue. Possible options for local flaps include the anterior interosseous perforator flap or the superior epigastric artery perforator flap.[1,11] For optimal aesthetic results in this location, distal flaps such as the mini-SIEA or mini-DIEP can be especially beneficial. The choice of these two options depends on the available vascular supply, but a SIEA flap can be performed if the artery is at least 1.3 mm and anastomosis to an internal mammary artery perforator permits improved size match. The benefits of choosing an abdominally based flap include an acceptable donor site scar and improved abdominal wall contour from removal of redundant tissue.[13] However, this does restrict reconstructive options if the patient has a recurrence and requires mastectomy

at a future date. Patients need to be informed about these issues in detail before this option is chosen.[2,13] Less commonly employed options for reconstructing these areas include anterior intercostal perforator flaps and distally based latissimus flaps.[1,11]

Fat grafting is a more controversial option for volume replacement and may require multiple treatment sessions.[14,15] It is a relatively simple technique with minimal morbidity.[14,16] Yet, there are concerns about adipocytes promoting malignant change and subsequent mammographic changes that may prompt biopsy and make cancer detection more difficult. Close oncologic follow-up is therefore mandatory for these patients.[14,15] The American Society of Plastic Surgeons has stated that fat grafting is a safe adjunct for post-mastectomy patients as there is no residual breast tissue, but considers this procedure to remain experimental in other situations.[17] Implants can also be utilized for partial breast reconstruction, but only improve distributed volume and are poor at correcting localized volume or skin shortage. This option therefore rarely offers a good aesthetic result and there is minimal literature supporting implant use in this setting. Moreover, there are inevitably higher rates of capsular contracture and infection in an area that has been radiated.[1]

Severe defects resulting from attempts at breast conservation are best managed with conversion to completion mastectomy and total breast reconstruction.[1] This is the author's preferred technique for significant defects, as frequently the same donor site for mastectomy reconstruction would be used and the aesthetic result is superior (especially with nipple-sparing mastectomy). Completion mastectomy in these circumstances has the added benefit of removing remaining breast tissue and diminishing the risk of recurrent disease.[1] Options for autologous reconstruction include DIEP, SIEA, superior gluteal artery perforator flaps, and profunda artery perforator flaps.

Many of these patients may also suffer from lymphedema. When conservative management with physiotherapy and compression garments fails, these patients may benefit from autologous lymph node transfer.[18,19] Lymph nodes can be harvested from the superficial circumflex iliac pedicle and transferred at the same time as microvascular breast reconstruction.[20] Most patients show a decreased arm circumference and many no longer require physiotherapy and compression after successful treatment.[18,20] Our preferred reconstructive algorithm is shown in **Figure 14.2.1.1.**

In conclusion, there are many options for delayed partial breast reconstruction. The nature of the defect must be taken into account to determine whether the patient would benefit from volume rearrangement, volume replacement, or conversion to mastectomy and total breast reconstruction.

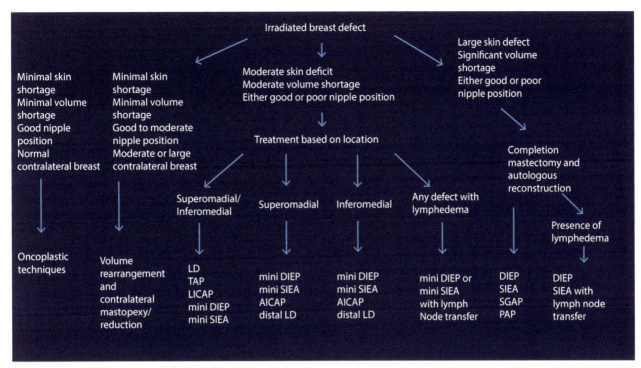

14.2.1.1 Treatment Algorithm for Irradiation Breast Defects.

REFERENCES

1. Hamdi M, Wolfli J, Van Landuyt K. Partial mastectomy reconstruction. *Clin Plast Surg.* 2007; 34(1): 51–62.
2. Kronowitz SJ, Kuerer HM, Buchholz TA, Valero V, Hunt KK. A management algorithm and practical oncoplastic surgical techniques for repairing partial mastectomy defects. *Plast Reconstr Surg.* 2008; 122(6): 1631–1647.
3. Iwuchukwu OC, Harvey JR, Dordea M, Critchley AC, Drew PJ. The role of oncoplastic therapeutic mammoplasty in breast cancer surgery–A review. *Surg Oncol.* 2012; 21(2): 133–141.
4. Kronowitz SJ, Feledy JA, Hunt KK, Kuerer HM, Youssef A, Koutz CA, Robb GL. Determining the optimal approach to breast reconstruction after partial mastectomy. *Plast Reconstr Surg.* 2006; 117(1): 1–11.
5. Churgin S, Isakov R, Yetman R. Reconstruction options following breast conservation therapy. *Cleve Clin J Med.* 2008; 75(Suppl 1): S24–S29.
6. Clough KB, Kaufman GJ, Nos C, Buccimazza I, Sarfati IM. Improving breast cancer surgery: A classification and quadrant per quadrant atlas for oncoplastic surgery. *Ann Surg Oncol.* 2010; 17(5): 1375–1391.
7. Munhoz AM, Aldrighi CM, Montag E, Arruda E, Brasil JA, Filassi JR, Aldrighi JM, Gemperli R, Ferreira MC. Outcome analysis of immediate and delayed conservative breast surgery reconstruction with mastopexy and reduction mammaplasty techniques. *Ann Plast Surg.* 2011; 67(3): 220–225.
8. Roughton MC, Shenaq D, Jaskowiak N, Park JE, Song DH. Optimizing delivery of breast conservation therapy: A multidisciplinary approach to oncoplastic surgery. *Ann Plast Surg.* 2012; 69(3): 250–255.
9. Patel KM, Hannan CM, Gatti ME, Nahabedian MY. A head-to-head comparison of quality of life and aesthetic outcomes following immediate, staged-immediate, and delayed oncoplastic reduction mammaplasty. *Plast Reconstr Surg.* 2011; 127(6): 2167–2175.
10. Rose JF, Colen JS, Ellsworth WA. Reduction and mastopexy techniques for optimal results in oncoplastic breast reconstruction. *Semin Plast Surg.* 2015; 29: 102–109.
11. Losken A, Hamdi M. Partial breast reconstruction: Current perspectives. *Plast Reconstr Surg.* 2009; 124(3): 722–736.
12. Levine JL, Soueid NE, Allen RJ. Algorithm for autologous breast reconstruction for partial mastectomy defects. *Plast Reconstr Surg.* 2005; 116(3): 762–767.
13. Spiegel AJ, Eldor L. Partial breast reconstruction with mini superficial inferior epigastric artery and mini deep inferior epigastric perforator flaps. *Ann Plast Surg.* 2010; 65(2): 147–154.
14. Petit JY, Lohsiriwat V, Clough KB, Sarfati I, Ihrai T, Rietjens M, Veronesi P, Rossetto F, Scevola A, Delay E. The oncologic outcome and immediate surgical complications of lipofilling in breast cancer patients: A multicenter study–Milan-Paris-Lyon experience of 646 lipofilling procedures. *Plast Reconstr Surg.* 2011; 128(2): 341–346.

15. Claro F Jr, Figueiredo JC, Zampar AG, Pinto-Neto AM. Applicability and safety of autologous fat for reconstruction of the breast. *Br J Surg.* 2012; 99(6): 768–780.
16. Coleman SR, Saboeiro AP. Fat grafting to the breast revisited: Safety and efficacy. *Plast Reconstr Surg.* 2007; 119(3): 775–785.
17. ASPS Position Statement. 2015. Post-Mastectomy Fat Graft/Fat Transfer ASPS Guiding Principles. http://www.plasticsurgery.org/Documents/Health-Policy/Principles/principle-2015-post-mastectomy-fat-grafting.pdf.

18. Mehrara BJ, Zampell JC, Suami H, Chang DW. Surgical management of lymphedema: Past, present, and future. *Lymphat Res Biol.* 2011; 9(3): 159–167.
19. Becker C, Assouad J, Riquet M, Hidden G. Postmastectomy lymphedema: Long-term results following microsurgical lymph node transplantation. *Ann Surg.* 2006; 243(3): 313–315.
20. Saaristo AM, Niemi TS, Viitanen TP, Tervala TV, Hartiala P, Suominen EA. Microvascular breast reconstruction and lymph node transfer for postmastectomy lymphedema patients. *Ann Surg.* 2012; 255(3): 468–473.

14.2.2 Our approach (Europe)

Charles M. Malata, Alexandra Bucknor, and Chidi Ekwobi

SUMMARY

The reconstruction of partial breast defects following radiotherapy presents surgical challenges, not only because of the complex effects of radiotherapy on the tissues, but also due to the reluctance of many patients to undergo further surgery which may be extensive and lead to patient concerns about its impact on their cancer status. The primary motivation for these patients when initially choosing breast-conserving surgery was to avoid extensive surgery with the expectation of a favorable aesthetic outcome which is safe from an oncological perspective.

A number of innovative techniques have been developed in Europe for partial breast reconstruction in the immediate setting. These techniques have also been applied to a variable extent for managing delayed partial breast reconstruction after radiotherapy. There are several options for delayed partial breast reconstruction including: (a) parenchymal rearrangement and breast remodeling (volume/tissue displacement), (b) standard local flap techniques (volume/tissue replacement), (c) mastopexy procedures, (d) modern perforator flap techniques, (e) autologous fat transfer (lipofilling), (f) use of prostheses, and (g) distant flap salvage (totally autologous replacement). Other modalities for delayed repair include local scar revision procedures and breast augmentation. These techniques may be used singly, in combination, or sequentially. Operative strategies to achieve optimum cosmetic results and symmetry may involve the ipsilateral, contralateral, or both breasts. An important consideration is whether the patient received whole or partial breast irradiation after their breast-conserving surgery. In general, delayed repair after whole breast irradiation is not ideal and often the only practical options are autologous fat grafting, contralateral symmetrizing surgery, or the use of a flap—the latter serving to both replace the breast skin and provide volume. Recipients of partial breast irradiation are more suited to standard reconstructive techniques listed above for partial breast defects similar to those used when immediate repair is performed.

INTRODUCTION

It is estimated that between 20% and 40% of women undergoing breast-conservation surgery for cancer have a residual deformity or breast asymmetry.[1–3] These result from the combined effects of tumor resection and adjuvant radiotherapy (whole breast external beam radiotherapy with or without a boost to the tumor site after lumpectomy reduces the risk of local recurrence)[4]. Although post-lumpectomy cosmetic deformities have been reduced by introduction of various oncoplastic techniques for immediate reconstruction of partial breast defects, these have not been universally adopted and deformities can occur following a formal oncoplastic repair. Additionally, there remains a pool of patients who underwent treatment prior to the advent of these techniques for partial breast reconstruction. There are four main issues: lack of volume, lack of aesthetically acceptable contouring, contracted skin, and the presence of irradiated, fibrotic tissue. The reconstructive surgeon needs to address these various elements taking into account the timing of any intervention with respect to postoperative radiotherapy.

In this chapter, we discuss some of the key operative techniques available to the reconstructive surgeon when confronted with an irradiated partial breast defect.

CLASSIFICATION

The cosmetic sequelae after breast-conserving therapy have been elegantly classified into three types:

Type 1: No localized volume loss; the main problem is volume and shape asymmetry between the 2 breasts.
Type 2: Localized volume loss; obvious deformity with asymmetry and characterized by:
   a. A localized glandular defect
   b. Skin sequelae
   c. Nipple-areola complex deviation
Type 3: Gross deformity; the breast is not salvageable and requires completion mastectomy with immediate breast reconstruction

The reasons for suboptimal cosmetic sequelae after breast-conserving therapy are multifactorial. Wide local excision of a tumor produces distortion, retraction, and potential volume changes in the breast. Alterations in the position of the nipple-areola complex may accentuate any intrinsic asymmetry of breast volume and shape. Postoperative radiotherapy has profound effects on the breast with initial generalized edema and skin erythema followed by hypo- or hyperpigmentation, telangiectasia, and atrophy. The breast parenchyma undergoes fibrosis and retraction in response to radiotherapy. Reconstructive options depend on the ratio of the volume of the defect to that of the remaining breast tissue, the location of the defect, and the available local tissues.[5–7]

An important principle for management of postradiation deformities after breast-conserving therapy is to avoid surgery on the irradiated breast wherever possible due to a high rate of complications and poor cosmetic results. Instead, contralateral symmetrization surgery with mastopexy or reduction should be considered, and this often yields excellent (and more predictable) results. Additionally recruitment of non-irradiated tissue, including use of myocutaneous and perforator flaps, either alone or in combination with an implant can be a useful option in these circumstances. Transfer of a local flap has three key advantages:

1. Encourages healing within irradiated breast tissue
2. Provides missing volume
3. Provides skin replacement to counter the contracted deformity (which happens whether skin was resected or not)

Augmentation of the irradiated breast is useful and may be achieved through lipofilling or implant-based reconstruction (preferably subpectoral). Staged autologous fat grafting (lipofilling) also serves to improve the scarring by releasing tight deforming bands. Prosthetic breast augmentation is often preferential to address volume asymmetry, but the patient should be warned about the high likelihood of capsular contracture on the irradiated side.

After partial breast irradiation, more options are available for reconstruction of the partial breast defect as local non-irradiated breast tissue rearrangements can be used without incurring the high complication rates associated with whole breast radiotherapy.[8–10] This scenario is less commonly encountered in Europe and the United Kingdom than the United States of America.

This chapter subsection is presented under the following headings:

1. Local reshaping procedures
2. Restoration of volumetric symmetry of post-radiotherapy defects after breast-conserving surgery
3. Correction of partial defects based on anatomical location using flaps
4. Completion mastectomy and immediate reconstruction
5. Comments about the future

GENERAL

The techniques used for delayed breast reconstruction after BCS and radiotherapy are similar to those used in the immediate setting. They are varied, and determinants of the technique selected[6,9]. Most notable are whether the patient presents before or after breast-conserving surgery and, if following surgery, whether it is before or after radiotherapy which may have been administered to the whole breast or only part of it. A self-explanatory and invaluable algorithm has been presented by the MD Anderson group.[6]

FACTORS DETERMINING TECHNIQUE SELECTION IN PARTIAL BREAST RECONSTRUCTION

PATIENT FACTORS

- MDT decision and patient choice
- Breast size (and shape)
- Location and size of the defect
- Patient characteristics

TUMOR FACTORS

- Size of the tumor versus the size of the breast
- The tumor margin status

SURGICAL FACTORS

- The timing of the reconstruction in relation to radiotherapy
- The extent of breast skin resection
- The surgeon's experience

LOCAL RESHAPING PROCEDURES

1. *Simple local reshaping procedures*
   These involve gland undermining (conservatively) from the underlying fascia, followed by mobilization of the breast tissues and layered suturing (**Figure 14.2.2.1**).
2. *Complex reshaping procedures*
   These involve larger procedures such as mammoplasty (inferior, superior [superolateral/ superomedial] or central pedicle techniques) and usually involve volumetric symmetrization procedures. Included in this category is centralization of the areola—using a keyhole or other mastopexy pattern in a manner akin to breast reduction. The concentric mastopexy is a widely applicable procedure for immediate repair, but may not be so useful in delayed repair in view of the contracted skin.

RESTORATION OF VOLUMETRIC SYMMETRY OF POST-RADIOTHERAPY DEFECTS AFTER BCS

1. *Contralateral symmetrizing surgery*
   If the main issue is a size mismatch, a viable option for symmetrization is contralateral breast reduction. This avoids the risks of poor healing, fat necrosis, and local complications associated with operating on irradiated tissue. A contralateral breast reduction and can be used alone, or in conjunction with other techniques.
2. *Bilateral mammoplasty (reduction/ lift/augmentation)*
   Sometimes it is desirable to operate on both breasts, depending on the degree of ptosis and the magnitude of volume asymmetry (**Figure 14.2.2.2**). A relative contraindication for such breast parenchymal rearrangement surgery ("therapeutic mammaplasty") is

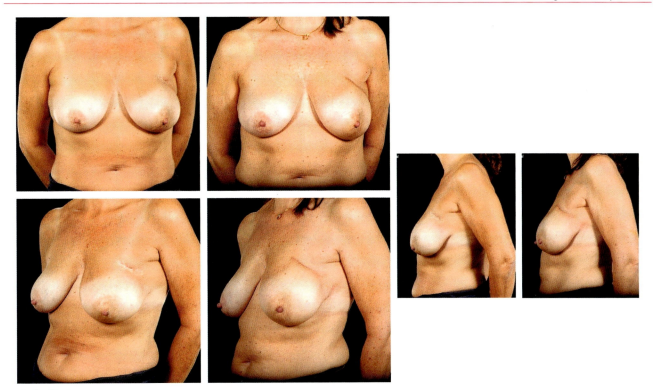

14.2.2.1 A 52-year-old woman had undergone a wide local excision of a grade III invasive carcinoma of the upper outer quadrant of the left breast 18 months earlier followed by chemotherapy and radiotherapy presented with a painful, tender, tethered, and deformed lumpectomy scar. She underwent full thickness resection of the scar tissue to correct the contour deformity and resect the dense scar tissue. The resultant defect was corrected parenchymal mobilisation/advancement. Histology revealed scar tissue with foreign body giant cell reaction. No evidence of malignancy.

a large volume defect-to-breast ratio. Recruitment of non-breast tissue is required when presented with this scenario and completion mastectomy with immediate whole breast reconstruction should be considered. Such bilateral surgery seldom results in perfect symmetry (**Figure 14.2.2.2**), and it is difficult to avoid wound healing problems in the ipsilateral breast. By combining breast-conservation therapy with breast reconfiguration or reduction in large-breasted women, multiple benefits are derived. Larger segmental or partial mastectomies can be performed without disfigurement risk, ensuring adequate surgical margins. Reconfiguration of the breast with reduction of the contralateral side creates symmetric, aesthetically pleasing breasts, allows contralateral breast tissue to be evaluated, and spares women any further operative procedures. Such a coordinated program gives women an important boost, both physically and psychologically, during management of their breast cancer.[9]

Occasionally, differential breast augmentation may reduce the asymmetry resulting from previous lumpectomy and radiotherapy. We favor the use of subpectoral augmentation, so as to reduce the risk of capsular contracture and minimize the interference with subsequent radiological surveillance of the breast. The patients are warned about the increased risk of capsular contracture on the irradiated side (**Figure 14.2.2.3**).

In the delayed setting, breast augmentation can also be undertaken using fat grafting (large volume lipofilling) into the conserved breast.

3. *Fat transfer or lipofilling*

Autologous fat grafting for those patients with post-radiotherapy defects after breast-conserving surgery has gained widespread popularity in recent years.[11,12] In addition to volumetric correction of the lumpectomy defect, ameliorating the irradiated skin quality, and improving the scarring, there are added advantages of reduced morbidity compared to flap harvest, use of autologous, non-irradiated tissue, and technically less complex surgery than flap transfer. Fat grafting is indicated in volume restoration for patients who decline or are not suitable for the above two techniques, implant-based or flap reconstruction. Nonetheless, caution

178 Delayed oncoplastic repair—after radiotherapy

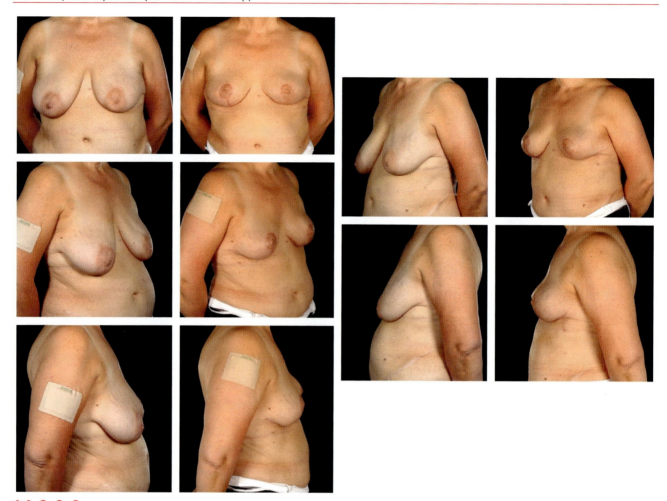

14.2.2.2 Correction of post-lumpectomy and post-radiotherapy asymmetry by mammaplasty: A 69-year-old woman was referred by the oncological breast surgeons for correction of acquired breast asymmetry following a left lumpectomy and radiotherapy for grade 3 DCIS 11 years earlier. This was achieved by a right superomedial T-scar breast reduction and a left superomedial T-scar mastopexy. The resection specimens weighed 85 g on the left and 310 g on right. Histology was unremarkable showing only minor fibrocystic changes in both breasts.

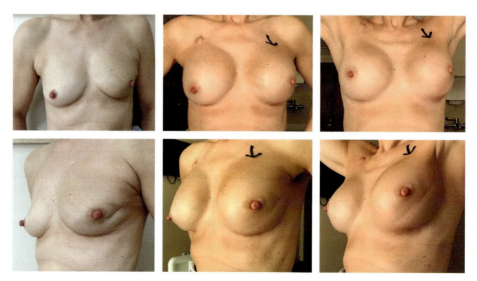

14.2.2.3 Correction of lumpectomy asymmetry by bilateral augmentation: A 55-year-old woman had undergone a left lumpectomy and irradiation. Her breast asymmetry was corrected by inframammary subpectoral breast augmentation with form-stable cohesive silicone gel implants. The appearances postoperatively are 1 year later when she needed resection of an axillary recurrence.

should be exercised and the cancer recurrence risk determined before embarking on any surgery.[13]

The method used for fat transfer is based on the techniques originally described by Coleman[14,15] and outlined in a previous publication book chapter.[11] After local infiltration of the donor sites with tumescent fluid, the fat is harvested with use of a micro-aspiration needle with 10 cc Luer-Lock syringes. Having "pre-tunneled" the recipient site in a multi-planar and multi-directional manner and following centrifugation and separation of fat, the latter is injected with a micro-injection cannula.[16] *See Section 13.4.3 for further details.*

4. *Autologous techniques including local flaps and regional flaps*

Delayed repair of radiation fibrosis and contour deformity can be performed with a partial mastectomy and flap reconstruction.[17–20]

1. Volume displacement techniques—These involve breast parenchymal rearrangement and are not frequently used for delayed repair. There is risk of compromised vascularity of the breast parenchymal flap during mobilization as a consequence of scarring secondary to previous lumpectomy and radiotherapy.

2. Volume replacement techniques are used following very wide excisions or based on the location of the defect. The latissumus dorsi (LD) muscle is commonly used.[17,21–25] Enajat and colleagues reported on delayed reconstruction of larger partial mastectomy defects.[20] Often importation of skin is needed, so non de-epithelialized (traditional myocutaneous or adipocutaneous) LD myocutaneous or thoracodorsal artery perforator (TDAP) flaps are appropriate in these circumstances.

CORRECTION OF PARTIAL DEFECTS BASED ON ANATOMICAL LOCATION USING FLAPS

Defects that are not suitable for mammoplasty techniques may be amenable to correction using local, regional, and, occasionally, distant flaps. The choice of flap largely depends on the anatomical location of the defect. The overriding principle is the recruitment of non-irradiated tissue be this from myocutaneous, fasciocutaneous, or perforator flaps. Local flaps (**Figure 14.2.2.4**) have been employed for this purpose for several decades, but it is only recently that algorithmic approaches have been proposed.[26] The most common regional flap employed for this purpose is the latissimus dorsi myocutaneous flap. The advent of perforator flaps without muscle sacrifice overcame one of the main drawbacks from use of myocutaneous flaps and paved the way for their widespread adoption in reconstruction of partial breast defects—especially in the context of radiotherapy.

As for myocutaneous flaps, perforator flaps are particularly useful in reconstruction of small- to moderate-sized breasts, which are not amenable to any therapeutic mammoplasty-type reconstructive options.[27,28] Furthermore, they avoid the use of glandular flaps which might lead to fat necrosis, which is an ever-present risk in recipients of prior breast radiotherapy.

The following flaps may be used[29] based on the site of the defect to be reconstructed:

1. *Lateral quadrants*: Tissue from the sub-axillary region is useful and available as either a lateral intercostal artery perforator flap or serratus anterior artery perforator flap. The advantages of these two options are that in the event of salvage breast reconstruction, the latissimus dorsi myocutaneous flap is preserved.[27,30,31] Abdominal-based free flaps can be used for defects in this region, but are generally reserved for the more challenging defects located in the medial breast. The latissimus dorsi muscle is versatile in this location due to its proximity (**Figure 14.2.2.5**).

2. *Medial quadrants*: A paucity of locally available tissue, coupled with the inherent cosmetic sensitivity of the area renders reconstruction of medially placed defects a challenge. Furthermore, any technique for reconstruction should ensure that the position of the nipple areola complex is maintained. Options include the anterior intercostal artery perforator flap and the superficial epigastric artery perforator flap, but the latissimus dorsi myocutaneous (**Figure 14.2.2.6**) and thoracodorsal artery perforator flaps can provide sufficient reach in this region.[27] Abdominal-based free flaps can be useful for reconstruction of these medial defects.[32]

In addition, the transverse upper gracilis (TUG) flap may yield a superior donor site scar[33] and can be especially useful in small-breasted women.

An alternative, less-commonly used flap, which has both free and pedicled options is the omental flap.[34] However, as the volume of omentum cannot be predicted, this particular flap is an unsuitable choice for very large defects.[35]

Finally, the superior epigastric artery perforator flap[36,37] can be employed for medial defects as well as for resurfacing procedures.

3. *All breast quadrants*, except medial quadrants: a thoracodorsal artery perforator flap.

4. *Superior partial defects*: In conjunction with the natural ptosis that occurs with age, superior defects are likely to become less noticeable than those elsewhere in the breast. Although latissimus dorsi[38,39] and even abdominal-based free flaps may be employed in this setting; these particular defects are likely to respond well to fat transfer unless very large (**Figure 14.2.2.7**). Thoracodorsal artery and lateral intercostal artery perforator flaps can also be used for this area (especially laterally). In the delayed setting, these flaps are used with the skin paddles to provide skin replacement for the contracted deformity caused by radiotherapy.

Often these superior defects can readily be reconstructed at the time of the primary surgery with a glandular rotation-advancement and give good results in patients with large and/or ptotic breasts.

5. *Inferior partial defects*: These have historically led to very poor cosmetic results and indeed prompted innovations in immediate partial breast reconstructions.[40] However, they still occur and are difficult deformities to correct (**Figure 14.2.2.8**). A range of flaps including thoracodorsal, lateral intercostal, lateral thoracic artery perforator, and inferior adipofascial tissue flaps may be used to reconstruct these inferior partial breast defects.

6. *Central defects*: Patients with central defects are relatively uncommon as these would usually be managed at the time of primary surgery—either with mastectomy (due to poor cosmetic outcomes associated with resection of the nipple-areolar complex) or with immediate oncoplastic surgery.[41–44] The latter could involve a Grisotti advancement rotation flap, which uses an inferiorly based dermal glandular pedicle to reconstruct the central defect, while the E/3 modification acts to relieve tension on the inferior suture line, improving rates of wound dehiscence.[43] Therapeutic mammoplasty has also proven useful in the immediate setting for central defects and can be combined with simultaneous contralateral symmetrizing surgery (reduction mammaplasty).[44] The lower pole tissue and associated skin paddle is used to fill the central defect, enabling immediate areolar reconstruction.[45]

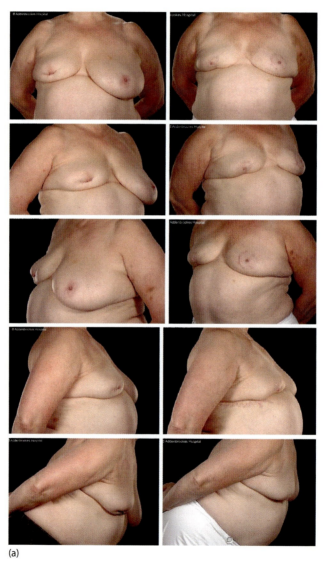

(a)

14.2.2.4 (a) Delayed partial breast reconstruction of an infra-areolar lumpectomy deformity using a medially based local transposition fasciocutaneous flap and a simultaneous contralateral superomedial T-scar breast reduction in a 60-year-old patient. Note the improved overall symmetry and the acceptable correction of the lumpectomy deformity. The scar is disguised in a horizontal skin crease.

(*Continued*)

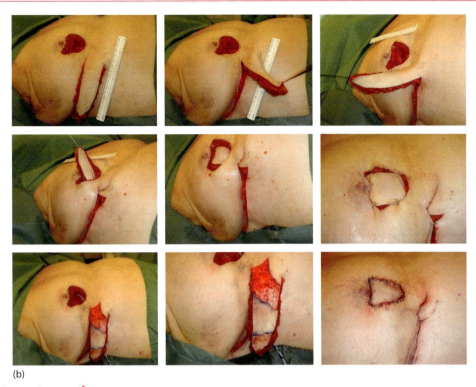

(b)

14.2.2.4 (Continued) (b) Delayed partial breast reconstruction of an infra-areolar lumpectomy deformity using a medially based local transposition fasciocutaneous flap—intraoperative sequence: the lumpectomy defect is recreated by resection of the postsurgical/postradiation scar tissue. This invariably results in a larger three-dimensional defect compared to what is suggested by the preoperative appearances due to the combined effects of postsurgical and post-radiotherapy scarring and tissue contraction. The flap (length about 10 cm) is shown in its native position at the end of harvest prior to transposition. It is then transposed clockwise 90° via an ample subparenchymal tunnel and initially stapled in place to determine the exact location and dimensions of the necessary skin paddle. The distal part (to be used for supporting the nipple-areola and providing bulk) and the part which will be buried under the tunnel are de-epithelialized. Final images showing the flap sutured in place after loose inset under a suction drain.

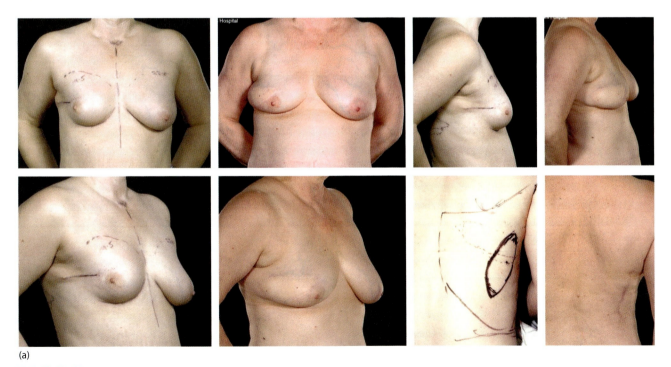

(a)

14.2.2.5 (a) Delayed reconstruction of a lateral near-quadrantectomy defect with an LD flap. 15 years after the reconstruction.

(*Continued*)

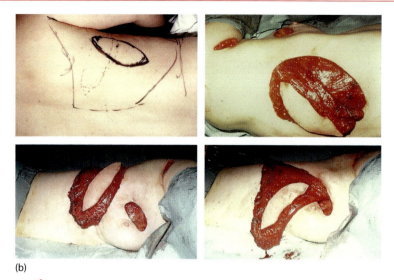

(b)

14.2.2.5 (Continued) (b) Operative sequence: An oblique skin paddle was designed (top left). The muscle and skin harvested with the assistance of a posterior axillary fold incision (top right). The defect has been recreated and the muscle shown prior to transposition through the tunnel (bottom left). After transposition into the defect and prior to "Swiss-rolling" the muscle under the skin flap. The flap harvested is much larger than the defect in order to compensate for postoperative muscle atrophy.

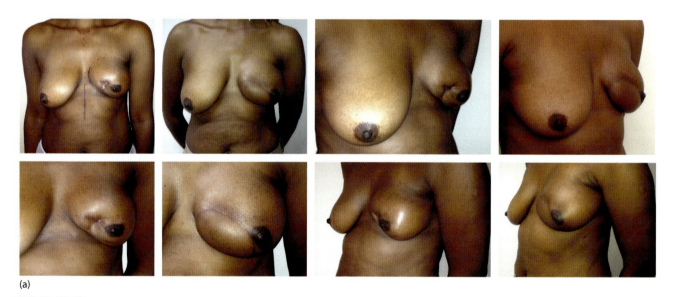

(a)

14.2.2.6 Delayed partial reconstruction of an inferomedial resection defect with an LD flap. 46-year-old patient with a deformed shrunken left breast following a large lumpectomy and postoperative radiation. Note the distortion of the nipple. This was not suitable for local flaps. (a) 14-month postoperative appearances show improvement in the volume deficit, better nipple position, and the need for a large skin paddle to compensate for the contracted native breast.

(*Continued*)

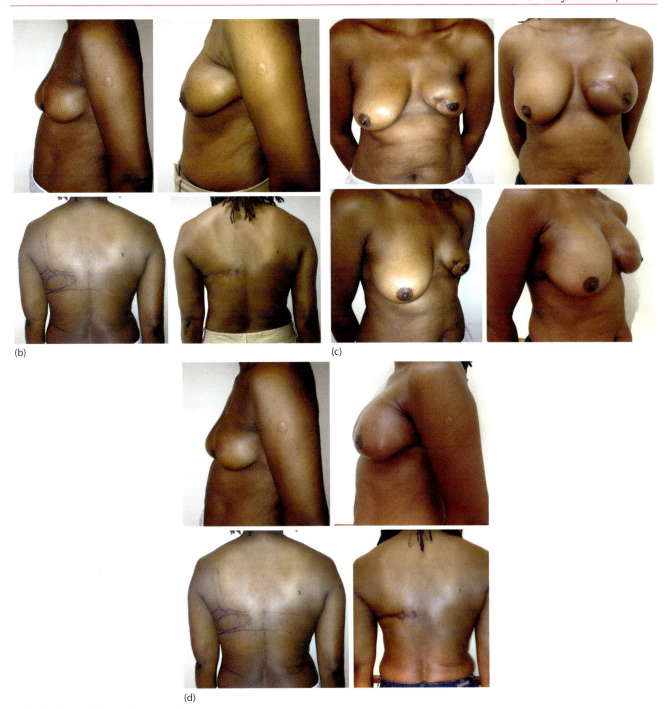

14.2.2.6 (Continued) Delayed partial reconstruction of an inferomedial resection defect with an LD flap. 46-year-old patient with a deformed shrunken left breast following a large lumpectomy and postoperative radiation. Note the distortion of the nipple. This was not suitable for local flaps. (b) There is better contour of the left breast which is now bigger and thus obscures the opposite normal breast on the lateral views. The donor site scar is well hidden in the bra strap line with minimal contour change of the back. (c) 18-month appearances: Three months after subpectoral differential breast augmentation via inframammary fold incisions. (d) The donor site scar, though stretched, is well hidden in the bra strap line with minimal contour deformity of the back.

184 Delayed oncoplastic repair—after radiotherapy

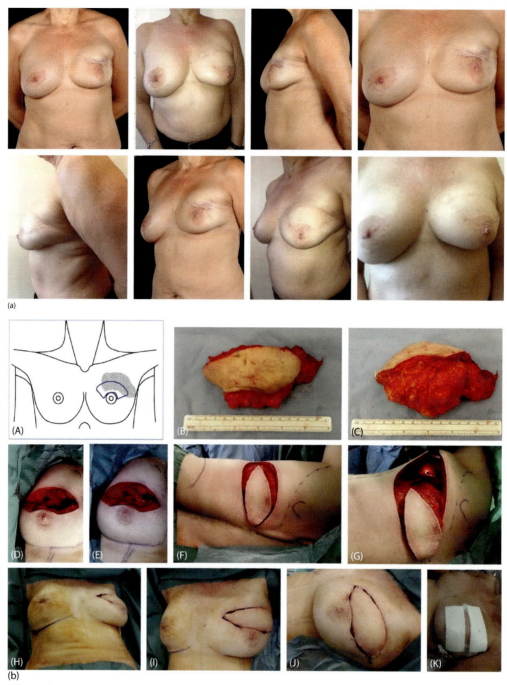

14.2.2.7 LD flap to large superior defect: (a) A 54-year-old patient had undergone a left wide local excision followed by radiotherapy a few years prior to referral. She presented with an indurated mass superiorly with gross distortion of the breast and significant radiotherapy skin changes. The large mass was excised down to the pectoralis muscle and the defect reconstructed with a latissimus dorsi flap with a large skin paddle to replace the abnormal skin (see intraoperative sequence). The resection specimen 10 × 10 × 3.5 cm and weighed 138 g. Histological examination of the mass showed fibrous scar and chronic inflammation with foreign body type giant cell reaction consistent with previous surgical procedure. There was no atypia and no evidence of malignancy. Two years after surgery she has acceptable cosmetic results and is symptom free. There is better symmetry and correction of the asymmetric nipple positions. (b) Intraoperative sequence of LD flap to large superior lumpectomy defect with extensive scarring and induration: This series illustrates the planning of the resection of the abnormal indurated and scarred tissue to recreate the defect and the shape of the skin paddle (line diagram A). The resection specimen measured 10 × 10 × 3.5 cm (B & C) leaving a significant defect (D & E) which was reconstructed with an LD flap with a large skin paddle (F & G) which enabled lowering on the nipple-areola. Images H, I, and J show the flap inset while K is the final appearance at the end of surgery with a water proof dressing in situ.

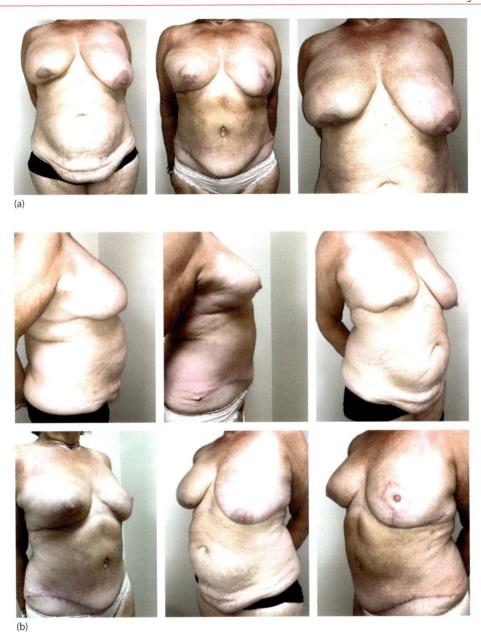

14.2.2.8 Significant inferior defect—corrected by mammaplasty: (a) A 64-year-old woman with a grossly deformed right breast following an inferior lumpectomy and radiotherapy. There was significant asymmetry and gross distortion of the tissues. There is substantial tissue deficit, scarring and distortion of the nipple in the presence of ptosis, and macromastia. The closeup view shows the gross distortion of the nipple which points vertically downward. Note the persistent patent blue dye staining of the skin. (b) The patient opted for a breast reduction and tissue rearrangement rather than tissue replacement. Therefore a superior pedicle breast reduction was performed on the right and a superomedial pedicle breast reduction on the left. The resection specimens were 164 g on the right (postsurgical changes only) and 317 g on the left (normal tissue). There was an improvement in symmetry and relative nipple positions.

COMPLETION MASTECTOMY AND IMMEDIATE RECONSTRUCTION

The option of completion mastectomy and immediate reconstruction should be borne in mind, especially when the volume ratio of the defect to the remaining breast tissue is high and/or radiotherapy changes are severe.[46–48] This salvage reconstruction is akin to totally autologous reconstruction for failed prosthetic reconstructions.[46] However, this option has a number of drawbacks including increased operative time, morbidity, and costs. Options include a free flap, latissimus dorsi flap, and other autologous techniques (**Figures 14.2.2.9 and 14.2.2.10**). Autologous non-implant-based techniques are preferred for these "salvage" reconstructions as implant reconstructions are likely to result in wound dehiscence, infection and implant exposure.

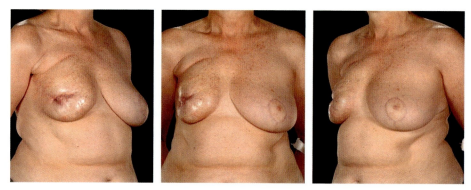

14.2.2.9 Salvage of deformed breasts from previous lumpectomies and radiotherapy necessitated mastectomy and autologous reconstruction with a DIEP flap (Figure 14.2.2.9) and a totally autologous LD flap (Figure 14.2.2.10). Autologous non-implant-based techniques are preferred for these "salvage reconstructions." This 55-year-old patient had undergone a lumpectomy followed by breast radiotherapy 13 years earlier. She suffered from severe radiotherapy reaction, extensive scarring, and gross deformation of her left breast. This necessitated a completion mastectomy (mastectomy weight 540 g) and immediate breast reconstruction with a DIEP flap. This and the next case (Figure 14.2.2.10) are the typical Krishna Clough Type 3 cosmetic sequelae of breast-conservation therapy.

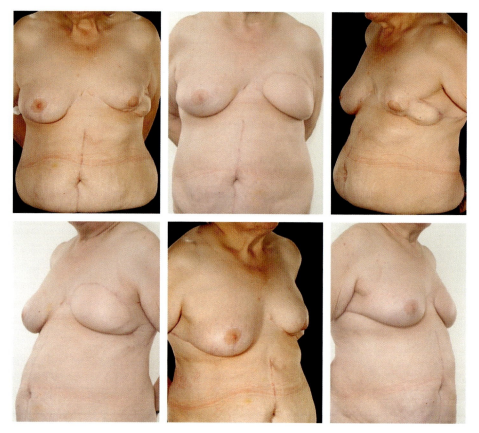

14.2.2.10 Salvage of deformed breasts from previous lumpectomies and radiotherapy necessitated mastectomy and autologous reconstruction with a DIEP flap (Figure 14.2.2.9) and a totally autologous LD flap (Figure 14.2.2.10). Autologous non-implant-based techniques are preferred for these "salvage reconstructions." A 59-year-old diabetic with a previous (6 years earlier) lumpectomy and RT and who had developed healing problems and severe scarring treated using a local flap 2 years earlier underwent left salvage/completion mastectomy + breast mound reconstruction with an autologous LD flap with an implant. She developed donor site wound breakdown and implant infection necessitating explantation. Her postoperative appearances 4 years later are shown.

CONCLUSION

Selecting the correct method for delayed repair of partial breast defects is challenging. When addressing reconstruction of these partial defects, it is crucial to thoroughly assess the underlying cosmetic issues and to consider this as part of a spectrum of defects as outlined in this chapter. It is important to understand the effects of radiotherapy on the breast and its status as a risk factor for future complications in the event that further surgery is to be undertaken. Any surgery for breast reconstruction should not occur within 6 months after completion of radiotherapy in order to minimize these risks. Fresh, non-irradiated tissue should be recruited where possible and completion mastectomy with free flap reconstruction should be included among the reconstructive options discussed. For delayed repair, local parenchymal rearrangements are eschewed and use of fat grafting encouraged with liberal use of contralateral balancing surgery.

There is greater adoption of techniques for accelerated partial breast irradiation worldwide among women with early breast cancer and this will change the nature of reconstruction of partial breast defects.[49–52] It is anticipated that demand for reconstruction of partial breast defects will increase as more women opt for breast-conserving surgery.

REFERENCES

1. Clarke, D., Martinez, A., Cox, RS. (1983) Analysis of cosmetic result and complications in patients with stage I and II breast cancer treated by biopsy and irradiation. *Int. J. Radiat. Oncol. Biol. Phys.* 9:1807–1813.
2. Pearl, RM., Wisnicki, J. (1985) Breast reconstruction following lumpectomy and irradiation. *Plast. Reconstr. Surg.* 76(1):83.
3. Matory Jnr, WE., Wertheimer, M., Fitzgerald, TJ., Walton, RL., Love, S., Matory, WE. (1990) Aesthetic results following partial mastectomy and radiation therapy. *Plast. Reconstr. Surg.* 85(5):739–746
4. National Institute for Clinical Excellence. (2009) Early and locally advanced breast cancer: Diagnosis and treatment. February 2009, pp. 16–17. NICE Clinical Guidelines. nice.org.uk/guidance/cg80.
5. Clough, KB., Lewis, JS., Couturaud, B., Fitoussi, A., Nos, C., Falcou, M. (2001) Oncoplastics techniques allow extensive resection for breast conserving therapy of breast carcinomas. *Ann. Surg.* 237(1):26–34.
6. Kronowitz, S., Kuerer, H., Buchholz, T., Valero, V., Hunt, K. (2008) A management algorithm and practical oncoplastic surgical techniques for repairing partial mastectomy defects. *Plast. Reconstr. Surg.* 122(6):1631–1647.
7. Lee, J., Kim, M., Park, H., Yang, J. (2014). Oncoplastic volume replacement techniques according to the excised volume and tumour location in small- to moderate-sized breasts. *Gland Surg.* 3(1):14–21.
8. Kronowitz, SJ., Robb, GL. (2004) Breast reconstruction with post-mastectomy radiation therapy: Current issues. *Plast. Reconstr. Surg.* 114(4):950–960.
9. Kronowitz, SJ., Feledy, JA., Hunt, KK., Kuerer, HM., Youssef, A., Koutz, CA., Robb, GL. (2006) Determining the optimal approach to breast reconstruction after partial mastectomy. *Plast. Reconstr. Surg.* 117(1):1–11; discussion 12–14.
10. Kronowitz, SJ. (2015) State of the art and science in post-mastectomy breast reconstruction. *Plast. Reconstr. Surg.* 135(4):755e–771e.
11. Spear, SL., Pelletiere, CV., Wolfe, AJ., Tsangaris, TN., Pennanen, MF. (2003) Experience with reduction mammaplasty combined with breast conservation therapy in the treatment of breast cancer. *Plast. Reconstr. Surg.* 111(3):1102–1109.
12. Patel, AJ., Benson, JR., Malata, CM. The science of autologous fat grafting. In: Querci della Rovere, G., Benson, JR., & Nava, M. (Eds.), *Oncoplastic & Reconstructive Surgery of the Breast.* 2nd ed, Informa Healthcare Publishers, London, UK, 2010, Chapter 29. pp. 223–233.
13. Pérez-Cano, R., Vranckx, JJ., Lasso, JM., Calabrese, C., Merck, B., Milstein, AM., Sassoon, E., Delay, E., Weiler-Mithoff, EM. (2012) Prospective trial of adipose-derived regenerative cell (ADRC)-enriched fat grafting for partial mastectomy defects: The RESTORE-2 trial. *Eur. J. Surg. Oncol.* 38(5):382–389.
14. Ihrai, T., Charalambos, G., Machiavello, JC., Chignon-Sicard, B., Figi, A., Raoust, I., Yveline, B., Fouche, Y., Flipo, B. (2013) Autologous fat grafting and breast cancer recurrences: Retrospective analysis of a series of 100 procedures in 64 patients. *J. Plast. Surg. Hand Su.* 47(4):273–275.
15. Coleman, S. (2001). Structural fat grafts–The ideal filler? *Clin. Plast. Surg.* 28(1):111–119.
16. Pu, L., Coleman, S., Cui, X., Ferguson, R., Vasconez, H. (2008). Autologous fat grafts harvested and refined by the Coleman technique: A comparative study. *Plast. Reconstr. Surg.* 122(3):932–937.
17. Coleman, S. (1997) Facial recontouring with lipostructure. *Clin. Plast. Surg.* 24(2):347–367.
18. van Geel, AN., Lans, TE., Haen, R., Tjong, Joe Wai R., Menke-Pluijmers, MB. (2011) Partial mastectomy and m. latissimus dorsi reconstruction for radiation-induced fibrosis after breast-conserving cancer therapy. *World J. Surg.* 35(3):568–572.
19. Munhoz, AM., Montag, E., Arruda, E., Pellarin, L., Filassi, JR., Piato, JR., de Barros, AC., Prado, LC., Fonseca, A., Baracat, E., Ferreira, MC. (2008) Assessment of immediate conservative breast surgery reconstruction: A classification system of defects revisited and an algorithm for selecting the appropriate technique. *Plast. Reconstr. Surg.* 121(3):716–727.
20. Kronowitz, SJ. (2007) Immediate versus delayed reconstruction. *Clin. Plast. Surg.* 34:39–50.
21. Enajat, M., Rozen, WM., Whitaker, IS., Smit, JM., Van Der Hulst, RR., Acosta, R. (2011) The deep inferior epigastric artery perforator flap for autologous reconstruction of large partial mastectomy defects. *Microsurgery.* 31(1):12–17.

22. Parmar, V., Hawaldar, R., Badwe, RA. (2010) Safety of partial breast reconstruction in extended indications for conservative surgery in breast cancer. *Indian J. Surg. Oncol.* 1(3):256

23. El-Marakby, HH., Kotb, MH. (2011) Oncoplastic volume replacement with latissimus dorsi myocutaneous flap in patients with large ptotic breasts. Is it feasible? *J. Egypt Natl. Canc. Inst.* 23(4):163–169.

24. Nano, MT., Gill, PG., Kollias, J., Bochner, MA. (2004) Breast volume replacement using the latissimus dorsi miniflap. *ANZ J. Surg.* 74(3):98–104.

25. Hernanz, F., Regaño, S., Redondo-Figuero, C., Orallo, V., Erasun, F., Gómez-Fleitas, M. (2007) Oncoplastic breast-conserving surgery: Analysis of quadrantectomy and immediate reconstruction with latissimus dorsi flap. *World J. Surg.* 31(10):1934–1940.

26. Munhoz, AM., Montag, E., Fels, KW., Arruda, EG., Sturtz, GP., Aldrighi, C., Gemperli, R., Ferreira, MC. (2005) Outcome analysis of breast-conservation surgery and immediate latissimus dorsi flap reconstruction in patients with T1 to T2 breast cancer. *Plast. Reconstr. Surg.* 116(3):741–752.

27. Hamdi, M. Pedicled perforator flap reconstruction. In: Losken, A., Hamdi, M. (Eds.), *Partial Breast Reconstruction: Techniques in Oncoplastic Surgery.* Quality Medical Publishing, St Louis, MI, 2009, Chapter 21. pp. 375–400.

28. Hamdi, M., Van Landuyt, K., Monstrey, S., Blondeel, P. (2004) Pedicled perforator flaps in breast reconstruction: A new concept. *Br. J. Plast. Surg.* 57(6): 531–539.

29. Munhoz, AM., Montag, E., Arruda, E., Brasil, JA., Aldrighi, JM., Gemperli, R., Filassi, JR., Ferreira, MC. (2011) Immediate conservative breast surgery reconstruction with perforator flaps: New challenges in the era of partial mastectomy reconstruction? *Breast.* 20(3):233–240.

30. Hamdi, M., Van Landuyt, K., Ulens, S., Van Hedent, E., Roche, N., Monstrey, S. (2009) Clinical applications of the superior epigastric artery perforator (SEAP) flap: Anatomical studies and preoperative perforator mapping with multidetector CT. *J. Plast. Reconstr. Aesthet. Surg.* 62(9):1127–1134.

31. Hamdi, M., Van Landuyt, K., de Frene, B., Roche, N., Blondeel, P., Monstrey, S. (2006) The versatility of the intercostal artery perforator (ICAP) flaps. *J. Plast. Recontr. Aesthet. Surg.* 57(6):644–652.

32. McCulley, S., Schaverien, M., Tan, V., Macmillan, R. (2015) Lateral thoracic artery perforator (LTAP) flap in partial breast reconstruction. *J. Plast. Reconstr. Aesthet. Surg.* 68(5):686–691.

33. Spiegel, A., Eldor, L. (2010) Partial breast reconstruction with mini superficial inferior epigastric artery and mini deep inferior epigastric perforator flaps. *Ann. Plast. Surg.* 65(2):147–154.

34. McCulley, SJ., MacMillan, RD., Rasheed, T. (2011) Transverse Upper Gracilis (TUG) flap for volume replacement in breast conserving surgery for medial breast tumours in small to medium sized breasts. *JPRAS.* 64:1056–1061.

35. Cothier-Savey, I., Tamtawi, B., Dohnt, F., Raulo, Y., Baruch, J. (2001) Immediate breast reconstruction using a laparoscopically harvested omental flap. *Plast. Reconstr. Surg.* 107(5):1156–1163.

36. Zaha, H., Onomura, M., Nomura, H., Umekawa, K., Oki, M., Asato, H. (2012) Free omental flap for partial breast reconstruction after breast-conserving surgery. *Plast. Reconstr. Surg.* 129(3):583–587.

37. Rizzuto, RP., Allen, RJ. (2004) Reconstruction of a partial mastectomy defect with the superficial inferior epigastric artery (SIEA) flap. *J. Reconstr. Microsurg.* 20(6):441–445; discussion 446.

38. Monticciolo, DL., Ross, D., Bostwick, J 3rd., Eaves, F., Styblo, T. (1996) Autologous breast reconstruction with endoscopic latissimus dorsi musculosubcutaneous flaps in patients choosing breast-conserving therapy: Mammographic appearance. *Am. J. Roentgenol.* 167(2):385–389.

39. Rainsbury, RM. (2002) Breast-sparing reconstruction with latissimus dorsi miniflaps. *Eur. J. Surg. Oncol.* 28(8):891–895.

40. Shestak, K., Johnson, R., Greco, R., Williams, S. (1993) Partial mastectomy and breast reduction as a valuable treatment option for patients with macromastia and carcinoma of the breast. *Surg. Gynaecol. Obstet.* 177(1):54–56.

41. Galimberti, V., Zurrida, S., Zanini, V., Callegari, M., Veronesi, P., Catania, S., Luini, A., Greco, M., Grisotti, A. (1993) Central small size breast cancer: How to overcome the problem of nipple and areola involvement. *Eur. J. Cancer.* 29A(8):1093–1096.

42. Grisotti, A., Calabrese C. Conservative treatment of breast cancer: Reconstructive problems. In: Spear, SL. (Ed.), *Surgery of the Breast: Principles and Art*, 1st ed, Lippincott Williams and Wilkins, Philadelphia, 1998, pp. 147–178.

43. Della Rovere, GQ., Pillarisetti, RR., Bonomi, R., Benson, J. (2007) Oncoplastic surgery for retro areolar breast cancer – A technical modification of the Grisotti flap. *Indian J. Surg.* 69(4):160–162.

44. McCulley, SJ., Durani, P., Macmillan, RD. (2006) Therapeutic mammoplasty for centrally located breast tumors. *Plast. Reconstr. Surg.* 117(2):366–373.

45. Munhoz, A., Aldrighi, C. (2007) A novel reconstructive technique following central lumpectomy. *Plast. Reconstr. Surg.* 119(2):750–751.

46. Rabey, N., Lie, K., Kumiponjera, D., Erel, E., Simcock, J., Malata, C. (2013) Salvage of failed prosthetic breast reconstructions by autologous conversion with free tissue transfers. *Eplasty.* 20(13):e32.

47. Mohan, A., Al-Ajam, Y., Mosahebi, A. (2013) Trends in tertiary breast reconstruction: Literature review and single centre experience. *Breast.* 22(2):173–178.

48. Visser, NJ., Damen, TH., Timman, R., Hofer, SO., Mureau, MA. (2010) Surgical results, aesthetic outcome, and patient satisfaction after microsurgical autologous breast reconstruction following failed implant reconstruction. *Plast. Reconstr. Surg.* 126(1):26–36.

49. Vaidya, JS., Wenz, F., Bulsara, M., Tobias, JS., Joseph, DJ., Keshtgar, M., Flyger, HL. et al. (2014) Risk-adapted targeted intraoperative radiotherapy versus whole-breast radiotherapy for breast cancer: 5-year results for local control and overall survival from the TARGIT-A randomised trial. *Lancet.* 383(9917):603–613.

50. Coles, C., Brunt, A., Wheatley, D., Mukesh, M., Yarnold, J. (2013) Breast radiotherapy: Less is more? *Clin. Oncol.* 25(2):127–134.

51. van der Leij, F., Bosma, S., van de Vijver, M., Wesseling, J., Vreeswijk, S., Rivera, S. et al. (2015) First results of the preoperative accelerated partial breast irradiation (PAPBI) trial. *Radiother. Oncol.* 114(3):322–327.

52. Berrino, P., Campora, E., Santi, P. (1993) Reconstruction of the radiated partial mastectomy defect with autogenous tissues. *Plast. Reconstr. Surg.* 92(2):380–381.

EDITORIAL COMMENTARY

Chapter 14 concludes with outstanding chapter sections by Dr. Charles Malata who discusses the complicated scenario of repairing partial mastectomy defects after radiation therapy. Besides the use of flaps described above, both Malata and myself are leading advocates for serial percutaneous needle release and autologous fat grafting. Complete release of an irradiated deformed breast is essential, not just in the region of the deformity, because a localized deformity is created from global contractile forces distributed throughout the irradiated breast. Likewise, it is imperative to fat graft the deformed breast in entirety and not just the grossly evident locally deformed region. This will ensure that the radiation damage is repaired with fat grafted stem cells throughout the breast which is exposed in entirety to whole breast irradiation after partial mastectomy. As pointed out by Malata, partial breast irradiation after breast-conserving surgery creates a perfect opportunity to perform dermoglandular repair (even delayed) after radiation without incurring high complication rates as most of the surrounding breast parenchyma does not receive radiation injury. However, we are still awaiting long-term outcomes of recurrence before these newer radiation techniques are widely adopted by the radiation community.

SECTION IV

Skin-sparing and nipple-sparing mastectomy

Chapter 15. Mastectomy and whole breast reconstruction: skin-sparing and nipple-sparing mastectomy   193

Chapter 16. Nipple-sparing mastectomy   205

15

Mastectomy and whole breast reconstruction: skin-sparing and nipple-sparing mastectomy

AT A GLANCE

Indications for nipple-sparing mastectomy continue to evolve with an increasing number of patients undergoing this technique. Although positive postoperative nipple margins can occur, especially in patients with ductal carcinoma in situ (DCIS), nipple-sparing mastectomy has significantly improved the outcomes of breast reconstruction. Nonetheless, patients for a nipple-sparing technique should be carefully selected.

15.1 ONCOLOGICAL ASPECTS

Gerald Gui

General considerations

In an age of early cancer detection, breast conservation is the gold standard surgical approach.[1,2] Up to 75% of screen-detected cancers can be managed by breast conservation,[3] and oncoplastic techniques are likely to further reduce mastectomy recommendations.[4] Larger tumors may be successfully downsized by primary chemotherapy to enable breast conservation to be considered. The ability to achieve complete pathological response in recent years has been more promising than ever, particularly with the introduction of primary anti-HER2 therapy using trastuzumab and pertuzumab.[5,6]

Mastectomy remains unavoidable in certain circumstances, perhaps most commonly in patients with multicentric disease at presentation. With enhanced imaging techniques including MRI-guided biopsy, it is likely that the diagnosis of multifocality will increase.[7,8] Failed breast conservation leading to mastectomy as a second operation may occur at two levels; the first after incomplete margins of excision at initial surgical management and the second after previous completed breast-conservation therapy with local recurrence detected at surveillance. The latter group differs by having received radiotherapy, which may impact on recommendations for reconstruction.

The number of risk-reducing mastectomies are likely to increase after lowering thresholds for gene testing (high-risk breast cancer predisposition genes) and the acceptance of surgery purely for risk-reduction.[9,10] Contralateral mastectomy in women at standard breast cancer risk should be weighed against competing cancer survival.[11] Overall contralateral prophylactic mastectomy rates have increased by 10% in the last decade.[12]

Oncologic considerations of skin-sparing mastectomy

As conservative management of the breast and axilla evolved, less radical approaches to mastectomy followed. The skin-sparing mastectomy described by Toth and Lappert[13] was popularized to become the mainstay of immediate breast reconstruction. As initial fears of oncologic safety subsided, patient selection criteria were refined.[14–21] Skin-sparing mastectomy provides the basis for immediate breast reconstruction by implant alone, autologous tissue, or a combination of both with good long-term oncological and aesthetic outcomes. The aim is to remove maximal parenchymal breast tissue while preserving the overlying skin of the breast envelope.

When performing a skin-sparing mastectomy, many surgeons are guided by a fascial plane, loosely corresponding to the superficial lamella that can be highly variable in continuity within the same breast, let alone in consistency between patients. It often comes to within 1 mm of the skin surface and appears unrelated to age, body mass index, and size of breast.[22–24] A compromise is often reached when raising skin flaps to balance completeness of a mastectomy with the vascularity of the overlying skin. This anatomical unpredictability in addition to operator variability[25] can lead to substantial differences in the amount of retained breast tissue that might contain occult disease or in which future cancer could form. While theoretical increases in local recurrence risk might be expected after non-skin-sparing mastectomy, mature studies with careful patient selection show equivalence of outcome compared with simple mastectomy.[26–28] The retrospective nature of these studies are subject to surgeon, case selection, and publication bias. Nonetheless, the overall trends in the existing literature, including a meta-analyses by Lanitis and colleagues comparing skin-sparing to non-skin-sparing mastectomy found no difference in locoregional recurrence rates between the two techniques.[29] The local recurrence rates with careful patient selection for skin-sparing mastectomy (1.9%–7.1%) compared with simple mastectomy (1.7%–9.5%) therefore allows for equipoise of choice.[14–18,26–28] Changing patterns of detecting early disease either at initial presentation or recurrence are likely to lead to higher rates of disease-free survival than in the past. Surveys of American plastic surgeons report the widespread use of the skin-sparing approach with overall agreement on oncological adequacy and superiority of aesthetic outcome.[30,31]

Oncological considerations of nipple-sparing mastectomy

Nipple preservation is an extension of the skin-sparing concept and represents the next step in conservative forms of mastectomy.[32–34] The skin of the nipple originates from the ectodermal embryological layer, but its contents are derived from mesenchymal structures of the mammary ridge which remain dormant until puberty. The developing nipple bud links the terminal duct lobular units to the lactiferous sinuses to open into the nipple orifices. Between 6 and 12 major ducts drain the majority of the lactational systems. Breast cancer forms in the terminal duct lobular-unit, and these structures are rarely found in the nipple.[35,36] The risk of cancer forming de novo in the nipple is thus unlikely, making this form of mastectomy ideal for risk-reducing surgery. The technique requires more careful consideration when applied to therapeutic nipple-sparing mastectomy as cancer forming in more proximal sites of the ductal-lobular system may affect the nipple by cancerization of the lobules from an extensive intraduct component.[37,38]

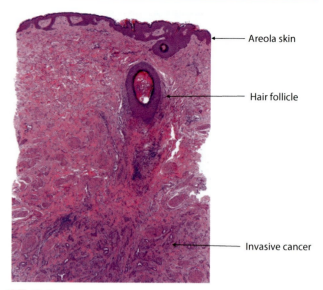

15.1.1 Photomicrograph of section through areola skin, showing breast cancer infiltrating the underlying tissue immediately deep to areolar smooth muscle bundles. Hematoxylin and eosin at magnification x20. (Courtesy of Dr. Ashutosh Nerurkar, Royal Marsden NHS Trust, London, UK.)

The two principle concerns in nipple-sparing mastectomy are retention of occult disease in the nipple core (**Figure 15.1.1**) and the risk of future disease forming within the preserved nipple. Studies that report the histological presence of cancer within the nipple removed as part of a routine mastectomy can be as high as 50%,[39–45] but cannot be directly applied to patients specifically selected for nipple-sparing mastectomy by their surgeons. Patient series that included women with obvious nipple involvement at the time of mastectomy have little relevance to clinical decision making as nipple-sparing mastectomy is clearly contraindicated. Nonetheless, even after exclusion of, there remains an occult cancer prevalence on histological examination of the nipple of up to 31%.[46–49] Differences in methods of pathological processing and preparation further influence the reported prevalence of occult disease identified within the nipple. Studies in keeping with contemporaneous practice estimate the risk of occult malignancy within the nipple to be closer to 10%.[50]

Risk factors associated with occult nipple involvement are summarized in **Table 15.1.1**. Clinical predictors of occult nipple disease need to be based on parameters that can be reliably assessed before surgery. Standard imaging by mammography and ultrasound are routinely used with further information provided by MRI,[51–53] but none provide sufficient sensitivity or specificity for the presence of cancer within the nipple.

Table 15.1.1 Predictors of nipple involvement with microscopic malignancy

Factors associated with occult nipple involvement

Tumor distance to nipple <2 cm

Tumor size greater than 5 cm

Multifocal disease

Extensive associated DCIS

Cancerization of the lobules

Invasive lobular cancer

Positive lymph nodes

Presence of vascular invasion

ER negativity

Her-2 positivity

Intraoperative assessment of the nipple

The lactiferous ducts within the nipple are arranged as a central bundle[54] and, while this is indistinguishable as a surgical plane, this anatomical feature allows for separation of the central core containing the ducts, leaving a fibrous margin with a minimal amount of at-risk ductal content. Intraoperative frozen section of the nipple base or core to confirm a clear margin of resection can be helpful, but has a false-negative rate of 1%–13%.[55–58] There are practical limitations of intraoperative frozen section: reacting to an unexpected positive result could mean an on-table change of plan which must be pre-agreed with the patient. Removing the nipple-areola complex causes tension at skin-closure, distorts the shape of the breast mound, and can add to a surgical scar if a remote incision site (such as the inframammary crease) has already been started. Despite a negative frozen section result, final clinical decisions are dependent on paraffin-fixed sections of the nipple base.[59]

Adjuvant treatment to the retained nipple

The role of focal radiotherapy to treat the retained nipple in therapeutic mastectomy is uncertain. A review by Janssen and colleagues of adjuvant radiotherapy after nipple-sparing mastectomy shows wide variation.[60] Controversy remains as whether to apply the same principles to nipple-sparing mastectomy as to simple or modified radical mastectomy. Petit and colleagues at the European Institute of Oncology employed intraoperative electron beam radiotherapy to preserve retroareolar parenchyma without compromising oncological outcome. The local recurrence rate in the retained nipple was 0.8% in those patients with invasive cancer, but significantly higher (2.9%) in ductal carcinoma in situ. Moreover, in a subset of 76 patients with negative frozen section, but positive disease on definitive histology, there were no cases of recurrence in the nipple.[61]

The same criteria for postmastectomy radiotherapy should apply to nipple or skin-sparing mastectomy as for any other form of mastectomy. A clear nipple margin can reasonably be considered to have been treated by the underlying resection alone. As intraoperative radiotherapy is not currently standard of care in the mastectomy setting, histologically proven cancer extension into the nipple at the time of surgery is best treated by nipple resection. Preservation of the areola with excision of the nipple alone may be an alternative option[62] to empirical consideration of targeted external beam radiotherapy to the retained nipple-areola complex.

Recurrence risk following nipple-sparing mastectomy

Studies of oncological outcome after nipple-sparing mastectomy are limited by differences in patient selection criteria, duration of follow-up, and variation in adjuvant treatment regimens. Earlier studies appear to report a higher incidence of subsequent cancer within the nipple of 5%–12%,[63,64] while there is a trend in more recent studies for lower rates of subsequent cancer incidence within the nipple of around 5%,[32,56,65–68] which may reflect more refined case selection for nipple preservation. Thus, with appropriate patient assessment, the overall incidence of nipple recurrence is small. Contemporary studies of patients with nipple-preservation in skin-sparing series show similar rates of local recurrence of 4% to 11.5%, with recurrence confined to the nipple areola-complex in less than 5% of cases.[50,69,70] Moreover, overall survival rates accounting for stage are comparable between nipple-sparing and skin-sparing techniques.[57,58,70]

CONCLUSION

Skin-sparing and nipple-sparing mastectomy are part of the armamentarium of reconstructive breast surgery after cancer, but require careful patient selection. Nipple-sparing is ideally suited for risk-reducing mastectomy. Improved outcome with modern adjuvant therapies and enhanced surveillance protocols are likely to see broader indications and acceptance of nipple-sparing techniques.

REFERENCES

1. Veronesi U, Cascinelli N, Marubini E et al. Twenty-year follow-up of a randomized study comparing breast-conserving surgery with radical mastectomy for early breast cancer. *N Engl J Med* 2002; 17: 1227–1232.
2. Fisher B, Anderson S, Bryant J et al. Twenty-year follow-up of a randomized trial comparing total mastectomy, lumpectomy, and lumpectomy plus irradiation for the treatment of invasive breast cancer. *New Engl J Med* 2002; 347: 1233–1241.
3. Kummerow KL, Du L, Penson DF et al. Nationwide trends in mastectomy for early-stage breast cancer. *JAMA Surg* 2015; 150: 9–16.
4. Crown A, Wechter DG, Grumley JW. Oncoplastic breast-conserving surgery reduces mastectomy and post-operative excision rates. *Ann Surg Oncol* 2015; 22: 3363–3368.
5. Advani P, Cornell L, Chumsri S, Moreno-Aspitia A. Dual HER2 blockade in the neoadjuvant and adjuvant treatment of HER2-positive breast cancer. *Breast Cancer* 2015; 7: 321–335.
6. Puglisi F, Fontanella C, Amoroso V et al. Current challenges in HER2-positive breast cancer. *Crit Rev Oncol Hematol* 2016; 98: 211–221.
7. Lehman CD, Gatsonis C, Kuhl CK et al. MRI evaluation of the contralateral breast in women with recently diagnosed breast cancer. *N Engl J Med* 2007; 356: 1295–1303.
8. Katipamula R, Degnim AC, Hoskin T et al. Trends in mastectomy rates at the Mayo Clinic Rochester: Effect of surgical year and preoperative magnetic resonance imaging. *J Clin Oncol* 2009; 27: 4082–4088.
9. Kwon JS, Gutierrez-Barrera AM, Young D, Sun CC, Daniels MS, Lu KH, Arun B. Expanding the criteria for BRCA mutation testing in breast cancer survivors. *J Clin Oncol* 2010; 28: 4214–4220.
10. Balmaña J, Díez O, Castiglione M, ESMO Guidelines working group. BRCA in breast cancer: ESMO clinical recommendations. *Ann Oncol* 2009; 20(Suppl 4): 19–20.
11. Jin J. Women with breast cancer who opt for contralateral prophylactic mastectomy may overestimate future risk. *JAMA* 2013; 310: 1548.
12. Tuttle TM, Habermann EB, Grund EH et al. Increasing use of contralateral prophylactic mastectomy for breast cancer patients: A trend toward more aggressive surgical treatment. *J Clin Oncol* 2007; 25: 5203–5209.
13. Toth BA, Lappert P. Modified skin incisions for mastectomy: The need for plastic surgical input in preoperative planning. *Plast Reconstr Surg* 1991; 87: 1048–1053.
14. Carlson GW, Bostwick J III, Wood WC et al. Skin-sparing mastectomy. Oncologic and reconstructive considerations. *Ann Surg* 1997; 225: 570–575.
15. Simmons RM, Fish SK, Osborne MP et al. Local and distant recurrence rates in skin-sparing mastectomies compared with non-skin sparing mastectomies. *Ann Surg Oncol* 1999; 6: 676–681.
16. Kroll SS, Khoo A, Singletary SE et al. Local recurrence risk after skin-sparing mastectomies compared with non-skin sparing mastectomies. *Ann Surg Oncol* 1999; 6: 676–681.
17. Slavin SA, Schnitt SJ, Duda RB et al. Skin-sparing mastectomy and immediate reconstruction: Oncologic risks and aesthetic results in patients with early-stage breast cancer. *Plast Reconstr Surg* 1998; 102: 49–62.

18. Greenway RM, Schlossberg L, Dooley WC. Fifteen-year series of skin-sparing mastectomy for stage 0 to 2 breast cancer. *Am J Surg* 2005; 190: 918–922.
19. Spiegel AJ, Butler CE. Recurrence following treatment of ductal carcinoma in situ with skin-sparing mastectomy and immediate breast reconstruction. *Plast Reconstr Surg* 2003; 111: 706–711.
20. Downes KJ, Glatt BS, Kanchwala SK et al. Skin-sparing mastectomy and immediate reconstruction is an acceptable treatment option for patients with high-risk breast carcinoma. *Cancer* 2005; 103: 906–913.
21. Medina-Franco H, Vasconez LO, Fix RJ et al. Factors associated with local recurrence after skin-sparing mastectomy and immediate breast reconstruction for invasive breast cancer. *Ann Surg* 2002; 235: 814–819.
22. Beer GM, Varga Z, Budi S et al. Incidence of the superficial fascia and its relevance in skin-sparing mastectomy. *Cancer* 2002;94: 1619–1625.
23. Larson DL, Basir Z, Bruce T. Is oncologic safety compatible with a predictably viable mastectomy skin flap? *Plast Reconstr Surg* 2011; 127: 27–33.
24. Ho CM, Mak CK, Lau Y et al. Skin involvement in invasive breast carcinoma: Safety of skin-sparing mastectomy. *Ann Surg Oncol* 2003; 10: 102–107.
25. Robertson SA, Rusby JE, Cuttress RI. Determinants of optimal mastectomy skin flap thickness. *Br J Surg* 2014; 10: 899–911.
26. Horiguchi J, Iino JH, Takei H et al. A comparative study of subcutaneous mastectomy with radical mastectomy. *Anticancer Res* 2001; 21: 2963–2967.
27. Ueda S, Tamaki Y, Kano K et al. Cosmetic outcome and patient satisfaction after skin-sparing mastectomy for breast cancer with immediate reconstruction of the breast. *Surgery* 2008; 143: 414–425.
28. Yi M, Kronowitz SJ, Meric-Bernstam F et al. Local, regional, and systemic recurrence rates in patients undergoing skin-sparing mastectomy compared with conventional mastectomy. *Cancer* 2011; 117; 916–924.
29. Lanitis S, Tekkis PP, Sgourakis G et al. Comparison of skin-sparing mastectomy versus non-skin-sparing mastectomy for breast cancer. *Ann Surg* 2010; 251: 632–639.
30. Shen J, Ellenhorn J, Qian D et al. Skin-sparing mastectomy: A survey based approach to defining standard of care. *Am Surg* 2008; 74: 902–905.
31. Ibrahim AM, Koolen PG, Ashraf AA, Kim K, Mureau MA, Lee BT, Lin SJ. Acellular dermal matrix in reconstructive breast surgery: Survey of current practice among plastic surgeons. *Plast Reconstr Surg Glob Open.* 2015: 3: e381.
32. Sacchini V, Pinnotti JA, Banos AC et al. Nipple sparing mastectomy for breast cancer and risk reduction: Oncologic or technical problem? *J Am Coll Surg* 2006; 203: 704–714.
33. Chung AP, Sacchini V. Nipple-sparing mastectomy: Where are we now? *Surg Oncol* 2008; 17: 261–266.
34. Adam H, Bygdeson M, de Boniface J. The oncological safety of nipple-sparing mastectomy – A Swedish matched cohort study. *Eur J Surg Oncol* 2014; 40: 1209–1215.

35. Rosen PP, Tench W. Lobules in the nipple. Frequency and significance for breast cancer treatment. *Pathol Annu* 1985; 20 Pt 2: 317–322.

36. Stolier AJ, Wang J. Terminal duct lobular units are scarcein the nipple: Implications for prophylactic nipple-sparing mastectomy: Terminal duct lobular units in the nipple. *Ann Surg Oncol* 2008; 15: 438–442.

37. Collins LC, Achacoso N, Nekhlyudov L, Fletcher SW, Haque R, Quesenberry CP Jr et al. Relationship between clinical and pathologic features of ductal carcinoma in situ and patient age: An analysis of 657 patients. *Am J Surg Pathol* 2009; 33: 1802–1808.

38. Go EM, Chan SK, Vong JS et al. Predictors of invasion in needle core biopsies of the breast with ductal carcinoma in situ. *Mod Pathol* 2010; 23: 737–742.

39. Smith J, Payne WS, Carney JA. Involvement of the nipple and areola in carcinoma of the breast. *Surg Gynecol Obstet* 1976; 143: 546–548.

40. Andersen JA, Gram JB, Pallesen RM. Involvement of the nipple and areola in breast cancer. Value of clinical findings. *Scand J Plast Reconstr Surg* 1981; 15: 39–42.

41. Lagios MD, Gates EA, Westdahl PR et al. A guide to the frequency of nipple involvement in breast cancer. A study of 149 consecutive mastectomies using a serial subgross and correlated radiographic technique. *Am J Surg* 1979; 138: 135–142.

42. Wertheim U, Ozzello L. Neoplastic involvement of nipple and skin flap in carcinoma of the breast. *Am J Surg Pathol* 1980; 4: 543–549.

43. Quinn RH, Barlow JF. Involvement of the nipple and areola by carcinoma of the breast. *Arch Surg* 1981; 116: 1139–1140.

44. Parry RG, Cochran TC Jr, Wolfort FG. When is there nipple involvement in carcinoma of the breast? *Plast Reconstr Surg* 1977; 59: 535–537.

45. Verma GR, Kumar A, Joshi K. Nipple involvement in peripheral breast carcinoma: A prospective study. *Indian J Cancer* 1997; 34: 1–5.

46. Morimoto T, Komaki K, Inui K et al. Involvement of nipple and areola in early breast cancer. *Cancer* 1985; 55: 2459–2463.

47. Santini D, Taffurelli M, Gelli MC et al. Neoplastic involvement of nipple-areolar complex in invasive breast cancer. *Am J Surg* 1989; 158: 399–403.

48. Laronga C, Kemp B, Johnston D et al. The incidence of occult nipple-areola complex involvement in breast cancer patients receiving a skin-sparing mastectomy. *Ann Surg Oncol* 1999; 6: 609–613.

49. Rusby JE, Brachtel EF, Othus M et al. Development and validation of a model predictive of occult nipple involvement in women undergoing mastectomy. *Br J Surg* 2008; 95: 1356–1361.

50. Mallon P, Feron JG, Couturaud B et al. The role of nipple-sparing mastectomy in breast cancer: A comprehensive review of the literature. *Plast Reconstr Surg* 2013; 131: 969–984.

51. Friedman EP, Hall-Craggs MA, Mumtaz H et al. Breast MR and the appearance of the normal and abnormal nipple. *Clin Radiol* 1997; 52: 854–861.

52. Ponzone R, Maggiorotto F, Carabalona S et al. MRI and intra-operative pathology to predict nipple-areola complex (NAC) involvement in patients undergoing NAC-sparing mastectomy. *Eur J Cancer* 2015; 51: 1882–1889.

53. D'Alonzo M, Martincich L, Biglia N et al. Clinical and radiological predictors of nipple-areola complex involvement in breast cancer patients. *Eur J Cancer* 2012; 48: 2311–2318.

54. Rusby JE, Brachtel EF, Michaelson JS et al. Breast duct anatomy in the human nipple: Three-dimensional patterns and clinical implications. *Breast Cancer Res Treat* 2007; 106: 171–179.

55. Vlajcic Z, Zic R, Stanec S et al. Nipple-areola complex preservation: Predictive factors of neoplastic nipple-areola complex invasion. *Ann Plast Surg* 2005; 55: 240–244.

56. Crowe JP, Patrick RJ, Yetman RJ et al. Nipple-sparing mastectomy update: One hundred forty-nine procedures and clinical outcomes. *Arch Surg* 2008; 143: 1106–1110.

57. Petit JY, Veronesi U, Rey P et al. Nipple-sparing mastectomy: Risk of nipple-areola recurrences in a series of 579 cases. *Breast Cancer Res Treat* 2009; 114: 97–101.

58. Benediktsson KP, Perbeck L. Survival in breast cancer after nipple-sparing subcutaneous mastectomy and immediate reconstruction with implants: A prospective trial with 13 years median follow-up in 216 patients. *Eur J Surg Oncol* 2008; 34: 143–148.

59. Wijayanayagam A, Kumar AS, Foster RD et al. Optimizing the total skin-sparing mastectomy. *Arch Surg* 2008; 143: 38–45.

60. Janssen S, Holz-Sapra E, Rades D, Moser A, Studer G. Nipple-sparing mastectomy in breast cancer patients: The role of adjuvant radiotherapy (Review). *Oncol Lett.* 2015; 9: 2435–2441.

61. Petit JY, Veronesi U, Orecchia R et al. Risk factors associated with recurrence after nipple-sparing mastectomy for invasive and intraepithelial neoplasia. *Ann Oncol* 2012; 23: 2053–2058.

62. Simmons RM, Brennan M, Christos P et al. Analysis of nipple/areola involvement with mastectomy: Can the areola be preserved? *Ann Surg Oncol* 2002; 9: 165–168.

63. Kissin MW, Kark AE. Nipple preservation during mastectomy. *Br J Surg* 1987; 74: 58–61.

64. Bishop CC, Singh S, Nash AG. Mastectomy and breast reconstruction preserving the nipple. *Ann R Coll Surg Engl* 1990; 72: 87–89.

65. Gerber B, Krause A, Reimer T et al. Skin-sparing mastectomy with conservation of the nipple-areola complex and autologous reconstruction is an oncologically safe procedure. *Ann Surg* 2003; 238: 120–127.

66. Caruso F, Ferrara M, Castiglione G et al. Nipple sparing subcutaneous mastectomy: Sixty-six months follow-up. *Eur J Surg Oncol* 2006; 32: 937–940.

67. Paepke S, Schmid R, Fleckner S et al. Subcutaneous mastectomy with conservation of the nipple-areola skin: Broadening the indications. *Ann Surg* 2009; 250: 288–292.

68. Amara D, Peled AW, Wang F, Ewing CA, Alvarado M, Esserman LJ. Tumour involvement of the nipple in total skin-sparing mastectomy: Strategies for management. *Ann Surg Oncol* 2015; 22: 3803–3808.

69. Boneti C, Yuen J, Santiago C et al. Oncologic safety of nipple skin-sparing or total skin-sparing mastectomies with immediate reconstruction. *J Am Coll Surg* 2011; 212: 686–693.

70. Gerber B, Krause A, Dietrich M et al. The oncological safety of skin sparing mastectomy with conservation of the nipple-areola complex and autologous reconstruction: An extended follow-up study. *Ann Surg* 2009; 249: 461–468.

15.2 RECONSTRUCTIVE ASPECTS

Gerald Gui

The evolution of skin-sparing mastectomy

The skin-sparing approach lends itself well to immediate breast reconstruction utilizing the preserved skin envelope following removal of the breast. Early skin-sparing methods included excision of the nipple-areola complex,[1] and as the technique became more formalized, various classification systems developed,[2] commonly incorporating a lateral radial incision as a racquet handle to excise the nipple. Where excision biopsies were performed, scars exposed on the breast mound were included in the resection. As needle biopsy techniques evolved and excision biopsies became much less common, the skin-sparing approach allowed the aesthetic planning of surgical incisions, avoiding scars on exposed areas of the breast with shorter incisions compared with simple or modified radical mastectomy.

A fundamental technical difference between immediate and delayed reconstruction is the loss of skin that needs to be replaced at the time of delayed reconstruction. This is achieved either by tissue expansion of the existing postmastectomy chest wall skin or by incorporation of the skin overlying the autologous tissue harvested to replace the volume of the missing breast. Tissue expansion may be compromised by previous radiotherapy, whereby the expansion process is restricted by radiation fibrosis, higher complication rates associated with poor wound healing, and subsequent capsule formation.

The transition to nipple-retaining mastectomies

In women who have had their nipple removed, nipple reconstruction and micropigmentation is usually the final part of the reconstructive process when the optimum breast mound and symmetrization surgery, where required, is complete. The majority of patients who have lost their nipple-areola complex as part of the mastectomy subsequently undergo nipple reconstruction.[3] There are imperfections of a reconstructed compared with a natural nipple (**Figure 15.2.1**), among which are loss of projection over time, the requirement to tattoo the reconstructed nipple that may subsequently fade, and the lack of sensation.[4,5] The nipple reconstruction lacks erectability and skin rugosity created by smooth muscle or the appearance of Montgomery's tubercles that may be prominent in certain areola types. Maintaining the natural nipple at skin-sparing mastectomy has a positive effect on psychological adjustment, perception of body image, and patient-reported satisfaction.[6–10] The preserved nipple often retains some sensation and erectile capability while maintaining the features of the areola and, hence, the identity of the original breast.

The trend toward nipple-sparing gained popularity as mastectomy procedures became more conservative. Apart

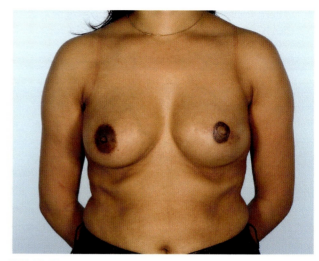

15.2.1 While nipple reconstruction can give excellent results, unilateral nipple reconstruction (in this example, the left) in time commonly results in visual differences compared with the natural (right) nipple. This patient has had a nipple-sparing mastectomy on the right and skin-sparing mastectomy with nipple excision on the left.

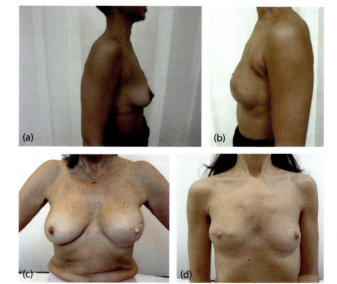

15.2.2 (a, b) Excising the nipple-areola complex results in a flattening and rounding-off where the natural breast peaks. (c) Especially with tissue expansion techniques, the scar to excise the nipple can rise to lie exposed on the superior breast mound cranial to the desired nipple position. (d) The length of a short transverse elliptical incision is often longer than the projected areola disc.

from the visual impact, removing the nipple-areola complex results in skin tightening causing distortion of the reconstructed breast mound. This flattens the appearance of the skin sparing compared with nipple-sparing mastectomy (**Figure 15.2.2a and b**). With tissue expansion, the final position of the nipple scar often lies cranial to the desired site of the subsequent nipple reconstruction (**Figure 15.2.2c**). A short ellipse to excise the nipple-areola complex is generally longer than the diameter of the areola (**Figure 15.2.2d**). While nipple reconstruction could soften the visual impression, the aesthetic outcome of nipple-sparing mastectomy is superior. The principle considerations in patient selection for nipple preservation are oncologically driven followed by patient choice. A group that lends itself well to nipple-sparing mastectomy are women who have risk reduction mastectomy as carriers of a high-risk breast cancer predisposition gene such as BRCA1/2.[11,12]

Surgical planning of skin and nipple–sparing mastectomy

The principle considerations in surgical decision making are summarized in **Table 15.2.1**. Preoperative assessment and skin marking is performed in the upright position. Useful landmarks are the midline, the breast meridian, and

Table 15.2.1 Factors in the surgical planning of nipple- and skin-sparing mastectomy

General	Body habitus
	Work, leisure, and sports
	Comorbid factors: smoking, diabetes, hypertension, and coagulopathy
Oncologic	Therapeutic or risk reduction
	Unilateral or bilateral
	Tumor size
	Proximity to skin and nipple
	Extensive intraduct component with cancerization of lobules
	Previous or planned radiotherapy
	Locally advanced disease and inflammatory presentation
Local tissue	Breast size, shape, and ptosis
	Skin properties including tissue elasticity
	Pre-existing scars
	Skin envelope maintenance, expansion, or reduction
	Contralateral breast properties and symmeterization requirements
Reconstruction	Implant alone, autologous, or combination
	Donor site quality, quantity, and impact of scars
Patient choice	Understanding
	Expectations
	Informed consent

the inframammary crease. Measurements of the sternal-notch nipple distance, inframammary crease-nipple distance, midline-nipple distance, transverse breast width, vertical breast height, and projection together with the preoperative photographs form an essential part of the patient's medical record.

Examples of skin-sparing mastectomies are shown in **Figure 15.2.3**. Pre-existing scars may need to be excised if the anterior margin is involved when breast conservation is being converted to a mastectomy or if the local recurrence involves the pre-existing scar. The advantages of being able to leave a pre-existing scar is the ability to plan the skin-sparing mastectomy undistracted. This is particularly useful when a nipple-sparing mastectomy is approached through a remote incision such as the inframammary crease or the lateral breast fold. Particular care has to be taken when there has been a recent periareolar incision, as the blood supply to the nipple may be compromised. A recent circumareolar scar may be a contraindication to preserve the nipple-areola complex; a longstanding circumareolar scar, for example, after a previous mastopexy some years before, is not.

Raising the skin flap

At surgery, the subcutaneous plane is developed with the intention of removing maximal breast parenchymal tissue. Great care must be taken to avoid injury to the subdermal tissue and to protect the integrity of the vascular plexus on which the skin flaps depend. Preoperative marking of the upper limit of the breast is helpful to avoid over-dissection into the subcutaneous non-breast tissue. When the subcutaneous plane has been developed, the breast can be dissected off the pectoralis major muscle. Delivering the breast through the incision may facilitate the final stages of the dissection.

Hydrodissection is increasingly being used as a technique to raise mastectomy flaps.[13,14] It is particularly useful in conjunction with remote incisions such as access through the inframammary crease. A typical hydrodissection solution would consist of one liter of normal saline, local anesthetic (e.g., 30 mL of 0.5% chirocaine), and adrenaline (e.g., 0.5 mL of 1:1000 adrenaline), from which up to 500 mL may be used per breast. The dermal blood supply must be protected by avoiding the creation of an unnatural subcutaneous plane that could lead to mastectomy flap necrosis. Hydrodissection is an effective technique of dissecting the nipple-areola complex.[15]

Nipple–sparing mastectomy as an extension of skin preservation

Good breast form and symmetry can be obtained with nipple-sparing mastectomy techniques to give satisfactory results with implant alone, autologous only, and combined autologous

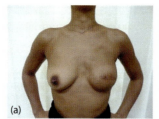 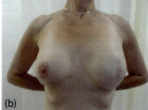 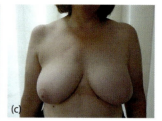

15.2.3 Examples of skin-sparing mastectomy incisions with excision of the nipple areola complex: (a) left central transverse skin crease; (b) left vertical incision; (c) left circumareolar approach to incorporate autologous donor site skin paddle for subsequent nipple reconstruction.

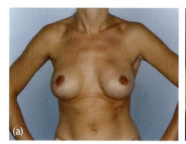 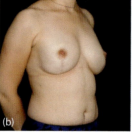 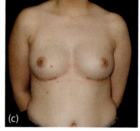 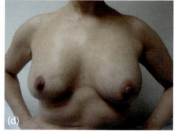

15.2.4 Bilateral nipple-sparing mastectomies through (a) inferior periareolar with lateral extension; (b) inferior periareolar with vertical extensions; (c) and (d) inframammary crease incisions.

and implant breast reconstructions.[16,17] Aesthetic satisfaction with nipple-sparing mastectomy is high and can be superior to skin-sparing methods without nipple preservation.[18,19] Nipple-sparing mastectomy can be performed through a range of surgical incisions (**Figure 15.2.4**). Lateral radial extensions may be associated with a lower risk of ischemia.[20,21] The vertical extension has the aesthetic advantage of being incorporated into the surgical incision of any future secondary procedure to resemble that of a mastopexy. Lateral breast fold or inferior mammary crease incisions provide excellent access to the breast and avoids incisions on the breast mound itself. Careful attention to safeguarding the anterior intercostal perforators and the integrity of the subareolar vascular plexus is integral to maintaining the nipple blood supply.[22,23]

Skin-reducing mastectomy

In women with larger and ptotic breasts, the use of a skin-reduction approach based on a Wise pattern[24] provides excellent access for mastectomy (**Figure 15.2.5**). This approach corrects for ptosis and forms a smaller breast. With appropriate planning and skin marking, it is usually possible to proceed directly to a fixed volume implant of the planned breast size. The procedure is well suited to bilateral cases. In unilateral cases, the contralateral breast will usually require a reduction mammoplasty for symmetry. The inferior mastectomy flap is dissected in the subcutaneous plane down to the inframammary crease, the only difference in thickness to a standard mastectomy flap being the de-epithelialized external skin surface. This dermal sling acts as an autologous internal tissue flap to provide lower implant cover. Axillary surgery can usually be accessed through the same breast incisions. It is essential that the vascularity of the de-epithelialized dermal flap is maintained through the subdermal vasculature entering from the inframammary crease to avoid ischemic necrosis. The risk of ischemic necrosis of the skin flaps can be minimized by meticulous technique. An interesting development in recent years has been the introduction of fluorescein dye and indocyanine green angiography to assess mastectomy skin-flap vascularity.[25–27]

A further level of complexity can be added to this skin reduction approach by nipple conservation.[28] The nipple blood supply can be maintained on either the superior-medial or superior-lateral dermal flaps (**Figure 15.2.6**). The superior-medial is often preferable, as preservation of the anterior intercostals are more consistent and tumors of the breast occur more commonly in the upper outer quadrant. The greater the distance of the nipple transposition, the higher the risk of nipple necrosis. When nipple repositioning exceeds distances greater than 3 cm, it may be better to consider planned excision of the nipple and delayed reconstruction or nipple grafting techniques.

Nipple necrosis following nipple-sparing mastectomy

Nipple necrosis rates vary widely, most studies reporting up to 10%, but some studies in excess of 50%.[6,7,29–37] With careful patient selection and surgical technique, full thickness rates of nipple-areola necrosis should be less than 5% and partial thickness ischemia below 10%.

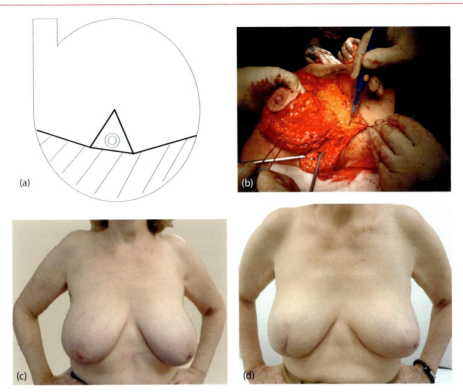

15.2.5 Wise pattern skin-reducing mastectomy with de-epithelialized lower mastectomy flap for lower implant cover. (a) Schematic diagram showing mark-up, with the cross-hatched area representing the de-epithelialised dermal sling; (b) Raising the mastectomy flaps with generous access; (c) and (d) Pre and postoperative photographs.

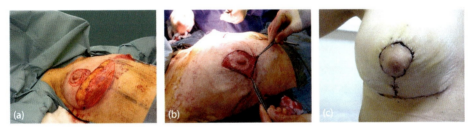

15.2.6 Skin-reduction pattern mastectomy with nipple preservation. (a) De-epithelialized area defines the pillars supporting the nipple and the inferior dermal sling. If the nipple needs to move cranially by a short distance, the vascularity can be maintained on both the superior-medial and superior lateral dermal bridges. (b) In this case, the blood supply of the nipple is maintained through the superior lateral dermal bridge to allow rotation to a more cranial position. (c) Early postoperative appearance.

Most nipple ischemia can be managed conservatively, the dry gangrene acting as its own dressing. When the eschar lifts off in partial-thickness necrosis, the granulation process is often complete. Lifting off the mature eschar in full-thickness necrosis where the base is still granulating shifts the requirement to active dressings.[28] In full thickness nipple loss, early nipple excision could avoid prolonged dressing requirements.

CONCLUSION

Patient selection is the key to safe skin-sparing and nipple-sparing mastectomy. Meticulous surgical technique to avoid complications and audit of outcome will continue to ensure low recurrence rates and to offer patients an informed mastectomy choice.

REFERENCES

1. Toth BA, Lappert P. Modified skin incisions for mastectomy: The need for plastic surgical input in preoperative planning. *Plast Reconstr Surg* 1991; 87: 1048–1053.
2. Carlson GW, Bostwick J III, Wood WC et al. Skin-sparing mastectomy. Oncologic and reconstructive considerations. *Ann Surg* 1997; 225: 570–575.
3. Nahabedian MY, Tsangaris TN. Breast reconstruction following subcutaneous mastectomy for cancer: A critical appraisal of the nipple-areola complex. *Plast Reconstr Surg* 2006; 117: 1083–1090.

4. Jabor MA, Shayani P, Collins DR Jr et al. Nipple-areola reconstruction: Satisfaction and clinical determinants. *Plast Reconstr Surg* 2002; 110: 457–463.

5. Shestak KC, Gabriel A, Landecker A et al. Assessment of long-term nipple projection: A comparison of three techniques. *Plast Reconstr Surg* 2002; 110: 780–786.

6. Denewer A, Farouk O. Can nipple-sparing mastectomy and immediate breast reconstruction with modified extended latissimus dorsi muscular flap improve the cosmetic and functional outcome among patients with breast carcinoma? *World J Surg* 2007; 31: 1169–1177.

7. Petit JY, Veronesi U, Orecchia R et al. Nipple-sparing mastectomy in association with intra operative radiotherapy (ELIOT): A new type of mastectomy for breast cancer treatment. *Breast Cancer Res Treat* 2006; 96: 47–51.

8. Gerber B, Krause A, Dietrich M et al. The oncological safety of skin sparing mastectomy with conservation of the nipple-areola complex and autologous reconstruction: An extended follow-up study. *Ann Surg* 2009; 249: 461–468.

9. Temple-Oberle C, Ayeni O, Webb C, Bettger-Hahn M, Ayeni O, Mychailyshyn N. Shared decision-making: Applying a person-centered approach to tailored breast reconstruction information provides high satisfaction across a variety of breast reconstruction options. *J Surg Oncol* 2014; 110: 796–800.

10. Sisco M, Johnson DB, Wang C, Rasinski K, Rundell VL, Yao KA. The quality-of-life benefits of breast reconstruction do not diminish with age. *J Surg Oncol* 2015; 111: 663–668.

11. Hartmann LC, Schaid DJ, Woods JE et al. Efficacy of bilateral prophylactic mastectomy in women with a family history of breast cancer. *New Engl J Med* 1999; 340: 77–84.

12. Ashikari RH, Ashikari AY, Kelemen PR et al. Subcutaneous mastectomy and immediate reconstruction for prevention of breast cancer for high-risk patients. *Breast Cancer* 2008; 15: 185–191.

13. Vargas CR, Koolen PG, Ho OA, Ricci JA, Tobias AM, Lin SJ, Lee BT. Tumescent mastectomy technique in autologous breast reconstruction. *J Surg Res* 2015; 198: 525–529.

14. Samper A, Blanch A. Improved subcutaneous mastectomy with hydrodissection of the subcutaneous space. *Plast Reconstr Surg* 2003: 112: 694–695.

15. Folli S, Curcio A, Buggi F et al. Improved sub-areolar breast tissue removal in nipple-sparing mastectomy using hydrodissection. *Breast* 2012; 21: 190–193.

16. Mori H, Umeda T, Osanai T et al. Esthetic evaluation of immediate breast reconstruction after nipple-sparing or skin-sparing mastectomy. *Breast Cancer* 2005; 12: 299–303.

17. Mosahebi A, Ramakrishnan V, Gittos M et al. Aesthetic outcome of different techniques of reconstruction following nipple-areola-preserving envelope mastectomy with immediate reconstruction. *Plast Reconstr Surg* 2007; 119: 796–803.

18. Salgarello M, Visconti G, Barone-Adesi L. Nipple-sparing mastectomy with immediate implant reconstruction: Cosmetic outcomes and technical refinements. *Plast Reconstr Surg* 2010; 126: 1460–1471.

19. Yueh JH, Houlihan MJ, Slavin SA et al. Nipple-sparing mastectomy: Evaluation of patient satisfaction, aesthetic results, and sensation. *Ann Plast Surg* 2009; 62: 586–590.

20. Wijayanayagam A, Kumar AS, Foster RD et al. Optimizing the total skin-sparing mastectomy. *Arch Surg* 2008; 143: 38–45.

21. Regolo L, Ballardini B, Gallarotti E et al. Nipple sparing mastectomy: An innovative skin incision for an alternative approach. *Breast* 2008; 17: 8–11.

22. Nakajima H, Imanishi N, Aiso S. Arterial anatomy of the nipple-areola complex. *Plast Reconstr Surg* 1995; 96: 843–845.

23. Matsen CB, Mehrara B, Eaton A et al. Skin flap necrosis after mastectomy with reconstruction: A prospective study. *Ann Surg Oncol* 2016; 23: 257–264.

24. Nava MB, Ottolenghi J, Pennati A et al. Skin/nipple preserving mastectomies and implant-based breast reconstruction in patients with large and ptotic breast: Oncological and reconstructive results. *Breast* 2012; 21: 267–271.

25. Losken A, Styblo TM, Schaefer TG, Carlson GW. The use of fluorescein dye as a predictor of mastectomy skin-flap viability following autologous tissue reconstruction. *All Plast Surg* 2008; 61: 24–29.

26. Phillips BT, Lanier ST, Conkling N, Wang ED, Dagum AB, Ganz JC, Khan SU, Bui DT. Intraoperative perfusion techniques can accurately predict mastectomy skin flap necrosis in breast reconstruction: Results of a prospective trial. *Plast Reconstr Surg* 2012; 129: 778–788.

27. Rinker B. A comparison of methods to assess mastectomy flap viability in skin-sparing mastectomy and immediate reconstruction: A prospective cohort study. *Plast Reconstr Surg* 2016; 137: 395–401.

28. Rusby JE, Gui GP. Nipple sparing mastectomy in women with large or ptotic breasts. *J Plast Reconstr Aesthet Surg* 2010; 63: 754–755.

29. Crowe JP, Patrick RJ, Yetman RJ et al. Nipple-sparing mastectomy update: One hundred forty-nine procedures and clinical outcomes. *Arch Surg* 2008; 143: 1106–1110.

30. Caruso F, Ferrara M, Castiglione G et al. Nipple sparing subcutaneous mastectomy: Sixty-six months follow-up. *Eur J Surg Oncol* 2006; 32: 937–940.

31. Sacchini V, Pinotti JA, Barros AC et al. Nipple-sparing mastectomy for breast cancer and risk reduction: Oncologic or technical problem? *J Am Coll Surg* 2006; 203: 704–714.

32. Margulies AG, Hochberg J, Kepple J et al. Total skin-sparing mastectomy without preservation of the nipple-areola complex. *Am J Surg* 2005; 190: 907–912.

33. Psaila A, Pozzi M, Barone Adesi L et al. Nipple sparing mastectomy with immediate breast reconstruction: A short term analysis of our experience. *J Exp Clin Cancer Res* 2006; 25: 309–312.

34. Stolier AJ, Sullivan SK, DellaCroce FJ. Technical considerations in nipple-sparing mastectomy: 82 consecutive cases without necrosis. *Ann Surg Oncol* 2008; 15: 1341–1347.

35. Roco N, Catanuto G, Nava MB. What is the evidence behind conservative mastectomies? *Gland Surgery* 2015; 4: 506–518.

36. Mallon P, Feron JG, Couturaud B et al. The role of nipple-sparing mastectomy in breast cancer: A comprehensive review of the literature. *Plast Reconstr Surg* 2013; 131: 969–984.

37. Colwell AS, Tessler O, Lin AM et al. Breast reconstruction following nipple-sparing mastectomy: Predictors of complications, reconstruction outcomes, and 5-year trends. *Plast Reconstr Surg* 2014; 133: 496–506.

EDITORIAL COMMENTARY

The evolution of skin-sparing mastectomy continues reductionist approaches to breast and axillary surgery. Skin-sparing forms of mastectomy have developed rapidly since the mid-1990s in parallel with techniques for breast-conserving surgery and immediate breast reconstruction. Preservation of much of the breast skin envelope while removing parenchymal tissue together with the nipple-areola complex has revolutionized immediate breast reconstruction and avoids the need for skin augmentation through either tissue expansion or a myocutaneous flap with "sculpturing" of imported skin into the shape of a breast. Essentially, skin-sparing mastectomy leaves a bag of skin that is subsequently filled with an implant, autologous tissue, or an implant-assisted latissimus dorsi flap. The advent of skin-sparing mastectomy with minimal scarring and a preserved breast skin envelope has greatly enhanced cosmetic results which are much superior to cases involving extensive skin sacrifice. Skin-sparing mastectomy demands a meticulous surgical technique with dissection maintained in the oncological plane. The latter can usually be identified in most patients especially younger ones with denser breast parenchyma. This plane lies just on the surface of the breast parenchyma and determines individual patient flap thickness. If dissection is too superficial, there is a risk of damage to the subdermal vascular plexus with compromise of flap viability. Conversely, if the flaps are too thick, excessive breast tissue will be retained on the undersurface of the flaps. It is important that all parenchymal tissue is removed at the periphery of the breast, especially superiorly and toward the axilla when an inframammary incision is used. Initial concerns about skin sparing mastectomy have now been assuaged, and several large retrospective single institution studies and a meta-analysis confirm comparable rates of local recurrence for appropriately selected cases of skin sparing compared to conventional mastectomy. The precise surgical approach and skin incision for skin-sparing mastectomy may need to be adapted if there is clinical evidence of skin involvement or a tumor lies very superficial. Under these circumstances, it may be necessary to excise additional skin with an extended periareolar incision.

As an unqualified term, skin-sparing mastectomy implies removal of the nipple-areola complex. A subcutaneous mastectomy aims to preserve a thin sliver of breast tissue in order to ensure viability of the nipple-areola complex but can leave up to 15% of residual breast tissue. This operation is often undertaken in younger women with dense breast tissue that can be difficult to dissect off the undersurface of the nipple-areola complex without compromise of vascular supply.

Nipple-sparing mastectomy extends the concept of skin-sparing mastectomy and aims to preserve the ectodermal component of the nipple but removes the central core of lactiferous ducts that are derived from the mesenchyme. No terminal duct lobular units are present within this core tissue of the nipple thus underpinning any oncological rationale for nipple-sparing mastectomy in both a prophylactic and therapeutic context. Nipple-sparing mastectomy is a potentially curative procedure for established malignancy within the breast and aims for extirpation of all glandular tissue—it should be noted that these patients will not routinely receive adjuvant radiotherapy to the chest wall tissues which might otherwise treat any residual foci of breast tissue. As emphasized by Dr. Gerald Gui, nipple-sparing mastectomy must be used judiciously in patients with established breast cancer as the nipple could become involved secondary to cancerization of lobules from an extensive in situ component. It is imperative that nipple-sparing mastectomy is safe from an oncological perspective and not associated with higher rates of local recurrence compared with conventional or skin-sparing mastectomy without nipple preservation. Seminal breast-conservation therapy trials have confirmed that preservation of the nipple-areola complex as part of breast-conserving surgery does not compromise overall survival, and rates of local recurrence are acceptable when the remaining breast tissue is irradiated. For appropriate selected patients, the estimated risk for occult nipple involvement at the time of nipple-sparing mastectomy for cancer is about 10%. Some surgeons routinely perform intraoperative frozen section of tissue at the nipple base/core but this has variable false-negative rates (up to 13%) as do random core needle biopsies of retro-areola tissue taken preoperatively.

Selection of breast cancer patients for whom nipple-sparing mastectomy is oncologically safe is crucial together with attention to surgical technique—the latter aims to minimize risk of local recurrence and ischemic changes within the retained nipple-areola complex. Nipple-sparing mastectomy presents several technical challenges relating to choice of skin incision, avoiding necrosis of the skin or nipple-areola complex, and managing large or ptotic breasts that may require skin reduction. The surgical approach and type of incision must be individually chosen to optimize cosmetic results and maximize levels of patient satisfaction. Nipple-areola complex preservation maintains some nipple sensation plus erectile capacity and can reduce psychological distress, enhance body image, and improve overall satisfaction with results of breast surgery. These benefits should not be offset by fear of recurrence due to retention of the nipple-areola complex.

There is currently no evidence to support the routine use of adjuvant radiotherapy after nipple-sparing mastectomy and in particular any form of intraoperative radiotherapy; those patients with histological involvement of the nipple should be managed with excision of the nipple-areola complex rather than external irradiation thereof. Rates of local recurrence and survival outcomes in patients undergoing nipple-sparing mastectomy are similar to skin-sparing mastectomy with most cases of local recurrence not directly involving the nipple-areola complex ($<5\%$).

16

Nipple-sparing mastectomy

AT A GLANCE

The decision to perform nipple-sparing mastectomy is often not oncologic related and patients with ptotic breasts for example have typically been excluded from nipple-sparing procedures. However, techniques of pre- and post-mastectomy mastopexy have increased the eligibility range for nipple-sparing mastectomy which now includes those with ptotic breasts.

16.1 INCISIONS FOR NIPPLE-SPARING MASTECTOMY

Sirwan M. Hadad and Jennifer E. Rusby

There has been an evolution in approaches to nipple-sparing mastectomy which has occurred in parallel with increasing confidence in nipple-sparing as an oncologically safe procedure. Moreover, this has coincided with the integration of acellular dermal matrix into routine breast reconstructive practice. Early attempts at nipple preservation extrapolated from routine incisions for skin-sparing mastectomy. In contrast to a complete circumareolar incision with removal of the nipple-areola complex, an incision involving part of the circumference with lateral extension was often used.

The key criteria for a nipple-sparing mastectomy incision are as follows:

1. Provision of adequate access to all breast tissue to permit a thorough mastectomy from an oncological perspective

   For example, there is general agreement that inframammary fold incisions give adequate access to perform nipple-sparing mastectomy in small breasts only. Those patients with larger and more ptotic breasts require different approaches

2. Avoid compromising the blood supply to the nipple-areola complex

   Incision placement was identified early on as a key determinant of nipple viability and will be discussed in more detail below.

3. Produces a cosmetically acceptable result

A large number of incisions have been described in the literature including:

(1) Periareolar with lateral extension; (2) omega; (3) transareolar; (4) transnipple; (5) radial (any direction from NAC); (6) italic S; (7) vertical; (8) lazy S vertical; (9) parametric; (10) lateral inframammary fold; and (11) inframammary fold. A recent case series and literature review[1] described the following incisions (with reference to a previous review[2]):

1. Periareolar incision (along the supra- or infra-areolar margin) with lateral extension. This incision allows good exposure to retroareolar tissue and the lateral breast and permits access to raise the pectoralis major muscle to create a pocket. However, there is a risk of compromising blood supply to the areolar skin especially in larger ptotic breasts and smokers.

2. Transareolar incision with peri-nipple and lateral and/or medial extension; although this incision may reduce the risk of ischemia to the lower half of the areola, there is a risk of distortion and loss of nipple projection caused by peri-nipple scar formation.

3. Transnipple with medial or lateral extension. Bivalving the nipple is not thought to compromise the vascularity of nipple or areola and provides good access to the retroareolar tissue.

4. Inframammary fold or lateral inframammary fold (for 8–10 cm) can give excellent cosmetic results as long as the condensation of fibrous bands in this region are not violated. Access to the parasternal and subclavicular regions can be challenging, and this coupled with nipple necrosis and placement issues limit its use in women with large breasts.
5. Italic S incision: from 1 cm lateral to areolar edge extending radially upward is preferred by some surgeons.

Crowe and colleagues published the first case series in the revival of nipple-sparing mastectomy and reported 54 procedures in 44 patients (of which 17 were therapeutic and 37 prophylactic resections). Only three patients had complete loss of the nipple-areola complex and of note all of these were done through a medial incision.[3] In another review of 20 patients, nipple necrosis was significantly more likely when a periareolar approach was used compared to others.[4] Similarly, Garwood and colleagues reported that restricting the incision to one-third or less of the areolar circumference decreased nipple loss rates from 20% to 5% with an associated reduction in the rate of implant loss (31%–10%).[5] Chen and colleagues used a mainly periareolar incision with lateral extension in a series of 115 patients undergoing nipple-sparing mastectomy. Inframammary fold, omega type, and transareolar incisions were used in some cases.[6] They reported complete nipple loss in 3.5% and partial nipple loss in 13% of cases, with the latter being successfully treated conservatively.

Several of the larger more recent series[7,8] report use of inframammary fold incisions which are associated with low complication rates and good aesthetic outcomes. For example, Colwell reported use of an inframammary fold incision which was associated with a reduction in complication rates over time (ischemic nipple complications in 4.4%; explantation in 1.9%).[10] Similarly, Salzberg et al. reported an implant loss rate of 1.3% in a series of 466 breasts (68% for risk-reduction) in which an framammary fold incision was used for the subset of patients without macromastia undergoing nipple-sparing mastectomy. Conversely, it has been reported that the incidence of wound breakdown, and potential removal of implant, in patients undergoing post-mastectomy radiotherapy is higher in women with an inframammary fold incision compared to non-inframammary approach (21% vs 10%). Therefore, the likelihood of requiring irradiation postoperatively should be taken into account when considering incision placement.[9]

Recent technological advances permit intraoperative evaluation of skin-flap blood supply. For example, Proano and Perbeck measured skin circulation in 69 patients using laser Doppler and fluorescein flowmetry. They were able to compare skin circulation between cases with inframammary fold and those with lateral lazy S incisions. Skin circulation within the nipple-areola complex and the area of skin directly above was similar, but significantly lower blood flow to an area of skin 2 cm below the nipple-areola complex was seen, but only when this was measured by fluorescein flowmetry. Furthermore, no skin necrosis was seen in either group of patients, but the clinical significance of these findings is not clear,[11] nor whether insertion of implants would have any effect on blood flow to the lower skin flaps.

A number of additional considerations deserve special mention:

1. Access to vessels for free-flap reconstruction.
   When a free-flap reconstruction is undertaken, atraumatic access to the recipient vessels is essential, and if this is via the mastectomy incision, then this must be considered in preoperative planning. In a series of 19 patients with large ptotic breasts undergoing nipple-sparing mastectomy and immediate free-flap reconstruction, Schneider and colleagues[12] could successfully access the perforator vessels through two types of incisions: vertical (68%) and lateral (32%) incisions. No case of flap necrosis was seen in this series; however, their patient population did not include patients with a history of smoking, diabetes, or other factors that may negatively impact mastectomy skin-flap viability.
2. Ptosis: Approaches to nipple-sparing mastectomy in patients with ptotic breasts are discussed in another chapter, but suffice it to say that this requires skin reduction and repositioning of the nipple either simultaneously or prior to nipple-sparing mastectomy.
3. Endoscopic approaches to nipple-sparing mastectomy have been pioneered in Japan where the population generally has small breast volumes and scars are considered culturally unacceptable.[13] This technique involves two small incisions: one placed in the axilla and the second periareolar.[14] Various instruments have been developed to facilitate dissection under direct vision and include a 30° endoscope[15] and round balloon dissector.[16] Carbon dioxide is employed for insufflation and an appliance is available for pulling the skin—which collectively secure the virtual cavity of the operation. One example of such a retractor is the Kirschner two wire retractor.[17] Endoscopic mastectomy has not been adopted in the USA or Europe and while the procedure appears to be safe, there is limited data on oncological outcomes, and no convincing evidence that aesthetics are superior to open surgery.[18,19] Furthermore, expensive equipment is required and the procedure takes longer than a conventional open approach. Finally, there may be fewer implications of scarring in Western populations.

The literature is very heterogeneous in terms of type of incision, pathology, and reconstruction. It is therefore difficult to produce clear guidance on the most appropriate incision. However, with careful surgical technique[20] and adherence to the criteria listed above, nipple-sparing mastectomy can be performed in the majority of women in whom it is oncologically appropriate, with good aesthetic results.

REFERENCES

1. Rossi, C. et al. Nipple areola complex sparing mastectomy. *Gland Surg*, 2015. 4(6): 528–540.
2. Sacchini, V. et al. Nipple-sparing mastectomy for breast cancer and risk reduction: Oncologic or technical problem? *J Am Coll Surg*, 2006. 203(5): 704–714.
3. Crowe, J.P. et al. Nipple-sparing mastectomy update: One hundred forty-nine procedures and clinical outcomes. *Arch Surg*, 2008. 143(11): 1106–1110; discussion 1110.
4. Rawlani, V. et al. The effect of incision choice on outcomes of nipple-sparing mastectomy reconstruction. *Can J Plast Surg*, 2011. 19(4): 129–133.
5. Garwood, E.R. et al. Total skin-sparing mastectomy: Complications and local recurrence rates in 2 cohorts of patients. *Ann Surg*, 2009. 249(1): 26–32.
6. Chen, C.M. et al. Nipple-sparing mastectomy and immediate tissue expander/implant breast reconstruction. *Plast Reconstr Surg*, 2009. 124(6): 1772–1780.
7. Colwell, A.S. et al. Retrospective review of 331 consecutive immediate single-stage implant reconstructions with acellular dermal matrix: Indications, complications, trends, and costs. *Plast Reconstr Surg*, 2011. 128(6): 1170–1178.
8. Salzberg, C.A. et al. An 8-year experience of direct-to-implant immediate breast reconstruction using human acellular dermal matrix (AlloDerm). *Plast Reconstr Surg*, 2011. 127(2): 514–524.
9. Peled, A.W. et al. Impact of total skin-sparing mastectomy incision type on reconstructive complications following radiation therapy. *Plast Reconstr Surg*, 2014. 134(2): 169–175.
10. Colwell, A.S. et al. Breast reconstruction following nipple-sparing mastectomy: Predictors of complications, reconstruction outcomes, and 5-year trends. *Plast Reconstr Surg*, 2014. 133(3): 496–506.
11. Proano, E. and L.G. Perbeck. Influence of the site of skin incision on the circulation in the nipple-areola complex after subcutaneous mastectomy in breast cancer. *Scand J Plast Reconstr Surg Hand Surg*, 1996. 30(3): 195–200.
12. Schneider, L.F. et al. Nipple-sparing mastectomy and immediate free-flap reconstruction in the large ptotic breast. *Ann Plast Surg*, 2012. 69(4): 425–428.
13. Sakamoto, N. et al. Early results of an endoscopic nipple-sparing mastectomy for breast cancer. *Ann Surg Oncol*, 2009. 16(12): 3406–3413.
14. Owaki, T. et al. Present status of endoscopic mastectomy for breast cancer. *World J Clin Oncol*, 2015. 6(3): 25–29.
15. Yamashita, K. and K. Shimizu. Transaxillary retromammary route approach of video-assisted breast surgery enables the inner-side breast cancer to be resected for breast conserving surgery. *Am J Surg*, 2008. 196(4): 578–581.
16. Ito, K. et al. Endoscopic-assisted skin-sparing mastectomy combined with sentinel node biopsy. *ANZ J Surg*, 2008. 78(10): 894–898.
17. Owaki, T. et al. Endoscopic quadrantectomy for breast cancer with sentinel lymph node navigation via a small axillary incision. *Breast*, 2005. 14(1): 57–60.
18. Keshtgar, M.R. and E. Fukuma. Endoscopic mastectomy: What does the future hold? *Womens Health (Lond Engl)*, 2009. 5(2): 107–109.
19. Leff, D.R. et al. Endoscopic breast surgery: Where are we now and what might the future hold for video-assisted breast surgery? *Breast Cancer Res Treat*, 2011. 125(3): 607–625.
20. Stolier, A.J. and E.A. Levine. Reducing the risk of nipple necrosis: Technical observations in 340 nipple-sparing mastectomies. *Breast J*, 2013. 19(2): 173–179.

16.2 NIPPLE-SPARING MASTECTOMY IN BREAST PTOSIS

Sirwan M. Hadad and Jennifer E. Rusby

Early publications on nipple-sparing mastectomy[1,2] stated that breast ptosis is a contraindication to this procedure, based on an increased risk of nipple necrosis consequent to long, poorly perfused skin flaps, and the inability to control the final nipple position on the breast mound.[1] The nipple is such a focal point on the breast that a preserved nipple which is badly positioned may look worse than a correctly positioned, good quality nipple reconstruction.

However, as expertise and confidence has increased, surgeons have successfully extended the role of nipple-sparing mastectomy to women with large or ptotic breasts.

The methods described in the literature can be classified into four categories:

1. *Staged*: Skin reduction and repositioning of the nipple are performed initially, and mastectomy and reconstruction follows after a period.
2. *Simultaneous*: Skin reduction is combined with mastectomy and immediate reconstruction.
3. *Subsequent*: Mastopexy is performed 4–6 months after mastectomy and reconstruction.
4. Free nipple grafting.

Staged

The original protagonist of the staged option was Scott Spear who described a number of reduction techniques which could precede mastectomy for those who do not meet anatomical criteria for standard nipple-sparing mastectomy.[3] Stage one involved mastopexy or reduction mammoplasty, followed 3–4 weeks later by stage two, nipple-sparing mastectomy and placement of an expander through the same incision. Final reconstruction followed as a third procedure. In this series of 15 patients (24 breasts), 8% developed skin-flap necrosis and 13% developed minor degrees of partial nipple-areola complex necrosis. The reduction procedure was done through a circum-vertical or Wise-pattern skin incision, maintaining the majority of the circumference of the periareolar dermis, particularly superiorly between the 9 o'clock and 3 o'clock positions. This left the sub-dermal vasculature of the superior de-epithelialized skin intact and parenchymal excision from the central inferior wedge was then performed, if necessary.

The mastectomy stage was carried out 3–4 weeks later, or in the event of neoadjuvant chemotherapy, 4–6 weeks after completion of chemotherapy. Nipple-sparing mastectomy was performed either through the vertical limb or the inframammary fold scar and implant-based reconstruction was carried out at the same time. This technique is most suited to women undergoing risk-reducing surgery and although it can be used in women prior to neoadjuvant systemic therapy, it is not widely offered in the setting of cancer.

Simultaneous

Simultaneous mastopexy and nipple-sparing mastectomy with immediate breast reconstruction has been reported in the literature with variable success. Thus Rivolin and colleagues described a modified nipple-sparing mastectomy technique that allows transposition/centralization of the nipple-areola complex at the same time as mastectomy, which they referred to as periareolar-pexy nipple-sparing mastectomy. This procedure was offered to patients with a longer sternal notch to nipple distance for which the mean value was 22.6 cm in their case series of 22 patients. They had one case of total nipple-areola complex necrosis and a partial nipple-areola complex necrosis rate of 13.6%. Nipple-sparing mastectomy was performed through an S-italic shape lateral incision extending from the edge of the areola to the axilla.[4] Rusby and Gui used a wise pattern approach, relying on the de-epithelialized skin in the periareolar region to maintain the nipple-areola blood supply and reported a single case of nipple necrosis in a series of 17 breasts in the first 11 patients.[5]

Al-Mufarrej and colleagues described two techniques for immediate mastopexy at the time of nipple-sparing mastectomy: doughnut and vertical mastopexy. The first method involves de-epithelialization of a doughnut of skin around and including an outer portion of the areola (depending on the size of the areola) with a nipple-sparing mastectomy performed through an inframammary fold incision. For the second method, the preoperative marking is identical as for a standard wise pattern incision, but de-epithelialization of the area around the nipple-areola complex continues vertically downward to the inframammary fold. Therefore access to the breast for a nipple-sparing mastectomy is essentially through a medial and lateral triangle, and this method is known as the "bucket handle" technique. In their case series of 64 mastopexies (25% doughnut and 75% vertical pedicle), these authors reported wound complications in 10.9% of patients: one patient developed bilateral nipple loss, four unilateral partial necrosis, and one unilateral partial mastectomy flap necrosis. All those patients with partial necrosis only responded to conservative management and recovered fully. Patient factors such as smoking were thought to be a contributory factor for nipple-areola complex necrosis.[4,6,7]

Subsequent

Schneider and colleagues describe the process for an immediate free-flap reconstruction with subsequent skin reduction 4–6 months after nipple-sparing mastectomy. This approach was used in 5 of 19 patients in a series of women with breast cup size C or larger, sternal notch to nipple distance of more than 24 cm, and grade 2/3 ptosis.

Detailed information on this approach is lacking as it represents a small subset of the cohort, but despite this limitation, this is an interesting alternative.[8]

DellaCroce and colleagues advocate mastopexy and repositioning of the nipple-areola complex using a complete periareolar incision some 6 months following nipple-sparing mastectomy and immediate perforator flap breast reconstruction. In their series of 116 patients, 3.4% of patients developed variable degrees of skin necrosis after the initial mastectomy, but no cases of nipple-areola complex necrosis were reported following the second procedure.[9]

Free nipple graft

Free nipple grafting at the time of skin-sparing mastectomy and autologous flap reconstruction has been reported in two case series.[10,11] One of these included a patient with partial nipple-areola complex necrosis who recovered with conservative management and the other reported successful graft take in more than 90% of cases albeit with some loss of projection and hypopigmentation. While this is a safe approach, and more commonly employed in breast reduction,[12] the aesthetic outcomes are variable and it has not been widely used in the setting of nipple-sparing mastectomy. Aesthetic results for free nipple grafting should be compared with nipple reconstruction before it is undertaken more frequently.

The gradual evolution of techniques to preserve the nipple means that nipple-sparing mastectomy is no longer reserved for those women with an "ideal" breast shape preoperatively.[13] Moreover, the opportunity to improve breast aesthetics is considered by some patients as "the silver lining" to their diagnosis and treatment.

REFERENCES

1. Sacchini, V. et al., Nipple-sparing mastectomy for breast cancer and risk reduction: Oncologic or technical problem? *J Am Coll Surg*, 2006. **203**(5): 704–714.

2. Caruso, F. et al., Nipple sparing subcutaneous mastectomy: Sixty-six months follow-up. *Eur J Surg Oncol*, 2006. **32**(9): 937–940.

3. Spear, S.L. et al., Breast reconstruction using a staged nipple-sparing mastectomy following mastopexy or reduction. *Plast Reconstr Surg*, 2012. **129**(3): 572–581.

4. Rivolin, A. et al., Nipple-areola complex sparing mastectomy with periareolar pexy for breast cancer patients with moderately ptotic breasts. *J Plast Reconstr Aesthet Surg*, 2012. **65**(3): 296–303.

5. Rusby, J.E. and G.P. Gui, Nipple-sparing mastectomy in women with large or ptotic breasts. *J Plast Reconstr Aesthet Surg*, 2010. **63**(10): e754–e755.

6. Al-Mufarrej, F.M., J.E. Woods, and S.R. Jacobson, Simultaneous mastopexy in patients undergoing prophylactic nipple-sparing mastectomies and immediate reconstruction. *J Plast Reconstr Aesthet Surg*, 2013. **66**(6): 747–755.

7. Folli, S. et al., Nipple-sparing mastectomy: An alternative technique for large ptotic breasts. *J Am Coll Surg*, 2015. **220**(5): e65–e69.

8. Schneider, L.F. et al., Nipple-sparing mastectomy and immediate free-flap reconstruction in the large ptotic breast. *Ann Plast Surg*, 2012. **69**(4): 425–428.

9. DellaCroce, F.J. et al., Nipple-sparing mastectomy and ptosis: Perforator flap breast reconstruction allows full secondary mastopexy with complete nipple areolar repositioning. *Plast Reconstr Surg*, 2015. **136**(1): 1e–9e.

10. Chidester, J.R. et al., Revisiting the free nipple graft: An opportunity for nipple sparing mastectomy in women with breast ptosis. *Ann Surg Oncol*, 2013. **20**(10): 3350.

11. Doren, E.L. et al., Free nipple grafting: An alternative for patients ineligible for nipple-sparing mastectomy? *Ann Plast Surg*, 2014. **72**(6): S112–S115.

12. Basaran, K. et al., The free-nipple breast-reduction technique performed with transfer of the nipple-areola complex over the superior or superomedial pedicles. *Aesthetic Plast Surg*, 2014. **38**(4): 718–726.

13. Mallucci, P. and O.A. Branford, Concepts in aesthetic breast dimensions: Analysis of the ideal breast. *J Plast Reconstr Aesthet Surg*, 2012. **65**(1): 8–16.

EDITORIAL COMMENTARY

Dr. Slavin tackles the difficult clinical scenario of reconstructive surgeons being faced with patients who may require radiation, but a final decision cannot be made until results of permanent pathology become available (usually about 1 week after mastectomy). What should we do? Options include nothing, placement of an expander, or performing definitive reconstruction. Even since my group published the initial approach of delayed-immediate reconstruction, the indications for postmastectomy radiation therapy have broadened and the threshold lowered because postmastectomy radiation therapy was found to be associated with a survival advantage. He points out that proponents of immediate reconstruction even in the setting of postmastectomy radiation therapy are more frequently adamant that the impact is modest on the reconstructed breast and willingly accept the risks. It is also re-emphasized that about half of patients who receive an expander upfront were found not to require postmastectomy radiation therapy in the original patient series of delayed-immediate reconstruction. However, I would warn readers that this data is now old and may not be relevant, as the indications for postmastectomy radiation therapy is more frequently applied depending on the radiation oncologist and the medical institution. Furthermore, recent trials have found that treating the internal mammary nodes may improve survival. As the push for irradiating the internal mammary nodes increases, immediate reconstruction with anything other than a deflatable expander will not be possible because it will not allow the geometry required to treat the medially located nodes. Dr. Slavin expertly informs the reader of the potential problems and studies of radiation for each method of reconstruction. He concludes with a leaning toward a position of immediate reconstruction in patients who may need postmastectomy radiation therapy, but in the context of an excellent and thorough discussion.

Dr. Garvey takes on a more clear-cut scenario as there is no chance these patients will not require postmastectomy radiation therapy. Nonetheless, the timing and approach to reconstruction in patients who will definitely require postmastectomy radiation therapy after mastectomy remain a very controversial topic. He begins by reviewing the history behind the implementation of expanders in the setting of radiation in the early 2000s and discusses delayed-delayed reconstruction. Many surgeons are confused between the terms delayed-immediate and delayed-delayed. The difference is that delayed-immediate patients may or may not require postmastectomy radiation therapy, and delayed-delayed patients are known preoperatively to require postmastectomy radiation therapy. Delayed-delayed patients go down the same algorithmic pathway as delayed-immediate patients who are found to require postmastectomy radiation therapy after review of their permanent pathology. Interestingly, Garvey discusses the optimal timing for delayed reconstruction after postmastectomy radiation therapy and details the two most relevant studies in the published literature. Not surprisingly, both these studies found conflicting outcomes of whether waiting 12 months or not to perform delayed reconstruction influences the rate of complications. He also discusses whether ADMs have any impact on complication rates when using radiation and cites studies that show they do not; however, rates for needing autologous tissue flap salvage are reduced by half. This is a noteworthy chapter that will leave the reader well-informed on the topic of radiation in the setting of mastectomy and breast reconstruction.

SECTION V

Mastectomy and whole breast reconstruction (timing and patient selection)

Chapter 17. Timing of reconstruction   213

Chapter 18. How to choose the optimal method of whole breast reconstruction   227

17

Timing of reconstruction

AT A GLANCE

There have been several approaches to the management of these patients who in a sense are on the fence. Some surgeons place an expander to scaffold the breast skin envelope at the time of mastectomy, and if postmastectomy radiotherapy (PMRT) is required, will use the irradiated breast skin for delayed reconstruction. These surgeons defer the definitive reconstruction until the need for PMRT is known. It is imperative to preserve the breast skin in order not to lose the opportunity for an optimal aesthetic outcome. Other surgeons perform the definite reconstruction at the time of mastectomy regardless of the need for PMRT. They do not consider a two-stage approach to be warranted because they have not found that radiation has a significant enough impact on the outcome of breast reconstruction. On the other hand, some surgeons prefer to delay reconstruction altogether.

17.1 PATIENTS WHO MAY REQUIRE POSTMASTECTOMY IRRADIATION

Sumner Slavin

Immediate reconstruction

CURRENT RELEVANCE

In recent years, the indications for postmastectomy radiation therapy have been broadening. While postmastectomy radiotherapy had previously been reserved for patients with four or more positive lymph nodes, positive margins, and T3 tumors, several trials have now demonstrated improved locoregional recurrence and survival in favor of postmastectomy radiotherapy for all node-positive stage II disease.[1–4] However, radiation can negatively impact breast reconstruction. Problematic sequelae include burns, hyperpigmentation, fibrosis, telangiectasias, and tissue contracture that can cause asymmetry. Numerous reports suggest increased complications and inferior cosmetic outcomes when radiation therapy is administered to the reconstructed breast mound.[5–7]

Whether or not a patient will require postmastectomy radiotherapy cannot be definitively known at the time of mastectomy and must be based on review of the permanent tissue sections. Thus, the clinical scenario of how to optimize the reconstructive plan for these patients has become an increasingly challenging area of discussion.

Optimal timing of breast reconstruction in this setting remains controversial. Proponents of immediate reconstruction believe that the potential deleterious effects of any subsequent postmastectomy radiotherapy on the final outcome of the reconstruction are modest and willingly accept this trade-off for the benefits of immediate reconstruction.

BENEFITS OF IMMEDIATE RECONSTRUCTION

Immediate reconstruction has multiple benefits, which include improvement of psychological well-being and quality of life.[8,9] There is also an added advantage of avoiding additional procedures, recuperation, cost, and an extended reconstructive process.[10]

In patients anticipating autologous reconstruction, preservation of the skin envelope and breast shape are optimized if reconstruction is performed in the immediate setting. In a delayed setting, even if a tissue expander is used to maintain the skin envelope during irradiation, the irradiated breast pocket is often distorted or constricted, resulting in a compromised aesthetic outcome.[10] In a delayed-immediate setting, patients must also endure a tight and often uncomfortable tissue expander in place during adjuvant therapy. Delaying autologous free flap reconstruction until after postmastectomy radiotherapy also increases the risk of potential radiation damage to recipient vessels that can make microvascular anastomoses more difficult.[11]

Finally, many patients who are considered potential candidates for postmastectomy radiotherapy ultimately do not require postmastectomy radiotherapy.[10] In fact, in the series of Kronowitz and colleagues, more than half of patients subjected to this algorithm of delayed-immediate reconstruction did not require radiotherapy and underwent the process unnecessarily.[12,13]

GENERAL CONSIDERATIONS

Not all patients are suitable for immediate reconstruction and standard principles apply for patient selection. Age, medical comorbidities, and anticipated operative time will all influence the timing and method of reconstruction selected.[14] Regardless of postmastectomy radiotherapy status, there are a few factors that have been associated with a higher risk for reconstructive failure in the immediate setting. Several studies suggest that patients with risk factors of smoking, obesity, or diabetes are poor candidates for immediate reconstruction due to increased rates of skin necrosis, infection, wound healing problems, and fat necrosis which may result in delayed adjuvant treatment and compromise aesthetic outcomes after postmastectomy radiotherapy.[10,15–17]

POTENTIAL CONCERNS

Although immediate breast reconstruction is an ideal option for many patients, there are several concerns which should be addressed. First, is it oncologically safe? The oncological validity of immediate reconstruction has been evaluated in several studies which confirm that detection of local recurrence, disease-free survival, and overall survival are not adversely affected—even in those women with invasive carcinoma. In addition, the presence of the reconstructed breast mound does not interfere with the timing or efficacy of adjuvant treatment.[18–23]

Another concern is that the reconstructed breast mound complicates and impairs the delivery of postmastectomy radiotherapy[6] by causing technical problems with design of the radiation fields.[2,3,24,25] This may require adoption of alternative radiation techniques leading to either exclusion of critical internal mammary nodes or increased irradiation of normal tissues such as heart and lungs.[6] This factor has not led to impaired outcomes for postmastectomy radiotherapy in terms of locoregional recurrence or survival rates, but it does make delivery of postmastectomy radiotherapy more problematic.

Lastly, it has been reported that postmastectomy radiotherapy may adversely affect the aesthetic outcome of an immediate breast reconstruction, whether autologous or implant based (**Figure 17.1.1**). Published data are of mixed opinion, however, with recent studies suggesting better results for postmastectomy irradiation. At present, there

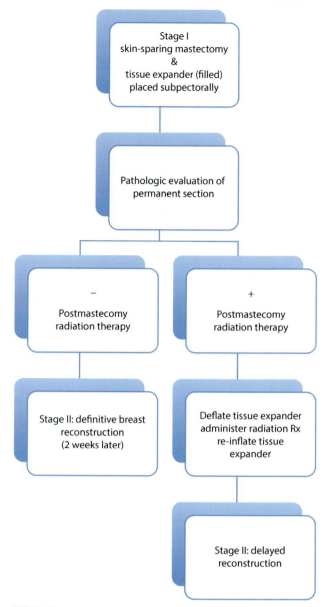

17.1.1 Necrosis of the native skin envelope following postmastectomy radiotherapy (PMRT).

remains controversy regarding the degree of radiation effect and whether outcomes can be optimized with newer radiation protocols and/or operative techniques. Ultimately, it is a subjective decision whether the risk:benefit ratio for postmastectomy radiotherapy is clinically acceptable.

AUTOLOGOUS APPROACH

There is general consensus in the literature that transposed autologous tissue is more tolerant of radiation than implant-based reconstruction, and the former has therefore been acknowledged as the preferred method when postmastectomy radiotherapy is anticipated.[14,26]

Although the detrimental effects of postmastectomy radiotherapy on pedicled and free flap reconstructions have

17.1.2 PMRT in a patient who had immediate breast reconstruction with latissimus dorsi myocutaneous flap and sub-latissimus implant.

been well documented (**Figure 17.1.2**), not all studies comparing irradiated to non-irradiated autologous reconstructions have shown an increase in the rates of complications such as fat necrosis or flap contracture, with similar cosmetic outcomes reported for irradiated and non-irradiated groups. This applies particularly to those situations with modification of radiotherapy regimes.[8,27–30] Indeed, many surgeons are now performing immediate tissue-based reconstruction before postmastectomy radiotherapy with reasonable rates of complications and good cosmetic outcomes.[10] Moreover, these trends are being seen with both pedicled and free flap reconstruction.

Carlson and colleagues examined the effect of timing of radiation on pedicled transverse rectus abdominis myocutaneous (TRAM) flap reconstruction and found that while radiation decreased the overall aesthetic outcome (**Figure 17.1.3a and b**), the effect was similar whether radiation was administered before or after TRAM flap reconstruction (**Figure 17.1.4**).[16] Another study by Soong and colleagues found that satisfactory cosmetic results and local control could be achieved after immediate autologous breast reconstruction using both pedicled TRAM and latissimus dorsi flaps for women requiring postmastectomy radiotherapy in a randomized trial setting.[31] Based on these studies, a possible need for postmastectomy radiotherapy should not exclude the choice of immediate breast reconstruction in otherwise suitable patients.

Similar findings have also been observed in free-flap breast reconstruction. Clarke-Pearson and colleagues described a systematic approach that mitigated the deleterious effects of postmastectomy radiotherapy on deep inferior epigastric perforator flap (DIEP) flap reconstruction which included the following interventions: (1) routine use of preoperative magnetic resonance angiography, (2) preferential use of flap zones 1 and 2, (3) "de-skinning" rather than de-epithelializing flaps to minimize residual dermal elements that may lead to fibrosis and contracture after radiation, (4) minimizing dead space around the flap to prevent uncontrolled contracture and distortion after radiation, and (5) delivery of postmastectomy radiotherapy using 3-D conformal techniques that reduce exposure to adjoining normal tissue structures.[10] They reported satisfactory aesthetic outcomes in all patients at 18 months, with no increase in rates of fat necrosis and only a slight loss of volume and mild increase in firmness in irradiated flaps. Overall, there was minimal distortion of breast shape and any deficits were usually readily corrected with minor outpatient revision. The latter involved a small reduction to the non-irradiated breast, with or without fat grafting to the radiated breast. It was concluded that immediate reconstruction with DIEP flaps could be performed successfully in patients who require postmastectomy radiotherapy when steps were taken to ensure flap vascularity, minimize fibrosis, optimize contour, and modulate radiation dosing.

In another prospective cohort study of 112 patients conducted over 2 years, Taghizadeh and colleagues found no increase in rates of fat necrosis, surgery for removal of fat necrosis, volume loss requiring surgery, wound complications, and flap survival in patients undergoing immediate DIEP

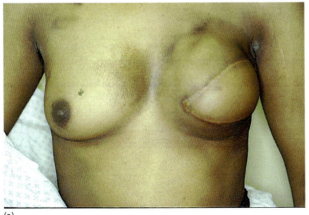 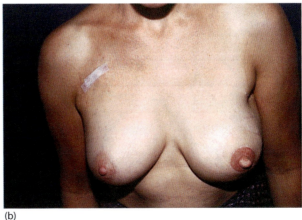

(a) (b)

17.1.3 (a) Postoperative appearance after left immediate TRAM flap. (b) Appearance 9 months after postoperative radiation therapy.

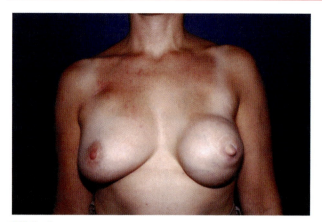

17.1.4 Local effects of postmastectomy radiotherapy to a TRAM flap include fat necrosis, macro and microcalcifications, clinical firmness, and muscle and soft tissue atrophy.

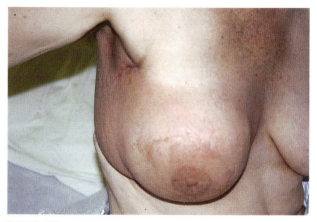

17.1.5 Impending exposure/extrusion of an implant following immediate implant to breast reconstruction and postmastectomy radiotherapy (PMRT).

reconstruction receiving postmastectomy radiotherapy.[32] These studies support decisions to offer immediate autologous-based breast reconstruction with acceptance of risk: benefit profiles for this procedure.

IMPLANT-BASED APPROACH

The deleterious impact of radiation on immediate implant-based breast reconstruction is well documented, with numerous studies citing increases in both early and late complications including capsular contracture, seroma, tissue ulceration, implant exposure requiring implant removal and reconstructive failure, revision surgeries, and overall decreased patient satisfaction.[1,4,6,7,33] However, some studies suggest that implant-based techniques represent an acceptable surgical option even when postmastectomy radiotherapy is administered.

Some groups have reported on the potentially protective effect of an autologous tissue flap (latissimus dorsi myocutaneous flap) in conjunction with an implant for immediate reconstruction. Thus, using this approach, Pinsolle and colleagues found that the rates of capsular contracture were less frequent than for use of implants alone, with a difference of more than three-fold (6.8% vs 25%). This effect was attributed to the thickness of the myocutaneous flap which allowed for placement of a correspondingly smaller implant located more deeply and away from the skin.[15]

There has been a shift in thinking in recent years which highlights how both general and aesthetic outcomes are not significantly different for immediate breast reconstruction with postmastectomy radiotherapy despite issues of capsule formation and complication rates.[1,34,35] There is an acceptance of recognized risks for radiation effects on immediate implant-based breast reconstruction which must be weighed against overall rates of success. Many surgeons willingly accept potentially suboptimal aesthetic outcomes, manage complications as they occur, and believe rates of revision to be relatively low and worth the benefits of immediate breast reconstruction (**Figure 17.1.5**).

Cordeiro and colleagues reported increased capsular contracture in patients receiving radiation after immediate implant-based reconstruction compared to those who did not (68% vs 40%). Nonetheless, the overall success rate in the irradiated group remained high (90% vs 99%) and was associated with corresponding high levels of patient satisfaction.[4] Recently, Cordeiro's group published the largest prospective long-term study of immediate implant-based breast reconstruction and postmastectomy radiotherapy with 2133 cases and a mean follow-up of 56.8 months. Results showed that 92% of irradiated patients had good to excellent aesthetic results and 94.2% of patients would choose implant-based reconstruction again.[36] Krueger and colleagues similarly found that although irradiated patients had a higher rate of reconstructive failure and rates of complications than non-irradiated patients, general and aesthetic patient satisfaction rates were similar across groups.[1]

Behranwala and colleagues reported that capsule formation is three times more likely to occur after immediate implant-based reconstruction when associated with irradiation. However, within their series, more than 60% of patients did not actually develop capsular problems after 4 years despite radiation therapy, and these results were felt to validate immediate implant-based breast reconstruction as a viable option.[37] Furthermore, Anderson and colleagues have asserted that immediate implant-based breast reconstruction with postmastectomy radiotherapy is not associated with any increase in overall rates of major or minor complications compared to non-irradiated patients.[38] Most recently, a systematic review by Ribuffo and colleagues based on data from 2012 to 2014 concluded that postmastectomy radiotherapy is not an absolute contraindication to immediate implant-based breast reconstruction and emphasized that newer techniques are allowing better results.[39]

Conclusion

In conclusion, immediate breast reconstruction in the context of postmastectomy radiotherapy represents an area of controversy and challenge. There are several benefits to the immediate approach, and both autologous and implant-based reconstruction are increasingly being shown as safe, reliable, and acceptable options for patients who receive postmastectomy radiotherapy, which may possibly be due to newer radiation modalities and improved surgical techniques. When minor revision is required, surgeons who are proponents of this approach find this to be a small price to pay. In view of the physical, economic, and psychological advantages of immediate breast reconstruction, this remains a valuable and worthwhile approach for many women which compensates for any uncertainties relating to the need for postmastectomy radiotherapy in individual patients.

Delayed-immediate reconstruction

IMMEDIATE VERSUS DELAYED RECONSTRUCTION

As discussed in the previous section, the benefits of immediate reconstruction include enhanced aesthetic outcome[40] and psychological benefits from not experiencing loss of a breast and the consequent negative effects on body image, sexuality, and sense of femininity.[41,42] However, in those patients who require postmastectomy radiotherapy after implant-based immediate reconstruction, the chance of immediate and late complications such as capsular contracture, implant extrusion, and eventual removal is increased significantly.[6,33,43] This results in loss of intended aesthetic goals and can lead to reconstructive failure. If autologous tissue is utilized for immediate reconstruction, postoperative radiotherapy can adversely affect aesthetic goals as a result of radiation-induced fibrosis.[39,44]

There are potential disadvantages from delayed reconstruction and although techniques using autologous tissue are preferred after radiotherapy, aesthetic outcomes are satisfactory at best (even for experienced surgeons).[40,42] On the other hand, when breast reconstruction is unnecessarily delayed due to suspected need for postmastectomy radiation therapy, the loss of breast shape and skin envelope from an absent scaffold often equates with a poor aesthetic outcome and represents a missed opportunity among those patients who ultimately do not require postmastectomy irradiation.[43]

A NOVEL APPROACH: DELAYED-IMMEDIATE RECONSTRUCTION

A two-staged approach called delayed-immediate reconstruction was developed over a decade ago for those patients whose status for postmastectomy radiation therapy was unknown (**Figure 17.1.6**).[12,13,43,45,46] This approach permits an optimal outcome that can equal that of an immediate

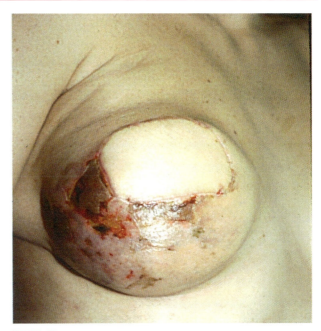

17.1.6 Delayed-immediate breast reconstruction algorithm.

reconstruction without postmastectomy radiation therapy. Moreover, this approach optimizes radiation delivery if this modality of treatment is found to be necessary after review of permanent pathology.

Kronowitz first reported on outcomes from delayed-immediate breast reconstruction as far back as 2004.[12,13,43,45,46] With this approach, a tissue expander filled to the manufacturer's recommended volume is placed subpectorally at the time of mastectomy and acts as a scaffold to preserve the initial shape, thickness, and dimensions of the breast skin envelope. Care must be taken not to overfill the implant with saline so that excess volume does not compromise vascularity of the mastectomy flaps. The final pathologic analysis then becomes available and serves as the key branching point in this algorithm. If a patient is found not to require postmastectomy radiation therapy, definitive breast reconstruction is performed approximately 2 weeks after the first stage to take advantage of the preserved skin envelope and uphold the greatest likelihood for aesthetic outcomes similar to immediate breast reconstruction.[13,45,46] Stage 2 reconstruction at this time is also vital to avoid any delays in adjuvant chemotherapy,[13] although systematic studies have already shown that a time delay of up to 12 weeks has no clinically relevant effect on survival rates.[47]

For those patients who will require postmastectomy radiation therapy, the tissue expander is fully deflated before the start of radiotherapy. Radiation therapy is planned typically 4–6 weeks after the first stage in order to allow for stability of capsule formation while the tissue expander is at the saline fill volume.[13] After deflation, a flat chest wall surface will facilitate modern, three-beam radiation delivery by creating favorable geometry for radiation oncologists to design a treatment regimen that is more precise in terms of medial and lateral radiation

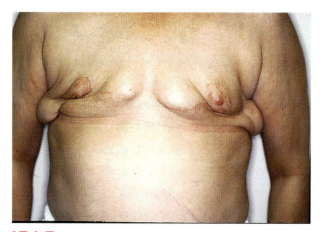

17.1.7 Poor cosmetic result following temporary deflation of a tissue expander used as a spacer prior to PMRT.

fields.[13,33] This allows for localized treatment to internal mammary nodes without excessive exposure and injury to the heart or lungs.[12] Two weeks after completion of postmastectomy radiotherapy, the tissue expander is re-inflated to the previous (pre-deflation) volume. It is imperative not to wait longer than 2 weeks after completion of radiotherapy for re-inflation to avoid flattening of the lower pole and maintain preservation of the breast skin envelope (**Figure 17.1.7**).[13] In addition, maintenance of the initial thickness of breast flaps after mastectomy results in better tolerance of the inflammatory effects of postmastectomy radiation therapy because the normal architecture of the dermis is preserved.[45]

COMPLICATIONS OF DELAYED-IMMEDIATE RECONSTRUCTION

The ultimate benefit of delayed-immediate reconstruction is to have an aesthetic outcome approaching immediate reconstruction in the setting of uncertainty about postmastectomy radiotherapy. However, this sequencing of events is not without complications. The placement of a tissue expander during the first stage of the reconstruction process carries the risk of infection, flap necrosis, hematoma, seroma, capsular contracture, implant exposure, implant rupture, and nipple necrosis[48] with postmastectomy radiation therapy having an additive effect. In one of the first studies to investigate this algorithm, Kronowitz and colleagues reported that out of 16 patients, only two developed mastectomy skin necrosis after the first stage.[12] Both required postmastectomy radiation therapy, where one necessitated explantation of the tissue expander, while the other only required local wound care since the tissue expander was covered by a subpectoral pocket. Among the patients who did not require radiotherapy and therefore moved on to the second stage of delayed-immediate reconstruction with autologous tissue, complications of tissue expander infection were probably minimized by their temporary nature. Hence, these implants were only in place for an average period of 13.4 days (11–22 days), which would not have allowed enough time for an infection to become established. With longer term follow-up, the main reasons for tissue expander loss were found to be mastectomy skin necrosis (56%), infection (33%), and expander exposure through skin during re-inflation after radiation therapy (11%).[13]

OUTCOMES OF DELAYED-IMMEDIATE RECONSTRUCTION

One of the key advantages of immediate over delayed reconstruction is that preservation of the skin envelope leads to a more optimal aesthetic outcome.[40] Delayed-immediate reconstruction supports preservation of the skin envelope by placement of a tissue expander during the first stage. However, it is difficult to know if this translates into the same optimal outcome as if this were an immediate reconstruction. One study attempted to compare aesthetic outcomes specifically between delayed and delayed-immediate reconstruction groups who all underwent postmastectomy radiation therapy.[49] To objectively come to a conclusion, comparisons of the following outcome parameters between both groups were used: skin quality, scar formation, superior pole contour, inferior pole contour, and overall aesthetic outcomes. The results showed that the delayed-immediate cohort group scored statistically superior to the delayed cohort in all five categories.

Delayed-immediate breast reconstruction combines these aesthetic outcomes while minimizing any adverse effects caused by radiation therapy. Patel and colleagues compared outcomes between the same two cohorts of patients, delayed-immediate versus delayed autologous.[50] This study concluded that flap related complications such as infection, seroma, necrosis, and flap failure were comparable between both cohorts. However, the rate of revisions was found to be significantly lower for delayed-immediate reconstruction patients. This included a decrease in skin contouring, soft tissue rearrangement/contouring, and fat grafting for contour abnormalities, further emphasizing the improved aesthetic outcomes in delayed-immediate reconstruction.

REFERENCES

1. Krueger EA, Wilkins EG, Strawderman M, Cederna P, Goldfarb S, Vicini FA et al. Complications and patient satisfaction following expander/implant breast reconstruction with and without radiotherapy. *International Journal of Radiation Oncology, Biology, Physics.* 2001;49(3):713–721.
2. Overgaard M, Hansen PS, Overgaard J, Rose C, Andersson M, Bach F et al. Postoperative radiotherapy in high-risk premenopausal women with breast cancer who receive adjuvant chemotherapy. Danish breast cancer cooperative group 82b trial. *New England Journal of Medicine.* 1997;337(14):949–955.
3. Ragaz J, Jackson SM, Le N, Plenderleith IH, Spinelli JJ, Basco VE et al. Adjuvant radiotherapy and chemotherapy in node-positive premenopausal women with breast cancer. *New England Journal of Medicine.* 1997;337(14):956–962.

4. Overgaard M, Jensen MB, Overgaard J, Hansen PS, Rose C, Andersson M et al. Postoperative radiotherapy in high-risk postmenopausal breast-cancer patients given adjuvant tamoxifen: Danish breast cancer cooperative group DBCG 82c randomised trial. *Lancet.* 1999;353(9165):1641–1648.

5. Rogers NE, Allen RJ. Radiation effects on breast reconstruction with the deep inferior epigastric perforator flap. *Plastic and Reconstructive Surgery.* 2002;109(6):1919–1924; discussion 25–26.

6. Spear SL, Onyewu C. Staged breast reconstruction with saline-filled implants in the irradiated breast: Recent trends and therapeutic implications. *Plastic and Reconstructive Surgery.* 2000;105(3):930–942.

7. Cordeiro PG, Pusic AL, Disa JJ, McCormick B, VanZee K. Irradiation after immediate tissue expander/implant breast reconstruction: Outcomes, complications, aesthetic results, and satisfaction among 156 patients. *Plastic and Reconstructive Surgery.* 2004;113(3):877–881.

8. Irvine D, Brown B, Crooks D, Roberts J, Browne G. Psychosocial adjustment in women with breast cancer. *Cancer.* 1991;67(4):1097–1117.

9. Stevens LA, McGrath MH, Druss RG, Kister SJ, Gump FE, Forde KA. The psychological impact of immediate breast reconstruction for women with early breast cancer. *Plastic and Reconstructive Surgery.* 1984;73(4):619–628.

10. Clarke-Pearson EM, Chadha M, Dayan E, Dayan JH, Samson W, Sultan MR et al. Comparison of irradiated versus nonirradiated DIEP flaps in patients undergoing immediate bilateral DIEP reconstruction with unilateral postmastectomy radiation therapy (PMRT). *Annals of Plastic Surgery.* 2013;71(3):250–254.

11. Fosnot J, Fischer JP, Smartt JM, Jr., Low DW, Kovach SJ, 3rd, Wu LC et al. Does previous chest wall irradiation increase vascular complications in free autologous breast reconstruction? *Plastic and Reconstructive Surgery.* 2011;127(2):496–504.

12. Kronowitz SJ, Hunt KK, Kuerer HM, Babiera G, McNeese MD, Buchholz TA et al. Delayed-immediate breast reconstruction. *Plastic and Reconstructive Surgery.* 2004;113(6):1617–1628.

13. Kronowitz SJ. Delayed-immediate breast reconstruction: Technical and timing considerations. *Plastic and Reconstructive Surgery.* 2010;125(2):463–474.

14. Benson JR, Taylor J, Loh S. Complications and contraindications to breast reconstruction. In: Querci della Rovere G, Benson JR, Nava M (Eds.). *Oncoplastic and Reconstructive Surgery of the Breast.* Second ed. New York: Informa Healthcare; 2011. pp. 18–32.

15. Pinsolle V, Grinfeder C, Mathoulin-Pelissier S, Faucher A. Complications analysis of 266 immediate breast reconstructions. *Journal of Plastic, Reconstructive & Aesthetic Surgery: JPRAS.* 2006;59(10):1017–1024.

16. Carlson GW, Page AL, Peters K, Ashinoff R, Schaefer T, Losken A. Effects of radiation therapy on pedicled transverse rectus abdominis myocutaneous flap breast reconstruction. *Annals of Plastic Surgery.* 2008;60(5):568–572.

17. Cowen D, Gross E, Rouannet P, Teissier E, Ellis S, Resbeut M et al. Immediate post-mastectomy breast reconstruction followed by radiotherapy: Risk factors for complications. *Breast Cancer Research and Treatment.* 2010;121(3):627–634.

18. Noone RB, Frazier TG, Noone GC, Blanchet NP, Murphy JB, Rose D. Recurrence of breast carcinoma following immediate reconstruction: A 13-year review. *Plastic and Reconstructive Surgery.* 1994;93(1):96–106; discussion 7–8.

19. Johnson CH, van Heerden JA, Donohue JH, Martin JK, Jr., Jackson IT, Ilstrup DM. Oncological aspects of immediate breast reconstruction following mastectomy for malignancy. *Archives of Surgery.* 1989;124(7):819–823; discussion 23–24.

20. Noguchi M, Fukushima W, Ohta N, Koyasaki N, Thomas M, Miyazaki I et al. Oncological aspect of immediate breast reconstruction in mastectomy patients. *Journal of Surgical Oncology.* 1992;50(4):241–246.

21. Missana MC, Levy C, Barreau-Pouhaer L, Janin N. Radiotherpay and immediate breast reconstruction with myocutaneous flap in breast cancer of reserved prognosis. *Annales de Chirurgie Plastique et Esthetique.* 2000;45(2):83–89.

22. Furey PC, Macgillivray DC, Castiglione CL, Allen L. Wound complications in patients receiving adjuvant chemotherapy after mastectomy and immediate breast reconstruction for breast cancer. *Journal of Surgical Oncology.* 1994;55(3):194–197.

23. Tran NV, Chang DW, Gupta A, Kroll SS, Robb GL. Comparison of immediate and delayed free TRAM flap breast reconstruction in patients receiving postmastectomy radiation therapy. *Plastic and Reconstructive Surgery.* 2001;108(1):78–82.

24. Buchholz TA, Kronowitz SJ, Kuerer HM. Immediate breast reconstruction after skin-sparing mastectomy for the treatment of advanced breast cancer: Radiation oncology considerations. *Annals of Surgical Oncology.* 2002;9(8):820–821.

25. Strom E. Radiation therapy for early and advanced breast disease. In: Hunt KK, Robb GL, Strom EA, Ueno NT (Eds.). *Breast Cancer.* New York: Springer-Verlag; 2001.

26. Chawla AK, Kachnic LA, Taghian AG, Niemierko A, Zapton DT, Powell SN. Radiotherapy and breast reconstruction: Complications and cosmesis with TRAM versus tissue expander/implant. *International Journal of Radiation Oncology, Biology, Physics.* 2002;54(2):520–526.

27. Wong JS, Ho AY, Kaelin CM, Bishop KL, Silver B, Gelman R et al. Incidence of major corrective surgery after post-mastectomy breast reconstruction and radiation therapy. *The Breast Journal.* 2008;14(1):49–54.

28. Chatterjee JS, Lee A, Anderson W, Baker L, Stevenson JH, Dewar JA et al. Effect of postoperative radiotherapy on autologous deep inferior epigastric perforator flap volume after immediate breast reconstruction. *The British Journal of Surgery.* 2009;96(10):1135–1140.

29. Berry T, Brooks S, Sydow N, Djohan R, Nutter B, Lyons J et al. Complication rates of radiation on tissue expander and autologous tissue breast reconstruction. *Annals of Surgical Oncology.* 2010;17 Suppl 3:202–210.

30. Crisera CA, Chang EI, Da Lio AL, Festekjian JH, Mehrara BJ. Immediate free flap reconstruction for advanced-stage breast cancer: Is it safe? *Plastic and Reconstructive Surgery.* 2011;128(1):32–41.

31. Soong IS, Yau TK, Ho CM, Lim BH, Leung S, Yeung RM et al. Post-mastectomy radiotherapy after immediate autologous breast reconstruction in primary treatment of breast cancers. *Clinical Oncology.* 2004;16(4):283–289.

32. Taghizadeh R, Moustaki M, Harris S, Roblin P, Farhadi J. Does post-mastectomy radiotherapy affect the outcome and prevalence of complications in immediate DIEP breast reconstruction? A prospective cohort study. *Journal of Plastic, Reconstructive & Aesthetic Surgery: JPRAS.* 2015;68(10):1379-1385.

33. Motwani SB, Strom EA, Schechter NR, Butler CE, Lee GK, Langstein HN et al. The impact of immediate breast reconstruction on the technical delivery of postmastectomy radiotherapy. *International Journal of Radiation Oncology, Biology, Physics.* 2006;66(1):76-82.

34. Alderman AK, Wilkins EG, Kim HM, Lowery JC. Complications in postmastectomy breast reconstruction: Two-year results of the Michigan Breast Reconstruction Outcome Study. *Plastic and Reconstructive Surgery.* 2002;109(7):2265-2274.

35. Ramon Y, Ullmann Y, Moscona R, Ofiram E, Tamir A, Har-Shai Y et al. Aesthetic results and patient satisfaction with immediate breast reconstruction using tissue expansion: A follow-up study. *Plastic and Reconstructive Surgery.* 1997;99(3):686-691.

36. Cordeiro PG, Albornoz CR, McCormick B, Hu Q, Van Zee K. The impact of postmastectomy radiotherapy on two-stage implant breast reconstruction: An analysis of long-term surgical outcomes, aesthetic results, and satisfaction over 13 years. *Plastic and Reconstructive Surgery.* 2014;134(4):588-595.

37. Behranwala KA, Dua RS, Ross GM, Ward A, A'Hern R, Gui GP. The influence of radiotherapy on capsule formation and aesthetic outcome after immediate breast reconstruction using biodimensional anatomical expander implants. *Journal of Plastic, Reconstructive & Aesthetic Surgery: JPRAS.* 2006;59(10):1043-1051.

38. Anderson PR, Hanlon AL, Fowble BL, McNeeley SW, Freedman GM. Low complication rates are achievable after post-mastectomy breast reconstruction and radiation therapy. *International Journal of Radiation Oncology, Biology, Physics.* 2004;59(4):1080-1087.

39. Ribuffo D, Monfrecola A, Guerra M, Di Benedetto GM, Grassetti L, Spaziani E et al. Does postoperative radiation therapy represent a contraindication to expander-implant based immediate breast reconstruction? An update 2012-2014. *European Review for Medical and Pharmacological Sciences.* 2015;19(12):2202-2207.

40. Kroll SS, Coffey JA, Jr., Winn RJ, Schusterman MA. A comparison of factors affecting aesthetic outcomes of TRAM flap breast reconstructions. *Plastic and Reconstructive Surgery.* 1995;96(4):860-864.

41. Gopie JP, Hilhorst MT, Kleijne A, Timman R, Menke-Pluymers MB, Hofer SO et al. Women's motives to opt for either implant or DIEP-flap breast reconstruction. *Journal of Plastic, Reconstructive & Aesthetic Surgery: JPRAS.* 2011;64(8):1062-1067.

42. Miller MJ, Rock CS, Robb GL. Aesthetic breast reconstruction using a combination of free transverse rectus abdominis musculocutaneous flaps and breast implants. *Annals of Plastic Surgery.* 1996;37(3):258-264.

43. Kronowitz SJ, Kuerer HM. Advances and surgical decision-making for breast reconstruction. *Cancer.* 2006;107(5):893-907.

44. Berbers J, van Baardwijk A, Houben R, Heuts E, Smidt M, Keymeulen K et al. Reconstruction: Before or after postmastectomy radiotherapy? A systematic review of the literature. *European Journal of Cancer.* 2014;50(16):2752-2762.

45. Kronowitz SJ, Robb GL. Radiation therapy and breast reconstruction: A critical review of the literature. *Plastic and Reconstructive Surgery.* 2009;124(2):395-408.

46. Kronowitz SJ. Current status of implant-based breast reconstruction in patients receiving postmastectomy radiation therapy. *Plastic and Reconstructive Surgery.* 2012;130(4):513e-523e.

47. Xavier Harmeling J, Kouwenberg CA, Bijlard E, Burger KN, Jager A, Mureau MA. The effect of immediate breast reconstruction on the timing of adjuvant chemotherapy: A systematic review. *Breast Cancer Research and Treatment.* 2015;153(2):241-251.

48. Adkinson JM, Miller NF, Eid SM, Miles MG, Murphy RX, Jr. Tissue expander complications predict permanent implant complications and failure of breast reconstruction. *Annals of Plastic Surgery.* 2015;75(1):24-28.

49. Albino FP, Patel KM, Smith JR, Nahabedian MY. Delayed versus delayed-immediate autologous breast reconstruction: A blinded evaluation of aesthetic outcomes. *Archives of Plastic Surgery.* 2014;41(3):264-270.

50. Patel KM, Albino F, Fan KL, Liao E, Nahabedian MY. Microvascular autologous breast reconstruction in the context of radiation therapy: Comparing two reconstructive algorithms. *Plastic and Reconstructive Surgery.* 2013;132(2):251-257.

17.2 PATIENTS WHO WILL REQUIRE POSTMASTECTOMY RADIATION

Margaret S. Roubaud and Patrick B. Garvey

AT A GLANCE

Patients who will require postmastectomy radiation therapy (PMRT) have benefited most from the increasing use of skin preservation during mastectomy. In addition, several studies have shown that preserving the breast skin in patients with stage III breast cancer does not appear to increase recurrence. Many patients with stage III breast cancer now awake from mastectomy with a breast and have the opportunity for much better aesthetic outcomes with less complicated reconstructive techniques. A paradigm shift is occurring in the management of this group of patients.

Delayed-delayed reconstruction (with skin preservation)

In many instances, the need for postmastectomy adjuvant radiation in patients with stage II breast cancer cannot be determined until review of permanent sections of breast pathology. In early 2000, a practice of "delayed-immediate" and "delayed-delayed" breast reconstruction that allowed placement of a tissue expander at the time of mastectomy, without knowledge of final pathology.[1] In this two-stage approach, all early-stage patients desiring tissue expander-based reconstruction received a saline-filled tissue expander at the time of mastectomy. The definitive reconstructive decision was delayed until final pathology results were available 2 weeks later. If the patient did not qualify for radiation treatment, they went on to receive "delayed-immediate" reconstruction with an implant or autologous tissue. If a patient required adjuvant radiation, they retained their expanders which remained inflated for 4 weeks to 6 weeks during treatment planning, then completed their adjuvant therapy with the tissue expander deflated. After completion of radiation, they received "delayed-delayed reconstruction" with serial re-expansion and an implant with autologous tissue or autologous tissue alone.

Early dogma in plastic surgery forbid the use of implants in an irradiated field due to a high rate of implant exposure and infection. Current literature continues to demonstrate an increased risk of complications with combined radiation and tissue expanders, regardless of whether pre- or post-reconstruction.[2,3] However, many surgeons consider that the aesthetic advantage of preserving the skin envelope with a tissue expander at the time of mastectomy outweighs the potential risk. Ho and colleagues recently published their results with a delayed-delayed implant reconstructive protocol at the University of British Columbia.[4] Patients receiving tissue expander-implant delayed-delayed reconstruction were studied against a control group not receiving radiation. Patients were irradiated once tissue expansion was complete and implant exchange was performed 6 months after radiation completion. This study found an increased odds ratio of 4.2 for major complications in the irradiated group as well as a significantly higher rate of Baker grade III and IV capsular contracture (approximately 27%). However, the authors note that revision rates were lower than expected for the radiated group (21%) and maintained that delayed-delayed reconstruction is a reasonable surgical option in many patients. It is incumbent on the plastic surgeon to understand the risks and benefits when choosing this technique and council the patient accordingly.

Of particular note, it is important for patient and surgeon to agree on a timeline based on recognized best practice. The optimal outcome of "delayed-delayed" reconstruction is heavily influenced by the timing of radiation and the resultant tissue response. The "delayed-delayed" reconstruction timeline includes initiation of re-expansion of the tissue expander 2 weeks after completion of radiation therapy and final reconstruction 3 months after completion of radiation.[5] Those patients who required adjuvant chemotherapy prior to adjuvant irradiation maintained inflation of the tissue expander during chemotherapy. An implant capsule is formed in the time period between mastectomy and onset of radiation therapy and contributes to improved re-expansion post-irradiation.

Delayed-delayed reconstructive timing with radiation and implants

It is well known that the effects of radiation on the soft tissues of the chest wall continue to develop and evolve after the completion of radiation therapy, although the exact timescale is unknown.[6–8] Delayed-delayed reconstruction seems a viable surgical algorithm for some patients, but the optimal timing remains unclear. For implant-based reconstruction, optimal timing is focused on tissue expander to implant exchange.

Peled and colleagues examined complication rates and implant loss among patients who underwent expander-implant exchange less than 6 months or more than 6 months from completion of radiation. They reported complication rates equivalent between the two groups, but total implant loss was significantly higher in the group exchanged before 6 months.[9] When the time intervals were analyzed in more detail, there was decreased chance of implant loss with increased delay of exchange, with an interval of at least 6 months being most protective.

Additionally, the delayed-delayed reconstructive algorithm may be challenged by whether the expander or implant performs better with radiation treatment.

Nava and colleagues examined rates of contracture and failed reconstruction in relation to irradiation of either the tissue expander or permanent implant in two-stage implant breast reconstruction.[10] Rates of total reconstruction failure were significantly higher in the radiated tissue expander group compared to the implant and control group. Moreover, the capsular contracture rate was significantly higher in both the irradiated implant and tissue expander group versus control.

Similarly, Cordeiro and colleagues recently published the largest single-surgeon series evaluating long-term outcomes in patients with two-stage implant breast reconstruction and radiation.[11] For this population, all patients received adjuvant radiation therapy to the permanent breast implant 4 weeks after tissue expander exchange. Reconstructive failure was 9.1% for the irradiated group compared to 0.5% for the non-radiated group. Rates of conversion to autologous flap and severe grade IV capsular contracture were also significantly higher in the radiated group, although relatively low at 1.9% and 6.9%, respectively. For long-term outcomes, Kaplan-Meier analysis was employed to predict implant loss rate at 12 years. These yielded a 17.5% loss rate for irradiated patients and 2.0% for non-radiated patients. Despite the increased complication and loss rate for irradiated patients, patient-reported outcomes remained high for the majority of patients, leading the authors to conclude that implant-based reconstruction with postmastectomy radiation is validated and advocated irradiation of the permanent implant over the tissue expander.

Of note, these studies by Cordeiro and Ho did not include patients undergoing reconstruction with the use of a dermal matrix. In 2012, Scott Spear published outcomes of two-stage prosthetic breast reconstruction using acellular dermal matrix and different timings of radiotherapy.[12] Three groups were evaluated and included: (1) patients who received radiation prior to mastectomy, (2) those who received radiation during the expansion process, and (3) those who received no radiation. Rates of Baker III and IV capsular contracture were highest in the radiation during expansion group, followed by the pre-mastectomy radiation group. Those patients irradiated during expansion also had the highest rates of capsular contracture (unsalvageable by capsule modification alone) as well as total implant failure. While these results confirmed that prosthetic breast reconstruction with acellular dermal matrix was not completely protective against capsular contracture and implant failure, a total failure rate of 21% in irradiated patients is much improved compared to published rates of up to 40%–60% without use of acellular dermal matrix.[4,10] Furthermore, the need for non-elective autologous tissue salvage was reduced from 30% to 16.1% when compared to a previous study by the same authors evaluating radiation and expanders without dermal matrix. In patients undergoing the delayed-delayed reconstructive protocol, with irradiation of either the expander or implant, acellular dermal matrix may be an important adjunct to improve outcomes.

Delayed–delayed reconstructive timing with radiation and autologous tissue

In patients who undergo delayed-delayed reconstruction with autologous tissue, the timing of autologous reconstruction must also be considered. The optimal timing of this tissue transfer has been debated in the literature, but nearly all studies suggest that a waiting period between 3 months and 12 months is required to decrease perioperative complications after radiation.

In 2011, Baumann and colleagues reported a significant difference in complication rates between patients reconstructed with free abdominal tissue less than and more than 12 months following postmastectomy radiation.[13] Rates of flap loss and re-operation were significantly higher in the group treated less than 12 months following radiation, with the highest level of complications occurring in patients undergoing reconstruction less than 6 months from radiation. Furthermore, this earlier group showed a trend toward a high incidence of microvascular thrombosis, infection, and wound dehiscence. Patel and colleagues recently evaluated two reconstructive algorithms in microsurgical autologous breast reconstruction and radiotherapy.[14] In the first algorithm, consistent with a delayed-delayed timeline, patients had a tissue expander placed at the time of mastectomy, underwent radiation, and then underwent autologous reconstruction at various intervals thereafter. The second algorithm included patients treated with standard delayed reconstruction. There was no significant difference in perioperative complications or total flap loss between the two groups. On subset analysis, when evaluating the delayed-delayed autologous cohort, those having reconstruction more than 12 months after radiation therapy had decreased complication rates compared to those having reconstruction within 12 months of completing radiation treatment (37.5% vs 8% , respectively, p = 0.04). Interestingly, the revisional surgery rates were significantly decreased in the delayed-delayed autologous group versus the standard delayed autologous group (60.8% vs 78.8% respectively, p = 0.008).

Moreover, the current authors advocate an additional maneuver that may decrease the risk of tissue expansion and radiation while preserving skin. At the University of Texas MD Anderson, we have started placing subcutaneous expanders at the time of mastectomy in patients who have a high likelihood of needing radiation, but would also benefit from skin envelope preservation. See **Figure 17.2.1**. Avoiding dissection of the subpectoral pocket limits chest wall morbidity and avoids capsule formation and scarring directly above the internal mammary vessels, which may be needed in future reconstruction. It also allows preservation of the skin envelope in those patients who may otherwise be limited in their delayed reconstructive options. Although tissue expanders placed in the subcutaneous pocket are susceptible to higher rates of complications during radiation, the morbidity or potential loss of the implant is still lower than for a violated subpectoral space

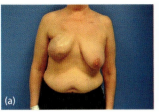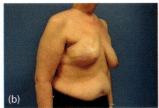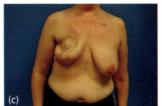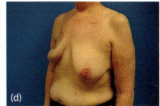

17.2.1 Example of a subcutaneous tissue expander, placed for skin preservation without subpectoral dissection. (a and b) Fully inflated subcutaneous expander, (c and d) deflated tissue expander demonstrating preservation of lower pole skin.

or the aesthetic compromise of complete skin retraction. In patients who do not require radiation, the subcutaneous expander can be easily converted to a subpectoral implant or prepectoral autologous tissue. In patients requiring postmastectomy radiation, the subcutaneous implant is expanded in the prepectoral space, radiated, and then removed in delayed fashion for autologous reconstruction. A meta-analysis published in 2011 found that patients who underwent autologous reconstruction had one-fifth the risk of adverse events of patients who underwent implant-based reconstruction when postmastectomy radiotherapy was delivered after immediate reconstruction.[15] This argues in favor of maintaining the capacity to provide an autologous reconstruction whenever feasible.

CONCLUSION

The optimal timing of radiation delivery, volume replacement with an implant or autologous tissue, and the use of dermal matrix remain controversial. Additionally, many outcomes are influenced by a center's radiation protocol, specifically including or excluding routine radiation to internal mammary nodes and using hypofractionated or intensity-modulated therapy. The surgeon must weigh the benefits of skin envelope preservation and implant reconstruction with the inevitable increased risk of complications from radiation.

Standard delayed reconstruction (without skin preservation)

In previous decades, postmastectomy breast reconstruction was often delayed due to concerns that reconstruction would interfere with chest wall surveillance. Over the past two decades, several studies have validated the efficacy and safety of immediate breast reconstruction, without evidence of any significant detriment to detection of local recurrence nor survival outcomes.[16–21]

The timing of standard delayed reconstruction depends on completion of adjuvant therapies and, in particular, radiation treatment. For most cases of delayed reconstruction, the skin envelope of the breast is lost due to resection and/or contraction after mastectomy. Delayed reconstruction usually requires use of pedicled or free autologous tissue transfer to replace soft tissue losses (including skin).

Immediate autologous reconstruction followed by radiation therapy is not ideal for the majority of patients. Tran and colleagues published outcomes for a series of patients irradiated within 6 months of autologous pedicled and microvascular reconstruction. Within this study, 78% of patients lost symmetry, 56% had a firm reconstruction, 37% had hyperpigmentation, 34% had palpable fat necrosis, and 24% required an additional flap.[22] Carlson and colleagues also found radiation to have deleterious effects on aesthetic coutcomes for pedicled transverse rectus abdominis myocutaneous (TRAM) flaps.[23] Garvey et al. published a similar study documenting much higher rates of fat necrosis in irradiated flaps and noted no differences in the protective effects between muscle-sparing TRAM and deep inferior epigastric perforator (DIEP) reconstructions against potential radiation damage.[24] Chang and colleagues also found no differences in rates of complications nor revision of radiated flaps based on the number of perforating vessels or amount of muscle included in the flap.[25]

The smaller diameter of the left internal mammary vein renders it more susceptible to irradiation damage and fibrosis, leading to increased complication rates in left-sided reconstruction.[13] Fosnot and colleagues examined the rate of vascular complications in free autologous breast reconstruction in patients who had or had not received previous chest wall irradiation.[26] Vascular complications were more prevalent in the irradiated group (17.3% vs 9.6%; $p = 0.001$) and radiation therapy was identified as an independent risk factor.

As previously discussed, there are increased rates of microvascular and wound complications in patients undergoing microvascular autologous reconstruction performed less than 1 year after radiation therapy and this is most evident in less than 6 months. Momoh and colleagues carried out a retrospective analysis of 199 patients undergoing delayed autologous reconstruction among whom half (100 patients) had previous radiation therapy.[27] These authors found that irradiated patients were more likely to have postoperative complications, including problems with wound healing and infection. Complication rates in irradiated patients were also analyzed based on timing of reconstruction and included 17 patients operated on within 6 months and 83 patients after 6 months of radiation treatment. No significant difference in overall rates of complication was found between these groups. When further subset analysis was performed with stratification into reconstruction within 12 months and reconstruction after 12 months, once again, significant differences were found. Interestingly, the authors noted an unusually high complication rate (60%) among five patients reconstructed within 3 months of postmastectomy radiation therapy. Momoh and colleagues have suggested waiting between 0 months and 3 months after radiation therapy before performing autologous reconstructive surgery which allows time for any acute inflammatory effects of radiation to subside. However, they argue that radiation changes are not finite and waiting for prolonged periods of time "may not provide significant benefit." The ideal timing of reconstruction may also change as radiation protocols and delivery advance.

Prospective studies are needed to evaluate the optimal time period between radiation and free flap reconstruction. Clinical factors, such as degree of skin desquamation, erythema, and tenderness provide clues as to tissue recovery after radiation, and sound clinical judgment is crucial. Based on current data, the safest time to reconstruct patients may still be after 12 months have passed since radiation, although more and more evidence suggests acceptable safety and outcomes after 6 months.

There are an increasing number of patients undergoing radiation therapy for early forms of breast cancer, and recent studies have documented the safety and efficacy of delayed breast reconstruction for high-risk groups, including inflammatory breast cancer.[28] There are major psychosocial benefits of breast reconstruction even when performed as a delayed procedure, and this should not be avoided due to innate fear of either physician or patient.[29]

CONCLUSION

Autologous reconstruction after mastectomy, when performed in a standard delayed fashion, is both safe and important to the patient's psychosocial benefit. Current studies suggest waiting 6 months to a year after radiation is complete to minimize perioperative morbidity and complications. Reconstruction following mastectomy for locally advanced cancers which are in remission is both safe and worthwhile for many patients.

REFERENCES

1. Kronowitz, S.J., Hunt, K.K., Kuerer, H.M., Babiera, G., McNeese, M.D., Bucholz, T.A., Strom, E.A., and Robb, G.L. Delayed-immediate breast reconstruction, *Plastic and Reconstructive Surgery* 113 (2004): 1617–1628.

2. Momoh, A.O., Ahmed, R., Kelley, B.P., Aliu, O., Kidwell, K.M., Kozlow, J.H., and Chung, K.C. A systematic review of complications of implant-based breast reconstruction with prereconstruction and postreconstruction radiotherapy, *Annals of Surgical Oncology* 21 (2014): 118–124.

3. Berry, T., Brooks, S., Sydow, N., Djohan, R., Nutter, B., Lyons, J., and Dietz, J. Complication rates of radiation on tissue expander and autologous tissue breast reconstruction, *Annals of Surgical Oncology* 17 (2010): S202–S210.

4. Ho, A.L., Bovill, E.S., Macadam, S.A., Tyldesley, S., Giang, J., and Lennox, P.A. Postmastectomy radiation therapy after immediate two-stage expander/implant breast reconstruction: A University of British Columbia perspective, *Plastic and Reconstructive Surgery* 134 (2014): 1e–10e.

5. Kronowitz, S.J. Delayed-immediate breast reconstruction: Technical and timing considerations, *Plastic and Reconstructive Surgery* 125 (2010): 463–474.

6. Archambeau, J.O., Pezner, R., and Wasserman, T. Pathophysiology of irradiated skin and breast, *International Journal of Radiation Oncology, Biology, Physics* 31 (1995): 1171–1185.

7. Hopewell, J.W., Campling, D., Calvo, W., Rcinhold, H.S., Wilkinson, J.H., and Yeung, T.K. Vascular irradiation damage: Its cellular basis and likely consequences, *British Journal of Cancer* 53 (1986): 181–191.

8. Peters, M.E., Fagerholm, M.I., Scanlan, K.A., Voegeli, D.R., and Kelcz, F. Mammographic evaluation of the postsurgical and irradiated breast, *Radiographics* 8 (1988): 873–899.

9. Peled, A.W., Foster, R.D., Esserman, L.J., Park, C.C., Hwang, E.S., and Fowble, B. Increasing the time to expander-implant exchange after postmastectomy radiation therapy reduces expander-implant failure, *Plastic and Reconstructive Surgery* 130 (2012): 503–509.

10. Nava, M.B., Pennati, A.E., Lozza, L., Spano, A., Zambetti, M., and Catanuto, G. Outcome of different timings of radiotherapy in implant-based breast reconstruction, *Plastic and Reconstructive Surgery* 128 (2011): 353–359.

11. Cordeiro, P.G., Albornoz, C.R., McCormick, B., Hu, Q., Van Zee, K. The impact of postmastectomy radiotherapy on two-stage implant breast reconstruction: An analysis of long-term surgical outcomes, aesthetic results, and satisfaction over 13 years, *Plastic and Reconstructive Surgery* 134 (2014): 588–595.

12. Spear, S.L., Seruya, M., Rao, S.S., Rottman, S., Stolle, E., Cohen, M., Rose, K.M., Parikh, P.M., and Nahabedian, M.Y. Two-stage prosthetic breast reconstruction using alloderm including outcomes of different timings of radiotherapy, *Plastic and Reconstructive Surgery* 130 (2012): 1–9.

13. Baumann, D.P., Crosby, M.A., Selber, J.C., Garvey, P.B., Sacks, J.M., Adelman, D.M., Villa, M.T., Feng, L., and Robb, G.L. Optimal timing of delayed free lower abdominal flap breast reconstruction after postmastectomy radiation therapy, *Plastic and Reconstructive Surgery* 127 (2011): 1100–1106.

14. Patel, K.M., Albino, F., Fan, K.L., Liao, E., and Nahabedian, M.Y. Microvascular autologous breast reconstruction in the context of radiation therapy: Comparing two reconstructive algorithms, *Plastic and Reconstructive Surgery* 132 (2013): 251–257.

15. Barry, M., Kell, M.R. Radiotherapy and breast reconstruction: A meta-analysis, *Breast Cancer Research and Treatment* 127 (2011): 15–22.

16. Feller, W.F., Holt, R., Spear, S., Little, J.W. Modified radical mastectomy with immediate breast reconstruction, *The American Surgeon* 52 (1986): 129–133.

17. Georgiade, G., Georgiade, N., McCarty, K.S., Seigler, H.F. Rationale for immediate reconstruction of the breast following modified radical mastectomy, *Annals of Plastic Surgery* 8 (1982): 20–28.

18. Langstein, H.N., Cheng, M.-H., Singletary, S.E., Robb, G.L., Hoy, E., Smith, T.L., and Kroll, S.S. Breast cancer recurrence after immediate reconstruction: Patterns and significance, *Plastic and Reconstructive Surgery* 111 (2003): 712–720.

19. Slavin, S.A., Love, S.M., and Goldwyn, R.A. Recurrent breast cancer following immediate reconstruction with myocutaneous flaps, *Plastic and Reconstructive Surgery* 93 (1994): 1191–1204.

20. Howard, M.A., Polo, K., Pusic, A.L., Cordeiro, P.G., Hidalgo, D.A., Mehrara, B., and Disa, J.J. Breast cancer local recurrence after mastectomy and TRAM flap reconstruction: Incidence and treatment options, *Plastic and Reconstructive Surgery* 117 (2006): 1381–1386.

21. Noone, R.B., Frazier, T.G., Noone, G.C., Blanchet, N.P., Murphy, J.B., and Rose, D. Recurrence of breast carcinoma following immediate reconstruction: A 13-year review, *Plastic and Reconstructive Surgery* 93 (1994): 96–106.

22. Tran, N.V., Evans, G.R.D., Kroll, S.S., Baldwin, B.J., Miller, M.J., Reece, G.P., and Robb, G.L. Postoperative adjuvant irradiation: Effects on transverse rectus abdominis muscle flap breast reconstruction, *Plastic and Reconstructive Surgery* 106 (2000): 313–317.

23. Carlson, G.W., Page, A.L., Peters, K., Ashinoff, R., Schaefer, T., and Losken, A. Effect of radiation therapy on pedicled transverse rectus abdominis myocutaneous flap breast reconstruction, *Annals of Plastic Surgery* 60 (2008): 568–572.

24. Garvey, P.B., Clemens, M.W., Hoy, A.E., Smith, B., Zhang, H., Kronowitz, S.J., and Butler, C.E. Muscle-sparing TRAM does not protect breast reconstruction from postmastectomy radiation damage compared to DIEP flap, *Plastic and Reconstructive Surgery* 133 (2014): 223–233.

25. Chang, E.I., Liu, T.S., Festekjian, J.H., Da, L., Andrew, L., and Crisera, C.A. Effects of radiation therapy for breast cancer based on type of free flap reconstruction, *Plastic and Reconstructive Surgery* 131 (2012): 1e–8e.

26. Fosnot, J., Fischer, J.P., Smartt Jr, J.M., Low, D.W., Kovach III, S.J., Wu, L.C., and Serletti, J.M. Does previous chest wall irradiation increase vascular complications in free autologous breast reconstruction? *Plastic and Reconstructive Surgery* 127 (2011): 496–504.

27. Momoh, A.O., Colakoglu, S., de Blacam, C., Gautam, S., Tobias, A.M., and Lee, B.T. Delayed autologous breast reconstruction after postmastectomy radiation therapy: Is there an optimal time? *Annals of Plastic Surgery* 69 (2011): 14–18.

28. Chang, E.I., Chang, E.I., Ito, R., Zhang, H., Nguyen, A.T., Skoracki, R.J., Hanasono, M.M., Crosby, M.A., Ueno, N.T., and Hunt, K.K. Challenging a traditional paradigm: A 12-year experience with autologous free flap breast reconstruction for inflammatory breast cancer, *Plastic and Reconstructive Surgery* 135 (2015): 262e–269e.

29. Wellisch, D.K., Schain, W.S., Noone, R.B., and Little III, J.W., Psychosocial correlates of immediate versus delayed reconstruction of the breast, *Plastic and Reconstructive Surgery* 76 (1985): 713–718.

EDITORIAL COMMENTARY

The most startling difference in whole breast reconstruction following mastectomy between practices in the United States and other regions of the world, such as South America and Europe, is the availability of acellular dermal matrix (ADM) products which may be limited because of high costs. Although the use of synthetic mesh has become a popular alternative to ADM for breast reconstruction outside of the United States, it does not incorporate physiologically into mastectomy skin flaps, and perforations within the mesh products do not provide the same protection as a sheet of ADM from exposure of the expander in the event that mastectomy skin necrosis occurs. At the time when ADMs were becoming widely used in the United States, other areas of the world were increasing utilization of autologous tissue flaps with a move away from the more commonly used latissimus dorsi flap. The latter was most popular in Europe and other countries for many years at a time when the use of autologous flap reconstruction was widespread in the United States. The impact of ADMs on the practice of single-stage, direct-to-implant, immediate breast reconstruction has been significant with a notable decrease in popularity of autologous tissue flap breast reconstruction in the United States. It appears that the availability of ADMs in South America and Europe is slowly improving, although a variety of mesh products are resulting in a trend away from autologous tissue flaps and toward implant-based reconstruction. Indeed, this is analogous to what has occurred in the United States over the last 10 years or so since the advent of ADMs.

18

How to choose the optimal method of whole breast reconstruction

AT A GLANCE

Many factors such as patient anatomy and personal desires as well as the need for radiotherapy have typically been used to choose the best method of whole breast reconstruction. The advent of acellular dermal matrices and fat grafting has increased the use of implant-based reconstruction, even among those patients requiring radiotherapy. Although autologous tissue flaps are still commonly used in the setting of radiation, their popularity has decreased in recent years. The increase in demand for bilateral mastectomy, especially nipple-sparing mastectomy, has probably played a role in reduction of use of autologous tissue flaps for breast reconstruction. This change has been most apparent for the latissimus dorsi flap, with decreased use evident in both the United States and Europe.

18.1   MY APPROACH (USA)

Steven J. Kronowitz

Selecting the optimal timing and technique for breast reconstruction after mastectomy requires knowledge of any anticipated oncology treatment. Key oncology considerations include: (1) whether the patient is a candidate for nipple sparing mastectomy (extensive ductal carcinoma in situ (DCIS) and close proximity of tumor to the nipple is a contraindication), (2) the timing of chemotherapy (neoadjuvant or adjuvant), and (3) the likelihood of postmastectomy radiation therapy. Breast anatomy as well as autologous tissue donor availability are also important considerations. Is the patient large-breasted with ptosis or small-breasted and non-ptotic? Is the candidate for a deep inferior epigastric perforator (DIEP) flap or other anatomic regional flap? Preoperative consideration of these factors will guide the reconstructive surgeon toward the most appropriate reconstructive option for each individual patient.

Two-stage implant reconstruction: tabbed tissue expander and acellular dermal matrix placement followed by exchange of the expander for a permanent breast implant along with fat grafting

The advent of tabbed tissue expanders, acellular dermal matrix (ADM), and autologous fat grafting has enhanced the outcomes of implant-based breast reconstruction. Tissue expanders are now available with suture-secure tabs to suture to the chest wall to prevent postoperative displacement. Increasingly, surgeons are using ADM to provide coverage for the lower pole of the expander with reliance on the pectoralis major muscle for the upper pole. A recent trend is provision of complete coverage of the expander with ADM to potentially decrease occurrence of capsular contracture. Using this technique, the entire expander is covered with a large sheet of ADM, and the pectoralis major muscle is sewn over the ADM in a vest-over-pants fashion (**Figure 18.1.1**). Because ADM allows for intraoperative saline filling of the

228 How to choose the optimal method of whole breast reconstruction

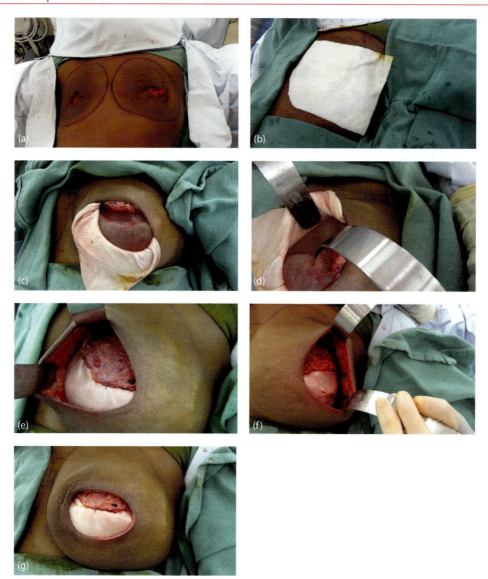

18.1.1 (a) Intraoperative views of a technique for providing complete coverage of the expander with ADM to potentially decrease the occurrence of capsular contracture in a 23-year-old woman undergoing bilateral skin-sparing mastectomy. (b) A large sheet of ADM is tailored to the dimensions of the footprint of the left breast. (c) The ADM is initially tacked at the medial and inframammary fold. (d) The tissue expander is then placed underlying the ADM and sutured to the chest wall using suture-secure tabs and is filled with saline. (e) The superior and lateral aspects of the ADM are sewn to the chest, providing complete coverage of the expander with ADM. (e–g) The previously dissected left pectoralis major muscle (released medially to the third intercostal space, inferiorly and laterally, with a pocket created posteriorly) is then draped overlying the ADM and sewn with full-muscle excursion (left arm by the patient's side) to the ADM. The last step in the technique is not shown in this figure: the inferior breast skin flap is sewn to the inferior edge of the pectoralis muscle so the mastectomy incision closure will be overlying the pectoralis muscle, which will assist in healing.

expander, a more ptotic-shaped breast can be reconstructed that enables more easily achieved symmetry with the contralateral native breast and reduces the number of postoperative expansion visits.[1] Before the advent of ADM with intraoperative saline filling, symmetry could be achieved only with bilateral implant-based breast reconstruction.

The increasing use of autologous fat grafting has also contributed to enhanced aesthetic outcomes using implant-based breast reconstruction.[2–5] Fat grafting can be performed at the time of exchange of the expander for a permanent implant. The ADM that is inserted during the first stage (placement of the tissue expander) allows for injection of fat grafts into the lower mastectomy flap. This maneuver is not always possible without ADM and accommodates a more secure closure of the mastectomy incision. Surgeons have begun performing fat grafting as a preliminary step after radiotherapy and before exchange for the permanent implant. The aim is to decrease subsequent wound healing problems and implant dehiscence during the second stage (exchange for the permanent implant). Future research should focus on the ideal timing for application of fat grafting to a reconstructed breast. Often, surgeons perform additional fat grafting at the same time as any subsequent revisional surgery or as dictated by patient needs.

The advent of ADM and fat grafting has decreased the need for utilization of a local flap such as latissimus dorsi or thoracodorsal artery perforator flap to reconstruct a ptotic-shaped and aesthetically pleasing implant-based breast. These adjuvant procedures have also changed the approach to revision of implant-based reconstruction. Thus, ADM allows for repositioning of an implant, and both ADM and fat grafting correct some of the adverse aesthetic effects of implant rippling.

One-stage implant reconstruction

The safety of nipple-sparing mastectomy has led to increased use of this surgery in patients seeking risk-reducing mastectomy and for selected patients with early-stage breast cancer.[3,6] The indications for nipple-sparing mastectomy will likely broaden in the near future. Preserving the nipple-areola complex maintains the three-dimensional shape of the breast skin envelope and allows for immediate insertion of a permanent implant. Implant-based reconstruction in conjunction with nipple-sparing mastectomy is preferred because it allows the mastectomy incision to be camouflaged in the lateral breast crease or inframammary fold. These incision locations do not provide access to the internal mammary blood vessels to serve as recipient vessels for microvascular breast reconstruction. Moreover, mastectomy incisions radial to the nipple-areola complex that displace nipple position, and those that interfere with blood supply to the nipple-areola complex should be avoided. In addition, patients who undergo nipple-sparing mastectomy have early-stage breast cancer and usually undergo sentinel lymph biopsy only. Therefore, use of the thoracodorsal vessels to serve as recipients for microvascular breast reconstruction necessitates dissection of the axilla, which may predispose the patient to lymphedema.

Nipple-sparing mastectomy together with ADM more readily promotes symmetry with the contralateral normal breast when unilateral implant-based breast reconstruction is undertaken. The addition of an ADM sling to support the permanent implant can reduce compression of the blood supply to the preserved breast skin and nipple-areola complex. Intraoperative fluorescence imaging can help determine whether adequate perfusion is retained to the breast skin envelope for immediate insertion of the permanent breast implant. Although the one-stage approach allows for reconstruction with a single surgical procedure, there is increased potential for complications. On the other hand, one-stage implant reconstruction is less costly than a two-stage option and tends to better maintain the ptotic shape of the breast, resulting in a more natural-appearing reconstructed breast (**Figure 18.1.2**).[2]

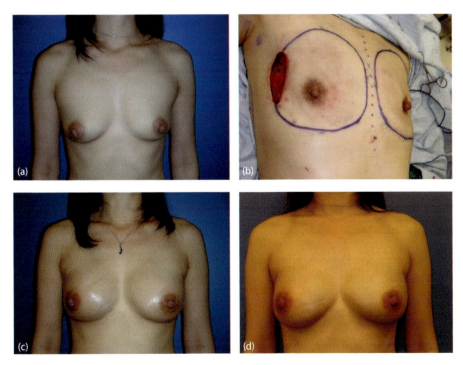

18.1.2 (a) A 39-year-old woman with right ductal carcinoma in situ. (b) The patient underwent bilateral nipple-sparing mastectomy using lateral breast incisions. Immediate one-stage breast implant reconstruction was performed along with acellular dermal matrix. (c) 3 months after one-stage breast implant reconstruction. (d) 10 months after one-stage implant breast reconstruction.

Muscle-only latissimus dorsi (LD) or thoracodorsal artery perforator (TAP) flap

The use of a latissimus dorsi myocutaneous flap for reconstruction after mastectomy has become less necessary with increasing use of ADM and breast-skin-preserving techniques. However, a muscle-only latissimus dorsi flap and the de-epithelialized thoracodorsal artery perforator flap continue to have important roles in postmastectomy reconstruction. These flaps are good options for obese patients, in whom it may not be safe to perform an implant-only reconstruction due to risk of infection. These flaps are also suitable for patients who have undergone radiotherapy for whom additional blood supply to the reconstructed breast can assist in healing through transfer of non-irradiated cellular elements to the radiated breast. The muscle-only latissimus dorsi and de-epithelialized thoracodorsal artery perforator flaps can help reabsorb postoperative inflammatory fluid, which can otherwise serve as a source for infection and subsequent implant loss (especially in patients who have undergone extensive lymphadenectomy).

Deep inferior epigastric perforator (DIEP) flap

In those clinical practices that routinely perform Deep inferior epigastric perforator (DIEP) flap breast reconstruction, use of computed tomography angiography can serve as a so-called road map to optimally position the flap overlying the perforating blood vessels and to hasten selection and dissection of perforating blood vessels. For patients who have received radiotherapy without any skin preservation and undergo delayed reconstruction (so-called standard delayed reconstruction after XRT) or thin patients without suitable gluteal tissue, a modification of a bipedicled DIEP flap (**Figure 18.1.3**) can provide an aesthetically pleasing breast reconstruction (referred to as the double-DIEP flap).

The double-DIEP is versatile and can be folded (vertical folded) or rotated (horizontally rotated) to increase, respectively, either projection or width (skin replacement) of the reconstructed breast. The double-DIEP also can provide axillary fill volume (horizontally folded with axillary extension) in patients who have undergone extensive nodal dissection. The innovative approach to insetting the double-DIEP allows for use of both antegrade and retrograde internal mammary blood vessels without the need for vein grafts or cumbersome microsurgery. The double-DIEP is especially useful for thin patients who need additional volume to reconstruct the breast or for irradiated patients who need a large area of skin replacement. The double-DIEP has become a commonly used and valuable option in the author's practice. The three most commonly used insets for the double-DIEP flap are explained in the following.

Rotated Inset: The rotated inset (upper row) is most useful for patients who need extensive skin replacement, such as those undergoing delayed reconstruction after PMRT. The rotated inset is also useful for patients with wide breasts, including those undergoing immediate reconstruction after skin-sparing mastectomy, who do not need skin replacement. The rotated inset is not used in patients who need axillary tissue replacement as a result of axillary nodal resection. For such patients, the rotated inset with axillary extension (see the next section) is preferred.

The suture plication of the two sides of the double-DIEP flap is usually positioned superiorly on the reconstructed breast, and the resultant overlapping tissue in the central region of the reconstructed breast is de-epithelialized and invaginated upon itself to create a more full-appearing breast. The contralateral side of the double-DIEP flap becomes the medial aspect of the reconstructed breast, and the ipsilateral side of the double-DIEP flap becomes the lateral aspect of the reconstructed breast. After the flap is suture plicated and secured to the chest wall, the contralateral side deep inferior epigastric artery (DIEA) and deep inferior epigastric vein (DIEV) are in the direct vicinity of the recipient antegrade internal mammary artery and vein vessels, and the ipsilateral side DIEA and DIEV are near the recipient retrograde internal mammary vessels.

Rotated Inset with Axillary Extension: The rotated inset with axillary extension (middle row) is similar to the rotated inset, except that zone 2 of the ipsilateral side of the flap is only partially suture plicated to the contralateral side of the flap and is de-epithelialized and placed within an axillary subcutaneous pocket. The axillary extension restores axillary volume that is lost when the axillary fat pad is resected during axillary nodal dissection. Consequently, the rotated inset with axillary extension can be ideal for patients undergoing delayed reconstruction after modified postmastectomy radical mastectomy (PMRT).

Vertical Folded Inset: The vertical folded inset (lower row) is well-suited for patients who do not need substantial replacement of breast skin and for those who undergo axillary sentinel lymph node biopsy without subsequent resection of the axillary fat pad. The vertical folded inset is most commonly used for thin patients with medium to large breasts who undergo immediate breast reconstruction after total mastectomy and axillary sentinel lymph node biopsy and for those who have not received preoperative radiation therapy and are not expected to require PMRT.

The contralateral side of the flap is positioned superficially to the ipsilateral side of the flap, which is folded under the contralateral side of the flap directly onto the chest wall and pectoralis major muscle. The vertical folded inset increases the projection of the lower

18.1 My approach (USA) 231

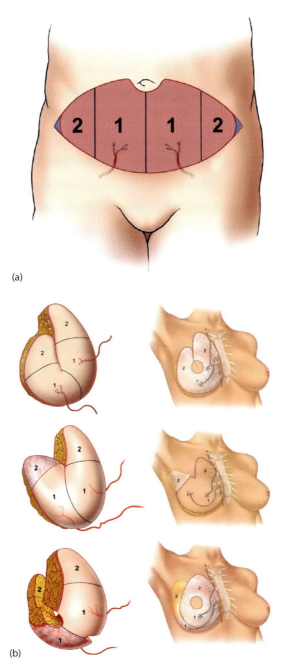

18.1.3 (a) Harvest of each side of a double-DIEP flap (Figure 18.1.1) is the same as harvest of a standard unipedicle DIEP flap with the exception of a few technical details. The flap harvest procedure described here is used for the three most common insets performed by the author, all of which involve positioning of zone 2 of each side of the flap superiorly on the reconstructed breast (Figure 18.1.2). If the surgeon prefers the suture closure to be positioned inferiorly on the reconstructed breast to conceal the scar, the steps below should be reversed. For delayed reconstruction after postmastectomy radiation therapy (PMRT), placement of the suture closure should be positioned superiorly on the reconstructed breast because this allows for zone 2 of the ipsilateral half of the DIEP flap (which will become the lateral aspect of the reconstructed breast) to be de-epithelialized and placed within an axillary subcutaneous pocket to replace the axillary fat pad that is resected as part of a nodal dissection. In addition, when the suture closure is positioned superiorly, the resulting invagination pushes the central de-epithelialized region of the flap inferiorly, increasing the lower pole projection of the reconstructed breast.
(b) These are the three most commonly used insets for the double-DIEP flap. However, for any of these options, the inset can be rotated 180° to position the suture closure of the ipsilateral and contralateral sides of the flap on the inferior, rather than the superior, aspect of the reconstructed breast to conceal the scar.

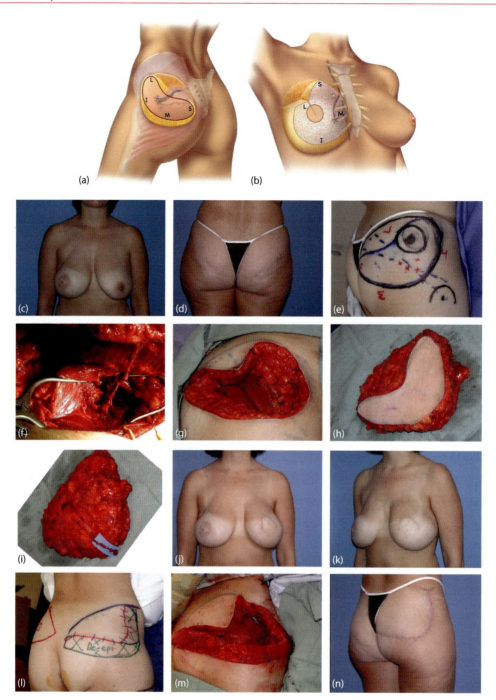

18.1.4 The boomerang flap. (a) The boomerang is harvested from the contralateral buttock and can be supplied by either the superior or inferior gluteal vessels and includes a subscarpa's fascia component that maintains a circumferential blood supply to the curvilinear-shaped flap. (b) The flap inset on the chest wall positions the perforator near the internal mammary blood vessels, which provides for long vascular pedicle length and ease of microsurgery. The boomerang requires only minimal plication to form the ideal breast shape and provides volume for both the superior and lateral aspects of the breast with a natural tapering contour.

An example is this: (c) 40-year-old, large-breasted woman who underwent a previous transverse rectus abdominis myocutaneous flap. Afterward, she was found to have the BRCA gene mutation and chose to undergo a risk-reducing mastectomy. She wanted to avoid implants and asked her surgeon to match her large contralateral transverse rectus abdominis myocutaneous flap. (d and e) Flap design on the contralateral buttock. (f) Extended pedicle dissection is important for arterial diameter, which can determine flap success or failure. (g–i) Although the skin island is curvilinear, the flap is a circumferential piece of tissue, which is important to ensure blood supply to all regions of flap. (j and k) 3 months after immediate reconstruction of the left breast with a redesigned gluteal artery perforator flap. (l and m) Revision involves recreation of the defect with superior advancement and de-epithelialization of the inferior gluteal skin. (n) Postoperative views several months after revision of the gluteal donor site.

pole of the reconstructed breast; this can be helpful for patients with a full contralateral native breast or a contralateral native breast that has previously been augmented with a breast implant.

Because the vascular pedicles from both sides of the double-DIEP flap are in close proximity to the internal mammary recipient vessels, the length of the vascular pedicles of the flap is not an issue. However, two rib cartilage segments are still removed to ensure adequate recipient vessel length and avoid tension on the vascular pedicles attributable to gravity when the patient is upright. In patients for whom a vertical folded inset is ideal, after microvascular reperfusion—but before placement of the flap within the breast skin envelope—the ipsilateral side of the flap, which will be positioned posteriorly, is de-epithelialized. This avoids the need to remove the flap from the breast skin pocket after the desired inset has been achieved. It is imperative that the perforators and vascular pedicle of the posterior aspect of the reconstructed breast (ipsilateral side of the flap) are not compressed by the overlying anterior aspect of the reconstructed breast (contralateral side of the flap).

The boomerang flap

Another commonly used option for breast reconstruction is a redesign of the gluteal artery perforator flap that is referred to as the "boomerang flap" (**Figure 18.1.4**).[7] The standard elliptical-shaped gluteal artery perforator flap was redesigned to be a more reliable option for breast reconstruction and to improve cosmetic outcomes, especially in large-breasted patients. This boomerang flap provides a larger volume of tissue for both the superior and lateral aspects of the reconstructed breast. Although many reconstructive surgeons still consider gluteal flaps to be a second-line option for autologous breast reconstruction, use of these flaps is increasing. This applies especially to: (1) patients who have already undergone transverse rectus abdominis flap reconstruction for contralateral breast cancer with a new ipsilateral breast cancer (or are found afterward to have the BRCA gene mutation), (2) those with a failed transverse rectus abdominis flap reconstruction, (3) those who underwent a previous aesthetic abdominoplasty, or (4) patients who have little abdominal subcutaneous tissue or no laxity in the abdominal musculofascial system. In these scenarios, the boomerang flap is useful, especially for patients who have received prior radiotherapy to the chest wall, in which case breast implants may be a less suitable option.

REFERENCES

1. Kim JY, Davila AA, Persing S, Connor CM, Jovanovic B, Khan SA, Fine N, Rawlani V. A meta-analysis of human acellular dermis and submuscular tissue expander breast reconstruction. *Plast Reconstr Surg.* 2012;129(1):28–41.

2. Spear SL, Rottman SJ, Seiboth LA, Hannan CM. Breast reconstruction using a staged nipple-sparing mastectomy following mastopexy or reduction. *Plast Reconstr Surg.* 2012;129(3):572–581.

3. Sarfati I, Ihrai T, Kaufman G, Nos C, Clough KB. Adipose-tissue grafting to the post-mastectomy irradiated chest wall: Preparing the ground for implant reconstruction. *J Plast Reconstr Aesthet Surg.* 2011;64(9):1161–1166.

4. Salgarello M, Visconti G, Barone-Adesi L. Fat grafting and breast reconstruction with implant: Another option for irradiated breast cancer patients. *Plast Reconstr Surg.* 2012;129(2):317–329.

5. Khouri RK, Eisenmann-Klein M, Cardoso E, Cooley BC, Kacher D, Gombos E, Baker TJ. Brava® and autologous fat transfer is a safe and effective breast augmentation alternative: Results of a 6-year, 81-patient, prospective multicenter study. *Plast Reconstr Surg.* 2012;129(5):1173–1187.

6. de Alcantara Filho P, Capko D, Barry JM, Morrow M, Pusic A, Sacchini VS. Nipple-sparing mastectomy for breast cancer and risk-reducing surgery: The Memorial Sloan-Kettering Cancer Center experience. *Ann Surg Oncol.* 2011;18(11):3117–3122.

7. Kronowitz SJ. Redesigned gluteal artery perforator flap for breast reconstruction. *Plast Reconstr Surg.* 2008;121(3):728–734.

18.2 OUR APPROACH (SOUTH AMERICA)

Alexandre Mendonça, Munhoz,

João Carlos Sampaio Goés, and Rolf Gemperli

Introduction

One of eleven women in Brazil will develop breast cancer in their lifetime.[1,2] Although conservative breast surgery is an important part of early breast cancer treatment, some patients are not satisfied with the aesthetic outcome.[3] Modified radical mastectomy and skin-sparing mastectomy continue to play an important role in the treatment algorithm of breast cancer.[4] The development of nipple-areola sparing mastectomy has improved aesthetic results, and these improvements are related to preservation of the inframammary fold and use of the native breast skin for reconstruction.[5-9]

Breast reconstruction is becoming increasingly popular and many options are available with choice of reconstructive technique based on surgeon experience, hospital resources, and patient preference.[10] Options for breast reconstruction include alloplastic techniques such as tissue expander/implant or autologous flap-based techniques. Planning and selection of the optimum method should take account of the breast volume, degree of ptosis, tumor location, the extent of skin resected, and the nuances of individual reconstructive requirements. Evaluation of reconstruction must subsequently incorporate fundamental aspects and guide usage of the proper technique at an appropriate time.

Timing of reconstruction

An in-depth dialogue concerning options for reconstruction should be undertaken with each patient, including the risks and beneficial aspects of immediate versus delayed and delayed-immediate reconstruction.[4,10] With immediate reconstruction, the surgical process is smoothened with both procedures being carried out in one operative setting. Nonetheless, total surgical time is lengthened and potential complications might adversely affect the outcome. By contrast, delayed reconstruction can be technically difficult, due to scarring of tissue as a result of previous radiotherapy,[4] and this group of patients present with a variety of chest wall deformities which need to be addressed on an individual basis.

Techniques

ALLOPLASTIC TECHNIQUES

Alloplastic tissue offers a reconstruction involving a less extensive procedure without the negative aspects of donor site morbidity. Two-stage expander-to-implant reconstruction is currently the most frequently used technique in many countries. According to the Brazilian Society of Plastic Surgery Report, almost 75% of breast reconstructions were done using expanders (**Figure 18.2.1**). More recently, reconstruction with single-stage implant placement (direct to implant) has become popular particularly with the introduction of nipple-sparing mastectomy.[9,11] Indeed, the single-stage concept has permitted immediate breast reconstruction without necessity for temporary expanders to augment overlying soft tissue or a second-stage exchange procedure. However, single-stage reconstruction may be associated with increased risks for some patients as this relies on the quality of the skin flaps without allowing for postoperative volume management. Furthermore, the quality of skin-flap coverage may ultimately limit the size of the implant which can feasibly be employed, and this may not accord with the patients' expectations. In the authors' experience, the one-stage approach has been a less successful procedure, mainly because of upper pole fullness and the need for surgical revisions[9] (**Figure 18.2.2**).

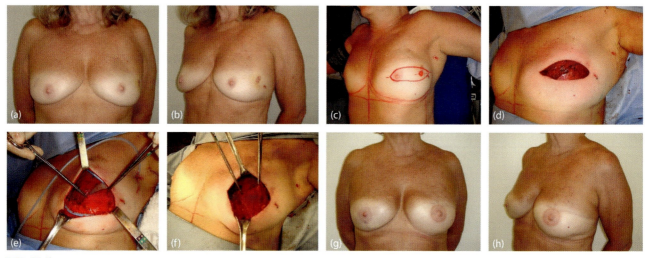

18.2.1 A 59-year-old patient with invasive ductal carcinoma (2.9 cm) of the left breast (a–b). The patient underwent a left skin-sparing mastectomy and sentinel lymph node biopsy; a total of 405 g was removed from the left breast (c–d). The patient underwent a reconstruction with total submuscular tissue expander (e–f). Two years postoperative appearance with a very good outcome (g–h).

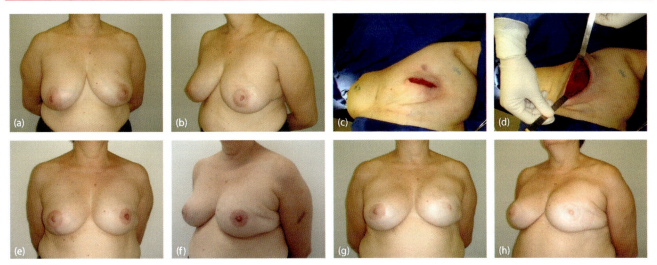

18.2.2 A 49-year-old patient with invasive ductal carcinoma (3.9 cm) of the left breast (a–b). The patient underwent a left skin-sparing mastectomy and sentinel lymph node biopsy; a total of 605 g was removed from the left breast (c–d). The patient underwent a reconstruction with dual-plane submuscular biodimensional implant-expander system with a very good outcome (e–f). Five years postoperative appearance with upper pole fullness and lack of ptosis on the left side (g–h).

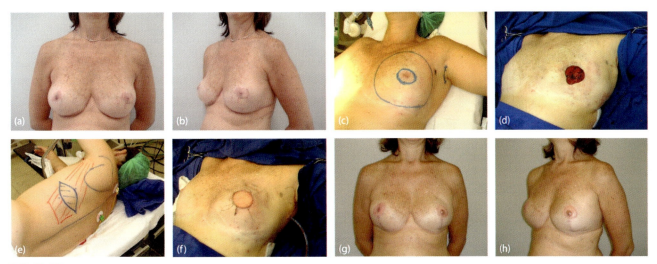

18.2.3 A 40-year-old patient with invasive and in situ ductal carcinoma (3.9 cm) of the left breast (a–b). The patient presented a previous reduction mammaplasty with inverted "T"scar. The patient underwent a left periareolar skin-sparing mastectomy and sentinel lymph node biopsy; a total of 475 g was removed from the left breast (c–d). The patient underwent a reconstruction with a latissimus dorsi myocutaneous flap for implant-expander coverage (e–f). Three years postoperative appearance with a very good outcome (g–h).

By contrast, the two-stage expander method gives the breast a more natural shape with the highest levels of patient satisfaction.[12–14] However, mastectomy flap complications can be expected and are best avoided by placing the implant under a partial or total submuscular pocket.[8,12] Regardless of the favorable results observed with total muscular coverage, this can constrain lower pole expansion and result in a high-riding device with implant malposition.[8] A technical alternative is medial coverage with the pectoralis muscle and lateral coverage with an acellular dermal matrix.[15,16] However, due to cost limitations and the lack of availability of this product in some countries, there is greater reliance on a muscular pocket, but a partially resorbable synthetic mesh is a potential alternative in these circumstances.[17] In some cases, a double approach is advocated using a combination of a latissimus dorsi myocutaneous flap and alloplastic material for implant coverage[8] (**Figure 18.2.3**).

In the authors' experience, these techniques are particularly beneficial in bilateral reconstruction and in patients with a small/medium breast size without ptosis.[4,10] The disadvantages are related to long-term aesthetic outcome due to capsular contracture and/or implant failure. For cases of unilateral reconstruction, it is a more complex process to match the ptosis and symmetry of the contralateral breast. In addition, there is a tendency for secondary ptosis in the long term (**Figure 18.2.2**).

Autologous techniques

Although autologous techniques remain less common in Brazil and many other countries, there are some positive aspects of using a patient's own tissue for breast reconstruction.[4,10] Thus techniques using abdominal wall tissues have the benefit of a concomitant abdominoplasty, especially for reconstruction using free deep inferior epigastric perforator (DIEP) and superficial inferior epigastric artery (SIEA) flaps.[18,19] The negative aspects relate to a more complex operation with donor site morbidity and a longer recovery time.[4] In addition, perforator flaps require microsurgical expertise and detailed knowledge of perforator anatomy compared with traditional transverse rectus abdominis myocutaneous (TRAM) flap or implant reconstruction. Nonetheless, these types of reconstruction can give a more natural appearing breast with durable outcomes and less donor site morbidity than non-perforator flap reconstruction.

According to the Brazilian Society of Plastic Surgery Report, reconstruction using abdominal flaps is the most frequent type of autologous technique performed in this South American country. With a pedicled TRAM flap, the lower part of the rectus muscle is transected creating a superiorly based vascular pedicle for a myocutaneous flap which is transferred up to the chest wall defect. The free TRAM and muscle-sparing alternatives (muscle-sparing 1 or 2) or DIEP (muscle-sparing 3) flaps involve some disruption of muscle fibers, but the DIEP flap is a true perforator flap which maintains integrity of the anterior abdominal wall musculature[4,18,19] (**Figure 18.2.4**). The SIEA flap is a modification and uses the superficial vessels rather than their deep counterparts. The advantages of this flap is that the abdominal wall fascia is totally preserved, leaving fascia and muscle completely intact. In the authors' experience, the SIEA pedicle is not sufficiently robust to support an entire infraumbilical abdominal flap.[20]

The latissimus dorsi flap remains an important option for autologous reconstruction and also serves as a salvage flap in cases of previous reconstructive failure or as part of a combination approach with alloplastic tissue[8] (**Figure 18.2.3**). Recently, the thoracodorsal artery perforator flap has attracted much interest because it offers several advantages, including a long pedicle and preservation of function of the latissimus dorsi muscle.[21,22] Thus, the authors consider the thoracodorsal artery perforator flap to be superior to other flaps from the region of the lateral thoracic wall, including not only the latissimus dorsi flap, but also the scapular and parascapular flaps.[4]

Although a more in-depth analysis of this issue is not appropriate here, other choices of free autologous tissue include gluteal flaps, the transverse upper gracilis flap, and the lateral thigh flap. These are typically considered as second/third options or for salvage procedures. The authors have used these techniques in patients who have undergone a previous TRAM flap procedure and develop a contralateral breast cancer or in patients who desire an autologous breast reconstruction, but have inadequate abdominal tissue.

CONCLUSION

Breast reconstruction can present challenges for both the oncological and plastic surgeon and demands meticulous understanding of basic principles and technical ability in reconstructive methods. Optimal treatment should be preventive by performing immediate reconstruction and addressing individual requirements, thereby enabling each patient to receive a "custom-made" reconstruction.

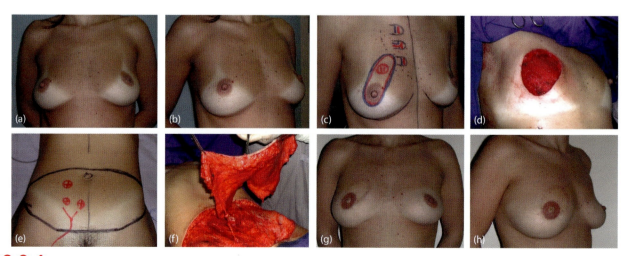

18.2.4 A 32-year-old patient with in situ ductal carcinoma (4.1 cm) of the right breast (a–b). The patient underwent a right skin-sparing mastectomy and sentinel lymph node biopsy; a total of 315 g was removed from the right breast (c–d). The patient underwent a reconstruction with a free DIEP flap (e–f). One-year postoperative appearance with a very good outcome (g–h).

REFERENCES

1. Ministério da Saúde (BR). Instituto Nacional do Câncer. Estimativas 2010: incidência de câncer no Brasil. Rio de Janeiro: INCA; 2009.
2. Paulinelli, R.R., Freitas, J.R., Curado, M.P., Souza, A.A. A Situação do Câncer de Mama em Goiás, no Brasil e no Mundo: Tendências Atuais para a Incidência e a Mortalidade. *Rev Bras Saude Mater Infant* 3 (2003): 17-24.
3. Wang, H.T., Barone, C.M., Steigelman, M.B., et al. Aesthetic outcomes in breast conservation therapy. *Aesthet Surg J* 28 (2010): 165-170.
4. Serletti, J.M., Fosnot, J., Nelson, J.A., Disa, J.J., Bucky, L.P. Breast reconstruction after breast cancer. *Plast Reconstr Surg* 127 (2011): 124e-135e.
5. Toth, B.A., Lappert, P. Modified skin incisions for mastectomy: The need for plastic surgical input in preoperative planning. *Plast Reconstr Surg* 87 (1991): 1048-1053.
6. Singletary, S.E. Skin-sparing mastectomy with immediate breast reconstruction: The MD Anderson Cancer Center experience. *Ann Surg Oncol* 3 (1996): 411-416.
7. Munhoz, A.M., Arruda, E., Montag, E., Aldrighi, C., Aldrighi, J.M., Gemperli, R., Ferreira, M.C. Immediate skin-sparing mastectomy reconstruction with deep inferior epigastric perforator (DIEP) flap. Technical aspects and outcome. *Breast J* 13 (2007): 470-478.
8. Munhoz, A.M., Aldrighi, C., Montag, E., Arruda, E.G., Aldrighi, J.M., Filassi, J.R., Ferreira, M.C. Periareolar skin-sparing mastectomy and latissimus dorsi flap with biodimensional expander implant reconstruction: Surgical planning, outcome, and complications. *Plast Reconstr Surg* 119 (2007): 1637-1649.
9. Munhoz, A.M., Aldrighi, C.M., Montag, E., Arruda, E.G., Aldrighi, J.M., Gemperli, R., Filassi, J.R., Ferreira, M.C. Clinical outcomes following nipple-areola-sparing mastectomy with immediate implant-based breast reconstruction: A 12-year experience with an analysis of patient and breast-related factors for complications. *Breast Cancer Res Treat* 140 (2013): 545-555.
10. Nahabedian, M.Y. Breast reconstruction: A review and rationale for patient selection. *Plast Reconstr Surg* 124 (2009): 55-62.
11. Agusti, A., Ward, A., Montgomery, C., Mohammed, K., Gui, G.P. Aesthetic and oncologic outcomes after one-stage immediate breast reconstruction using a permanent biodimensional expandable implant. *J Plast Reconstr Aesthet Surg* 69 (2016): 211-220.
12. Cordeiro, P.G., McCarthy, C.M. A single surgeon's 12-year experience with tissue expander/implant breast reconstruction: Part II. An analysis of long-term complications, aesthetic outcomes, and patient satisfaction. *Plast Reconstr Surg* 118 (2006): 832-839.
13. Spear, S.L., Onyewu, C. Staged breast reconstruction with saline-filled implants in the irradiated breast: Recent trends and therapeutic implications. *Plast Reconstr Surg* 105 (2000): 930-942.
14. Collis, N., Sharpe, D.T. Breast reconstruction by tissue expansion: A retrospective technical review of 197 two-stage delayed reconstructions following mastectomy for malignant breast disease in 189 patients. *Br J Plast Surg* 53 (2000): 37-41.
15. Sbitany, H., Sandeen, S.N., Amalfi, A.N., Davenport, M.S., Langstein, H.N. Acellular dermis-assisted prosthetic breast reconstruction versus complete submuscular coverage: A head-to-head comparison of outcomes. *Plast Reconstr Surg* 124 (2009): 1735-1740.
16. Nahabedian, M.Y. alloderm performance in the setting of prosthetic breast surgery, infection, and irradiation. *Plast Reconstr Surg* 124 (2009): 1743-1753.
17. Goés, J.C.S., Macedo, A.L. Immediate reconstruction after mastectomy using a periareolar approach with an omental flap and mixed mesh support. *Perspect Plast Surg* 10 (1996): 69-81.
18. Selber, J.C., Nelson, J., Fosnot, J., et al. A prospective study comparing the functional impact of SIEA, DIEP, and muscle-sparing free TRAM flaps on the abdominal wall: Part I. Unilateral Reconstruction. *Plast Reconstr Surg* 126 (2010): 1142-1153.
19. Wu, L.C., Bajaj, A., Chang, D.W., Chevray, P.M. Comparison of donor-site morbidity of SIEA, DIEP, and muscle-sparing TRAM flaps for breast reconstruction. *Plast Reconstr Surg* 122 (2008): 702-709.
20. Munhoz, A.M., Pellarin, L., Montag, E., Filassi, J.R., Tachibana, A., Gebrim, H., Gemperli, R., Ferreira, M.C. Superficial inferior epigastric artery (SIEA) free flap using perforator vessels as a recipient site: clinical implications in autologous breast reconstruction. *Am J Surg* 202 (2011): 612-617.
21. Hamdi, M., Salgarello, M., Barone-Adesi, L., et al. Use of thoracodorsal artery perforator (TDAP) flap with implant in breast reconstruction. *Ann Plast Surg* 61 (2008): 143-146.
22. Hamdi, M., Rasheed, M.Z. Advances in autologous breast reconstruction with pedicled perforator flaps. *Clin Plast Surg* 39 (2012): 477-490.

Mastectomy and whole breast reconstruction (methods and techniques)

Chapter 19. Implant-based whole breast reconstruction (without irradiation)	241
Chapter 20. Implant-based whole breast reconstruction (with irradiation)	279
Chapter 21. Fat grafting exclusively for whole breast reconstruction	301
Chapter 22. Standard autologous tissue flaps for whole breast reconstruction	309
Chapter 23. Advanced autologous tissue flaps for whole breast reconstruction	339

19

Implant-based whole breast reconstruction (without irradiation)

19.1 ONE-STAGE IMPLANT RECONSTRUCTION

AT A GLANCE

Nipple-sparing mastectomy is the ideal scenario for one-stage implant breast reconstruction, usually along with an acellular dermal matrix sling. However, a reliable mastectomy is extremely important so that the implant does not compress the blood supply to the breast skin and nipple. Many surgeons are also concerned that if radiation is needed after review of permanent sections from the mastectomy that the implant may interfere with radiation delivery. The economics of one-stage implant reconstruction is very appealing and can be an excellent choice for many patients. One surgery and done.

19.1.1 Our approach (USA)

Andrew Salzberg and Jordan Jacobs

The evolution in surgical treatment of breast cancer from Halsted's radical mastectomy to the present day skin-sparing and nipple-sparing techniques has provided the reconstructive surgeon with more options.[1–3] The resultant larger skin envelope is able to support immediate breast reconstruction, provided skin flaps are healthy.[4,5] The single-stage, direct-to-implant approach overcomes the limitations of a two-stage, expander approach and represents the ultimate simplicity in breast reconstruction.

The feasibility of a single-stage implant approach has been greatly facilitated by the introduction of acellular dermal matrices (ADMs) in reconstructive breast surgery.[6] These structurally intact tissue matrices provide the biologic scaffold necessary for tissue in-growth and cellular repopulation. They have been utilized to specifically provide coverage of the implant or expander at the inferolateral pole,[7–14] thus eliminating the need for recruitment of neighboring muscle and/or fascia for this purpose.[10] ADM use at the inferolateral pole also allows better control of the inframammary fold, improves lower pole projection, and reduces expander or implant migration.[8,10] Collectively, these benefits of ADM can lead to improved aesthetic results.[10,15]

PREOPERATIVE PLANNING

Preoperative assessment to determine whether the patient is a candidate for direct-to-implant reconstruction focuses on the patient's body habitus, the ablative component of the surgery, and the specific desires of the patient for contralateral breast symmetry. Coordination between plastic surgeon and surgical oncologist will help ensure a clear understanding of the planned surgical strategy. The ideal candidate for a direct-to-implant technique is a patient with a medium or small breast size, grade 1–2 ptosis, and good skin quality. Patients with a history of smoking must abstain for at least 4 weeks prior to and after surgery. Morbidly obese patients are generally poor candidates for implant reconstruction because of an increased risk of postoperative complications.[16]

Although the quality of the skin flaps after mastectomy is a critical component for a successful outcome, choosing an appropriately sized implant to fill the space beneath these flaps is also an important consideration. The patient's chest wall dimensions are carefully measured and an array of sizers is used preoperatively to gauge the anticipated volume that will be required. In addition, a three-dimensional volumetric computer program is commonly used to assist with implant selection. A notable point is to have an implant base width that complements the chest diameter, as a concave lateral chest contour will result if the implant is of insufficient width. Saline implants are not routinely recommended because they often produce a suboptimal aesthetic shape in a reconstructed breast and are prone to greater visibility and palpability as well.

MASTECTOMY AND RECONSTRUCTION

The reconstructive surgeon needs to be an active participant during the mastectomy, thereby assuring careful handling of the skin and the avoidance of traction or thermal injury to the flaps. If electrocautery is used for flap elevation, low settings are monitored and used on low cutting to reduce the risk of tissue damage. Scalpel or more recent radiofrequency devices (Peak™ Surgical, Palo Alto, CA) may also be used for surgical development of skin flaps.

Critical for immediate reconstruction with a direct-to-implant technique is utilizing ADM to extend the submuscular plane, support the implant in its anatomic position, and define the inferior and lateral folds of the breast. The technique begins by creating a subpectoral pocket extending from the second rib superiorly, medially to the origin of the pectoralis major muscle at the sternum, and laterally to the lateral mammary fold. Elevation of a portion of the infero-medial muscle to allow anatomic placement of the implant is also performed. The ADM is introduced at the inferior pole (**Figure 19.1.1.1**) and is sutured in a running fashion to the pectoralis major muscle along its entire lower course from medial to lateral and then around and down to the lateral mammary fold.

No elevation of muscle is necessary at the serratus margin and direct suturing of the ADM to the chest wall with absorbable suture material defines and sets the limit of the lateral fold. The appropriately sized implant is confirmed by surgical judgment as well as by the weight of the mastectomy specimen. A modest over correction is added to the final implant volume to accommodate the anticipated release of the skin elasticity following mastectomy. After placing the implant beneath the muscle-ADM layer, continued suturing of the ADM directly to the inframammary fold at its desired position—without expectation of migration—is performed, completely covering the implant. Direct conformation of the skin envelope to the lower pole will decrease the chance of seroma formation. A "perfect" shape should be achieved at this point and postoperative settling should not be planned. Two suction drains are placed in the subcutaneous plane through separate stab incisions followed by skin closure.

Typically, patients remain in hospital for approximately 48 hours. Upon discharge, drains covered with occlusive dressings are maintained for 7–14 days, with removal determined by the amount and quality of their output. A supportive surgical bra with an additional superior pole pectoralis strap is worn for a minimum of 3 weeks to assist in the optimal positioning of the implants in the pocket. The patients are encouraged to do gentle exercise to improve range-of-motion of the arm and to perform gentle massaging of their breasts to prevent development of axillary contracture.

OUTCOMES

This technique can be successfully performed in patients with a variety of breast sizes and varying degrees of ptosis. Moreover, these techniques are suitable for patients undergoing nipple-sparing or skin-sparing mastectomy for either oncologic or prophylactic reasons. The principles for clinical decision making in the context of single-stage implant reconstruction with ADM are summarized in **Figure 19.1.1.2**.

Over a 14-year period, low rates of complications and good aesthetic outcomes (**Figures 19.1.1.3 and 19.1.1.4**) have been consistently obtained. Major complications include

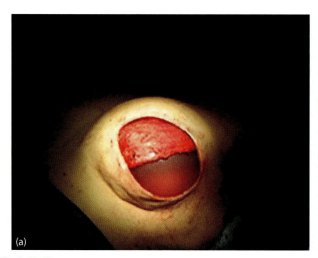
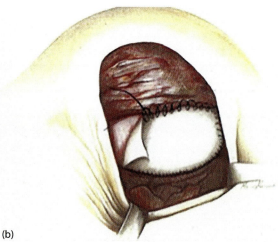

19.1.1.1 (a) Suture and (b) Lateral muscle.

19.1 One-stage implant reconstruction 243

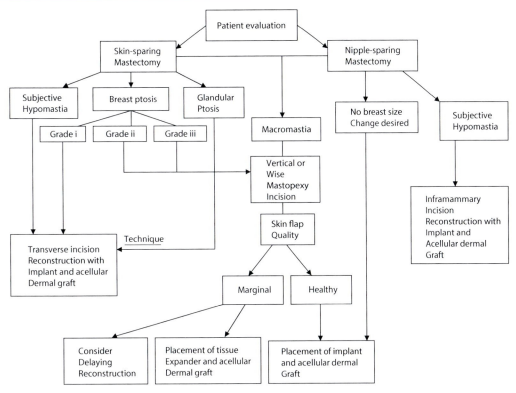

19.1.1.2 Clinical decision-making in direct-to-implant reconstruction with acellular dermal matrix.

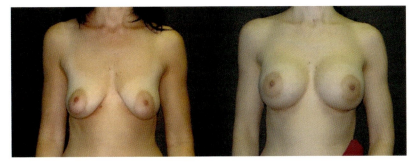

19.1.1.3 Preoperative front view (left) and postoperative (right).

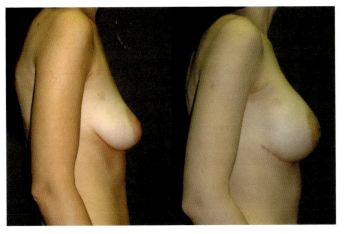

19.1.1.4 Preoperative lateral view (left) and postoperative view (right).

implant loss (1.4%), skin necrosis requiring re-operation (1.1%), infection (0.9%), hematoma (0.6%), seroma (0.5%), and capsular contracture (0.5%). Other minor issues related to suture exposure, wound healing delay, superficial epidermolysis, and non-infectious redness of the skin have been noted in up to 1% of patients.

The decision to perform this technique in the setting of adjuvant radiotherapy requires careful consideration. Significant skin changes from prior radiation with a firm and non-expansive skin envelope are indications for autologous reconstruction. In patients who have mild skin changes, incorporation of the ADM into the radiated-skin milieu has been shown to be successful. A total of 32 patients in the author's series have received either pre- or postoperative radiation treatments, with complications occurring in four of them (infection, ADM exposure, or implant malposition). In patients who are scheduled to receive adjuvant radiation therapy, and who have declined an autologous tissue option, immediate-implant insertion can still be successfully performed.

If there are any doubts about the preoperative quality or intraoperative viability of the skin flaps, then the planned procedure should be modified and an expander placed in the submuscular-ADM pocket. A limited volume can then be injected into the expander—which is just sufficient to gently fill the skin envelope ("hand in glove" fit).

Special consideration should be given to those patients presenting for prophylactic mastectomy who also desire a significant reduction in their breast size. In this situation, a staged breast reduction followed by a nipple-sparing mastectomy and implant reconstruction is a good option—with a minimum of 3 months between the two stages. Alternatively, a skin pattern reduction utilizing either a vertical or Wise-pattern with free nipple grafting can be performed at the time of mastectomy.

CONCLUSION

The introduction of ADM in breast surgery has allowed improved definition of the implant pocket with better support of the device in the proper position. One-stage, direct-to-implant reconstruction in properly selected patients reduces intraoperative time, postoperative visits, and the need for a secondary surgery. Clinical experience with this technique over the last 14 years has demonstrated the effectiveness of the procedure, the long-term safety, and aesthetic benefits of this approach.

REFERENCES

1. Halstead W. The results of operations for the cure of cancer of the breast performed at The Johns Hopkins Hospital from June 1889 to January 1894. *Johns Hopkins Bull.* 1894;4:297.
2. Kroll SS et al. The oncologic risks of skin preservation at mastectomy when combined with immediate reconstruction of the breast. *Surg Gynecol Obstet.* 1991;172:17–20.
3. Crowe JP Jr, Kim JA, Yetman R, Banbury J, Patrick RJ, Baynes D. Nipple-sparing mastectomy: Technique and results of 54 procedures. *Arch Surg.* 2004;139:148–150.
4. Foster RD, Esserman LJ, Anthony JP, Hwang ES, Do H. Skin-sparing mastectomy and immediate breast reconstruction: A prospective cohort study for the treatment of advanced stages of breast carcinoma. *Ann Surg Oncol.* 2002;9:462–466.
5. Ashikari RH, Ashikari AY, Kelemen PR, Salzberg CA. Subcutaneous mastectomy and immediate reconstruction for prevention of breast cancer for high-risk patients. *Breast Cancer.* 2008;15:185–191.
6. Duncan DI. Correction of implant rippling using allograft dermis. *Aesthetic Surg J.* 2001;21:81–84.
7. Salzberg CA. Nonexpansive immediate breast reconstruction using human acellular tissue matrix graft (AlloDerm). *Ann Plast Surg.* 2006:57:707–711.
8. Breuing KH, Colwell AL. Inferolateral AlloDerm hammock for implant coverage in breast reconstruction. *Ann Plast Surg.* 2007;59:250–255.
9. Zienowicz RJ, Karacaoglu E. Implant-based breast reconstruction with allograft. *Plast Reconstr Surg.* 2007;120:373–381.
10. Spear SL, Parikh PM, Reisin E, Menon NG. Acellular dermis-assisted breast reconstruction. *Aesthetic Plast Surg.* 2008;32:418–425.
11. Preminger BA, McCarthy CM, Hu QY, Mehrara BJ, Disa JJ. The influence of AlloDerm on expander dynamics and complications in the setting of immediate tissue expander/implant reconstruction: A matched-cohort study. *Ann Plast Surg.* 2008;60:510–513.
12. Losken A. Early results using sterilized acellular human dermis (Neoform) in post-mastectomy tissue expander breast reconstruction. *Plast Reconstr Surg.* 2009;123:1654–1658.
13. Becker S, Saint-Cyr M, Wong C et al. AlloDerm versus DermaMatrix in immediate expander-based breast reconstruction: A preliminary comparison of complication profiles and material compliance. *Plast Reconstr Surg.* 2009;123:1–6.
14. Rawlani V, Buck DW 2nd, Johnson SA, Heyer KS, Kim JY. Tissue expander breast reconstruction using prehydrated human acellular dermis. *Ann Plast Surg.* 2011;66:593–597.
15. Vardanian AJ, Clayton JL, Roostaeian J et al. Comparison of implant-based immediate breast reconstruction with and without acellular dermal matrix. *Plast Reconstr Surg.* 2011;128:403e–410e.
16. McCarthy CM, Mehrara BJ, Riedel E et al. Predicting complications following expander/implant breast reconstruction: An outcomes analysis based on preoperative clinical risk. *Plast Reconstr Surg.* 2008;121:1886–1892.

19.1.2 My approach (Europe)

Pierluigi Santi

Breast cancer surgery affects the daily and the social life of a woman as well as her job and her relationships, so immediate reconstruction is preferable except for the most advanced oncological stages. There is not a "correct" reconstructive solution for all patients, but each case requires a careful assessment and a multidisciplinary approach. This is essential to guarantee that every woman is offered the most appropriate reconstruction in accordance with her clinical and personal needs.

Instead of using autologous tissues, the author prefers implant-based reconstruction (expander or prosthesis) that permits rapid recovery, fewer days of hospitalization, less donor site morbidity, and which is well-suited for the majority of patients.

Immediate implant-based reconstruction represents about 90% of all reconstructive procedures undertaken in the IRCCS San Martino–IST Plastic Breast Surgery Department according to data compiled by both European and international case series.[1]

During the past 10 years, there has been significant improvements in skin-sparing, nipple-sparing, and skin-reducing forms of mastectomy together with the development of prosthesis technology. This has led to the availability of a range of implants of different shapes and sizes, which has spurred interest in and augmented popularity of one-stage reconstruction with a direct-to-implant (DTI) approach.

DIRECT-TO-IMPLANT RECONSTRUCTION

This surgical technique consists of the placement of a definitive breast prosthesis at the time of mastectomy and immediate breast reconstruction and is usually undertaken in conjunction with the use of a biological or synthetic mesh and possible concomitant symmetrization of the contralateral breast (**Figures 19.1.2.1 through 19.1.2.6**).

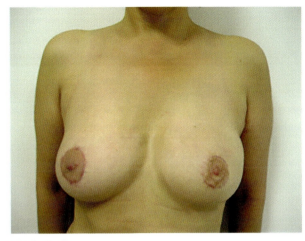

19.1.2.2 Immediate one-stage bilateral reconstruction with anatomical implant after radical mastectomy.

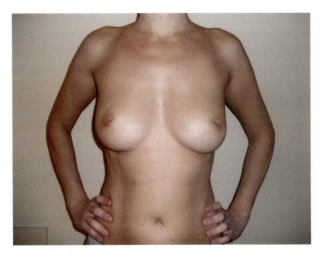

19.1.2.3 Preoperative.

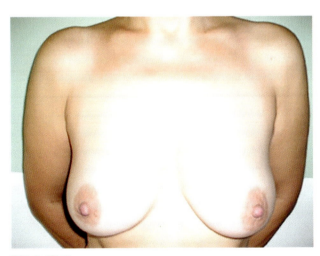

19.1.2.1 Preoperative.

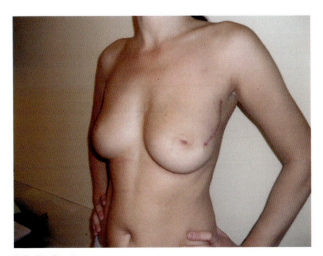

19.1.2.4 Immediate one-stage monolateral reconstruction with anatomical implant after nipple-sparing mastectomy.

Alternatively, a definitive expandable mammary prosthesis could be inserted whose use is limited to a group of older patients, for whom use of DTI reconstruction is not recommended due to clinical and morphological characteristics (**Figures 19.1.2.7 and 19.1.2.8**).

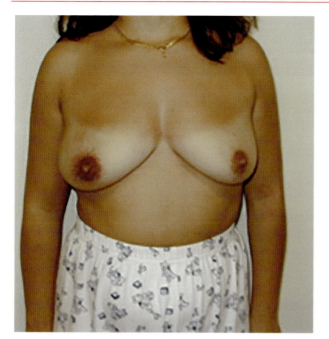

19.1.2.5 Preoperative.

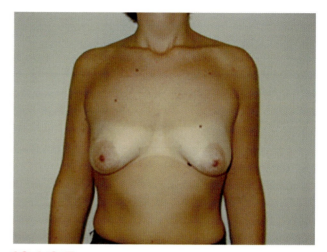

19.1.2.7 Preoperative.

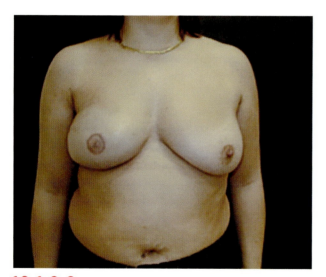

19.1.2.6 Immediate one-stage reconstruction with anatomical implant after skin-sparing mastectomy and nipple reconstruction.

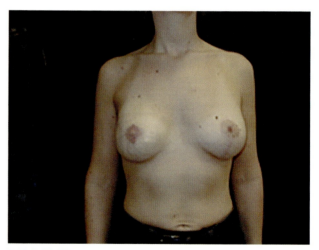

19.1.2.8 Immediate one-stage monolateral reconstruction and contralateral mastoplasty with permanent expander after radical mastectomy and nipple reconstruction.

Immediate two-stage breast reconstructions (Figures 19.1.2.9 through 19.1.2.15)

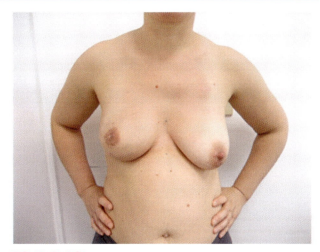

19.1.2.12 Postoperative implant replacement.

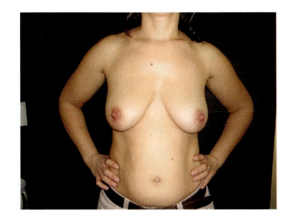

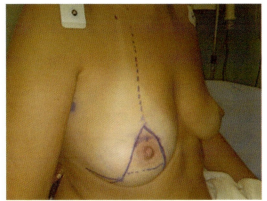

19.1.2.9–19.1.2.10 Preoperative skin marking.

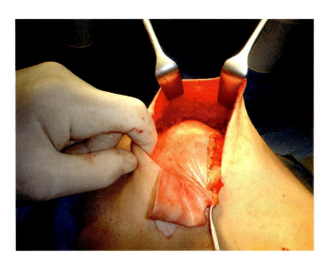

19.1.2.13 ADM and tissue expander.

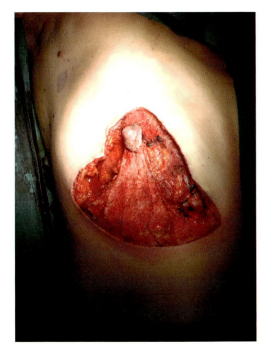

19.1.2.11 Intraoperative two-stage reconstruction after nipple-sparing mastectomy (inferior dermal flap and tissue expander).

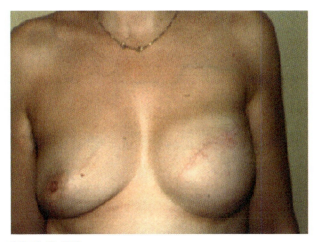

19.1.2.14 Postoperative appearance with expander.

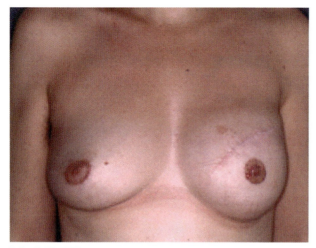

19.1.2.15 Implant replacement with anatomical prosthesis.

Delayed-breast reconstruction
(Figures 19.1.2.16 through 19.1.2.20)

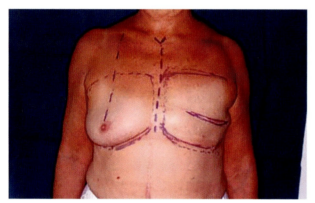

19.1.2.16 Preoperative markings.

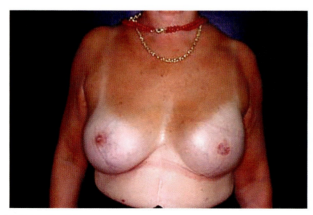

19.1.2.17 Delayed one-stage reconstruction with prosthesis.

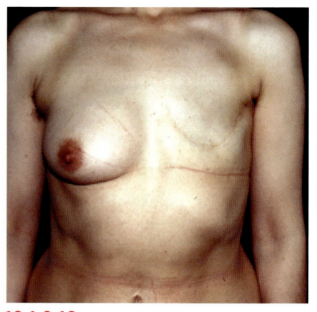

19.1.2.18 Preoperative appearance.

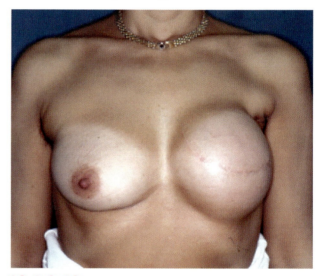

19.1.2.19 Delayed expander insertion.

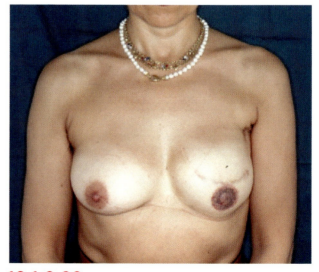

19.1.2.20 Replacement with anatomical prosthesis.

Direct-to-implant reconstruction 249

19.1 One-stage implant reconstruction 251

Combined reconstruction (DTI reconstruction + lipofilling) (**Figures 19.1.2.21 through 19.1.2.27**)

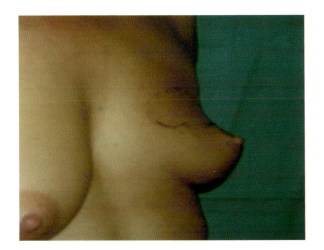

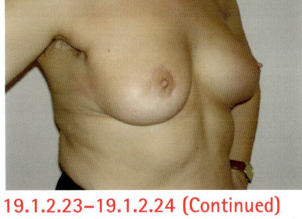

19.1.2.23–19.1.2.24 (Continued) Immediate combined reconstruction used to improve volume and contours of the breast, cover of the prosthesis, and the thickness of the subcutaneous tissue in nipple-sparing mastectomy.

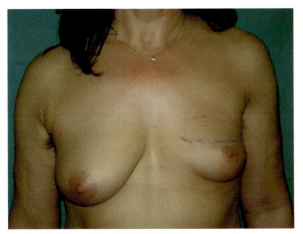

19.1.2.21–19.1.2.22 Preoperative appearance.

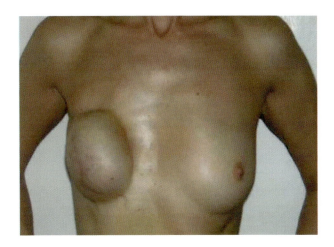

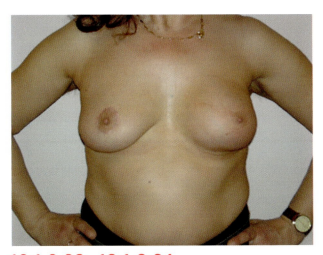

19.1.2.23–19.1.2.24 Immediate combined reconstruction used to improve volume and contours of the breast, cover of the prosthesis, and the thickness of the subcutaneous tissue in nipple-sparing mastectomy. (*Continued*)

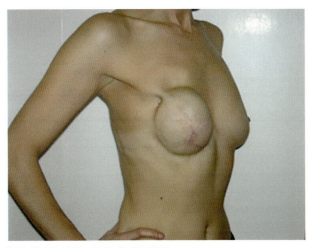

19.1.2.25–19.1.2.26 Lipofilling between expander insertion (19.1.2.25–19.1.2.26) and prosthesis replacement (19.1.2.27a–b).

250 Implant-based whole breast reconstruction (without irradiation)

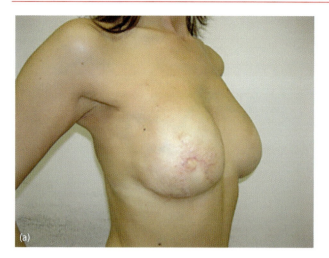

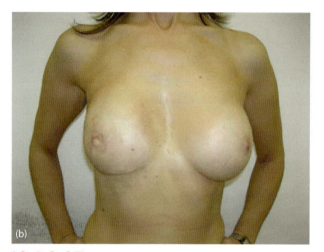

19.1.2.27 Lipofilling between expander insertion (19.1.2.25–19.1.2.26) and prosthesis replacement (19.1.2.27a–b).

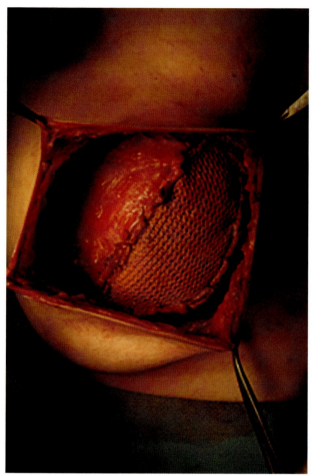

19.1.2.28 Synthetic mesh.

SURGICAL TECHNIQUE

In the preoperative phase, the incision site, the type of mastectomy (skin-sparing, nipple-sparing, skin-reducing), and the possible need for contralateral breast symmetrization is determined.

On completion of the mastectomy, if the skin flaps are healthy, then it is safe to proceed with one-stage reconstruction. The prosthetic pocket is created below the pectoralis major muscle that is detached from its inferolateral and medial insertions. The author often uses a sizer to aid in the selection of a prosthesis whose size and shape best suits the patient.

Prophylactic antibiotics containing cefazolin is administered and 1–2 drains are positioned in the prosthetic pocket and the axilla. Optimal results can be obtained by enhancing the subpectoral pocket at the level of the lateral inferior quadrant with use of a biological or synthetic mesh, which allows the inframammary fold to be defined more precisely (**Figures 19.1.2.28 through 19.1.2.30**).

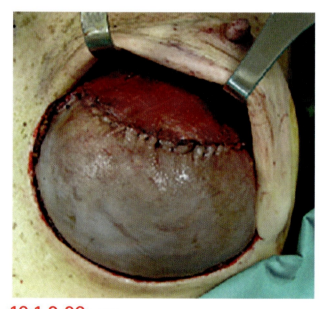

19.1.2.29 ADM.

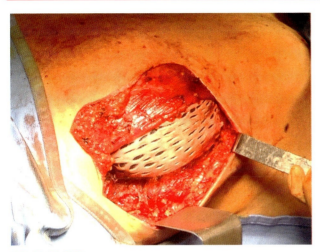

19.1.2.30 Mesh of homologous dermis.

In Italy and Europe, there are different types of biological and synthetic materials (matrices, meshes), although it remains unclear which material is preferable and any particular choice depends mainly on the experience of the individual surgeon.[2]

SELECTION OF PATIENTS

Reconstruction using DTI techniques is indicated for patients with the following characteristics:

1. Expectation of rapid resumption of activity
2. Small-medium-sized breasts and adequate amounts of overlying tissue
3. Early stage of disease
4. Skin-sparing mastectomy, nipple-sparing mastectomy, prophylactic mastectomy and healthy intraoperative mastectomy flaps

ADVANTAGES AND DISADVANTAGE OF DTI RECONSTRUCTION

A direct-to-implant approach allows a shortened reconstructive pathway favoring an earlier return to normal daily activities and arguably involves less psychological trauma for the patient. Several studies have attempted to compare one-stage and two-stage reconstruction based on complications, cosmetic results, and costs.[3-5] Most of these studies have shown no significant difference between DTI and two-stage in terms of postoperative complications such as skin necrosis, exposure, infection, hematoma, and seroma rates. However, it is known that DTI procedures are more prone to implant loss and temporary failure of the reconstruction. There are clinical challenges with effectively treating complications in the setting of implant-based reconstruction and, in particular, immediately following DTI approaches. The most worrying problem is necrosis of the mastectomy flaps that can be aggravated by placement of an implant of fixed volume and can result in exposure, infection, and loss of the implant itself.

By contrast, an advantage of reconstruction using expansion is the possibility of adjusting the volume according to local tissue conditions that can increase the chance of healing without implant loss.

According to the published literature on this subject, the final aesthetic results are comparable for the two groups, although in the author's opinion, a two-stage reconstruction improves symmetry and is associated with improved levels of patient satisfaction. The potential advantages of DTI in terms of costs need careful health and economic assessments. Apart from the benefit of a single operation, the additional expense related to the management of complications and any subsequent surgical revision must be taken account of and may render overall costs comparable to a two-stage reconstruction.

DTI reconstruction can be an alternative reconstruction option based on levels of patient satisfaction and aesthetic results provided costs can be contained and patients are carefully selected.

Given the high risk of implant loss and need for subsequent surgical revisions with an increase in healthcare costs, the two-stage reconstruction is generally safer and recommended in patients previously treated with radiotherapy and who are deemed to be at high risk for postsurgical complications. This includes smokers (current and recent) and those women with a high body mass index.

REFERENCES

1. Lee KT, Mun GH Comparison of one-stage vs two-stage prosthesis-based breast reconstruction: A systematic review and meta-analysis. *Am J Surg.* 2015;212(2):336–344.
2. Dieterich M, Faridi A Biological matrices and synthetic meshes used in implant-based breast reconstruction—A review of products available in Germany. *Geburtshilfe Frauenheilkd.* 2013;73(11):1100–1106.
3. Colwell AS Current strategies with 1-stage prosthetic breast reconstruction. *Gland Surg.* 2015;4(2):111–115.
4. Wink JD, Fischer JP, Nelson JA, Serletti JM, Wu LC Direct-to-implant breast reconstruction: An analysis of 1612 cases from the ACS-NSQIP surgical outcomes database. *J Plast Surg Hand Surg.* 2014;48(6):375–381.
5. Davila AA, Mioton LM, Chow G, Wang E, Merkow RP, Bilimoria KY, Fine N, Kim JY Immediate two-stage tissue expander breast reconstruction compared with one-stage permanent implant breast reconstruction: A multi-institutional comparison of short-term complications. *J Plast Surg Hand Surg.* 2013;47(5):344–349.

19.2 TWO-STAGE IMPLANT RECONSTRUCTION

AT A GLANCE

Despite the recent popularity of one-stage implant breast reconstruction, the two-stage approach continues to be the predominant method of implant-based reconstruction. The reliability of the blood supply to the mastectomy skin flaps and in the case of nipple-sparing mastectomy (NSM) the nipple areolar complex are concerns for many reconstructive surgeons, who prefer to avoid any pressure on the often tenuous breast skin flaps. In addition, the spectrum of skin-sparing mastectomy is broad and many extirpative surgeons continue to remove a significant portion of the native breast skin which requires expansion to achieve an adequate breast skin envelope for reconstruction. It remains unclear whether two stages are better than one and a recent randomized controlled trial (BRIOS) failed to confirm superiority of one-stage direct-to-implant over two-stage reconstruction.

19.2.1 Our approach (USA)

Patrick Maxwell and Allen Gabriel

INTRODUCTION

Implant-based breast reconstruction is the most frequently performed reconstructive technique following breast ablative surgery. The techniques and technologies have evolved over the years, which has allowed surgeons to continue improving reconstructive outcomes.

Use of regenerative scaffolds of acellular matrices and regenerative cells of physiologically processed fat has changed the face of breast enhancement and breast reconstruction. No longer is an implant alone the sole factor in replacing the female breast form, but soft tissue cover overlying the implant can now be enhanced, which not only supplements volume and shape, but further alters how recipient host tissue responds to the foreign body implant. This powerful combination of constructs better allows the ultimate goal of breast reconstruction to be achieved—the recreation of a breast that appears and feels like a natural breast.

The application of this concept of utilizing a combination of form-stable and/or higher fill implants, regenerative dermal matrices, and fat grafting[1] (otherwise known as the bioengineered breast) allows predictable results to be obtained using both the pre-pectoral and dual plane approaches.[1]

CONCEPT/RATIONALE

The rationale for bioengineered breasts originated with the observation that commonly encountered complaints of women who have undergone implant-based breast reconstruction often relate to insufficient soft tissue. Problems of implant visibility, implant rippling/wrinkling, and/or hollowing/depression of the skin that often appear in the vicinity of the upper pole of the breast are related to inadequate upper pole soft tissue coverage and inadequate upper pole fullness.

SURGICAL TECHNIQUE

Within our practice, bioengineered breasts are typically created in a two-stage expander/implant procedure (Figure 19.2.1.1), although the technique can also be performed as a one-stage, direct-to-implant reconstruction. The authors' personal preference is for the two-stage technique.

Stage 1

The first stage is identical to a standard acellular matrix-assisted tissue expander reconstruction in which the expander is placed subpectorally with its lower third covered by a sheet of acellular matrix (usually either AlloDerm or Strattice [LifeCell Corporation, Branchburg, New Jersey] in our practice).[2,3] Medium or short-high projection expanders are preferable and allow maximal expansion of the lower pole. Attention to best practice to minimize risk of complications with acellular dermal matrix-assisted reconstruction is crucial and include: (1) infection control (i.e., prophylactic antibiotic use, single-touch technique when handling expander); (2) seroma formation (i.e., proper drain usage with adequate drainage); and (3) skin necrosis (i.e., trimming of compromised tissue, optimal intraoperative expansion).[4,5] "Pie crusting" the acellular matrix during the first stage of reconstruction is a preferred maneuver.

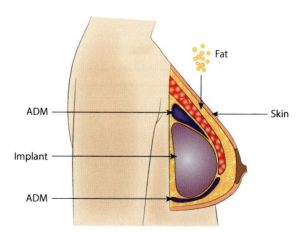

19.2.1.1 Bioengineered breast. Acellular dermal matrix and autologous fat are used to create a bioengineered breast.

Stage 2

The second stage of reconstruction involves placement of a further piece of acellular dermal matrix subpectorally (inside the breast pocket) at the upper pole in a select group of patients, namely, those with lower body mass index and inadequate soft tissue thickness. This is followed by autologous fat injections in the subcutaneous space at the upper pole and medial and lateral contours of the reconstructed breast as needed. If the pocket lies in a pre-pectoral location, then fat grafting is performed during this stage only in those circumstances when no additional capsulotomies are performed.

In a patient for dual plane reconstruction, preoperative marking of the skin includes: (1) the breast boundary; (2) the location of planned capsulotomy at the upper pole; and (3) the location of acellular matrix to be placed under the pectoral muscle at the upper pole (**Figure 19.2.1.2**). A sheet of relatively high thickness acellular matrix is prepared according to manufacturer's instructions. If using an acellular matrix that has a backing paper, then the matrix and its backing paper must be trimmed to the desired shape. For a previously hydrated acellular matrix that lacks a backing paper, a glove wrapper can be used as a satisfactory alternative. Three to five anchor points for suturing are marked on the acellular matrix and backing paper. The anchor point markings on the backing paper are transferred onto the upper pole skin where the acellular matrix will be inset under the pectoralis muscle. The purpose of using a backing or glove paper is to avoid using the acellular matrix to mark the suture points on the skin.

After these preliminary steps, the tissue expander is accessed and removed via an inframammary incision. A superomedial capsulotomy is performed and the posterior capsule is scored vertically and medially in several places to allow subcutaneous tissue to penetrate the capsule and potentially provide more robust vascularity. Alternatively, a complete capsulotomy may be performed or a segment of the anterior capsule can be removed to allow for greater surface contact between acellular dermal matrix and muscle. The anchor points on the acellular matrix are secured to the corresponding anchor points on the skin using 2-0 prolene sutures and Keith needles (**Figure 19.2.1.3**). Note that if AlloDerm is employed, the dermal surface should be facing upward. After placement of sutures at the anchor points, sutures on the skin are pulled up at the same time to parachute the acellular matrix into the pocket for positioning under the pectoralis muscle. The acellular matrix is smoothed out so as to lay flat against the muscle with elimination of any gross wrinkles or creases. "Stay stitches" are placed at the lateral and medial corners of the acellular matrix to prevent the corners from folding in. The corners should lay flat and be in direct contact with the overlying pectoralis muscle. If a superomedial capsulotomy was performed, the superior one-third of the acellular matrix will drape over the implant, while the inferior two-thirds will drape over the capsule. Any drains, should be carefully placed prior to introducing the implant to avoid potential trauma thereto. We recommend that one drain between the acellular matrix and the skin flap. In addition, small perforations can be made in the acellular matrix to reduce fluid accumulation between

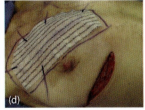

19.2.1.2 Preoperative markings. (a) Breast boundary markings; (b) location of planned capsulotomy at the upper pole and location of acellular matrix to be placed under the pectoral muscle at the upper pole marked on the breast skin; (c) anchor points markings on acellular matrix and backing paper; and (d) transfer of anchor point markings from backing paper to upper pole where the acellular matrix will be inset under the pectoralis muscle.

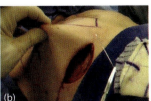
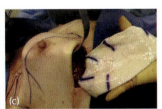

19.2.1.3 Intraoperative steps. (a) Sutures are placed at the anchor points on the acellular matrix. (b) Each anchor point suture on the matrix is secured to the corresponding anchor point on the skin. (c) All sutures on the skin are pulled at the same time to parachute the acellular matrix into the pocket to position it under the pectoralis muscle.

254 Implant-based whole breast reconstruction (without irradiation)

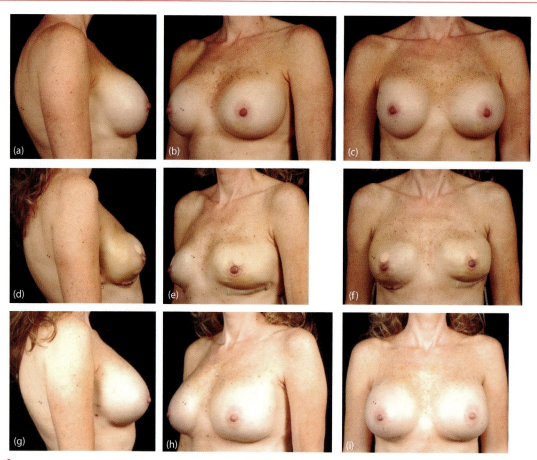

19.2.1.4 (a-c) Preoperative view of a patient who underwent immediate acellular matrix-assisted tissue expander reconstruction at stage 1 followed by implant exchange; upper pole tissue supplementation with acellular matrix; and autologous fat grafting at the upper, medial, and lateral poles. (d-f) After stage 1 tissue expander reconstruction; and (h-i) 1 year after stage 2 reconstruction.

the acellular matrix and the pectoralis muscle. An implant which is preferably an anatomical, form-stable, silicone implant is introduced into the pocket and incision closure is performed in standard fashion. The anchoring sutures at the upper pole are pulled snugly, air tied about 2 inches away from the skin, and taped to the skin using Tegaderm (3M, St. Paul, MN). Autologous fat injection is performed in the subcutaneous plane from medial to lateral, sweeping across the upper pole (**Figure 19.2.1.4**).

DISCUSSION

Bioengineered breasts represent an evolution of the reconstructive process that aims to augment the soft tissue envelope of reconstructed breasts to produce breasts that not only look like, but also feel like natural breasts. Upper pole submuscular acellular matrix placement coupled with autologous fat grafting where necessary provides a degree of soft tissue volume which adequately addresses tissue deficits that are often encountered after implant-based breast reconstruction. Placement of a complete acellular matrix covered implant in a pre-pectoral location supplemented with fat can also be undertaken using these bioengineered concepts. We believe that the two-stage technique provides more opportunity to enhance soft tissue coverage by either use of additional dermal matrices and/or fat grafting. Tissue supplementation not only improves the overall aesthetic outcome, but may also mitigate the risk of implant-related complications. The technique is safe and is associated with minimal postoperative complications.

REFERENCES

1. Maxwell GP, Gabriel A. Bioengineered breast: Concept, technique, and preliminary results. *Plast Reconstr Surg.* 2016;137(2):415–421.
2. Bindingnavele V, Gaon M, Ota KS, Kulber DA, Lee DJ. Use of acellular cadaveric dermis and tissue expansion in postmastectomy breast reconstruction. *J Plast Reconstr Aesthet Surg.* 2007;60(11):1214–1218.
3. Breuing KH, Colwell AS. Inferolateral AlloDerm hammock for implant coverage in breast reconstruction. *Ann Plast Surg.* 2007;59(3):250–255.
4. Adams WP, Jr., Rios JL, Smith SJ. Enhancing patient outcomes in aesthetic and reconstructive breast surgery using triple antibiotic breast irrigation: Six-year prospective clinical study. *Plast Reconstr Surg.* 2006;117(1):30–36.
5. Ganske I, Verma K, Rosen H, Eriksson E, Chun YS. Minimizing complications with the use of acellular dermal matrix for immediate implant-based breast reconstruction. *Ann Plast Surg.* 2013;71(5):464–470.

19.2.2 Our approach (South America)

Alberto Rancati, Claudio Angrigiani, Marcelo Irigo, and Agustin Rancati

Implant-based breast reconstruction is currently the most widely used form of immediate breast reconstruction in many parts of the world. It provides a satisfactory result in most cases and is the optimal choice for many women seeking breast reconstruction and for whom radiotherapy is not anticipated.

A two-stage approach allows symmetrization of the contralateral breast at the time of the second stage, resulting in a more predictable outcome.

It is generally accepted that the most suitable patients for a staged implant-based breast reconstruction are those with small or medium-sized breasts. In addition, a well-defined body shape, minimal breast ptosis, and minimal or no skin resection with symmetric breasts is desirable. Large-breasted women usually require skin resection that must be planned prior to mastectomy.

It is the authors' opinion that evaluation of breast volume alone is insufficient for patient selection and optimizing technique. Mastectomy flap thickness is also an important factor when planning immediate breast reconstruction, and there is no direct relationship between breast volume and flap thickness.

Digital mammography allows appropriate preoperative evaluation, not only in terms of tumor detection, but also for improved prediction of the resultant flap thickness and viability after mastectomy,[1–2] thereby improving patient safety.

Standard film-screen mammograms do not allow clear identification and measurement of non-glandular breast tissue coverage. By contrast, digital mammography distinguishes glandular tissue density from tegument and fat; this preoperative assessment can indicate the coverage thickness[3,4] (i.e., the distance between breast skin and Cooper's ligaments that cover the gland) **Figure 19.2.2.1**.

Rational use of materials is favoured by adequate assessment of each individual patient, and not just by breast volume, surgeon experience, or comfort.[5,6]

Flap necrosis or impaired viability after mastectomy is a feared complication of immediate breast reconstruction.[7–9] Preoperative measurement of breast tissue coverage and evaluation of flap thickness on digital mammography should be taken into account during surgical planning; the proposed classification may help to identify patients at higher risk for flap ischemia/necrosis independent of breast volume. Thus, preoperative communication between reconstructive and oncologic surgeon concerning placement of incisions and integumentary preservation based on digital mammogram findings may lead to improved outcomes with a lower rate of complications.

Planning of incisions, surgical technique, and choice of reconstructive procedure are related to several factors including breast volume, tumor characteristics, surgeon preference, and patient wishes. Preoperative information

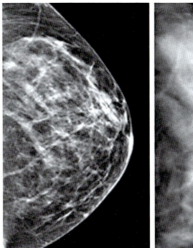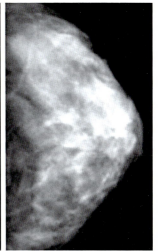

19.2.2.1 Difference of density between digital and standard (film) mammograms of a same patient.

regarding breast tissue coverage thickness may help predict any postmastectomy flap problems and help with the planning process.[3]

Of particular note is the observation that breast tissue coverage is independent of breast volume, and large breasts (C, D, E cup) can have poor tissue coverage. By contrast, some patients with small breasts (A, B cup), can achieve good tissue coverage (**Figure 19.2.2.2**).

Data are provided of non-glandular breast tissue coverage in a wide range of breast volumes and a three-type classification of breast coverage thickness is described. This can offer a baseline for further studies examining the importance of breast tissue coverage while planning conservative mastectomy procedures with immediate breast reconstruction with the aim of reducing postoperative complications.[10,11]

Based on the range of coverage values derived, the authors have proposed a Type 1-2-3 breast tissue coverage classification as follows. Type 1: Up to 1 cm (poor coverage), Type 2: between 1 cm and 2 cm (medium coverage), and Type 3: more than 2 cm (good coverage) (**Table 19.2.2.1**).

According to this classification, for those patients in the poor coverage group (type 1), it would be appropriate to add supplementary coverage for the reconstruction, that is, ADM, retropectoral implant placement, and possibly delayed fat grafting. In the medium coverage group (type 2), a two-stage reconstruction should be recommended to avoid tension over flap closure; while with good coverage (type 3), a one-stage reconstruction using implant only could be carried out.

A two-stage approach is preferred by many surgeons for implant-based whole breast reconstruction (without irradiation). Preoperative planning and careful selection is essential for each individual patient. Selection is based not only on breast volume, but the associated tissue coverage which can be evaluated using digital mammography.

256 Implant-based whole breast reconstruction (without irradiation)

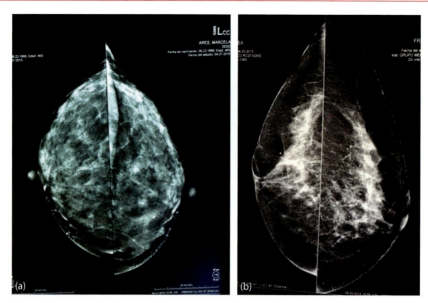

19.2.2.2 Preop, digital mammograms, breast volume between 500 cc showing different flap thickness in breast tissue coverage on two different patients with medium breast volume.

Table 19.2.2.1 Breast tissue coverage classification

TYPE 1	Up to 1 cm	Poor Coverage
TYPE 2	Between 1 and 2 cm	Medium Coverage
TYPE 3	More than 2 cm	Good Coverage

REFERENCES

1. Kuhl C. The current status of breast MR imaging. Part I. Choice of technique, image interpretation, diagnostic accuracy, and transfer to clinical practice. *Radiology* 2007;244:356–378.
2. Kuhl CK. Current status of breast MR imaging. Part 2. Clinical applications. *Radiology* 2007;244:672–691.
3. Zenn MR. Staged immediate breast reconstruction. *Plast Reconstr Surg* 2015;135:976–979.
4. Lalardrie JP, Jouglard JP. *ChirurgiePlastique du Sein.* Paris, France: Masson; 1973.
5. Phillips BT, Lanier ST, Conkling N et al. Intraoperative perfusion techniques can accurately predict mastectomy skin flap necrosis in breast reconstruction: Results of a prospective trial. *Plast Reconstr Surg* 2012;129:778e–788e.
6. Chu C, Carlson G. Techniques and outcomes of nipple sparing mastectomy in the surgical management of breast cancer. *Curr Breast Cancer Rep* 2013;5:118–124.
7. Gerber B, Krause A, Dieterich M, Kundt G, Reimer T. Theoncological safety of skin sparing mastectomy with conservation of the nipple-areola complex and autologous reconstruction: An extended follow-up study. *Ann Surg* 2009;249:461–468.
8. Mallon P, Feron JG, Couturaud B et al. The role of nipple-sparing mastectomy in breast cancer: A comprehensive review of the literature. *Plast Reconstr Surg* 2013;131:969–984.
9. Salgarello M, Visconti G, Barone-Adesi L. Nipple-sparing mastectomy with immediate implant reconstruction: Cosmetic outcomes and technical refinements. *Plast Reconstr Surg* 2010;126:1460–1471.
10. Scott SL, Willey SC, Feldman ED et al. Nipple-sparing mastectomy for prophylactic and therapeutic indications. *Plast Reconstr Surg* 2011;128:1005–1014.
11. Cordeiro PG, Pusic AL, Disa JJ, McCormick B, VanZee K. Irradiation after immediate tissue expander/implant breast reconstruction: Outcomes, complications, aesthetic results, and satisfaction among 156 patients. *Plast Reconstr Surg* 2011;113:877–881.

19.3 ACELLULAR DERMAL MATRIX WITH IMPLANTS

AT A GLANCE

Aside from nipple-sparing mastectomy and fat grafting, acellular dermal matrices (ADMs) have significantly changed the clinical practice of implant-based breast reconstruction. ADMs have allowed expanders to be inflated intraoperatively and the implant to be placed at the time of mastectomy. ADMs add another layer of dermis that not only improves the aesthetics by decreasing the visibility of the underlying implant, but also protects against implant exposure and has significantly decreased the need for explantation. There is also increasing evidence that ADMs decrease the cellularity of the radiation inflammatory response and pseudocapsule formation, at least during the initial 3–6 months following radiotherapy that may decrease capsular contracture.

19.3.1 My approach (USA)

Hani Sbitany

Traditional techniques for implant-based breast reconstruction have included complete or partial submuscular coverage of tissue expanders or permanent implants inserted at the time of mastectomy for immediate breast reconstruction. This usually involves elevation of the pectoralis major muscle together with either the serratus anterior muscle or fascia for lateral implant coverage.[1] In recent years, addition of acellular dermal matrices (ADMs) have offered many advantages relative to the more conventional techniques.[2] When used to assist in tissue expander or implant coverage, ADM offers increased control over definition and placement of the inframammary fold and device position. Moreover, a larger pocket allows for greater on-table expansion, more rapid completion of tissue expansion, and reduced lateral intercostal nerve pain from avoidance of serratus elevation.[3]

Acellular dermal matrices also offer the potential advantage of improved cosmesis through maximized use of preserved mastectomy skin, and this applies especially in the context of nipple-sparing mastectomy where aggressive skin excision and contouring is not possible.[4] Furthermore, ADM favors consistency in achievement of excellent cosmetic results, allowing for greater control over the entire positioning of the breast. The latter is due to precise control of the inframammary and lateral folds and improved lower pole projection.

Recent research has shown that use of ADM in tissue expander coverage can also reduce complication rates in the setting of postmastectomy radiation therapy.[5,6] Specifically,

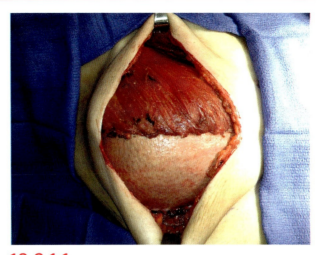

19.3.1.1 Breast reconstruction with ADM-assisted coverage of the tissue expander.

this is associated with reduced rates of expander extrusion and removal relative to purely submuscular coverage techniques.[7]

The author's preferred technique is immediate tissue expander reconstruction involving elevation and inferior disinsertion of the pectoralis major muscle from the 6th to 8th ribs. The pectoralis muscle covers the upper half of the prosthesis, and ADM is placed as a lower pole inferolateral hammock to cover the lower half of the device (**Figure 19.3.1.1**). Inferiorly, the ADM is sutured to the chest wall approximately 1 cm below the planned inframammary fold of the reconstructed breast. Laterally, the ADM is sutured to the serratus fascia along the planned lateral fold of the reconstructed breast. Finally, the superior border of the ADM is sutured to the disinserted inferior border of the pectoralis major muscle. A tissue expander is placed under this partial submuscular/partial ADM pocket. Suture tabs on the tissue expander are advisable, as this allows for complete control over position of both the expander and the overlying pocket. In this way, the best and most predictable aesthetic outcomes are achieved.

Intraoperative expansion is subsequently performed and is limited in degree only by tension on the overlying mastectomy skin flaps. Ideally, expansion is performed until there is no open space between the ADM and the underside of the mastectomy flap. At this juncture, the mastectomy skin should be devoid of wrinkles, but remain loose and soft to avoid skin-flap necrosis. This apposition of ADM to the skin flaps allows for direct contact and in turn improved revascularization potential for the ADM. Furthermore, obliteration of this space overlying the ADM also reduces rates of seroma formation as there is less space for fluid to collect.[8] At this point, further intraoperative expansion should be avoided. Both seroma rates and mastectomy skin-flap necrosis rates are minimized when these placement techniques are adhered to.

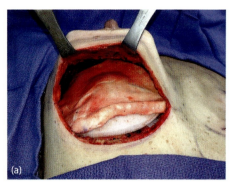
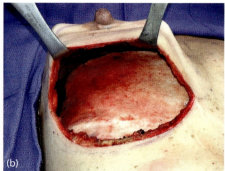

19.3.1.2 (a and b) Breast reconstruction with complete ADM (prepectoral) coverage of the tissue expander, before (a) and after (b) the inferior border of the ADM is sutured to the chest wall in the location of the planned inframammary fold (IMF).

When using the ADM as an inferolateral hammock, one drain is placed between the ADM and the overlying skin flaps. Generally, there is no need for a drain deep to the ADM, as there is no space around the prosthetic device (when expansion is carried out adequately).

Using these techniques the author and others have achieved reproducible results with low complication profiles. When compared to complete submuscular coverage techniques, patients undergoing ADM-assisted tissue expander coverage have no statistically significant differences in complication rates (infection, partial nipple necrosis, nor overall reoperative rates).[9] Furthermore, the author's practice leads to a much higher mean intraoperative fill volume for ADM-based reconstruction versus submuscular coverage alone (205 cc vs 52 cc, p = 0.0001). Thus, ADM allows for greater on-table fill and thereby capitalizes on preservation of mastectomy skin flaps and shape of the breast envelope.

A meta-analysis published by Sbitany and Serletti in 2011 pooled data from nine publications comparing conventional submuscular expander coverage to ADM assisted coverage[10] and found rates of seroma to be the only statistically significant complication rate that was increased in the ADM cohort (4.3% vs 8.4%, p = 0.03). However, with proper management of seromas including aspiration and drain care, overall infection rates together with rates of explantation were statistically equivalent between the two groups. Thus, proper management of these patients is associated with low complication rates, which are comparable for these two groups of patients.

More recently, novel techniques for tissue expander coverage at the time of mastectomy, involving complete coverage with ADM, have been successfully employed.[11] These techniques avoid elevation of pectoralis major muscle for superior expander coverage. By placing the expander in a pre-pectoral position, there is a reduction in immediate postoperative pain and hyperanimation deformity of the reconstructed breast is eliminated.[12] When this technique is carried out, the entire anterior face of the tissue expander and all other sides are enveloped with ADM (**Figure 19.3.1.2a and b**). Thus, no part of the expander is in the immediate submuscular position.

When considering pre-pectoral expander placement with complete ADM coverage, the surgeon must adhere to strict patient selection criteria. Currently, it is not recommended that this approach be used in any patient for whom postmastectomy radiotherapy is either necessary or anticipated. Furthermore, neither is this technique recommended in patients with unduly thin or compromised mastectomy skin flaps.

When performed in the appropriately selected patient, this technique can offer an aesthetically pleasing reconstruction without any muscle tightness or contraction over the prosthetic device. It should be noted that implant sizing needs to be precise with this technique to prevent rippling. Without the pectoralis major muscle overlying the upper pole of the implant, there is less tissue available for fat grafting to treat postoperative rippling. Thus, a precise "hand-in-glove" fit of the final implant into the expanded breast pocket is critical to prevent aesthetic contour deformities which may be unacceptable to the patient.

REFERENCES

1. Serletti JM, Fostnot J, Nelson JA, Disa JJ, Bucky LP. Breast reconstruction after breast cancer. *Plast Reconstr Surg.* 2011;127(6):124e–135e.
2. Sbitany H, Sandeen SN, Amalfi AN, Davenport MS, Langstein HN. Acellular dermis-assisted prosthetic breast reconstruction versus complete submuscular coverage: A head-to-head comparison of outcomes. *Plast Reconstr Surg.* 2009;124(6):1735–1740.
3. Sbitany H, Langstein HN. Acellular dermal matrix in primary breast reconstruction. *Aesthet Surg J.* 2011;31(7 Suppl):30S–37S.

4. Nahabedian MY. Acellular dermal matrices in primary breast reconstruction: Principles, concepts, and indications. *Plast Reconstr Surg*. 2012;130(5 Suppl 2):44S–53S.

5. Sbitany H, Wang F, Peled AW, Lentz R, Alvarado M, Ewing CA, Esserman LJ, Fowble B, Foster RD. Immediate implant-based breast reconstruction following total skin-sparing mastectomy: Defining the risk of preoperative and postoperative radiation therapy for surgical outcomes. *Plast Reconstr Surg*. 2014;134(3):396–404.

6. Seth AK, Hirsch EM, Fine NA, Kim JY. Utility of acellular dermis-assisted breast reconstruction in the setting of radiation: A comparative analysis. *Plast Reconstr Surg*. 2012;130(4):750–758.

7. Nava MB, Pennati AE, Lozza L, Spano A, Zambetti M, Catanuto G. Outcome of different timings of radiotherapy in implant-based breast reconstructions. *Plast Reconstr Surg*. 2011;128(2): 353–359.

8. Sbitany H. Techniques to reduce seroma and infection in acellular dermis-assisted prosthetic breast reconstruction. *Plast Reconstr Surg*. 2010;126(3):1121–1122.

9. Sbitany H, Wang F, Peled AW, Alvarado M, Ewing CA, Esserman LJ, Foster RD. Tissue expander reconstruction after total skin-sparing mastectomy: Defining the effects of coverage technique on nipple/areola preservation. *Ann Plast Surg*. 2014;77(1):17–24.

10. Sbitany H, Serletti JM. Acellular dermis-assisted prosthetic breast reconstruction: A systematic and critical review of efficacy and associated morbidity. *Plast Reconstr Surg*. 2011;128(6):1162–1169.

11. Becker H, Lind JG 2nd, Hopkins EG. Immediate implant-based prepectoral breast reconstruction using a vertical incision. *Plast Reconstr Surg Glob Open*. 2015;3(6):e412.

12. Sbitany H. Management of the post-breast reconstruction "hyperanimation deformity." *Plast Reconstr Surg*. 2014;133(6):897e–898e.

19.3.2 Our approach (Europe)

Alexandra Molina and Jian Farhadi

Since their introduction in 2005, acellular dermal matrices have been increasingly adopted as an adjunct to prosthetic breast reconstruction. The matrix, or mesh, is placed at the lower pole of the reconstructive pocket in order to act as a sling between the lower border of the pectoralis major muscle and the inframammary fold. This allows the reconstructive surgeon to place a definitive implant (direct-to-implant reconstruction) in cases where previously a two stage approach using an expander would have been necessary. The current market is dominated by biologically derived products known as acellular dermal matrices, but synthetic mesh alternatives are also available. Overall complication rates for matrix or mesh-assisted prosthetic reconstructions are purported to be increased. Nonetheless, due to lack of level I evidence and reporting bias, the magnitude of this effect remains unclear. Prospective randomized-controlled trials are needed to investigate this in greater detail, but it is becoming clear that patient selection is paramount when using this reconstructive technique. Thus far, the best aesthetic results achieved have been observed in healthy women with a low body mass index (BMI) opting for implant reconstruction.

INTRODUCTION TO ACELLULAR DERMAL MATRICES IN BREAST RECONSTRUCTION

Acellular dermal matrices (ADMs) were first introduced to the breast reconstruction market in the form of a human-derived ADM, Alloderm (LifeCell Corp., Branchburg, NJ, USA). Two papers published in 2005 and 2006 by Breuing and Salzburg, respectively,[1,2] reviewed case series using Alloderm in single stage implant breast reconstruction. These original descriptions highlighted that the reconstructive process could be shortened from two stages to a single stage by using this novel technique. Single stage techniques benefit patients by circumventing the need for repeated outpatient appointments for expansion and also avoiding second surgery to exchange an expander for a definitive prosthesis.

Since their introduction to the market, ADMs have been increasingly used in patients undergoing skin-sparing mastectomy[3,4] and more recently nipple-sparing mastectomy.[5] Matrices have also been used in two stage expander-based reconstruction,[6,7] potentially allowing greater initial expander fill and more rapid tissue expansion. However, the primary goal when using ADM in our practice remains the facilitation of single stage, direct-to-implant reconstruction.

TYPES OF MATRICES USED IN BREAST RECONSTRUCTION

The terms mesh and matrix when applied to breast reconstruction are generally in reference to the composition of the material used in the manufacture of the product. The term "matrix" usually refers to a product derived from biological sources (most commonly dermis), whereas "mesh" refers to a product wholly manufactured from synthetic materials (e.g., polypropylene). With the exception of SERI (Allergan Medical, Medford, USA), which is made from silk-derived bioprotein, the majority of products used in breast reconstruction can be divided into matrices and meshes.

Biological ADMs may be classified according to a variety of properties, most commonly their human or animal source. Alloderm, as previously mentioned, is human-derived, while Strattice (LifeCell Corp., Branchburg, NJ, USA) is derived from porcine dermis. Surgimend (TEI Biosciences Inc, Boston, MA, USA) originates from a bovine dermal source. Meso BioMatrix (DSM Biomedical, Exton, PA, USA) originates from porcine mesothelium and is thinner and more pliable than the dermis-derived products.

In contrast to the biological ADMs, TiLOOP Bra (Pfm Medical Ag, Koln, Germany) is a synthetic mesh composed of titanized polypropylene. A vast number of other synthetic meshes are in existence, but their use is generally being superseded by biological ADMs in breast reconstruction and is outwith the scope of this chapter.

TECHNIQUE

In the authors' practice, ADM is used primarily to allow single stage, definitive implant reconstruction. The matrix (or mesh) is placed at the inferior border of the reconstructive pocket after elevation and release of the pectoralis major muscle, which continues to provide coverage for the prosthesis superiorly. The implant is placed in the subpectoral plane and the inferior border of the matrix is sutured along the inframammary fold. Excess ADM can then be trimmed, and its superior border is sutured to the inferior border of the pectoralis major to achieve complete implant coverage, as well as inframammary fold definition. A combination of interrupted and continuous sutures may be used to secure the hammock of mesh, in which the lower pole of the prosthesis should sit snugly.

It is important to ensure that the matrix is also secured laterally to control outward migration of the implant. Although many products are already porous to some extent, certain surgeons will perforate the matrix to minimize fluid pooling in the pocket,[8] and this may reduce seroma rates.[9] It is common practice to place a vacuum drain between the mastectomy skin flap and the mesh/matrix to reduce the potential dead space between the layers and facilitate contact for revascularization where appropriate. Some surgeons will site an additional drain in the implant pocket itself, deep to the matrix. Drains should be left in situ until there is minimal drainage (less than 30 mL in 24 hours) to reduce the likelihood of seroma formation. Compression dressing or sports bras can also be employed to this end in the immediate postoperative period.

ADVANTAGES OF ACELLULAR DERMAL MATRIX FOR BREAST RECONSTRUCTION

1. Acting as a sling between pectoralis major and the inframammary fold

   This is the primary advantage of the use of ADM. The surgeon is able to release the pectoralis major muscle without being concerned with regard to lower pole implant coverage. This is especially useful in patients in whom the muscle is high on the chest wall, or in whom the pectoralis muscle is tight, which would limit the achievable volume of the reconstruction.[10] The use of a matrix or mesh enables a greater implant or expander volume to be placed at the initial operation, allowing either a shortened expansion process or ideally obviating the need for second stage surgery altogether.[11–13] In patients with large and/or ptotic breasts, there is often a discrepancy between the skin envelope of the breast and the underlying subpectoral pocket. The use of an ADM can help to redress this imbalance and improve projection of the breast.[10,14] However, we would generally recommend caution in the use of meshes and matrices in obese or large breasted patients (see "Patient Selection").

2. Control of the reconstructive pocket

   Securing the matrix along the inframammary fold allows the surgeon to crisply define the inferior border of the reconstructive pocket and thus accurately place the footprint of the reconstructed breast. This control can prevent inferior implant migration, and clear definition of the IMF improves aesthetic outcomes.[15–18] Furthermore, the ADM acts as a hammock to support the implant, allowing the maintenance of lower pole projection and a natural aesthetic breast mound shape. A case series of 38 patients compared ADM reconstruction patients with controls using blinded surgeon assessors. The authors reported improvements in breast contour, lower pole projection, implant placement, and inframammary fold (IMF) definition in those patients where ADM was used.

3. Additional soft tissue coverage of the prosthesis

   In contrast to the extensive musculofascial dissection often performed before the introduction of ADMs, the breast reconstruction surgeon can now confer "made-to measure" soft tissue coverage in the lower pole of the reconstructed breast. By increasing the soft tissue coverage, particularly in thin patients where the mastectomy flaps are relatively devoid of subcutaneous fat, contour irregularities and implant palpability may be reduced. There is some evidence that the increased soft tissue coverage can also result in lower than expected rates of capsular contracture.[19,20]

4. Biological meshes may improve neovascularization of the mastectomy skin envelope

   ADMs act as a stimulus to the surrounding host tissue, inducing growth factors such as vascular endothelial growth factors, basic fibroblast growth factor, and transforming growth factor beta 1.[21] In vivo, in a porcine model, angiogenesis was demonstrated at 4 weeks postimplantation on the skin-flap surface of the ADM, while established vasculature on both surfaces was observed at 8 weeks.[22]

COMPLICATION PROFILE OF ACELLULAR DERMAL MATRIX BREAST RECONSTRUCTION

There is a lack of level I evidence in the literature to evaluate whether the use of ADM in addition to an implant increases the complication profile. A systematic review comparing ADM assisted reconstructions to expander/implant reconstruction without ADM found significantly higher rates of seroma, infection, and reconstructive failure in the ADM group.[19] However, the authors were unable to separate the source data into single stage versus two stage reconstructions and acknowledge that the overall quality of outcome data included was low. If matrices are used to achieve single stage reconstruction, an increased complication rate is arguably expected, as the increased volume will inevitably place more strain on the mastectomy skin flaps.

Looking at individual studies, one large analysis of 415 implant reconstructions found that the use of ADM increased the risk of infection five-fold.[23] The increased infection rate was not so marked in another similar-sized study,[24] where ADM was found to increase the risk of wound infection and overall complications—but not to increase the risk of major infections. By contrast, another review of 276 irradiated patients with implant-based reconstruction with or without ADM found no difference in overall complication profile between patients with and without ADM[25] (Clemens).

RISK FACTORS FOR COMPLICATIONS IN ACELLULAR DERMAL MATRIX BREAST RECONSTRUCTION

A consensus is developing as to certain risk factors, particularly patient factors, which may lead to an unacceptably high complication rate when using ADM. The authors' own two center study of 200 ADM breast reconstructions using Strattice-linked smoking, BMI >30, and mastectomy weight >600 g with a significantly increased risk of complications.[26] Interestingly, this cohort was divided into two separate time periods with modifications to the surgical technique introduced between the two periods. Strattice was washed in antibiotic solution instead of saline, mastectomy skin flaps were trimmed if necessary after careful assessment of viability, and drains were tunneled subcutaneously to reduce potential communication between the ADM and external sources of infection. Rates of infection, implant exposure, and implant loss decreased significantly between the two time periods, illustrating that surgical technique remains a critical factor in addition to patient selection.

A study from the United States found that age, body mass index, and axillary dissection were all linked with an increased risk of complications in ADM breast reconstruction.[27] In addition to these three risk factors, postoperative chemotherapy was associated with an increased risk of reconstructive failure specifically. A previously quoted analysis of 470 reconstructions identified smoking, high BMI, and higher initial volume or implant size as factors increasing the risk of complications across both ADM and non-ADM prosthetic reconstructions.

PATIENT SELECTION FOR OPTIMAL RESULTS

In view of the above proven risk factors for complications, in particular implant loss, it is becoming abundantly clear that careful patient selection is paramount in achieving acceptable outcomes in ADM breast reconstruction. The ideal candidate for the use of ADM would have the following characteristics:

- Small- to medium-breasted without significant ptosis
- No adjuvant radiotherapy planned
- Non-smoker
- Not diabetic
- Body mass index <30
- Good skin quality
- Preference for single-stage implant reconstruction
- Awareness of complications and lifespan of implant reconstruction

CONCLUSION

The introduction of acellular dermal matrices was initially viewed by some as the "holy grail" in breast reconstruction. As with many new devices in surgery, enthusiasm for their use was initially unbridled, and some surgeons felt they could dispense with the former workhorse flaps such as the latissimus dorsi.

Now with growing experience and knowledge of their complication profile, indications for the use of ADM have narrowed significantly. There seems little justification for the use of ADMs in combination with tissue expanders as a two stage procedure. ADMs should be viewed as a tool to achieve single stage implant reconstruction in the carefully selected patient. In our practice, we now limit their use to the small to medium size breast in a patient who is a non-smoker, not diabetic, and with no prior radiotherapy. A near perfect mastectomy is also a pre-requisite to ensure that skin-flap necrosis does not occur, resulting in exposure of the ADM and inevitably the implant itself.

REFERENCES

1. Breuing KH, Warren SM. Immediate bilateral breast reconstruction with implants and inferolateral Alloderm slings. *Ann Plast Surg.* 2005;55:232–239.
2. Salzberg CA. Nonexpansive immediate breast reconstruction using human acellular tissue matrix graft (Alloderm). *Ann Plast Surg.* 2006;57:1–5.
3. Govshievich A, Somogyi RB1, Brown MH. Conservative mastectomies and immediate reconstruction with the use of ADMs. *Gland Surg.* 2015;4(6):453–462.
4. Nahabedian MY. Acellular dermal matrices in primary breast reconstruction: Principles, concepts, and indications. *Plast Reconstr Surg.* 2012;130:44S.
5. Colwell AS, Tessler O, Lin AM, Liao E, Winograd J, Cetrulo CL, Tang R, Smith BL, Austen WG Jr. Breast reconstruction following nipple-sparing mastectomy: Predictors of complications, reconstruction outcomes, and 5-year trends. *Plast Reconstr Surg.* 2014;133(3):496–506.
6. Weichman KE, Wilson SC, Weinstein Al. *et al.* The use of acellular dermal matrix in immediate two-stage tissue expander breast reconstruction. *Plast Reconstr Surg.* 2012;129:1049–1058.
7. Kim JY, Connor CM. Focus on technique: Two-stage implant based breast reconstruction. *Plast Reconstr Surg.* 2012;130:104S.
8. Martin JB, Moore R, Paydar KZ *et al.* Use of fenestrations in acellular dermal allograft in two-stage tissue expander/implant breast reconstruction. *Plast Reconstr Surg.* 2014;134(5):901–904.
9. Palaia DA, Arthur KS, Cahan AC, Rosenberg MH. Incidence of seromas and infections using fenestrated versus nonfenestrated acellular dermal matrix in breast reconstructions. *Plast Reconstr Surg Glob Open.* 2015;3(11):e569. doi:10.1097/GOX.0000000000000559.
10. Masden RJ Jr, Chim J, Ang B *et al.* Variance in the origin of the pectoralis major muscle: Implications for implant based reconstruction. *Ann Plast Surg.* 2015;74:111–113.
11. Vu MM, Kim JY. Current opinions on indications and algorithms for acellular dermal matrix use in primary prosthetic breast reconstruction. *Gland Surg.* 2015;4(3):195–203.
12. Lee KT, Mun GH. Updated evidence of acellular dermal matrix use for implant-based breast reconstruction: A meta-analysis. *Ann Surg Oncol.* 2015.
13. Rodriguez-Feliz J, Codner MA. Embrace the change: Incorporating single-stage implant breast reconstruction into your practice. *Plast Reconstr Surg.* 2015;136(2):221–231.
14. Ganske I, Verma K, Rosen H *et al.* Minimising complications with the use of acellular dermal matrix for immediate implant-based breast reconstruction. *Ann Plast Surg.* 2013;71:464–470.
15. Forsberg CG, Kelly DA, Wood BC *et al.* Aesthetic outcomes of acellular dermal matrix in tissue expander/implant-based breast reconstruction. *Ann Plast Surg.* 2014;72(6):S116–S120.

16. Topol BM, Dalton EF, Ponn T *et al*. Immediate single-stage breast reconstruction using implants and human acellular dermal tissue matrix with adjustment of the lower pole of the breast to reduce unwanted lift. *Ann Plast Surg*. 2008;61:494–499.

17. Vardanian AJ, Clayton JL, Roostaeian J *et al*. Comparison of implant-based immediate breast reconstruction with and without acellular dermal matrix. *Plast Reconstr Surg*. 2011;128(5):403e–410e.

18. Ibrahim AM, Koolen PG, Ganor O *et al*. Does acellular dermal matrix really improve aesthetic outcome in tissue expander/implant-based breast reconstruction? *Aesthetic Plast Surg*. 2015;39(3):359–368.

19. Ho G, Nguyen TJ, Shahabi A *et al*. A systematic review and meta-analysis of complications associated with acellular dermal matrix-assisted breast reconstruction. *Ann Plast Surg*. 2012; 68(4):346–356.

20. Salzberg CA, Ashikari AY, Koch RM *et al*. An 8-year experience of direct-to-implant immediate breast reconstruction using human acellular dermal matrix (AlloDerm). *Plast Reconstr Surg*. 2011;127(2):514–524.

21. Carruthers CA, Dearth CL, Reing JE. Histologic characterization of acellular dermal matrices in a porcine model of tissue expander breast reconstruction. *Tissue Eng Part A*. 2015;21(1–2):35–44.

22. Garcia O Jr, Scott JR. Analysis of acellular dermal matrix integration and revascularization following tissue expander breast reconstruction in a clinically relevant large-animal model. *Plast Reconstr Surg*. 2013;131(5):741e–751e.

23. Chun YS, Verma K, Rosen H, Lipsitz S, Morris D, Kenney P, Eriksson E. Implant-based breast reconstruction using acellular dermal matrix and the risk of postoperative complications. *Plast Reconstr Surg*. 2010;125(2):429–436.

24. Liu AS, Kao HK, Reish RG, Hergrueter CA, May JW Jr, Guo L. Postoperative complications in prosthesis-based breast reconstruction using acellular dermal matrix. *Plast Reconstr Surg*. 2011;127(5):1755–1762.

25. Clemens MW, Kronowitz SJ. Acellular dermal matrix in irradiated tissue expander/implant-based breast reconstruction: Evidence-based review. *Plast Reconstr Surg*. 2012;130(5 Suppl 2):27S–34S.

26. Lardi AM, Ho-Asjoe M, Mohanna PN, Farhadi J. Immediate breast reconstruction with acellular dermal matrix: Factors affecting outcome. *J Plast Reconstr Aesthet Surg*. 2014;67(8):1098–1105.

27. Antony AK, McCarthy CM, Cordeiro PG, Mehrara BJ, Pusic AL, Teo EH, Arriaga AF, Disa JJ. Acellular human dermis implantation in 153 immediate two-stage tissue expander breast reconstructions: Determining the incidence and significant predictors of complications. *Plast Reconstr Surg*. 2010;125(6):1606–1614.

19.4 FAT GRAFTING WITH IMPLANTS

AT A GLANCE

The adjunct of fat grafting to implant-based reconstruction, usually in conjunction with acellular dermal matrix has decreased the use of the latissimus muscle for breast reconstruction. Although, some surgeons have been unable to obtain significant volumetric increases within a reconstructed breast, fat grafting (vascular stroma and adult bone-derived stem cells within the lipoaspirate) can improve the qualitative appearance of the breast skin and decrease the visibility of the underlying implant. Fat grafts can replenish and heal the subcutaneous tissue layer and hence enhance the quality of implant reconstruction.

19.4.1 Our approach (Europe)

Pietro Berrino and Valeria Berrino

Fat transfer is currently widely used in breast reconstructive surgery for the treatment of radiotherapy tissue damage,[1] for site preparation before alloplastic reconstruction after radiation therapy,[2] or in women with thin, scarred skin at the mastectomy site with missing pectoralis major muscle. It is also used for correction of contour irregularities after breast implant reconstruction and for correction of certain sequelae of conservative treatment.[3-5]

In this section we shall describe:

1. How to use fat grafting for the "preconditioning" of the mastectomy site in order to make it more suitable for implant placement
2. How to use fat grafting in order to improve and refine outcomes after implant placement in "difficult" patients
   a. Patients with thin and/or irradiated skin at the mastectomy site and with a missing or atrophic pectoralis muscle have traditionally been considered poor candidates for implant reconstruction and are usually reconstructed using distant autologous flaps. "Preparation" of the mastectomy site makes these women potentially suitable candidates for implant

placement (**Figure 19.4.1.1**). The procedure consists of one to three lipostructure sessions, dependent on the original defect. Indeed, when the recipient subcutaneous fat layer is very thin (e.g., 1–3 mm), only a small amount of fat can be injected in order to ensure proper distribution of the graft. After the first fat injection, the recipient fat layer is thicker, and it can thereafter receive a larger volume of injected fat. The procedure is repeated until a 5-mm thick subcutaneous layer is obtained. During "preconditioning" sessions, lipostructure can also be carried out in areas that will benefit from a thicker subcutaneous layer once the implant is in place (e.g., the lower breast pole, the upper quadrant, or the axillary tail). Areas where the skin is dystrophic and adherent to the chest cage can be excised during these lipostructure sessions, such that by the end of the "preparation" stages, an almost ideal mastectomy site for implant placement is created (**Figure 19.4.1.2**). We use a simple "decantation" technique: after infiltration of the donor area with "Klein solution" (for each 500 cc of saline solution, 0.5 cc adrenaline, 12 cc xylocayne 2%, 8 cc sodium bicarbonate), a 2 mm cannula connected to a 10 mL syringe is used for harvesting the fat graft. The syringe is then left to rest vertically on the table for approximately 10 minutes while harvesting proceeds. The fluid portion of the fat graft, which spontaneously separates from the fat is discarded, and the graft is transferred into 1 mL or 2.5 mL syringes. During this maneuver, the "oil" is left in the first syringe and discarded. In the authors' experience, this procedure is fast, effective, relatively cheap, and provides a "fluid" graft which can be easily injected through a 1.5 mm injection cannula. The preferred donor areas are the flanks, the inner aspect of the knees, the lateral thighs, and lateral buttocks. The abdomen is not a first choice donor site since irregularities and skin emptiness are not infrequent, and damage to the perforators must be avoided in case of need for an abdominal flap in the future. A minimal waiting period of 3 months is mandatory between sessions, and this allows for graft stabilization. Injections are carried out in two layers, that is, an immediately subdermal plane and a further plane immediately above the rib cage (or the pectoral major muscle if present). Small lines of harvested fat are delivered in a radial fashion, while injecting from opposite points. Since tiny lines of adipocytes must be distributed into a well vascularized environment, 0.1 mL–0.2 mL are injected at each passage

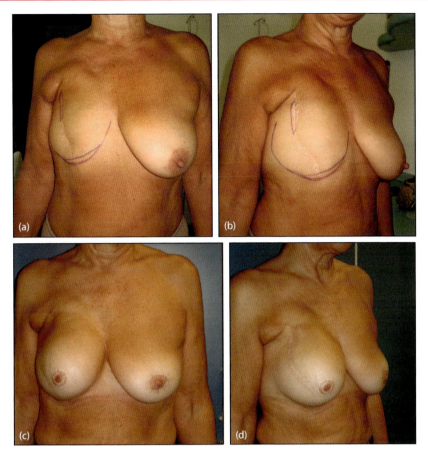

19.4.1.1 (a,b) Preoperative views of a 54-year-old woman showing a Halsted mastectomy defect: she underwent mastectomy site "preparation" by lipostructure. (c,d) Postoperative view after expansion, positioning of a final implant, periprosthetic lipostructure, and contralateral periareolar pexy.

in multiple retrograde paths. Fat injection at the mastectomy site increases the thickness of the subcutaneous layer, so that an implant can be placed with better cosmetic results and lower complication rates. Moreover, lipostructure makes scarred and retracted tissue more elastic and pliable and improves the quality of irradiated tissues. In our series "preconditioning," the mastectomy site by multiple lipostructure sessions has dramatically reduced complication rates in "difficult" patients.

b. When the implant is finally in place, several refinements can be done using fat injections. Four months should elapse after implant placement before making any final decision on where the fat is to be injected. Lipostructure is most often used for the correction of contour deformities in the upper quadrants, where the subcutaneous layer can be particularly thin (**Figure 19.4.1.3**). Within this area, the implant often requires a smoother cleavage into the subclavicular area despite being anatomical in shape. The inferior pole often needs to be more rounded to simulate a degree of some ptosis, and fat injection can provide a relatively simple solution for these difficult defects (**Figure 19.4.1.4**). Local liposuction and fat injections can be used for correction of subcutaneous irregularities and retractions due to unequal resection of tissue at various margins (**Figure 19.4.1.5**). Construction of a lateral breast tail, simulation of an anterior axillary pillar, and correction of implant rippling are also tasks that can be accomplished by fat injections. All these modifications and refinements from fat injection can change a poor result with visible implant contours into a more natural-looking breast.

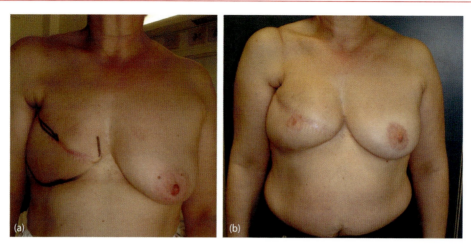

19.4.1.2 (a) Preoperative view of a 34-year-old woman showing radiated mastectomy site: the whole mastectomy area was fat grafted. (b) Postoperative view after expansion, positioning of a permanent implant, contour refinements by fat grafting, and contralateral periareolar pexy.

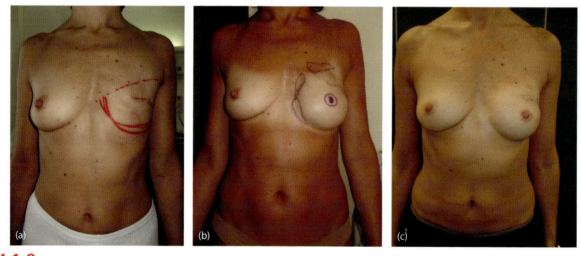

19.4.1.3 (a) Preoperative view of a 43-year-old woman showing radical mastectomy with scar thin: the mastectomy area was "prepared" by fat grafting. (b) The result after expansion and placement of the final implant is poor: contour refinements by fat grafting at the upper and inner quadrants are planned. (c) The final outcome shows the improvements obtained by lipostructure in this difficult case.

Fat injection is a simple procedure associated with minimal risks and morbidity and therefore indications for more traumatic and extensive procedures such as transfer of distant flaps can be confined to "salvage" conditions (e.g., recurrent implant complications). In the authors' practice, lipostructure is carried out at some stage along the reconstructive route in 85% of postmastectomy patients.

Patient compliance with these fat grafting procedures is high, and they can be carried out on an outpatient basis with minimal interference with social activities; moreover, the woman is involved in the decision-making process and correction of any defects which she finds disturbing as soon as they are perceived.

Fat grafting plays a strategic role in breast reconstruction for mastectomy patients and has arguably changed the surgical approach by converting "difficult" patients requiring major procedures into women who are candidates for implant-based reconstruction and other less intrusive surgical procedures.

19.4 Fat grafting with implants 267

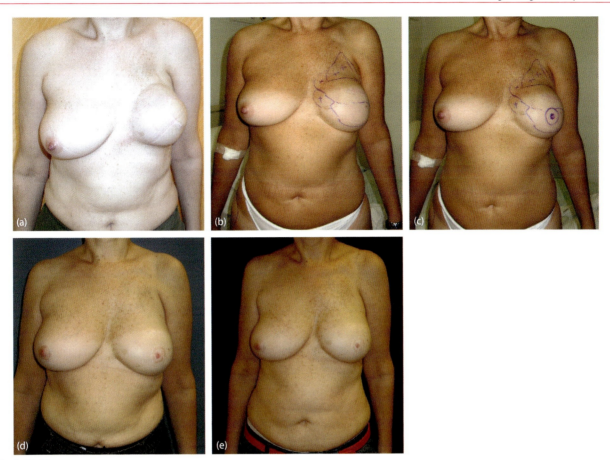

19.4.1.4 (a) Preoperative view of a 52-year-old woman who had Poland's syndrome and developed breast cancer: she had been treated by radical mastectomy and simultaneous LD myocutaneous flap transfer and a permanent implant, with a poor aesthetic outcome. (b) After implant replacement and excision of the poorly positioned LD skin island, lipostructure at upper quadrants and lower pole was planned. (c) The final stage is planned: NAC reconstruction and additional fat grafting at the upper quadrants and inferior breast pole. (d) The outcome 1 year later. (e) The outcome at the 6-year follow-up.

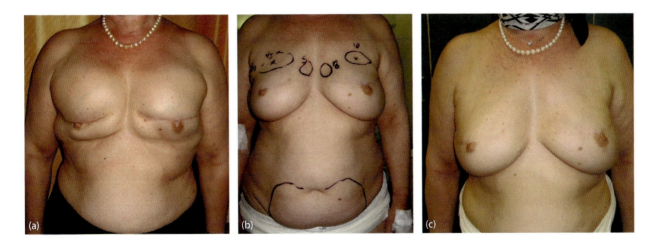

19.4.1.5 (a) A 64-year-old woman with a poor result after bilateral mastectomy and poorly positioned implants. (b) After implant replacement and repositioning and simultaneous fat grafting, most subcutaneous irregularities have improved. Final refinement by lipostructure at the upper quadrants is planned. (c) The final outcome showing smooth contours and rounded lower poles.

REFERENCES

1. Rigotti G, Marchi A, Galie` M, Baroni G, Benati D, Krampera M, Pasini A, Sbarbati A. Clinical treatment of radiotherapy tissue damage by lipoaspirate transplant: A healing process mediated by adipose-derived adult stem cells. *Plast Reconstr Surg* 119 (5):1409–1422; 2007.

2. Salgarello M, Visconti M, Tarallo E. Autologous fat graft in radiated tissue prior to alloplastic reconstruction of the breast: Report of two cases. *Aesth Plast Surg* 34 (1):5–10; 2009.

3. Spear SL, Wilson HB, Lockwood, MD. Fat injection to correct contour deformities in the reconstructed breast. *Plast Reconstr Surg* 5:1300–1305; 2005.

4. Kanchwala SK, Glatt BS, Conant EF, Bucky LP. Autologous fat grafting to the reconstructed breast: The management of acquired contour deformities. *Plast Reconstr Surg* 124(2):409–418; 2009.

5. Berrino P. Operative strategies in breast plastic surgery. *SEE-Firenze* 380–382; 2007.

19.4.2 My approach (Europe)

Alessandra Marchi

Fat transplantation was first introduced by Neuber at the end of the nineteenth century and, following standardization of techniques by Coleman, it was widely utilized in plastic surgery as a filler procedure to correct soft tissue defects.[1] The treatment of radiotherapy tissue damage with lipoaspirate and the strikingly beneficial effects of fat grafting on these radiation-induced lesions have prompted a conceptual change from simple filling of defects, toward one of regeneration.[2,3] In the author's practice, the majority of patients with implant-based reconstruction will subsequently undergo a variable number of fat grafting procedures with different aims and purposes. Our first reconstructive choice of whole breast reconstruction is with fat grafting without use of implants or matrices.[4] Recent studies confirm the oncological safety of this procedure.[5–9]

SURGICAL TECHNIQUE

The goal is to achieve maximal uniformity with regards to distribution of the lipoaspirate and to limit areas where there is overlap and gaps in tissue deposition.[10]

The selected donor areas are first infiltrated with cold Klein solution. Fat tissue is harvested using a multihole 2 mm diameter blunt-tip cannula, in order to obtain smaller clusters of lipoaspirate so improving fat take.[11] The syringe containing the lipoaspirate is placed in a bowl for decantation; the middle fraction, with potentially viable fatty tissue, is transferred into a 3 cc syringe for injection. Coleman type II and III cannulas are mainly used for fat distribution. Fat is placed in any available plane, with different entry points and many passes, in order to inject minimal quantities of fat with each pass.[12,13] The uniformity of distribution and contact with the surrounding tissue is crucial to facilitate graft take. The number of procedures required is strictly case dependent.[14,15] In order to release fibrotic scar tissue or tight retracting fibers, *Rigottomies* are performed, with a 14 gauge needle. This surgical step should be undertaken very carefully with avoidance of extensive resection or detachment of tissue that would lead to liponecrosis and formation of oil cysts.[4,16]

The following series of patients presented with a range of problems affecting their reconstructive outcome from surgery carried out previously in various different hospitals.

CLINICAL CASES

CASE 1: 31 year old—Contour deformity

Patient with irregularity and upper pole right breast defect (**Figures 19.4.2.1 through 19.4.2.3**). Three sessions of fat grafting were performed. The lipoaspirate was grafted in the plane between the capsule and the skin and in the pectoralis muscle.

Figures 19.4.2.4 through 19.4.2.6 confirm stability of results, after a period of 7 years. The breast displays a natural contour with no recurrence of volume defects.

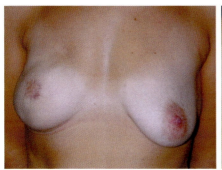 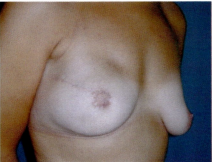 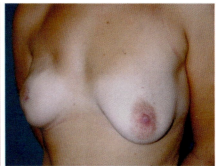

19.4.2.1–19.4.2.3 Breast reconstruction with implant after right mastectomy. Patient shows skin irregularity and upper pole right breast defect.

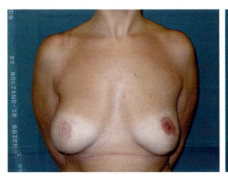 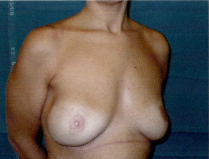 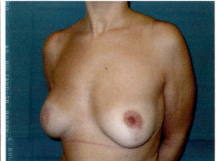

19.4.2.4–19.4.2.6 Stability of the result, after a period of 7 years. Three sessions of fat grafting were performed. The lipoaspirate was grafted in the plane between the capsule and the skin and in the pectoralis muscle.

CASE 2—58 year old: Contour defect and capsular retraction

Patient with left capsular retraction mostly situated in the lower outer quadrant after reconstruction with latissimus dorsi flap and implant (**Figures 19.4.2.7 through 19.4.2.9**). The defects were corrected with fat grafting exactly in the required areas. **Figures 19.4.2.10 through 19.4.2.12** show results at 2 years after only two fat grafting sessions. Adipose tissue helped to fill the lateral quadrants, to improve capsular contracture, and promoted downward shifting of the implant.

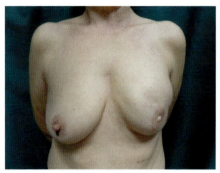
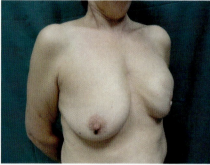
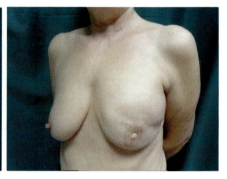

19.4.2.7–19.4.2.9 Patient with left capsular retraction mostly situated in the lower external quadrant after reconstruction with latissimus dorsi flap and implant.

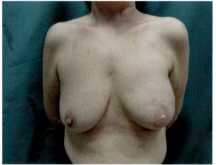
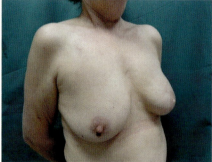
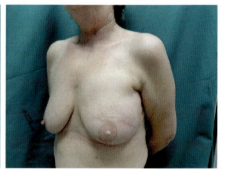

19.4.2.10–19.4.2.12 Results after 2 years and two fat grafting sessions. Adipose tissue aided to fill the lateral quadrants, to improve the capsular contracture, and helped the downward shifting of the implant.

CASE 3—55 year old: Shape deformity and capsular contracture

Painful and worsening capsular retraction, Baker II, after immediate reconstruction with an Allergan style 410 MF 255 g implant (**Figures 19.4.2.13 through 19.4.2.15**). Four fat grafting sessions were performed (160 cc, 150 cc, 130 cc, 110 cc). An improvement in contour and pain symptoms were evident immediately following the first graft (**Figures 19.4.2.16 through 19.4.2.18**). After the next operation, volume was restored and the retraction was no longer present. Results after 5 years show stability and a progressive improvement in contour and softness of the breast (**Figures 19.4.2.19 through 19.4.2.21**). No contralateral reshaping was necessary.

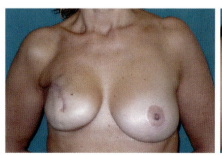
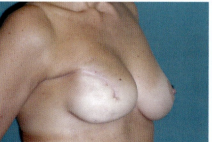
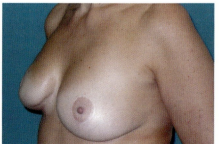

19.4.2.13–19.4.2.15 Painful and worsening capsular retraction, Baker II, after an immediate reconstruction with an Allergan style 410 MF 255 g implant.

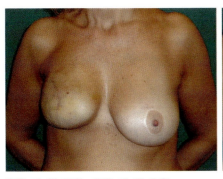 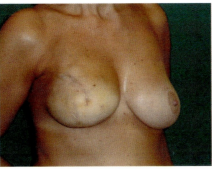 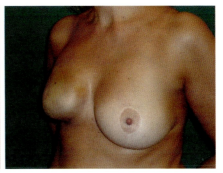

19.4.2.16–19.4.2.18 An improvement in contour and pain relief was evident immediately after the first graft.

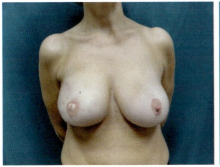 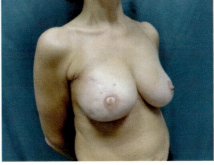 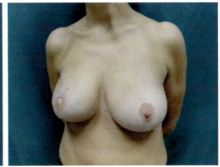

19.4.2.19–19.4.2.21 Four fat grafting sessions were performed (160, 150, 130, and 110 cc). The results after 5 years show the stability and the progressive improvement in contour and softness of the breast. No contralateral reshaping was necessary.

CASE 4—50 year old: Volume defect

Patient with painful, but minimal degree of capsular retraction (**Figures 19.4.2.22 through 19.4.2.24**). The patient sought improvement of her breast contour, but mainly to increase volume. No replacement of the implants was necessary. Three surgical sessions of lipostructural fat grafting (150 cc, 250 cc, and 200 cc) were performed from April 2008 to June 2010. Results after 1 year are shown in **Figures 19.4.2.25 through 19.4.2.27** and after an increase in body weight 4 years later (**Figures 19.4.2.28 through 19.4.2.30**). Both breasts had a consensual increase in volume and behaved just like normal breasts.

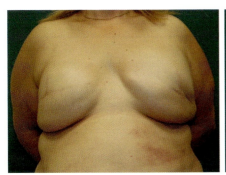 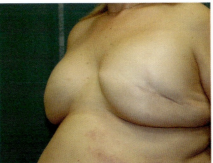 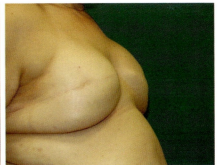

19.4.2.22–19.4.2.24 Bilateral mastectomy and reconstruction with implant. Patient with a not painful slight capsular retraction. The patient asked to improve her breast contour, but mostly to increase the volume.

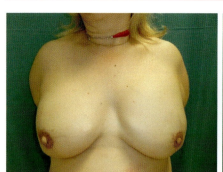
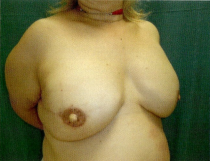
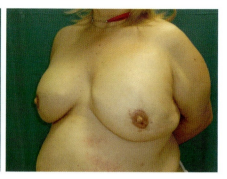

19.4.2.25–19.4.2.27 Three surgical sessions of lipostructural fat grafting (150, 250, and 200 cc) were performed. No replacement of the implants was necessary. Results after 1 year.

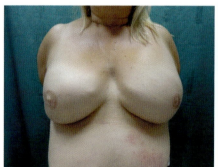
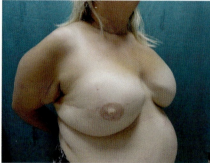
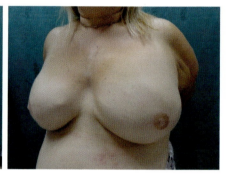

19.4.2.28–19.4.2.30 4-year follow-up. Body weight gain. Both breasts increase consensually their volume, behaving just like normal breasts.

CASE 5—33 year old—Implant malpositioning

This patient presented after a skin reducing mastectomy for an invasive carcinoma with immediate implant insertion (**Figures 19.4.2.31 through 19.4.2.33**).

Two fat grafts (155 and 200 cc) were distributed around the entire breast surface, in the plane between capsule and skin, in order to obtain a thicker and softer subcutaneous layer (**Figures 19.4.2.34 through 19.4.2.36**). The existing implant was then replaced with a smaller, adjustable volume one, and a third graft of 280 cc was performed simultaneously (**Figures 19.4.2.37 through 19.4.2.39**). Six months later, the original nipple-areola complex was removed due to its aberrant position, and a new nipple was reconstructed at the correct site. A final fat graft of 200 cc was performed at this time.

There was a progressive improvement in shape and natural ptosis and results after 2 years are shown in **Figures 19.4.2.40 through 19.4.2.42**.

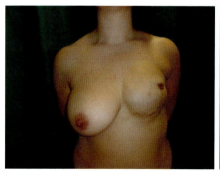
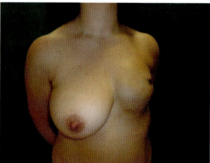

19.4.2.31–19.4.2.33 This woman came to a consultation after a skin reducing mastectomy for an invasive DCIS carcinoma with immediate implant insertion. Implant malpositioning.

19.4 Fat grafting with implants 273

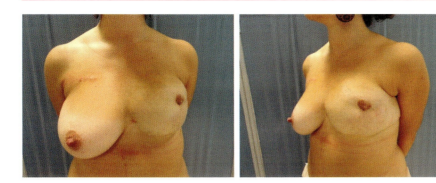
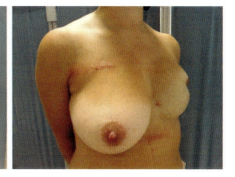

19.4.2.34–19.4.2.36 Two fat grafts, 155 and 200 cc, were distributed around the whole breast surface, between the capsular plane and the skin, in order to obtain a thicker and softer subcutaneous layer.

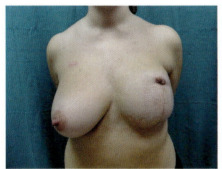
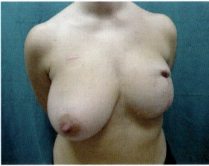
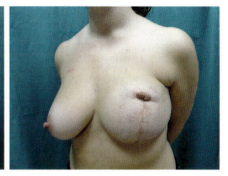

19.4.2.37–19.4.2.39 Implant replacement with a smaller, adjustable volume one and a simultaneous third graft of 280 cc.

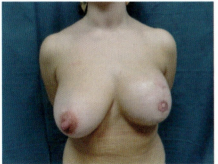
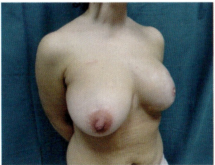
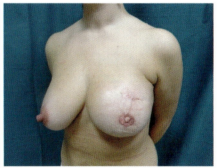

19.4.2.40–19.4.2.42 Results after 2 years. Progressive improvement in shape and natural ptosis. The original NAC was removed, and a new NAC was reconstructed in the correct situation. Consensually, a last fat graft, of 200 cc was performed.

CASE 6—50 year old—Delayed reconstruction

This patient presented after expander extrusion consequent to infection (**Figures 19.4.2.43 through 19.4.2.45**). Three small volume fat grafts (60 cc–80 cc) were performed with time intervals of 3 months from each other. The retracting scars were gradually released with use of the Rigottomies technique: keeping the scarred skin under tension with the aid of a hook and using a 14 gauge needle, a subcutaneous tissue release, in multiple planes and on multiple levels, was gradually obtained in the constricted areas (**Figures 19.4.2.46 through 19.4.2.48**). The resulting soft tissue allowed insertion of a new expander which was then replaced with an Allergan 410 MX 410 g implant (**Figures 19.4.2.49 through 19.4.2.51**). Three more grafts were subsequently performed. Results at 1 year follow-up are shown in **Figures 19.4.2.52 through 19.4.2.54** and at a 9 years follow-up (**Figures 19.4.2.55 through 19.4.2.57**). It should be noted how breast volume, contour, softness, and symmetry are maintained over time.

274 Implant-based whole breast reconstruction (without irradiation)

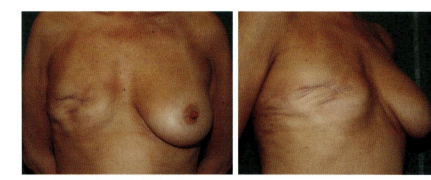
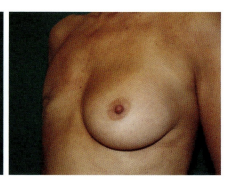

19.4.2.43–19.4.2.45 This patient presented after expander extrusion due to infection.

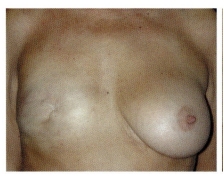
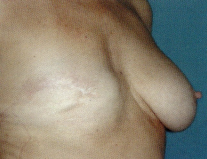
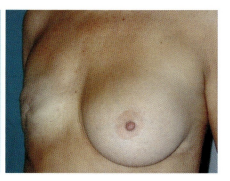

19.4.2.46–19.4.2.48 Three fat grafts of small amount (60–80 cc) were performed with time intervals of 3 months from each other. The retracting scars were gradually released thanks to the *Rigottomies* technique.

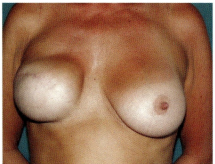
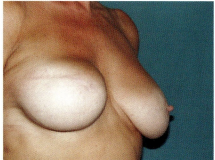
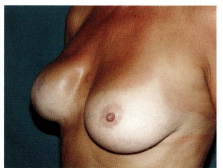

19.4.2.49–19.4.2.51 The resulting soft tissue allowed the insertion of a new expander.

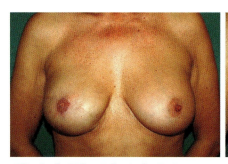
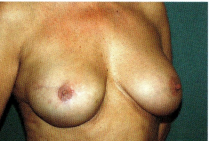
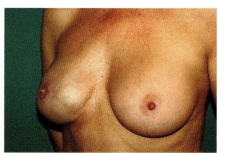

19.4.2.52–19.4.2.54 Results at 1-year follow-up. The expander was replaced with an Allergan 410 MX 410 g implant and three more grafts were performed.

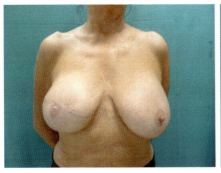 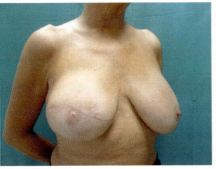 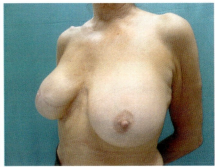

19.4.2.55–19.4.2.57 9-year follow-up. The breast volume, contour, softness, and symmetry are maintained along time.

CASE 7: 50 year old—Salvage procedure

Fat grafting can be extremely useful in salvage procedures where it allows reconstruction to be completed without the need for invasive surgery.

This patient presented with a wide skin opening and implant exposure through the gap (**Figures 19.4.2.58 and 19.4.2.59**). She had not been irradiated and scar dehiscence was probably due to excessive tension from high implant volume. Microbiological culture was mandatory. No bacterial growth was detected and therefore it was decided not to replace the implant. The skin opening was sutured during the first operation at the same time as fat grafting and implant deflation. The patient had an adjustable volume implant which was gradually deflated during the subsequent three procedures, and the volume was replaced with the fat grafting for a total amount of 240 cc (**Figures 19.4.2.60 and 19.4.2.61**). The lipoaspirate was injected in a very thin layer between skin and capsule. Moreover, the procedure was carried out very carefully in order not to damage the underlying implant. A progressive improvement of the skin texture was evident over time (**Figures 19.4.2.62 and 19.4.2.63**).

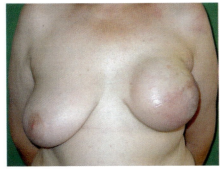 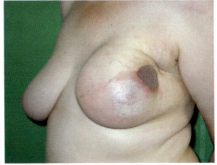

19.4.2.58 AND 19.4.2.59 Left breast reconstruction after mastectomy. Skin gap and implant exposure. She was not a radiated patient and probably the scar dehiscence was due to excessive implant volume.

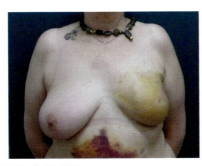 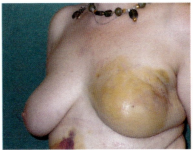

19.4.2.60 AND 19.4.2.61 The skin gap was sutured during the first operation along with fat grafting and implant deflation.

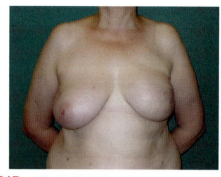
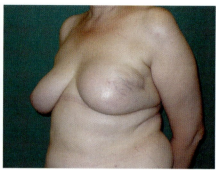

19.4.2.62 AND 19.4.2.63 The patient had an adjustable volume implant which was gradually deflated during the subsequent three procedures and the volume was replaced with the fat grafting for a total amount of 240 cc. The lipoaspirate was injected in a very thin layer between skin and capsule. A progressive improvement of the skin texture was evident for a long time.

REFERENCES

1. Coleman SR, Saboeiro AP. Fat grafting to the breast revisited: Safety and efficacy. *Plastic and Reconstructive Surgery.* 2007;119(3):775–785.
2. Rigotti G, Marchi A, Galiè M, Baroni G, Benati D, Krampera M et al. Clinical treatment of radiotherapy tissue damage by lipoaspirate transplant: A healing process mediated by adipose-derived adult stem cells. *Plastic and Reconstructive Surgery.* 2007;119(5):1409–1422.
3. Rigotti G, Marchi A, Sbarbati A. Adipose-derived mesenchymal stem cells: Past, present, and future. *Aesthetic Plastic Surgery.* 2009;33(3):271–273.
4. Rigotti G, Marchi A, Khouri R. Minimally invasive autologous mastectomy incisionless reconstruction; external expansion fat grafting and percutaneous scar release: A multicenter experience. 2009.
5. Rigotti G, Marchi A, Micciolo PR, Baroni PG. On the safety of autologous fat grafting for breast reconstruction. *Plastic and Reconstructive Surgery.* 2012;130(1):206e–207e.
6. Rigotti G, Marchi A, Stringhini P, Baroni G, Galiè M, Molino AM et al. Determining the oncological risk of autologous lipoaspirate grafting for post-mastectomy breast reconstruction. *Aesthetic Plastic Surgery.* 2010;34(4):475–480.
7. Klopp AH, Gupta A, Spaeth E, Andreeff M, Marini F. Concise review: Dissecting a discrepancy in the literature: Do mesenchymal stem cells support or suppress tumor growth? *Stem Cells.* 2011;29(1):11–19.
8. Petit JY, Maisonneuve P, Rotmensz N, Bertolini F, Clough KB, Sarfati I et al. Safety of lipofilling in patients with breast cancer. *Clinics in Plastic Surgery.* 2015;42(3):339–344.
9. Kronowitz SJ, Mandujano CC, Liu J, Kuerer HM, Smith B, Garvey P et al. Lipofilling of the breast does not increase the risk of recurrence of breast cancer: A matched controlled study. *Plastic and Reconstructive Surgery.* 2016;137(2):385–393.
10. Rigotti G. Discussion: The volumetric analysis of fat graft survival in breast reconstruction. *Plastic and Reconstructive Surgery.* 2013;131(2):192–193.
11. Mashiko T, Yoshimura K. How does fat survive and remodel after grafting? *Clinics in Plastic Surgery.* 2015;42(2):181–190.
12. Pu LLQ, Yoshimura K, Coleman SR. Fat grafting: Current concept, clinical application, and regenerative potential, part 1. *Clinics in Plastic Surgery.* 2015;42(2):ix–x.
13. Pu LLQ, Yoshimura K, Coleman SR. Fat grafting: Current concept, clinical application, and regenerative potential, Part 2. Preface. *Clinics in Plastic Surgery.* 2015;42(3):xiii–xiv.
14. Khouri RK, Khouri RK, Rigotti G, Marchi A, Cardoso E, Rotemberg SC et al. Aesthetic applications of Brava-assisted megavolume fat grafting to the breasts: A 9-year, 476-patient, multicenter experience. *Plastic and Reconstructive Surgery.* 2014;133(4):796–807.
15. Khouri RK, Rigotti G, Khouri RK, Cardoso E, Marchi A, Rotemberg SC et al. Tissue-engineered breast reconstruction with Brava-assisted fat grafting: A 7-year, 488-patient, multicenter experience. *Plastic and Reconstructive Surgery.* 2015;135(3):643–658.
16. Khouri RK, Smit JM, Cardoso E, Pallua N, Lantieri L, Mathijssen IMJ et al. Percutaneous aponeurotomy and lipofilling: A regenerative alternative to flap reconstruction? *Plastic and Reconstructive Surgery.* 2013;132(5):1280–1290.

EDITORIAL COMMENTARY

Chapters 18 and 19 provide important perspective on patients who may and may not require postmastectomy radiotherapy following implant-based whole breast reconstruction. Some of the world's leading breast reconstructive surgeons discuss their approaches and techniques for incorporation of acellular dermal matrix (ADM) and fat grafting. The utilization of ADM and fat grafting has particularly increased in the context of postmastectomy irradiation and attention is now focused on determining the optimal timing and sequencing of these adjuvant methods. Dr. Salzberg is a pioneer in use of ADM for breast reconstruction and describes in particular his technique for one-stage direct-to-implant reconstruction and selection of the ideal candidate for this approach. Meanwhile Dr. Santi provides the European perspective on direct-to-implant reconstruction emphasizing that their European counterparts often use synthetic meshes instead of ADM due to cost issues. Dr. Maxwell, a great innovator in techniques of breast reconstruction discusses his concept of the bioengineered breast using a two-stage technique that he finds preferable to a single stage approach. Dr. Rancati provides input from South America and discusses how he makes use of preoperative imaging with mammography to predict the surgical outcome of breast skin flaps following skin-sparing mastectomy; this determines his two-stage approach to implant-based breast reconstruction. Meanwhile, Dr. Sbitany discusses the benefits of ADM for implant-based reconstruction, pointing out the merits of intraoperative expansion, more rapid completion of expansion and decreased lateral intercostal pain from avoiding any surgical disruption of serratus anterior muscle. However, perhaps the most significant advantage of ADM reconstruction is reduced chance of expander explantation compared to a dual plane technique. Dr. Farhadi from London also describes how surgeons in Europe often use synthetic mesh rather than biological materials because of financial constraints and lack of insurance coverage for these more expensive adjuvant options. Nonetheless, he cautions the use of mesh in obese patients who have been reported in general to have higher rates of complications from implant-based reconstructions. Dr. Berino from Genoa in Italy describes a novel and interesting technique for pre-conditioning the mastectomy site to render it more suitable for implant breast reconstruction. His compatriot Dr. Marchi emphasizes that fat grafting as an adjunct to implant-based reconstruction has dramatically reduced usage of the latissimus dorsi flap. Dr. Mehara from Memorial Sloan Kettering Cancer Center (MSKCC) in New York opens the discussion of implant-based reconstruction in the setting of postmastectomy radiotherapy. He describes the timing of the MSKCC algorithm and presents important data published from that institution. Dr. Catanuto continues the discussion by considering how multiple fat grafting sessions can ameliorate the sequelae of radiation-induced tissue damage. Of note, he identifies four clinical scenarios where use of fat grafting can potentially limit the detrimental effects of radiation therapy on implant-based breast reconstruction. It should be noted that both Dr. Cordeiro from the United States and Dr. Spano from Europe chose to exchange the tissue expander for a permanent implant prior to any postmastectomy radiation therapy. Several surgeons have expressed a preference for pre-fat grafting in advance of delayed implant-based breast reconstruction to prepare the recipient site. Perhaps more controversially, Dr. Martin and myself discuss how use of both ADM and fat grafting can lower complication rates and improve surgical and patient-reported outcomes for implant-based reconstruction in the context of postmastectomy radiotherapy. There are some technical variations; I prefer Alloderm while Dr. Martin commonly uses TiLoop. Dr. Martin has alluded to several distinct trends in breast reconstruction evident in the United Kingdom over the past couple of decades. Firstly, the rate of immediate breast reconstruction more than doubled (from 13% to 28%) over the period 2000–2012, and more recently increased use of ADM has coincided with a reduction in numbers of implant-assisted latissimus dorsi flap reconstruction. Nonetheless, both myself and others continue to emphasize how the "interval fat grafting" approach is complicated in the irradiation breast reconstruction.

20

Implant–based whole breast reconstruction (with irradiation)

AT A GLANCE

There are currently three timing approaches to implant reconstruction in patients requiring radiotherapy. Some surgeons perform a one-stage immediate reconstruction, some perform a two-stage approach with exchange for a permanent implant prior to radiotherapy, while the majority of surgeons perform two-stage with exchange for the permanent implant after radiotherapy. Fat grafting has very low complication rates and may decrease the complications associated with acellular dermal matrix (ADMs) with and without radiotherapy. Indeed, the use of ADMs and/or fat grafting lowers the rates of complications compared to the use of implant-only reconstruction without these adjunct procedures. Furthermore, the potential of ADMs and fat grafting to decrease capsular contracture has exciting implications. Implant reconstruction in the setting of radiotherapy has higher complications than autologous tissue; however, it is more practical in the private practice setting and advances in matrix technology, and fat grafting may enhance its safety and improve the outcomes.

20.1 TIMING OF RECONSTRUCTION

20.1.1 Our approach (USA)

Claudia R. Albornoz and Babak Mehrara

INTRODUCTION

Radiotherapy to the chest wall and regional lymph nodes following mastectomy is now an important component of breast cancer treatment for some patients and has been shown to both increase survival and decrease locoregional relapse rates.[1-3] Although previously reserved for patients with locally advanced tumors (tumor size >5 cm or four or more positive lymph nodes or invasion of skin/muscle), indications for postmastectomy radiation (PMRT) have been expanded, and it is now recommended for some patients with smaller tumors or involvement of only 1–2 lymph nodes.[4-10] This upward trend in use of PMRT has coincided with an increase of more than 200% in use of immediate implant-based reconstruction over the past year.[11,12] As a result, it is likely that more patients who are reconstructed with implants will receive PMRT. Therefore, it is incumbent on reconstructive surgeons to

identify reliable algorithms for reconstruction in this particular setting.

In the past, those patients who required PMRT were generally not considered good candidates for immediate breast reconstruction. However, these viewpoints have evolved in many institutions such that PMRT is no longer considered a contraindication for immediate implant reconstruction in selected cases.[13,14] Thus, although it is clear that patients who undergo implant-based reconstruction and receive PMRT have higher rates of early and late complications as compared to non-irradiated patients, several studies have reported that the majority of carefully selected patients have reasonable long-term outcomes and successful reconstruction despite the negative effects of radiation.[15-19]

ALGORITHMS FOR IMPLANT RECONSTRUCTION IRRADIATION

Researchers led by Peter Cordeiro at Memorial Sloan Kettering Cancer Center (MSKCC) have published the largest series of patients who underwent immediate implant-based reconstruction and were later treated with PMRT.[15,16,18,19] Following total mastectomy and immediate

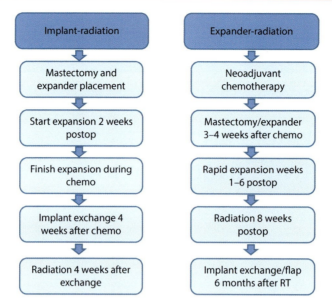

20.1.1.1 MSKCC algorithms for implant and tissue expander (TE) irradiation. (From Cordeiro, P.G. et al., *Plast. Reconstr. Surg.*, 135, 1509–1517, 2015.)

implant reconstruction, there are basically two options for radiation therapy: either to irradiate the tissue expander prior to exchange for a permanent implant, or to irradiate the permanent implant after exchange. The MSKCC algorithm proposes irradiation of the permanent implant (**Figure 20.1.1.1**).[19] In this scenario, patients undergo total mastectomy with immediate submuscular placement of a tissue expander and intraoperative filling. Two weeks after surgery, expansion begins weekly or as time permits with a volume of 60–100 cc/session until an acceptable volume is reached. A small amount of over-expansion (5%–10%) is used in some cases to achieve a more ptotic appearance and match the contralateral breast. Four weeks after the final cycle of chemotherapy, exchange to a permanent implant is performed, and the patient is allowed to recover. Drains are removed after 1 week and the patient is simulated by the 3rd postoperative week, followed by initiation of radiation therapy which is ideally performed 4 weeks after surgery. Radiation is administered to the chest wall, locoregional, and paraclavicular lymph nodes. Internal mammary and axillary nodes are not routinely irradiated at MSKCC, unless they are confirmed to be involved by pathologic findings and/or preoperative imaging. From 2002 onward, intensity-modulated tangent beams have been used to achieve dose homogeneity. The prescribed energy is usually 6 MV photons, with a higher energy beam for large breasted patients. A daily bolus of 0.5 cm is delivered over the chest-wall fields only to ensure adequate dose to the skin surface and mastectomy scar.[19]

The second option is to irradiate the tissue expander (Figure 20.1.1.1). At MSKCC, this option is usually employed when radiotherapy is recommended as a neoadjuvant treatment. In this algorithm, patients receive chemotherapy before mastectomy, and then undergo total mastectomy with immediate placement of a tissue expander. The tissue expander is intraoperatively filled as much as possible and rapid expansion begins promptly 2 weeks after surgery with a goal of finishing expansion within 6–8 weeks of surgery. Radiotherapy to the tissue expander starts after the completion of expansion, and the patients are monitored for healing/infection. The exchange for a permanent implant is usually performed 4–6 months following completion of radiation therapy. Radiation energy used for this approach is 15 MV photons to minimize "scatter" dose off the magnetic tissue expander valve, and the bolus is increased to 1 cm. Radiation fields are similar to those previously described for implant radiation. The tissue expander is deflated neither before nor during radiation therapy.[19]

OUTCOMES FOR THE DIFFERENT ALGORITHMS

Outcomes reported in the literature are variable, focus mainly on tissue expander or implant loss, have small numbers of cases, and fail to incorporate aesthetic outcomes.[20] For the purpose of this chapter, more uniform outcomes will be analyzed as reported by MSKCC.[18,19] In a study published in June 2015, Cordeiro and colleagues analyzed long-term outcomes for 210 patients with irradiated implants and 94 patients with tissue expander irradiation. These were compared to 1486 non-irradiated implant-based reconstructions operated on between 2003 and 2012. Patients were followed up annually and outcomes were registered in a prospective database.[19]

- *Failure rates*: Patients who underwent irradiation of a tissue expander had higher reconstructive failure rates (18% vs 12%) compared with those in whom radiation was delivered to a permanent implant. Furthermore, radiation in either scenario (i.e., to the implant or the tissue expander) as well as time to follow-up were independent risk factors for reconstructive failure in a multivariate model of patients who underwent implant-based reconstruction (tissue expander radiation: Odds Ratio (OR) 5.75, p < 0.01; permanent implant irradiation OR 5.19, p < 0.01). Since patients with tissue expander irradiation had shorter follow-up times than patients with implant irradiation, a Kaplan-Meier analysis was used to better account for this difference. Kaplan-Meier analysis allows for prediction of progressive events (e.g., reconstructive failure) at different times, including data from patients who are currently in follow-up and those who were lost to follow-up before the occurrence of the event. This analysis showed that predicted reconstructive loss is higher for irradiation of tissue expanders (32% at 6 years) than for patients with implant irradiation (16.3%).

- *Capsular contracture*: Patients who underwent irradiation of the permanent implant had higher long-term capsular contracture rates (grade III/IV) as compared with patients who underwent irradiation of the tissue expander (50% vs 17%). This difference is likely related to capsulectomy/capsulotomy in irradiated patients who have exchange of their irradiated tissue expander for an implant.
- *Aesthetic outcomes*: Over 90% of patients in the implant-irradiated group had a good to excellent result when evaluated by their surgeon. These results are comparable to those of patients with tissue expander-irradiation.
- *Patient satisfaction*: Patient satisfaction is one of the most important outcomes in breast reconstruction and can now be objectively measured using the BREAST-Q. Patients with an irradiated reconstruction have lower levels of satisfaction irrespective of radiation timing compared to patients without radiation. However, no meaningful difference was found in the BREAST-Q scales when comparing irradiation of the implant versus the tissue expander.

CONCLUSION

Good cosmetic results and high levels of patient satisfaction can be expected with implant-based reconstruction even in the setting of radiation therapy. The authors' preference is for radiation to the permanent implant, since there is an increased risk of failure for tissue expander irradiation. Coordination between the surgical, oncology, and radiation team is necessary in order to achieve a successful reconstruction.

REFERENCES

1. Ragaz J, Jackson SM, Le N et al. Adjuvant radiotherapy and chemotherapy in node-positive premenopausal women with breast cancer. *N Engl J Med.* 1997;337(14):956–962.
2. Overgaard M, Hansen PS, Overgaard J et al. Postoperative radiotherapy in high-risk premenopausal women with breast cancer who receive adjuvant chemotherapy. Danish breast cancer cooperative group 82b trial. *N Engl J Med.* 1997;337(14):949–955.

3. Overgaard M, Jensen MB, Overgaard J et al. Postoperative radiotherapy in high-risk postmenopausal breast-cancer patients given adjuvant tamoxifen: Danish breast cancer cooperative group DBCG 82c randomised trial. *Lancet.* 1999;353(9165):1641–1648.
4. National Institutes of Health Consensus Development P. National institutes of health consensus development conference statement: Adjuvant therapy for breast cancer, 2000. *J Natl Cancer Inst.* 2001(30):5–15.
5. Taghian A, Jeong JH, Mamounas E et al. Patterns of locoregional failure in patients with operable breast cancer treated by mastectomy and adjuvant chemotherapy with or without tamoxifen and without radiotherapy: Results from five national surgical adjuvant breast and bowel project randomized clinical trials. *J Clin Oncol.* 2004;22(21):4247–4254.
6. Chua B, Olivotto IA, Weir L, Kwan W, Truong P, Ragaz J. Increased use of adjuvant regional radiotherapy for node-positive breast cancer in British Columbia. *Breast J.* 2004;10(1):38–44.
7. Trovo M, Durofil E, Polesel J et al. Locoregional failure in early-stage breast cancer patients treated with radical mastectomy and adjuvant systemic therapy: Which patients benefit from postmastectomy irradiation? *Int J Radiat Oncol Biol Phys.* 2012;83(2):e153–e157.
8. Tendulkar RD, Rehman S, Shukla ME et al. Impact of postmastectomy radiation on locoregional recurrence in breast cancer patients with 1–3 positive lymph nodes treated with modern systemic therapy. *Int J Radiat Oncol Biol Phys.* 2012;83(5):e577–e581.
9. Recht A, Edge SB, Solin LJ et al. Postmastectomy radiotherapy: Clinical practice guidelines of the American society of clinical oncology. *J Clin Oncol.* 2001;19(5):1539–1569.
10. Harris JR, Halpin-Murphy P, McNeese M, Mendenhall NP, Morrow M, Robert NJ. Consensus statement on postmastectomy radiation therapy. *Int J Radiat Oncol Biol Phys.* 1999;44(5):989–990.
11. Albornoz CR, Bach PB, Mehrara BJ et al. A paradigm shift in U.S. breast reconstruction: Increasing implant rates. *Plast Reconstr Surg.* 2013;131(1):15–23.
12. Albornoz CR, Matros E, Lee CN et al. Bilateral mastectomy versus breast-conserving surgery for early-stage breast cancer: The role of breast reconstruction. *Plast Reconstr Surg.* 2015;135(6):1518–1526.
13. Albornoz CR, Cordeiro PG, Farias-Eisner G et al. Diminishing relative contraindications for immediate breast reconstruction. *Plast Reconstr Surg.* 2014;134(3):363e–369e.
14. Albornoz CR, Cordeiro PG, Pusic AL et al. Diminishing relative contraindications for immediate breast reconstruction: A multicenter study. *J Am Coll Surg.* 2014;219(4):788–795.
15. Cordeiro PG, McCarthy CM. A single surgeon's 12-year experience with tissue expander/implant breast reconstruction: Part I. A prospective analysis of early complications. *Plast Reconstr Surg.* 2006;118(4):825–831.
16. Cordeiro PG, McCarthy CM. A single surgeon's 12-year experience with tissue expander/implant breast reconstruction: Part II. An analysis of long-term complications, aesthetic outcomes, and patient satisfaction. *Plast Reconstr Surg.* 2006;118(4):832–839.

17. Nava MB, Pennati AE, Lozza L, Spano A, Zambetti M, Catanuto G. Outcome of different timings of radiotherapy in implant-based breast reconstructions. *Plast Reconstr Surg.* 2011;128(2):353–359.

18. Cordeiro PG, Albornoz CR, McCormick B, Hu Q, Van Zee K. The impact of postmastectomy radiotherapy on two-stage implant breast reconstruction: An analysis of long-term surgical outcomes, aesthetic results, and satisfaction over 13 years. *Plast Reconstr Surg.* 2014;134(4):588–595.

19. Cordeiro PG, Albornoz CR, McCormick B et al. What is the optimum timing of postmastectomy radiotherapy in two-stage prosthetic reconstruction: Radiation to the tissue expander or permanent implant? *Plast Reconstr Surg.* 2015;135(6):1509–1517.

20. Lam TC, Hsieh F, Boyages J. The effects of postmastectomy adjuvant radiotherapy on immediate two-stage prosthetic breast reconstruction: A systematic review. *Plast Reconstr Surg.* Sep 2013;132(3):511–518.

20.1.2 My approach (Europe)

Giuseppe Catanuto

INTRODUCTION

Although breast reconstruction with implants can be offered to most women undergoing mastectomy and immediate breast reconstruction, the possibility of delayed reconstruction or use of autologous tissue is discussed with patients when radiotherapy is involved.[1] High failure rates for reconstruction with prostheses have been demonstrated by several authors in the setting of radiotherapy, although the poor results can be partially addressed by appropriate timing of surgery, systemic treatment, and radiotherapy.[2–4]

For the above reasons, patients must be warned that the combination of oncological therapies and reconstructive procedures may increase the overall length of the treatment process. The authors usually perform two-stage breast reconstruction, although, in selected cases, use a one-stage technique.[5,6] Multiple fat grafting can be a useful tool for treatment of radiation-induced tissue sequelae.[7–9] Four possible scenarios for radiotherapy in the setting of breast reconstruction can be identified:

1. Breast reconstruction after previous radiation (salvage mastectomy or other)
2. Postmastectomy radiotherapy after neoadjuvant chemotherapy, mastectomy, and tissue expander
3. Postmastectomy radiotherapy after mastectomy and tissue expansion followed by adjuvant chemotherapy
4. Postmastectomy radiotherapy in the setting of locally advanced breast cancer

BREAST RECONSTRUCTION AFTER PREVIOUS RADIATION

Breast reconstruction with implants for patients who have already received radiotherapy (either for previous breast cancer or for other diseases) has been investigated by several authors.[10–12] Despite many studies being substantially biased with poor quality evidence, there is a clear trend toward higher complication rates with radiation therapy. For instance, Persichetti and colleagues compared patients who had radiotherapy to a non-radiotherapy group and found overall complication rates of 75% (25% minor, 50% major) versus 49%, respectively with corresponding capsular contracture rates of 40% (grade III/IV) versus 6.9%.[12]

More recently, Cordeiro and colleagues compared a large series of patients who had breast reconstruction without radiotherapy (1578 patients) to that of a group with previous irradiation (121 patients). These authors confirmed with larger numbers a higher complication rate in the irradiated cohort (29.7% vs 15.5%; $p \leq 0.001$) with a prevalence of flap necrosis. A significantly higher proportion of results rated as excellent were reported for the non-irradiated group.[10]

Complications may compromise either the reconstructive or the oncological outcomes of treatment with poor results or delays in administrations of adjuvant treatments. Therefore, it is the authors' preferred practice to offer delayed reconstruction to this subset of patients.[13] In order to improve final cosmetic results, multiple fat grafting is performed as there is robust evidence that this procedure can increase aesthetic results and treat radiation-induced tissue damage.[7–8]

A proposed schedule of the treatment for these patients is shown in **Figure 20.1.2.1**.

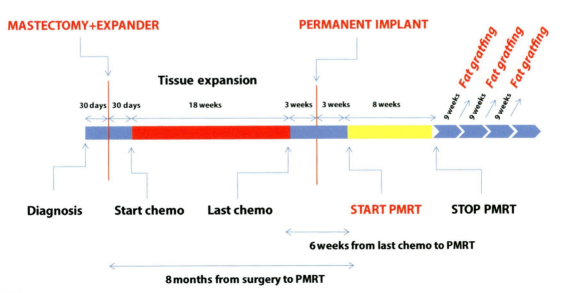

20.1.2.1 Postmastectomy radiotherapy: On permanent implant.

Breast reconstruction with implants in patients requiring postmastectomy radiotherapy

Postmastectomy radiotherapy has proven efficacy in the setting of patients with four or more positive nodes. However, indications for postmastectomy radiotherapy are likely to be broadened to include patients with 1–3 positive nodes based on emerging data.[14–16]

When patients decide to undergo breast reconstruction, the need for radiotherapy cannot be always anticipated and radiation effects may interfere with the reconstructive process. The authors' group demonstrated that administering radiotherapy to the permanent implant after completion of tissue expansion improves final reconstructive outcomes.[2] These results have subsequently been confirmed in a larger series published by Cordeiro and colleagues from Memorial Sloan Kettering Cancer Center.[3–4]

For these reasons, the period of adjuvant chemotherapy can be used to execute tissue expansion. Three weeks after the end of chemotherapy, second stage surgery is performed with the insertion of a permanent implant. Moreover, 8 weeks after completion of surgery postmastectomy radiotherapy can be performed. In the study comparing irradiation of tissue expanders (TE) with irradiation of permanent implants (PI) or no radiotherapy (no RT), the second approach improved the Baker IV capsular contracture rates (RT+ TE = 13.3% versus RT+ PI 10.1% versus no RT = 0) and increased long-term reconstruction survival (RT+ TE = 68% versus RT+ PI = 83.6% versus no RT = 94.5%). However, it is evident that despite relatively favorable results, chronic radiation-induced damage to tissue is still present. The latter can be treated by administering a triple course of fat grafting (3 months after RT, one graft every 3 months for three times according to clinical response and fat availability). These treatment schedules are summarized in **Figure 20.1.2.2**.

Breast reconstruction in patients who had neoadjuvant chemotherapy

Neoadjuvant chemotherapy has been shown to reduce mastectomy rates and can test the effectiveness of systemic treatments in vivo.[17–26] Nonetheless, a significant proportion of patients still require removal of all breast tissue. In these circumstances, when postmastectomy radiotherapy is required and a tissue expander is in situ, there is no opportunity to perform tissue expansion during chemotherapy. Instead, radiotherapy to the chest wall is administered 8 weeks after surgery to replace the tissue expander with a permanent implant. Patients are warned about the possible need to switch to a flap-based procedure due to reconstructive failure (implant loss, poor cosmetic results, or capsular contracture) in up to 60% of the cases.[2] Before insertion of the permanent implant, the standard three sessions of fat grafting is done followed by the second surgical stage (**Figure 20.1.2.3**).

Breast reconstruction in locally advanced breast cancer

Patients with locally advanced breast cancer at presentation require upfront chemotherapy, mastectomy, and axillary dissection. The indications for chest wall radiotherapy are usually clear at the time of diagnosis although a decision for regional nodal irradiation may be made subsequently. The authors do not offer immediate reconstruction in this setting unless specifically requested by the patient and there has been a very good clinical response to chemotherapy. In these circumstances, the authors follow a similar schedule as for patients having neoadjuvant chemotherapy for large (but not locally advanced) cancers not suitable for breast conservation (see Figure 20.1.2.3). These patients are warned about the increased risk of complications and the impact this may have on the timing of oncological treatments.

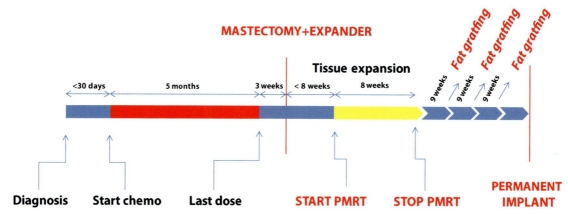

20.1.2.2 Postmastectomy radiotherapy: On expander.

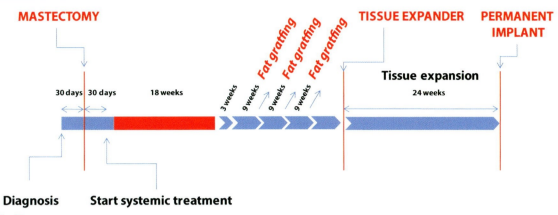

20.1.2.3 Previous radiotherapy: Delayed reconstruction.

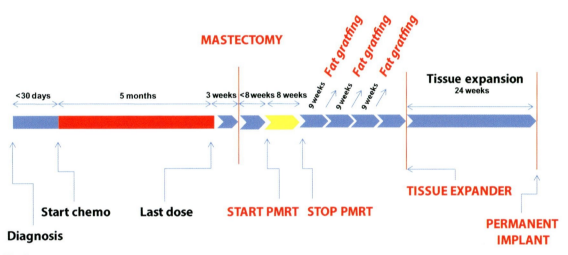

20.1.2.4 Locally advanced breast cancer: Delayed reconstruction.

If a delayed breast reconstruction has to be performed after radiotherapy, the authors' preference is for an autologous deep inferior epigastric perforator flap, but if a less aggressive surgical approach is contemplated, fat grafting can be used to treat radiation-induced damage (three courses every 3 months), and then a temporary expander inserted that will be replaced by a permanent implant after a minimum of 6 months. The whole treatment pathway will last not less than 67 weeks (**Figure 20.1.2.4**).

REFERENCES

1. Barry M, Kell M. Radiotherapy and breast reconstruction: A meta-analysis. *Breast Cancer Res Treat* 2011;127(1):15–22.
2. Nava MB, Pennati AE, Lozza L, Spano A, Zambetti M, Catanuto G. Outcome of different timings of radiotherapy in implant-based breast reconstructions. *Plast Reconstr Surg.* 2011;128(2):353–359.

3. Cordeiro PG, Albornoz CR, McCormick B, Hu Q, Van Zee K. The impact of postmastectomy radiotherapy on two-stage implant breast reconstruction: An analysis of long-term surgical outcomes, aesthetic results, and satisfaction over 13 years. *Plast Reconstr Surg.* 2014;134(4):588–595.

4. Cordeiro PG, Pusic AL, Disa JJ, McCormick B, Van Zee K. Irradiation after immediate tissue expander/implant breast reconstruction: Outcomes, complications, aesthetic results, and satisfaction among 156 patients. *Plast Reconstr Surg.* 2004;113(3):877–881.

5. Nava MB, Cortinovis U, Ottolenghi J, Riggio E, Pennati A, Catanuto G, Greco M, Rovere GQ. Skin-reducing mastectomy. *Plast Reconstr Surg.* 2006;118(3):603–610.

6. Nava MB, Ottolenghi J, Pennati A, Spano A, Bruno N, Catanuto G, Boliglowa D, Visintini V, Santoro S, Folli S. Skin/nipple sparing mastectomies and implant-based breast reconstruction in patients with large and ptotic breast: Oncological and reconstructive results. *Breast.* 2012;21(3):267–271.

7. Rigotti G, Marchi A, Galiè M, Baroni G, Benati D, Krampera M, Pasini A, Sbarbati A. Clinical treatment of radiotherapy tissue damage by lipoaspirate transplant: A healing process mediated by adipose-derived adult stem cells. *Plast Reconstr Surg.* 2007;119(5):1409–1422; discussion 1423–1424.

8. Serra-Renom JM, Muñoz-Olmo JL, Serra-Mestre JM. Fat grafting in postmastectomy breast reconstruction with expanders and prostheses in patients who have received radiotherapy: Formation of new subcutaneous tissue. *Plast Reconstr Surg.* 2010;125(1):12–18.

9. Riggio E, Bordoni D, Nava MB. Oncologic surveillance of breast cancer patients after lipofilling. *Aesthetic Plast Surg.* 2013;37(4):728–375.

10. Cordeiro PG, Snell L, Heerdt A, McCarthy, C. Immediate tissue expander/implant breast reconstruction after salvage mastectomy for cancer recurrence following lumpectomy/irradiation. *Plast Reconstr Surg.* 2012;129(2):341–350.

11. Kronowitz SJ. Delayed-immediate breast reconstruction: Technical and timing considerations. *Plast Reconstr Surg.* 2010;125(2):463–474.

12. Cagli B, Barone M, Ippolito E, Cogliandro A, Silipigni S, Ramella S, Persichetti P. Ten years experience with breast reconstruction after salvage mastectomy in previously irradiated patients: Analysis of outcomes, satisfaction and well-being. *Eur Rev Med Pharmacol Sci.* 2016;20(22):4635–4641.

13. Rocco N, Catanuto G, Nava MB. Radiotherapy and breast reconstruction. *Minerva Chir.* 2018;73(3):322–328. doi:10.23736/S0026-4733.18.07615-0.

14. Fowble B, Gray R, Gilchrist K, et al. Identification of a subgroup of patients with breast cancer and histologically positive axillary nodes receiving adjuvant chemotherapy who may benefit from postoperative radiotherapy. *J Clin Oncol.* 1988;6(7):1107–1117.

15. Overgaard M, Hansen PS, Overgaard J, et al. Postoperative radiotherapy in high-risk premenopausal women with breast cancer who receive adjuvant chemotherapy. Danish Breast Cancer Cooperative Group 82b Trial. *N Engl J Med.* 1997;337(14):949–955.

16. McGale P, Taylor C, Correa C, et al. Effect of radiotherapy after mastectomy and axillary surgery on 10-year recurrence and 20-year breast cancer mortality: meta-analysis of individual patient data for 8135 women in 22 randomised trials. *Lancet.* 2014;383(9935):2127–2135.

17. Mauri D, Pavlidis N, Ioannidis JP. Neoadjuvant versus adjuvant systemic treatment in breast cancer: A meta-analysis. *J Natl Cancer Inst.* 2005;97(3):188–194.

18. Bear HD, Anderson S, Brown A, et al. The effect on tumor response of adding sequential preoperative docetaxel to preoperative doxorubicin and cyclophosphamide: Preliminary results from National Surgical Adjuvant Breast and Bowel Project Protocol B-27. *J Clin Oncol.* 2003;21(22):4165–4174.

19. Smith IE, Dowsett M, Ebbs SR, et al. Neoadjuvant treatment of postmenopausal breast cancer with anastrozole, tamoxifen, or both in combination: The Immediate Preoperative Anastrozole, Tamoxifen, or Combined with Tamoxifen (IMPACT) multicenter double-blind randomized trial. *J Clin Oncol.* 2005;23(22):5108–5116.

20. Cortazar P, Zhang L, Untch M, et al. Pathological complete response and long-term clinical benefit in breast cancer: The CTNeoBC pooled analysis. *Lancet.* 2014;384(9938):164–172.

21. Smith IC, Heys SD, Hutcheon AW, et al. Neoadjuvant chemotherapy in breast cancer: Significantly enhanced response with docetaxel. *J Clin Oncol.* 2002;20(6):1456–1466.

22. von Minckwitz G, Kümmel S, Vogel P, et al. Intensified neoadjuvant chemotherapy in early-responding breast cancer: Phase III randomized GeparTrio study. *J Natl Cancer Inst.* 2008;100(8):552–562.

23. Fisher B, Bryant J, Wolmark N, et al. Effect of preoperative chemotherapy on the outcome of women with operable breast cancer. *J Clin Oncol.* 1998;16(8):2672–2685.

24. Fisher ER, Wang J, Bryant J, et al. Pathobiology of preoperative chemotherapy: Findings from the National Surgical Adjuvant Breast and Bowel (NSABP) protocol B-18. *Cancer.* 2002;95(4):681–695.

25. Rastogi P, Anderson SJ, Bear HD, et al. Preoperative chemotherapy: Updates of National Surgical Adjuvant Breast and Bowel Project Protocols B-18 and B-27. *J Clin Oncol.* 2008;26(5):778–785.

26. van der Hage JA, van de Velde CJ, Julien JP, et al. Preoperative chemotherapy in primary operable breast cancer: Results from the European Organization for Research and Treatment of Cancer trial 10902. *J Clin Oncol.* 2001;19(22):4224–4237.

20.2 TECHNIQUE FOR RECONSTRUCTION

20.2.1 Our approach (USA)

Sophocles H. Voineskos and Peter G. Cordeiro

GENERAL APPROACH

Radiotherapy has become an essential component in the multimodal treatment of locally advanced breast cancer. Indications for radiotherapy are broadening[1] and may be beneficial for patients with one to three positive axillary nodes.[2] Irrespective of the method of reconstruction chosen or the timing of reconstruction, radiotherapy creates a challenging environment in which to reconstruct a natural appearing, soft, symmetrical breast mound.

Patients offered implant-based whole breast reconstruction are generally those who desire an expander/implant reconstruction or who are unable to undergo an autologous reconstruction (no available donor tissue, high-risk surgical patients). Patients should be counseled that alloplastic reconstruction failure rates are significantly higher for patients who require radiotherapy.[3] In the setting of radiotherapy, reconstructive surgeons are faced with performing alloplastic reconstruction in two main groups of patients: those who will complete their tissue expansion before radiotherapy, and those who will require tissue expansion in a previously irradiated field. Previously irradiated chest wall tissue is fibrotic and non-compliant, and the authors therefore rarely recommend attempting tissue expansion in a delayed fashion. Successful reconstruction in these circumstances can be facilitated with use of a latissimus dorsi flap as a "combined" alloplastic/autologous technique which introduces healthy, non-irradiated tissue to the chest wall.

This section will focus on approaches to implant-based whole breast reconstruction with irradiation as practiced at Memorial Sloan Kettering Cancer Center with a description of immediate two-stage prosthetic reconstruction in the setting of radiotherapy.

RADIOTHERAPY TO THE TISSUE EXPANDER VERSUS THE PERMANENT IMPLANT

When a patient decides to proceed with immediate two-stage prosthetic reconstruction and requires adjuvant radiotherapy, the reconstructive surgeon must decide whether to recommend radiotherapy of the tissue expander or the permanent implant following an exchange procedure. Typically, this decision is related to the amount of time available before radiotherapy. At Memorial Sloan Kettering, the precise timing and sequence of mastectomy, reconstruction, chemotherapy, and radiotherapy are often dependent on whether patients undergo neoadjuvant chemotherapy. When a neoadjuvant

schedule is employed, radiotherapy is delivered before the exchange for a permanent implant, for example, while the tissue expander remains in the breast. The exchange procedure is then performed on a delayed basis, 6 months later. If adjuvant chemotherapy is required, the exchange procedure is performed and radiotherapy is delivered after exchange to the permanent implant. The protocol for immediate implant-based whole breast reconstruction with irradiation is illustrated in **Figure 20.2.1.1**.

OUR APPROACH FOR RADIATION TO THE TISSUE EXPANDER

Patients undergo total mastectomy and insertion of a tissue expander 3 to 4 weeks after the completion of chemotherapy. The expander is immediately placed in the submuscular plane at the time of total mastectomy. Approximately 50% of tissue expansion is performed intraoperatively. Complete musculofascial coverage is used and sentinel lymph node biopsy/axillary lymph node dissection is performed as appropriate. Rapid weekly expansion commences 10–14 days postoperatively, with the goal of achieving the final volume by 6 weeks postoperatively. At 8 weeks, with the tissue expander fully inflated, radiotherapy is administered to the chest wall and regional lymph nodes. Six months after radiotherapy is complete, an extensive capsulotomy is performed at the time of the exchange procedure, and the permanent device is subsequently inserted.

OUR APPROACH FOR RADIATION TO THE PERMANENT IMPLANT

For patients receiving radiotherapy to the permanent implant, tissue expansion is performed weekly and is continued during chemotherapy. Exchange of the tissue expander for a permanent implant is performed 4 weeks after completion of chemotherapy. Irradiation of the permanent implant commences 4 weeks after the exchange procedure. The radiation field consistently includes the paraclavicular nodal region and a decision is made whether to irradiate the internal mammary chain and the axillary nodes based on preoperative imaging and/or pathologic evaluation.

DISCUSSION

It is clear that administration of radiotherapy will negatively affect the long-term survival and aesthetic outcomes of an immediate alloplastic breast reconstruction. When radiotherapy is required, the optimal timing of administration remains unresolved from the point of view of the reconstructive surgeon. When a tissue expander is irradiated, loss rates of 32%[4] and 40%[5] have been reported. By contrast, when a permanent implant is irradiated, reconstructive failure rates are much lower (6.4%,[5] 9.1%,[6] and 16%[3]).

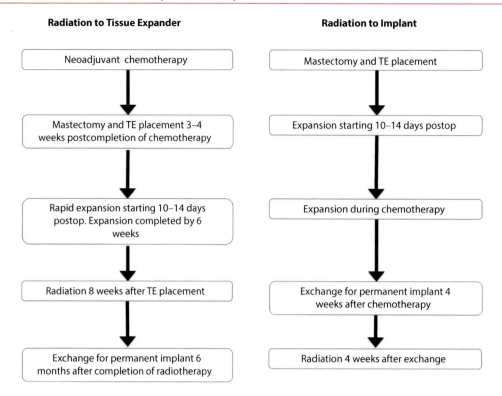

20.2.1.1 Memorial Sloan Kettering protocol for immediate implant-based whole breast reconstruction with irradiation.

A systematic review by Lam and colleagues[7] attempted to establish the optimal timing of radiotherapy with respect to the two stages of tissue expander/implant reconstruction. They concluded that radiotherapy administered to the tissue expander resulted in a higher risk of reconstructive failure,[7] although these authors acknowledged that most studies reviewed were retrospective with small case numbers and some lacked appropriate control groups. Following publication of this systematic review,[7] Cordeiro and colleagues[3] reported data for the largest, prospectively collected evaluation of surgical, aesthetic, and patient-reported outcomes in patients undergoing immediate alloplastic reconstruction with radiotherapy. Patients undergoing radiotherapy to the tissue expander were significantly more likely to lose the expander than those receiving radiotherapy to the permanent implant (6-year predicted failure rate of 32% vs 16%, respectively).[3] Nonetheless, those patients with irradiation of the tissue expander had slightly better aesthetic outcomes and lower rates of grade III and grade IV contracture.[3] Outcomes measured using the BREAST-Q were similar between the two groups.[3]

CONCLUSION

Radiotherapy presents a major obstacle to achieving alloplastic reconstructions with comparably favorable cosmetic outcomes to women who do not receive radiotherapy. However, immediate alloplastic reconstruction in patients who require radiotherapy can be worthwhile. The protocol outlined in Figure 20.2.1.1 provides useful guidance in this challenging area. The authors believe that when this approach is used for two-stage reconstruction and postmastectomy radiotherapy, acceptable rates of capsular contracture, aesthetic outcomes, and patient satisfaction are attainable. It is likely that techniques in alloplastic reconstruction and the timing and administration of radiotherapy for this complex subset of breast cancer patients will continue to evolve.

REFERENCES

1. Recht A, Edge SB, Solin LJ, Robinson DS, Estabrook A, Fine RE et al. Postmastectomy radiotherapy: Clinical practice guidelines of the American society of clinical oncology. *J Clin Oncol* 2001;19(5):1539–1569.
2. McGale P, Taylor C, Correa C, Cutter D, Duane F, Ewertz M et al. Effect of radiotherapy after mastectomy and axillary surgery on 10-year recurrence and 20-year breast cancer mortality: Meta-analysis of individual patient data for 8135 women in 22 randomised trials. *Lancet* 2014;383(9935):2127–2135.
3. Cordeiro PG, Albornoz CR, McCormick B, Hudis CA, Hu Q, Heerdt A et al. What is the optimum timing of post-mastectomy radiotherapy in two-stage prosthetic peconstruction: Radiation to the tissue expander or permanent implant? *Plast Reconstr Surg* 2015;135(6);1509.

4. Kronowitz SJ, Lam C, Terefe W, Hunt KK, Kuerer HM, Valero V et al. A multidisciplinary protocol for planned skin-preserving delayed breast reconstruction for patients with locally advanced breast cancer requiring postmastectomy radiation therapy: 3-year follow-up. *Plast Reconstr Surg* 2011;127(6):2154–2166.

5. Nava MB, Pennati AE, Lozza L, Spano A, Zambetti M, Catanuto G. Outcome of different timings of radiotherapy in implant-based breast reconstructions. *Plast Reconstr Surg* 2011;128(2):353–359.

6. Cordeiro PG, Albornoz CR, McCormick B, Hu Q, Van Zee K. The impact of postmastectomy radiotherapy on two-stage implant breast reconstruction: An analysis of long-term surgical outcomes, aesthetic results, and satisfaction over 13 years. *Plast Reconstr Surg* 2014;134(4):588–595.

7. Lam TC, Hsieh F, Boyages J. The effects of postmastectomy adjuvant radiotherapy on immediate two-stage prosthetic breast reconstruction: A systematic review. *Plast Reconstr Surg* 2013;132(3):511–518.

20.2.2 Our approach (Europe)

Andre Spano, Stefano Avvedimento, and Secondo Folli

Implant-based breast reconstruction in patients that have received or for whom receiving postmastectomy radiotherapy is anticipated presents challenges due to higher rates of implant-related complications, including capsular contracture and implant extrusion that collectively result in a poor cosmetic outcome and have a significant negative impact on patient satisfaction.[1–3] Currently, there is a lack of consensus about surgical protocols and guidelines on timing of reconstructive procedures in relation to radiotherapy.

The authors prefer to perform the second stage of reconstruction (placement of the permanent implant) before postmastectomy radiotherapy. In a recent study, it has been shown that the risk of reconstructive failure is significantly higher for patients with irradiation of a tissue expander compared to patients with an irradiated permanent implant.[4,5] However, there are two circumstances when postmastectomy radiotherapy is not administered on permanent implants (i) in the case of delayed breast reconstruction when radiotherapy is carried-out before reconstruction has started and (ii) in case of immediate two-stage reconstruction when radiotherapy is given immediately after the placement of the expander to avoid any delay in initiation of radiotherapy that could be associated with an increase in locoregional recurrence of breast cancer.[6]

DELAYED RECONSTRUCTION

In patients who have received postmastectomy radiotherapy before reconstruction and who are not candidates for or decline autologous reconstruction, the authors use a multi-staged approach (**Figures 20.2.2.1 and 20.2.2.2**). Patients undergo serial sessions of fat grafting (from 1 to 4) with a minimum interval of 3 months between one and the other in order to prepare the recipient site for definitive reconstruction thus enhancing general skin quality and thickness of the mastectomy flaps and having a regenerative effect on the recipient site.[7–9]

Fat is usually harvested from the flanks, inner thigh, knees, or trochanteric area according to patient's characteristics and preferences. Harvesting of fat from the abdomen should be avoided at this stage since it can be a relative contraindication for any future salvage autologous procedure employing an abdominal flap. Local anesthesia with sedation is used with a tumescent technique, and fat harvest is done using a 3 mm two-holed blunt harvesting cannula attached to a 40-ml Luer-Lock syringe. The harvested fat is then centrifuged at 3000 rpm for 1 minute, discarded from the oil, blood, and infiltration liquids, and then transferred to 3-ml syringes. Before fat infiltration, scars and any fibrotic adherent tissue are released with a 16G needle to allow enlargement of the surface area of the recipient bed. Fat is injected using a blunt Coleman infiltration cannula attached to a 3-mm syringe between the overlying breast skin and the pectoralis major muscle in a multi-directional fashion.

After 3 months of each fat graft session, patients are evaluated in terms of skin elasticity, thickness of the mastectomy flap, fibrosis, atrophy, and pain. Once local conditions are favorable, a two-stage breast reconstruction is performed (expander insertion at the first stage and thereafter expander/implant exchange at the second stage).

IMMEDIATE RECONSTRUCTION

When an immediate reconstruction is planned, two basic principles are followed: (1) it is preferable to irradiate an implant rather than an expander[4,5] and (2) delays in radiotherapy of more than 6 months after the mastectomy should be avoided to reduce the risk of locoregional recurrence.[6]

For patients who undergo a one-stage implant-based reconstruction, radiotherapy is normally administered after mastectomy and insertion of the implant. Nevertheless, this subgroup represents a minority of patients in the authors' institution as they are more likely to need revision and have poorer aesthetic outcomes.

In two-stage implant reconstruction, it is important to initially assess the need for adjuvant chemotherapy. Under these circumstances, there is sufficient time to inflate the expander during the interval between chemotherapy cycles and to exchange for a permanent implant before postmastectomy radiation therapy starts. If chemotherapy is not indicated, a complete alloplastic reconstruction in two-stages is not feasible as this takes on average 9 months and would incur excessive delay with postmastectomy radiotherapy. In this case, postmastectomy radiotherapy is started 4 weeks after mastectomy and expander insertion.

Three months following completion of postmastectomy radiotherapy, serial sessions of free fat grafting are carried out (numbering from 1 to 4 according to the local tissue conditions). In some circumstances, deflating the expander before a lipofilling session can help to reduce tissue pressure on the graft and increase take. When an adequate result is judged to have been obtained (at least 3 months after the last fat graft procedure), exchange of the expander for the permanent implant is done. Through the lateral end of the previous mastectomy scar, a complete anterior capsulectomy is performed without removing the expander that remains attached to the capsule and helps with the identification of the correct plane of dissection. After removal of the capsule and the expander, release of the pectoralis major from the pectoralis minor and defining the inframammary fold are the key elements for obtaining complete tissue coverage of the implant. Particular attention should be paid to releasing any attachments of the pectoralis major infero-medially and dividing the superficial fascia at the level of the inframammary fold. The lower edge of the superficial fascia is then sutured to the chest wall musculature using continuous sutures of strong absorbable material to better define

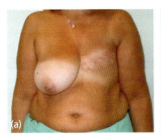 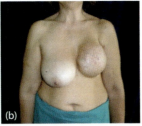 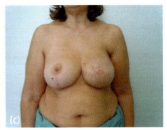

20.2.2.1 56-year-old patient that underwent delayed multi-staged reconstruction (three session of fat graft-expander/implant exchange) after previous mastectomy and radiotherapy for an invasive lobular carcinoma of the left breast. (a) 6 months after two sessions of fat graft to the left breast. (b) 3 months after three sessions of fat graft and left breast expander insertion. (c) 6 months after left breast expander replacement and contralateral reduction mammoplasty.

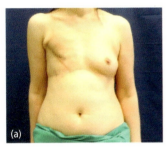 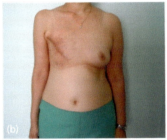 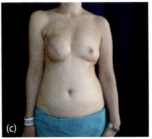 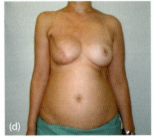

20.2.2.2 42-year-old patient that underwent right mastectomy and RT for a locally advanced breast cancer at another institution 1 year earlier. Complete reconstruction was done after three sessions of fat graft and expander/implant exchange. (a) Preoperative frontal view. (b) 3 months after three sessions of fat graft to the right breast. (c) 6 months after expander insertion and complete expansion of the right breast. (d) 6 months after expander/implant replacement of the right breast. Patient refused to undergo any procedure of symmetrization to the left breast.

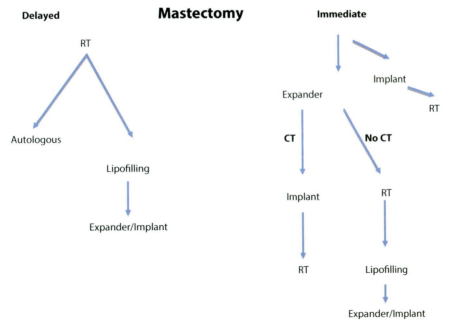

20.2.2.3 Algorithm of implant-based reconstruction in irradiated patients.

the new inframammary fold and to enhance the natural ptosis of the reconstructed breast.

Although the use of autologous tissue should be considered as the gold standard for reconstruction of a previously irradiated breast, the use of fat grafting after irradiation of a reconstructed breast can yield promising results. A multi-staged approach with serial sessions of fat grafting before (delayed reconstruction) or after (immediate reconstruction) expander placement in two-stage breast reconstruction reduces the risk of implant-related complications which in turn enhances the cosmetic outcomes and may reduce the incidence of capsular contracture (**Figure 20.2.2.3**).[10,11]

Notwithstanding this, one-stage breast reconstruction is generally discouraged in patients receiving postmastectomy radiotherapy due to higher rates of surgical revision and poorer cosmetic outcomes.[12]

REFERENCES

1. Barry M, Kell MR. Radiotherapy and breast reconstruction: A meta-analysis. *Breast Cancer Res Treat* 2011;127(1):15e22.
2. Cowen D, Gross E, Rouannet P, Teissier E, Ellis S, Resbeut M *et al.* Immediate post-mastectomy breast reconstruction followed by radiotherapy: Risk factors for complications. *Breast Cancer Res Treat* 2010;121(3):627e34.
3. Kronowitz SJ. Current status of implant-based breast reconstruction in patients receiving postmastectomy radiation therapy. *Plast Reconstr Surg.* 2012 ;130(4):513e–523e.
4. Nava MB, Pennati AE, Lozza L, Spano A, Zambetti M, Catanuto G. Outcome of different timings of radiotherapy in implant-based breast reconstructions. *Plast Reconstr Surg.* 2011;128(2):353–359.

5. Cordeiro PG, Albornoz CR, McCormick B, Hudis CA, Hu Q, Heerdt A, Matros E. What is the optimum timing of postmastectomy radiotherapy in two-stage prosthetic reconstruction: Radiation to the tissue expander or permanent implant? *Plast Reconstr Surg.* 2015;135(6):1509–1517.
6. Huang J, Barbera L, Brouwers M, Browman G, Mackillop WJ J Clin Oncol. Does delay in starting treatment affect the outcomes of radiotherapy? *A Systematic Review.* 2003; 21(3):555–563.
7. Sarfati I, Ihrai T, Kaufman G, Nos C, Clough KB. Adipose-tissue grafting to the post-mastectomy irradiated chest wall: Preparing the ground for implant reconstruction. *J Plast Reconstr Aesthet Surg.* 2011;64(9):1161–1166.
8. Rigotti G, Marchi A, Galie M *et al.* Clinical treatment of radiotherapy tissue damage by lipoaspirate transplant: A healing process mediated by adipose-derived adult stem cells. *Plast Reconstr Surg* 2007;119:1409e22.
9. Salgarello M, Visconti G, Barone-Adesi L. Fat grafting and breast reconstruction with implant: Another option for irradiated breast cancer patients. *Plast Reconstr Surg.* 2012;129(2):317–329.
10. Panettiere P, Marchetti L, Accorsi D. The serial free fat transfer in irradiated prosthetic breast reconstructions. *Aesth Plast Surg* (2009) 33:695–700.
11. Serra-Renom JM, Muñoz-Olmo JL, Serra-Mestre JM. Fat grafting in postmastectomy breast reconstruction with expanders and prostheses in patients who have received radiotherapy: Formation of new subcutaneous tissue. *Plast Reconstr Surg.* 2010;125(1):12–18.
12. Roostaeian J, Pavone L, Da Lio A, Lipa J, Festekjian J, Crisera C. Immediate placement of implants in breast reconstruction: Patient selection and outcomes. *Plast Reconstr Surg.* 2011;127(4):1407–1416.

20.3 IMPACT OF ACELLULAR DERMAL MATRICES (ADMs) AND FAT GRAFTING ON IRRADIATED BREAST RECONSTRUCTION

20.3.1 My approach (USA)

Steven J. Kronowitz

Breast implants can develop severe contracture from radiation therapy and subsequently require excision of breast skin with loss of cosmetic benefit from skin-sparing mastectomy. These secondary reconstructions often necessitate a complex flap procedure for salvage, usually with a suboptimal outcome. Consensus within the published literature is that irradiation generally increases the rate of reconstructive complications, including capsular contracture. The negative impact of irradiation is especially pronounced for implant-based reconstruction with complication rates upward of 40% or greater. Up to one-third of patients who receive irradiation of breast implant-based reconstructions develop Baker grade III or IV capsular contracture. Anecdotal and preliminary data suggest that use of acellular dermal matrices (ADM) may contribute to a reduced frequency of capsular contracture. However, much of the enthusiasm for this approach has been tempered by costs and additional complications.

In 2014, Losken and colleagues studied the effect of radiation on ADM and capsule formation in breast reconstruction.[1] They evaluated clinical outcomes and performed a histologic analysis from the peri-prosthetic capsules of six patients. Irradiated native capsules had more elastin fibers and a 2-fold increase in cellular infiltrate. However, there were no differences in cellular counts between the native capsule and ADM capsule. Irradiation of the ADM capsule did not alter the architecture or cellular components of the ADM capsules. Irradiated ADMs had similar cell counts as non-irradiated ADM, and cell counts were higher in irradiated native capsules than in irradiated ADM. Cellular counts in the peri-implant capsule are greatly increased by irradiation.

Although no difference in cell counts between native and ADM capsule was observed, architectural makeup showed a 5-fold reduction in macrophages and 2.5-fold increase in elastin in ADM capsules compared with native capsules with minimal histologic differences between irradiated and non-irradiated ADM. Irradiated ADM showed less peri-implant inflammation and non-vascular alpha smooth actin then irradiated capsules. The authors concluded that tissue expander breast reconstruction with radiation is associated with a high rate of failure, but this is not directly caused by ADM.

Patients receiving radiation after ADM reconstructions have significantly higher complication rates than non-irradiated ADM reconstructions. Although reports vary from 4- to 11-fold increase in rates of complications, these are most likely related to the radiation itself and not the presence of ADM. Interesting scientific findings from animal studies include the following: (a) no difference in ADM thickness between irradiated and non-irradiated ADM, (b) diminished cellular invasion for irradiated implants with ADM compared to no irradiation, and (c) radiation-related inflammation is decreased by ADM, which also delays or diminishes pseudoepithelium formation in irradiated implant breast reconstruction.[2–5] However, many of these changes occur in the short term without evidence of any long-term impact on implant capsule formation. Furthermore, postmastectomy radiation therapy does not appear to decrease incorporation of the ADM into the undersurface of the breast skin envelope (**Figure 20.3.1.1**).

If ADM provides healing advantages and might reduce occurrence or severity of capsular contracture, it would seem logical to achieve complete coverage of the implant with ADM rather than limiting this to the lower pole of the breast reconstruction (which is most commonly practiced). Over the last 8 years, the author has utilized complete coverage of a tissue expander or implant with ADM with a large sheet of ADM. In some patients, especially those undergoing nipple-sparing mastectomy, the prosthesis is placed in a prepectoral position, while in other patients, the pectoralis major muscle is sewn over the

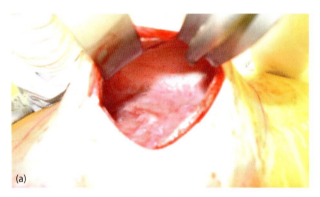

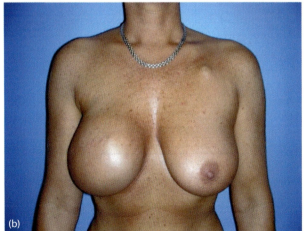

20.3.1.1 ADM integration after postmastectomy radiation therapy. (a) Intraoperative view of radiated breast skin with integrated human acellular dermal matrix (HADM). (b) Postoperative after implant placement into HADM-lined breast envelope. Contralateral symmetry procedure planned.

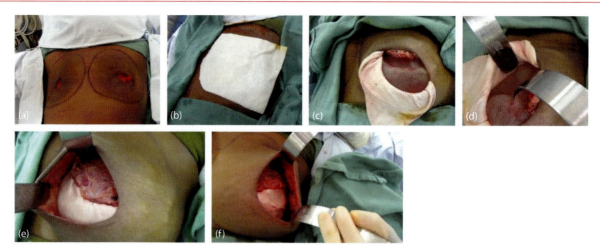

20.3.1.2 The Kronowitz expander insertion technique (intraoperative views). (a) After the completion of bilateral skin-sparing mastectomy. (b) HADM contoured to footprint of the left breast and chest wall. (c and d) The HADM has been sutured to the medial and inferior chest wall. The tissue expander has placed on the chest wall using suture-secure tabs and filled with saline. Notice the pectoralis major muscle has been released from its inferior, lateral, and medial (below 3rd intercoastal space [ICS]) attachments. (e and f) The HADM has now also been sutured to the superior and lateral chest wall providing complete coverage overlying the tissue expander. The pectoralis muscle under full excursion has been sutured to the HADM in a vest-over-pants manner. Notice that there is no tension placed on the breast skin envelope.

ADM in a vest-over-pants fashion (**Figure 20.3.1.2**) (the reasoning behind this technique is that, if ADM decreases capsular contracture, then complete coverage should decrease the incidence of severe capsular contracture).

ADM also permits intraoperative saline filling of the expander, which facilitates a more ptotic-shaped breast after radiotherapy. This subsequently enables placement of an implant directly into the breast skin pocket. ADM-enabled intraoperative saline filling of the expander also avoids the need for postoperative expansion and delayed initiation of radiotherapy in patients who receive neoadjuvant chemotherapy. The ADM not only increases the thickness of mastectomy skin flaps directly, but use of intraoperative saline filling avoids potential compromise of already thin mastectomy skin flaps (which can be treacherous in patients undergoing radiotherapy). At stage 2, during exchange for a permanent implant, the thicker radiated mastectomy skin will provide better implant coverage than without ADM. The thicker mastectomy skin flaps attained with ADM along with fat grafting has decreased the need for employment of a flap (such as latissimus dorsi flap) for implant-based breast reconstruction when radiotherapy is anticipated. Nonetheless, an equivalent safety profile has not yet been conclusively shown.

Use of ADM can provide other advantages for implant-based breast reconstruction. Placement of ADM with a tissue expander at the first stage of a two-stage implant-based breast reconstruction creates a tissue plane for injection of fat grafts into the lower mastectomy skin flap during stage 2 (exchange for permanent implant). This is not always possible in the absence of ADM. Fat grafting shows promise in terms of decreasing potential morbidity and improving outcomes of implant-based reconstruction in the setting of radiation.

So, what happens when we perform fat grafting in the breasts of our patients? The healing properties of lipoaspirate have been studied in irradiated tissue models. Thus, in 2007, Rigotti elucidated that lipoaspirate promoted healing of irradiated tissue by a process mediated by adipose-derived adult stem cells.[6] Ultrastructural analyses of the lipoaspirate revealed preservation of the stromal vascular component, but healthy adipocytes were virtually absent. The cytologic characterization of the lipoaspirate by in vitro expansion of the mesenchymal stem cells corresponded to that of bone marrow-derived mesenchymal stem cells. Rigotti injected lipoaspirate into radio-damaged subcutaneous tissue of humans, that was fibrotic and microangiopathic. Photomicrographs of subcutaneous tissue taken at 1 month and 2 months after lipofilling damaged irradiated tissue were characterized by signs of both removal of the injected material and regeneration. Two months after treatment, any injected material had completely gone, with complete absence of cellular debris. The overall picture indicated that regenerative phenomena with healing of irradiated fibrotic skin were at an advanced stage. At 4 months to 6 months after treatment, adipocytes appeared normal and microvessels exhibited normal ultrastructure. Finally, at 1 year or more after treatment, the picture was essentially unchanged with gross and microscopic evidence of regenerative changes to the irradiated fibrotic tissue and healing of an osteoradionecrotic wound.

Probably the most important question is whether fat grafting increases the rate of local recurrence of breast cancer. Although fat grafting continues to gain in popularity, little is known about interactions between grafted fat and the prior oncological environment. The "tumor stromal interaction" or paracrine action of the injected fat may affect recurrence rates. This applies especially to ipsilateral breast tumor recurrence following conservation therapy, where dormant tumor cells may exist within the breast parenchyma after completion of treatment. Hypothetically, the transfer of adipose-derived stem cells or adipose-derived mesenchymal stem cells could induce silent tumor cells to reproduce and predispose to recurrence. In vitro and animal studies are conflicting and show both positive and negative associations with breast cancer cell proliferation. To date, no clinical case series or studies have clearly demonstrated any association between fat grafting and breast cancer recurrence.

The most recent of these studies was published by the author and colleagues.[7] Although many plastic surgeons perform autologous fat grafting (lipofilling) as part of breast reconstruction after oncologic surgery, it has not been established whether this increases the risk of breast cancer recurrence. The study in question assessed the risk of locoregional (LRR) and systemic recurrence in patients undergoing lipofilling for breast reconstruction. The authors identified all patients who underwent segmental or total mastectomy for breast cancer (719 breasts), breast cancer risk reduction, or benign disease (305 cancer-free breasts) followed by breast reconstruction with lipofilling as an adjunct or primary procedure. A group of matched patients were also identified who had breast cancer treated with segmental or total mastectomy followed by reconstruction without lipofilling (670 breasts; controls). The probability of LRR was estimated by the Kaplan-Meier method. The mean follow-up times after mastectomy were 60 months for the cases, 44 months for the controls, and 73 months for the cancer-free breasts. LRR occurred in 1.3% (9/719) of the cases and 2.4% (16/670) of the controls. Breast cancer did not develop in any cancer-free breast. The cumulative 5-year LRR rates were 1.6% and 4.1%, for cases and controls, respectively. Systemic recurrence occurred in 2.4% of the cases and 3.6% of the controls ($p = 0.514$). There was no primary breast cancer in healthy breasts reconstructed with lipofilling. The results of this controlled study showed no increase in LRR, systemic recurrence, or second breast cancer and support the oncologic safety of lipofilling in breast reconstruction.

Scientific evidence therefore indicates that ADM used in conjunction with fat grafting is a promising method for improving the outcomes and safety of implant-based breast reconstruction, especially in the context of postmastectomy radiotherapy. The author employs a technique of interval fat grafting overlying the in situ tissue expander following radiotherapy, but before exchange for the permanent breast implant. This potentially holds great promise for improving the safety of two-stage breast implant reconstruction in the setting of radiotherapy (**Figure 20.3.1.3**). The fat graft is injected directly overlying the tissue expander on top of the ADM (placed during expander placement) after completion of radiotherapy. Several months are allowed for maturation of the injected fat graft within the irradiated breast skin, and therefore implant exchange is performed under optimal healing conditions. This will decrease the potential for peri-operative implant-related complications such as implant exposure and infection. Application of science to improve our outcomes in breast reconstruction will allow surgeons to continue achieving optimal outcomes

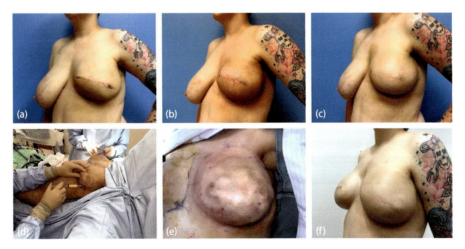

20.3.1.3 Kronowitz interval fat grafting. 35-year-old female with stage III left breast cancer who desires implant-based breast reconstruction. (a) Postoperative view: 4 weeks after placement of a HADM/subpectoral saline-filled tissue expander. (b) 2 weeks after the completion of postmastectomy radiation therapy. Approximately ½ the saline fill volume was removed from the tissue expander just prior to the initiation of radiation therapy. Shown is after re-instillation of the pre-radiation saline fill volume back into the tissue expander. (c) 3 months after the completion of radiation therapy with the expander in situ on chest wall. (d) Interval fat grafting being performed 3 months after radiation overlying the entirety of the tissue expander. (e) Intraoperative after completion of interval fat grafting. (f) Postoperative: 3 months after interval fat grafting. Ready for exchange of tissue expander for implant.

despite the challenges of newer oncological treatments in the years ahead.

REFERENCES

1. Moyer H, Pinell-White X, Losken A. The effect of radiation on acellular dermal matrix and capsule formation in breast reconstruction: Clinical outcomes and histologic analysis. *Plastic & Reconstructive Surgery.* 133(2):214–221, 2014.
2. Garcia O, Scott J. Analysis of acellular dermal matrix integration and revascularization following tissue expander breast reconstruction in a clinically relevant large-animal model. *Plastic & Reconstructive Surgery.* 131(5):741e–751e, 2013.
3. Dubin MG, Feldman M, Ibrahim HZ, et al. Allograft dermal implant (AlloDerm) in a previously irradiated field. *Laryngoscope.* 2000 ;110(6):934–937.
4. Ibrahim HZ, Kwiatkowski TJ, Montone KT, et al. Effects of external beam radiation on the allograft dermal implant. *Otolaryngol—Head and Neck Surgery.* 2000;122(2):189–194.
5. Komorowska-Timek E, Oberg KC, Timek TA, Gridley DS, Miles DA. The effect of alloderm envelopes on periprosthetic capsule formation with and without radiation. *Plastic and Reconstructive Surgery.* 2009;123(3):807–816.
6. Rigotti G, Marchi A, Galie M, Baroni G, Benati D, Krampera M, Pasini A, Sbarbati A. Clinical treatment of radiotherapy tissue damage by lipoaspirate transplant: A healing process mediated by adipose-derived adult stem cells. *Plastic and Reconstructive Surgery.* 2007;119(5):1409–1422.
7. Kronowitz, SJ, Cosman CM, Liu, J et al., Lipofilling of the breast does not increase the risk of recurrence of breast cancer: A matched controlled study. *Plastic and Reconstructive Surgery.* 2016;137(2):385–393.

20.3.2 Our approach (Europe)

Lee Martin and Sonia Bathla

Between 2000 and 2012, immediate reconstruction in the United Kingdom increased from 13% to 28%. Implant-based breast reconstruction is the most common approach to reconstruction of the breast, and latissimus dorsi flap-based reconstruction has become less favorable in recent years.[1] The use of either biological or synthetic acellular dermal matrices (ADMs) potentially enables immediate one-stage implant-based reconstruction by preserving the skin envelope and reproducing a natural ptosis with full implant coverage. These techniques using ADM are gaining popularity, despite limited long-term outcome data and concerns regarding high rates of complications. National guidelines (United Kingdom) recommend these techniques for patients with a normal body mass index, small to moderate volume breasts, and good soft tissue cover.[2] Increased complications have been noted in those patients undergoing axillary node clearance and when mastectomy volumes exceed 600 g. The use of ADMs in the United Kingdom is being prospectively audited as part of the iBRA study.

The indications for postmastectomy radiotherapy are increasing; radiotherapy has been shown to reduce locoregional recurrence by up to 28% and increase survival by at least 5%. Postmastectomy radiotherapy is indicated for high-risk cancers (tumors > 5 cm, $\geq$ 4 positive axillary nodes, involved resection margins, or 10-year locoregional recurrence risk of >20%). The results of the SUPREMO trial may further expand these indications (1–3 positive nodes and 10-year locoregional recurrence risk of <15%). This especially applies to pre-menopausal patients, the group who may psychologically benefit the most from immediate reconstruction.[3,4] The use of skin-sparing techniques may also result in increased use of postmastectomy radiotherapy depending on the radiation oncologists' view of close or involved anterior and posterior margins. The deleterious effects of postmastectomy radiotherapy on both implant and autologous flap-based reconstructions are well-documented with increased rates of complications and corresponding decreased patient satisfaction.

Professor Robert Mansel famously stated, "we have soft breasts, but no hard data." The senior author's own opinion is about informed patient choice with personal practice based on individual interpretation of published studies. However, the data are heterogenous for methods of implant-based breast reconstruction and timing of radiotherapy and conclusions difficult to draw. The authors have used both biological (Strattice) and synthetic ADM (TiLoop – titanium coated polypropylene mesh) with comparable and acceptable complication rates, low implant loss rates, and no significant delays in adjuvant therapy. TiLoop is cost-effective and is the authors' preferred material. Patient satisfaction and aesthetic results are better when using ADM than with standard expander techniques, and this is now the authors' standard method for all implant-based reconstruction. The use of ADM allows for direct-to-implant reconstruction, although for those patients likely to require radiotherapy, an anatomical expander with an integral port is used. The timing of radiotherapy can impact on outcomes; postmastectomy radiotherapy after placement of a permanent implant is associated with a complication rate of up to 33.3%, but acceptable cosmetic outcomes in 51% of patients[5,6] (most patients stating they would choose implant-based breast reconstruction again). Nonetheless, studies have described a significantly increased rate of revisional surgery and lower aesthetic scores in patients with an irradiated permanent implant.[7,8] Irradiating an expander and then waiting for the radiotherapy effects to settle is best suited to the authors' practice from the perspective of service delivery and allows for potential revision when undergoing exchange for a definitive implant.

Management of a tissue expander during radiotherapy is controversial. A study in rabbits suggested that deflation of the expander prior to radiotherapy increased the risk of skin damage.[9] However, there is concern that an inflated expander renders radiotherapy planning and accurate targeting more difficult, particularly on the left side. The use of an integral port may also result in radiotherapy scattering. Management of an expander should be based on local discussion with clinical oncologists. In the authors' unit, planning and delivery of radiotherapy is to the fully inflated expander. The presence of an implant or expander (including ADM) during postmastectomy radiotherapy does not impair efficacy of radiotherapy in terms of locoregional recurrence.[10,11]

Denying a patient reconstruction based on the need for postmastectomy radiotherapy is unnecessary, provided the patient understands and accepts the effects it can have. Although implant-based breast reconstruction may not give as good aesthetic results as autologous breast reconstruction, it is a shorter procedure which can be converted to an autologous reconstruction once the effects of radiotherapy have stabilized. Patients should be aware of the potential risks of increased complications (39.6%–67.5%)[12] and a two-fold elevated risk of re-operation. There is also an implant loss rate of 30% with potential long-term poor aesthetic outcomes. Implant loss is significantly higher in patients with T3 or T4 tumors and those with positive axillary nodes[13] who are the group most likely to receive postmastectomy radiotherapy.[14,15] Radiotherapy also has a deleterious effect on autologous tissue which can produce poor long-term aesthetic results. For these reasons, the authors would rather not irradiate a flap. Patients must be aware that access to autologous reconstruction can be available once adjuvant treatment is complete. It is important to empower patients at a psychologically distressing time. Although 50% of implant-based reconstructions will require revision at 5 years, an equal number of patients will find their reconstruction acceptable. The use of ADM-assisted reconstruction may improve these figures with optimal skin envelope preservation and ptosis, combined with autologous fat grafting.

The use of autologous fat grafting in the setting of post-mastectomy radiotherapy shows promising results. Diego Ribuffo and colleagues propose a protocol whereby expanders are placed under full muscle coverage at the time of mastectomy, and then rapidly expanded over a period of 2 months (100 cc per week) to full volume. Standard post-mastectomy radiotherapy is then delivered without deflation and lipofilling performed 6 weeks after completing radiotherapy. Implant exchange and low anterior capsulectomy is then performed after 3 months. These authors reported improved patient satisfaction and reduced major complication rates. Autologous fat grafting in the delayed-immediate approach has also been shown to improve cosmetic outcomes in the irradiated implant-based reconstructed breast.[16] The authors currently reserve lipomodeling for those patients who require additional volume or for treatment of radiotherapy effects of radiotherapy in implant-based reconstruction. It has been suggested immediate lipomodeling of the mastectomy flaps can improve outcomes (Michael Dixon, personal communication).

It must be remembered that patients undergoing radiotherapy are likely to be young and at higher risk for distant metastatic disease. It is the senior author's opinion that no patients should be refused reconstruction even when objective results may be suboptimal. The most important outcome is quality of life, which takes into account the patient's overall well-being and subjective view.

REFERENCES

1. Mennie J 2014: HES NHS data 2012.
2. ADM Assisted breast reconstruction procedures: Joint guidelines from the ABS & BAPRAS. *EJSO* 39 (2013) 425–429.
3. NICE guidelines CG80: Early and locally advanced breast cancer: Diagnosis and treatment. 2009.
4. SUPREMO – www.supremo-trial.com
5. Jhaveri JD, Rush SC, Kostroff K, Derisi D, Farber LA, Maurer VE, Bosworth JL. Clinical outcomes of postmastectomy radiation therapy after immediate breast reconstruction. *Int J Radiat Oncol Biol Phys.*; 2008 72(3):859–865.
6. Cordeiro, Peter G M.D.; Albornoz, Claudia R M.D., M.Sc.; McCormick, Beryl M.D.; Hu, Qunying M.D.; Van Zee, Kimberly M.D. The impact of postmastectomy radiotherapy on two-stage implant breast reconstruction: An analysis of long-term surgical outcomes, aesthetic results, and satisfaction over 13 years. *Breast J* 2014; 134:588–595.

7. Whitfield GA, Horan G, Irwin MS, Malata CM, Wishart GC, Wilson CB. Incidence of severe capsular contracture following implant-based immediate breast reconstruction with or without postoperative chest wall radiotherapy using 40 Gray in 15 fractions. *Radiother Oncol.*; 2009 90(1):141–147. Epub 2008 Nov 1. [PubMed: 18977547].
8. Hvilsom GB, Hölmich LR, Steding-Jessen M, Frederiksen K, Henriksen TF, Lipworth L, McLaughlin J, Elberg JJ, Damsgaard TE, Friis S. Delayed breast implant reconstruction: Is radiation therapy associated with capsular contracture or reoperations? *Ann Plast Surg.* 2011 E-pub.
9. Celet Ozden B, Guven E, Aslay I, Kemikler G, Olgac V, Soluk Tekesin M, Serarslan B, Tumerdem Ulug B, Biligin Karabulut A, Arinici A, Emekli U. Does partial expander deflation exacerbate the adverse effects of radiotherapy in two-stage breast reconstruction? *World J Surg Oncol* 2012; 10: 44.
10. Kronowitz SJ, Lam C, Terefe W, Hunt KK, Kuerer HM, Valero V, Lance S, Robb GL, Feng L, Buchholz TA. A multidisciplinary protocol for planned skin-preserving delayed breast reconstruction for patients with locally advanced breast cancer requiring postmastectomy radiation therapy: 3 year follow up. *Plast Reconstr Surg.*; 2011 127(6):2154–2166.
11. Kutcher L, Ballangrud A, Cordeiro PG, McCormick B, Hunt M, Van Zee KJ, Hudis C, Beal K. Post mastectomy intensity modulated radiation following immediate expander-implant reconstruction. *Radiother Oncol.*; 2010 94(3):319–323.
12. Kronowitz SJ. Current status of implant based breast reconstruction in patients receiving postmastectomy radiation therapy. *Plast Reconstr Surg.* 2012 130(4):513e–523e.
13. Gross E, Hannoun-Levi JM, Rouanet P, Houvenaeghel G, Teissier E, Ellis S, Resbeut M, Tallet A, Vaini Cowen V, Azria D, Cowen D. [Evaluation of immediate breast reconstruction and radiotherapy: Factors associated with complications]. *Cancer Radiother.*; 2010 14(8):704–710. Epub 2010 Aug 2. French. [PubMed: 20674442 – kron ref 8].
14. Baschnagel AM, Shah C, Wilkinson JB, Dekhne N, Arthur DW, Vicini FA. Failure rate and cosmesis of immediate tissue expander/implant breast reconstruction after post mastectomy irradiation. *Clin Breast Cancer* 2012; 12: 428–432.
15. Pestana IA, Campbell DC, Bhart G, Thompson JT. Factors affecting complications in radiated breast reconstruction. *Ann Plast Surg* 2013; 70: 542–545.
16. Panettiere P, Marchchetti L, Accorsi D. The serial free fat transfer in irradiated prosthetic breast reconstructions. *Aesthetic Plast Surg* 2009; 33(5): 695–700.

EDITORIAL COMMENTARY

The ability to reconstruct a whole breast solely using fat grafting techniques is desirable and research is advancing rapidly in this field. As Dr. Rubin points out, the current issues pertaining to reconstruction of a breast exclusively with fat grafting include the need for multiple-staged procedures and unpredictable absorption. Furthermore, although external expansion has been shown to be helpful in this process, this can be associated with problems of patient compliance and the lack of health insurance reimbursement. In addition, those with expertise in fat grafting alone (including Dr. Delay) often utilize a thoracic advancement flap along with multiple stages of fat grafting. Not only does this chapter include Delay's eloquent technique of fat grafting to reconstruct a breast in its entirety, but describes the amazing science underpinning these techniques and visions for the future. There is no doubt that breast reconstructive surgeons will soon be capable of harvesting fat and/or mesenchymal stems cells, enhancing or multiplying these cells, and subsequently storing them for serial office-based injection at a future date. Researchers are now able to clonally expand mesenchymal stem cells in vitro, which along with the vascularized stromal component of the lipoaspirate may be sufficient for breast growth, without the need for storage of the adipocytes for serial injections. Whichever techniques for enhancement prove to be successful in achieving whole breast reconstruction using lipoaspirate components alone, these are likely to become a principle method for routine breast reconstruction in the future.

21

Fat grafting exclusively for whole breast reconstruction

AT A GLANCE

The ability to create a whole breast purely from a process of repeat fat grafting is a huge advance in breast reconstruction. Nonetheless, despite impressive outcomes from several prominent surgeons, others have struggled to achieve satisfactory results, and this topic of exclusive fat grafting remains controversial. The use of the Brava® device (negative suction applied to chest wall) may significantly impact the engraftment of fat within the breast being reconstructed. This concept is interesting and may have implications in terms of reconstruction in other regions of the body. Some investigators strive to improve engraftment by the addition of growth factors to in vitro clonally expanded stem cell lines. In addition, the creation of three-dimensional scaffolds has received much attention and may at some stage in the future permit construction of a genuinely bioengineered breast.

21.1 OUR APPROACH (EUROPE)

Gilles Tousson and Emmanuel Delay

Introduction

Breast reconstruction has always been challenging surgery, and technical improvements coupled with creativity have been critical tools for breast plastic surgeons in the common goal of achieving the best possible result with the least scarring and functional impairment.

The ultimate achievement would be construction of a new breast mound without use of either foreign material nor any scarring from flaps. Patient selection is the key to success for these techniques, and the optimal results are only achievable if the following conditions are met:

- A small to moderate contralateral breast (low projection, cup A or B)
- Sufficient thoracic skin laxity to allow for an abdominal advancement flap technique to be performed

- Adequate areas of fat excess to be harvested in multiple stages
- A willing patient who is strongly motivated to accept multiple stage breast reconstruction

Patients, methods, and surgical technique

The reconstructed breast volume is achieved exclusively with the use of autologous fat (no implant or muscular flap is used). The principles of fat harvesting, processing, and injection are similar to those already described earlier in this section in delayed reconstruction, we firstly execute a thoraco-abdominal skin advancement flap technique[1] to expand the skin envelope and restore the breast footprint (submammary and lateral crease in particular). This technique can also be offered for immediate breast reconstruction, where the skin envelope is preserved and the shape of the breast is therefore improved.

During this same stage, the first fat transfer is performed within the pectoralis major muscle and the décolleté area (rather than beneath the undermined skin flaps).

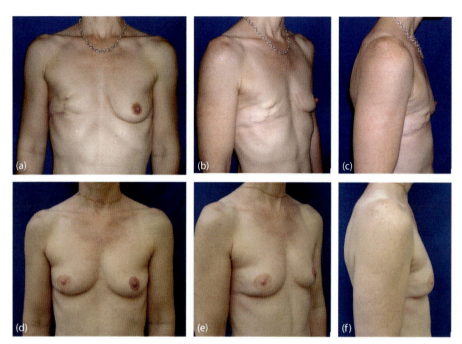

21.1.1 (a–c) Patient awaiting right breast reconstruction after an inverted "T" scar mastectomy and (d–f) final result after three sessions of lipomodeling (with a total 443 cm³ of purified fat). Contralateral p-xie and nipple-areola complex (NAC) reconstruction (nipple sharing and tattoo).

Multiple subsequent stages are necessary to achieve the desired volume and shape. Contralateral symmetrization is also undertaken during one of the last transfer sessions. A mean number of three (one to five) sessions are planned in typical cases with a minimum period of 3 months between subsequent procedures. Fat grafting procedures are usually carried out in a day case hospital setting (**Figure 21.1.1**).

It is crucial to adequately assess the skin quality at the mastectomy site and the potential fat donor sites for each particular patient. The fat transfer technique must be carried out with utmost care to maximize the transferred volume per session while minimizing rates of oil cyst formation and fat necrosis. In the authors' experience, a mean volume of 600 mL of purified fat must be transferred throughout the multiple stages for a unilateral breast reconstruction. Analysis of their first series[2] shows that the volume of transferred fat is nearly twice the amount used with latissimus reconstruction to obtain the same final volume. This is probably due to the lack of an adequate mechanical and vascular scaffold that is associated with a muscular flap.

CONCLUSION

The ability to reconstruct a full breast mound exclusively using multiple fat injections is testimony to the efficiency of fat transfer techniques. Most pathologic and morphologic conditions of the breast (including malignancy, hypoplasia, malformation, and chest wall deformities) can potentially benefit from the use of fat transfer either in association with other reconstructive techniques or as a stand-alone procedure.

REFERENCES

1. Delay E, Jorquera F, Pasi P, Gratadour AC. Autologous latissimus breast reconstruction in association with abdominal advancement flap: A new refinement in breast reconstruction. *Ann Plast Surg* 1999;42:67–75.
2. Delaporte T, Delay E, Tousson G et al. Reconstruction mammaire par transfert graisseux exclusif. A propos de 15 cas consécutifs. *Ann Chir Plast Esthet* 2009;54(4):303–316.

21.2 STEM CELL EXPANSION AND GROWTH FACTOR STIMULATION

Adam J. Reid

Despite refinements of clinical technique, objective measurements of fat resorption still approach 50% in large volume fat grafting for breast reconstruction.[1] Focus has now shifted to cellular manipulation of adipose tissue and its components in order to improve fat survival and feasibility of clinical translation.

Digestion of human lipoaspirate generates a pellet of cells termed the "stromal vascular fraction," which contains multipotent adipose-derived mesenchymal stem cells alongside fibroblasts, inflammatory, and hematopoietic cells.[2] Stromal vascular fraction-enriched fat grafting has been used clinically with reported success in cosmetic augmentation[3] and in reconstruction following breast-conserving oncological resections.[4] While these predominantly subjective studies utilize unrefined stromal vascular fraction cell populations, there is now good objective evidence for the use of laboratory expanded adipose-derived mesenchymal stem cells to improve small volume fat graft survival (greater than fourfold) in posterior arm deposits versus unenriched controls.[5]

In order to exploit adipose-derived mesenchymal stem cells fully, we need to understand better the complex interactions between adipose-derived mesenchymal stem cells, adipocytes, and the micro-environment. An exciting prospect is the potential selection of adipose-derived mesenchymal stem cell subpopulations with improved proliferative, adipogenic, angiogenic, or ischemia-resistant properties. Adipose-derived mesenchymal stem cell surface marker expression is of particular interest, a minimum preset of CD73/90/105 positivity in the absence of other key markers has been historically accepted as Mesenchymal Stem Cell (MSC) defining,[6] but the role of others is less clear. Sorting cell populations for the adhesion factor CD34 has demonstrated improved adipogenesis in vitro.[7-9] Other strategies include gene transfection of adipose-derived mesenchymal stem cell populations[10] and the manipulation of 3-D scaffolds to facilitate adipose-derived mesenchymal stem cell:adipocyte interaction.

Optimizing culture conditions for laboratory adipose-derived mesenchymal stem cell expansion with respect to proliferation, adipogenesis, and safety of clinical translation are critical. Use of xenogeneic animal-derived products, including bovine-derived serum, may carry a risk of transmitting infective disease or potentiate ethical conflict.[11] Commercially available serum-free xeno-free media alternatives have been shown to maintain multipotency and proliferation rates.[12,13] Others have adapted completely xeno-free protocols.[14] Human-derived alternatives including umbilical cord extracts,[15] platelet-rich plasma,[16] and pooled human platelet lysates[17] have demonstrated a variable response with equivalent or markedly reduced population doubling times, although platelet-rich plasma may improve adipogenic differentiation.[18]

The safety profile of this very promising therapy is yet to be fully elucidated; however, recent experimental studies suggest adipose-derived mesenchymal stem cells may incite breast cancer cells to potentiate a metastatic phenotype in vitro[19] and in vivo.[20] Oncological risk and the clinical efficacy of stem cell treatments will be best addressed with well-designed clinical studies; meanwhile, further academic and industrial laboratory-based research is required to demonstrate the safety and cost-effectiveness of these stem cell adjuvant treatments.

REFERENCES

1. Choi M, Small K, Levovitz C, Lee C, Fadl A, Karp NS. The volumetric analysis of fat graft survival in breast reconstruction. *Plast Reconstr Surg.* 2013, 131: 185–191.
2. Zuk PA, Zhu M, Mizuno H et al. Multilineage cells from human adipose tissue: Implications for cell-based therapies. *Tissue Eng.* 2001, 7: 211–228.
3. Yoshimura K, Sato K, Aoi N, Kurita M, Hirohi T, Harii K. Cell-assisted lipotransfer for cosmetic breast augmentation: Supportive use of adipose-derived stem/stromal cells. *Aesthetic Plast Surg.* 2008, 32: 48–55; discussion 6–7.
4. Perez-Cano R, Vranckx JJ, Lasso JM et al. Prospective trial of adipose-derived regenerative cell (ADRC)-enriched fat grafting for partial mastectomy defects: The RESTORE-2 trial. *Eur J Surg Oncol.* 2012, 38: 382–389.
5. Kolle SF, Fischer-Nielsen A, Mathiasen AB et al. Enrichment of autologous fat grafts with ex-vivo expanded adipose tissue-derived stem cells for graft survival: A randomised placebo-controlled trial. *Lancet.* 2013, 382: 1113–1120.
6. Dominici M, Le Blanc K, Mueller I et al. Minimal criteria for defining multipotent mesenchymal stromal cells. The international society for cellular therapy position statement. *Cytotherapy.* 2006, 8: 315–317.
7. De Francesco F, Tirino V, Desiderio V et al. Human CD34/CD90 ASCs are capable of growing as sphere clusters, producing high levels of VEGF and forming capillaries. *PLoS One.* 2009, 4: e6537.
8. Doornaert MA, Declercq H, Stillaert F et al. Intrinsic dynamics of the fat graft: In vitro interactions between the main cell actors. *Plast Reconstr Surg.* 2012, 130: 1001–1019.
9. Suga H, Matsumoto D, Eto H et al. Functional implications of CD34 expression in human adipose-derived stem/progenitor cells. *Stem Cells Dev.* 2009, 18: 1201–1210.
10. Lu F, Li J, Gao J et al. Improvement of the survival of human autologous fat transplantation by using VEGF-transfected adipose-derived stem cells. *Plast Reconstr Surg.* 2009, 124: 1437–1446.
11. Erickson G, Bolin S, Landgraf J. Viral contamination of fetal bovine serum used for tissue culture: Risks and concerns. *Dev Biol Stand.* 1991, 75: 173.
12. Lindroos B, Boucher S, Chase L et al. Serum-free, xeno-free culture media maintain the proliferation rate and multipotentiality of adipose stem cells in vitro. *Cytotherapy.* 2009, 11: 958–972.

13. Patrikoski M, Juntunen M, Boucher S et al. Development of fully defined xeno-free culture system for the preparation and propagation of cell therapy-compliant human adipose stem cells. *Stem Cell Res Ther.* 2013, 4: 27.

14. Escobedo-Lucea C, Bellver C, Gandia C et al. A xenogeneic-free protocol for isolation and expansion of human adipose stem cells for clinical uses. *PLoS One.* 2013, 8: e67870.

15. Kim SM, Moon SH, Lee Y, Kim GJ, Chung HM, Choi YS. Alternative xeno-free biomaterials derived from human umbilical cord for the self-renewal ex-vivo expansion of mesenchymal stem cells. *Stem Cells Dev.* 2013, 22(22): 3025–3038.

16. Kocaoemer A, Kern S, Kluter H, Bieback K. Human AB serum and thrombin-activated platelet-rich plasma are suitable alternatives to fetal calf serum for the expansion of mesenchymal stem cells from adipose tissue. *Stem Cells.* 2007, 25: 1270–1278.

17. Trojahn Kolle SF, Oliveri RS, Glovinski PV et al. Pooled human platelet lysate versus fetal bovine serum-investigating the proliferation rate, chromosome stability and angiogenic potential of human adipose tissue-derived stem cells intended for clinical use. *Cytotherapy.* 2013, 15: 1086–1097.

18. Cervelli V, Scioli MG, Gentile P et al. Platelet-rich plasma greatly potentiates insulin-induced adipogenic differentiation of human adipose-derived stem cells through a serine/threonine kinase Akt-dependent mechanism and promotes clinical fat graft maintenance. *Stem Cells Transl Med.* 2012, 1: 206–220.

19. Kuhbier JW, Bucan V, Reimers K et al. Observed changes in the morphology and phenotype of breast cancer cells in direct co-culture with adipose-derived stem cells. *Plast Reconstr Surg.* 2014, 134: 414–423.

20. Kamat P, Schweizer R, Kaenel P et al. Human adipose-derived mesenchymal stromal cells may promote breast cancer progression and metastatic Spread. *Plast Reconstr Surg.* 2015, 136: 76–84.

21.3 THE BIOENGINEERED BREAST

J. Peter Rubin

Fat grafting used exclusively for whole breast reconstruction is a great advance in restoring tissues with minimally invasive approaches. Reduced donor site morbidity and ability to achieve a complete breast mound with only minimal incisions and autologous tissue moves the field of breast reconstruction forward in a dramatic way. The downside is the need for multiple procedures to achieve the final result, coupled with an unpredictable resorption of the grafted fat volume. Moreover, while external expansion has been beneficial in facilitating this procedure, compliance issues can limit effectiveness. As these tremendous strides are made, surgeons can look foward to the future of tissue engineering for the next generation of breast reconstruction therapies. What will a therapy involving a "bioengineered breast" look like? As potential therapeutic models are explored, some approaches represent a more immediate jump in technology from current therapies, while others are more far reaching.

In the first category, the use of pharmacological agents, cells and biomaterials is envisioned to improve outcomes of injectable therapies to restore soft tissue. As applied to methods of autologous fat grafting, this would include agents that can facilitate greater retention of injected adipose tissue or even stimulate growth of adipose tissue. This falls in the category of "enhancers" for fat grafting and represents a concept that has been investigated by many in the field. One promising technology is the use of micro-encapsulated adipogenic agents mixed with fat grafts. Dexamethasone has very potent adipogenic effects; when dexamethasone was encapsulated in PLGA microspheres and implanted with human fat grafts in a nude mouse model, results at 6 months showed dramatic and statistically significant improvement in the survival of adipose tissue with dexamethasone treatment.[1] Other adipogenic agents such as insulin, as well as angiogenic agents such as vascular endothelial growth factor are potential candidates for this type of therapy. In the cell therapy arena, there has been much interest in use of concentrated adipose stem cells supplemented with fat grafts to increase bioactivity and survival. This effect has been demonstrated experimentally and more recently in a level-1 randomized trial by Kolle and colleagues.[2,3] New regenerative scaffolds, including acellular adipose tissue matrix, represent an "off-the-shelf" injectable matrix for generating new adipose tissue without any donor site.[4]

But what about more far reaching approaches? There are three potential options to consider. The first approach would be an off-the-shelf free flap implant that would be placed at the time of mastectomy for immediate breast reconstruction and form adipose tissue. Tissues grown ex-vivo in bioreactors have been in existence for some time and the rate limiting step is the vascular supply. Recent work with whole organ decellularization suggests an approach that can be used for the breast. Instead of harvesting a free flap for breast reconstruction, decellularized free flaps would be readily available for implantation in a range of sizes and shapes. As these organs are decellularized, they would not be at risk of immunologic rejection and be analogous to acellular dermal matrix. The vascular supply would be from anastomoses, just as is the case for a conventional free flap, but with no donor site. Of note, if the flap fails, it can readily be replaced with a new one. In this scenario, the decellularized tissue flap is repopulated by circulating host progenitor cells.[5] In another approach, a polymer disk containing adipogenic and angiogenic growth factors would be placed in the anterior chest wall tissues at the time of mastectomy. A vascular pedicle, derived either from the internal thoracic artery or an intercostal artery, would be immobilized and placed over the disk to enable a robust blood supply to the regenerating tissues. Different angiogenic and adipogenic growth factors would be released from this disk at various timepoints over a 6-month period. Chemo-attractants would draw in circulating progenitor cells through the overlying vascular pedicle and then induce these cells to form new adipose tissue. A cycle of angiogenic growth factors would then ensue to enrich the vascular supply, followed by a further cycle of adipogenesis, continuing until a breast mound is developed. The precise dose of growth factors would determine the final size and shape of the breast. In yet another approach, genetic transfection could be used to manipulate autologous host cells to an earlier stage in embryogenesis. Unlike the experiments of Yamanaka and colleagues,[6] these cells would be reprogrammed to a blastema stage for breast tissue generation. In essence, adult cells from a patient would be reprogrammed to form a breast bud and then be implanted back into the patient and over time generate the breast. Since these cells are derived from the same patient, they would be genetically predetermined for the native size and shape of the breast for that patient.

Fat grafting for whole breast reconstruction represents a significant technical advance for breast cancer patients, and plastic surgeons will continue to lead the scientific endeavors in the development of a bioengineered breast.

REFERENCES

1. Kelmendi-Doko A, Marra KG, Vidic N, Tan H, Rubin JP. Adipogenic factor-loaded microspheres increase retention of transplanted adipose tissue. *Tissue Eng Part A*. 2014;20(17–18):2283–2290.
2. Kølle SF, Fischer-Nielsen A, Mathiasen AB, Elberg JJ, Oliveri RS, Glovinski PV, Kastrup J et al. Enrichment of autologous fat grafts with ex-vivo expanded adipose tissue-derived stem cells for graft survival: A randomised placebo-controlled trial. *Lancet*. 2013;382(9898):1113–1120. doi:10.1016/S0140-6736(13)61410-5.
3. Rubin, JP, Marra KG. Invited discussion-Enrichment of autologous fat ex vivo expanded adipose tissue-derived stem cells for raft survival: A randomized placebo-controlled trial. *Lancet*. 2013;382(9898):1077–1079.

4. Brown BN, Freund JM, Li H, Rubin JP, Reing JE, Jeffries G, Wolf M, Tottey S, Barnes C, Ratner B, Badylak SF. Comparison of three methods for the derivation of a diologic scaffold composed of adipose tissue extracellular matrix. *Tissue Eng Part C.* 2011;17(4):411–421.

5. Ott HC, Matthiesen TS, Goh SK, Black LD, Kren SM, Netoff TI, Taylor DA. Perfusion-decellularized matrix: Using nature's platform to engineer a bioartificial heart. *Nat Med.* 2008;14(2):213–221.

6. Takahashi K, Yamanaka S. Induction of pluripotent stem cells from mouse embryonic and adult fibroblast cultures by defined factors. *Cell.* 2006;126(4):663–676.

EDITORIAL COMMENTARY

Despite the increasing use of implant-based breast reconstruction since the advent of acellular dermal matrices, autologous tissue reconstruction continues to be the gold standard with excellent long-term outcomes. There are many autologous tissue options that are utilized by reconstructive surgeons based on their ability and experience. Over the last 10 years, there has been a decline in the use of the latissimus dorsi flap for breast reconstruction. This change has been most evident in the United Kingdom where the latissimus flap was the mainstay of breast reconstruction until recent years. However, thanks to information accruing from publications of Dr. Delay and Dr. Saint-Cyr, our knowledge of the anatomy of the back region has improved. This has allowed surgeons to harvest more fat with the latissimus flap, along with the concept of using the latissimus dorsi flap as a vessel to increase the surface area for fat grafting a whole breast reconstruction. This has to some extent re-invigorated the latissimus dorsi flap as a desirable option for autologous breast reconstruction. The opportunity to avoid the need for a breast implant by employing either an autologous latissimus flap or serial fat grafting of a flap transferred to the chest wall has undoubtedly increased patients interest in this method of breast reconstruction.

Despite the predominance of the deep inferior epigastric perforator (DIEP) flap in terms of publications and presentations at symposia, all three types of abdominal-based autologous tissue reconstructions (pedicled TRAM, free TRAM, and DIEP flap) are currently being used around the world based on surgeon ability and experience. It is evident that each of these three methods of breast reconstruction can result in excellent cosmetic outcomes with minimal morbidity. In this chapter, some of those acknowledged as masters of their art describe their techniques for these flaps in a manner which will benefit the reader and ultimately improve the knowledge and understanding as well as the outcomes of this approach to breast reconstruction.

22

Standard autologous tissue flaps for whole breast reconstruction

AT A GLANCE

Although the deep inferior epigastric perforator (DIEP) flap has become an excellent choice of reconstruction for selected patients with adequate perforators for perfusion of the lower abdominal tissue, the muscle sparing transverse rectus abdominis myocutaneous (TRAM) flap is probably used more commonly in clinical practice. Although the use of the latissimus flap has remained stable or decreased in frequency over the past few years, inclusion of the subcutaneous adipose tissue to circumvent the need for an implant has become a popular option, especially in obese patients. Thus, despite much attention being focused on advanced perforator flaps, the latissimus dorsi flap and TRAM flap continue to be used with significant frequency.

22.1 LATISSIMUS DORSI FLAP (WITH IMPLANT)

Michel Hector Saint–Cyr

Introduction

The pedicled latissimus dorsi (LD) flap was initially described by Tansini and colleagues in 1906 for reconstruction of mastectomy defects.[1] It is considered a workhorse flap in breast reconstruction, but can be limited by its inability to provide sufficient volume, especially when compared to abdominal-based flaps. The traditional method to augment volume remains use of an LD flap in conjunction with implants; however, newer techniques to augment volume have been described which include harvesting an extended LD flap and fat grafting (both immediate and delayed).[2]

Anatomy and technique

BLOOD SUPPLY AND INNERVATION

The LD muscle is a broad, flat muscle measuring up to 25 cm × 35 cm located in the postero-inferior aspect of the trunk. It originates from the iliac crest, lower six thoracic vertebrae, and the lower four ribs and inserts into the inter-tubercular groove of the humerus. It is classified as a Mathes type V muscle with a primary blood supply from the thoracodorsal artery along with secondary segmental pedicles from perforators of the posterior intercostal arteries and the lumbar arteries.[3] It is innervated by the thoracodorsal nerve, the vascular pedicle is usually accompanied by two veins, and pedicle length is around 8 cm.

FLAP HARVEST

The LD flap can be harvested with or without a skin paddle. Skin requirement depends on the amount of skin resected at the time of mastectomy. Since volume is important in breast reconstruction, the LD flap is usually harvested with a large skin paddle from the lower back even when minimal amounts of skin are needed as in skin-sparing mastectomy. The patient is marked in the standing position. The lateral border of the LD muscle is initially marked, and the superior edge of the flap is marked at the level of the scapular spine. The skin island can be designed laterally, obliquely, or transversely. Studies have shown that designing a low skin paddle with the scar below the inframammary fold is associated with improved patient satisfaction.[4] Flap harvest is performed in the lateral decubitus position. The skin island is incised, and the dissection is carried out deep to the superficial fascia leaving the deep fat on the muscle. The lateral border of the muscle is identified; inferiorly, the muscle is divided from the lumbosacral and paraspinous fascia and, medially, the attachments to the vertebrae are divided. Large perforating branches are carefully ligated. The pedicle is identified proximally, and the thoracodorsal nerve can be clipped if desired. A subcutaneous tunnel is subsequently created high in the axilla, and the flap is transferred into the mastectomy defect with closure of the donor site. Quilting sutures are used to obliterate dead space and relieve tension at the time of closure.[5] The patient is then repositioned in the supine position in preparation for the inset.

LOW EXTENDED LD FLAP TO AUGMENT VOLUME

Various modifications of the extended LD flap have been described based on the fat compartment theory of the back.[6] Aggressive subcutaneous harvest of the parascapular and scapular fat and also lumbar fat have been described and while they do increase flap volume, they are sometimes associated with contour abnormalities and donor site morbidity.[7] We use the low extended LD flap where a transverse skin paddle is marked with the patient in the standing position by grabbing the lumbo-thoracic and the lumbar fat compartments simultaneously with the "double bubble" pinch test.[8] Placing the skin paddle in the lower back where the maximum fat is found helps to increase volume of the flap and in some patients with small to medium breast, this may help avoid using an implant. The authors have been able to design skin paddles up to 31 cm × 20 cm. However, the extended LD flap is limited by patient body habitus and most patients with larger breasts and smaller body habitus will still require an underlying implant to augment volume (**Figure 22.1.1**).

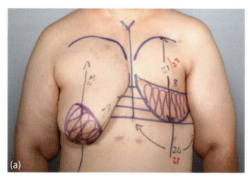

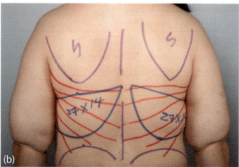

22.1.1 (a–b) Preoperative markings for low extended LD flap with transverse skin paddle.

TISSUE EXPANDER VERSUS IMPLANT

If immediate breast reconstruction is being performed, a tissue expander can be placed at the time of the mastectomy under the muscle. If used in skin-sparing mastectomy, a small central skin island is designed and the flap is usually placed directly under the skin. The expander is usually placed between the pectoralis major (left intact on the chest wall) and the latissimus dorsi muscle. Use of an expander helps to better control volume and has been shown to be associated with better patient outcomes.

Delayed breast reconstruction is usually planned in patients where immediate postoperative radiotherapy is planned to avoid irradiating the muscle.[9,10] In this situation, the muscle is used mainly for inferior pole fullness and for coverage of an expander or implant. An implant can be used directly in this situation and the volume of the implant is chosen based on what is needed to achieve symmetry with the other breast. Usually in delayed reconstruction, a larger skin paddle is required as most of the patients are lacking skin after initial mastectomy. The skin paddle is usually inset along the inframammary fold to provide lower pole volume, and the implant is placed between the pectoralis major and the latissimus dorsi muscle (**Figure 22.1.2**).

SECONDARY PROCEDURES

Patients who have tissue expanders placed under the LD flap usually undergo tissue expansion starting at 2 weeks when the incisions are healed. And in about 3 months, these patients usually have the expanders changed to permanent implants. Other secondary procedures that may be needed include thoracodorsal nerve division, nipple reconstruction, and contralateral procedures for symmetry.

Current role in breast reconstruction

With the evolution of breast reconstruction techniques and in particular the advent of free tissue transfer, there remains a limited role for use of the LD flap in breast reconstruction. Common indications include:

1. Patients who are not candidates for abdominal-based free tissue transfers including transverse rectus abdominis myocutaneous (TRAM) /deep inferior epigastric perforator (DIEP) flaps
2. Patients with failed abdominal-based autologous reconstruction
3. Irradiated thin patients
4. Partial mastectomy defects, for example, to replace dead space after lumpectomy
5. Thin skin flaps after skin-sparing mastectomy (LD flap provided extra coverage over implant/expander)

In summary, the LD flap is a versatile, reliable, and robust flap that remains a "workhorse" in breast reconstruction. Use in conjunction with an implant is often needed for volume augmentation, and this has been associated with a slightly higher rate of infective complications especially for irradiated patients. However, specific indications for an LD flap with an

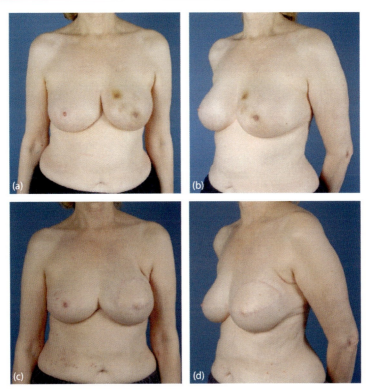

22.1.2 (a–b) Preoperative views: 56-year-old female patient with breast cancer who underwent skin-sparing mastectomy followed by immediate tissue expander-based breast reconstruction. (c–d) Patient eventually required a left latissimus dorsi flap due to skin-flap loss. Below are patient pictures at 12 months s/p LD flap and 2 months s/p nipple reconstruction.

implant seem to be diminishing given that newer techniques of fat grafting for volume augmentation are taking precedence. This can lead to avoidance of an implant altogether.

REFERENCES

1. Maxwell GP. Iginio Tansini and the origin of the latissimus dorsi musculocutaneous flap. *Plast Reconstr Surg* 1980;65:686–692.
2. Zhu L, Mohan AT, Vijayasekaran A et al. Maximizing the volume of latissimus dorsi flap in autologous breast reconstruction with simultaneous multisite fat grafting. *Aesthet Surg J* 2016;36:169–178.
3. Mathes SJ, Nahai F. Classification of the vascular anatomy of muscles: Experimental and clinical correlation. *Plast Reconstr Surg* 1981;67:177–187.
4. Bailey S, Saint-Cyr M, Zhang K et al. Breast reconstruction with the latissimus dorsi flap: Women's preference for scar location. *Plast Reconstr Surg* 2010;126:358–365.
5. Bailey SH, Oni G, Guevara R, Wong C, Saint-Cyr M. Latissimus dorsi donor-site morbidity: The combination of quilting and fibrin sealant reduce length of drain placement and seroma rate. *Ann Plast Surg* 2012;68:555–558.
6. Hammond DC. Latissimus dorsi flap breast reconstruction. *Plast Reconstr Surg* 2009;124:1055–1063.
7. Chang DW, Youssef A, Cha S, Reece GP. Autologous breast reconstruction with the extended latissimus dorsi flap. *Plast Reconstr Surg* 2002;110:751–759; discussion 60–61.
8. Bailey SH, Saint-Cyr M, Oni G et al. The low transverse extended latissimus dorsi flap based on fat compartments of the back for breast reconstruction: Anatomical study and clinical results. *Plast Reconstr Surg* 2011;128:382e–394e.
9. Spear SL, Onyewu C. Staged breast reconstruction with saline-filled implants in the irradiated breast: Recent trends and therapeutic implications. *Plast Reconstr Surg* 2000;105:930–942.
10. Thomson HJ, Potter S, Greenwood RJ et al. A prospective longitudinal study of cosmetic outcome in immediate latissimus dorsi breast reconstruction and the influence of radiotherapy. *Ann Surg Oncol* 2008;15:1081–1091.

22.2 TOTALLY AUTOLOGOUS LATISSIMUS DORSI FLAP

Eva Weiler-Mithoff and James Mansell

Introduction

Recent evidence demonstrates increasing use of mastectomy in the management of patients with early breast cancer and as part of a risk reduction strategy.[1,2] It is now widely accepted that breast reconstruction should be offered to all suitable women who require mastectomy for surgical treatment of breast cancer.[3] The versatility and reliability of the autologous latissimus dorsi (ALD) flap can be a useful technique in both immediate and delayed breast reconstruction (**Figure 22.2.1** and **Figure 22.2.2**).

Originally described by Tansini in 1896 as a method for covering defects resulting from radical mastectomy, evolution of its application throughout the 1970s and 1980s culminated in description of the ALD reconstruction by Delay in 1998.[4,5] This involved harvesting fat from six additional zones at or below the level of Scarpa's fascia, thereby increasing flap volume (**Figure 22.2.3**). Further series have since been published which have established the ALD flap as an effective method for breast reconstruction.[6,7]

ADVANTAGES

There is reasonably consistent anatomy of the neurovascular pedicle which renders the ALD flap extremely reliable and robust. It precludes the need for implant placement and thus avoids any associated complications with fewer additional procedures being required following ALD reconstruction.[8] Compared with autologous free tissue transfer from the abdomen, the ALD flap has lower morbidity, shorter hospital stay, and may be more cost-effective.[9,10] In addition, it is a safe procedure to use in obese women.[11,12]

DISADVANTAGES

The ALD flap may not be ideal for those women who rely on upper body strength such as wheelchair users and elite athletes. Donor site morbidity can be significant with a long scar and frequent seroma formation which often requires repeated aspiration. Furthermore, the color and texture match of the skin between the back and breast may be suboptimal. The ALD is more appropriate for immediate reconstruction because the total amount of skin and fat may be limited.

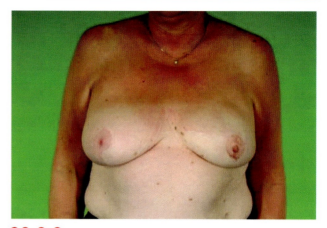

22.2.2 Delayed breast reconstruction requires more extensive skin replacement and has a higher incidence of symmetry surgery to the other breast. Delayed left breast reconstruction and right breast reduction.

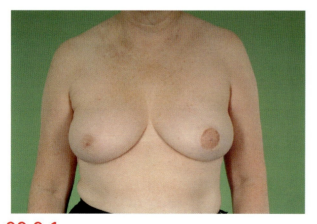

22.2.1 Immediate breast reconstruction with the autologous LD flap allows preservation of breast skin and facilitates a more cosmetic result. Immediate left breast reconstruction with autologous LD flap after skin-sparing mastectomy.

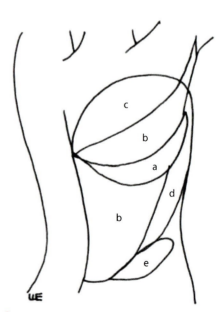

22.2.3 Six additional zones of fat harvest increase the volume of the autologous LD flap. (a) Fat under the skin island; (b) Fat overlying the muscle surface; (c) Para-scapular adipo-fascial extension; (d) Fat anterior to muscle; (e) Supra-iliac "love-handles;" (f) Fat underneath the muscle (not shown).

PREOPERATIVE PLANNING

PATIENT SELECTION

Women who desire an autologous reconstruction and have small to moderate-sized breasts or larger breasts but a desire for a contralateral reduction are well-suited to ALD reconstruction. This technique is especially useful in the context of postmastectomy radiotherapy where implant reconstruction is often avoided and abdominal tissue transfer procedures delayed. Other indications include patients with non-expansible chest wall skin, breast hypoplasia, and salvage procedures following prior reconstructive failure (**Figure 22.2.4**). The ALD flap is well-suited to bilateral breast reconstruction because it can be performed as either a synchronous or metachronous procedure in the context of contralateral breast cancer or risk reduction (**Figure 22.2.5**).

Women who have undergone prior posterior thoracotomy cannot usually have ALD flap breast reconstruction and those with prior axillary surgery/radiotherapy should be carefully assessed to establish an intact thoracodorsal pedicle. Imaging with ultrasound-assisted doppler or Computed Tomography (CT) angiography should be considered. Those women who rely on upper abdominal strength for various activities relating to mobility, sport, or employment should be counseled regarding any potential impact on shoulder function.

MARKING

Markings are made anteriorly and posteriorly as shown (**Figure 22.2.6**). In the delayed setting, the outline of the contralateral breast is transposed to the chest wall. The skin ellipse is ideally centered over the fat roll on the back, orientated within relaxed skin tension lines and is typically 6–9 cm wide.

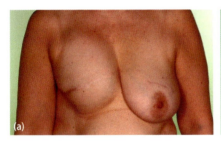
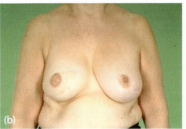

22.2.4 Replacement of a breast implant with the autologous LD flap in case of recurrent capsular contracture after implant based breast reconstruction. (a) Preoperative appearance. (b) Stable reconstruction 7 years postoperatively.

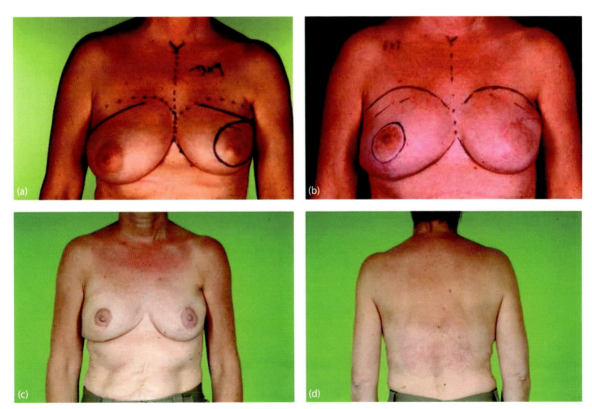

22.2.5 (a–d) Bilateral metachronous breast reconstruction with the autologous LD flap.

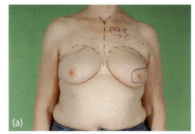
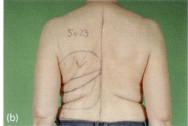

22.2.6 (a) Important preoperative markings on the breast include the area of skin excision, the breast base, the take-off point of the breast, and the anterior axillary fold. (b) Preoperative markings on the back show the limits of the LD muscle, the skin ellipse which will allow direct closure of the donor site and areas of additional soft tissue harvest.

Operative approach

FLAP HARVEST

In most cases, the patient can be placed in the lateral decubitus position and the mastectomy and flap harvest performed simultaneously (**Figure 22.2.7**).

Preinfiltration of the subcutaneous plane with local anesthetic reduces postoperative pain and facilitates dissection. The skin flaps are initially raised just beneath Scarpa's fascia. This level of dissection is maintained throughout for smokers, bilateral breast reconstructions, and other patients at risk of poor healing. Otherwise, a 2cm strip of Scarpa's fascia is raised to support wound closure (**Figure 22.2.8**). The remainder of the skin flap is raised in the suprafascial plane maximizing soft tissue volume. At the outer boundary of soft tissue harvest, the dissection is deepened at 45° circumferentially. The subcutaneous fat overlying the trapezius muscle is raised along with the adipofascial parascapular extension revealing the posterior border of the latissimus dorsi. A thin layer of fat covering the inferior angle of the scapula should be left to avoid adherent scarring (**Figure 22.2.9**). The anterior edge of the latissimus dorsi muscle is dissected and identified in the proximal third. Dissection over the proximal part of the latissimus dorsi to the tendinous insertion is performed avoiding additional fat harvest to minimize bulkiness in the axillary tunnel (**Figure 22.2.10**). The medial and inferior origins of the latissimus dorsi muscle are released to allow elevation

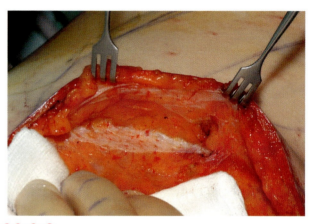

22.2.8 The skin flaps are raised at the level of Scarpa's fascia.

of the flap from distal to proximal. On the deep aspect of the muscle, substantive intercostal and lumbar perforators should be controlled. Care is taken to avoid inadvertent raising of the serratus anterior and posterior muscles or of any interdigitating slips of the external oblique muscle inferolaterally. Additional fat can be harvested along the posterior border of the serratus anterior and the under surface of the latissimus dorsi (**Figure 22.2.11**). It is important to stay within the areolar plane between the latissimus dorsi and serratus anterior to protect the vascularity of both muscles. As the two muscles are separated, the thoracodorsal neurovascular pedicle supplying the latissimus

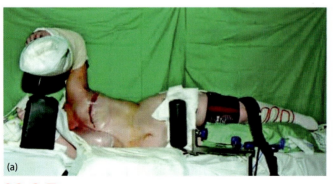
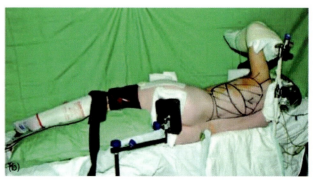

22.2.7 (a) The anterior aspect of the patient positioned intraoperatively with an anterior table support, a guttered wedge to take the pressure of the dependent shoulder, and a pillow between the legs. (b) The posterior aspect shows the posterior table support and a well padded arm support in order to position the arm at 90° of shoulder abduction and elbow flexion for easier access to the axilla.

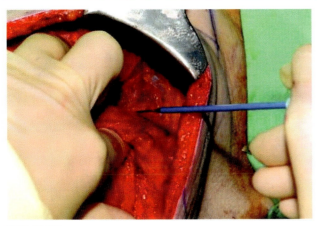

22.2.9 The parascapular adipo-fascial flap of approximately 1 cm thickness has been lifted and folded back. The diathermy tip is pointing to a thin layer of fat which has been left over the tip of the scapula.

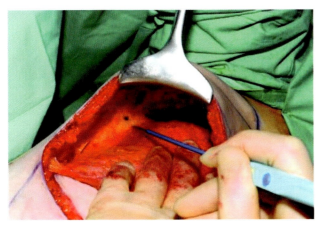

22.2.10 The anterior border of the LD muscle is identified in the proximal third of the muscle and followed cranially to the tendineous insertion on the humerus.

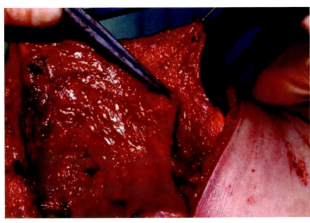

22.2.11 Additional fat deposits on the under-surface of the LD muscle and along the posterior border of the Serratus anterior muscle can be dissected along with the LD flap.

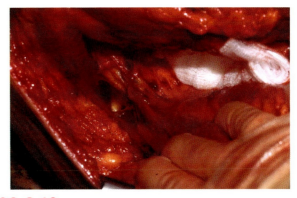

22.2.12 The Thoracodorsal neurovascular pedicle and the serratus branch are identified and preserved.

dorsi and the serratus branch are identified and preserved (**Figure 22.2.12**).

The upper posterior border of the latissimus dorsi muscle is detached from the teres muscles. Overall a significant volume of additional fat can be harvested with the latssimus dorsi muscle (**Figure 22.2.13**). This tunnel has to be sufficiently wide to prevent any constriction and placed high enough to avoid bulkiness of tissue on the lateral chest wall (**Figure 22.2.14**). The latissimus dorsi tendon and the serratus branch are left intact and the thoracodorsal nerve

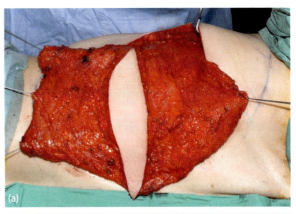

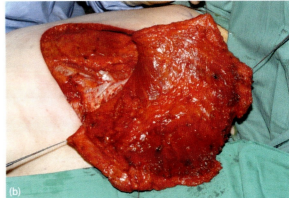

22.2.13 (a) The outer surface of the autologous LD shows the extent of the additional fat harvest. (b) The under-surface of the flap shows the extent of muscle harvest and fat deposits deep to the muscle.

22.2.14 The flap has been transferred through a high axillary tunnel onto the anterior chest wall. There is no tension on the thoracodorsal neurovascular bundle.

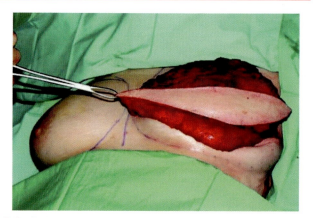

22.2.17 The parascapular flap from the upper pole is folded underneath to create projection of the inferior pole of the new breast. Folding the flap in this way provides a natural profile to the reconstructed breast.

is preserved. Quilting of the flaps is performed and suction drains are placed at the donor site.

FLAP INSET

This is performed in the supine position with the arms partially abducted and the upper trunk tilted head-up about 30°–45° (**Figure 22.2.15**). The inframammary fold and the lateral border of the breast are secured in their original anatomical position. The latissimus dorsi tendon is routed parallel to the pectoralis major tendon, and the upper part of the latissimus dorsi muscle is sutured to the lateral border of the pectoralis major muscle and the flap rotated 180° (**Figure 22.2.16**). The parascapular extension is folded under the larger upper segment of the latissimus dorsi to create central projection and the lower pole (**Figure 22.2.17**). The flap is sutured to the margins of the mastectomy defect. The inferior aspect of the reconstructed mound is sutured precisely along the inframammary fold while the cleavage inset is carried out last after elimination of gravity. Any excess skin remaining on the ALD flap is de-epithelialized with fine tuning of shape using plication sutures. Skin-sparing mastectomy necessitates replacement of a disc of skin, and a small skin island only can be harvested from the back (**Figure 22.2.18**). A Wise

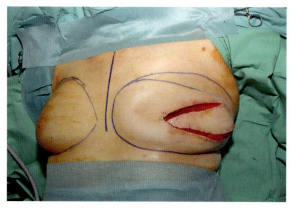

22.2.15 The patient has been turned supine, re-prepped, and re-draped.

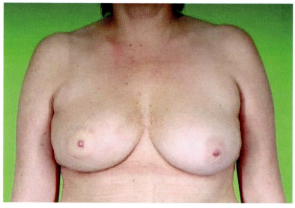

22.2.18 Skin-sparing mastectomy in a non-ptotic breast requires insertion of a small skin island in the area of the NAC only.

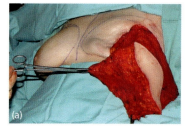 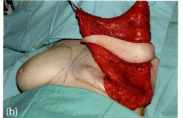

22.2.16 For insetting the flap is rotated through 180°. The most distal part of the LD flap becomes the upper pole of the reconstructed breast. The retractors are attached to the most distal part of the ALD. (a) Before the rotation and (b) after the rotation.

pattern may be useful if a concomitant reduction of the opposite breast is planned (**Figures 22.2.19**). If the breast volume is acceptable, but both breasts could benefit from a mastopexy, the whole flap can be de-epithelialized and buried to create a less ptotic breast (**Figure 22.2.20**). The volume of the reconstructed breast should ideally be about 25% greater than the contralateral side as postoperative atrophy will occur especially if adjuvant radiotherapy is planned.

Postoperative outcomes

RECOVERY

Patients are transferred to a high dependency facility for flap monitoring. A supportive brasserie without underwiring is recommended. A program of shoulder physiotherapy is commenced from day 1. Hospital stay is usually 3–5 days and may be less than this in motivated patients with multimodal perioperative analgesia.

COMPLICATIONS

Complications include hematoma, infection, mastectomy skin-flap necrosis, delayed healing, and partial or total flap-loss. The incidence of partial flap necrosis is

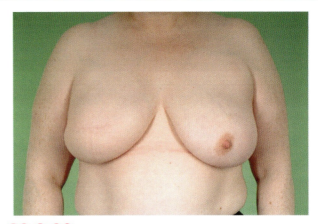

22.2.20 If the breast volume is acceptable but both breasts could benefit from a mastopexy, the whole flap can be de-epithelialized and buried completely under the breast skin leaving a transverse scar only.

less than 5%–7% and total flap loss occurs in approximately 0.2% of cases.[5,13,14]

Donor site hematoma and seroma after ALD is more common than after conventional latissimus dorsi with implant.[13] Seroma formation at the donor site after extended latissimus dorsi harvest occurs in up to 80% of cases, and this may require

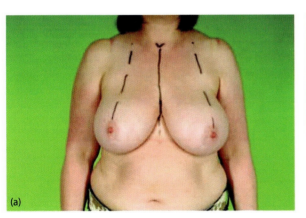

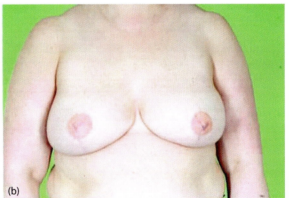

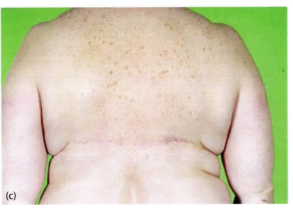

22.2.19 A Wise pattern mastectomy can be used for reconstruction of a smaller breast in a patient with large and ptotic breast if a contralateral reduction is planned. This allows complete de-epithelialization of the autologous LD flap. This figure shows a patient with bilateral risk-reducing mastectomy: (a) Preoperative breast appearance, (b) postoperative breast appearance, (c) postoperative appearance of back donor site.

repeated aspiration if symptomatic. Spontaneous resolution usually occurs by the 6th week. The reaccumulation of seroma post-aspiration and time course to resolution can be significantly reduced by intracavity injection of Triamcinolone.[15] Preventative techniques include the use of quilting sutures or fibrin sealants during donor site closure.[16–18]

SHOULDER FUNCTION

The ALD flap can lead to impairment of shoulder function, but usually causes minimal long-term difficulty with return of shoulder strength and no significant difficulty with activities of daily living.[19–21] Nonetheless, significant functional deficit is likely in the context of specific sporting activities (e.g., swimming, golf, mountain climbing). It should be noted that donor site quilting does not adversely affect shoulder function.[17]

RADIOTHERAPY

Postmastectomy chest wall radiotherapy inevitably leads to collateral irradiation of the ALD with associated volume loss often most prominent in the upper pole. There is atrophy of the subcutaneous fat, latissimus dorsi, and pectoralis major muscles. Despite this, the overall cosmetic outcome remains of sufficient quality and levels of patient satisfaction are high irrespective of radiotherapy usage (**Figure 22.2.21**).[22,23]

SECONDARY PROCEDURES

In an audit by the author of 500 ALD flap breast reconstructions undertaken between 1995 and 2005, symmetrizing surgery was performed following immediate and delayed breast reconstruction in 20% and 60% of cases, respectively.[24] Volume deficiencies within the ALD flap which are either focal or global can be corrected using fat transfer.[25] The autologous tissue of the reconstructed breast is a perfect recipient for microdroplet fat grafting, which can often restore skin suppleness and soften the reconstruction following radiotherapy.

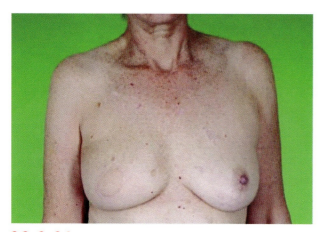

22.2.21 Immediate breast reconstruction with autologous LD flap after adjuvant radiotherapy.

CONCLUSION

The ALD can be used to create a moderate-sized breast often without the need for contralateral symmetry surgery. Rates of morbidity are low and aesthetic outcomes are consistent and durable even despite any requirement for adjuvant radiotherapy. With increasing patient expectations coupled with the need for cost-effective surgical practice, the ALD should be considered as a major option for the majority of breast reconstructions.

REFERENCES

1. Kummerov KL, Du L, Penson DF, Shyr Y, Hooks MA. Nationwide trends in mastectomy for early breast cancer. *JAMA Surg* 2015;150(1):9–16.
2. Lucas DJ, Sabino J, Shriver CD, Pawlik TM, Singh DP, Vertrees AE. Doing more: Trends in breast cancer surgery, 2005 to 2011. *Ann Surg* 2015;81(1):74–80.
3. Rainsbury D. and A. Willett *Oncoplastic Breast Reconstruction: Guidelines for Best Practice*. London, UK: ABS, BAPRAS; 2012.
4. Maxwell GP. Iginio tansini and the origin of the latissimus dorsi musculocutaneous flap. *Plast Reconstr Surg* 1980;65:686–692.
5. Delay E, Gounot N, Bouillot A et al. Autologous latissimus breast reconstruction: A 3 year clinical experience with 100 patients. *Plast Reconstr Surg* 1998;102:1461–1478.
6. Chang DW, Youssef A, Cha S et al. Autologous breast reconstruction with the extended latissimus dorsi flap. *Plasr Reconstr Surg* 2002;110:751–759.
7. Fatah MFT. Extended latissimus dorsi flap in breast reconstruction. In: Cuthbertson JH, Jones G, ed. *Operative Techniques in Plastic and Reconstructive Surgery*. Philadelphia, PA: WB Saunders, 1999: 38–49.
8. Fischer JP, Fox JP, Nelson JA, Kovach SJ, Serletti JM. A longitudinal assessment of outcomes and healthcare resource utilization after immediate breast reconstruction comparing implant-based and autologous based breast reconstruction. *Ann Surg* 2015;262(4):692–699.
9. Masoomi H, Wirth GA, Paydar KZ, Salibian AA, Mowlds DS, Evans GR. Comparison of perioperative outcomes of autologous breast reconstruction surgeries. *J Plast Reconstr Aesthet Surg* 2015, doi:10.1016/j.bjps.2015.05.023.
10. Grover R, Padula WV, Van Vliet M, Ridgway EB. Comparing five alternate methods of breast reconstruction surgery: A cost - effectiveness analysis. *Plast Reconstr Surg* 2013;132(5):709e–723e.
11. Hanwright PJ, Davila AA, Hirsch EM, Khan SA, Fine NA, Bilimoria KY, Kim JY. The differential effect of BMI on prosthetic versus autogenous breast reconstruction: A multivariate analysis of 12,986 patients. *Breast* 2013;22(5):938–945.
12. Yeshelyev M, Duggal CS, Carlson GW, Losken A. Complications of latissimus dorsi flap breast reconstruction in overweight and obese patients. *Ann Plast Surg* 2013;70(5):557–562.
13. Roy MK, Shrotia S, Holcombe C et al. Complications of latissimus dorsi myocutaneous flap breast reconstruction. *Eur J Surg Oncol* 1998;24:162–165.

14. National mastectomy and breast reconstruction audit 3rd report. http://www.ic.nhs.uk/webfiles/Services/NCASP/audits%20and%20reports/NHS%20IC%20MBR%202010%20Audit%20Interactive%2024-06-10%20final.pdf

15. Taghizadeh R, Shoaib T, Hart AM et al. Triamcinolone reduces seroma re-accumulation in the extended latissimus dorsi donor site. *J Plast Reconstr Aesthet Surg* 2008;61(6):636–642.

16. Titley OG, Spyrou GE, Fatah MFT et al. Preventing seroma in the latissimus dorsi flap donor site. *Br J Plast Surg* 1997;50:106–108.

17. Button J, Scott JR, Taghizadeh R, Weiler-Mithoff E, Hart AM. Shoulder function following autologous latissimus dorsi breast reconstruction. A prospective three year observational study comparing quilting and non-quilting donor site techniques. *J Plast Reconstr Aesthet Surg* 2010;63(9):1505–1512.

18. Weinrach JC, Cronin ED, Smith BK et al. Preventing seroma in the latissimus dorsi flap donor site with fibrin sealant. *Ann Plast Surg* 2004;53:12–16.

19. Clough KB, Louis-Sylvestre C, Fitoussi A, Couturaud B, Nos C. Donor site sequelae after autologous breast reconstruction with an extended latissimus dorsi flap. *Plast Reconstr Surg* 2002;109:1904–1911.

20. Lee KT, Mun GH. A systematic review of functional donor site morbidity after latissimus dorsi muscle transfer. *Plast Reconstr Surg* 2014;134(2):303–314.

21. Yang JD, Huh JS, Min YS, Kim HJ, Park HY, Jung TD. Physical and functional ability recovery patterns and quality of life after immediate autologous latissimus dorsi breast reconstruction: A 1 year prospective observational study. *Plast Reconstr Surg* 2015. doi:10.1097/PRS.0000000000001769.

22. McKeown DJ, Hogg FJ, Brown IM et al. The timing of autologous latissimus dorsi breast reconstruction and effect of radiotherapy on outcome. *J Plast Reconstr Aesthet Surg* 2009; 62(4):488–493.

23. Thomson HJ, Potter S, Greenwood RJ, Bahl A, Barker J, Cawthorn SJ, Winters ZE. A prospective longitudinal study of cosmetic outcome in immediate latissimus dorsi breast reconstruction and the influence of radiotherapy. *Ann Surg Oncol* 2008;15(4):1081–1091.

24. Cortufo S, Rickard RF, Weiler-Mithoff EM. Autologous latissimus dorsi breast reconstruction: A technique for all occasions. International Meeting of Oncoplastic and Reconstructive Breast Surgery, 2008, Nottingham, UK.

25. Delay E. Lipomodelling of the reconstructed breast. In: Spear SL, Ed. *Surgery of the Breast, Principles and Art.* 2nd ed. Philadelphia, PA: Lippincott-Raven, 2006:930.

22.3 PEDICLED TRANSVERSE RECTUS ABDOMINIS MYOCUTANEOUS (TRAM) FLAP

Jean-Yves Petit, Maria Rietjens, and Andrea Manconi

The transverse rectus abdominis myocutaneous (TRAM) flap is a myocutaneous flap based on one or two rectus abdominis muscles, allowing the transfer of an island of skin and fat taken horizontally below the level of the umbilicus. The pedicle TRAM flap allows reconstruction of the breast even in circumstances where local conditions are compromised such as radio dystrophy, resection of the pectoralis muscle (Halsted mastectomy), or extensive integument resection (**Figure 22.3.1**). Despite advances in microsurgical techniques using free TRAM flaps, the pedicled TRAM remains an option for single (**Figure 22.3.2**) or bilateral (**Figure 22.3.3**) breast reconstruction, especially when micro-surgical facilities are not available.[1–4]

Anatomy

The skin paddle is taken from the lower abdomen and includes 1 or 2 cm of tissue above the umbilicus (**Figure 22.3.4**). This area is supplied with blood by five vascular systems:[3]

1. Superior epigastric vessels coming from the internal mammary vessels
2. Deep inferior epigastric vessels
3. Superficial inferior epigastric vessels
4. Intercostal segmental vessels
5. Superficial and deep circumflex iliac vessels

The dominant blood supply comes from the deep inferior epigastric vessels which are connected with the superior epigastric vessels. The latter will be the sole vascular pedicle supplying blood to the flap after section of the inferior epigastric vascular pedicle.

The superior vessels reach the upper insertion of the rectus muscle approximately 1 or 2 cm lateral to a line drawn above the xiphoid. Here, the vessels penetrate the muscle or remain on its deep surface, decreasing progressively in diameter.

Miller described a macroscopic communication between the upper and lower systems in 40%–50% of cases with around 60% of patients having microscopic choke vessels.[5] The inferior epigastric vessels enter the postero-lateral margin of the rectus muscle between the arcuate line and the crural arcade. The two systems anastomose in the periumbilical area.

The inferior system is dominant and therefore when the flap is raised, the venous drainage has to reverse and follow the superior venous system. This reverse venous flow may take few a minutes and explains the temporary venous stasis within the flap. Arterial perforators are located laterally near the margins of the muscle (lateral row of the perforators), while a second row of perforators can be found more medially, approximately 1–2 cm from the linea alba.

The anterior rectus fascia is adherent to the muscle and the tendinous intersections. The fascia is formed from two layers provided by the external and internal oblique muscles in the lower rectus muscle and by a single layer in the upper muscle. During dissection of the muscle, it is possible to retain a thin layer of fascia to protect the small vessels inside the muscle and to make the muscular pedicle more resilient when transposing onto the thorax. To reinforce the quality of the parietal closure, it is worthwhile separating the fascia from the muscle and preserving this for the closure.

Four different zones are described on the paddle of the TRAM (Figure 22.3.4) which indicate the quality of the blood supply according to the distance from the vascular pedicle. After revision of the first description by Hartrampf, zones 1 and 2 are located on the same side as the muscular pedicle and zones 3 and 4 are on the opposite side.

To increase the quality of the blood supply and reduce the risk of necrosis, Moon and Taylor[3] recommend a surgical delay of 1 week before definitive elevation of the flap. Embolization or ligation of the inferior epigastric vessels is undertaken 1 or 2 weeks before the reconstruction.

Surgical technique

Preoperative evaluation of the abdominal integument is fundamental for ensuring quality of the final reconstruction with a TRAM flap be this either an immediate or delayed reconstruction. The amount of redundant tissue can be evaluated with the patient in a sitting position. The quantity of skin

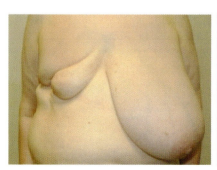
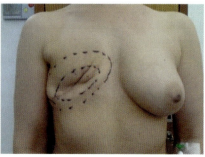
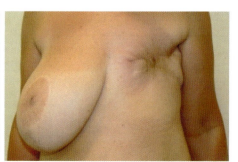

22.3.1 Local thoracic defects are an indication for TRAM flap reconstruction.

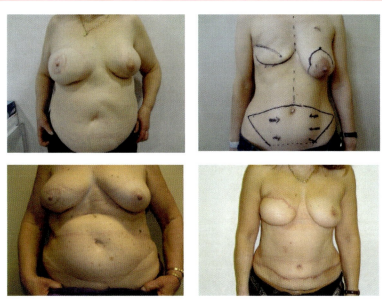

22.3.2 Preoperative drawings.

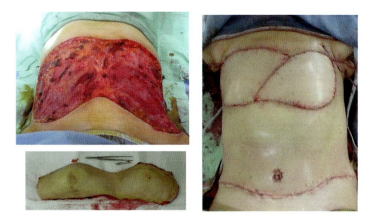

22.3.3 Localization of the perforators with ultrasound.

and fat available can be measured using the pinch test, with squeezing of abdominal skin between the fingers. The markings should be done in a standing position (Figure 22.3.4) after evaluation of the quantity of tissue which is available for the flap. These markings should start in the midline by drawing a line from the sternal notch to the pubic crest. The upper limit of the flap is then carefully drawn so as to be symmetrical in relation to the midline. In the region of the midline, the marking should be 1–2 cm above the umbilicus. Laterally, the marking should reach as far as the iliac crests at equal distance from the midline and also should be at the same level as the iliac crest to ensure perfect symmetry of the abdominal scar. The inferior line can be drawn based on the pinch test, but the final placement of the incision should be decided intraoperatively once the upper abdominal skin has been undermined. The skin margins are stretched down to the limit which allows closure of the abdominal defect without excessive tension. Perforator sites can be located with a Doppler. In the case of an immediate breast reconstruction, mastectomy will be done after marking the inframammary fold of both breasts. Lateral to the xiphoid, the boundaries of the thoracic cage determine location of the rectus muscle insertion and can be drawn on the skin to mark the limits of the muscle. In the case of delayed reconstruction, the inframammary fold of the contralateral breast should be marked in order to determine position of the inframammary fold in the reconstructed breast. The skin excision along the mastectomy scar is outlined depending on the laxity of the skin and on the size of the flap. If the scar lies high on the thorax, it will not be possible to draw the inferior limit of the excision at the level of the sulcus corresponding to the other breast. It is usually advisable not to draw the inferior limit of the skin resection 1–2 cm above the sulcus, as tension from the abdominal skin closure will pull down the position of this suture line. In the case of a vertical mastectomy scar, the paddle of the flap can be orientated either vertically or horizontally without regard for the vertical scar. If the skin is tight, it may be necessary to use a horizontal scar together with a short incision of the vertical scar to open it above the flap. This will facilitate a natural shape to the upper part of the reconstructed breast. It is worthwhile removing the radio-dystrophic scar on the thorax if the size of the flap is sufficient.

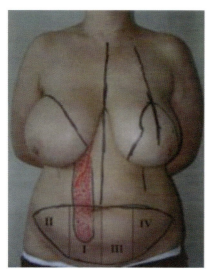

22.3.4 Lateral dissection of the skin flap with localization of the lateral perforators.

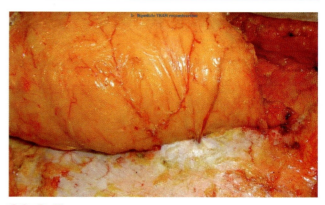

22.3.5 Dissected muscle with ligature of the inferior epigastric vessels.

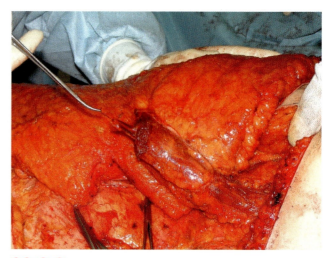

22.3.6 Closure of the fascia with a mersilene mesh.

Perioperative assessment implies heparin prophylaxis together with pneumatic leg pumps. Antibiotics should be given every 4 hours during surgery, but not postoperatively. The need for blood transfusion will depend upon blood loss during the operation and be guided by anaesthetic evaluation. The patient is positioned on an operating table with a break to assist with abdominal closure at the end of the operation.

Surgery begins by undermining the epigastric flap above the muscle fascia. The incision is inclined at 45° in order to include as many perforators within the flap as possible. In most cases, the decision will be for a single pedicle TRAM, with choice of muscle dependent on the quality of the lateral perforators at the end of the dissection. Both rectus muscles are dissected up to the ribs and xiphoid. A tunnel is then undermined between the costal insertions of the rectus muscle and the breast.

Flap dissection continues with suprafascial dissection of the skin paddle from lateral to medial. The perforators are identified at the lateral border of the muscle (**Figure 22.3.5**). The quality of these perforators will determine choice of muscle; an ipsilateral pedicle avoids a bulge in the epigastric area due to rotation of the contralateral pedicle.

The rectus sheath is next incised along the lateral border of the muscle which is dissected from the overlying fascia. Intercostal segmental vessels and nerves are ligated. The main vessels can usually be seen beneath the muscle. The inferior epigastric pedicle is then divided 4–5 cm from the pubic insertion. The fascia can then be incised 2–3 cm from the linea alba up to the xiphoid process. As much fascia as possible is spared along the linea alba so as to allow easier repair of the fascial defect. Muscle perfusion should be checked; the color of the tip of the muscle is usually darker for 2 to 3 cm. It is useful at this stage to remove temporarily the ligature around the vessels to verify arterial flow and to deal with venous stasis (**Figure 22.3.6**). In case of poor blood supply to the muscle, it is possible to perform a bipedicled TRAM, but usually local perfusion at the tip of the muscle gradually improves with opening up of the choke vessels.

The umbilicus is isolated, the cutaneous palette is dissected, and the perforators of the contralateral muscle are cut. It is important to divide the 8th intercostal nerve to avoid unpleasant contractions of the muscle in the future. The authors recommend not cutting the blood supply to the opposite rectus before completion of harvesting the chosen rectus muscle. This will enable use of the contralateral muscle in case of any problems with the blood supply to the first muscle.

DONOR SITE REPAIR AND ABDOMINAL CLOSURE

Abdominal closure should be methodical with suturing of the different fascia layers with non-absorbable material. It is essential to include both internal and external oblique aponeuroses into sheath closure. To reinforce strength of the closure, a Mersilene mesh is recommended (**Figure 22.3.7**), especially in the case of a bipedicled TRAM. In some cases, closure can be performed without any mesh when laxity of the abdominal fascia is sufficient to avoid excessive tension and increased pressure in the abdominal cavity. The latter can restrict respiratory capacity during the postoperative period leading to bronchial stasis and basal atelectasis which increases the risk of pulmonary infection and impaired blood supply to the flap. The mesh can be fixed with a single layer of continuous suture medially to the remaining rectus fascia and

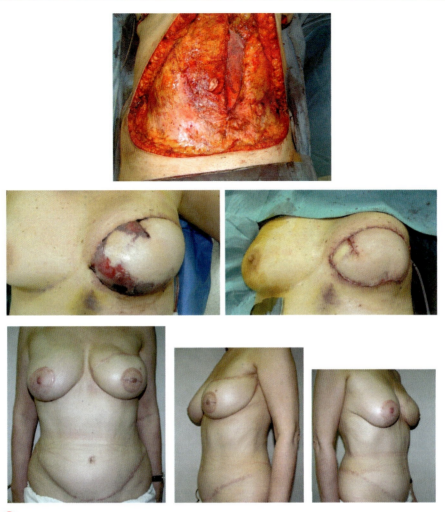

22.3.7–22.3.9 Examples of breast reconstruction with monopedicle TRAM flap.

laterally to the external oblique muscle. Due to vertical closure of the rectus fascia after harvesting of the flap, the umbilicus is displaced slightly and should be fixed with small stitches to the fascia in the midline before closure of the abdominal skin flaps. Once the flap has been transposed to the chest wall, the abdominal skin closure can be done. The patient should be raised to a semi sitting position to avoid excessive tension on the skin flaps. A triple layer of sutures should be done after fixing a double suction drain. The umbilicus is sutured within the midline after making an appropriately positioned hole in the midline at a level which avoids distortion of the umbilical position.

FLAP REMODELING

Whatever the choice of rectus pedicle (ipsi- or contralateral), it is important to avoid too much tension on the muscle within the epigastric tunnel. Sufficient laxity is required to avoid problems with the flap blood supply.

With the patient remaining in a sitting position, the flap is rotated carefully to determine the optimal position to reproduce the natural shape of the reconstructed breast. It is recommended that the less vascularized area of the flap is placed close to the axilla. In the event of partial necrosis, the repair is in a less conspicuous location than if the necrosis lies close to the sternal area (**Figure 22.3.8**). In delayed reconstruction, excision of the mastectomy scar will remove skin down to the future sulcus of the breast. In case of radiodystrophic sequelae along the mastectomy scar, all affected skin should be removed. Suturing of the flap should start with the inferior incision to reconstruct optimum appearance of the sulcus. If the mastectomy scar lies high on the thoracic wall, the inferior incision of the flap will not reach the sulcus, and this will be obtained by undermining of the native skin and refill by the de-epithelized inferior part of the flap. Experienced surgeons with TRAM flap reconstruction will be aware that reshaping of the flap is a crucial step in the reconstruction and there are no simple tricks for doing this well. It is always advisable to assess the blood supply to the reconstructed breast at least half an hour from completion of transposition. Any margins which are blue or do not readily bleed (red blood) should be discarded. It is preferable to obtain a good shape to the reconstruction immediately rather than to leave any improvements for a second stage operation. The upper part of the reconstructed breast should be symmetrical with the opposite breast. This is achieved by burying the upper margin of the flap under the skin after de-epitheliazation (**Figure 22.3.9**). In the case of immediate reconstruction with nipple-sparing mastectomy, the flap should be totally buried beneath the skin envelope after total de-epithelialization. A drain should be placed deep to the flap.

COMPLICATIONS

In the authors' institution, complications among 420 pedicled TRAM flap breast reconstructions have been evaluated.[7,8]

Abdominal cosmetic results were evaluated with photographs. Immediate and delayed complications were rated, and a total of 139 patients operated on between 2000 and 2001 were asked to evaluate abdominal wall symptoms (**Figures 22.3.10 through 22.3.12**).

PATIENT EVALUATION

This group of non-selected patients[7] were asked two questions: "Do you feel any abdominal disturbance?" "Based on your experience, would you undergo this operation again?" 64% of patients reported they had no abdominal disturbance, 20% reported slight disturbance, and 16% reported moderate or severe disturbance. Of the 110 patients who answered the second question, 97 said "yes" (88.2%) and 13 said "no" (11.8%).

Taking into account what is known about decrease of abdominal wall strength[9] from studies undertaken by the authors and others, indications for bipedicle flaps (35.5% versus

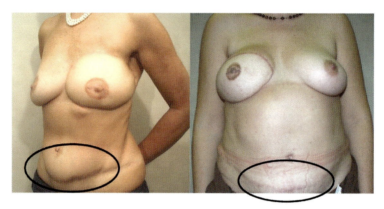

22.3.10 Previous midline scar (sub-umbilical) does not jeopardize a TRAM flap reconstruction.

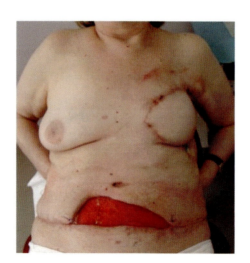

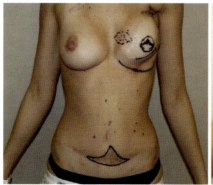 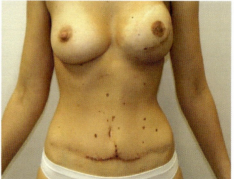

22.3.11–22.3.12 Partial flap necrosis and repair.

more than 50%) have reduced significantly in recent years. A contralateral mammoplasty has been performed more frequently (58.8% versus 30%) and some surgeons have reduced the use of mesh (less than 20% for monopedicled flaps in a recent period). A hernia rate of 2.6% is comparable to the rate observed in the literature. Interestingly, the rate of hernia formation was similar for bipedicled flaps with mesh and monopedicled flaps with or without mesh. Therefore, abdominal repair with mesh is strongly recommended in the case of bipedicled flaps. Body mass index is correlated with a higher incidence of hernia, especially in patients who smoke. Of note, more than 80% of the patients questioned in the follow-up reported normal physical activity, although 16% complained of medium to severe abdominal disturbance.

TRAM flap reconstruction and pregnancy: An overview of the literature by Eskandari and colleagues[13] revealed that uneventful pregnancy and delivery is well tolerated in breast cancer survivors who have undergone abdominal flap-based breast reconstruction, and these patients report minor adverse effects in terms of either the breast or the abdomen.

REFERENCES

1. Hartrampf CR, Scheflan M, Black PW. (1982) Breast reconstruction with a transverse abdominal island flap. *Plast. Reconstr. Surg* 69:216–224.
2. Scheflan M, Hatrampf CR, Black PW. (1982) Breast reconstruction with a transverse abdominal island flap. *Plast Reconstr Surg* 69(5)908–909.
3. Moon HK, Taylor GI (1988) The vascular anatomy of rectus abdominis musculocutaneous flap based on the deep superior epigastric system. *Plast Reconstr Surg* 82(5):815–832.
4. Elliott LF, Eskenazi L, Beegle PH et al (1993) Immediate TRAM flap breast reconstruction – 128 consecutive cases. *Plast. Reconstr. Surg* 92:217–227.

5. Miller LB et al. (1988)The superiorly based rectus abdominis flap: Predicting and enhancing its blood supply based on an anatomic and clinical stidy. *Plast Reconstr Surg* 81(5):713–724.
6. Losken A, Carlson GW, Jones GE et al. (2002) Significance of intraabdominal compartment pressures following TRAM flap breast reconstruction and the correlation of results. *Plast Reconstr Surg* 109:2257–2264.
7. Petit JY, Rietjens M, Ferreira MAR et al. (1997) Abdominal sequelae after pedicled TRAM flap breast reconstruction. *Plast. Reconstr. Surg* 99:723–729.
8. Petit JY, Rietjens M, Garusi C et al. (2003) Abdominal complications and sequelae after breast reconstruction with pedicled TRAM flap: Is there still an indication for pedicled TRAM in the year 2003? *Plast. Reconstr. Surg* 112:1063–1065.
9. Lejour M, Dome M. (1991) Abdominal – wall function after rectus – abdominis transfer. *Plast. Reconstr. Surg* 87:1054–1068.
10. Kroll, SS, Schusterman, MA, Reece, GP, Miller, MJ, Robb, G, and Evans, G. Abdominal wall strength, bulging, and hernia after TRAM flap breast reconstruction. *Plast. Reconstr. Surg.* 96: 616, 1995.
11. Spear SL, Ducic I, Low M et al. (2005) The effect of radiation on pedicle TRAM flap breast reconstruction: Outcomes and implications. *Plast. Reconstr. Surg* 115:84–95.
12. Clough KB, O'Donoghue JM, Fitoussi AD et al. (2001) Prospective evaluation of late cosmetic results following breast reconstruction: II. TRAM flap reconstruction. *Plast. Reconstr. Surg* 107:1710–1716.
13. Eskandari A, Alipour S. Systematic review of effects of pregnancy on breast and abdominal contour after TRAM/DIEP breast reconstruction in breast cancer survivors. *Breast Cancer Res Treat.* 2015;152(1):9–15.
14. Petit JY, Rietjens M, Manconi A et al., *Department of Plastic Surgery Department of Plastic and Reconstructive Surgery* Milan, Italy: European Institute of Oncology.

22.4 FREE TRANSVERSE RECTUS ABDOMINIS MYOCUTANEOUS (TRAM) FLAP

Charles M. Malata and Georgette Oni

Introduction

First described in 1979 by Holmstrom, the inferiorly based free TRAM flap relies on the more robust deep inferior epigastric vessels.[1] It obviates the need for subcutaneous tunneling which can lead to unsightly bulging in the epigastric region, but involves an element of microsurgery, which carries its own inherent risks (**Table 22.4.1**). This free flap reliably harvests a larger amount of skin and subcutaneous fat than the pedicled TRAM flap. It is therefore desirable when large volumes of tissue are required to reconstruct the breast and delayed or bipedicled techniques are neither feasible nor desirable. It is the TRAM flap of choice in patients with a variety of risk factors including obesity, smoking, diabetes, peripheral vascular, autoimmune, and cardiovascular disease. Moreover, a free TRAM flap is well suited to those patients who have abdominal scars, especially across the upper abdomen, which might have transected the superior epigastric vascular pedicle in the case of a pedicled TRAM flap. Although abdominal-based autologous reconstruction is considered a gold standard for breast reconstruction, the TRAM donor site can be fraught with complications including weakness of the remaining muscle, abdominal bulging, and herniation.[2–4] In attempts to minimize this, several modifications were proposed which utilized varying degrees of muscle and rectus sheath harvest.[5–7] More recently, Nahabedian and colleagues have published a classification based on the amount of muscle spared during harvest (**Table 22.4.2**), so-called muscle-sparing TRAM.[8]

Indications and contraindications

Free TRAM flaps can be used for both unilateral and bilateral breast reconstruction and in the immediate, delayed, or delayed-immediate settings with respect to the mastectomy. In addition, these flaps can also be employed in tertiary forms of breast reconstruction as a salvage procedure following failed/suboptimal autologous or implant reconstructions.

In general, patients with a lower anterior abdominal wall pannus that has no/favorable scarring and who have minimal comorbidities and are non-smokers are the best candidates for this surgery (**Table 22.4.3**). In addition, nuances relating to whether it is a unilateral or bilateral reconstruction, current breast size and shape, patient's wishes with regard to breast size, and oncological status together with planned adjuvant therapy need to considered.

Relative contraindications include smoking, body mass index greater than 35, abdominal scars (e.g., appendicectomy, Pfannensteil, or Kocher's incisions) and comorbidities rendering prolonged anesthesia unsafe. Furthermore, factors which affect microsurgical transfer such as clotting disorders, pre- and post-oncological adjuvant therapies, as well as the patient's psychological status will influence whether this is an appropriate reconstructive option for that individual. Absolute contraindications include documented

---

Table 22.4.2 Classification of free TRAM flaps

Type	Muscle preserved
MS-0	Full width, partial length
MS-1	Preservation of lateral segment
MS-2	Preservation of lateral and medial segment
MS-3 (DIEP)	Preservation of entire muscle

Source: Nahabedian, M.Y. *et al., Plast. Reconstr. Surg.,* 110, 466–475, 2002.

Table 22.4.1 Advantages of free TRAM flap over pedicled TRAM flap in breast reconstruction

Better blood supply as based on deep inferior epigastric vessels

Bigger skin and fat paddle

Reduced fat necrosis

Better flap inset

Reduced donor site morbidity: hernias, functional weakness

Fewer contraindications: e.g., can be used in smokers, diabetics, previous abdominal scars

No epigastric bulge caused by folded rectus muscle pedicle

No violation of the inferior mammary fold as no tunneling required

---

Table 22.4.3 Current indications for free TRAM flap breast reconstruction

Preoperative

CT/MR angiogram demonstrates poor perforators

Extensive scarring making DIEP flap unpredictable

Surgical preference/unfamiliarity with perforator flap harvest

Patient comorbidities

Intraoperative

Difficult dissection

Small perforators <1 mm with unfavorable locations

Inadvertent damage to perforators

Perforator anatomy means it will entail extensive muscle/nerve damage

22.4 Free transverse rectus abdominis myocutaneous (TRAM) flap

Table 22.4.4 Contraindications for free TRAM flap breast reconstruction

Absolute
Previous division of the deep inferior epigastric vessels, CT angiography shows DIEVs not in continuity, injury to vessels
Significant co morbidities: e.g., ischemic heart disease, pulmonary disease, clotting problems
Previous abdominoplasty/apronectomy
Relative
Smoking: increased risk of partial flap necrosis/fat necrosis, pulmonary complications
Previous abdominal scars
Extensive abdominal scarring
Previous liposuction

injury to the deep inferior epigastric vessels or previous abdominoplasty or apronectomy as these procedures would likely have transected perforating vessels supplying the flap (**Table 22.4.4**).

Preoperative investigations and surgical technique

PREOPERATIVE

Standard preoperative checks aimed at assessing fitness for a prolonged general anesthesia should be undertaken. A clotting and thrombophilia screen is recommended and essential if there is any suggestion of a family or personal history of blood dyscrasias. Specific preoperative planning investigations pertaining to TRAM flap microsurgical transfer vary from one unit to another. In the authors' unit, computed tomography (CT) angiography is routinely employed to delineate the anterior abdominal wall vasculature. This provides information on where the perforators are concentrated and therefore guides the approach for optimal muscle harvest. Additional information relates to hernia, and patterns of superficial versus dominant circulation can be elucidated. Nonetheless, many units employ no preoperative imaging and rely on use of a hand held Doppler when marking the patient prior to surgery.

The patient is marked in both standing and supine positions. The midline of the patient is initially marked followed by the inframammary fold, breast height, and breast base width. This information is used to plan the volume and dimensions of subcutaneous tissue required for the free flap which will determine the amount of overlying abdominal skin that needs to be included. Scar placement should be as low as possible and take account of existing scars (especially Pfannensteil incisions), together with the location of perforators, which will be included in the myocutaneous flap. The flap design is basically similar to an aesthetic abdominoplasty (see **Figure 22.4.1**).

INTRAOPERATIVE SURGICAL TECHNIQUE: FLAP HARVEST

The superior and inferior skin incisions are made and care taken to identify the superficial inferior epigastric vein and artery. When the corresponding artery and vein are average size of more than 1.5 mm and pulsatile, this suggests that the superficial system is dominant and a superficial epigastric artery flap may be warranted at this stage, but otherwise these vessels are ligated. The umbilicus is carefully isolated and the upper incision is beveled outward to increase the amount of fat harvested and thus the vertical dimensions of the flap. The skin incisions are subsequently deepened to the level of the abdominal wall fascia/muscles.

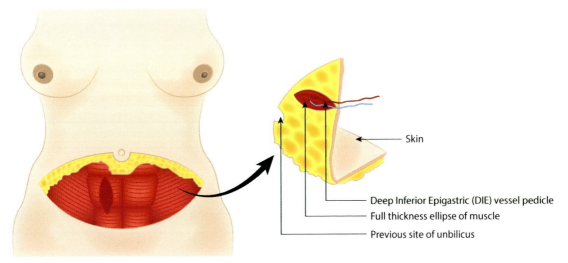

22.4.1 Schematic diagram showing the design of a muscle-sparing free TRAM flap. It also illustrates the variable amount of muscle harvested and the deep inferior epigastric vessels on the undersurface of the rectus abdominis muscle. (Drawn by Dr. Yahan Yu, MD, Taiwan.)

The next stage involves raising the flap from lateral to medial in the loose areolar tissue plane just above the fascia. This dissection can proceed swiftly to the lateral edge of the rectus muscle (semilunaris) and at this point careful dissection is required to identify the medial and lateral row of perforators. This procedure is carried out on both sides and from inferior to superior with dissection stopping at the points when the perforators are visualized. A central tunnel of dissection is also performed from inferior to the umbilicus with careful preservation of the medial perforators on either side. On the side of muscle harvest, the precise ellipse of sheath and underlying muscle is outlined. The anterior sheath is incised with a no. 15 blade along these boundaries to expose the underlying rectus muscle. Typically the segment of muscle used is the contralateral periumbilical rectus, where the largest perforators are usually concentrated. The full thickness of muscle is divided along these boundaries using monopolar diathermy taking care to avoid damage to the perforators and the main pedicle of the deep inferior epigastric vessels (**Figure 22.4.1**). The incision in the anterior rectus sheath is then continued in a J-shaped fashion toward Hasselbach's triangle with the lower limit of incision defined by the muscle fibers of the internal oblique muscle. The lateral border of the rectus muscle is then freed from the lateral and posterior rectus sheath which allows the rectus muscle to be reflected medially in order to identify and expose the deep inferior epigastric vein and artery. The deep inferior epigastric pedicle can be found entering the lateral border of the rectus muscle. At this point, a key decision has to be made on whether the entire width of the muscle needs to be harvested or a muscle sparing variant is appropriate. This decision is usually made at the time of exposure of the perforators, but can be refined at this stage. Often a variable portion of the lateral part of the rectus muscle is spared based on location of the perforators and the principle branches of the main deep inferior epigastric pedicle. The muscle to be harvested is isolated taking especial care not to damage the perforators or the pedicle. The rectus muscle is divided longitudinally just lateral to the lateral row of perforators. The cranial part of the pedicle is divided along with the rectus muscle to be taken with the perforators. A useful tip is to suture the sheath to the muscle to prevent any shearing injury to the perforators. The lower rectus is then divided transversely caudal to the entry point of the pedicle into the muscle, and it is particularly important not to damage the pedicle during this muscle division. The medial part of the rectus is then divided longitudinally, and a medial strip of muscle may be spared depending on the location of the perforators. Following these maneuvers, the main deep inferior epigastric pedicle is dissected caudally down to its origin from the external iliac vessels.

Pedicle length is determined by choice of recipient vessels, with a longer pedicle required if the thoracodorsal vessels are to be used and a free TRAM as opposed to a deep inferior epigastic perforator flap. Ideally, the whole length of the donor vascular pedicle is harvested with routine dissection stopping 1 cm or so caudal to the confluence of the deep inferior epigastric artery venae comitantes. The flap is now ready for microsurgical transfer. The authors prefer the contralateral side for TRAM flaps as this facilitates flap inset and microvascular anastomoses irrespective of the recipient vessels being the internal mammary or the thoracodorsal-subscapular systems.

INTRAOPERATIVE SURGICAL TECHNIQUE: MICROVASCULAR ANASTOMOSES AND DONOR SITE CLOSURE

Microvascular anastomoses are performed to the recipient vessels in a standard manner. For most surgeons, including the authors, the preferential recipient vessels are the internal mammary artery and vein.[9] Likewise, a popular technique is to use a venous coupler with a hand-sewn arterial anastomosis. If the thoracodorsal-subscapular system is used, the anastomosis must be done above the branch to the serratus anterior to allow retrograde filling and therefore preservation of the latissimus dorsi flap pedicle in case of abdominal flap failure.

The abdominal wall defect closure is ideally performed at the same time as the microvascular anastomoses to shorten operative time. The anterior sheath is repaired either directly where possible (two layer plication with looped 0 nylon sutures) or with use of an inlay mesh (prolene/vicryl). Standard abdominoplasty closure is then employed.

INTRAOPERATIVE SURGICAL TECHNIQUE: FLAP INSET

Flap inset and shaping are performed according to standard techniques. The contralateral flap is rotated 180° on the chest wall so that the umbilical area is at about the 5 o'clock or 7 o'clock position for right and left breasts, respectively. After trimming the flap to leave the desired amount of skin and subcutaneous tissue, the flap is inset by suturing its Scarpa's fascia or dermis to the pectoral fascia. Care must be taken during flap inset and shaping not to inadvertently avulse the microvascular anastomoses.

The flap is inset starting at the inner upper quadrant to protect the vascular anastomoses and ensure adequate recreation of medial fullness and cleavage. The process of insetting then proceeds in both an anticlockwise and clockwise manner. It is important to address the infraclavicular hollow as well as any depression caused by axillary clearance with insetting at the anterolateral border of the pectoralis major muscle and leaving a small amount of the flap to "rest" in the axillary hollow. For delayed reconstruction, the medial inset of the flap is very important to avoid a breast mound that is too laterally positioned. After securing the medial part of the flap, this should then be secured to the inframammary fold starting medially and proceeding laterally. Additionally it is important to minimize skin de-epithelialization until the stage of flap inset as there is always a reasonable native breast skin deficit. The upper part of the inset flap is de-epithelialized and secured under the superior mastectomy flap, whereas the inferior skin is used to replace the deficit and help create the correct degree of ptosis.

Perioperative management

Microsurgical free flap monitoring protocols are employed that ensure the patient is kept warm, well hydrated, and pain free. The authors have a very low threshold for flap exploration if there is any suspicion of vascular compromise and recommend a minimum urine output of 0.5 mL/kg/hour–1 mL/kg/hour in the first 24 hours (measured via catheter) and intravenous fluids are administered for the first 72 hours. TED stockings, low molecular weight heparin, and abdominal binders are routinely used as is mobilizing the patient the next day with a physiotherapist. Many units no longer routinely use aspirin, dextran 40, dipyridamole, or intravenous heparin to alter the coagulability of the blood unless there was a problem with the microvascular anastomoses or prolonged ischemia time. Patients are expected to be discharged within 5–7 days, although there are currently moves toward enhanced recovery protocols and earlier discharge times on day 4.

Short-term and long-term outcomes

Success rates for TRAM flap reconstruction are generally high in many centers with low re-exploration/failure rates quoted in the literature. The chances of total flap failure are 5%–6%, with a re-exploration rate of 10%–15%.[10,11] With increasing experience of the operating team, these values should decrease to <1% and <10%, respectively.[8,12,13] The complications of free TRAM flaps are similar to those of pedicled TRAMs and DIEP flaps, with potential problems at both the donor site and the recipient sites (Table 22.4.5). A notable advantage of free TRAMs over pedicled TRAMs and DIEP flaps is improved vascularity and possibly lower rates of fat necrosis within the flap.[14–16] However, there is no clear advantage for a free TRAM flap in terms of tolerability to subsequent irradiation compared to a DIEP flap.[17]

Patient satisfaction from this autologous procedure is well documented compared to implant-based reconstruction,[18] and this is largely attributable to the excellent cosmetic results achieved (Figures 22.4.2 and 22.4.3). Refinements such as nipple reconstruction, donor site scar revision, adjustment to the flap (e.g., liposuction), or a contralateral balancing procedure may be needed (as with other reconstructive techniques). However, in contrast to implant-based procedures, little or no maintenance is required long term for free TRAM flap reconstruction.

The main concern with harvesting part of the rectus abdominus muscle is donor site morbidity and whether

Table 22.4.5 Advantages of free TRAM over DIEP flap in breast reconstruction

Quicker to raise: no intramuscular dissection needed
Less fat necrosis: due to excellent blood supply of multiple perforators
Applicable to those with poor perforator anatomy: size/location/scarring
Fewer contraindications
More predictable in obese and morbidly obese patients, e.g., flap size >800 g

this is similar to the relatively low rates seen with DIEP flaps. Abdominal wall integrity following this operation has been extensively researched, and there is some debate as to whether the risk of postoperative donor site morbidity is low and has similar rates when compared to the DIEP flap (Table 22.4.6). Some studies have shown that the rates are comparable,[19,20] while others suggest that the DIEP flap has a lower abdominal bulge rate[2,3] and is more likely to retain superior abdominal wall function than the TRAM flap.[21] Rates of hernia formation are also much less for a free TRAM than when a pedicled flap is used as noted in the authors' series of rectus muscle harvests.

CONCLUSION

Free TRAM flap for breast reconstruction has been practiced for more than 25 years. It represents a predictable option for postmastectomy breast reconstruction and along with other lower abdominal free flap variants, shares several clear benefits compared to the pedicled TRAM. In particular, its muscle-sparing variants may have a donor site profile similar to a DIEP flap, and a free TRAM flap remains a technically simpler option for microsurgical breast reconstruction versus the perforator flaps. Nonetheless, it is being superseded by DIEP flaps as the favored option in many centers[22] although a free TRAM remains an intraoperative "backup" option in circumstances where a DIEP flap is not feasible. As with all microsurgical techniques, success is dependent on a combination of factors and it is imperative that the operating surgeon should familiarize themselves with these in order to optimize clinical outcomes and patient satisfaction.

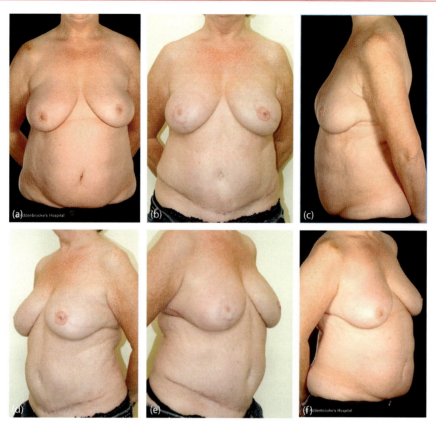

22.4.2 Immediate muscle-sparing free TRAM flap left breast reconstruction after nipple reconstruction and tattooing. As with all free TRAM flaps. There is no outward difference in appearance compared to a DIEP flap.

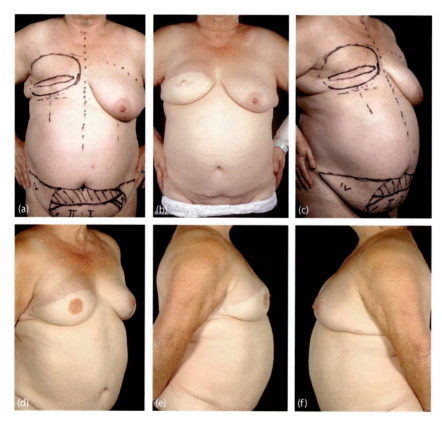

22.4.3 Delayed right breast reconstruction with a muscle-sparing free TRAM flap with subsequent nipple reconstruction before and after tattooing and contralateral mastopexy. Note the excellent symmetry achieved after staged surgery.

Table 22.4.6 Comparison of free TRAM, pedicled TRAM, and DIEP flaps in breast reconstruction

Parameter	Free TRAM	Pedicled TRAM	DIEP flap
Failure rate	5%–6% (historical)	rare	1%–2%
Fat necrosis	7% (historical)	13%–41%	7.3%
Hernia	3%–6% (historical)	12%	<1%
Effect of radiotherapy	Least	Maximal	Better than pedicled

Multiple historical references.

REFERENCES

1. Holmstrom H. The free abdominoplasty flap and its use in breast reconstruction. An experimental study and clinical case report. *Scand J Plast Reconstr Surg.* 1979;13(3):423–427.

2. Egeberg A, Rasmussen MK, Sorensen JA. Comparing the donor-site morbidity using DIEP, SIEA or MS-TRAM flaps for breast reconstructive surgery: A meta-analysis. *J Plast Reconstr Aesthet Surg.* 2012;65(11):1474–1480.

3. Man LX, Selber JC, Serletti JM. Abdominal wall following free TRAM or DIEP flap reconstruction: A meta-analysis and critical review. *Plast Reconstr Surg.* 2009;124(3):752–764.

4. Wan DC, Tseng CY, Anderson-Dam J, Dalio AL, Crisera CA, Festekjian JH. Inclusion of mesh in donor-site repair of free TRAM and muscle-sparing free TRAM flaps yields rates of abdominal complications comparable to those of DIEP flap reconstruction. *Plast Reconstr Surg.* 2010;126(2):367–374.

5. Elliott LF, Seify H, Bergey P. The 3-hour muscle-sparing free TRAM flap: Safe and effective treatment review of 111 consecutive free TRAM flaps in a private practice setting. *Plast Reconstr Surg.* 2007;120(1):27–34.

6. Arnez ZM, Khan U, Pogorelec D, Planinsek F. Rational selection of flaps from the abdomen in breast reconstruction to reduce donor site morbidity. *Br J Plast Surg.* 1999;52(5):351–354.

7. Kroll SS, Marchi M. Comparison of strategies for preventing abdominal-wall weakness after TRAM flap breast reconstruction. *Plast Reconstr Surg.* 1992;89(6):1045–1051; discussion 52–53.

8. Nahabedian MY, Momen B, Galdino G, Manson PN. Breast reconstruction with the free TRAM or DIEP flap: Patient selection, choice of flap, and outcome. *Plast Reconstr Surg.* 2002;110(2):466–475; discussion 76–77.

9. Malata CM, Moses M, Mickute Z, Di Candia M. Tips for successful microvascular abdominal flap breast reconstruction utilizing the "total rib preservation" technique for internal mammary vessel exposure. *Ann Plast Surg.* 2011;66(1):36–42.

10. Serletti JM, Moran SL. Free versus the pedicled TRAM flap: A cost comparison and outcome analysis. *Plast Reconstr Surg.* 1997;100(6):1418–1424; discussion 25–27.

11. Arnez ZM, Bajec J, Bardsley AF, Scamp T, Webster MH. Experience with 50 free TRAM flap breast reconstructions. *Plast Reconstr Surg.* 1991;87(3):470–478; discussion 9–82.

12. Baldwin BJ, Schusterman MA, Miller MJ, Kroll SS, Wang BG. Bilateral breast reconstruction: Conventional versus free TRAM. *Plast Reconstr Surg.* 1994;93(7):1410–1416; discussion 7.

13. Damen TH, Morritt AN, Zhong T, Ahmad J, Hofer SO. Improving outcomes in microsurgical breast reconstruction: Lessons learnt from 406 consecutive DIEP/TRAM flaps performed by a single surgeon. *J Plast Reconstr Aesthet Surg.* 2013;66(8):1032–1038.

14. Kroll SS. Fat necrosis in free transverse rectus abdominis myocutaneous and deep inferior epigastric perforator flaps. *Plast Reconstr Surg.* 2000;106(3):576–583.

15. Baumann DP, Lin HY, Chevray PM. Perforator number predicts fat necrosis in a prospective analysis of breast reconstruction with free TRAM, DIEP, and SIEA flaps. *Plast Reconstr Surg.* 2010;125(5):1335–1341.

16. Serletti JM. Breast reconstruction with the TRAM flap: Pedicled and free. *J Surg Oncol.* 2006;94(6):532–537.

17. Garvey PB, Clemens MW, Hoy AE, Smith B, Zhang H, Kronowitz SJ et al. Muscle-sparing TRAM flap does not protect breast reconstruction from postmastectomy radiation damage compared with the DIEP flap. *Plast Reconstr Surg.* 2014;133(2):223–233.

18. Yueh JH, Slavin SA, Adesiyun T, Nyame TT, Gautam S, Morris DJ et al. Patient satisfaction in postmastectomy breast reconstruction: A comparative evaluation of DIEP, TRAM, latissimus flap, and implant techniques. *Plast Reconstr Surg.* 2010;125(6):1585–1595.

19. Chun YS, Sinha I, Turko A, Yueh JH, Lipsitz S, Pribaz JJ et al. Comparison of morbidity, functional outcome, and satisfaction following bilateral TRAM versus bilateral DIEP flap breast reconstruction. *Plast Reconstr Surg.* 2010;126(4):1133–1141.

20. Macadam SA, Zhong T, Weichman K, Papsdorf M, Lennox PA, Hazen A et al. Quality of life and patient-reported outcomes in breast cancer survivors: A multicenter comparison of four abdominally based autologous reconstruction methods. *Plast Reconstr Surg.* 2016;137(3):758–771.

21. Seidenstuecker K, Legler U, Munder B, Andree C, Mahajan A, Witzel C. Myosonographic study of abdominal wall dynamics to assess donor site morbidity after microsurgical breast reconstruction with a DIEP or an ms-2 TRAM flap. *J Plast Reconstr Aesthet Surg.* 2016;69(5):598–603.

22. Pien I, Caccavale S, Cheung MC, Butala P, Hughes DB, Ligh C et al. Evolving trends in autologous breast reconstruction: Is the deep inferior epigastric artery perforator flap taking over? *Ann Plast Surg.* 2016;76(5):489–493.

22.5 DEEP INFERIOR EPIGASTRIC PERFORATOR (DIEP) FLAP

Edward Wayne Buchel and Nakul Gamanlal Patel

Introduction

The deep inferior epigastric artery perforator (DIEP) flap is an evolution on the transverse rectus abdominis myocutaneous (TRAM) flap, in which a single or multiple perforators of the deep inferior epigastric artery and accompanying veins are dissected through the rectus abdominis muscle. This preserves fascia and innervated muscle, hence easing abdominal closure and reducing donor site morbidity.[1] First described in 1992, the DIEP flap is now becoming the gold standard for autologous breast reconstruction[2,3] (**Figure 22.5.1**).

Vascular anatomy of the abdomen

The deep inferior epigastric artery and venae originate from the external iliac artery, enter the deep lateral surface of the lower third of the rectus muscle, and divide into a series of vertical rows within the substance of the muscle. These rows give off perforating vessels that travel through the muscle and into the overlying fascia fat and skin. Hartrampf originally described four zones of perfusion to the lower abdomen for pedicled TRAM flaps: zone I directly over the ipsilateral rectus muscle; zone II across the midline over the contralateral muscle; zone III lateral to the ipsilateral muscle; and zone IV is the remaining area lateral to the contralateral rectus abdominis muscle.[4] Greatest perfusion was thought to be in zones I and II, with lesser perfusion in zone III, and least perfusion in IV (**Figure 22.5.2**).

Holm proposed swapping zones II and III to better represent perfusion of the DIEP flap[5] (Figure 22.5.2).

Wong and colleagues demonstrated that both the Hartrampf and Holm's zones of perfusion were accurate depending on the perforator location.[6] They introduce the concept of "perforasomes" to the DIEP flap, which is the block of tissue supplied by each perforator. Further understanding of perforator anatomy and perfusion has been elucidated by the work of Saint-Cyr.[7] His work shed light on the importance of linking vessels between perforators and the concepts of "hot" and "cold" perforator zones in the body.[7,8]

Advantages

Donor site weakness, bulging, and hernia are reduced compared to the TRAM flap.[9] The preservation of innervated muscle and fascia as a consequence of only harvesting the dominant perforator(s) is a major advantage of the DIEP flap. In bilateral breast reconstructive cases, direct fascial closure is only possible for the DIEP flap.

In comparison to non-autologous methods, the DIEP flap breast reconstruction provides a lifelong reconstruction which does not require ongoing revision. This leads to high levels of patient satisfaction for longer periods in this group of patients.[10,11]

Drawbacks

The DIEP flap is a technically more challenging flap to raise and hence can take longer for surgeons not familiar with perforator flap dissection. In particular, damage to a main perforator can result in partial or complete flap loss.

The DIEP flap does have slightly reduced perfusion when compared to free-TRAM flaps and may be associated with an increased rate of fat necrosis and partial flap loss (in areas outside zones I/II).[12] Increased rates of venous congestion necessitates secondary venous drainage in a limited number of cases[13] (**Figure 22.5.3**).

It should be noted that raising a DIEP flap via a long full thickness incision in the rectus muscle will inevitably transect motor nerves and de-innervate muscle. This will negate any benefit in terms of abdominal wall morbidity which the DIEP flap is designed to achieve.

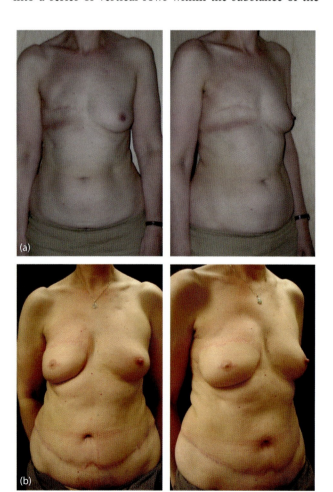

22.5.1 Right delayed breast reconstruction with DIEP flap: (a) preoperative and (b) postoperative photographs.

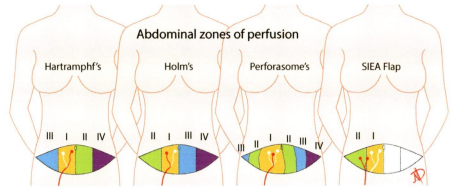

22.5.2 Abdominal zones of perfusion: (i) Hartrampf's pedicled TRAM, (ii) Holm's DIEP, (iii) Perforasome's, and (iv) SIEA flap.

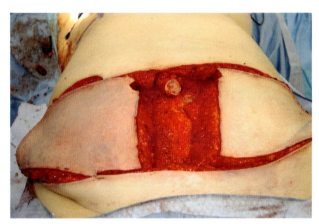

22.5.3 Right and left hemi-abdomen raised as DIEP flaps on single perforators on each side. The right DIEP flap showing signs of venous congestion requiring secondary drainage via the superficial inferior epigastric vein.

Indications

Almost all patients with adequate abdominal tissue are potential candidates for DIEP flap breast reconstruction. It is ideal for both immediate and delayed breast reconstruction and is particularly helpful in failed implant-based reconstructions (**Figure 22.5.4**). Indications are similar to those for the free TRAM flap. Patients undergoing postoperative radiotherapy benefit from autologous reconstruction over implant-based reconstructions, but should be counseled regarding increased rates of fat necrosis, mastectomy skin tightening, volume loss, and potential revision surgery which may subsequently be required to improve breast shape and symmetry postradiation.

Contraindications include significant comorbidities preventing a safe general anesthetic, and those patients who have undergone an abdominoplasty or resection of the lower abdominal wall tissue. Relative contraindications include previous abdominal scars and coagulopathies. Smoking, poorly controlled diabetes, and obesity have a negative impact on the donor site and mastectomy skin flaps.[14,15]

For those patients who have limited abdominal tissue, techniques have been described in the following

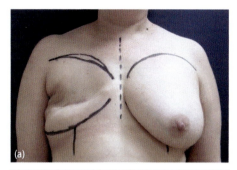
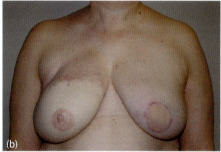

22.5.4 Right delayed breast reconstruction and left skin-sparing mastectomy and immediate breast reconstruction with DIEA flaps: (a) preoperative and (b) postoperative photographs.

chapters to utilize and recruit tissue from adjacent areas. Combining flaps also helps increase tissue volume, such as bipedicled abdominal flaps to one breast, DIEP-DCIA/SGAP combined flaps, and DIEP-TUG stacked flaps[16–18] (**Figure 22.5.5**).

Imaging modalities

Although not essential, imaging provides a roadmap to the largest perforators and can lead to faster intraoperative decision-making. Various vascular imaging modalities including duplex Doppler, computed-tomography angiography, and magnetic resonance angiography have been used[19] (**Figure 22.5.6**). However, these are expensive, time-consuming procedures and are not without risk. Computed-tomography angiography specifically exposes

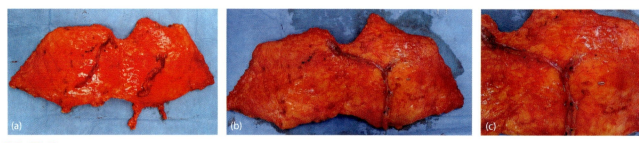

22.5.5 (a-c) Bipedicled abdominal allow greater volume to reconstruct a single breast flap.

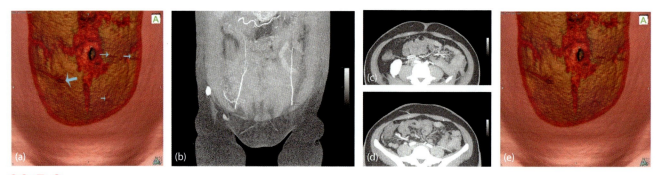

22.5.6 (a-e) CT angiography to map out the abdominal wall perforators. Right hemi-abdomen has a large infra-umbilical perforator and the left has three smaller perforators. Three-dimensional reconstructions.

the patient to significant radiation doses and carries a carcinogenic risk.[20]

Laser angiography using indocyanine green is a useful intraoperative vascular imaging modality that can be used to assess the physiological zone of perfusion of the DIEP flap and also be helpful in assessing the vascularity of mastectomy skin flaps.[21]

Flap harvest

Preoperative markings focus on designing the flap(s) on the lower abdomen while incorporating periumbilical perforators. Flap harvest begins with the inferior incision and dissection of the superficial vein and identification of the superficial inferior epigastric artery (SIEA), if present, with up to one-third of patients being suitable for SIEA flaps. The superficial inferior epigastric vein is dissected in all available cases as a secondary venous drainage option for the DIEP flap. The superior incision is then made, the umbilicus is freed, and the abdominal flap above the umbilicus raised to the xiphisternum. The DIEP flap is then raised from lateral to medial with the identification of the largest lateral row of perforator(s). In bilateral cases, the midline infra-umbilical incision is made and the medial row of perforators is identified. If imaging has located a dominant perforator, this is dissected out to the level of the fascia. Otherwise intraoperative dissection locates the dominant medial row of perforators. Once the dominant perforator is located, all other remaining perforators are temporarily clamped and perfusion to the flap evaluated. The fascia around the dominant perforator is split and the perforator is dissected through the rectus abdominis muscle to obtain a suitable length and caliber of vessel. Once verification of perfusion on the dominant perforator is assured, the remaining perforators are cut and the flap harvested (**Figures 22.5.7 and 22.5.8**). If perfusion is insufficient, secondary perforators are dissected to connect to the main perforator.

Simultaneously, recipient vessels are prepared from either the internal mammary or thoracodorsal systems. In the chest, the internal mammary vessels are used unless large internal mammary perforators are present. The flap is anastomosed to the recipient vessels and fashioned into a breast mound. The abdominal fascial opening is repaired with a 0 looped ethilon, and the superior abdominal flap may be quilted to the anterior rectus abdominal fascia with a barbed suture prior to incision closure in layers with absorbable sutures. The umbilicus is brought out through a new opening in the pulled down abdominal flap (Figure 22.5.7).

Evolution of abdominal flaps

The abdominal donor site has evolved from TRAM flaps, to muscle-sparing variant TRAM flaps, to the DIEP flap in an effort to reduce donor site morbidity. Nevertheless, all of these require an incision through the anterior rectus fascia and dissection through the muscle with possible injury to the intercostal nerves supplying the rectus abdominis muscle (**Figure 22.5.9**).

22.5 Deep inferior epigastric perforator (DIEP) flap 335

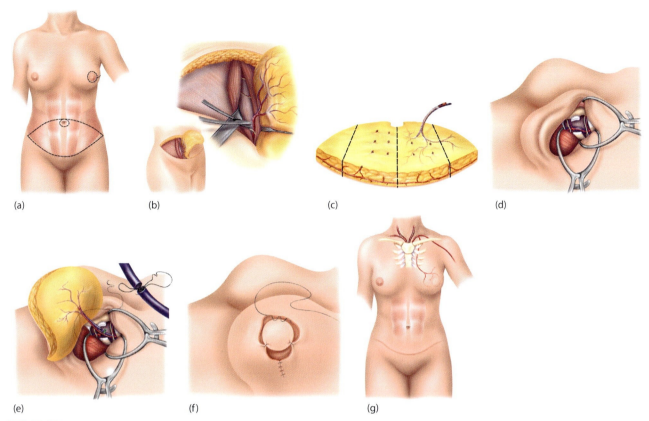

22.5.7 Illustrative steps of DIEP flap harvest and inset: (a) preoperative marking, (b) intramuscular dissection of the flap, (c) raised flap, (d) internal mammary vessel (IMA/V) prepartion with costal cartilage resection, (e) microsurgical anastomosis of the DIEA/V to IMA/V, (f) flap inset, and (g) postoperative outcome.

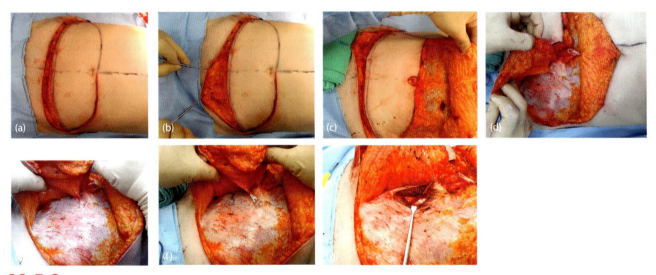

22.5.8 Intraoperative photographs of DIEP flap harvest: (a) caudal incision, (b) dissection of SIEA/V, (c) dissection of abdominal flap above the umbilicus up to the xiphisternum, (d) dissection of medial and lateral row perforators, (e) clamps allied to smaller perforators, and (f) intramuscular dissection of selected (medial) row perforator.

The SIEA flap is advantageous given that it does not involve dissection through the rectus abdominis muscle or fascia. Unfortunately, the small caliber vessels, high incidence of vessel transection from previous lower abdominal wall surgery, and unreliable perfusion to the contralateral abdomen have limited its use[22–24] (Figure 22.5.5).

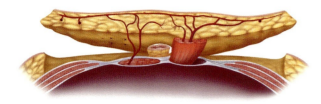

22.5.9 Illustration comparing the DIEP and TRAM flaps.

CONCLUSION

The DIEP flap is the gold standard autologous breast reconstructive option. It can be used in immediate and delayed breast reconstruction and for correction of failed implant-based reconstruction. The DIEP flap provides a consistent and reliable method of creating a breast mound which is long-lasting and natural in appearance, limiting abdominal wall morbidity, and often improving abdominal contour (**Figure 22.5.10**).

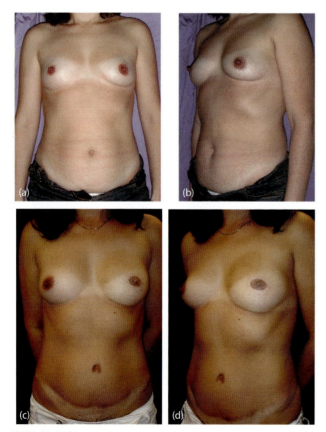

22.5.10 Left skin-sparing mastectomy and immediate breast reconstruction with DIEP flap: (a,b) preoperative and (c,d) postoperative photographs following nipple reconstruction and tattooing.

REFERENCES

1. Wang, X.L. et al. Meta-analysis of the safety and factors contributing to complications of MS-TRAM, DIEP, and SIEA flaps for breast reconstruction. *Aesthetic Plast Surg*, 2014. 38(4): pp. 681–691.
2. Allen, R.J. and P. Treece. Deep inferior epigastric perforator flap for breast reconstruction. *Ann Plast Surg*, 1994. 32(1): pp. 32–38.
3. Healy, C. and R.J. Allen, Sr. The evolution of perforator flap breast reconstruction: Twenty years after the first DIEP flap. *J Reconstr Microsurg*, 2014. 30(2): pp. 121–125.
4. Hartrampf, C.R., M. Scheflan, and P.W. Black. Breast reconstruction with a transverse abdominal island flap. *Plast Reconstr Surg*, 1982. 69(2): pp. 216–225.
5. Holm, C. et al. Perfusion zones of the DIEP flap revisited: A clinical study. *Plast Reconstr Surg*, 2006. 117(1): pp. 37–43.
6. Wong, C. et al. Perforasomes of the DIEP flap: Vascular anatomy of the lateral versus medial row perforators and clinical implications. *Plast Reconstr Surg*, 2010. 125(3): pp. 772–782.
7. Mohan, A.T. and M. Saint-Cyr. Anatomic and physiological fundamentals for autologous breast reconstruction. *Gland Surg*, 2015. 4(2): pp. 116–133.
8. Saint-Cyr, M. et al. The perforasome theory: Vascular anatomy and clinical implications. *Plast Reconstr Surg*, 2009. 124(5): pp. 1529–1544.
9. Man, L.X., J.C. Selber, and J.M. Serletti. Abdominal wall following free TRAM or DIEP flap reconstruction: A meta-analysis and critical review. *Plast Reconstr Surg*, 2009. 124(3): pp. 752–764.
10. Yueh, J.H. et al. Patient satisfaction in postmastectomy breast reconstruction: A comparative evaluation of DIEP, TRAM, latissimus flap, and implant techniques. *Plast Reconstr Surg*, 2010. 125(6): pp. 1585–1595.
11. Atherton, D.D. et al. The economic viability of breast reconstruction in the UK: Comparison of a single surgeon's experience of implant; LD; TRAM and DIEP based reconstructions in 274 patients. *J Plast Reconstr Aesthet Surg*, 2011. 64(6): pp. 710–715.
12. Mulvey, C.L. et al. Increased flap weight and decreased perforator number predict fat necrosis in DIEP breast reconstruction. *Plast Reconstr Surg Glob Open*, 2013. 1(2): pp. 1–7.
13. Rozen, W.M. and M.W. Ashton. The venous anatomy of the abdominal wall for deep inferior epigastric artery (DIEP) flaps in breast reconstruction. *Gland Surg*, 2012. 1(2): pp. 92–110.
14. Parrett, B.M. et al.. DIEP flaps in women with abdominal scars: Are complication rates affected? *Plast Reconstr Surg*, 2008. 121(5): pp. 1527–1531.
15. Klasson, S. et al. Smoking increases donor site complications in breast reconstruction with DIEP flap. *J Plast Surg Hand Surg*, 2016: pp. 1–5.
16. Patel, N.G. et al. Stacked and bipedicled abdominal free flaps for breast reconstruction: Considerations for shaping. *Gland Surg*, 2016. 5(2): pp. 115–121.
17. DellaCroce, F.J. et al. Body lift perforator flap breast reconstruction: A review of 100 flaps in 25 cases. *Plast Reconstr Surg*, 2012. 129(3): pp. 551–561.
18. Rozen, W.M., N.G. Patel, and V.V. Ramakrishnan. Increasing options in autologous microsurgical breast reconstruction: Four free flaps for "stacked" bilateral breast reconstruction. *Gland Surg*, 2016. 5(2): pp. 255–260.

19. Rozen, W.M. et al. Stereotactic image-guided navigation in the preoperative imaging of perforators for DIEP flap breast reconstruction. *Microsurgery*, 2008. 28(6): pp. 417–423.
20. Smith-Bindman, R. et al., Radiation dose associated with common computed tomography examinations and the associated lifetime attributable risk of cancer. *Arch Intern Med*, 2009. 169(22): pp. 2078–2086.
21. Gurtner, G.C. et al. Intraoperative laser angiography using the SPY system: Review of the literature and recommendations for use. *Ann Surg Innov Res*, 2013. 7(1): 1.
22. Antia, N.H. and V.I. Buch. Transfer of an abdominal dermo-fat graft by direct anastomosis of blood vessels. *Br J Plast Surg*, 1971. 24(1): pp. 15–19.
23. Grotting, J.C. The free abdominoplasty flap for immediate breast reconstruction. *Ann Plast Surg*, 1991. 27(4): pp. 351–354.
24. Buchel, E.W., K.R. Dalke, and T.E. Hayakawa. Rethinking the superficial inferior epigastric artery flap in breast reconstruction: Video demonstration of a rapid, reliable harvest technique. *Can J Plast Surg*, 2013. 21(2): pp. 99–100.

EDITORIAL COMMENTARY

Chapter 22 presents advanced options for autologous tissue breast reconstruction by the actual developers or the world experts in performing these advanced flaps who provide summarized details on how they perform these flaps for breast reconstruction. These chapters will provide imperative information for the reader to integrate the use of these advanced flaps into their clinical practice.

The transverse rectus abdominis myocutaneous (TRAM) flap and the deep inferior epigastric perforator (DIEP) flap continue to be the predominant autologous tissue options for breast reconstruction after mastectomy because they provide the ideal donor sites, resulting in a cosmetic improvement of the abdomen with a reliable and consistent blood supply. Of course, there are several methods of increasing the use of the abdominal based flaps in patients with limited abdominal adipose tissue. These include the use of a double-DIEP flap, where the flaps are either perfused as a chain based chimeric flap or by using two separate recipient vessels, like the antegrade and retrograde internal mammary vessels. A more recent and popular option is to use the transferred TRAM or DIEP flap as a conduit for subsequent serial fat transfer to optimize the volume of the reconstructed breast by providing fat from all regions of the body, not limiting the reconstruction to abdominal adipose tissue.

However, many patients are still not candidates for a TRAM or DIEP flap. Patients who have already had a TRAM or DIEP flap and need another breast reconstruction or anatomy-related issues often require tissue from other body regions. The creativity of plastic surgeons has lead to other autologous free tissue transfer options for these patients based on the anatomical fat distribution. Many patients who lack abdominal fat deposit fat in their buttocks, which can serve as an excellent option for breast reconstruction. An interesting variant in the gluteal artery perforator (GAP) flap, referred to as the boomerang flap, has increased the widespread use of buttock tissue for breast reconstruction. Drs. Allen and Dr. Levine continue to expand the use of the profunda artery perforator (PAP) flap. The authors describe their flap elevation technique, provide surgical tips, flap insetting options, and reconstructive outcomes in more than 300 PAP flaps they have performed. The transverse upper gracilis (TUG) flap is very useful but has been limited by its small size and poor cosmetic donor site outcome. However,

many experts who routinely perform this flap, like Dr. Buntic, utilize the TUG flap for breast reconstruction with incredible cosmetic outcomes. Dr. Buntic and colleagues provide a very descriptive chapter on "how-to" perform the TUG flap, especially shaping and insetting and how to minimize the deformity to the medial thigh donor site. The details provided within this chapter should provide the reader with the confidence and knowledge to use this workhorse flap in their breast reconstructive practice. Dr. Hamdi has recently published the largest experience with use of the lumbar artery perforator (LAP) flap for breast reconstruction. He presents a step-by-step chapter including potential perils and pitfalls of this free flap that was first described in 2003, including figures for planning and surgical dissection.

All advanced flaps for breast reconstruction are not free tissue transfers. The thoracodorsal artery perforator (TAP) flap has brought back the use of the back for breast reconstruction. Techniques for partial breast reconstruction using these chest wall perforator flaps (TDAP and LICAP variants) are succinctly outlined by Dr. Agrigiani. These flaps are particularly useful for larger breast excisions confined to the upper outer and lateral aspects of the breast and can avoid the need for mastectomy and whole breast reconstruction. The latissiumus dorsi myocutaneous flap has suffered a decline in usage since the advent of acellular dermal matrices (ADMs) products in breast reconstruction. The TAP flap, which avoids the transfer of the back muscle, can be limited by mainly providing skin replacement to the breast reconstruction. However, the amount of fat that can be transferred with the TAP flap can be extended which can add significant volume for a TUG flap only reconstruction, avoiding the need for a breast implant. Despite the popularity of the TAP flap and the obvious benefit of avoiding transfer of the latissimus muscle, circumstances still exist that the latissimus muscle only flap can be the best option for breast reconstruction. In the circumstance of delayed-immediate reconstruction, when the expander is exchanged for a permanent breast implant after radiation, covering the implant with a latissimus muscle only flap can be ideal for healing and cosmetic outcome. Dr. Selber has developed and continues to utilize a robotic approach to harvest of the latissimus muscle, which minimizes adverse cosmetic and functional outcomes of the back donor site.

23

Advanced autologous tissue flaps for whole breast reconstruction

AT A GLANCE

Perforator flaps for breast reconstruction along with preoperative imaging with both computed tomography and magnetic resonance imaging has opened a Pandora's box of new flap options, including the profunda artery perforator (PAP) flap. In addition, the increasing use of robotic surgery has now carried over to breast reconstruction, potentially with increasing applications in the future. Innovative approaches to bipedicled deep inferior epigastric perforator (DIEP) flaps have expanded the indications for DIEP reconstruction in thin patients. The transverse upper gracilis (TUG) flap is gaining in popularity as a secondary option for reconstruction instead of the gluteal flap. These alternative flaps and methods of harvest continue to invigorate the field of microsurgical breast reconstruction.

23.1 THORACODORSAL PERFORATOR (TAP) FLAP

Claudio Angrigiani, Alberto Rancati, and Marcelo Irigo

Introduction

The thoracodorsal artery perforator (TDAP) flap was originally described in 1992[1] and involves harvesting the skin and a subcutaneous island in the territory of a traditional latissimus dorsi (LD)-musculocutaneous flap, but without inclusion of muscle. This flap was initially promoted as a supplementary flap for breast reconstruction,[2–3] although it has recently been used for complete autologous breast reconstruction.[4] There is evidence from several studies demonstrating that the TDAP flap is both a reliable and safe option for breast reconstruction.[4–6]

The blood supply of the TDAP flap is based on the proximal perforator of the descending branch of the thoracodorsal artery, which has a consistent anatomical presence.[7–8] When additional volume is needed without muscle, the superior (scapular) and inferior (lumbar) fat compartments can be partially captured and supplied by this proximal muscle perforator as an extended TDAP flap (**Figure 23.1.1**).[9] Using this technique, sufficient volume can be obtained to reconstruct a B-cup-sized breast with a totally or partially de-epithelialized flap (**Figures 23.1.2 and 23.1.3**).

Indications

The TDAP flap should be considered as a reconstructive option when an autologous procedure is required and a conventional abdominal donor site is not available, or this approach, is declined by the patient and/or surgeon.

Additionally, the TDAP flap may be indicated when microsurgical techniques are not available. Based on the authors, own experience, autologous breast reconstruction with a TDAP is the first choice when a volume comparable to that of the contralateral breast can be obtained via a single operative procedure. Avoidance of microsurgery, a relatively short procedure duration, reliability, low morbidity of the donor area, and efficacy of the technique are the main advantages of a TDAP flap reconstruction. Furthermore, compared to the LD myocutaneous flap, there is low morbidity associated with the donor site.

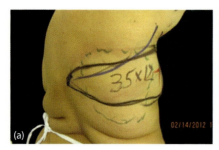
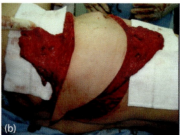
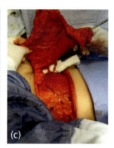

23.1.1 (a) The flap is designed on the back; (b) The incision is extended with part of the scapular and lumbar fat compartments; and (c) The flap is elevated, and the perforator is observed.

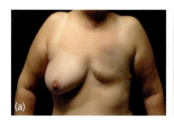

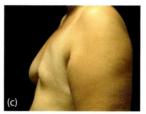

23.1.2 Breast reconstruction in a 54-year-old woman who had undergone mastectomy and radiotherapy. (a) Preoperative frontal view; (b) 6-month postoperative frontal view of the breast reconstructed with a thoracodorsal artery perforator flap; (c) Preoperative lateral view; and (d) 6-month postoperative lateral view.

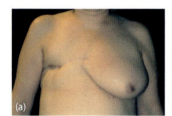
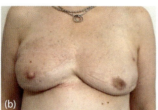
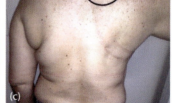
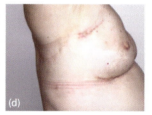

23.1.3 Breast reconstruction in a 48-year-old woman who had undergone mastectomy and radiotherapy. (a) Preoperative frontal view; (b) 12-month postoperative frontal view of the breast reconstructed with an extended thoracodorsal artery perforator flap; (c) 12-month postoperative back view of the donor area; and (d) 12-month postoperative lateral view.

Surgical technique

FLAP DESIGN

The flap is planned with the patient in the standing position, with arms at the side, and hands on the waist. The patient is asked to actively contract the back muscles, at which time the antero-lateral border of the LD muscle is clearly defined under the skin and is marked with an indelible pen. The absence of any obvious contraction of this muscle in postmastectomy cases is highly suggestive of damage to the latissimus dorsi neurovascular pedicle. Although this finding is indicative of a nerve lesion, it is also frequently associated with a vascular lesion. The possibility of harvesting a LD-musculocutaneous flap with "compensatory" blood supply has been reported; however, other options are recommended in order to minimize the risk of flap loss.

A point "A" is marked on the anterolateral muscle line 8 cm below the axillary fold. The descending branch of the proximal perforator artery runs parallel and approximately 2 cm lateral to this line. The point at which the perforator (or cutaneous branch) pierces the flap tissue should be identified and included in the flap design to ensure vascularization.

The full length of the flap extends to the junction of the lateral three-quarters of the back with the most medial quarter of the back. The flap width is designed so as to allow direct closure of the donor site. The skin and the associated subcutaneous tissue are pinched with the thumb and index finger to mark the desired width.

FLAP ELEVATION

The flap is raised in a distal to proximal direction, superficial to the deep fascia, while protecting the fascia overlying the LD muscle. At the same time, the perforator arteries are carefully identified using 4× loop magnification. Continuous and progressive control of the amount of bleeding from the end of the flap is an ideal way for monitoring the presence of good perforating vessels. If the flap maintains excellent perfusion when it is partially separated from the LD muscle, then the perforator is likely to be adequate with a diameter of at least 0.5 mm. By contrast, if the perfusion decreases markedly when the flap is partly raised and the medial intercostal perforators sectioned, then the procedure should be postponed to avoid flap loss.

The medial part of the flap is expanded superiorly and inferiorly with incorporation of part of the scapular and lumbar fat compartments. It is essential to maintain a minimum (3–5 mm) thickness for the remaining parts of the flap to avoid tissue damage at the donor site.

Once the perforator has been clearly identified, the following options can be used to develop the flap:

1. Rotate the flap by 180° as a propeller on to the anterior chest wall.[9] This procedure is very simple; however, the perforator does not reach as far anterior as a conventional perforator. This technique is indicated for partial reconstruction of lateral breast defects.[10]
2. Turn the flap over (flip over) as a muscle sparing technique. This procedure requires de-epithelialization of the flap because the dermis remains in the deep part of the breast. This option is indicated when volume replacement is required.
3. Perform complete dissection of the perforator through the muscle (conventional TAP flap) and transposition with complete preservation of the muscle fibers. Although this procedure is complex, it provides a flap with the most distal reaching point and is indicated for complete autologous breast reconstruction.

FLAP INSETTING

The cutaneous part of the flap is positioned to cover the skin defect. In delayed breast reconstruction, it is convenient to recreate the round shape of the wound edges by transforming the Stewart type scar into a round scar. The flap is then tailored accordingly, avoiding the sharp triangular shape of the final scar. In immediate breast reconstruction, the skin sparing technique is recommended for mastectomy in order to achieve an optimal final aesthetic result.

SURGICAL TIPS

Thoracodorsal artery muscle perforators are universally present in all individuals. Nonetheless, in cases of delayed breast reconstruction, these perforators should be carefully

evaluated preoperatively to assess any damage that might have resulted from a more aggressive initial surgical procedure. Although acoustic Doppler is an important aid for the surgeon, it might not be sufficient to determine the presence of a good perforator.

Direct intraoperative evaluation through an inferior surgical approach is advisable until the perforators have been visualized. Larger perforators seen during flap elevation should be preserved until the selected perforator has been confidently identified.

REFERENCES

1. Angrigiani C, Grilli D, Siebert J. Latissimus dorsi musculocutaneous flap without muscle. *Plast Reconstr Surg.* 1995;96:1608–1614.
2. Hamdi M, Van Landuyt K, Hijjawi JB et al. Surgical technique in pedicled thoracodorsal artery perforator flaps: A clinical experience with 99 patients. *Plast Reconstr Surg.* 2008;121:1632–1641.
3. Hamdi M, Salgarello M, Barone-Adesi L et al. Use of the thoracodorsal artery perforator (TDAP) flap with implant in breast reconstruction. *Ann Plast Surg.* 2008;61:143–146.
4. Santanelli F, Longo B, Germano S et al. Total breast reconstruction using the thoracodorsal artery perforator flap without implant. *Plast Reconstr Surg.* 2014;133:251–254.
5. Ortiz CL, Mendoza MM, Sempere LN et al. Versatility of the pedicled thoracodorsal artery perforator (TDAP) flap in soft tissue reconstruction. *Ann Plast Surg.* 2007;58:315–320.
6. Guerra AB, Metzinger SE, Lund KM et al. The thoracodorsal artery perforator flap: clinical experience and anatomic study with emphasis on harvest techniques. *Plast Reconstr Surg.* 2004;114:32–41;discussion 42–43.
7. Lin CT, Huang JS, Yang KC et al. Reliability of anatomical landmarks for skin perforators of the thoracodorsal artery perforator flap. *Plast Reconstr Surg.* 2006;118:1376–1386;discussion 1387.
8. Schaverien M, Wong C, Bailey S et al. Thoracodorsal artery perforator flap and latissimus dorsi myocutaneous flap--anatomical study of the constant skin paddle perforator locations. *J Plast Reconstr Aesthet Surg.* 2010;63:2123–2127.
9. Angrigiani C, Rancati A, Escudero E et al. Extended thoracodorsal artery perforator flap for breast reconstruction. *Gland Surg.* 2015;4:519–527.
10. Thomsen JB, Bille C, Wamberg P et al. Propeller TAP flap: is it usable for breast reconstruction? *J Plast Surg Hand Surg.* 2013;47:379–382.

23.2 ROBOTIC LATISSIMUS DORSI MUSCLE HARVEST

Karim A. Sarhane, Amir E. Ibrahim, and Jesse C. Selber

Introduction

Since its revolution in the late 1980s and early 1990s,[1,2] robotic surgery has spread across various surgical fields including, gynecology, otorhinolaryngology, urology, vascular, gastrointestinal, and cardiothoracic surgery.[3] With its enhanced precision, greater degrees of freedom, superior three-dimensional vision, improved resolution, and tremor elimination, it has permeated the field of plastic surgery and is becoming more widely used in reconstructive cases. In this chapter, we discuss the clinical application and surgical technique for robotic harvest of the latissimus dorsi muscle flap.

Traditional harvest of the latissimus dorsi muscle flap requires an incision on the back that ranges between 15 and 40 cm, in addition to an axillary incision for pedicle isolation and transfer.[4,5] A technique that eliminates the incisional morbidity associated with a back incision is desirable. Although semi-open and endoscopic approaches were conceived for that purpose, they did not gain widespread use due to technical challenges and lack of adequate instruments. However, the robotic approach (owing to the multiple advantages of its platform) has been successful in safely and reliably harvesting the muscle-only latissimus dorsi flap.

This novel technique was first tested in a cadaver model in 2010 by the senior author.[6] It was then first used clinically in 2011 in a series of eight patients,[7] and has since been used in over 40 latissimus harvests at the senior author's institution. It is a safe procedure with diminished donor site morbidity and no major complications. The entire muscle can be harvested and transposed through a small hidden incision and has many uses as a pedicled and free flap, including partial breast reconstruction, implant coverage, chest wall reconstruction, together with free flap applications. Its major indications for breast reconstruction include reconstruction of lateral defects following partial mastectomy, implant-based reconstruction following nipple areola complex sparing mastectomy, and in secondary reconstruction in patients with expanders who received adjuvant radiotherapy (delayed-immediate protocol) (**Figure 23.2.1**).

OPERATIVE PROCEDURE
Patient positioning and landmark marking

The patient is positioned in the lateral decubitus position with the ipsilateral arm prepped and placed on a sterile Mayo stand. An axillary roll is placed to avoid contralateral brachial plexopathy. The boundaries of the latissimus dorsi muscle are marked.

Incision and port placement

The mastectomy incision is often the only incision used for the harvest. When an additional sentinel lymph node incision is created, this can also be used. Three ports are then planned; these are placed at 6–8 cm intervals starting at the posterior axillary fold and 3–4 cm anterior to the anterior border of the muscle.

The surgery begins with the open dissection through existing incisions. The muscle is identified and dissected along its anterior surface. The thoracodorsal vessels are isolated and tagged with a vessel loop. The subcutaneous space anterior to the muscle is dissected; this dissection will allow the placement of additional ports. The subcutaneous space of all three ports must be continuous to allow an adequate working space. The muscle is dissected as much as possible through existing incisions. "Marionette" sutures are then used to suspend the muscle to the skin to facilitate the first part of the robotic dissection. Ports are then placed under direct vision (one 12 mm port in the middle for the endoscope and two 8 mm ports on either side).

Robotic docking and dissection

After port placement is completed, the robot is introduced posterior to the patient, with the two surgical arms and the endoscope extending over the back and in line with the ports. The ports are docked to the arms and insufflation is started.

Dissection commences on the undersurface of the muscle. After this is completed up to the borders, the "marionette" sutures are cut to allow the edge of the muscle to fall down into view. The grasper is used to direct the anterior edge of the muscle toward the chest wall, and dissection is performed over the superficial surface of the muscle. Once the dissection in both the deep and superficial planes is finished, the muscle is released at the inferoposterior border. It is then easily accessible through the axillary incision.

Undocking and extraction of the muscle

Once the muscle is completely released, the robot is undocked. The muscle is then extracted from the axillary incision. The tendinous insertion can be fully or partially divided to help mobilise the pedicle for any additional excursion. Drains are positioned in the donor site.

Technical considerations

Set up time (axillary incisions, port placement, and robot docking) is approximately 30 minutes. The harvest time is a little over 60 minutes. No conversion to open technique had to be performed in the authors' series, with all flaps harvested and transferred in their totality. There were a few morbidities with one seroma and one infection, but no patients developed capsular contracture, hematoma, dehiscence, or overlying skin injury. However, like any other new technique, robotic harvest of the latissimus dorsi flap has a long learning curve before it can be performed efficiently.

23.2 Robotic latissimus dorsi muscle harvest

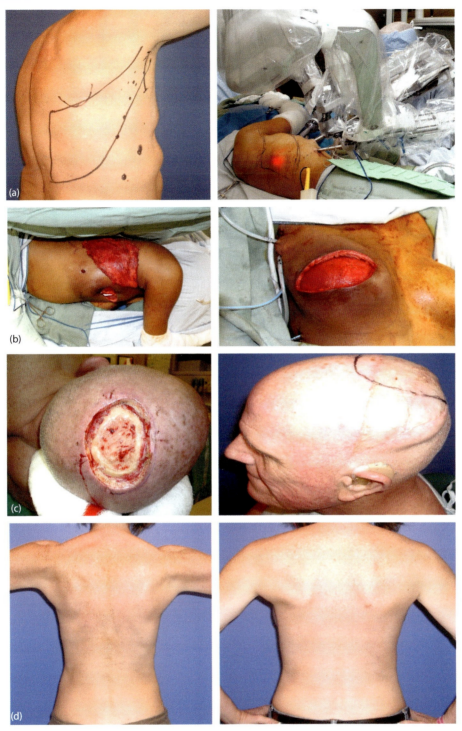

23.2.1 (a) *Left*. Markings and port placement. The borders of the latissimus dorsi muscle are marked according to anatomic landmarks. An axillary incision is then marked. For breast reconstruction, the sentinel lymph node incision is used. If a free flap is planned, then an incision is made that will facilitate pedicle dissection, dissection of the subcutaneous space anterior to the muscle, and placement of a port at the inferior end. Two additional ports are marked 8 cm from the end of the axillary incision and anterior to the muscle, and 8 cm distal to the second port and anterior to the muscle. *Right*. After port placement, the robotic side cart is positioned posterior to the patient with two robotic arms and the endoscope extending over the patient in proximity to the ports. (b) Intraoperative views *Left*. Transposition of latissimus dorsi muscle underneath a subcutaneous skin bridge. *Right*. Latissimus dorsi muscle achieves total muscle coverage over a permanent silicone-shaped implant. (c) *Left*. 90 cm² scalp defect from resection of a squamous cell carcinoma. *Right*. Three weeks postoperatively, his flap is well healed, and he is marked for radiation simulation. (d) Case of immediate breast reconstruction following a right nipple-areola complex–sparing mastectomy. Besides a very minor contour defect, there is little appreciable difference in the appearance of the donor site before (*Left*) and after (*Right*) surgery.

CONCLUSION

Robotic technology is the next step in the evolution of minimally invasive techniques. Robotic harvest of the latissimus dorsi muscle flap is a safe and reliable option for a multitude of reconstructive purposes. In addition to improved cosmesis, this approach demonstrates reduced patient discomfort, decreased seroma formation, and shortened length of stay compared to the open procedure.

REFERENCES

1. Kwoh YS, Hou J, Jonckheere EA, Hayati S. A robot with improved absolute positioning accuracy for CT guided stereotactic brain surgery. *IEEE Trans Biomed Eng* [Internet]. 1988;35(2):153–160. Available from: http://www.ncbi.nlm.nih.gov/pubmed/3280462

2. Davies BL, Hibberd RD, Ng WS, Timoney AG, Wickham JE. The development of a surgeon robot for prostatectomies. *Proc Inst Mech Eng H* [Internet]. 1991;205(1):35–38. Available from: http://www.ncbi.nlm.nih.gov/pubmed/1670073

3. Lanfranco AR, Castellanos AE, Desai JP, Meyers WC. Robotic surgery: A current perspective. *Ann Surg* [Internet]. 2004;239(1):14–21. Available from: http://www.pubmedcentral.nih.gov/articlerender.fcgi?artid=1356187&tool=pmcentrez&rendertype=abstract

4. Maxwell GP, Manson PN, Hoopes JE. Experience with thirteen latissimus dorsi myocutaneous free flaps. *Plast Reconstr Surg* [Internet]. 1979;64(1):1–8. Available from: http://www.ncbi.nlm.nih.gov/pubmed/377326

5. Maxwell GP, McGibbon BM, Hoopes JE. Vascular considerations in the use of a latissimus dorsi myocutaneous flap after a mastectomy with an axillary dissection. *Plast Reconstr Surg* [Internet]. 1979;64(6):771–780. Available from: http://www.ncbi.nlm.nih.gov/pubmed/117475

6. Selber JC, Baumann DP, Holsinger CF. Robotic harvest of the latissimus dorsi muscle: Laboratory and clinical experience. *J Reconstr Microsurg* [Internet]. 2012;28(7):457–464. Available from: http://www.ncbi.nlm.nih.gov/pubmed/22744894

7. Selber JC, Baumann DP, Holsinger FC. Robotic latissimus dorsi muscle harvest: A case series. *Plast Reconstr Surg* [Internet]. 2012;129(6):1305–1312. Available from: http://www.ncbi.nlm.nih.gov/pubmed/22634647

23.3 DOUBLE-DIEP FLAP

Phillip Blondeel and Michel Moutran

Introduction

Autologous reconstruction of a breast is recreating a well-organized living structure in the three dimensions of space. This new structure should try to mimic the shape, volume, and texture of a normal breast. Autologous tissue transfer has become the gold standard in breast reconstruction and in creating this defined structure. Autologous reconstruction is preferred over implant reconstruction in an attempt to avoid the long-term complications of implant-based reconstruction. The use of perforator flaps provides additional advantages from reduction of donor site morbidity while providing the best volume and skin restoration. Reliability and versatility of this technique is well-established.[1] Regardless of the flap used for breast reconstruction, secondary procedures to the flap and to the contralateral breast are almost always needed to ultimately achieve satisfactory and symmetrical results.

Fat grafting has likewise become a more predictable technique in plastic surgery.[2-6] It can efficiently restore volume and improve shape. Furthermore, its use in whole breast reconstruction is gaining popularity.

A matrix is a three-dimensional structure that assists the process of reconstruction. It can serve as a scaffold on which tissues are engineered, and this concept is widely integrated in vitro. This concept can now be applied to an in vivo model at a macroscopical level, but instead of fat tissue, engineering clinicians are dealing with fat transfer. The adipocytes are not cultured, but are harvested from the patient and auto-grafted. The matrix is not a microscopic scaffold, but the host tissue. Its role remains nevertheless the same: offering the optimal soil for the grafted fat and supporting its organization and growth.

The volume of a flap transferred to the chest wall can sometimes be insufficient to provide a symmetrical result. Reducing the volume of the contralateral breast and augmenting the reconstructed breast in a second session are possible solutions. Augmentation can be done by placing an implant underneath the flap, by adding a second (pedicled) flap, or by lipofilling.

This chapter describes the authors' experience of the evolution from using lipofilling as a tool to create symmetry of volume to using this as a technique to augment bilateral breast volume and finally to a concept that changes the choice of primary free flap reconstruction.

Lower abdominal free flaps such as the transverse rectus abdominis musculocutaneous (TRAM) and deep inferior epigastric artery perforator (DIEP) flaps are preferred for their consistency, skin texture, and extent of the skin paddle. Lower abdominal flaps with insufficient volume occur in thin patients and after abdominal wall liposuction. TRAM and DIEP flaps are often abandoned in these cases in favor of secondary choices as superior gluteal artery perforator (SGAP), inferior gluteal artery perforator (IGAP), transverse musculocutaneous gracilis, lumbar artery perforator, anterior lateral thigh, and extended latissimus dorsi flaps. These flaps can be technically challenging, provide insufficient volume, and be difficult to shape. Another method to solve the shortage of volume is harvesting Siamese type flaps such as double-pedicled TRAM or DIEP flaps or transferring multiple flaps in one procedure, stacking them on top of each other.

Harvesting these more "exotic" flaps (for which even senior surgeons may have little experience) involves performing lengthy procedures with multiple vascular anastomoses thereby increasing the risk of microsurgical complications. The authors are convinced that with increasing experience of fat grafting, applying the principle of vascularized matrix transplantation is safer and easier.

The vascularized matrix principle

This involves the surgeon harvesting a small volume flap that they are most familiar with (usually lower abdominal flaps) and transferring this onto the footprint of the proposed reconstructed breast. The transplanted tissue is not intended to re-create the entire volume of the breast, but is placed in position where it will serve as a recipient bed or matrix for fat grafts. This will better be done as a second procedure (3 months to 6 months later).

Time is the fourth dimension in breast reconstruction. Reconstructing a breast is a dynamic procedure, and the initial appearance of the reconstructed breast evolves with time, due to gravity and healing process. Complementary procedures also tend to modify the final appearance of the breast. This dynamic aspect has to be integrated into the surgical plan for the patient. Hence, the aim of the first stage when the free "matrix" flap is transferred to the breast is to achieve adequate shape and contour while bearing in mind that the volume restoration can be dealt with secondarily.

The three-step principle is followed during the first procedure,[7] with the borders of the footprint surgically (re-)defined and the footprint covered by a free flap. It is imperative that this free flap covers the entire footprint. The volume of the conus at this point is of less importance, but the best possible shape is given to the small conus. Therefore, the breast is initially "too small," but has an acceptable shape. Lipofilling of the mastectomy flaps can be considered at the same time as transfer of the free flap.

With regards to the envelope, a sufficient amount skin is left at the first stage to create a large enough skin envelope that will be needed in later stages. All essential components of the breast are in place at this time and the flap as the "vascularized matrix" that is ready to accept a fat grafting performed as a second procedure. This represents the final component to be added to complete the reconstruction.[8] The flap is no more than a three-dimensional construct of vessels together with a collagenous framework that lacks volume, but is an ideal recipient bed for subsequent lipofilling.

Adding volume to the conus by fat grafting is relatively easy to perform as fat can be injected throughout the flap's full thickness, which can therefore accept large volumes in one single surgical step. Additionally, the shape of the conus can be optimized by selective volume injections.

The fat graft

The specific characteristics of fat grafts are essential for success of the procedure. This includes a clear protocol for fat harvesting. The infiltration solution, cannulas used for harvesting, the negative pressure applied, processing of the graft (filtration, rinsing, centrifugation), cannulas used to re-inject the graft, and the amount of fat transferred at once (total volume) are all factors determining the quality of the end results.

As a graft, contact between adipocytes and the host is important to facilitate sufficient imbibition for initial survival of the fat. When the fat particles are relatively small, contact is spherical and therefore optimal. By contrast with larger particles, the core of the spheres will not make contact with the micro-environment. This results in fat necrosis within the core together with oil cyst formation.[9,10] This issue can be addressed by using small cannulas for harvesting of fat and for the fat transfer.

The pressure applied to the fat can be detrimental to the survival of adipocytes. Experimental studies tend to recommend use of moderate negative pressure harvesting.

The amount of fat transferred in each passage of the cannula is limited to 0.2° cc per tunnel, and there is a change of tunnel with each passage. This aims to limit the amount of fat per tunnel and prevents extensive undermining whereby fat would be deposited without thorough contact with its environment.

There is much variation in technique, and the authors recommend that each surgeon uses a technique with which they are familiar and is proven to give good clinical results.

The host

Because of reduced donor site morbidity, the authors have tended to prefer use of perforator flaps over myocutaneous flaps. Moreover, perforator flaps have certain characteristics that make them more suitable as a vascularized matrix.

Perforator flaps are mainly harvested from the lower abdomen (DIEP flaps), from the lumbar (LAP), or from the gluteal region (SGAP and IGAP). They are adipocutaneous flaps with the adipose layer divided by the fascia superficialis. The suprafascial fat is generally thicker than the subfascial fat. Any fat transfer beneath the fascia superficialis will elevate the fascia and the fat layer above leading to a global volume augmentation. By contrast, fat transfer above the superficial fascia will result in elevation of skin and a change in contour.

These characteristics of perforator flaps will be utilized when performing the secondary fat grafting to the breast. When the goal is volume enhancement, fat injection is done in the deeper planes of the matrix. When the goal is mainly enhancement of contour or shape enhancement, the fat injection is done within the superficial layers in those areas requiring treatment. This is the basis of the matrix concept.

The contours of the breast are mainly curves that change direction in different quadrants. Liposuction can also be employed to define these contours by creating depressions where appropriate. These depressions can outline any curve creation by fat transfer when located before or after the curve. Liposuction can also be used to correct excessive augmentation.

Perforator flaps are most commonly vascularized by a single perforator. This perforator is anastomosed to recipient vessels that have a high flow rate (internal mammary artery). After the delay phenomenon and opening of the choke vessels, the subdermal and deep plexus are widely recruited to perfuse the entire flap. The vascular supply to the fat and to the skin is augmented compared to perfusion before isolation of the perforators. This transforms the flap into a "vascular sponge." The perforator flap becomes a highly vascularized matrix and provides a very suitable blood supply to any fat grafted within it. This in turn optimizes the take of the graft.

Free perforator flaps are the authors' first choice as a matrix, but if microsurgery is not appropriate, a pedicled (extended) latissimus dorsi flap or thoracodorsal artery perforator flap are great alternatives. The challenge with these flaps is to center them correctly on the footprint of the breast, to avoid lateral bulging and to provide sufficient skin in case of secondary breast reconstruction. The skin from the back tends to be thicker and less elastic.[5] Some surgeons have tried the reversed abdominoplasty flap in combination with an latissimus dorsi or thoracodorsal artery perforator flap in order to increase the surface of the skin envelope.

Small flaps that have been irradiated or flaps with an initial normal volume that have lost volume due to irradiation are still candidates for lipofilling. However, it is advisable to perform lipofilling in multiple smaller steps. In the first procedure, small amounts of fat are injected very close to the skin. As expansion of an irradiated breast is limited, small amounts need to be injected to avoid total necrosis of the injected fat. Clinical experience has shown that those fat grafts injected very close to the dermis are more likely to improve the color, texture, elasticity, and general appearance of the breast skin. The precise mechanism of this beneficial effect is unknown, but is useful for permitting later expansion of the skin envelope. In subsequent interventions, more fat should be injected in the deeper layers of the reconstructed breast to augment volume and improve the shape. Each fat grafting session has limited volume due to irradiated tissue having less elasticity and laxity. But with each session, the volume can be increased as tissues regain their natural expandability.

Finally, it should be considered whether a free flap transfer to the footprint of the breast is really necessary. If sufficient subcutaneous fat and skin remains on mastectomy flaps after the ablative procedure, fat grafting can commence in the subcutaneous fat layers that are then considered to be the initial host or matrix. This applies especially when the natural borders of the footprint can be clearly identified (i.e., the inframammary crease and lateral border). If the patient is content with a small- to medium-sized breast and there is sufficient expansion of the skin and matrix, maximal fat grafting can be performed. If insufficient breast volume is obtained, a small central implant or a secondary free or pedicled flap can be considered.

The main disadvantage of multiple lipofilling sessions (often 3 months to 6 months apart) is that it takes a long time to reach the final result. The patient also needs to sacrifice sufficient fat deposits throughout her body to serve as a donor area. Approximately 50% of the fat transferred is lost and therefore the strategy of multiple harvesting needs to be well thought out and explained to the patient before starting. Instructions to the patient on postoperative care include avoiding pressure on the recipient site and wearing of a lipopanty for 4 weeks to 6 weeks after every session. These must be clearly explained as part of fully informed consent and indeed patient compliance is a key to obtaining a good result.

Results

Before the advent of lipofilling, a free flap for breast reconstruction had to simultaneously fulfill requirements of volume, shape, and skin replacement. The use of implants positioned below the flap as a second stage procedure has been practiced, but defeats the purpose of providing the patient with a natural-looking and purely autologous reconstruction, thereby avoiding the side effects and long-term complications of breast implants.

In those patients where the lower abdominal tissue cannot be used (skinny patients, previous abdominal liposuction, multiple scarring, patients refusing abdominal scars, etc.), the authors have used other donor sites such as SGAP, IGAP, lumbar artery perforator, or any flap that would provide sufficient volume. However, many of these flaps have their own drawbacks: dissection is technically challenging, shaping is difficult because of firmer consistency of the flap, or vessel grafts are needed because of short flap pedicles. Perhaps the most important reason is that these are more "exotic" flaps that tend to be otherwise used as secondary solutions. These flaps are therefore used less frequently and surgeons have less experience with them. This potentially increases complication rates both for the microsurgical aspects as well as for shaping of the breast. These procedures can also create unnecessary stress for the surgical team.

Alternatively, volume can be gained by using Siamese type flaps such as bilateral DIEP or TRAM flaps. These are large flaps taken over the midline that need two feeding vessels. The DIEP is usually taken on one side and for the other side, the DIEP can also be taken or possibly the SIEA. These pedicles are then either connected to each other and anastomosed to the internal mammary vessels or both pedicles are connected to the internal mammary vessels (both to the cranial end of the internal mammary vessels or one to the cranial and the other to the distal part). This technique allows volume to be increased drastically, but restricts mobility of the flap during the shaping process. Moreover, operating time is prolonged significantly and the risk of vascular thrombosis much higher. Furthermore, donor site morbidity from sacrificing both rectus abdominis muscles with bilateral TRAM flaps for construction of a single breast is unacceptably high and suitable alternatives exist to solve the problem of flap volume.

Another option for gaining volume is combining multiple separate "smaller" free flaps into one single breast. This so-called stacking of two or more flaps can be considered, but has several disadvantages: shaping might be a challenge (especially in secondary reconstruction cases) and the need for multiple vascular anastomoses increases risk of thrombosis and prolongs operating time.

Using a single flap that surgeons are familiar with is associated with low complication rates and shorter procedure times.[11] Nine out of ten patients require a secondary procedure after 6 months for nipple reconstruction, adjustments to the ipsi- and/or contralateral breast, or corrections to the donor site. Lipofilling at the same time can easily be performed. In contrast to lipo-augmentation of a normal breast where lipo-injection is limited to the subglandular and subcutaneous areas only, the previously transplanted flap can be injected in different directions and multiple layers including the subcutaneous and pre-pectoral layers. The presence of abundant skin will allow sufficient "space" for lipofilling and expansion of the conus. Moreover, lipofilling is regularly used today to augment the volume or improve the shape of the contralateral breast.

Even when liposuction has been performed to the lower abdominal wall or any other free flap donor site, the flap can still be safely harvested, provided suitable sized perforator vessels can be visualized on the preoperative angio-CT scan.[12] The scarring of the fat tissue above and below the superficial fascia will affect advancement of the lipofilling canula in the second stage, but still allows full three-dimensional expansion of the flap.

CONCLUSION

The principle of the vascular matrix combines use of a free flap as a first step with intra-flap lipofilling as a second step to provide a safe, reliable, and reproducible technique in breast reconstruction. This can avoid use of more exotic flaps that surgeons are less familiar with and represents both a surgical challenge and risk to patients.

REFERENCES

1. Matros, E. et al. Cost-effectiveness analysis of implants versus autologous perforator flaps using the BREAST-Q. *Plast Reconstr Surg*, 2015. 135(4): pp. 937–946.
2. Kaoutzanis, C. et al. Autologous fat grafting after breast reconstruction in postmastectomy patients: Complications, biopsy rates, and locoregional cancer recurrence rates. *Ann Plast Surg*, 2016. 76(3): pp. 270–275.
3. Gentile, P. et al. Breast reconstruction with enhanced stromal vascular fraction fat grafting: What is the best method? *Plast Reconstr Surg Glob Open*, 2015. 3(6): pp. e406.
4. Gabriel, A., M.C. Champaneria, and G.P. Maxwell. Fat grafting and breast reconstruction: Tips for ensuring predictability. *Gland Surg*, 2015. 4(3): p. 232–243.
5. Delay, E. and S. Guerid. The role of fat grafting in breast reconstruction. *Clin Plast Surg*, 2015. 42(3): pp. 315–323, vii.
6. Agha, R.A. et al. Use of autologous fat grafting for breast reconstruction: A systematic review with meta-analysis of oncological outcomes. *J Plast Reconstr Aesthet Surg*, 2015. 68(2): pp. 143–161.
7. Blondeel, P.N. et al. Shaping the breast in aesthetic and reconstructive breast surgery: An easy three-step principle. *Plastic and reconstructive surgery*, 2009. 123(2): pp. 455–462.
8. Blondeel, P.N. et al. Shaping the breast in aesthetic and reconstructive breast surgery: An easy three-step principle. Part II--Breast reconstruction after total mastectomy. *Plastic and reconstructive surgery*, 2009. 123(3): pp. 794–805.
9. Mashiko, T. and K. Yoshimura. How does fat survive and remodel after grafting? *Clin Plast Surg*, 2015. 42(2): pp. 181–190.
10. Doi, K. et al. Differential contributions of graft-derived and host-derived cells in tissue regeneration/remodeling after fat grafting. *Plast Reconstr Surg*, 2015. 135(6): pp. 1607–1617.
11. Seidenstuecker, K., Mahajan, A, Van Waes, C, Christoph, A and Blondeel, Ph, DIEAP flap for safe definitive autologous breast reconstruction. *The Breast*, 2016. accepted for publication.
12. De Frene, B. et al. Free DIEAP and SGAP flap breast reconstruction after abdominal/gluteal liposuction. *J Plast Reconstr Aesthet Surg*, 2006. 59(10): pp. 1031–1036.

23.4 PROFUNDA ARTERY PERFORATOR (PAP) FLAP

Joshua L. Levine and Robert J. Allen, Sr.

Introduction

The abdomen is the first choice as a donor site for most women seeking autologous breast reconstruction. The deep inferior epigastric perforator flap (DIEP) has become the gold standard because it allows for the use of extra abdominal tissue without sacrifice of underlying muscle. Some women, however, are not candidates for abdominal tissue harvest. Absolute contraindications for the use of the abdomen in autologous breast reconstruction include previous abdominoplasty, excessive abdominal surgery resulting in significant diminishment of blood flow to the lower abdomen, and inadequate abdominal fat volume for breast reconstruction. Prior to the advent of thigh flaps for breast reconstruction, the buttock flaps (GAP flaps) were the preferred and most common alternative donor sites for perforator flap breast reconstruction. The TUG (transverse upper gracilis) flap emerged as an alternative to buttock flaps, but requires muscle sacrifice, has a short pedicle, and is typically designed anteriorly on the inner thigh. This relative anterior placement on the thigh results in visible scaring and the risk of disruption of the saphenous vein and the lymphatics of the lower extremity. The profunda artery perforator (PAP) flap, based on the area perfused by the profunda femoris artery perforators to the posterior thigh, is an alternative thigh flap that overcomes the disadvantages of the TUG. The PAP vessels perforate through the abductor magnus immediately posterior to the gracilis muscle, and perfuse the area just below the buttock crease (commonly referred to as the "banana role"). The authors have used the PAP flap in over 300 cases in the past 4 years.

Indications

Any patient who is a candidate for a GAP or TUG flap is usually also suitable for a PAP flap. Ideal candidates are thinner women with inadequate abdominal pannus for breast reconstruction. Even those women who are extremely thin tend to have adequate posterior thigh volume for breast reconstruction, provided that expectations of breast reconstruction volume are reasonable. In other words, thin women with scant body fat who may not achieve a proportionately large breast reconstruction in one stage will nonetheless be candidates for PAP flap breast reconstruction. Thin women with a small cup size do not require much volume for breast reconstruction. Moreover, autologous breasts can always be enhanced at a second stage with fat injection, another flap, or implants.

Some women will have a genuine choice and have adequate volume for reconstruction from both the abdomen and the posterior thigh. These women should be made aware of the advantages and disadvantages of choosing the posterior thigh as the donor site for breast reconstruction.

Anatomy

The profunda femoral artery is a branch of the common femoral artery. As it descends within the medial thigh, it supplies a pedicle to the gracilis, followed by perforating branches that travel through the adductor magnus muscle. These perforators terminate in the skin of the posterior and medial thigh. One or more of these perforators can be used as the vascular pedicle to the PAP flap.

Preoperative planning

All patients undergo vascular imaging with magnetic resonance angiography or computerized tomographic angiography. Imaging is essential for planning this procedure because it is extremely important to know exactly where the primary perforator enters the flap. This point (or points) is designated by coordinates determined by the radiologist and confirmed by reviewing the imaging study. The coordinates of the perforators are established according to specific landmarks. The main perforators are identified in their vertical orientation by their distance caudal to the most inferior point of the infra-gluteal crease. Its distance from the midline establishes the perforator's horizontal orientation. This gives the surgeon two points of reference. With the patient prone, these points can be located with a tape measure and marked. The marked points of the perforators are then confirmed with a Doppler signal.

We have found that most large perforators are between 2 and 7 cm below the infra-buttock crease. Once the perforators have been marked, the flap is designed around the points. In thin women, it is advisable to harvest no more than 6 cm in the vertical orientation in order to limit tension on the closure of the donor site. The horizontal orientation can be 20 cm or more. The flap design becomes a crescent of tissue just below the infra-buttock crease, the anterior apex is in the inner thigh, posterior to the adductor tendon, and the lateral apex terminates approximately at the lateral infra-buttock crease. Since the vertical dimension of the flap is limited, it is essential that the marking is correct so that the key perforator is not missed.

It is also very important to become familiar with the course of the perforator as it travels through the magnus muscle. Details of its anatomy will be very useful during the dissection, and it is helpful to refer to the images of the vascular pattern during the procedure.

Operative technique

The patient is placed in the supine position. Her arms and legs are prepped and draped within the surgical field. Sequential compression devices are placed on the calves below the knees, and then wrapped in sterile sheets so that they can be prepped completely into the field. The legs are placed on sterile sheets. Two microsurgeons work simultaneously, one surgeon will be preparing the reception site in the chest, while the other is harvesting one of the flaps. The surgeon harvests the PAP flap from the opposite side of the patient's body. The leg is abducted and externally rotated (frog-legged). It is also very helpful to position the patient in Trendelenburg with slight rotation away from the surgeon in order to expose the inner thigh. An incision is then made at the anterior apex of the flap. The adductor longus tendon is identified, and the incision is taken down to its posterior edge. It is important to avoid the saphenous vein and lymph nodes that may occur anterior to the abductor tendon. There will be a venous branch from the saphenous vein that should be ligated. The dissection is then taken down to the gracilis muscle and the flap is elevated off this muscle. It is important to bevel when approaching the area of the perforator to be sure that the dominant perforator is contained within the harvested fat. Once the superior and inferior incisions have been made down to the muscle and to a point caudal to where the perforator is expected to enter the flap, the flap is elevated off the gracilis completely. The septum between the gracilis and the adductor longus is identified. The gracilis is reflected anteriorly, and the septum overlying the magnus is entered. This is a key point in the procedure and begins the search for the perforator. From this point in the operation loop, magnification is essential for the remainder of the dissection.

When the appropriate perforator is identified, the dissection then follows the perforating vessel into the magnus muscle all the way to its take off at the profundus vessels. The dissection requires multiple self-retaining retractors and frequent repositioning of both these and the patient.

It is important to pursue the dissection so far as the profunda vessels. At that point, a space will be entered where fatty tissue surrounds the take off of the perforators. It is at that point that the artery will be of adequate diameter for anastomosis to the internal mammary artery.

The pedicle is then dissected free from its deep muscular attachments such that it is connected now only to the profundus vessels and the flap tissue. At that point, the flap can be stapled back into position anteriorly so that the posterior flap harvest can be undertaken with the pedicle remaining intact. With experience, a surgeon gains the confidence to harvest the pedicle prior to removing the flap from its posterior muscular attachments. However, until several flaps have been completed successfully, it is recommended that the final pedicle ligation is done as the last step when harvesting the flap.

The posterior and lateral flap harvest is made by adducting and internally rotating the leg such that the lateral incision can be made more easily.

The PAP pedicle is typically 8–12 cm in length. The average arterial diameter is 2.2 mm and the vein is typically 2.7 mm in diameter. The internal mammary vessels are used as recipient vessels in the majority of cases.

Insetting of the PAP flap usually necessitates some manipulation of its shape. The long crescentic shape of the flap allows for a degree of coning and creating a breast with good projection. Harvest time is usually about 40 minutes to an hour.

The donor site is closed in a standard fashion over drains with antibiotic irrigation used prior to closure. The patient is sent to the recovery room for 2 hours, and then transferred to the ward for flap monitoring. The intravenous cannulae and Foley catheter are removed on the first postoperative day when the patient will be ambulating and discharge is between 2 and 4 days after surgery.

Clinical results

In more than 300 cases, the PAP flap has proven to be a very reliable and successful operation. The failure rate is less than 1%, and donor site problems occur in about 10%–15% of cases. These include infection, seroma, and wound breakdown. The authors have also seen areas of flap fat necrosis in about 10% of cases. PAP flaps can also be combined with other flaps when more volume is needed for breast reconstruction. Two flaps can be used for one breast, and a PAP flap can be combined with a hemi-abdominal DIEP flap or a lateral thoracic flap. These flaps can also be augmented with autologous fat injection. The pedicle length of the PAP flap is 10 cm on average and makes insetting uncomplicated. The crescent shape of the PAP flap allows for shaping and positioning of the flap for maximal projection and optimal shape. The authors have routinely been able to provide adequate flap volume relative to mastectomy weight in thinner women. By avoiding the inguinal area, no cases of lymphedema have been seen. On occasion, it has been possible to innervate the flap using a branch of the posterior femoral cutaneous nerve.

CONCLUSION

The PAP flap represents an excellent alternative option to using the abdomen for autologous breast reconstruction. The PAP flap has four main advantages over the TUG flap:

1. There is no muscle sacrifice.
2. The pedicle is consistently much longer; in the range of 8–14 cm.
3. The more posterior orientation of the PAP design avoids the saphenous vein and lymphatics of the lower extremity.
4. The more posterior orientation results in a more favorable scar.

23.5 BOOMERANG GLUTEAL ARTERY PERFORATOR (GAP) FLAP

Edward I. Chang and Steven J. Kronowitz

Introduction

While the abdomen continues to be the most popular donor site for autologous free flap breast reconstruction, there are a number of circumstances which may preclude the use of the abdomen as a donor site. Patients who lack sufficient abdominal tissue or who have undergone a prior abdominoplasty have often not been considered candidates for autologous reconstruction. Further, patients who may have already had an abdominal flap and develop contralateral disease or in the setting of a failed abdominal free flap also are in need of an alternate donor site. In such circumstances, the gluteal region represents one of the preferred donor sites which can provide sufficient soft tissue with minimal donor site morbidity.

At most institutions, the gluteal flaps tend to be a secondary flap due to less familiarity with the flap and perforator dissection and often a change in position that is necessary for flap harvest and the subsequent microvascular anastomosis and flap inset. Further, there are often concerns regarding pedicle length and caliber that make gluteal flaps less appealing as a primary donor site for autologous breast reconstruction.

The superior gluteal artery perforator (SGAP) flap has been well-described and is a perforator flap based on the superior gluteal artery. Others have also described flaps based off the inferior gluteal artery which is less commonly used. Since its inception, the design of the SGAP has undergone modifications, and here, we present the "boomerang" modification of the traditional SGAP flap with a novel design that has demonstrated improved donor site contour as well as increased flap volume to allow for coning of the flap to maximize breast projection.

Flap design and harvest

The flap design procedure is as follows: The location of the trochanter is demarcated with the patient standing (**Figure 23.5.1**). Then the patient is positioned prone. The inferior border of the flap (M, medial aspect of reconstructed breast) is marked at the level (horizontal plane) of the superior aspect of the trochanter. The medial border of the flap (S, superior aspect of reconstructed breast) is marked, and its medial extent is usually limited to avoid an undesirable elevation of the gluteal crease upon closure of the donor site.

The perforating blood vessels supplying the flap—usually a single artery and two venae comitantes that perforate through the gluteus muscles into the overlying subcutaneous tissue and skin (hereafter referred to as perforator)—are

delineated using a handheld Doppler probe. The most desirable perforator is one located at the inferolateral region of the flap—at the horizontal plane of the superior edge of the gluteal cleft—because it provides for a long vascular pedicle. Depending on the location of the selected perforator, either the superior or inferior gluteal vessels provide the blood supply to the flap. Although usually only one perforator is harvested, locating the exact position of the perforator can be difficult preoperatively, even with the handheld Doppler probe. Thus, a cluster of Doppler signals is obtained to mark the general location of the perforators so they will all be included within the inferolateral boundary of the flap.

After the perforator signals are identified, the lateral border of the flap (I, inferior aspect of reconstructed breast) is designed so that this surface of the flap will sit on the inframammary fold, like an anatomical shelf.

The superior border of the skin island (L, lateral region of reconstructed breast) is then marked to complete its curvilinear shape. It is important to distinguish the superior border of the skin island from the superior border of the flap. Although the skin island is curvilinear, the shape of the flap is circumferential. At the superomedial aspect of the flap, above the border of the skin island, adipose tissue is harvested from below the level of Scarpa's fascia along with the underlying gluteal muscle fascia, which creates a circumferential blood supply to the flap. Omission of this component can result in partial flap loss due to inadequate blood supply around the curvature of the flap.

The flap harvest procedure is as follows: After exposure of the internal mammary vessels with the patient in the supine position, the patient is repositioned prone for harvest of the R-GAP flap. The author prefers not to use the corkscrew position because the torsion it creates can lead to back-related ailments, especially if the position is maintained for an extended period. Also, the author prefers to determine the adequacy of the internal mammary vessels as recipient vessels prior to initiating the flap harvest. In addition, the internal mammary vessels can be injured during the dissection and become unsuitable to serve as recipient vessels.

Flap dissection begins with incision of the skin island and, with the exception of the superomedial aspect of the flap, located below Scarpa's fascia, includes all intervening adipose tissue with incision through the fascia of the gluteus maximus muscle. It is imperative to limit the dissection to the buttock proper. This can be done by limiting the flap harvest to only the tissue directly overlying the gluteus maximus muscle, especially during the lateral dissection, when the angle of dissection should be exaggerated inward to maintain the plane of dissection perpendicular to the patient's torso.

Incision of the gluteal muscle fascia allows for dissection of the perforators within the subfascial tissue plane, which allows for easier identification and isolation of the perforating vessels supplied from the underlying gluteal vessels. Subfascial dissection is usually initiated at the inferolateral aspect of the flap, the most desirable perforator location. Once the perforator is identified, the subfascial dissection

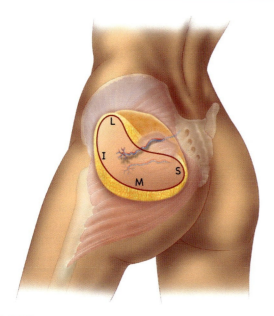 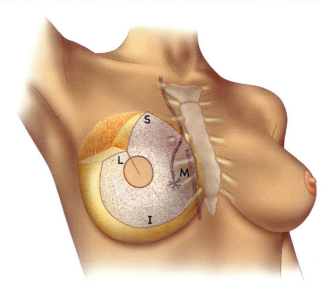

23.5.1 Design and harvest of the R-GAP flap. The R-GAP flap is designed on the buttock opposite the involved breast (i.e., right breast, left buttock) to allow for optimal flap orientation on the chest wall and to maintain the desired cascade of tissue thickness from thinnest in the superior breast to thickest in the inferolateral breast. The flap is designed directly over the gluteus maximus muscle, the boundaries of which are marked before the flap is designed. The flap must not be extended onto the region overlying the tensor fascia lata because doing so could result in an undesirable donor site deformity and this tissue tends to have a less reliable blood supply.

23.5.2 Insetting of the R-GAP flap onto the chest wall. After the flap is transferred to the chest wall, the flap is rotated 90° counterclockwise from its orientation on the contralateral buttock. This positions the medial border of the flap at the superior aspect of the reconstructed breast and the inferolateral border of the flap at the inferomedial aspect of the reconstructed breast. This orientation positions the perforator in the direct vicinity of the recipient vessels, the internal mammary artery and vein, which allows for a long pedicle and for the vascular pedicle to be placed within the hollow in the chest wall that is created by removal of the third intercostal cartilage to gain access to the internal mammary vessels. The superomedial border of the flap—the portion that includes only the adipose tissue below Scarpa's fascia and the fascia of the gluteus maximus muscle—is positioned within the axillary region of the reconstructed breast, where it provides cosmetic benefits by supplanting the axillary volume. To complete the breast shape, the superolateral border of the flap is rotated in a clockwise direction and plicated overlying the sub-Scarpa's fascia component to create the lateral aspect of the reconstructed breast.

can be completed expediently. Beginning dissection in the inferolateral aspect also provides for easier dissection than when dissection is begun in another region, where the connective tissue attachments between the fascia and muscle can be very adherent.

All perforators considered to be of adequate caliber are isolated underneath the dissected flap. The diameter of the perforators varies from patient to patient, so best practice is to not ligate any reasonably sized perforator until all perforators have been isolated. At that time, a perforator is chosen on the basis of caliber and flow as determined by the audible signal from a handheld Doppler and also on the basis of the location of the perforator in relation to the desired inferolateral position on the flap. Usually two or three perforators are considered adequate to supply the flap. Once the optimal perforator is selected, the remaining perforator(s) should be occluded with an Acland microsurgical vascular clamp during the remainder of the vascular dissection. Although retaining the secondary perforator(s) can make the vascular dissection more cumbersome, it preserves an additional option in case the selected perforator is injured during its dissection or the flap is found to be inadequately perfused by the selected perforator.

Although with a deep inferior epigastric perforator (DIEP) flap, more than one perforator may be needed to avoid fat necrosis, the R-GAP flap usually requires only a single perforator to adequately perfuse the flap. The author's clinical experience suggests that arterial inflow and venous drainage within the skin and subcutaneous tissues of the buttock region are adequate with only a single perforator as long as the flap includes only adipose tissue located directly overlying the gluteus maximus muscle. Incorporating more than one perforator often requires the destruction of gluteus maximus muscle, and the proximal dissection of the pedicle to the pelvic bone not uncommonly reveals an in continuity or requires ligation of the vascular branch supplying the second or third perforator. An additional perforator can also shorten the pedicle length, which can increase the difficulty of performing microsurgery and may lead to kinking of the perforator.

As the vascular dissection continues proximally, it becomes apparent whether the perforator originates from the superior or inferior gluteal vessels. Clinical experience

23.5 Boomerang gluteal artery perforator (GAP) flap   353

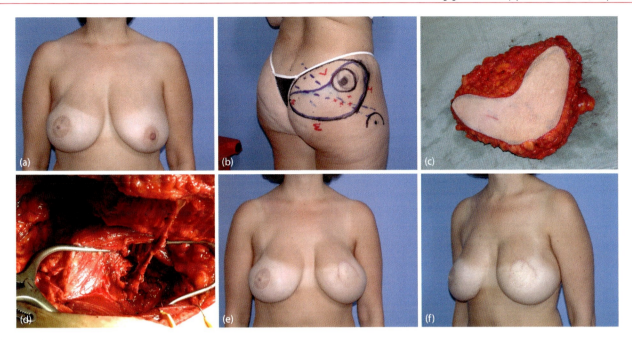

23.5.3 R-GAP flap breast reconstruction in a woman with previous contralateral TRAM flap breast reconstruction. (a) A 41-year-old-woman with 34D bra-cup size who had undergone right modified radical mastectomy with immediate pedicled TRAM flap reconstruction presented having recently tested positive for a BRCA mutation. Left risk-reducing mastectomy was planned. (b) Preoperative markings showing design of the right-sided R-GAP flap to be used for reconstruction of the left breast. (c, d) Intraoperative views of R-GAP flap dissection. (e, f) Postoperative views 3 months after R-GAP flap reconstruction.

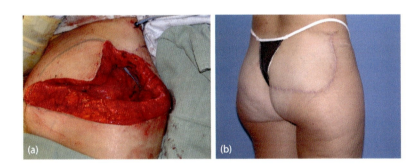

23.5.4 Buttock donor site revision after R-GAP flap breast reconstruction in the patient. (a) Intraoperative view: At time of revision of right buttock donor site, 12 months after R-GAP flap breast reconstruction. The extent to which donor site revision is required depends on the initial buttock size and the laxity of the buttock skin and subcutaneous tissues, but most patients undergoing R-GAP flap breast reconstruction require donor site revision. The author usually performs donor site revision at least 6 months after breast reconstruction to allow for laxity to develop in the skin and subcutaneous tissue inferior to the donor site incision. Often, donor site revision is performed at the same time as any revision of the reconstructed breast or symmetry procedure on the contralateral breast. When this is the case, donor site revision is performed before the breast procedures because prone positioning may disrupt the more delicate repairs to the breasts. Buttock revision usually involves recreation of the initial donor defect in the superior aspect of the buttock, located above the donor scar, with undermining at the level of the gluteus maximus muscle. In addition, the skin and subcutaneous tissue located below the donor scar are extensively undermined at the level of the gluteus maximus muscle to allow for superomedial advancement. The upper edge of the inferior advancement skin flap skin is de-epithelialized, advanced superomedially, and sutured to the gluteus maximus muscle, underlying the previously elevated superomedial skin flap located above the donor scar. The advanced de-epithelialized skin and subcutaneous tissue corrects the volume loss and contour deformity that resulted from initial flap harvest. After placement of a closed suction drain, the lower edge of the de-epithelialized region is incised to allow for a multiple layered closure with absorbable sutures. (b) Postoperative view: 3 months after donor site revision. In patients who undergo unilateral R-GAP flap breast reconstruction and have an intact native breast, the author prefers not to perform a symmetry procedure on the opposite buttock so that a second R-GAP flap will be available should one be required in the future. In contrast, in patients who have already undergone mastectomy with breast reconstruction on the contralateral breast and are satisfied with the outcome, a contralateral buttock symmetry procedure may be performed. However, it may be preferable to delay the contralateral symmetry procedure for at least 3 to 6 months after revision of the buttock donor site to allow for the gravitational effects to take effect.

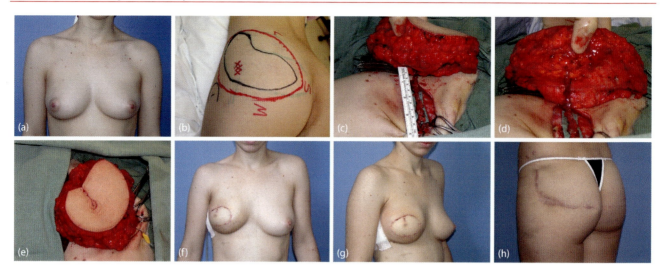

23.5.5 Skin-preserving delayed-immediate R-GAP flap breast reconstruction after modified radical mastectomy and PMRT. (a) A 26-year-old nulliparous woman with a 32C bra-cup size and minimal abdominal adipose tissue and laxity presented with right-sided stage IIA breast cancer. Modified radical mastectomy and delayed-immediate breast reconstruction were planned because the patient was at increased risk of requiring PMRT. After mastectomy and placement of a subpectoral fully inflated tissue expander (400 cc) to preserve the breast skin envelope, the review of permanent sections revealed that the patient would indeed require PMRT. During the 6-week interval between mastectomy and the start of PMRT, the tissue expander was left inflated. During PMRT, which lasted 6 weeks, the expander was completed deflated. Two weeks after the completion of PMRT, the expander was reinflated to 400 cc. At the time of R-GAP flap reconstruction, 6 months after the completion of PMRT, the expander was removed. (b) Intraoperative view of R-GAP flap design on left buttock. Black oval, outline of the skin island. Red oval, sub-Scarpa's-fascia superomedial extension and extension of the flap subcutaneously in the inferolateral aspects. Red X's, audible Doppler signals at the preferred perforator location within the flap. Black plus-mark on lateral hip, trochanter. The internal mammary vessels are not transected until after the patient is repositioned into the supine positioned for the microsurgery and insetting of the R-GAP flap. This way, if additional pedicle length is required, the fourth intercostal cartilage can also be removed to extend the length of the internal mammary vessels. Not dividing the internal mammary vessels until the time of the microsurgery also maintains flow through the vessels during the often lengthy flap harvest and avoids disruption of an Acland clamp while the patient is in the prone position, which can lead to uncontrollable hemorrhage. (c, d) The flap temporarily located in the axilla after completion of microsurgery. The long pedicle of the R-GAP flap allows the flap to be positioned within the axilla during microsurgery, which facilitates the microsurgery because the thick gluteal flap does not interfere with the delicate hand movements required. The long pedicle also allows for the use of other recipient vessels, like the thoracodorsal vessels, while still allowing the flap to be positioned medially on the chest wall. (e) The R-GAP flap on the chest wall during the insetting to create the breast form. The flap has been rotated 90° counterclockwise from its orientation on the contralateral buttock but has not yet been placed within the breast skin envelope. The superolateral border of the flap (buttock) has been rotated clockwise and plicated overlying the sub-Scarpa's-fascia component to the vertically oriented aspect of the flap to create the inferolateral aspect of the reconstructed breast. The superomedial aspect of the flap (buttock), the portion of the flap that includes only the tissue below Scarpa's fascia, will be positioned within the axillary region of the reconstructed breast, where it will replace the lost axillary volume in this patient, who underwent a level I and II axillary lymph node dissection as well as axillary irradiation. (f, g) Two weeks after breast reconstruction. (h) The unrevised left buttock donor site 10 months after breast reconstruction. The patient developed a postoperative seroma with a small region of wound dehiscence at the buttock donor site because of extensive undermining at the time of breast reconstruction. As a result of this complication, in subsequent cases, the inferior buttock skin and subcutaneous tissue was undermined only enough to allow for a tension-free closure of the donor site. A closed suction drain is used, usually for 2 to 3 weeks, because the gluteal region is densely enriched with lymphatic tissue, which makes it prone to seroma formation. Upon removal of the drain, the patient immediately begins wearing a girdle, which not only assists in recontouring the donor site but, more importantly, compresses the donor region to further prevent seroma formation.

with the R-GAP flap indicates that flap circulation is not affected by whether the perforator is supplied by the inferior or superior gluteal vessels. However, it is preferable to transect the gluteal vessels below the gluteal fascia, near the pelvic bone. If the gluteal vessels are transected before the gluteal fascia is penetrated, the resulting relatively short pedicle will require that the flap be tubed on itself to perform the microsurgery. Although this deep dissection can be precarious because of the large veins that are encountered, which can be difficult to encircle without injury, harvest of the gluteal artery at this proximal level, near the pelvic bone, provides for a larger luminal diameter that decreases the risk of vessel mismatch with the recipient artery and lessens the potential for microvascular thrombosis.

Often the large-caliber veins intertwined with each other at this level allow for ligation of only the proximal side of the vein during the flap harvest. Often, the distal side of the large vein branches cannot be transected until the vascular dissection is complete. After the perforator dissection is completed without injury and the flap appears adequately perfused, the secondary perforator(s) are ligated. Cold ischemia of the flap is utilized during the closure of the buttock donor site.

Any large distal side branches of the gluteal vein that were not ligated during flap harvest must be oversewed under direct visualization using surgical magnification, which avoids inadvertent occlusion of flow within the gluteal vein. Transection of the gluteal vessels so proximally, near the pelvic bone, allows the surgeon to select from several arterial and venous ostia for anastomosis to the internal mammary artery and vein. Most commonly, the choice of ostium is based on the luminal diameter and the positional relationship to the internal mammary vessels.

In the unusual instance in which an R-GAP flap exhibits signs of perforator compression, consideration should be given to releasing the encasing adventitia and fascia that surround the perforating vessels as they enter the adipose tissue. The encasing adventitia and fascia can be very thick and inelastic and can act as a constriction band, especially across the fragile venae comitantes that drain the venous blood from the flap.

Flap inset

The flap is rotated counterclockwise 90 degrees, placing the medial most portion of the flap superiorly (**Figure 23.5.2**). This allows for the most optimal orientation of the flap pedicle to the internal mammary vessels for the microvascular anastomosis. Once the microvascular anastomoses are completed, and the flap is adequately perfused, care is taken to position and shape the flap taking advantage of the "boomerang" design. Careful attention must be paid during the flap positioning and inset to make certain that there is no traction on the pedicle which can create a traction injury or avulse the pedicle from the internal mammary vessels. The medial most portion of the flap is placed superiorly, and the lateral most portion is sutured to the medial aspect of the flap reconstructing the lateral superior portion of the breast. By bringing the two ends of the "boomerang" together, the SGAP flap is effectively coned to maximize flap projection.

Outcomes

In comparison to the traditional SGAP flap, the "boomerang" technique allows for harvesting a flap of larger volume for autologous breast reconstruction (**Figures 23.5.3, 23.5.4, and 23.5.5**). The added volume allows for reconstruction of larger breasts to restore symmetry in larger breasted patients and therefore avoids the need for a contralateral procedure. The added volume and flap design also aids in maximizing the projection of the reconstructed breast and providing improved superior pole fullness compared to the traditional technique, thereby restoring a more aesthetic appearing breast with adequate fullness and projection.

Regarding the donor site, the "boomerang" skin paddle allows for easy re-approximation of the skin allowing for a tension free closure. Harvesting of additional tissue beyond the skin margins below the level of Scarpa's fascia preserves the subcutaneous fat which minimizes the contour deformity of the donor site. The final position of the donor site scar is easily concealed in clothing, while the traditional SGAP flap may have a scar that becomes apparent in bathing suits or other apparel.

CONCLUSION

The "boomerang" superior gluteal artery perforator flap is a novel modification of the traditional SGAP flap, allowing for added pedicle length and increased flap volume to optimize the shape and projection of the reconstructed breast.

BIBLIOGRAPHY

Allen RJ, Tucker C Jr. Superior gluteal artery perforator free flap for breast reconstruction. *Plast Reconstr Surg.* 1995;95(7):1207–1212.

Kronowitz SJ. Redesigned gluteal artery perforator flap for breast reconstruction. *Plast Reconstr Surg.* 2008;121(3):728–734.

Hamdi M, Andrades P, Thiessen F, Stillaert F, Roche N, Van Landuyt K, Monstrey S. Is a second free flap still an option in a failed free flap breast reconstruction? *Plast Reconstr Surg.* 2010;126(2):375–378.

Rozen WM, Ting JW, Grinsell D, Ashton MW. Superior and inferior gluteal artery perforators: In-vivo anatomical study and planning for breast reconstruction. *J Plast Reconstr Aesthet Surg.* 2011; 64(2):217–225.

Baumeister S, Werdin F, Peek A. The sGAP flap: Rare exception or second choice in autologous breast reconstruction? *J Reconstr Microsurg.* 2010;26(4):251–258.

23.6 TRANSVERSE UPPER GRACILIS (TUG) FLAP

Andrei Odobescu, Isak Goodwin, and Rudolf Buntic

Introduction

While the deep inferior epigastric perforator (DIEP) flap is often the first choice for autologous breast reconstruction, not all patients are suitable candidates. A number of alternative flaps have been described, such as the superficial inferior epigastric artery perforator (SIEA), superior gluteal artery perforator, inferior gluteal artery perforator, transverse upper gracilis (TUG), and popliteal artery perforator flaps. The TUG flap, first reported by Yousif and colleagues,[1] provides adequate tissue volume, reliable and straightforward pedicle dissection, a well-hidden donor scar, and often improved projection over the DIEP flap. Although not performed widely in the United States, it is an excellent choice for many patients and provides some of the best aesthetic results in the opinion of the authors.

Advantages of the TUG flap:

1. Superior breast shaping
2. Immediate nipple-areola complex reconstruction in some patients
3. Consistent blood supply
4. Donor site thigh lift
5. High success rate (in experienced hands)
6. Use in immediate or delayed reconstruction

Indications for TUG flap:

1. Patients intent upon avoiding abdominal scars
2. Athletic or thin patients who may have insufficient abdominal subcutaneous fat
3. Patients with previous abdominoplasty or abdominal surgery

Anatomy

The gracilis muscle lies medially beneath the fascia lata of the thigh. It arises from the ischiopubic ramus and inserts as the middle component of the pes anserinus on the medial tibial tuberosity. The muscle belly of the gracilis lies posterior to the adductor longus and sartorius muscles and anterior to the hamstrings (**Figure 23.6.1**).

The dominant vascular pedicle is located 8 to 10 cm distal to the pubic tubercle and travels between the adductor longus and adductor magnus to reach the undersurface of the gracilis muscle at a right angle to its axis. Secondary vascular pedicles are usually found distal to the dominant vessel, however, these are not adequate to support the flap. Musculocutaneous perforators supply the overlying skin

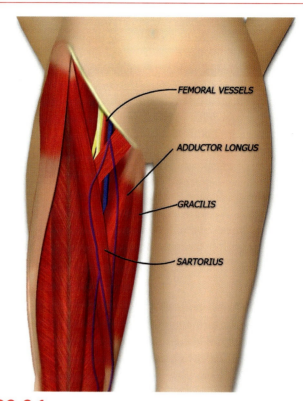

23.6.1 Anatomy of the gracilis muscle. The gracilis muscle originates from the body of the pubis and inserts on the medial aspect of the knee. It is located just posterior to the adductor longus muscle. The anterior and posterior branches of the saphenous vein are shown.

with a transversely oriented perforasome centered over the proximal one-third of the gracilis muscle.[1,2] The obturator nerve supplies the gracilis muscle with a single motor nerve. Unlike the vascular pedicle, the nerve enters the muscle at an oblique angle.

Flap design and dissection

The patient is placed in dorsal lithotomy position, allowing adequate access to the posterior incision (**Figure 23.6.2**).

The flap is marked in the inner thigh crease, just below the inguinal ligament, extending posteriorly in the inferior buttock crease. The skin paddle of the flap is marked with the widest point centered over the gracilis muscle. The skin paddle is ideally 8–12 cm wide, as closure under excessive tension can result in donor site breakdown, scar widening, and labial spreading. A pinch test of the inner thigh in the adducted position helps confirm the extent of skin that can be removed. The anterior extent of the incision should not exceed the adductor longus by more than 2–3 cm.[3] This hides the donor scar in the gluteal crease while avoiding an obvious anterior scar. Additionally, posterior incision placement minimizes dissection in the femoral triangle, decreasing the risk of lymphatic disruption.

23.6 Transverse upper gracilis (TUG) flap   357

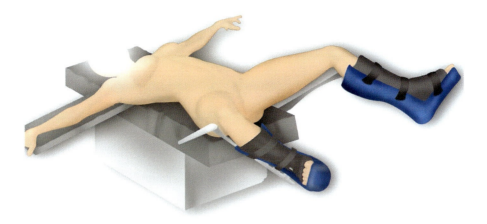

23.6.2 Lithotomy positioning of the patient. This allows for better exposure and dissection of the posterior aspect of the flap, which can be tedious in supine frog-leg position.

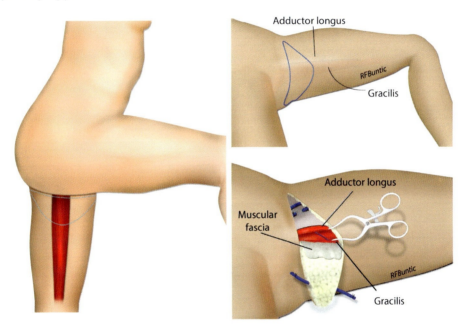

23.6.3 Flap markings and dissection. Left and top right: The skin paddle is centered over the proximal aspect of the gracilis muscle. Bottom right: The vascular pedicle can be visualized coursing on top of the adductor magnus muscle by retracting the adductor longus laterally. The posterior branch of the saphenous vein is often sacrificed with the flap. Once the pedicle is visualized and protected, the posterior aspect of the flap is raised safely.

The anterior flap is elevated first in a plane superficial to the muscular fascia of the adductor longus, sparing the anterior branch of the saphenous vein. The posterior branch of the saphenous vein travels within the flap and is ligated and divided. When the medial edge of the adductor longus is reached, the muscular fascia is incised and the pedicle to the gracilis is identified by retracting the adductor longus laterally. Once the pedicle is identified, the posterior flap can be elevated safely (**Figure 23.6.3**). The proximal and distal gracilis muscles are divided.[4] The pedicle is traced to its origin to gain length. The artery is generally of small diameter (2 mm), and its maximum length is 6 cm. Two venae comitantes accompany the artery, one often larger in diameter than the artery itself. The donor site is closed in layers over a suction drain.

Shaping and inset

Flap shaping is shown in **Figures 23.6.4 and 23.6.5**. Much like the DIEP flap for breast reconstruction, TUG flap shaping and inset will distinguish a good from an excellent result. While abdominal-based flaps are flat and provide projection only by means of the thickness of the pannus, the TUG flap is formed into a standing cone that more accurately mimics the shape of a breast. The projection is often superior to that created by DIEP and SIEA flaps. By using the crescent shape of the flap and folding to full advantage, the nipple-areola complex can be created in one stage. The naturally darker color of the inner thigh compared to the relatively pale breast skin color can give the areola superior pigmentation (**Figure 23.6.6**).

An inner thigh lift is performed, with the thigh donor site closed in layers with the thigh adducted. The patient avoids abducting her legs for several days, at which point the tension on the incision site begins to relax, and the patient resumes a recovery similar to the DIEP or SIEA flap patient.

Clinical cases are outlined in **Figures 23.6.7 and 23.6.8**.

Complications and donor site morbidity

Published rates of total flap failure for TUG flaps range from 2% to 6%, and partial flap loss is less (0%–1.3%). A steep learning curve for performing the TUG flap is widely accepted. Contour abnormality can be high (100% by some accounts) and is likely secondary to fat necrosis (3.9%–29%) and atrophy of the gracilis muscle. Contour deficits are reflected in the high rate of secondary fat grafting (57%). The average number of additional procedures per patient (not including nipple areola complex reconstruction) is as high as 3.9 (SD 2.9).[5]

Donor site complications include seroma (7%), wound breakdown/scar revision (6%), and sensory disturbances (4%).[6] Limiting the flap width to less than 8 cm reduces the dehiscence and infection rate from 28% to 9%. Donor site morbidity for the TUG flap is generally acceptable to patients and microsurgeons. It provides a good alternative to patients who seek autologous reconstruction, but have contraindications to abdominal-based breast reconstruction.[7]

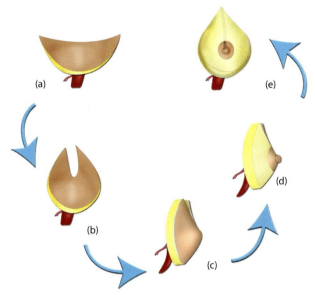

23.6.4 Shaping of the TUG flap. Once harvested, the crescent shape of the flap lends itself well to folding into a standing cone. The neo-nipple areola complex is marked, and the remaining flap is de-epithelialized for inset.

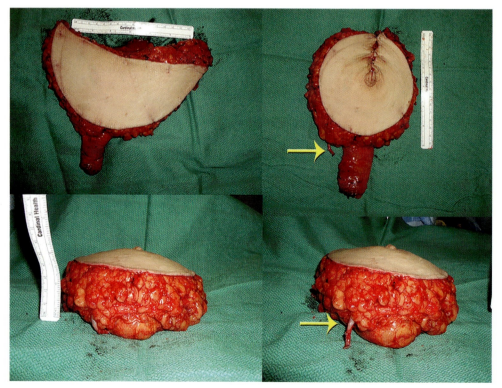

23.6.5 Flap shape after coning. Folding the flap into a standing cone gives additional projection of the central area, recreating well the shape of the breast. The projection in the central area is of 5 cm, tapering off toward the periphery. The exit of the pedicle (yellow arrow) determines the position the flap will be inset.

23.6 Transverse upper gracilis (TUG) flap 359

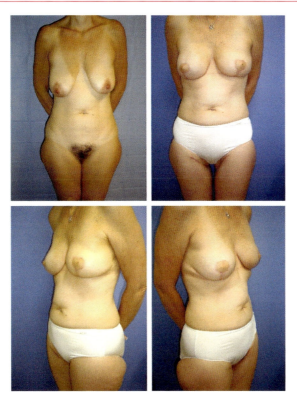

23.6.6 Clinical case showing the projection offered by the TUG flap. A 68-year-old female with left breast cancer opted for bilateral mastectomy and TUG reconstructions. Note that the nipple areola complex was reconstructed with the TUG skin at the same stage, with no additional tattooing. The bottom photographs show the projection and shape that can be accomplished with a TUG reconstruction.

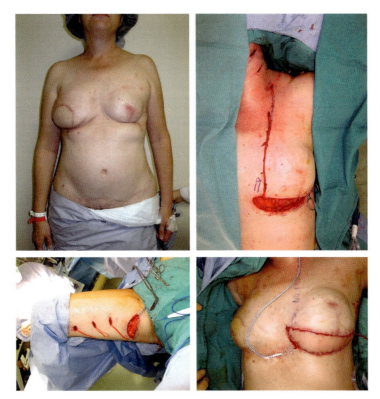

23.6.7 Modifications of the TUG design. This patient had previous failed bilateral transverse rectus abdominis myocutaneous flap (TRAM) reconstructions followed by bilateral superior gluteal artery perforator reconstruction. The left lower pole remained deficient and asymmetric. A TUG flap was done to give volume and coverage of the left lower pole. The posterior branch of the saphenous vein was dissected and anastomosed to a branch of the external jugular vein. The flap artery was anastomosed to the internal mammary artery.

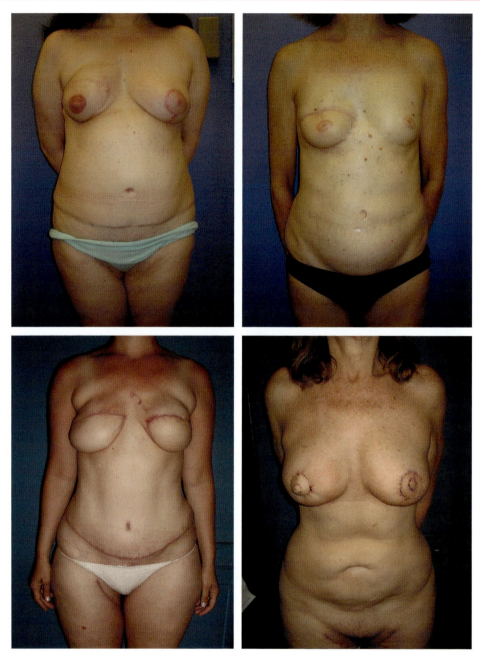

23.6.8 TUG flap breast reconstruction examples. Upper left: Patient following failed DIEP reconstruction who had TUG flap reconstruction and left breast reduction. Top right: TUG flap reconstruction of a previous failed TRAM flap. The gracilis muscle was used to obliterate the dead space from resection of rib osteoradionecrosis. Bottom left: Patient had previous DIEP reconstruction of the right breast. Patient then required left mastectomy which was reconstructed with a TUG flap from her right thigh. Bottom right: Bilateral breast reconstruction using TUG flaps. Note the substantial volume the flaps provide, as well as the immediate nipple-areola complex (NAC) reconstructions.

REFERENCES

1. Yousif NJ, Matloub HS, Kolachalam R, Grunert BK, Sanger JR. The transverse gracilis musculocutaneous flap. *Ann Plast Surg.* 1992;29(6):482–490.

2. Coquerel-Beghin D, Milliez PY, Auquit-Auckbur I, Lemierre G, Duparc F. The gracilis musculocutaneous flap: Vascular supply of the muscle and skin components. *Surg Radiol Anat.* 2006;28(6):588–595.

3. Craggs B, Vanmierlo B, Zeltzer A, Buyl R, Haentjens P, Hamdi M. Donor-site morbidity following harvest of the transverse myocutaneous gracilis flap for breast reconstruction. *Plast Reconstr Surg.* 2014;134(5):682e–691e.

4. Buntic RF, Horton KM, Brooks D, Althubaiti GA. Transverse upper gracilis flap as an alternative to abdominal tissue breast reconstruction: Technique and modifications. *Plast Reconstr Surg.* 2011;128(6):607e–613e.

5. Locke MB, Zhong T, Mureau MA, Hofer SO. Tug 'O' War: Challenges of transverse upper gracilis (TUG) myocutaneous free flap breast reconstruction. *J Plast Reconstr Aesthet Surg.* 2012;65(8):1041–1050.

6. Hunter JE, Lardi AM, Dower DR, Farhadi J. Evolution from the TUG to PAP flap for breast reconstruction: Comparison and refinements of technique. *J Plast Reconstr Aesthet Surg.* 2015;68(7):960–965.

7. Lakhiani C, DeFazio MV, Han K, Falola R, Evans K. Donor-site morbidity following free fissue harvest from the thigh: A systematic review and pooled analysis of complications. *J Reconstr Microsurg.* 2016;32(5):342–357.

23.7 LUMBAR ARTERY PERFORATOR (LAP) FLAP

Moustapha Hamdi and Randy De Baerdemaeker

Definition

The lumbar artery perforator (LAP) flap has been added to the group of flaps used for breast reconstruction in those cases where an abdominal donor site is unavailable.[1-8] De Weerd and colleagues published a case report in 2003 describing a free LAP flap for breast reconstruction.[1] This followed a fresh cadaver study by these authors on six hemicadavers. More recently, Peters and colleagues together with the author's group (both from Belgium) published the largest reported series of free LAP flaps used in breast reconstruction.[8,9]

Anatomy

The lumbar arteries arise from the posterior aspect of the aorta, four on each side of the body, and travel behind the psoas major muscle. The upper three lumbar arteries run laterally and backward between the quadratus lumborum muscle and the erector spinae musculature, while the lowest set of arteries normally run in front of the quadratus lumborum muscle (**Figure 23.7.1 A and B**). Not every lumbar artery gives origin to a perforating artery; L1 and L2 perforators are less common than L3 and L4 perforators while the fourth lumbar artery is the most reliable for having perforators. Cadaveric and imaging studies reveal a mean number of 6 + 2 lumbar artery perforators per patient.[7] It should be noted that the size, position, and course of the lumbar perforators can be somewhat variable.[1-3,6,7,9] The mean diameter of a lumbar vessel perforator (artery and vein) is 2.1 ± 0.5 mm.[7] The lower lumbar vessels give off more and slightly larger perforators, and the fourth lumbar perforators are more often septocutaneous. Sometimes (20% dominant perforators) the vessel diameter at the level of the transverse process is smaller than at the transition through the fascia into the subcutaneous tissue. This may happen because once the vessel has left the muscle, a surrounding counter pressure falls away and the vessel assumes a slightly larger diameter.[9] The mean point of perforation of the lumbar fascia by the lumbar vessel perforator lies 7.22 cm (range 5–9 cm) from the midline.[3] Bifurcation of the perforator itself at the level of the fascia is present in hardly any of the L1 and L2 perforators, but is more common in the L3 and L4 perforators. Further bifurcation at the level of the subcutaneous tissue is seldom present and only in the lower perforators.[9] Variations in vascular anatomy such as a second perforator arising from the same main artery or a large side branch from L2 taking the place of an absent L3 perforator are described.

Patient history and physical findings

Preoperative evaluation should include the same work-up as for any other free flap autologous breast reconstruction technique. Physical examination should include inspection of the skin of the lumbar region for scarring or previous incision sites and general tissue bulk is examined with a pinch test.

Imaging

All patients should undergo a preoperative computed tomographic angiography of the lumbar and thoracic regions showing the size (**Figure 23.7.2**), patency, and position of the lumbar perforators and the patency of the internal mammary recipient vessels.[4] The perforators are marked by the radiologist using a grid system in which the midline represents the Y-axis and the iliac crest being the X-axis. The dominant perforator is marked and confirmed by a unidirectional Doppler.

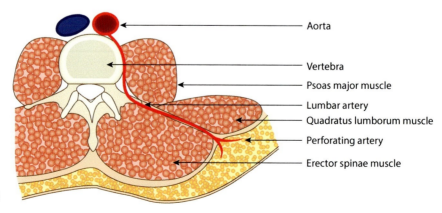

23.7.1 (A) Schematic drawing sagittal view of the origin and course of the lumbar artery and its perforator. (Continued)

23.7 Lumbar artery perforator (LAP) flap 363

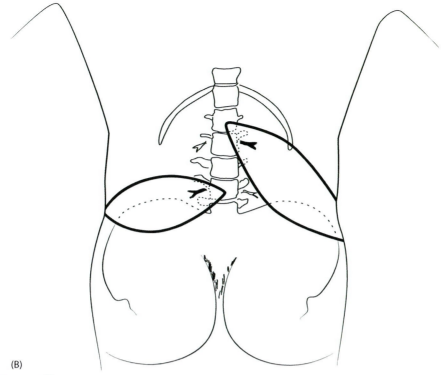

23.7.1 (Continued) (B) Schematic drawing of possible LAP flap design based on perforators of different levels.

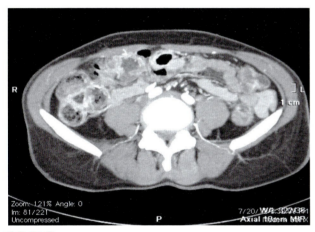

23.7.2 Computed tomographic angiography image of L4 perforators.

Surgical management

The LAP should be considered for unilateral or bilateral breast reconstruction in primary, secondary, or even tertiary cases where the abdominal donor site is unavailable. Bilateral cases are always performed in two stages. Indications for a LAP flap include insufficient abdominal tissue and previous abdominal surgery, for example, abdominoplasty or previous harvesting of a deep inferior epigastric perforator flap.

PREOPERATIVE PLANNING

Computed tomographic (CT) imaging should be carefully reviewed before surgery and the dominant LAP is selected. In general, an ipsilateral LAP flap is planned (**Figure 23.7.3**), but in the case of bilateral reconstruction, a sequential approach is employed with a minimum of 3 months between operations. Markings: The patient is marked in a standing position (**Figure 23.7.3a–c**). The posterior midline and iliac crest are marked initially, and then the dominant LAP is identified and confirmed by unidirectional Doppler. A fusiform skin island is drawn over the perforators with the long axis in a slightly medially pointing upward direction to resemble an upper-buttock lift scar (**Figure 23.7.3b and c**). The drawings do not pass the midline, and they are designed to eventually meet up with an abdominoplasty scar laterally. The size of the flap is judged using the pinch test. The thoracic region is marked.

POSITIONING

The flap can be harvested in either a prone position or in lateral decubitus position. Attention is paid to protection of all pressure points and placement of an arm roll is mandatory for patients positioned in lateral decubitus (**Figure 23.7.3d and e**).

APPROACH

Lateral decubitus: The flap is most easily harvested from the back toward the abdomen with the surgeon standing at the posterior side of the patient (posterior approach). The anterior approach is also used when the perforator is more laterally located. It allows a two-team approach for the simultaneous preparation of the mastectomy site and for harvesting of a deep inferior epigastric interposition graft if necessary.

Prone decubitus: The operation starts with the patient in supine decubitus while the mastectomy site is prepared, the recipient vessels are dissected and a deep inferior epigastric

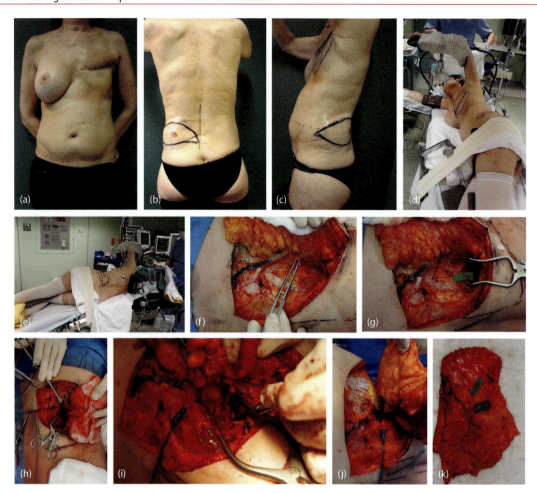

23.7.3 A 57-year-old patient who underwent left breast reconstruction with LAP flap 2 years after mastectomy and postoperative irradiation. (a) Preoperative views. (b, c) Planning of an ipsilateral flap: A fusiform skin island is drawn over the perforators with the long axis in a slightly medially pointing upward direction to resemble an upper-buttock lift scar (d, e) Patient's positioning on lateral decubitus which allows two-team approach for flap harvesting and preparing the recipient site. (f) The thoracolumbar fascia is opened medially over the erector spinae muscle. The fascia is elevated with a retractor to identify the sensory nerves and the perforators. The blue line is the iliac crest superior border. (g) The sensate nerve is followed for adequate length when a sensate LAP flap is planned. The arrow pointed where the lumbar perforator emerges through the deep fascia. (h) The selected perforator with its concomitant vein is dissected down between the erector spinae and quadratus lumborum muscles. (i) The pedicle is dissected between the muscle fibers until an adequate artery diameter and/or length of the pedicle is obtained. (j) Once the pedicle is completely dissected, the flap is then freed from the abdominal deep fascia anteriorly. (k) Flap is completely harvested with a sensate nerve (small green back-ground).

interpositional graft is harvested. Subsequently, the patient is turned to a prone position for flap dissection. The flap is harvested from the lateral to the medial with the surgeon standing at the ipsilateral side. While anastomosis of the interposition graft is performed, a second team closes the donor site and repositions the patient in a supine position for revascularization and shaping of the flap.[8,9] The dissection of the perforator and pedicle is similar with the flap usually based on a single perforator.

Techniques

After incising the skin and subcutaneous tissue, the thoracolumbar fascia is opened medially over the erector spinae muscle. The fascia is elevated with a retractor to identify the sensory nerves and the perforators (**Figure 23.7.3f and g**). While directly visualizing the perforators, the flap is elevated from anterolateral to medial in a subfascial plane (**Figure 23.7.3g**). To obtain sufficient pedicle length, the selected perforator with its concomitant vein is dissected down between the erector spinae and quadratus lumborum muscles (**Figure 23.7.3h and i**). To harvest more subcutaneous tissue, the flap is raised beveling superiorly and inferiorly creating a gluteal extension in the adipose tissue and the flap is then freed from the abdominal deep fascia (**Figure 23.7.3j**). Flap is harvested with a sensate nerve (**Figure 23.7.3k**). At this stage, the lumbar pedicle length and diameter are evaluated. It is advised to stop the dissection at the level of the processus transversus vertebrae to avoid injury to the spinal nerves. If the length is adequate (≥ 6 cm) and/or the artery diameter is more than 0.5 mm, the anastomosis is performed in a similar manner as for a deep inferior epigastric perforator flap. If the length or artery diameter of the pedicle is not suitable, a vascular interposition graft will be harvested from the deep inferior epigastric vessels through an extension of the incision or a separate Pfannensteil incision. The anastomoses between the vascular graft and the lumbar artery and vein are done on a separate surgical table. Harvesting the deep inferior epigastric segment is straightforward and allows a longer pedicle with a better size match to the diameter of the internal mammary (IM) vessels, and in particular, with the internal mammary artery (as it is shown in **Figure 23.7.6**). The recipient vessels are the internal mammary vessels, which are dissected simultaneously using a two-team approach. However, due to the short lumbar perforator length, the IM vessels are dissected over 3–4 cm after removal of one costal cartilage (**Figure 23.7.4a**). This makes the microanastomosis easier. The sensate nerve can be sutured to an intercostal nerve. Donor site closure is performed simultaneously during the microanastomosis. Limited undermining, mainly inferior, resembling an upper buttock lift, is required. Quilting sutures are used, as well as fibrin glue. Two suction drains are left in the donor site. Once the microanastomosis is done with the internal mammary vessels, the flap is fixed temporarily with surgical staples to the mastectomy skin. The patient is then turned to the supine position for shaping of the breast. The subcutaneous tissue is fixed to the pectoralis major muscle at the axillary side and to the inframammary fold. The flap is de-epithelialized, depending on the reconstruction type. In some cases, the entire flap is used, in others, the distal part of the flap is trimmed if there are signs of venous congestion or ischemia. The flap is used as a hammock within the mastectomy pocket without the need for folding the flap onto itself. Shaping the flap is simple because the fat tissue is quite supple and can be remodeled easily. Turning the flap 180°, the gluteal extension creates a nice fullness in the upper pole of the reconstructed breast (**Figure 23.7.4b**).

Pearls and pitfalls

Technique	• Surgical challenges consist of a careful dissection through the thoracolumbar fascia and tedious dissection of the perforator between the muscle.
	• Using a two-team approach, no time is lost with cartilage excision or vascular grafting. To the contrary, a longer vessel on the pedicle or recipient side facilitates the anastomosis.
Pedicle length and size mismatch	• Prepare for harvesting deep inferior epigastric pedicle graft (necessary in 50%–75% due to short pedicle (mean 5.25 cm[9]).
	• Remove partial or total costal cartilage at the 3rd or 4th rib.
Seroma	• More anterior flap design preserving the lymphatic drainage over the thick deep fascia over the paraspinal muscle.
	• Less flap skin harvesting.
	• Avoid aggressive denuding of the iliac crest, minimal undermining only.
	• Place quilting sutures and adequate wound drainage.
	• Fibrin glue.
	• Use compressive garments over the lumbar area.
Contour	• Only inferior undermining for donor site closure.
	• Contralateral liposuction in unilateral cases.
Hypoesthesia upper buttock/ Sensate flap	• Rarely bothersome to patient, but avoided by not injuring the nervi clunium superiors.
	• Anastomosing nervi clunium superiors to fourth intercostal nerve, only in specific cases.
High scar	• Difficult to be hidden in standard underwear or bikini suits.
	• Limits indications in young women, importance of patient selection.
	• Select lowermost suitable perforator.

Postoperative care

An abdominal binder or lipopanty is applied at the donor site for between 4 and 6 weeks postoperatively. Drains are left in the donor site until they produce less than 20 mL per 24 hours or for a maximum period of 10 days postoperatively.

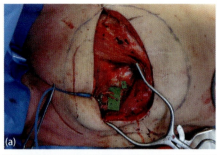
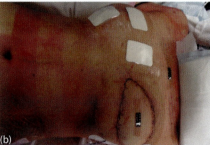

23.7.4 Preparation of recipient site. The caudal breast skin is mainly undermined and not de-epithelialized because the lumbar skin paddle is limited in width. (a) The internal mammary vessels are prepared. The rib cartilage is removed depending on the acquired lumbar pedicle. Cartilage resection is necessary when the lumbar pedicle length is short. The internal mammary vessels are dissected for 3–4 cm after removal of one costal cartilage to obtain easier microsurgical setup. (b) After the microanastomoses are done and the nerve was coapted to an intercostal nerve, the flap is fixed on the thoracic wall by few sutures.

Outcomes

The size of a LAP flap is usually ample to create a breast of sufficient volume (**Table 23.7.1**). The mean flap size is about 142 cm^2 (dimensions 22 × 5.28 × 6.5 cm) and mean flap weight 495–554g.[8] Additional lipofilling to improve breast contour can be used to improve the quality of skin damaged from preoperative irradiation (**Figure 23.7.5**). Compared to a transverse myocutaneous gracilis (TMG) flap (average 224 + 67 g for patients with a mean body mass index of 22 + 2 kg/m^2), the LAP flap provides correspondingly more tissue in patients with a similar body mass index (average 495 g, mean body mass index of 23 kg/m^2). In the study of Peters and colleagues involving 35 LAP flaps, 6 flaps had to be revised as a consequence of venous thrombosis (17%). This may be due to a larger series, a learning curve, or the interposition graft used. Flap necrosis occurred in three cases only (5.7%).[8] In the series of Hamdi and colleagues,[9] there were no cases requiring revision of microanastomoses and no cases of flap failure or necrosis. A high seroma rate at the donor site is relatively common, varying from 17% to 78%.[9] Moreover, the scar lies higher than for a superior/inferior gluteal artery perforator flap or profunda artery perforator (PAP) flap, but does not distort contour and does reshape a slim waist (**Figure 23.7.6**). Follow-up period ranged between 6 and 26 months (average 13 months) in the study of Hamdi and colleagues[9] and between 1 and 48 months (average 18 months) in the study of Peters and colleagues.[8] The LAP flap offers better fat quality, which tends to be much

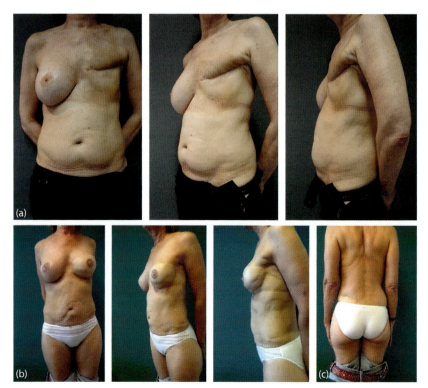

23.7.5 The outcome: A right mastopexy was done 5 months later with fat grafting under the skin on the reconstructed side. The results are presented after 30 months follow-up. (a) Preoperative views. (b) Postoperative views. (c) The donor site with the resulting scar.

23.7 Lumbar artery perforator (LAP) flap 367

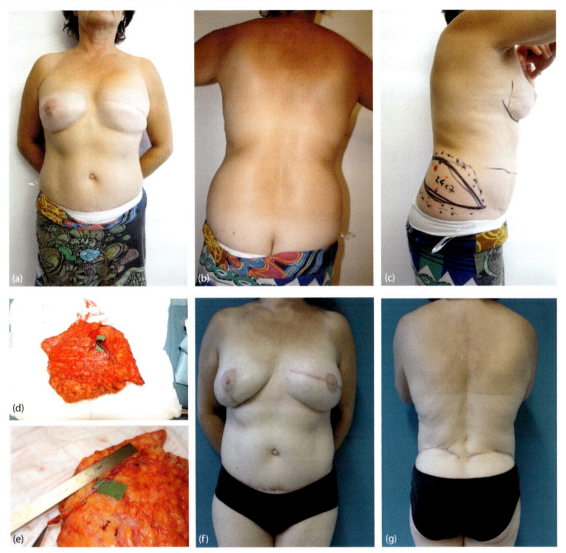

23.7.6 A 53-year-old patient who had previous abdominoplasty underwent sequential reconstruction with bilateral LAP flaps. (a) Preoperative view. (b) The donor site. (c) The flap's design was extended to the abdominoplasty scar. (d) The left LAP flap was harvested with pedicle length <6 cm and small artery diameter. (e) A vascular artery-vein bypass was harvested from the left DIE vessels, thereby creating a 12 cm pedicle length and better artery diameter match with the IM recipient artery. (f) Result with 2 years follow-up of sequential LAP flap breast reconstruction. (g) The donor site: Note the scar is above her underwear, but does not disrupt the buttocks and improves waistline contour.

softer and more pliable. Flap shaping is therefore easier and does not require further surgical revision. Furthermore, levels of patient satisfaction are high. Mean operating times vary between 6 hours 15 minutes[8] and 4 hours 20 minutes.[9]

Complications

Complications include revision surgery, partial/complete flap necrosis, and seroma formation. The latter can lead to prolonged drainage, serial aspiration, and need for excision of seroma capsule. Delayed wound healing can also be problematic and impact upon timing of adjuvant treatments. Quadriceps weakness or paresthesia in the territory of L3–L4[8] can be a consequence of LAP flap reconstruction (Table 23.7.1).

Table 23.7.1 Complications in author series[9]

	Flaps	Donor sites (/9)
Revision surgery	0/9	
Partial/complete flap necrosis	0/9	
Seroma		7/9
Prolonged drainage		4
Serial aspiration		1
Excision seroma capsule		2
+/− quilting sutures		

REFERENCES

1. de Weerd L, Elvenes OP, Strandenes E, Weum S. Autologous breast reconstruction with a free lumbar artery perforator flap. *Br J Plast Surg* 2003; 56(2):180–183.
2. Hamdi M, Van Landuyt K, Van Hedent E et al. Advances in autogenous breast reconstruction: The role of preoperative perforators mapping. *Ann Plast Surg* 2007; 58:18e–26e.
3. Kato H, Hasegawa M, Takada T, Torii S. The lumbar artery perforator based island flap: Anatomical study and case reports. *Br J PLast Surg* 1999; 52(7):541–546.
4. Kiil BJ, Rozen WM, Pan WR et al. The lumbar artery perforators: A cadaveric and clinical anatomical study. *Plast Reconstr Surg* 2009; 132:1229–1238.
5. Kroll SS, Rosenfield L. Perforator-based flaps for low posterior midline defects. *Plast Reconstr Surg* 1988; 81(4):561–566.
6. Lui KW, Hu S, Ahmad N, Tang M. Three-dimensional angiography of the superior gluteal artery and lumbar artery perforator flap. *Plast Reconstr Surg* 2009; 123(1):79–86.
7. Offman SL, Geddes CR, Tang M, Morris SF. The vascular basis of perforator flaps based on the source arteries of the lateral lumbar region. *Plast Reconstr Surg* 2005; 115(6):1651–1659.
8. Peters KT, Blondeel PN, Lobo F, Van Landuyt K. Early experience with the free lumbar artery perforator flap for breast reconstruction. *J Plast Reconstr Aesthet Surg* 2015; 68(8):1112–1119.
9. Hamdi M, Craggs, B, Carola Brussaard et al. Lumbar artery perforator flap: An anatomic study using multidetector CT Scan and surgical pearls for breast reconstruction. *Plast Reconstr Surg,* 2016 (in Press).

Revisional breast reconstruction (following both partial and whole breast reconstruction)

AT A GLANCE

Revision of a reconstructed breast can be more challenging than the reconstruction itself, especially after radiotherapy. Flaps such as the latissimus dorsi flap are typically used to salvage a poor outcome from an irradiated implant reconstruction. With increasing frequency, ADMs and fat grafting are used in revisional breast procedures. Perhaps the best approach to revision, in cases of partial mastectomy, is prevention. The need for revision is limited when immediate repair is performed before radiation. Notwithstanding, when considering revision of an irradiated partial breast deformity, several options are available, depending upon the complexity of the required repair, and the desires of the patient. In revisional surgery of whole breast reconstruction, it is important to follow a systematic method to optimize outcomes an ensure that the secondary reconstruction is performed safely and with predictive results. Implant-based reconstruction is one of the most common forms of breast reconstruction, following mastectomy. However, long-term results can be suboptimal, especially following radiotherapy. For implant-based procedures, there are several factors for consideration that can subsequently impact the risk and complexity of revisional surgery after radiation therapy to the breast. The procedure for revising an irradiated flap is not the same as revising a non-irradiated flap. The main difference lies in the ability of wounds to heal in the setting of reshaping a flap-based breast reconstruction. Irradiated flaps have lost the capacity for normal wound healing, and attempts at revision may lead to wound healing problems, and may require a vacuum-assisted closure device or even the fashioning of another flap. However, pre-surgical fat grafting can lead to successful revision of an irradiated breast reconstruction and potentially decrease the risk of subsequent contracture deformity and obviate the need for flap salvage. In summation, there are significant differences in the problems associated with a revision of an immediate compared with a delayed breast reconstruction. The major difference between revising an irradiated and non-irradiated breast reconstruction is related to wound healing issues. Revision of irradiated breast tissue is invariably associated with greater morbidity than revision of non-irradiated breast reconstructions. Moreover, irradiated tissue—regardless of whether this is breast after partial, or chest wall after total mastectomy—does not heal normally and is associated with significant morbidity. The complexity of performing these operations has led to textbooks dedicated solely to revising the reconstructed breast.

370 Revisional breast reconstruction (following both partial and whole breast reconstruction)

Chapter 24. Breast revision following breast conservation and oncoplastic repair   371

Chapter 25. Breast revision after implant-based breast reconstruction   379

Chapter 26. Breast revision after mastectomy, whole breast reconstruction, and postmastectomy radiation therapy   383

24

Breast revision following breast conservation and oncoplastic repair

STEVEN J. KRONOWITZ

REVISIONAL BREAST RECONSTRUCTION AFTER PARTIAL MASTECTOMY

Revisional breast reconstruction after irradiation can be extremely challenging. The major difference between revising an irradiated and non-irradiated breast reconstruction relate to issues of wound healing. Although there are differences dependent on whether revision is being undertaken on irradiated breast tissue, an irradiated breast implant, or an irradiated flap, these revisional procedures on previously irradiated tissue are invariably associated with increased morbidity than revision of non-irradiated breast reconstructions.[1–8] The timing of the breast reconstruction also has a significant impact on the outcomes. Thus, delayed reconstruction of an irradiated chest wall using a non-irradiated flap incurs much less morbidity than revision of a radiated flap. Revision of a delayed breast reconstruction after radiation performed using a latissimus dorsi flap and breast implant generally has fewer problems than a similarly irradiated implant construct without a flap. Furthermore, it should be noted that revision of an irradiated breast reconstruction, even when initially undertaken as a delayed procedure after radiation treatment, still has a potentially higher rate of complications than non-irradiated breast reconstructions because of irradiated chest wall tissues.[5,6,8] In general terms, addition of a breast implant to any reconstruction that involves prior radiation treatment carries increased morbidity compared to tissue-only based reconstructions.[3] Moreover, irradiated tissue regardless of whether this is breast after partial or chest wall after total mastectomy does not heal normally and is associated with significant morbidity.

Following breast-conserving surgery, extensive local repair can result in major problems with wound dehiscence and sometimes the need for a flap in order to achieve wound closure. Although the breast can appear suitable for a local rearrangement procedure (such as mastopexy) several years

after the completion of partial mastectomy and radiation therapy, delayed repair of these deformities can result in complication rates in excess of 50%.[9–12] Delayed repair of a partial mastectomy defect may appear to be the same as revising a repair that was performed before radiation, but these are quite different. Immediate repair of partial mastectomy defects before radiation is the preferred approach and usually limits the degree to which the breasts require revision after radiation. The safe performance of delayed reconstruction of partial mastectomy defects after radiation usually requires a flap procedure, and many of these patients are not interested in undergoing these more extensive procedures.

Perhaps the best approach to revision in cases of partial mastectomy is prevention. The need for revision is limited when immediate repair is performed before radiation. This approach usually minimizes the extent of revision required and often this is confined to minor skin tailoring and fat grafting.[9,12] Extensive percutaneous needle scar release with fat grafting can represent a safe alternative to formal surgical repair of these deformities, but multiple operative sessions are usually indicated and results can be suboptimal because of scarring within the dermis.[13] Some surgeons attempt to augment partial breast deformities using implants, but it should be emphasized that this procedure is associated with significant morbidity and exaggerates any overlying irregularity in the breast tissue, which can then appear more pronounced than was previously the case.

Notwithstanding these comments, when considering revision of an irradiated partial breast deformity several options are available. It should be noted that the simplest approach is to perform a contralateral symmetry procedure only, and for some patients, this is all they are seeking along with being be able to wear a brassiere satisfactorily. For example, if a mastopexy is performed to achieve symmetry, the position of the nipple areola complex does not necessarily have to be repositioned to the level of the inframammary fold, but rather just high enough to be symmetric with the nipple-areola complex of the ipsilateral irradiated breast. The next ascending level of complexity of surgical revision would involve performing a de-epithelialized repair of the irradiated partial breast deformity. This approach usually helps only with position of the nipple-areola complex, but can be optimally combined well with a contralateral mastopexy for symmetry. Although de-epithelialized repairs tend to heal better than those involving dissection deep within the radiated breast tissue, surgeons should resist the temptation to perform surgical forays into the deeper layers of radiated breast tissue. There is much evidence from published studies and surgeons' experience over time confirming these repairs to be fraught with postoperative wound healing problems.[9–13]

Another option of relatively low morbidity for revision of a prior partial mastectomy oncoplasty repair involves use of extensive percutaneous needle release of scar tissue within the breast resulting from the effects of radiation and primary surgery. It is imperative to release the breast in its entirety and not restrict this just to the region of a localized deformity (**Figure 24.1**).[13] Deformities in irradiated breasts containing residual native breast tissue relates to scarring throughout the breast consequent to fibrosis from whole breast irradiation as standard treatment.[13] The majority of patients undergoing breast conservation continue to receive whole breast irradiation as opposed to newer techniques of partial breast irradiation.

Although the fibrosis resulting from primary oncoplastic repair can be an additional factor that contributes to the need for revision, the purpose of primary repair of partial mastectomy defects before radiation therapy is to limit the extent of any localized deformity before delivery of radiation.[9,12,13] Breast irradiation can diffusely affect the breast tissue (especially the fatty component) leading to a global reduction in breast volume, especially the fatty component of the breast, and exacerbate any (unrepaired) localized deformities from surgical excision. Even in those circumstances of a prior primary oncoplastic repair, extensive percutaneous needle release of the entire breast is advisable. After performing scar release, fat grafting of the breast throughout its entirety is an essential next step in the revision process.[13] After approximately 3 months, the maturation process of the fat graft results in neovascularization and neoadipogenesis. Additional treatment cycles of both needle release and fat grafting are usually required to achieve the desired outcome.[13]

Surgical revision after partial mastectomy repair involves a major procedure that can be considered a secondary reconstruction due to the complexity of revision within an irradiated field. An assortment of local and distant flaps can be employed to revise poor outcomes after oncoplastic repair. These include local flaps such as the intercostal flap, epigastric flaps, thoracodorsal artery perforator flap, and the partial latissimus flap. Several flaps have been used for microvascular transfer, most recently thigh flaps from either the inner thigh (gracilis) or anterior thigh (anterior lateral thigh). Although some surgeons use the deep inferior epigastric perforator (DIEP) flap for revision after attempted oncoplastic repair and radiation therapy, it is probably sensible to preserve this particular flap for whole breast reconstruction. This DIEP flap has the advantage of providing extensive skin replacement for a delayed whole breast reconstruction (especially after radiation treatment).[5–7] Furthermore, in circumstances of severe deformation of the breast after partial mastectomy and oncoplastic repair, the most appropriate approach to revision may be completion mastectomy and whole breast reconstruction with a DIEP flap.

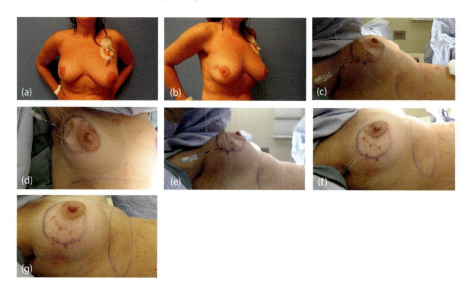

24.1 The Kronowitz stair-step approach to revising partial mastectomy defects. (a and b) A 38-year-old female who presents several years after a right partial mastectomy and whole breast radiation therapy. The patient has an upper outer tethering deformity that has created a contour deformity and a displaced nipple and areola complex that is asymmetric with the contralateral breast. (c–e) Intraoperative views. After placement of violin sutures along partial mastectomy scar to allow for counter traction for scar release. In a stair-step fashion from the chest wall to the skin, the entirety of the breast parenchyma is released using a large bore percutaneous spinal needle. Although not shown, the patient subsequently underwent fat grafting to the entirety of the breast. (f and g) After completion of delayed extensive percutaneous needle scar release and fat grafting of the entirety of the deformed breast after partial mastectomy and fat grafting.

As mentioned above, the best approach to revisional surgery after breast-conservation therapy is to either prevent or limit the extent of revision required after wide local excision and radiotherapy. There are several ways of achieving these objectives prior to irradiation for women with a variety of breast shapes and sizes.[9,12,13] For patients with A- and B-cup-sized breasts, and early-stage breast cancer (small tumors), nipple-sparing mastectomy with immediate breast reconstruction rather than partial mastectomy might be preferable (**Figure 24.2**).[12–14] This approach avoids the need for radiation therapy in patients who usually have limited autologous tissue options if a poor outcome ensures from primary oncoplastic surgery and radiation therapy. Moreover, nipple-sparing mastectomy in this patient population also retains the option for implant-based reconstruction as the use of implants in the setting of irradiation is generally not advisable.

These patients with C-cup-sized breasts can be divided into two groups: those with and without breast ptosis.[12] Patients with C-cup-sized breasts and no breast ptosis, but with an upper pole defect, can undergo oncoplastic repair using displacement concentric mastopexy (**Figure 24.3**). This technique works especially well for upper outer

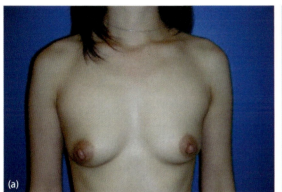
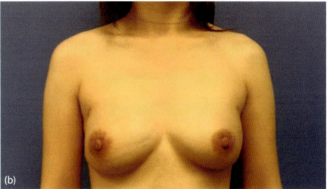

24.2 Preventing need for revision after partial mastectomy in small-breasted patient. (a) Preoperative view: 42-year-old female with B-cup-sized breasts with minimal ptosis who was referred for possible oncoplastic repair after partial mastectomy. (b) Postoperative view: Instead of performing a partial mastectomy followed by radiation in this small-breasted patient, she underwent nipple sparing mastectomy with one-stage direct-to-implant repair. This prevented the need for subsequent revision surgery, even if she would have undergone immediate oncoplastic repair after partial mastectomy.

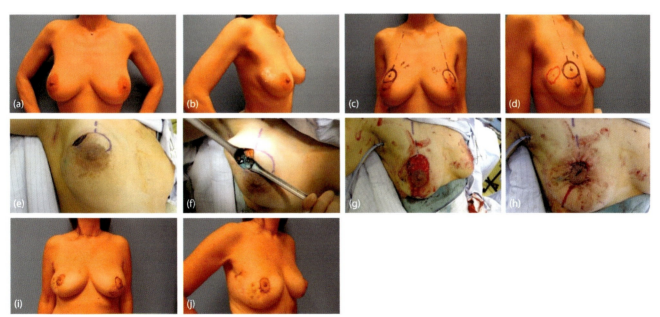

24.3 Preventing need for revision after partial mastectomy in large-breasted patient. Kronowitz displacement oncoplasty. Preoperative views: (a and b) 36-year-old female with D-cup-sized, minimally ptotic breasts. Breast tumor located in upper outer quadrant of right breast. (c and d) Markings for right displacement concentric mastopexy oncoplastic repair and left symmetry procedure. Red marking indicates tumor location. Intraoperative views: (e and f) Access incision along mastopexy marking to perform partial mastectomy. Large defect after tumor resection and negative intraoperative tumor margin. (g and h) Concentric displacement mastopexy performed displacing tissue superiorly and filling the defect. Postoperative views: (i and j) Several weeks after right oncoplastic repair using displacement mastopexy technique and a left concetric mastopexy for symmetry.

quadrant tumors, which is the most common site for breast cancer. Those patients with C-cup breasts without breast ptosis may be better candidates for nipple-sparing mastectomy, especially those patients with early-stage breast cancer who are unlikely to require radiation therapy after mastectomy.

Patients with C-cup breasts with ptosis can be ideal candidates for vertical oncoplasty techniques (**Figure 24.4 and 24.5**). Nonetheless, on account of their equivocal breast volume and volume losses occurring after radiation therapy, these patients can often benefit from fat grafting following breast irradiation, which will help restore any lost volume to at least baseline levels. The fat graft can also aid healing and soften the breast tissue after radiation therapy.

Patients with D-cup-sized breasts or larger often derive most benefit from immediate oncoplastic repair.[10,11] These patients not only have ample surrounding breast tissue to repair the tumor defect, but the oncoplasty hastens the delivery of radiation therapy. Hence, there is improved daily set-up for radiation delivery that can be very cumbersome in patients with large, ptotic-shaped breasts. Many of these patients also suffer from back pain and other related skeletal aches associated with large breasts. From the perspective of an oncoplastic surgical technique, these patients can conveniently be divided into two groups. First, there is a group of women who are wide-breasted, with extension of the breast into the axilla. By contrast, there exists a group of women with large breasts which are narrow and limited to the anterior chest wall with a clear delineation from the axillary tissue.

Those patients with D-cup-sized breasts or larger who are wide-breasted are ideal candidates for inferiorly based dermoglandular pedicles with a Wise skin pattern (**Figures 24.6 through 24.8**).[12] This approach provides great versatility for these patients and a reliable blood supply to the nipple-areola complex. For those patients with large breasts that are narrow-based, vertical oncoplasty is an excellent technique for oncoplastic repair. Superiorly based dermoglandular pedicles for upper pole and lower central defects along with a vertical skin pattern are an effective and reliable approach. For those patients with large breasts that are narrow with defects located in the lower inner or lower outer quadrants, a dual-dermoglandular approach can provide an optimal outcome. Although these techniques are effective in terms of limiting the extent of revision required after breast-conserving therapy, it is imperative that a multidisciplinary breast team plan the strategy prior to any surgical intervention in a coordinated, multidisciplinary approach.

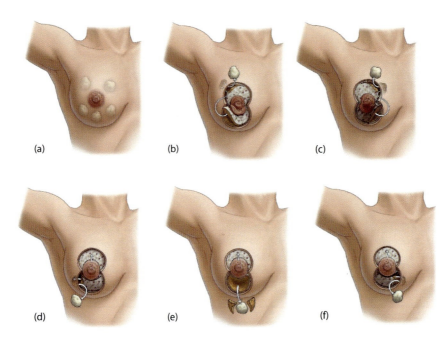

24.4 Kronowitz vertical oncoplasty. (a) Tumor locations that are amenable to repair using Kronowitz Vertical Oncoplasty. (b) Tumor defects located in the upper outer quadrant of the breast are repaired using a superiomedial dermoglandular pedicle rotated in a clockwise direction to fill the defect. (c) Tumor defects located in the upper inner aspect of the breast are repaired using a superiolateral dermoglandular pedicle rotated in a counter clockwise direction to fill the defect. (d) Tumor defects located in the lower outer quadrant are repaired using two dermoglandular pedicles. A standard superior dermoglandular pedicle is used to elevate the position of the nipple and areola complex, and a lower inferiomedial dermoglandular pedicle is advanced laterally to fill the defect. (e) Lower central tumor defects are amenable to repair using a standard superiorly based vertical dermoglandular pedicle. (f) Tumor defects located in the lower inner quadrant are repaired using two dermoglandular pedicles. A standard superior dermoglandular pedicle is used to elevate the position of the nipple and areola complex, and a lower inferiolateral dermoglandular pedicle is advanced medially to fill the defect.

Revisional breast reconstruction after partial mastectomy 375

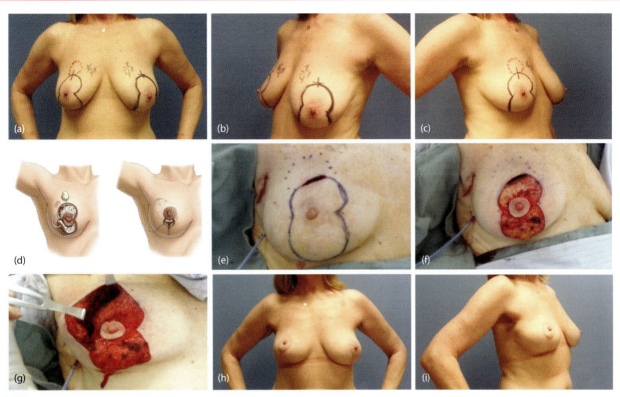

24.5 Preoperative views: (a–c) Preoperative views: 43-year-old female with C-cup-sized breasts with a breast tumor located in the upper outer quadrant of her right breast. (d) Schematic of proposed vertical oncoplasty repair using a superomedial dermoglandular pedicle with clockwise rotation and closure of the vertical skin pattern. Intraoperative views: (e) Surgical access used by breast surgeon to perform tumor extirpation. (f and g) After creation of the superomedial dermoglandular pedicle, but prior to clockwise rotation into upper outer breast defect. Postoperative views: (h and i) Six months after completion of radiotherapy to the right breast.

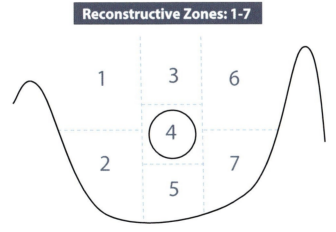

24.6 Kronowitz Wise pattern oncoplasty. Zone designations within the breast that correspond to dermoglandular designs for repair of the partial mastectomy defects.

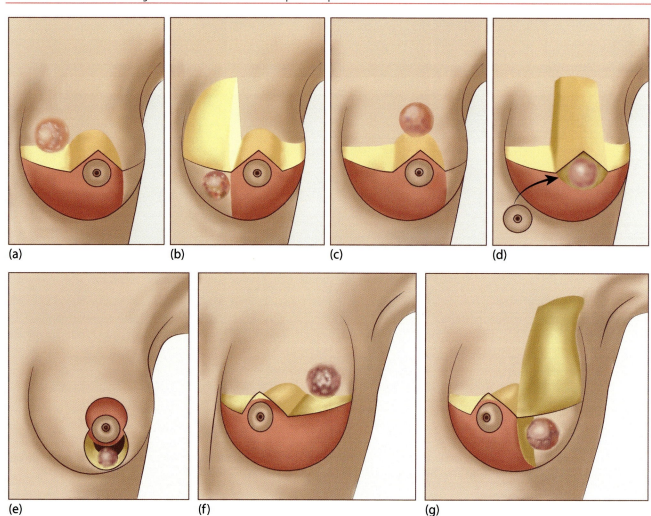

24.7 Kronowitz Wise pattern oncoplasty. Dermoglandular designs that are used to repair defects within the breast using Kronowitz Wise pattern oncoplasty. (a) Zone 1: Defects are repaired using a inferomedial dermoglandular pedicle. (b) Zone 2: Defects are repaired using an inferolateral dermoglandular pedicle, and the thickness of tissue on the medial one-third of the Wise skin pattern flap is not thinned, but kept thick to fill the defect upon closure of the Wise skin pattern. (c) Zone 3: Defects are repaired using an inferomedial dermoglandular pedicle design; the retained medial wedge adds blood supply to the nipple and areola, which is essential because tumor resection tends to follow the ductal system which can undermine the blood supply. The medial wedge also improves the cosmetic outcome by adding cleavage to the breasts. (d) Zone 4: Central defects that involve resection of the nipple and areola are repaired using an inferomediolateral dermoglandular pedicle, and the parenchymal tissue on the central one-third of the Wise skin pattern flap is kept thick to fill the defect upon closure. Nipple and areola reconstruction are required. (e) Zone 5: Lower central defects are more amenable to repair using a standard superiorly based dermoglandular pedicle along with a vertical skin resection pattern. (f) Zone 6: Defects are repaired using an inferomediolateral dermoglandular pedicle. The retained lateral wedge fills the defect, and the medial wedge is also retained to enhance blood supply and cleavage to the breasts. (g) Zone 7: Defects are repaired using the inferomedial dermoglandular pedicle, and the parenchyma on the lateral one-third of the Wise skin pattern flap is kept thick to fill the defect upon skin closure.

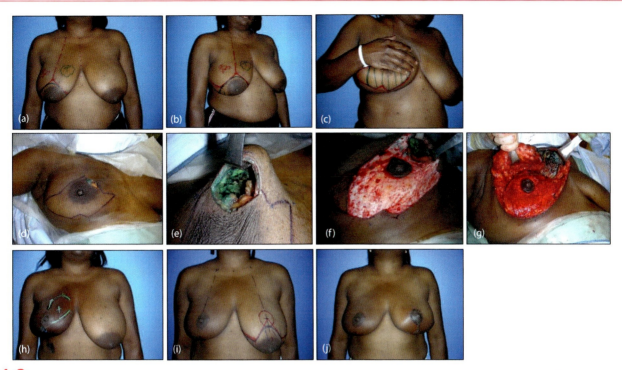

24.8 Kronowitz Wise pattern oncoplasty. (a–c) Preoperative views: 43-year-old female with stage 2 right breast cancer. Tumor located in zone 1 of right breast. Markings shown for repair using inferomedial dermoglandular pedicle and Wise skin pattern flap. (d–g) Intraoperative views: Access incision used for tumor resection and subsequent defect in zone 1 of right breast. After de-epithelialization of inferomedial dermoglandular pedicle in relation to tumor defect. Last, after dissection of the Wise skin pattern flap prior to skin closure. (h) During whole breast radiation and a boost to the tumor site. (i) Six months after the completion of radiation therapy to the right breast. Left breast shows markings for the contralateral symmetry procedure using the same inferomedial dermoglandular pedicle design. (j) One month after completion of the left symmetry procedure.

REFERENCES

1. Clemens MW, Kronowitz SJ. Current perspectives on radiation therapy in autologous and prosthetic breast reconstruction. *Gland Surg.* 2015 Jun;4(3):222–231.
2. Hubenak JR, Zhang Q, Branch CD, Kronowitz SJ. Mechanisms of injury to normal tissue after radiotherapy: A review. *Plast Reconstr Surg.* 2014 Jan;133(1):49e–56e.
3. Kronowitz SJ. Current status of implant-based breast reconstruction in patients receiving postmastectomy radiation therapy. *Plast Reconstr Surg.* 2012 Oct;130(4):513e–523e.
4. Kronowitz SJ. Current status of autologous tissue-based breast reconstruction in patients receiving postmastectomy radiation therapy. *Plast Reconstr Surg.* 2012 Aug;130(2):282–292.
5. Kronowitz SJ, Robb GL. Radiation therapy and breast reconstruction: A critical review of the literature. *Plast Reconstr Surg.* 2009 Aug;124(2):395–408.
6. Kronowitz SJ, Robb GL. Breast reconstruction with postmastectomy radiation therapy: Current issues. *Plast Reconstr Surg.* 2004 Sep 15;114(4):950–960.
7. Kronowitz SJ, Robb GL. Breast reconstruction and adjuvant therapies. *Semin Plast Surg.* 2004 May;18(2):105–115.
8. Adesiyun TA, Lee BT, Yueh JH, Chen C, Colakoglu S, Anderson KE, Nguyen MD, Recht A. Impact of sequencing of postmastectomy radiotherapy and breast reconstruction on timing and rate of complications and patient satisfaction. *Int J Radiat Oncol Biol Phys.* 2011 Jun 1;80(2):392–397.
9. Kronowitz SJ, Kuerer HM, Buchholz TA, Valero V, Hunt KK. A management algorithm and practical oncoplastic surgical techniques for repairing partial mastectomy defects. *Plast Reconstr Surg.* 2008 Dec;122(6):1631–1647.
10. Losken A, Hamdi M. Partial breast reconstruction: Current perspectives. *Plast Reconstr Surg.* 2009 Sep;124(3):722–736.
11. Losken A, Styblo TM, Carlson GW, Jones GE, Amerson BJ. Management algorithm and outcome evaluation of partial mastectomy defects treated using reduction or mastopexy techniques. *Ann Plast Surg.* 2007 Sep;59(3):235–242.
12. Kronowitz SJ, Feledy JA, Hunt KK, Kuerer HM, Youssef A, Koutz CA, Robb GL. Determining the optimal approach to breast reconstruction after partial mastectomy. *Plast Reconstr Surg.* 2006 Jan;117(1):1–11; discussion 12–14.
13. Kronowitz SJ. State of the art and science in postmastectomy breast reconstruction. *Plast Reconstr Surg.* 2015 Apr;135(4):755e–771e.
14. de Alcantara Filho P, Capko D, Barry JM, Morrow M, Pusic A, Sacchini VS. Nipple-sparing mastectomy for breast cancer and risk-reducing surgery: The Memorial Sloan-Kettering Cancer Center experience. *Ann Surg Oncol.* 2011 Breast reconstruction. *Plast Reconstr Surg.* 2008 Mar;121(3):728–734.

25

Breast revision after implant-based breast reconstruction

JOÃO CARLOS SAMPAIO GOÉS, ALEXANDRE MENDONÇA MUNHOZ, AND ROLF GEMPERLI

INTRODUCTION

Salvage or revision surgery may be required for complications of previously failed reconstruction, unsatisfactory outcomes from conservative breast surgery, or recurrent disease. Not infrequently, when these patients present for revisional surgery, there are several technical issues that may complicate the revision such as tissue thickness, capsular contracture, implant malposition, rippling, and even synmastia. Thus, the revision cases are challenging, require significant operative time, and can be associated with a higher complication rate.

The authors usually follow a systematic method in revisional surgery to optimize outcomes and ensure that the secondary reconstruction is performed safely and with predictable results. One of the major determinants of patient satisfaction relates to how closely the surgeon listens to the wishes and expectations of the patient. Once these have been clearly elucidated, it is important to decide which objectives are feasible and recognize those that are not possible. In the authors' experience involving reconstructive revisions, surgery is usually performed for one or more of the following indications: (1) local soft tissue deficiency/irregularities; (2) capsular contracture; (3) implant contour visibility; and (4) rippling.

REVISIONAL SURGERY FOLLOWING WHOLE BREAST RECONSTRUCTION

Implant-based reconstruction is one of the most common forms of breast reconstruction following mastectomy.[1] However, long-term results can be suboptimal, especially following radiotherapy. At 10 years after implant placement, Baker III/IV contracture was present in almost 60% of patients, with necessity for removal of implants in almost 45% of patients.[2]

As a result of these unsatisfactory outcome data, a significant number of patients exist who request removal of their implants in favor of alternative reconstructive techniques. As a further evolution of implant muscular coverage, synthetic meshes[3–6] and acellular dermal matrices[7–9] are being employed to provide supplemental tissue. In fact, these materials potentially reinforce the muscle as well as provide additional material in the space between the released pectoralis muscle and inframammary fold.[8,9] As a surgical adjunct to reconstruction, autologous fat aims to increase thickness of the covering tissue and correct surface irregularities[5,6] (**Figure 25.1a and b**). In the early stages of clinical experience with this scenario, the authors started with transfer of intra-abdominal fat through the omentum flap.[5,6] A laparoscopically harvested omental flap achieves sufficient volume with a single procedure without significant postoperative absorption.[5,6] Despite favorable results observed, certain limitations, in addition to a learning curve, exist. Inability to predict omentum size and those symptomatic hernia requiring repair have been reported as important limitations to its use in reconstruction. Additionally, laparoscopy may be contraindicated in some patients with a previous history of laparotomy.[10,11] In 2009, the American Society of Plastic Surgeons made consensus recommendations for the safe use of fat grafting to the breast.[12] Thus, from that time, the authors and others began acquiring clinical experience with fat grafting associated with a mixed mesh in both primary and revisional breast reconstructions (**Figure 25.2**). Employment of fat grafting as a tool for secondary breast reconstruction has become a useful and reliable procedure. The authors have observed a relatively

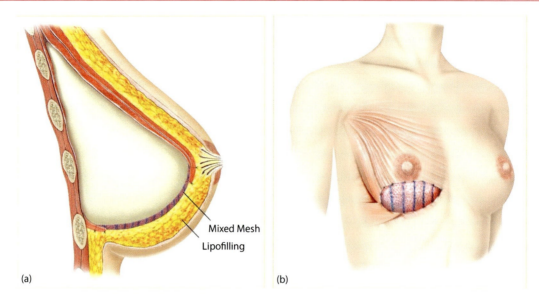

25.1 (a) Schematic and intraoperative view, reconstruction with silicone implant, mixed mesh, and lipofilling. (b) Breast implant placed under the pectoralis major muscle and mixed mesh covering the lower pole of the implant.

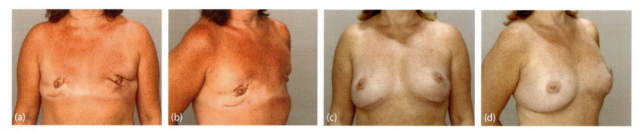

25.2 A 57-year-old patient with previous in situ ductal carcinoma and familial history of breast cancer. The patient underwent elsewhere a bilateral nipple-areola mastectomy and immediate reconstruction with bilateral implants and developed implant extrusion due to bilateral infection (a and b). The patient underwent a revisional reconstruction with form-stable anatomical shape silicone implant, mixed mesh, and lipofilling. Breast implant was placed under the pectoralis major muscle and mixed mesh covering the lower pole of the implant (c and d).

low rate of complications and a broadening of indications for use of fat grafting in revisional breast surgery.

PATIENT EVALUATION, INCISION, AND RECONSTRUCTIVE PROCEDURE SELECTION

Most candidates for revisional reconstruction can be successfully treated with present techniques. This group of patients frequently present with partial or total soft-tissue deficiency with visible implant contours, rippling, or capsular contracture. In patients with attenuated subcutaneous tissue, irregularities of the implant surface become noticeable. Thus, implant replacement and subcutaneous placement of autologous fat graft where needed provides extra soft tissue that reinforces thin tissue, thus masking surface irregularities. An anatomical textured silicone implant is selected preoperatively, according to the width and height of the breast. The implants are placed in a partially submuscular pocket associated with mixed mesh on the inferior edge of the pectoralis major muscle depending upon the patient's anatomy and condition of the muscle/skin flaps. The mixed mesh (ULTRAPRO, Johnson & Johnson) is sutured by separate 4.0 polypropylene stiches superiorly to the pectoralis major muscle, inferiorly next to the inframammary fold, and laterally to the serratus muscle. To maximize the aesthetic outcome, and potentially improve contour deformities, we utilize autologous fat transfer to fill localized soft tissue defects and to protect the mesh/implant. For this purpose, liposuction in the selected donor site was performed using a 2.4 mm diameter cannula. Lipofilling is performed in parallel tunnels in superficial and subdermal layers to increase the tissue coverage, correct subcutaneous irregularities, and avoid skin adhesions (**Figure 25.3**).

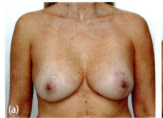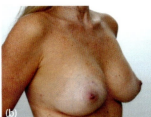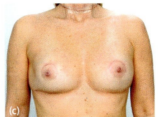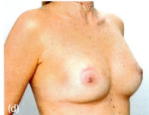

25.3 A 40-year-old patient with invasive (1.9 cm) of the left breast (a and b). The patient presented a previous reduction mammaplasty with periareolar scar and developed a local relapse. The patient underwent a bilateral periareolar nipple-areola-sparing mastectomy and revisional reconstruction with form-stable anatomical shape silicone implant, mixed mesh, and lipofilling (c and d).

REVISIONAL SURGERY FOLLOWING PARTIAL BREAST RECONSTRUCTION

Breast-conserving surgery is an important surgical component of early breast cancer treatment, with survival outcomes comparable to those of more radical procedures.[13,14] In spite of acceptance that most partial breast resections can be managed with primary closure, aesthetic outcomes may be unpredictable and sometimes related to the timing of reconstruction.[15,16] In fact, radiotherapy generally has negative effects on tissues, leading to tissue ischemia, enhanced fibrous tissue, and capsular contracture. The challenge for this reconstructive scenario relates to the skin and the remaining breast tissue having been previously irradiated. Thus, the use of implants may be contraindicated due to concerns about wound healing, capsular contracture, and fibrosis of the pectoralis muscle. As a result, these patients are generally offered autologous reconstruction techniques using either abdominal flap-based, or an implant-assisted latissimus dorsi myocutaneous flap.[17]

The choice of reconstructive procedure following previous breast-conserving surgery demands careful attention taking into account various factors, including: breast volume, degree of ptosis, patient preference/expectations, clinical factors, and surgeon's experience.[18,19] Although autologous tissue offers certain advantages, it is not appropriate for all patients. In these circumstances, alloplastic techniques can be used and involve a two-stage approach or one-stage reconstruction with conventional submuscular silicone implants. As a further evolution, synthetic meshes[3–6] can be employed to provide supplemental tissue and improve implant coverage. In the authors' clinical experience, the surgical approach is usually based on an anatomical implant in conjunction with mixed mesh. Similarly, as other authors have observed with acellular dermal matrix,[7–9] a mixed mesh can provide additional support and coverage of implants. As a surgical complement to the reconstruction, an omental flap or lipofilling of a skin flap aims to increase the thickness of mastectomy skin flaps and correct contour irregularities after breast-conserving surgery. Satisfactory results from the authors' practice support use of the present technique which when applied to revisional surgery after breast-conserving procedures is an effective method which avoids the necessity for additional donor sites in selected patients.

CONCLUSION

Previous failed implant reconstruction can provide a considerable challenge and is a complex scenario. The goal of revisional surgery is the complete restoration of a breast mound after previous unsatisfactory reconstruction and can be achieved with an implant, autologous tissue, or a combination of both. In general, choice of procedure following previous reconstructions requires careful consideration of various patient-related factors.

REFERENCES

1. Serletti, J.M., Fosnot, J., Nelson, J.A., Disa, J.J., Bucky, L.P. Breast reconstruction after breast cancer. *Plast Reconstr Surg* 127 (2011): 124e–135e.
2. Saline-filled breast implant surgery: Making an informed decision. Mentor Corporation; 2009. Available at: http://www.mentorcorp.com/pdf/ FinalInformedConsent.pdf.
3. Becker, H., Lind, J.G. The use of synthetic mesh in reconstructive, revision, and cosmetic breast surgery. *Aesth Plast Surg* 37 (2013): 914–921.
4. Dieterich, M., Paepke, S., Zwiefel, K. et al. Implant-based breast reconstruction using coated polypropylene mesh (TiLOOP Bra): A multicenter study of 231 cases. *Plast Reconstr Surg* 132 (2013): 8e–19e.
5. Goés, J.C.S., Macedo, A.L. Immediate reconstruction after mastectomy using a periareolar approach with an omental flap and mixed mesh support. *Perspectives Plast Surg* 10 (1996): 69–81.
6. Góes, J.C.S., Macedo, A.L.V. Immediate reconstruction after skin-sparing mastectomy using the omental flap and synthetic mesh. In: *Surgery of the Breast—Principles* and Art by Scott L. Spear–Third ed.–2012; Chap. 57.
7. Breuing, K.H., Warren, S.M. Immediate bilateral breast reconstruction with implants and inferolateral AlloDerm slings. *Ann Plast Surg* 55 (2005): 232–239.

8. Spear, S.L., Seruya, M., Clemens, M.W., Teitelbaum, S., Nahabedian, M.Y. Acellular dermal matrix for the treatment and prevention of implant-associated breast deformities. *Plast Reconstr Surg* 127 (2011): 1047–1058.

9. Salzberg, C.A. Nonexpansive immediate breast reconstruction using human acellular tissue matrix graft (AlloDerm). *Ann Plast Surg* 57 (2006): 1–5.

10. Das, S.K. The size of the human omentum and methods of lengthening it for transplantation. *Br J Plast Surg* 29 (1976): 170–244.

11. Saltz, R. Endoscopic harvest of the omental and jejunal free flaps. *Clin Plast Surg* 22 (1995): 747–754.

12. Gutowski, K.A. ASPS fat graft task force. Current applications and safety of autologous fat grafts: A report of the ASPS fat graft task force. *Plast Reconstr Surg* 124 (2009): 272–280.

13. Fisher B, Anderson S, Bryant J. et al. Twenty-year follow-up of a randomized trial comparing total mastectomy, lumpectomy, and lumpectomy plus irradiation for the treatment of invasive breast cancer. *N Engl J Med* 347 (2002): 1233–1239.

14. Veronesi, U., Cascinelli, N., Mariani, L. et al. Twenty-year follow-up of a randomized study comparing breast-conserving surgery with radical mastectomy for early breast cancer. *N Engl J Med* 347 (2002): 1227–1233.

15. Berrino, P., Campora, E., Santi, P. Postquadrantectomy breast deformities: Classification and techniques of surgical correction. *Plast Reconstruct Surg* 79 (1987): 567–572.

16. Clough, K.B., Cuminet, J., Fitoussi, A., Nos, C., Mosseri, V. Cosmetic sequel after conservative treatment for breast cancer: Classification and results of surgical correction. *Ann Plast Surg* 41 (1998): 471–479.

17. Munhoz, A.M., Aldrighi, C., Montag, E., Arruda, E.G., Aldrighi, J.M., Filassi, J.R., Ferreira, M.C. Periareolar skin-sparing mastectomy and latissimus dorsi flap with biodimensional expander implant reconstruction: Surgical planning, outcome, and complications. *Plast Reconstr Surg* 119 (2007): 1637–2149.

18. Slavin, S.A., Halperin, T. Reconstruction of the breast conservation deformity. *Sem Plas Surg* 18 (2004): 89–95.

19. Munhoz, A.M., Montag, E., Fels, K.W. et al. Critical analysis of reduction mammaplasty techniques in combination with conservative breast surgery for early breast cancer treatment. *Plast Reconstr Surg* 117 (2006): 1091–1099.

26

Breast revision after mastectomy, whole breast reconstruction, and postmastectomy radiation therapy

STEVEN J. KRONOWITZ

DIFFERENCES BETWEEN IMMEDIATE AND DELAYED BREAST RECONSTRUCTION

As for revision of a partial breast reconstruction, correctional surgery after whole breast reconstruction and radiation can be very complex if appropriate procedures have not been selected prior to the delivery of radiation. Implant replacement subsequent to radiation therapy is associated with high rates of complications including infection, seroma, wound dehiscence, and implant loss.[1,2] Revision of an irradiated flap often leads to poor healing because tissues have lost the capacity for normal fibrin deposition and healing secondary to dysfunctional fibroblast stem cells. Irradiation of a flap can defeat the purpose of transferring well-vascularized tissue to an irradiated chest wall, where the objective is to transfer non-irradiated cellular elements. Although, the optimal timing of flap transfer for a patient who will receive postmastectomy radiation remains a topic of debate,[1–4] there is general consensus that revisional surgery on an irradiated flap is a complicated procedure.

REFERENCES

1. Kronowitz SJ, Hunt KK, Kuerer HM, Babiera G, McNeese MD, Buchholz TA, Strom EA, Robb GL. Delayed-immediate breast reconstruction. *Plast Reconstr Surg.* 2004;113(6):1617–1628.
2. Kronowitz SJ, Lam C, Terefe W, Hunt KK, Kuerer HM, Valero V, Lance S, Robb GL, Feng L, Buchholz TA. A multidisciplinary protocol for planned skin-preserving delayed breast reconstruction for patients with locally advanced breast cancer requiring postmastectomy radiation therapy: 3-year follow-up. *Plast Reconstr Surg.* 2011;127(6):2154–2166.
3. Kronowitz SJ. Delayed-immediate breast reconstruction: Technical and timing considerations. *Plast Reconstr Surg.* 2010;125(2):463–474.
4. Mehrara BJ, Santoro TD, Arcilla E, Watson JP, Shaw WW, Da Lio AL. Complications after microvascular breast reconstruction: Experience with 1195 flaps. *Plast Reconstr Surg.* 2006;118(5):1100–1109.

AFTER IMPLANT-BASED PROCEDURES

For implant-based procedures, there are several premastectomy factors for consideration which can subsequently impact the risk and complexity of revisional surgery after radiation therapy to the breast. Whether it be the permanent implant or the tissue expander which is irradiated (then exchanged for a permanent implant), radiation therapy will inevitably affect any revision. When a permanent implant is inserted before radiation treatment, this can obviate the need for high-risk exchange of the tissue expander for an implant after radiation. However, irradiated permanent implants tend to be associated with higher rates of capsular contracture, which can potentially lead to more extensive revisional procedures at a later date.

Placement of acellular dermal matrices (ADMs) has been found to suppress the inflammatory process, decrease cellularity, and reduce rates of pseudo-capsule formation after radiation to an implant-based breast reconstruction.[1,2] Placement of an ADM in an implant-based reconstruction that will be irradiated may reduce the chance and extent of breast revision. Utilization of ADM can also render any revision more robust and safe by providing a strong layer for mastectomy wound closure in the event that an implant exchange is required. Moreover, it provides an adequate tissue layer in the lower mastectomy skin flap to allow fat grafting. In some patients who have minimal peri-implant capsule formation, it can be difficult to inject fat into the lower mastectomy skin flap which can be thinned from a combination of surgical dissection and radiation.

Patients not uncommonly present with contraction of a breast implant after breast-conservation surgery and radiotherapy performed in the context of prior implant augmentation. This is a particularly challenging reconstructive problem to correct with a high risk of implant loss secondary to attempted capsulectomy and implant exchange. A preferred approach is to consider these cosmetically augmented patients as being small breasted and instead of undertaking breast conservation, nipple-sparing mastectomy can be performed thereby avoiding radiation therapy. Most patients who undergo breast augmentation with implants have A- or B-cup-sized native breast tissue and in terms of breast reconstruction should be assessed accordingly. In addition, many small-breasted patients tend to be relatively thin with limited autologous tissue salvage options in the event that outcomes from breast-conservation therapy are poor.

REFERENCES

1. Clemens MW, Kronowitz SJ. Acellular dermal matrix in irradiated tissue expander/implant-based breast reconstruction: Evidence-based review. *Plast Reconstr Surg.* 2012;130(5 Suppl 2):27S–34S.
2. Kim JY, Davila AA, Persing S, Connor CM, Jovanovic B, Khan SA, Fine N, Rawlani V. A meta-analysis of human acellular dermis and submuscular tissue expander breast reconstruction. *Plast Reconstr Surg.* 2012;129(1):28–41.

AFTER FLAP-BASED PROCEDURES

The procedure for revising an irradiated flap is not the same as revising a non-irradiated flap (e.g., a deep inferior epigastric perforator (DIEP) flap). The main difference lies in the ability of wounds to heal in the setting of reshaping a flap-based breast reconstruction. Irradiated flaps have lost the capacity for normal wound healing, and attempts at revision may lead to wound healing problems. Thus, wounds can be very slow to heal or may require a vacuum-assisted closure device or even fashioning of another flap. Although, many surgeons prefer immediate flap reconstruction, even in patients for whom postmastectomy radiation is anticipated, others prefer an initial tissue expander and then perform transfer of a flap after radiation treatment, thereby avoiding radiation-induced injury to the flap.[1-3] With this latter approach, the flap allows transfer of non-irradiated cellular elements like fibroblasts that can assist in healing of any subsequent revisional surgery that involves this flap.[4]

Transposition of a flap such as the latissimus dorsi can be very useful for both revisional or salvage surgery for an irradiated implant reconstruction. However, another alternative has recently emerged. Fat grafting can be an essential element in revision after whole breast reconstruction, not only following implant-based reconstruction, but also when revising irradiated flaps (**Figure 26.1**).[5-7] This is irrespective of whether the revision involves: (1) a contracted implant in an augmented breast after breast-conservation therapy, (2) exchange of an irradiated breast implant after mastectomy, or (3) revision of an irradiated flap reconstruction (e.g., a DIEP flap). Fat grafting has become the first step in initiating healing prior to any surgical intervention for a failed irradiated reconstruction. Transfer of fat to an irradiated breast reconstruction will allow adipocyte deposition and new blood vessel formation with resolution of the fibrotic environment.[4-7] In some circumstances, multiple sessions of fat grafting are performed to the irradiated breast reconstruction prior to any attempts at revisional surgery. Although fat grafting does not eliminate inherent risks of surgical intervention within an irradiated surgical field, it can generally enhance healing of wounds and hasten the absorption of post-inflammatory surgical fluid within the compromised tissues and local environment of an irradiated breast reconstruction. Pre-surgical fat grafting can lead to successful revision of an irradiated breast reconstruction and potentially decrease the risk of subsequent contracture and deformity with radiated implant-based reconstructions.[4,6] In addition, fat grafting as a preliminary step in a revision program for an irradiated breast reconstruction may obviate the need for flap salvage using, for example, a latissimus flap to revise radiation-related deformities in both implant and flap reconstructions.

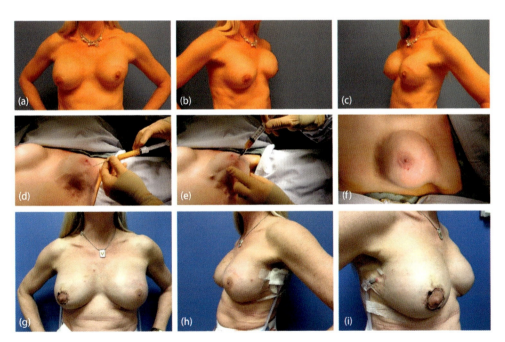

26.1 (A) Kronowitz Interval Fat Grafting. (a–c) Preoperative views: 47-year-old female with prior left partial mastectomy and radiation therapy. Patient had bilateral breast implant augmentation prior to breast cancer treatment. The patient developed severe grade 4 capsular contracture of the left breast implant. (d–f) Intraoperative views: Filtered fat being injected into the entirety of the radiated and contracted breast overlying the breast implant. Fat grafting to the left breast was performed two times, 3 months apart, and then a third fat grafting was performed at the implant exchange and capsulotomy which was performed 3 months after the second fat graft procedure. (g–i) Postoperative views: Several weeks after left implant exchange and a right mastopexy for symmetry. *(Continued)*

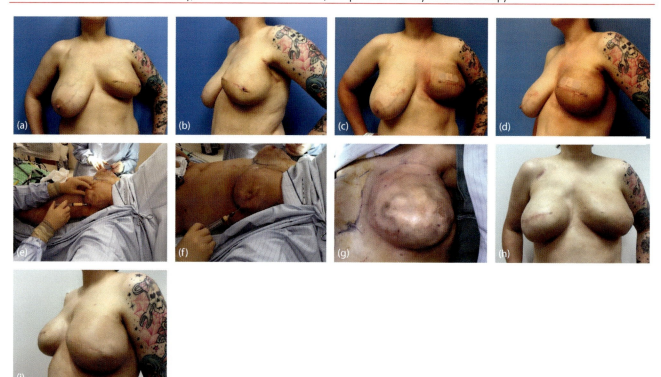

26.1 (Continued) (B) Kronowitz Interval Fat Grafting. (a and b) 41-year-old female shown 6 weeks after a left modified radical mastectomy for stage III breast cancer. The patient had immediate placement of a saline-filled tissue expander to preserve the breast skin envelope during postmastectomy radiation therapy. (c and d) Two weeks after the completion of postmastectomy radiation therapy, the tissue expander was re-inflated. The tissue expander was partially deflated during radiation to allow for radiation delivery. (e–g) Intraoperative views: Interval fat grafting being performed to the left breast 3 months after radiation before definitive breast reconstruction with the expander still in situ. (h–i) The entirety of the breast and axillary region is injected with fat.

REFERENCES

1. Kronowitz SJ, Hunt KK, Kuerer HM, Babiera G, McNeese MD, Buchholz TA, Strom EA, Robb GL. Delayed-immediate breast reconstruction. *Plast Reconstr Surg.* 2004;113(6):1617–1628.
2. Kronowitz SJ, Lam C, Terefe W, Hunt KK, Kuerer HM, Valero V, Lance S, Robb GL, Feng L, Buchholz TA. A multidisciplinary protocol for planned skin-preserving delayed breast reconstruction for patients with locally advanced breast cancer requiring postmastectomy radiation therapy: 3-year follow-up. *Plast Reconstr Surg.* 2011;127(6):2154–2166.
3. Kronowitz SJ. Delayed-immediate breast reconstruction: Technical and timing considerations. *Plast Reconstr Surg.* 2010;125(2):463–474.
4. Salgarello M, Visconti G, Barone-Adesi L. Fat grafting and breast reconstruction with implant: Another option for irradiated breast cancer patients. *Plast Reconstr Surg.* 2012;129(2):317–329.
5. Kronowitz SJ, Mandujano CC, Liu J, Kuerer HM, Smith B, Garvey P, Jagsi R, Hsu L, Hanson S, Valero V. Lipofilling of the breast does not increase the risk of recurrence of breast cancer: A matched controlled study. *Plast Reconstr Surg.* 2016;137(2):385–393.
6. Sarfati I, Ihrai T, Kaufman G, Nos C, Clough KB. Adipose-tissue grafting to the post-mastectomy irradiated chest wall: Preparing the ground for implant reconstruction. *J Plast Reconstr Aesthet Surg.* 2011;64(9):1161–1166.
7. Salgarello M, Visconti G, Barone-Adesi L. Fat grafting and breast reconstruction with implant: Another option for irradiated breast cancer patients. *Plast Reconstr Surg.* 2012;129(2):317–329.

EDITORIAL COMMENTARY

An overwhelming majority of breast reconstructions, whether these be oncoplastic repair after partial mastectomy or whole breast reconstruction after mastectomy will require some element of revision to optimize aesthetic outcome and symmetry. Revisional breast surgery can often be more challenging and fraught with complications than primary surgical procedures. It is intuitive to consider the defining differences in breast revisional surgery to be based on whether the primary reconstruction relates to the partial breast or whole breast. Nonetheless, experienced breast reconstructive surgeons understand that the major determinant of procedure complexity is whether the reconstructed breast has been irradiated.

The approach to revision of breast reconstruction has dramatically changed with the advent of autologous fat transfer. Fat transfer to the breasts serves a positive role for revision of both non-irradiated and irradiated reconstructions. However, strategies for utilization of fat transfer in revising irradiated breast reconstructions has dramatically changed surgeons approaches; these procedures were previously associated with an overwhelming propensity for poor wound healing following open surgical breast revision.

In the context of revising prior oncoplastic repairs, whereby any remaining breast tissue has received whole breast irradiation use of serial percutaneous needle release of internal scar tissue in conjunction with fat transfer has revolutionized approaches to these revisional procedures. These would previously not have been attempted or resulted in chronic open wounds. An important aspect of performing serial needle release and fat transfer is to treat the entirety of the breast, which needs to be released and fat grafted, not just the localized site of the visual deformity. Internal scarring resulting from whole breast irradiation produces tethering forces on the site of local resection. This requires needle release and fat grafting as an effective method for restoring softness to the entirety of the breast and obtaining optimal symmetry with the contralateral breast. Often radiation therapy delivered after partial mastectomy will further shrink the remaining breast tissue due to fat atrophy as a result of injury to the delicate stromal blood supply to adipocytes that make up the breast along with breast parenchyma.

The methodology of fat transfer in revising irradiated whole breast reconstruction varies depending on whether an implant was utilized in the primary breast reconstruction. In the case of autologous flap tissue reconstruction, fat transfer after irradiation can assist in providing non-irradiated cellular elements (such as fibroblasts)that can (a) improve the appearance of the breast reconstruction (b) soften a firm irradiated flap and (c) create a better local environment for further revisional surgery. Despite

being an area of controversy an area of controversy, the author prefers to avoid this particular situation and does not irradiate autologous tissue flap transfers. Instead, the author prefers instead to scaffold the preserved breast skin envelope with an inflated tissue expander during postmastectomy radiation and then replace this "babysitter" tissue expander with a non-irradiated autologous tissue flap after completion of radiation therapy.

Revision of an irradiated breast implant reconstruction is probably the most complex scenario for revisional breast reconstruction. This circumstance can occur in both the context of breast-conserving surgery in which a patient with cosmetic augmentation subsequently develops breast cancer and undergoes lumpectomy and breast irradiation without removal of the breast implant. Although there are varying approaches to revising these complex and invariably contracted breasts, the author has found pre-revisional serial fat transfers to be beneficial. These can be undertaken prior to open capsulectomy and implant exchange and creates a local environment that is more conducive to healing and appears to decrease the potential for postoperative wound healing problems (namely loss of exchanged implants and further development of capsular contracture). To reiterate, in the setting of primary breast implant reconstruction, it is not the author's practice to place a permanent implant in those patients who are anticipated to require postmastectomy radiation, but instead to place an inflated expander at the time of mastectomy. In those patients who are confirmed preoperatively or found to require postmastectomy radiation therapy after final pathology, the author performs serial fat transfer. This is undertaken prior to exchanging the expander for a permanent breast implant after the completion of radiation treatment and fat is deposited in tissues overlying the expander and surrounding areas of the chest wall. The author has found this approach leads to fewer complications and improved outcomes compared to proceeding directly to open surgical revision.

A further important point in revision of breast reconstructions is a readiness to use mastopexy whether this be after partial mastectomy repair or mastectomy reconstruction. Mastopexy with de-epithelized skin only in the setting of revisional procedures for irradiated partial mastectomy repairs can be very effective option and heal without compromise when used alongside fat transfer. Following both non-irradiated and irradiated total mastectomy, de-epithelized skin only mastopexy can likewise be very effective for improving the rather unattractive, boxy appearance that is often associated with primary whole breast reconstruction.

Techniques for delivery of radiotherapy

Chapter 27. Partial or whole breast radiotherapy after breast-conserving surgery?   391

Chapter 28. Postmastectomy radiotherapy after whole breast reconstruction   399

Chapter 29. Partial breast radiotherapy after breast-conserving surgery   405

Chapter 30. Whole breast radiotherapy (boost) after partial mastectomy   417

27

Partial or whole breast radiotherapy after breast-conserving surgery?

MUKESH BINDISH MUKESH AND CHARLOTTE COLES

AT A GLANCE

Partial breast irradiation has expanded rapidly over the 10 last years and can be delivered either intraoperatively or postoperatively with brachytherapy using an applicator or a linear accelerator. Many of these developments in the field of partial breast irradiation have been driven by new devices and technologies. However, there continues to be concerns regarding local recurrence rates for partial breast irradiation compared to whole breast radiotherapy. Of course, the range in oncoplastic options and timing for repair is notably different in partial versus whole breast irradiation and whether delivered intraoperatively or postoperatively.

ROLE OF RADIOTHERAPY AFTER BREAST-CONSERVING SURGERY

Adjuvant radiotherapy after breast-conserving surgery is the current standard of care for early breast cancer. The beneficial and adverse effects of radiotherapy are well documented by the Early Breast Cancer Trialists' Collaborative Group meta-analysis of >10,000 patients randomized into trials of breast-conserving surgery with or without radiotherapy over 30 years.[1] Addition of radiotherapy halves the rate of disease recurrence (local, regional, or distant) and reduces breast cancer death rate by about one-sixth (15%).

The Early Breast Cancer Trialists' Collaborative Group meta-analysis included trials where radiotherapy was delivered to the whole breast. Over the last three decades, the need for whole breast radiotherapy after breast-conserving surgery in all patients has been questioned, and the use of partial breast radiotherapy has been explored. In this chapter, we discuss the use of partial breast radiotherapy as an alternative to whole breast radiotherapy.

RATIONALE FOR PARTIAL BREAST RADIOTHERAPY

Partial breast radiotherapy involves targeting radiotherapy to the surgical cavity and a smaller volume of breast tissue around it, often referred to as the tumor bed. For early breast cancer, most cases of local recurrence appear in and around the tumor bed,[2,3] and the greatest benefits of radiotherapy are linked to irradiation of the tumor bed. Hence, local recurrence rates with partial breast radiotherapy are expected to be comparable to whole breast radiotherapy.

Women receiving whole breast radiotherapy are at risk of late side effects including breast shrinkage and suboptimal cosmesis, which can impair quality of life and cause psychological distress (although this risk is relatively low when the dose homogeneity is optimized).[4,5] Irradiation of a smaller volume of breast tissue with partial breast radiotherapy can potentially reduce the above mentioned side effects.[6] The total duration of whole breast radiotherapy has conventionally been 5–6 weeks, which can be stressful and inconvenient to those patients with limited access to radiotherapy facilities. In consequence, many patients choose to undergo mastectomy even though breast-conserving surgery is feasible.[7] Partial breast radiotherapy involves the delivery of radiotherapy over a shorter period of time and may be more acceptable to this group of patients.

RANDOMIZED CONTROLLED TRIALS COMPARING WHOLE VERSUS PARTIAL BREAST RADIOTHERAPY

Two randomized trials in the late 1980s reported inferior results for partial breast radiotherapy including higher rates of local recurrence and breast fibrosis compared to whole breast radiotherapy.[8,9] Neither of these trials used strict patient selection criteria, but nonetheless pioneered the concept of partial breast radiotherapy.

The efficacy of partial breast radiotherapy after breast-conserving surgery as compared to whole breast radiotherapy has been evaluated in several more recent randomized controlled trials using strict patient selection criteria and quality assurance procedures and are summarized in Table 27.1. These trials have utilized different modalities of radiotherapy techniques for partial breast radiotherapy including brachytherapy, intraoperative radiotherapy, three-dimensional (3-D)-conformal radiotherapy, and intensity-modulated

radiotherapy. These trials are quite heterogeneous with significant differences in radiation dose, dose per fraction, and volume of breast tissue irradiated in the partial breast radiotherapy arm.

The Cochrane review from 2014 found higher rates of local recurrence with partial breast radiotherapy as compared to whole breast radiotherapy, but was unable to make any definitive conclusions based on limited published data available at that time.[10] A more recent meta-analysis by Marta and colleagues,[11] involving 8653 patients confirmed that accelerated partial breast radiotherapy is associated with higher rates of local recurrence compared to whole breast radiotherapy, but there were no differences in rates of nodal recurrence, systemic recurrence, and overall survival.

Brachytherapy technique

Partial breast radiotherapy can be delivered by using either interstitial brachytherapy or intracavity brachytherapy catheters. Interstitial brachytherapy involves placement of 10–20 catheters in the tumor bed followed by temporary after-loading of radioactive sources in the catheter. Intracavity brachytherapy entails insertion of a single catheter (single/multilumen) within the tumor bed followed by temporary loading of radioactive sources.

A Hungarian trial randomized 258 patients with T1N0 grade I or II breast cancer to whole breast radiotherapy

Table 27.1 Randomized controlled trials comparing WBRT versus PBRT

Clinical trial	WBRT arm	PBRT arm	Number of patients (follow-up in years)	Efficacy results (local recurrence rates)	Toxicity results
Hungarian National Institute of Oncology trial[13]	50 Gy in 25 fractions over 5 weeks.	HDR Iridium-192 (85 pts) to a dose of 36.4 Gy in 7 fractions over 4 days or electrons (40 pts) to a dose of 50 Gy in 25 fractions prescribed to the 80% isodose.	258 (10.2 years)	10-year LR: 5.9% versus 5.1% in PBRT and WBRT arms.	10 years excellent-good cosmetic: 81 versus 63% in PBRT and WBRT arm (p < 0.01).
ELIOT trial[14]	50 Gy in 25 fractions with 10 Gy TB boost.	Intraoperative electrons 21 Gy in single fraction.	1305 (5.8 years)	5-year LR: 4.4 versus 0.4% in PBRT and WBRT arm.	Reduced skin toxicity in the PBRT arm. No difference in breast retraction and breast fibrosis.

(Continued)

Table 27.1 (*Continued*) Randomized controlled trials comparing WBRT versus PBRT

Clinical trial	WBRT arm	PBRT arm	Number of patients (follow-up in years)	Efficacy results (local recurrence rates)	Toxicity results
TARGIT-A trial[15]	40 Gy–56 Gy with optional TB boost of 10 Gy–16 Gy.	20 Gy single fraction using intraoperative 50 kV photons.	3451 (2.4 years)	5-year LR: 3.3 versus 1.3% in PBRT and WBRT arm.	Reduced grade 3–4 skin toxicity with PBRT: 0.2 versus 0.7%.
Florence trial[18]	50 Gy in 25 fractions with 10 Gy TB boost.	30 Gy in 5 fractions over 2 weeks using IMRT.	520 (5 years)	5-year LR: 1.5% in both PBRT and WBRT arm.	5 years excellent-good cosmesis: 100 versus 99.2% in PBRT and WBRT arm. Acute skin toxicity grade ≥ 2: 2 versus 37.7% favoring PBRT.
RAPID trial[19]	42.5 Gy in 16 fractions with optional 10 Gy TB boost.	38.5 Gy in 10 fractions twice daily over 5–8 days using 3D-CRT.	2135 (3 years)	Not reported.	5 years excellent-good cosmesis PBRT versus WBRT: Nurse assessment: 67.2 versus 86.6% Patient assessment: 67.6 versus 78.5% Physician photo assessment: 64.9 versus 83.4%
IMPORT-Low[26]	40 Gy in 15 fractions, no TB boost.	Arm 1: 40 Gy in 15 fractions to the index quadrant and 36 Gy in 15 fractions to the remaining breast Arm2 (PBRT): 40 Gy in 15 fractions to the index quadrant.	2018 (6 years)	5-year LR: 0.5% in PBRT (arm 2), 0.2% in arm 1 and 1.1% in WBRT arm.	Patient assessment: 5 years cumulative incidence of moderate to marked "change in breast appearance" 48% (WBRT), 37% (arm 1) and 27% (PBRT). 5 years cumulative incidence of moderate to marked "breast hardening/ firmness" 35% (WBRT), 21% (arm 1) and 15% (PBRT).
NSABP-B39/ RTOG 0413[27]	50 Gy–50.4 Gy in 25–28 fractions with optional 10 Gy–16 Gy TB boost.	34 Gy in 10 fractions over 5 days using single/multisource brachytherapy or 38.5 Gy in 10 fractions over 5 days using 3D-CRT.	4300 (NA)	Not reported.	Not reported.

(*Continued*)

Table 27.1 (*Continued*) Randomized controlled trials comparing WBRT versus PBRT

Clinical trial	WBRT arm	PBRT arm	Number of patients (follow-up in years)	Efficacy results (local recurrence rates)	Toxicity results
GEC-ESTRO[28]	50 Gy–50.4 Gy in 25–28 fractions with 10 Gy optional TB boost.	32 Gy in 8 fractions or 30.3 Gy in 7 fractions HDR or 50 Gy PDR.	1184 (5 years)	5-year LR: 1.4% versus 0.9% in PBRT and WBRT arm.	Physician assessment: 5 years cumulative incidence of grade 2-3 skin toxicity: 6.9% versus 10.7% in PBRT and WBRT arm.
IRMA[29]	45 Gy in 18 fractions or 50 Gy in 25 fractions or 50.4 Gy in 28 fractions with optional TB boost 10 Gy–16 Gy	38.5 Gy in 10 fractions twice daily over 5 days using 3D-CRT.	3302 (NA)	Not reported.	Not reported.
Danish Breast Cancer Cooperative Group[30]	40 Gy in 15 fractions.	40 Gy in 15 fractions using 3D-CRT.	628 (NA)	Not reported.	Not reported.
SHARE[31]	50 Gy in 25 fractions + 16 Gy TB boost or 40 Gy–42.5 Gy in 15–16 fractions without TB boost.	40 Gy in 10 fractions twice daily over 5–7 days using 3D-CRT.	2796 (NA)	Not reported.	Not reported.

WBRT: Whole breast radiotherapy
PBRT: Partial breast radiotherapy
IORT: Intraoperative radiotherapy
LR: Local recurrence
OS: Overall survival
HDR: High dose rate
PDR: Pulse dose rate
3D-CRT: Three-dimensional conformal radiotherapy
TB: Tumor bed

or partial breast radiotherapy after breast-conserving surgery. Whole breast radiotherapy was delivered using cobalt or photon beams to a total dose of 50 Gy in 2 Gy daily fractions. By contrast, partial breast radiotherapy was delivered using high dose rate Iridium-192 brachytherapy (85 patients) to a dose of 36.4 Gy in 5.2 Gy per fraction over 4 days or electrons (40 patients) to a dose of 50 Gy in 2 Gy daily fractions prescribed to the 80% isodose. At a median follow-up of 122 months, local recurrence rates were not significantly different in the two trial arms. However, the cosmetic results using Harvard criteria[12] were more favorable in the partial breast radiotherapy arm. The rate of excellent to good cosmesis was 81%

for the partial breast radiotherapy compared with only 63% for the whole breast radiotherapy.[13] It was acknowledged that this is a small single-center study, and results from large confirmatory trials are required.

The GEC-ESTRO trial randomized 1184 patients between whole breast radiotherapy and accelerated partial breast radiotherapy using high dose rate or pulse rate brachytherapy.[28] The partial breast radiotherapy was delivered in an accelerated manner with twice-daily fractionation. At median follow-up of 6.6-year follow-up, there were no differences in local recurrence, distant metastases and overall survival. The 5-year cumulative grade 2-3 late skin toxicity (including skin pigmentation and skin telangiectasia) were less commonly reported on clinician assessment in the accelerated partial breast radiotherapy arm as compared to whole breast radiotherapy. There was no significant difference between the two study arms for cumulative grade 2-3 subcutaneous toxicity, breast pain or grade 3 fibrosis. Most patients had excellent to good cosmetic results on both clinician and patient assessments with no difference between whole breast and accelerated partial breast radiotherapy.

Intraoperative technique

Intraoperative radiotherapy involves irradiating the surgical cavity immediately after removal of the tumor and has been evaluated in two randomized trials. The ELIOT trial randomized 1305 patients with tumor size $\leq$ 2.5 cm between whole breast radiotherapy and intraoperative radiotherapy using electrons.[14] Whole breast radiotherapy was delivered to a dose of 50 Gy in 25 fractions followed by tumor bed boost, and intraoperative radiotherapy was delivered as a single dose of 21 Gy to the tumor bed using electrons. The 5-year ipsilateral breast tumor recurrence rate was much higher in the intraoperative radiotherapy group as compared to the whole breast radiotherapy group (4.4% vs 0.4%; hazard ration 9.3). Nonetheless, fewer patients in the intraoperative radiotherapy group developed cutaneous side-effects and there was no difference in overall rates of 5-year survival. The TARGIT-A trial randomized 3451 patients with early breast cancer to either whole breast radiotherapy (40 Gy–56 Gy) with or without tumor bed boost or intraoperative radiotherapy using low energy x-rays (50 kV) to deliver a dose of 20 Gy to the tumor bed (attenuating to 5 Gy–7 Gy at a depth of 1 cm).[15] At a median follow-up of 2.4 years, the 5-year local recurrence was higher in the intraoperative radiotherapy arm compared to whole breast radiotherapy arm (3.3% vs 1.3%). A potential criticism of these results is that a median follow-up of 2.4 years is inadequate for patients with small estrogen receptor (ER)-positive cancers for whom the risk of local recurrence continues to increase linearly with time.[16] Haviland and colleagues[17] also highlighted that binomial analysis used in the trial is unsuitable when fewer than 700 patients had 5 years of follow-up. Instead, a Kaplan-Meier-based analysis should have been used which would take account of varying follow-up periods, timing of events, and incorporate censoring. At the present time, no definitive conclusions can be drawn about intraoperative radiotherapy within the context of the TARGIT trial.

Conformal radiotherapy/intensity–modulated radiotherapy

Partial breast radiotherapy can also be delivered with conformal radiotherapy or intensity-modulated radiotherapy which both use standard linear accelerators found in most radiotherapy departments.

A trial from Florence randomized 520 patients with tumors measuring $\leq$2.5 cm in size to either whole breast radiotherapy or partial breast radiotherapy using intensity-modulated radiotherapy techniques.[18] Patients in the partial breast radiotherapy arm received 30 Gy in 5 daily fractions over 2 weeks. At a median follow-up of 5 years, there were no differences in either ipsilateral breast recurrence nor overall survival. However, patients in the partial breast radiotherapy arm had more favorable acute and long-term toxicity including cosmetic outcomes. Notwithstanding these results, this study was underpowered with too few patients to detect a small difference between partial and whole breast radiotherapy.

The larger RAPID trial from the Ontario Cancer Group randomized more than 2000 patients between whole and partial breast radiotherapy administered with three-dimensional conformal radiotherapy (3-D CRT).[19] Patients in the whole breast radiotherapy arm received 50 Gy in 25 fractions with or without tumor bed boost, and those patients in the partial breast radiotherapy arm received 38.5 Gy in 10 fractions (twice daily) over 5–8 days. Data for breast cancer recurrence and overall survival have not been formally reported. However, at 3 years, those patients in the partial breast radiotherapy had worse cosmetic outcomes compared to patients receiving whole breast radiotherapy. This was contrary to expectations as partial breast radiotherapy involves irradiating a smaller volume of breast tissue. It had previously been commented by Bentzen and Yarnold that from a radio-biological perspective, a radiotherapy dose of 38.5 Gy in 10 fractions (twice daily) over 5–8 days might be equivalent to 65 Gy in normal 2 Gy fractionation.[20] A higher radiotherapy dosage would explain worse cosmetic outcomes in the partial breast radiotherapy arm and indicate that irradiation of a smaller volume of breast tissue cannot necessarily compensate for a higher radiotherapy dose overall.

The UK-based IMPORT LOW study randomized 2018 patients between whole breast radiotherapy, reduced dose group and partial breast radiotherapy.[26] All patients received 40 Gy in 15 fractions over 3 weeks using simple form of forward planned IMRT, with the volume of breast tissue radiated being the only randomized variable between the three arms of the study. There was no statistically significant difference between local recurrence or overall survival between the three arms of the study. The study looked at both clinician- and patient-based assessment for cumulative toxicity and additional photographic assessment. A stringent significance level of 1% was used to account for multiple testing. Using patient assessments, the 5-year cumulative incidence of "change in breast appearance" and "breast hardening/firmness" were less commonly reported in both partial breast and reduced dose radiotherapy arms as compared to whole breast radiotherapy. No significant difference was reported in other patient-reported domains, clinician assessments and photographic scoring.

Results are awaited from several other trials including the American NSABP-B39/RTOG 0413 and IRMA trial.

PATIENT SELECTION FOR PARTIAL BREAST RADIOTHERAPY

The various trials discussed above have shown either higher rates of local recurrence associated with partial breast radiotherapy or similar efficacy to whole breast radiotherapy. This could be explained by the use of different partial breast radiotherapy techniques, but is more likely related to eligibility criteria and selection of patients for each particular trial. Both ASTRO and GEC-ESTRO published consensus statements (2009–2010) on suitability of patients for partial breast radiotherapy in 2009–2010.[21,22] These recommendations[23] were predominantly based on results from feasibility and/or single center partial breast radiotherapy studies. Most of the randomized trials comparing partial and whole breast radiotherapy have been reported after publication of these consensus statements, which require periodic updates since knowledge and experience of partial breast radiotherapy has evolved.

SHOULD PARTIAL BREAST RADIOTHERAPY BE ROUTINELY USED IN LOW-RISK PATIENTS?

To date, only the small Hungarian partial breast radiotherapy trial has reported efficacy outcome at 10-years. Typically, low-risk estrogen receptor positive patients receiving endocrine treatment have been included in the partial breast radiotherapy trials and a minimum of 5-years trial follow-up is required to demonstrate non-inferiority. Longer duration of follow-up is desirable as the effects of radiotherapy on local recurrence continue to be manifest beyond 5 years as was evident in the CALGB 9343 trial.[16]

There are potential alternatives to partial breast radiotherapy for patients in whom 5–6 weeks of whole breast radiotherapy is inconvenient. A 3-week course of hypofractionated whole breast radiotherapy is now routinely used in Canada and the United Kingdom, and use of a more hypofractionated regimen over a period of 1 week is under investigation in the UK FAST FORWARD trial.[24] In accordance with trends toward personalized medicine, safe omission of radiotherapy may become an option for some patients.[25]

CONCLUSION

Partial breast radiotherapy is an emerging concept which can be delivered using several different techniques. Rates of local relapse associated with partial breast radiotherapy are higher than for whole breast radiotherapy, although absolute relapse rates remain low. Long-term results of the ongoing trials (Table 27.1) will provide robust scientific data and answer the important question of whether partial breast radiotherapy represents an acceptable and safe alternative to whole breast radiotherapy for low-risk groups of patients.

REFERENCES

1. Darby S, McGale P, Correa C et al. Effect of radiotherapy after breast-conserving surgery on 10-year recurrence and 15-year breast cancer death: Meta-analysis of individual patient data for 10,801 women in 17 randomised trials. *Lancet* 2011;378:1707–1716.
2. Vaidya JS, Vyas JJ, Chinoy RF, Merchant N, Sharma OP, Mittra I. Multicentricity of breast cancer: Whole-organ analysis and clinical implications. *Br J Cancer* 1996;74:820–824.
3. Baum M, Vaidya JS, Mittra I. Multicentricity and recurrence of breast cancer. *Lancet* 1997;349:208.
4. Hopwood P, Haviland JS, Sumo G, Mills J, Bliss JM, Yarnold JR. Comparison of patient-reported breast, arm, and shoulder symptoms and body image after radiotherapy for early breast cancer: 5-year follow-up in the randomised Standardisation of Breast Radiotherapy (START) trials. *Lancet Oncol* 2010;11:231–240.
5. Mukesh MB, Barnett GC, Wilkinson JS et al. Randomized controlled trial of intensity-modulated radiotherapy for early breast cancer: 5-year results confirm superior overall cosmesis. *J Clin Oncol* 2013;31:4488–4495.
6. Mukesh M, Harris E, Jena R, Evans P, Coles C. Relationship between irradiated breast volume and late normal tissue complications: A systematic review. *Radiother Oncol* 2012;104:1–10.
7. Nattinger AB, Kneusel RT, Hoffmann RG, Gilligan MA. Relationship of distance from a radiotherapy facility and initial breast cancer treatment. *J Natl Cancer Inst* 2001;93:1344–1346.
8. Ribeiro GG, Magee B, Swindell R, Harris M, Banerjee SS. The Christie Hospital breast conservation trial: An update at 8 years from inception. *Clin Oncol (R Coll Radiol)* 1993;5:278–283.
9. Dodwell DJ, Dyker K, Brown J et al. A randomised study of whole-breast vs tumour-bed irradiation after local excision and axillary dissection for early breast cancer. *Clin Oncol (R Coll Radiol)* 2005;17:618–622.
10. Lehman M, Hickey BE, Francis DP, See AM. Partial breast irradiation for early breast cancer. *Cochrane Database Syst Rev* 2014;6:CD007077.
11. Marta GN, Macedo CR, Carvalho Hde A, Hanna SA, da Silva JL, Riera R. Accelerated partial irradiation for breast cancer: Systematic review and meta-analysis of 8653 women in eight randomized trials. *Radiother Oncol* 2015;114:42–49.
12. Harris JR, Levene MB, Svensson G, Hellman S. Analysis of cosmetic results following primary radiation therapy for stages I and II carcinoma of the breast. *Int J Radiat Oncol Biol Phys* 1979;5:257–261.
13. Polgar C, Fodor J, Major T, Sulyok Z, Kasler M. Breast-conserving therapy with partial or whole breast irradiation: Ten-year results of the Budapest randomized trial. *Radiother Oncol* 2013;108:197–202.
14. Veronesi U, Orecchia R, Maisonneuve P et al. Intraoperative radiotherapy versus external radiotherapy for early breast cancer (ELIOT): A randomised controlled equivalence trial. *Lancet Oncol* 2013;14:1269–1277.
15. Vaidya JS, Joseph DJ, Tobias JS et al. Targeted intraoperative radiotherapy versus whole breast radiotherapy for breast cancer (TARGIT-A trial): an international, prospective, randomised, non-inferiority phase 3 trial. *Lancet* 2010;376:91–102.

16. Hughes KS, Schnaper LA, Bellon JR et al. Lumpectomy plus tamoxifen with or without irradiation in women age 70 years or older with early breast cancer: Long-term follow-up of CALGB 9343. *J Clin Oncol* 2013;31:2382–2387.

17. Haviland JS, Bliss JM, Bentzen SM, Cuzick J. The TARGIT-A trial: understanding non-inferiority and survival analysis. *Int J Radiat Oncol Biol Phys* 2015;92:954–955.

18. Livi L, Meattini I, Marrazzo L et al. Accelerated partial breast irradiation using intensity-modulated radiotherapy versus whole breast irradiation: 5-year survival analysis of a phase 3 randomised controlled trial. *Eur J Cancer* 2015;51:451–463.

19. Olivotto IA, Whelan TJ, Parpia S et al. Interim cosmetic and toxicity results from RAPID: A randomized trial of accelerated partial breast irradiation using three-dimensional conformal external beam radiation therapy. *J Clin Oncol* 2013;31:4038–4045.

20. Bentzen SM, Yarnold JR. Reports of unexpected late side effects of accelerated partial breast irradiation—Radiobiological considerations. *Int J Radiat Oncol Biol Phys* 2010;77:969–973.

21. Polgar C, Van Limbergen E, Potter R et al. Patient selection for accelerated partial-breast irradiation (APBI) after breast-conserving surgery: Recommendations of the Groupe Europeen de Curietherapie-European Society for Therapeutic Radiology and Oncology (GEC-ESTRO) breast cancer working group based on clinical evidence (2009). *Radiother Oncol* 2010;94:264–273.

22. Smith BD, Arthur DW, Buchholz TA et al. Accelerated partial breast irradiation consensus statement from the American Society for Radiation Oncology (ASTRO). *Int J Radiat Oncol Biol Phys* 2009;74:987–1001.

23. Leonardi MC, Maisonneuve P, Mastropasqua MG et al. Accelerated partial breast irradiation with intraoperative electrons: Using GEC-ESTRO recommendations as guidance for patient selection. *Radiother Oncol* 2013;106:21–27.

24. Coles CE, Brunt AM, Wheatley D, Mukesh MB, Yarnold JR. Breast radiotherapy: Less is more? *Clin Oncol (R Coll Radiol)* 2013;25:127–134.

25. Bellon JR. Personalized radiation oncology for breast cancer: The new frontier. *J Clin Oncol* 2015;33:1998–2000.

26. Coles CE, Griffin CL, Kirby AM et al. on behalf of the IMPORT Trialists. Partial-breast radiotherapy after breast conservation surgery for patients with early breast cancer (UK IMPORT LOW trial): 5-year results from a multicentre, randomised, controlled, phase 3, non-inferiority trial. *Lancet* 2017;390:1048–1060.

27. NSABP B-39, RTOG 0413: A randomized phase III study of conventional whole breast irradiation versus partial breast irradiation for women with stage 0, I, or II breast cancer. *Clin Adv Hematol Oncol* 2006;4:719–721.

28. Polgár C, Ott OJ, Hildebrandt G et al. Late side-effects and cosmetic results of accelerated partial breast irradiation with interstitial brachytherapy versus whole-breast irradiation after breast-conserving surgery for low-risk invasive and in-situ carcinoma of the female breast: 5-year results of a randomised, controlled, phase 3 trial. *Lancet Oncol* 2017;18:259–268.

29. Breast Cancer with Low Risk of Local Recurrence: Partial and Accelerated Radiation with Three-Dimensional Conformal Radiotherapy (3DCRT) vs. Standard Radiotherapy after Conserving Surgery (Phase III Study). Available from: https://clinicaltrials.gov/ct2/show/NCT01803958 (accessed October 1, 2015).

30. Danish Breast Cancer Co-operative Group. Partial breast versus whole breast irradiation in elderly women operated on for early breast cancer. http://clinicaltrials.gov/ct2/show/NCT00892814.

31. Belkacemi Y, Lartigau E. On behalf of federation nationale des centres de lutte contre le cancer. Standard or hypofractionated radiotherapy versus accelerated partial breast irradiation (APBI) for breast cancer (SHARE); 2010. http://clinicaltrials.gov/ct2/show/NCT01247233.

28

Postmastectomy radiotherapy after whole breast reconstruction

AT A GLANCE

The indications for postmastectomy radiotherapy (PMRT) have broadened in recent years with up to 30% of patients now being offered chest wall irradiation, although this is dependent on medical center with some persistent controversy. This shift in oncological strategy will impact on options for reconstruction in terms of both type and timing of reconstructive procedure. The effects of PMRT on longer term outcomes following whole breast reconstruction with implant-based techniques remain unclear, but data are now emerging on the impact of PMRT in the context of improvements in radiation techniques and implant design and incorporation of the latter into either implant-only (with or without acellular dermal matrix [ADM]) or implant-assisted latissimus dorsi (LD) flap reconstruction. There is general consensus that subpectoral tissue expanders should be avoided when PMRT is anticipated with no evidence for any radio-protective effect of ADM. Studies have now confirmed that PMRT worsens rates of capsular contracture for both implant-only and implant-assisted LD flap reconstruction, but some surgeons will offer the latter when PMRT is indicated with any subsequent implant exchange as necessary. Others prefer to use autologous tissue only (extended LD flap, free transverse rectus abdominis myocutaneous (TRAM) flap or deep inferior epigastric perforator (DIEP) flap), as transposed autologous tissue appears to be more tolerant of irradiation than implant-based reconstruction. Nonetheless, PMRT may prompt a "delayed immediate" breast reconstruction, whereby flap transfer is only undertaken after completion of PMRT and employment of an implant to act as a scaffold for skin-sparing mastectomy flaps. Radiotherapy after whole breast reconstruction is also a subject of controversy among radiation oncologists; some are of the opinion that a flap, implant, or inflated expander on the chest wall is a hindrance during radiotherapy and does not allow use of a three-beam technique to treat the internal mammary nodes without compromising the radiation field design (and risking overtreatment of the heart and/or lungs). Other radiation oncologists are prepared to deliver radiotherapy in the presence of any device or flap on the chest wall. Furthermore, there is continued concern regarding the metallic filling port within some types of tissue expanders.

28.1 POSTMASTECTOMY RADIOTHERAPY AFTER BREAST RECONSTRUCTION DOES NOT INTERFERE WITH RADIATION DELIVERY

Beryl McCormick

Women with breast cancer who opt for mastectomy, for whatever decision-making guidance they follow, frequently also want to hear about options for breast reconstruction. Thus, when I see a woman in consultation for possible postmastectomy radiation (PMRT), she is frequently in some stage of breast reconstruction. Does the presence of a reconstructed breast interfere with the delivery of any needed radiation? In my experience, this has not been a major issue, in terms of planning the actual delivery of the radiation, of dealing with the dosimetric challenges of an expander with a steel valve when present, or most importantly, in terms of patient outcomes as measured with the endpoints of local control and disease-specific survival.

To address the specific treatment planning issues, first consider what an optimal breast reconstruction restores, which is the shape of the human breast for the patient. When treatment is indicated postmastectomy, the beams utilized are essentially the same radiation beams as those which are used to treat a woman post lumpectomy, who also requires regional nodal radiation. All methods of reconstruction, including saline and silicone implants, or autologous reconstructions, are composed of what a medical physicist calls "tissue equivalent" material, in other words, of material similar in density to breast tissue for the purpose of planning the treatment. The only exception is the magnetized steel valve in expanders, which will be discussed.

TREATMENT PLANNING ISSUES

In 2005, Schechter et al. from the MD Anderson Cancer Center first reported that "immediate breast reconstruction may impose limitations on the treatment planning of PMRT." That study retrospectively reviewed standard PMRT treatment plans in 18 women with immediate reconstruction, concluding that only 4 of the plans achieved optimal coverage of the chest wall and internal mammary node (IMN) regions. The plans were scored for coverage of those regions by two radiation oncologists, using predetermined anatomic landmarks and a scoring system consisting of 1 point for no compromise, ½ point for moderate compromise, and 0 points for severe compromise.[1] The same MD Anderson group reported similar findings on a larger number of patients in 2006, concluding that "the potential for compromised PMRT planning should be considered when deciding between immediate and delayed reconstruction."[2]

The immediate years following those reports saw major advances in radiation treatment planning for breast cancer. The majority of patients were now planned using dedicated computed tomography (CT) simulators; the radiation oncologist had the tools with this new technology to contour organs at risk (OARS), like the heart and the lungs, as well as the target breast or chest wall tissue, and regional nodes when indicated. Sophisticated planning computers helped to calculate "safe" doses to defined volumes of the OARS, linking clinical outcomes with the information. In 2009, the RTOG Cooperative Group first presented a Breast Cancer Atlas specifically for contouring regional nodes, breast tissue and chest wall volumes (http://www.rtog.org), for use in designing fields for patients on protocols, and for general use in our specialty. That same year, Koutcher et al. from Memorial Sloan Kettering Cancer Center published a retrospective analysis of 41 PMRT treatment plans in women with tissue-expander or permanent implant reconstructions, addressing similar coverage issues as the MD Anderson paper. All patients were planned with a CT simulator, and the lungs and heart were contoured to analyze dose to those OARs, as well as coverage of chest wall and regional nodes. But in this study, not all patients received radiation to the IMNs. The study documented a slightly higher dose to the heart and lungs when IMN radiation was given, in addition to the chest wall and supra-clavicular regions, but the doses to those OARs met acceptable criteria in both types of plans. The authors concluded that "PMRT following immediate expander-implant reconstruction is a safe and reasonable option for patients."[3]

PMRT treatment plan techniques include three-dimensional photon beams with tangent fields, plans combining photon and electron coverage, intensity-modulated radiation and in selected cases where available, proton therapy. The optimal technique depends on the individual patient anatomy, targeted groups of regional nodes, and the technology available at the center. While it is beyond the scope of this chapter to review these in detail, **Figure 28.1.1** illustrates coverage to the reconstructed chest wall and IMNs at the level of the heart, in the same patient with several technologies. For this patient, the proton coverage on the right side of the figure, is most conformal. The partially wide tangent plan on the left side of Figure 28.1.1, because of

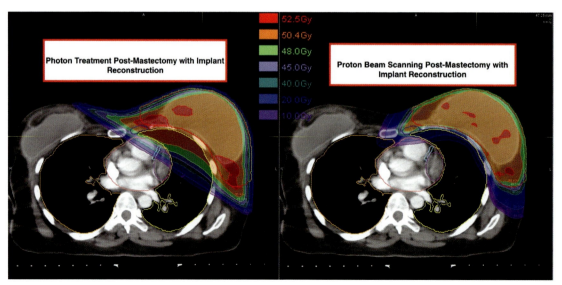

28.1.1 Standard photon field plan is shown on the left, and the more conformal proton plan on the right.

the location of the heart and the implant, is suboptimal with significantly higher volume of heart receiving a higher dose.[4]

How the expander does magnetized disc, for locating the injection port, effect PMRT dosimetry? The medical physics group at Memorial Sloan Kettering ran a series of radiation measurements with both low and high energy photon beams, so assess this. The transmission of the dose was 78% with the lower energy (6 MV) beam, and 84% with the 15 MV beam. Because the location of the magnetized disc changes each day, the study concluded that the "attenuation is small" and recommended treating such patients with 15 MV photons and appropriate bolus to address the skin dose with this beam.[5]

What are the oncologic clinical outcomes when patients have PMRT with reconstructions? A study from Taiwan comparing 191 patients with and without TRAM flap reconstruction, who underwent PMRT after appropriate systemic therapy found no differences in local or distant failure.[6] A study by Ho et al. looked at 151 women with tissue expander placement at surgery, which received chemotherapy, underwent an exchange for the implant, and then began PMRT on average 8 weeks from the last chemotherapy. With a median follow-up of 86 months, overall survival was 93% with no local failures at 7 years. 69% of the patients had stage III disease, with the remainder stage II. These outcomes are favorable for this population, reflecting the impact of both systemic and local-regional treatments.[7]

REFERENCES

1. Schechter N, Strom E, Perkins G, et al. Immediate breast reconstruction can impact postmastectomy irradiation. *Am J Clin Oncol* 2005; 28:485–494.
2. Motwani S, Strom E, Schechter N, et al. The impact of immediate breast reconstruction on the technical delivery of postmastectomy radiotherapy. *Int J Radiat Oncol Biol Phys* 2006; 66:76–82.
3. Koutcher L, Ballengrud A, Cordiero P, et al. Postmastectomy intensity modulated radiation therapy following immediate expander-implant reconstruction. *Radiother Oncol* 2010; 94:319–323.
4. MacDonald S, Patel S, Hickey S, et al. Proton therapy for breast cancer after mastectomy: Early outcomes of a prospective clinical trail. *Int J Radiat Oncol Biol Phys* 2013; 86:484–490.
5. Damast S, Beal K, Ballengrud A, et al. Do metallic ports in tissue expanders affect postmastectomy radiation deliver? *Int J Radiat Oncol Biol Phys* 2006; 66:305–310.
6. Huang C, Hou M, Lin S, et al. Comparison of local recurrence and distant metastases between breast cancer patients after postmastectomy radiotherapy with and without immediate TRAM flap reconstruction. *Plast Reconstr Surg* 2007; 118:1079–1086.
7. Ho A, Cordeiro P, Disa J, et al. Long-term outcomes in breast cancer patients undergoing immediate 2-stage expander/implant reconstruction and postmastectomy radiation. *Cancer* 2012; 118: 2552–2559.

28.2 POSTMASTECTOMY RADIOTHERAPY AFTER WHOLE BREAST RECONSTRUCTION: DOES BREAST RECONSTRUCTION INTERFERE WITH RADIATION DELIVERY?

Eric Strom and Wendy Woodward

Postmastectomy radiotherapy (PMRT) generally aims to deliver broad coverage of the chest wall, treat the ipsilateral supraclavicular fossa and axillary apex (level III), avoid the heart, and minimize the amount of lung tissue within the therapy field. Adequate chest wall coverage is commonly agreed to be the single most important target for PMRT. Controversy exists regarding the inclusion of the ipsilateral internal mammary chain (IMC) as a target in patients with stage II disease. However, every randomized trial demonstrating a survival benefit for PMRT included the ipsilateral internal mammary nodes within the target volumes.[1–4] Furthermore, recent data in early-stage patients also demonstrate a disease-free survival benefit from regional nodal irradiation.[5] Coverage of desired targets must be balanced with the need to spare normal tissue, particularly the heart where there is evidence to suggest a strong linear correlation between cardiac dose and cardiac toxicity.[5] Treatment of the IMC is not optional in patients with stage III breast cancer.

Our group has rigorously assessed the technical trade-offs and in some cases detriment to optimization of radiation treatment secondary to immediate reconstruction. Schechter and colleagues examined 18 different PMRT plans for patients who had undergone reconstruction prior to radiotherapy.[6] A score was developed and two board certified radiation oncologists specializing in breast radiotherapy reviewed all cases. For the purposes of this study, a plan was scored as being optimal and uncompromised if the chest wall was covered by at least 45 Gy to 50 Gy in 25 fractions from the midsternum medially, to the midaxillary line inferolaterally, the posteroaxillary line superolaterally, and 2 cm below the opposite inframammary fold inferiorly, with the superior border matched to the supraclavicular axillary apical field. A plan was scored as having adequate (uncompromised) ipsilateral IMC coverage if the internal mammary vessels were covered by at least 45 Gy to 50 Gy in the territory of the first three intercostal interspaces. A plan was scored as having adequate minimization of lung coverage if the quantity of lung within the chest wall tangential fields was 2 cm or less in maximal thickness. Finally, a plan was scored as having adequate avoidance of the heart if the heart and epicardial vessels were entirely excluded from the tangential fields. Only egregious deviations were scored as suboptimal. Only 4 of 18 plans were considered to be optimal. Twelve involved compromised coverage of the chest wall breadth medially and/or laterally, while nine provided no IMC coverage.

A larger study by Motwani and colleagues explicitly compared stage-matched plans after reconstruction to cases without reconstruction and attempted to provide more

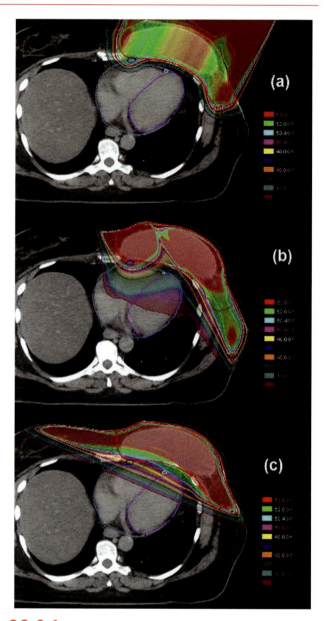

28.2.1 Geometric challenges treating internal mammary nodes with an implant or inflated expander. Optimal coverage is demonstrated with protons (a). Normal tissue dose is minimal while the target coverage including the internal mammary nodes is achieved. Using standard, readily available tools, photons and electrons (b) or photons alone (c) demonstrates the trade-offs of both approaches. Due to the geometry created by the implant, photon electron plans require high energy electrons and deliver significant non-target dose while leaving an untreated area at the match (b). This is oncologically acceptable when an implant or expander is post-pectoral, but could represent a geographic miss in a pre-pectoral implant or expander. Using only photons addresses this problem, but treats significantly more of the opposite breast (c).

granular data about type and degree of compromise when noted.[7] Using a similar approach to the previous study, an "optimal" plan achieved all objectives or otherwise had only a minor 0.5 point deduction. Those cases classified as having "moderately" compromised treatment plans had 1.0 or 1.5 point deductions while "major" compromised plans had ≥2.0 point deductions. Of the 112 PMRT plans scored after reconstruction, 52% had degrees of compromise compared with 7% of matched controls (p < 0.0001). Of the compromised plans after reconstruction, 33% were considered to be moderately compromised and 19% constituted major compromised treatment plans. Even chest wall coverage which is considered to be a primary goal of PMRT was compromised in 21% of reconstructed cases. IMC coverage was compromised in 55% and avoidable heart dose was observed in 16% of cases. These findings were statistically significant compared to controls and indeed, 67% of the "major" compromised radiotherapy plans were left-sided (p < 0.16).

Compromises occur because the presence of a reconstructed breast changes the target geometry (a mound instead of a surface) and impacts the techniques available for radiation planning. Photons (x-rays) are needed to penetrate tissue to a greater depth, but can lead to unnecessary dosage to non-target tissues because they penetrate completely through the patient. Increasing the size of a photon field to fully cover targets at depths created by the reconstruction can increase radiation doses to normal tissues (**Figure 28.2.1**). The practicing radiation oncologist must make a judgment regarding the technique for optimally treating the tumor-containing target while limiting radiation dose to adjacent structures. Without the distortions of shape induced by a completed reconstruction, multibeam techniques can be employed which improve the trade-offs between adequate coverage and reduced normal tissue dose.

The highest energy electrons cannot penetrate to adequately cover targets at depths of more than 5 cm and therefore tend not to be used in the setting of reconstruction. However, this limits techniques available to the treating physician and increases the necessity for trade-offs in the planning process (**Figure 28.2.2**). Whenever possible, either delayed reconstruction or placement of a deflatable tissue expander (with deflation during radiation therapy) is recommended for preventing avoidable compromises in radiotherapy.

Intensity-modulated radiation therapy is a technique that offers a potential solution to this anatomic dilemma. Because intensity modulated radiation therapy achieves conformality using photon beams only, low-dose irradiation is spread to structures not previously treated in patients with curable breast cancer including the opposite breast and lung. Indeed, the entire thorax may receive up to 5 Gy or more using this technique. With radiation-induced carcinogenesis occurring at thresholds of 1 Gy,[8] this technique should be approached cautiously in patients who are likely to be long-term survivors from breast cancer. Last, advances in reconstruction to improve patient comfort such as gas or air-filled expanders, or pre-pectoral placement can create new challenges for optimal radiotherapy. Non-tissue equivalent, such as air, in a pre-pectoral expander can limit dose build up and compromise the dose planning algorithms and should be avoided in patients who will receive PMRT. Multidisciplinary coordination between the surgeon, plastic surgeon, and radiation oncologist is critical to plan the optimal strategy to provide the best oncologic care and plastic surgery outcome, especially as new plastic surgery and radiotherapy techniques come into practice.

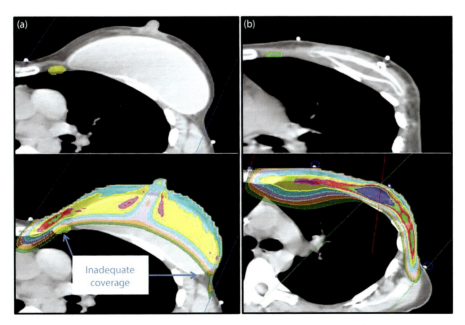

28.2.2 Electron options. Compare geometric issues using electrons in a case with an implant (or any reconstructed breast mound) in place (a) or a flat chest wall either without implant or with a deflated expander (b). Electrons have the advantage of limited penetration. With a reconstructed breast mound in place, even high energy electrons cannot penetrate adequately to cover the entire target (a, bottom) and are compromised even in coverage of the shallow IMC target (yellow shading) because of the rapidly sloping mound over the target. This means electrons cannot be used in this setting and photons such as in Figure 28.2.1 would be selected. Contrast B where the deflated expander makes electron coverage of the IMC and chest wall tightly conforming to the desired target without compromising on undesired normal tissue dose.

REFERENCES

1. Ragaz J, Olivotto IA, Spinelli JJ et al. Locoregional radiation therapy in patients with high-risk breast cancer receiving adjuvant chemotherapy: 20-year results of the British Columbia randomized trial. *Journal of the National Cancer Institute* 2005; **97**(2): 116–126.

2. Overgaard M, Hansen PS, Overgaard J et al. Postoperative radiotherapy in high-risk premenopausal women with breast cancer who receive adjuvant chemotherapy. Danish Breast Cancer Cooperative Group 82b Trial. *New England Journal of Medicine* 1997; **337**(14): 949–955.

3. Overgaard M. Overview of randomized trials in high risk breast cancer patients treated with adjuvant systemic therapy with or without postmastectomy irradiation. *Seminars in Radiation Oncology* 1999; **9**(3): 292–299.

4. Ebctcg, McGale P, Taylor C et al. Effect of radiotherapy after mastectomy and axillary surgery on 10-year recurrence and 20-year breast cancer mortality: Meta-analysis of individual patient data for 8135 women in 22 randomised trials. *Lancet* 2014; **383**(9935): 2127–2135.

5. Darby SC, Ewertz M, McGale P et al. Risk of ischemic heart disease in women after radiotherapy for breast cancer. *New England Journal of Medicine* 2013; **368**(11): 987–998.

6. Schechter NR, Strom EA, Perkins GH et al. Immediate breast reconstruction can impact postmastectomy irradiation. *American Journal of Clinical Oncology* 2005; **28**(5): 485–494.

7. Motwani SB, Strom EA, Schechter NR et al. The impact of immediate breast reconstruction on the technical delivery of postmastectomy radiotherapy. *International Journal of Radiation Oncology, Biology, Physics* 2006; **66**(1): 76–82.

8. Berrington de Gonzalez A, Curtis RE, Kry SF et al. Proportion of second cancers attributable to radiotherapy treatment in adults: A cohort study in the US SEER cancer registries. *Lancet Oncology* 2011; **12**(4): 353–360.

29

Partial breast radiotherapy after breast-conserving surgery

AT A GLANCE

A group of techniques collectively referred to as accelerated partial breast irradiation (APBI) decrease both the volume of breast irradiated and the duration of treatment. Most recurrences occur at the site of tumor excision, and whole breast irradiation (WBI) may be unnecessary. Techniques for APBI focus on the tumor bed and a zone of surrounding tissue of variable depth, and rates of local control to date appear comparable to WBI for matched and appropriately selected patients. The perceived complexity of brachytherapy may have detracted from its popularity, but novel methods for delivery of APBI are being pioneered. Intraoperative radiotherapy (IORT) delivers a high dose of irradiation as a single fraction at the time of surgery, allowing precise application to the target area and evidence to date suggests that the various forms of IORT are acceptable in terms of clinical effectiveness. TARGIT employs a low energy x-ray source (20 Gy) as opposed to electron beam therapy (ELIOT) delivered by a mobile linear accelerator. Postoperative brachytherapy can also be administered via a multi-lumen catheter placed within the surgical cavity using a remote afterloader (Iridium 192) or interstitial implantation over 4–5 days. External beam APBI yields less favorable cosmetic outcomes compared with TARGIT IORT which also results in less pain, better breast-related quality of life, less travel, less cost, and fewer deaths from heart attacks and other cancers. TARGIT IORT during lumpectomy can be more accurate than external beam APBI, especially when oncoplastic remodeling distorts the tumor bed (http://bit.ly/35BwojG).

29.1 TARGETED RADIOTHERAPY AS PART OF BREAST–CONSERVING THERAPY

Jayant S. Vaidya, Michael Douek, Nathan Coombs, Julian Singer, and Jeffrey S. Tobias

Randomized controlled trials and meta-analyses have demonstrated that the addition of radiotherapy to wide local excision/lumpectomy reduces rates of local recurrence. If this reduction exceeds an absolute value of 10% at 5 years, then a survival benefit of a quarter of the difference is expected.

Several clinical trials have questioned the extent of radiotherapy and provided insight into the natural history of the disease as well as guiding management decisions.

Increasing radiation

1. The EORTC trial[1] is the largest trial that has demonstrated a benefit for the addition of a tumor bed boost in terms of reducing local recurrence—the absolute reduction depends on the background risk, but there is no level of risk for which there is no reduction. Although this represents a desirable improvement in local control, there is no demonstrable improvement in survival.

2. Irradiation of the internal mammary chain and medial supraclavicular areas is associated with an improvement in disease-free and breast cancer-specific survival and a marginal improvement in overall survival.[2] In this trial from the Netherlands, 25% of patients underwent mastectomy and the majority of patients had node-positive disease.

3. TARGIT-B (www.targit.org.uk) is a health technology assessment funded randomized trial evaluating whether targeted radiation of the tumor bed during surgery improves local control. The trial uses intraoperative radiotherapy with Intrabeam™ and is currently recruiting in 35 centers worldwide. TARGIT IORT is accurately targeted and given at the right time without delay and could not only improve local control, by could also improve overall survival due to its abscopal effects.[14,15,21,22] Patients with higher-risk disease seem to benefit more from higher levels of irradiation, with benefits for breast cancer outcomes

being substantial for some patients and outweighing any toxicity from radiotherapy. Meanwhile, based on published data, TARGIT IORT with Intrabeam has become the standard of care in over 280 centers in thirty-eight counties.

Omitting radiation

The CALGB,[3] BASO II,[4] and PRIME II[5] trials have attempted to assess whether omission of radiation after breast conservation in highly selected lower-risk cohorts of patients can yield acceptable results. It has become clear that there is no defined cohort of patients for whom radiation does not improve local control. Omitting radiation therapy in highly selected low-risk patients increases the local recurrence rate to levels between 1 in 17 and 1 in 25. It appears that use of partial breast irradiation with techniques such as TARGIT IORT (using the TARGIT-A criteria) would lead to a meaningful improvement in local control. There would be an estimated recurrence rate of 1 in 71 by just applying one selection criteria of being ER (estrogen receptor) positive, without increasing patient burden nor cost to the healthcare system (**Table 29.1.1**).

Partial breast irradiation or targeted radiation to the tumor bed

Randomized trials conducted over the last two decades provide evidence supporting an original hypothesis[6,7] proposed more than 20 years ago.[8] A commentary[9] accompanying the first results of the TARGIT-A trial claimed partial breast irradiation to be a new standard of care for suitably selected patients. Published trials have confirmed that rates of local control lie within pre-defined non-inferiority margins. Details of relevant trials are provided below.

1. ***TARGIT-IORT***: In the TARGIT-A trial,[3,10–13] local control with targeted intraoperative radiotherapy (see **Figure 29.1.1**) was not statistically different from whole breast external beam radiotherapy at the pre-specified significance level (0.01). Non-inferiority was established for the whole trial with a margin of 2.5%. When TARGIT was given during lumpectomy, the 5-year local recurrence free survival was 93.9% (95% CI 90.9–95.9) for intraoperative radiotherapy and 92.5% (95% CI 89.7–94.6) for external beam radiotherapy (p = 0.35) (see **Figure 29.1.2a**). Interestingly, this was the first trial that found a statistically significant reduction in non-breast cancer mortality with targeted radiation.[14,15]

For the patients with screen-detected cancers in the TARGIT-A trial, there was a 2% improvement in overall survival (see **Figure 29.1.2b**). Using targeted intraoperative radiotherapy instead of external beam radiotherapy in appropriately selected patients can also significantly impact on the patient travel with implications for the environment. If widely available, 5 million miles (8,000,000 km) of travel, 170,000 woman-hours, and 1200 tons of CO_2 emissions (annual absorption by a forest of 100 hectares) would theoretically be saved annually in the United Kingdom.[16] Using TARGIT IORT has also been shown to have better breast-related quality of life compared with external beam radiotherapy and can be safely used in patients with preexisting breast implants.[25] TARGIT IORT is also less expensive than conventional treatment with savings for healthcare systems such as the NHS.[26]

2. ***IORT using NOVAC-7***: In the ELIOT trial, the 5-year event rate for ipsilateral breast tumor recurrence was significantly higher in the intraoperative radiotherapy group [4.4% (95% CI 2.7–6.1)] compared with the external radiotherapy group [0.4% (0.0–1.0)]. However, the difference was less than the pre-planned non-inferiority

Table 29.1.1 Local recurrence after omitting radiotherapy after breast conservation vs using TARGIT IORT during lumpectomy

	CALGB	BASO 2	PRIME 2	TARGIT–A Prepathology
Number	636	1135	1326	1625
Age	>=70	>=65	>=65	>=45
T Size	<=2 cm	<=2 cm	<=2 cm	Small T2, <=3.5 cm
Grade		Grade 1	Grade 1 or 2	No restriction
Nodes	Negative	Negative	Negative	No restriction
LV invasion		Negative	Negative	No restriction
ER status	Positive	Positive	Positive	No restriction
5–year local recurrence (LR)	4% vs 1% Stat Sig.	6% vs 2% Stat Sig.	4.1% vs 1.3% Stat Sig.	2.1% vs 1.1% overall
				1.4% vs 1.1% if ER Positive
				Both *not* statistically significant
5–year LR in experimental arm	1 in 25	1 in 17	1 in 25	1 in 48 overall
				1 in 71 if ER positive

29.1 Targeted radiotherapy as part of breast-conserving therapy 407

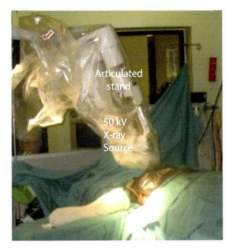
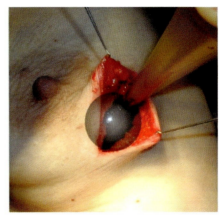

29.1.1 (a) Survival without local recurrence after TARGIT IORT during lumpectomy in the TARGIT-A trial. (b) Overall survival benefit of TARGIT IORT seen in the screen-detected population (n=2102) in the TARGIT-A trial.

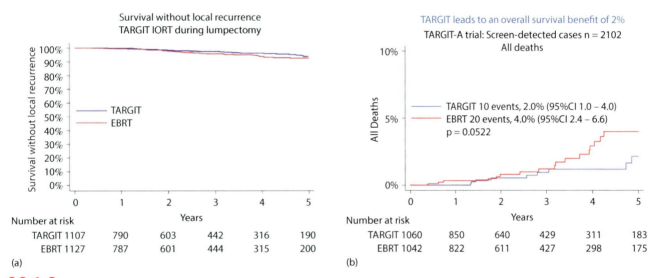

29.1.2 TARGIT IORT is given immediately after the lumpectomy is completed, under the same anaesthetic and in a standard operation theatre. A spherical applicator is inserted in the fresh tumor bed and apposed to the target tissues using purse-string sutures. Radiation is delivered over 20–30 minutes. The applicator is removed, and the wound closed as usual. The postoperative care is no different from the usual and the patient usually goes home the same day. (More information at https://www.targit.org.uk.)

margin of 7.5%. The difference between the groups was not statistically significant in the subgroup of patients with a favorable prognosis (e.g., luminal A).
3. The **GEC-ESTRO trial** assessed the effectiveness of partial breast irradiation with interstitial radiotherapy using radioactive wires (**Figure 29.1.3**) and found that local recurrence was non-inferior compared to whole breast irradiation. This study employed a non-inferior margin of 3%.[18] A meta-analysis of the GEC-ESTRO and TARGIT-A trials (**Figure 29.1.4**) has shown that local control is non-inferior with partial breast irradiation. Furthermore, there is evidence for reduction of non-breast cancer mortality.[19]
4. The **IMPORT LOW trial**[20] has also reported that local control is non-inferior when using intensity-modulated radiotherapy delivered daily over 3 weeks exclusively to the tumor bed compared with whole breast radiotherapy. To receive this treatment, patients must attend every day for 3 weeks, and intensity-modulated radiotherapy is significantly more expensive than traditional radiotherapy. In consequence, there may be no net savings to the National Health Service. Furthermore, only two quality-of-life outcome measures tested were found to be statistically better in favor of intensity-modulated radiotherapy.[24]

Survival benefit of targeted radiotherapy compared with whole breast radiotherapy

The much debated survival benefit of targeted radiotherapy first reported in the TARGIT-A trial has been confirmed in a meta-analysis of 5-year data from published

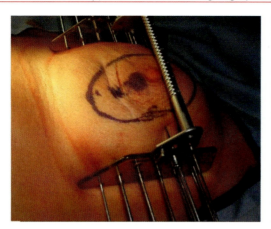
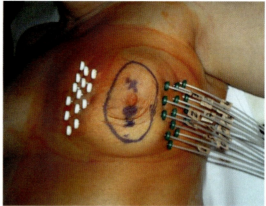

29.1.3 Interstitial brachytherapy as in the GEC-ESTRO trial is given a few weeks after surgery. Multiple plastic implantation needles (16–20 cm long) are inserted in the breast under local/general anaesthetic as shown in the figure. Radioactive wires are then inserted twice a day for 4–5 days. The patient is required to be in a radiation protected room during this period. Multiple CT scans are required to confirm positions. Due to uncertainty of localization, a much larger is irradiated than necessary as can be seen in this figure.

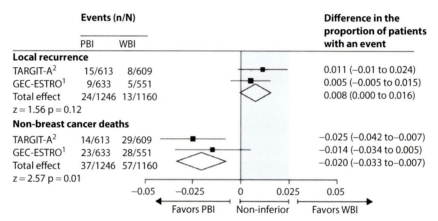

29.1.4 A meta-analysis of TARGIT-A and GEC-ESTRO trials: results show that with targeted radiotherapy, local recuerrnce is non-inferior and non-breast cancer deaths are signficantly reduced.

randomized trials including nearly 6000 patients evaluating partial breast irradiation alone (or within a risk adapted approach) versus whole breast irradiation for invasive breast cancer treated with lumpectomy[24] and the updated meta-anslysis including the IMPORT-Low data[23] (**Figure 29.1.5**). There was no difference in breast cancer mortality (n = 5574, difference 0.000% (95% CI −0.6 to +0.6) (p = 0.925). However, partial breast irradiation was better than whole breast irradiation for non-breast cancer mortality (n = 5832, difference 1.0% (95% CI −1.8% to −0.2%) (p = 0.015) and overall mortality (difference 1.1% (95% CI 2.2% to 0.0%) (p = 0.044), leading to a 25% relative risk reduction. Thus, in suitable patients, partial breast irradiation (using TARGIT IORT as a single intraoperative dose for example) reduces mortality, possibly by avoiding radiation exposure of vital organs (or some other mechanism[14,15,21]), while maintaining adequate cancer control.

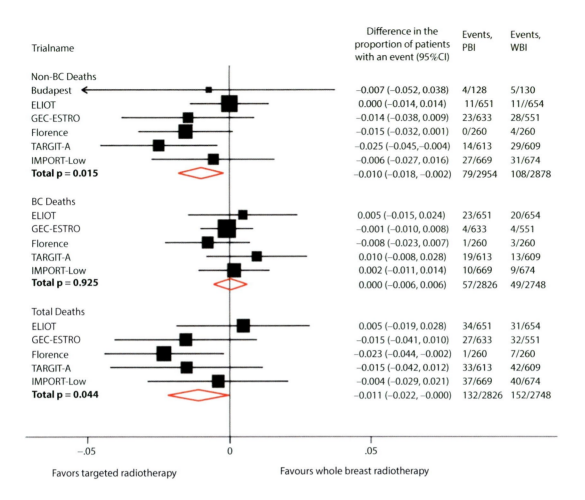

29.1.5 Improved overall survival with targeted radiotherapy: Forest plots representing meta-analysis of nearly 6000 patients in randomised trials of PBI showing the difference in mortality between PBI and WBI. The trials included were the Budapest,[1] TARGIT-A,[2] ELIOT,[3] Florence,[4] GEC-ESTRO,[5] and IMPORT- LOW.[6] The median follow-up duration of all these trials was 5–6 years. Data from only the initial 1222 patients in the TARGIT-A trial, whose median follow-up was 5 years, are included. BC deaths or total deaths were not available for the Budapest trial. There was no significant heterogeneity; p=0.546 for BC, p=0.447 for non-BC, and p=0.448 for total deaths, with Higgins I2 values of 0.0% for each. BC mortality was not significantly different (p=0.925). Compared with WBI, targeted radiotherapy resulted in a significant reduction in non-BC mortality by 1% (p=0.015) and overall mortality by 1.1% (p=0.044). PBI=partial breast irradiation. WBI=whole breast irradiation. BC=breast cancer.

CONCLUSION

1. Increasing the extent of irradiation improves outcomes in those with higher-risk disease. Efforts should be made to recruit patients into TARGIT-B.
2. Reducing the extent of irradiation with targeted approaches improves overall outcomes in suitable patients by reducing non-breast cancer mortality, while maintaining local control of breast cancer. TARGIT intraoperative radiotherapy is effective, safer, quicker; it most convenient to the patient, providing better quality of life and is the least expensive to healthcare providers as well as to insurance companies.
3. If omission of radiotherapy is considered, discussion with the patient before surgery must include potential benefits of partial breast irradiation of which TARGIT-IORT achieves better cancer control and being so conveniently delivered during surgery could be the patient's preferred choice.

REFERENCES

1. Bartelink H, Horiot JC, Poortmans PM et al. Impact of a higher radiation dose on local control and survival in breast-conserving therapy of early breast cancer: 10-year results of the randomized boost versus no boost EORTC 22881-10882 trial. *Journal of Clinical Oncology* 2007; 25(22): 3259–3265.
2. Poortmans PM, Collette S, Kirkove C et al. Internal mammary and medial supraclavicular irradiation in breast cancer. *New England Journal of Medicine* 2015; 373(4): 317–327.

3. Hughes KS, Schnaper LA, Bellon JR et al. Lumpectomy plus tamoxifen with or without irradiation in women age 70 years or older with early breast cancer: Long-term follow-up of CALGB 9343. *Journal of Clinical Oncology: Official Journal of the American Society of Clinical Oncology* 2013; **31**(19): 2382–2387.

4. Blamey RW, Bates T, Chetty U et al. Radiotherapy or tamoxifen after conserving surgery for breast cancers of excellent prognosis: British association of surgical oncology (BASO) II trial. *European Journal of Cancer* 2013.

5. Kunkler IH, Williams LJ, Jack WJ, Cameron DA, Dixon JM, investigators PI. Breast-conserving surgery with or without irradiation in women aged 65 years or older with early breast cancer (PRIME II): A randomised controlled trial. *Lancet Oncology* 2015; **16**(3): 266–273.

6. Vaidya JS, Vyas JJ, Mittra I, Chinoy RF. Multicentricity and its influence on conservative breast cancer treatment strategy. *Hongkong International Cancer Congress* 1995: Abstract 44.4.

7. Vaidya JS, Vyas JJ, Chinoy RF, Merchant N, Sharma OP, Mittra I. Multicentricity of breast cancer: Wole-organ analysis and clinical implications. *British Journal of Cancer* 1996; **74**(5): 820–824.

8. Baum M, Vaidya JS, Mittra I. Multicentricity and recurrence of breast cancer. *Lancet* 1997; **349**(9046): 208.

9. Azria D, Bourgier C. Partial breast irradiation: New standard for selected patients. *Lancet* 2010; **376**(9735): 71–72.

10. Vaidya JS, Joseph DJ, Tobias JS et al. Targeted intraoperative radiotherapy versus whole breast radiotherapy for breast cancer (TARGIT-A trial): An international, prospective, randomised, non-inferiority phase 3 trial. *Lancet* 2010; **376**(9735): 91–102.

11. Vaidya JS, Wenz F, Bulsara M et al. Risk-adapted targeted intraoperative radiotherapy versus whole-breast radiotherapy for breast cancer: 5-year results for local control and overall survival from the TARGIT-A randomised trial. *Lancet* 2014; **383**(9917): 603–613.

12. Vaidya JS, Bulsara M, Wenz F et al. Pride, Prejudice, or Science – attitudes towards the results of the TARGIT-A trial of targeted intraoperative radiotherapy for breast cancer. *International Journal of Radiation Oncology*Biology*Physics* 2015; **92**(3): 494–500.

13. Vaidya JS, Wenz F, Bulsara M et al. An international randomised controlled trial to compare TARGeted Intraoperative radioTherapy (TARGIT) with conventional postoperative radiotherapy after breast-conserving surgery for women with early-stage breast cancer (the TARGIT-A trial). *Health Technology Assessment* 2016; **20**(73): 1–188.

14. Vaidya JS, Bulsara M, Wenz F. Ischemic heart disease after breast cancer radiotherapy. *New England Journal of Medicine* 2013; **368**(26): 2526–2527.

15. Vaidya JS. The systemic effects of local treatments (Surgery and Radiotherapy) of breast cancer. In: Retsky M, Demichelli R, eds. *Perioperative Inflammation as Triggering Origin of Metastasis Development.* Cham, Switzerland: Nature, Springer; 2017.

16. Coombs NJ, Coombs JM, Vaidya UJ et al. Environmental and social benefits of the targeted intraoperative radiotherapy for breast cancer: Data from UK TARGIT-A trial centres and two UK NHS hospitals offering TARGIT IORT. *British Medical Journal Open* 2016; **6**(5): e010703.

17. Vaidya A, Vaidya P, Both B, Brew-Graves C, Bulsara M, Vaidya JS. Health economics of targeted intraoperative radiotherapy (TARGIT-IORT) for early breast cancer: A cost- effectiveness analysis in the United Kingdom. *British Medical Journal Open* 2017; **7**: e014944.

18. Strnad V, Ott OJ, Hildebrandt G et al. 5-year results of accelerated partial breast irradiation using sole interstitial multi-catheter brachytherapy versus whole-breast irradiation with boost after breast-conserving surgery for low-risk invasive and in-situ carcinoma of the female breast: A randomised, phase 3, non-inferiority trial. *Lancet* 2015.

19. Vaidya JS, Bulsara M, Wenz F, Tobias JS, Joseph D, Baum M. Partial breast irradiation and the GEC-ESTRO trial. *Lancet* 2016; **387**(10029): 1717.

20. Coles CE, Griffin CL, Kirby AM et al. Partial-breast radiotherapy after breast conservation surgery for patients with early breast cancer (UK IMPORT LOW trial): 5-year results from a multicentre, randomised, controlled, phase 3, non-inferiority trial. *Lancet* 2017.

21. Vaidya JS, Bulsara M, Wenz F et al. The lower non-breast cancer mortality with TARGIT in the TARGIT-A trial could be a systemic effect of TARGIT on tumor microenvironment. *International Journal of Radiation Oncology, Biology, Physics* 2013; **87**(2): S240.

22. Kolberg HC, Loevey G, Akpolat-Basci L, Stephanou M, Fasching PA, Untch M, Liedtke C, Bulsara M, Vaidya JS. Targeted intraoperative radiotherapy tumour bed boost during breast-conserving surgery after neoadjuvant chemotherapy. *Strahlentherapie und Onkologie* 2017; **193**(1): 62–69.

23. Vaidya JS, Bulsara M, Wenz F et al. Targeted radiotherapy for early breast cancer. *Lancet* 2018; **391**(10115): 26–27.

24. Vaidya JS, Wenz F, Tobias JS. Trial supports targeted radiotherapy for early breast cancer but protocol still requires 3 weeks of daily therapy. *BMJ Evidence-Based Medicine* 2018; **23**(1): 38–39.

25. Corica T, Nowak AK, Saunders CM, et al. Cosmetic outcome as rated by patients, doctors, nurses and BCCT.core software assessed over 5 years in a subset of patients in the TARGIT-A trial. *Radiation Oncology* 2018; **13**(1): 68.

26. Kolberg HC, Uhl V, Massarut S, et al. Targeted intraoperative radiotherapy during breast-conserving surgery for breast cancer in patients after implant augmentation. *Anticancer Research* 2019; **39**(8): 4215–4218.

29.2 POSTOPERATIVE RADIOTHERAPY

29.2.1 Brachytherapy

Nicholas Serrano and Douglas W. Arthur

Historically, lumpectomy followed by whole breast irradiation has been the foundation of breast-conservation therapy and provides an acceptable alternative to mastectomy in the management of early-stage breast cancer.[1–3] Evolution of radiation treatment techniques has moved from open field whole breast treatment delivered over 6–7 weeks to individualized treatment options which include both accelerated whole breast and partial breast techniques. Success in radiation treatment delivery and outcomes have become increasingly dependent on the ability to identify a partial breast target defined as the lumpectomy cavity plus an immediate zone of surrounding normal breast tissue. Identification of this partial breast target is crucial irrespective of treatment with accelerated partial breast irradiation (APBI) or a boost dose following whole breast irradiation. Therefore, collaboration between the surgeon and radiation oncologist is essential for creation of a recognizable treatment target particularly when oncoplastic techniques are employed that can re-distribute at-risk tissue to remote and unidentifiable locations within the breast.[4,5] APBI is an acceptable treatment option for appropriately selected patients. Published patient selection guidelines are available and are categorized as conservative with characteristically older women (>50–60 years old) with node-negative tumors less than 3 cm being represented in guidelines from the American Society of Radiation Oncology,[6] the American Brachytherapy Society,[7] the Groupe Européen de Curiethérapie and the European Society for Radiotherapy & Oncology,[8] and the American Society of Breast Surgeons.[9] Although specific details vary between these four guidelines, they are all similar in approach and additional information is awaited from maturing multiple phase III trials investigating APBI. The latter might suggest the need for guideline refinements based on emergent outcome data.

APBI techniques include interstitial multi-catheter brachytherapy, single entry intracavitary, and 3D-conformal external beam techniques (3D-CRT).[10–15] Innovation over the past few years has enhanced each of these treatment techniques to improve reproducibility and outcome. Continued evaluation includes a multi-institutional trial reducing the APBI treatment scheme from the standard ten to three fractions which is presently enrolling.[16] Additionally, a non-invasive breast brachytherapy approach using the AccuBoost system is under investigation and has the advantage of avoiding the invasive component of brachytherapy and decreases treatment time to only five daily schedules.[17]

However, it should be noted that when coupling oncoplastic surgery with APBI techniques, single entry intracavitary breast irradiation is problematic. This technique requires an intact lumpectomy cavity that reliably identifies the treatment target and provides a location to place the intracavitary treatment device. By definition, oncoplastic procedures disrupt this essential structure and thereby negate the ability to use this APBI technique. Instead, alternative techniques such as multi-catheter brachytherapy or 3D-CRT should be considered for these patients.

The utilization of oncoplastic surgery has increased in recent years and maximizes cosmetic results in women undergoing breast conservation.[18] The most challenging task is determination of the target volume for APBI. There have been several published reports on the difficulties of identifying and contouring tumor beds following oncoplastic procedures.[19–21] One meta-analysis systemically examined 24 studies involving 1933 patients undergoing oncoplastic surgery and external beam whole breast irradiation.[22] It was concluded that improved communication between disciplines could allow for better tumor bed identification and reduced treatment volumes.

A retrospective series analyzed 136 low-risk breast cancers among 134 patients receiving breast-conserving oncoplastic surgery.[23] The authors performed an interstitial multi-catheter implant approximately 3 weeks after surgery and targeted the volume defined by surgical clips with an additional margin. APBI was administered with either a pulse dose rate of 50.4 Gy or a high dose rate of 32 Gy over 4 days. The median follow-up time was 39 months with a range of 4–106 months. Three in-breast recurrences, one marginal-miss, and two in-breast recurrences in different quadrants were reported, and the authors concluded that multi-catheter APBI after oncoplastic breast-conserving surgery was a feasible technique in selected low-risk breast cancer patients.

Tumor bed visualization prior to and leading up to an APBI procedure is essential to achieve the goals of local control and limited toxicity. One group of authors examined 31 patients treated with lumpectomy of which 18 had oncoplastic techniques.[24] Preoperative and postoperative CT scans were obtained. It was found that the use of more than three clips (associated with pre- to postoperative CT image registration) allowed for better optimization of the topographic definition of tumor bed after oncoplastic surgical procedures. With tumor bed identification established as an important step, innovative 3-D marking devices are under development which can be placed at the time of lumpectomy, thus facilitating target definition for radiation boost delivery and APBI. One example, the BioZorb tissue marker, allows for simultaneous closure of the cavity with fiducial marker placement that provides a method of 3-D tumor bed identification. As seen in **Figure 29.2.1.1**, the use of this tissue marker allows for easy identification of the treatment target after an oncoplastic closure, providing the opportunity for safe and effective APBI with a multi-catheter approach.

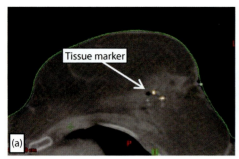  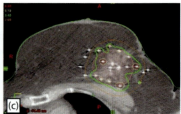

29.2.1.1 (a) BioZorb tissue marker with cavity edges surgically approximated following lumpectomy and oncoplastic closure guiding multi-catheter brachytherapy implant extent, and location. (b) Following catheter placement, APBI treatment target identification and delineation for CT-based treatment planning. (c) APBI dose distribution depicting accurate coverage of partial breast target.

CONCLUSION

The use of oncoplastic breast surgery is increasing and allows the breast surgeon to achieve both negative surgical margins and an acceptable cosmetic outcome. When oncoplastic techniques are utilized, tumor bed identification can be problematic. Thus, efforts toward target creation and appropriate delineation allowing for accurate delivery of targeted radiotherapy are necessary. This remains important for all patients receiving postoperative radiotherapy whether delivering treatment with APBI or as boost treatment following whole breast irradiation. Goals can be achieved through communication and placement of multiple surgical clips or the use of emerging 3-D cavity identification devices. While APBI techniques may be limited after an oncoplastic closure, APBI can still be considered in appropriately selected patients using an interstitial multi-catheter or 3D-CRT approach.

REFERENCES

1. Fisher B, Anderson S, Bryant J et al. Twenty-year follow-up of a randomized trial comparing total mastectomy, lumpectomy, and lumpectomy plus irradiation for the treatment of invasive breast cancer. *N Engl J Med.* 2002;347(16):1233–1241.
2. Veronesi U, Cascinelli N, Mariani L et al. Twenty-year follow-up of a randomized study comparing breast-conserving surgery with radical mastectomy for early breast cancer. *N Engl J Med.* 2002;347(16):1227–1232.
3. Darby S, McGale P, Correa C et al. Effect of radiotherapy after breast-conserving surgery on 10-year recurrence and 15-year breast cancer death: Meta-analysis of individual patient data for 10,801 women in 17 randomised trials. *Lancet.* 2011;378(9804):1707–1716.
4. Anderson BO, Masetti R, Silverstein MJ. Oncoplastic approaches to partial mastectomy: An overview of volume-displacement techniques. *Lancet Oncol.* 2005;6(3):145–157.
5. Clough KB, Lewis JS, Couturaud B, Fitoussi A, Nos C, Falcou MC. Oncoplastic techniques allow extensive resections for breast-conserving therapy of breast carcinomas. *Ann Surg.* 2003;237(1):26–34.
6. Smith BD, Arthur DW, Buchholz TA et al. Accelerated partial breast irradiation consensus statement from the American society for radiation oncology (ASTRO). *Int J Radiat Oncol Biol Phys.* 2009;74(4):987–1001.
7. Shah C, Vicini F, Wazer DE, Arthur D, Patel RR. The American brachytherapy society consensus statement for accelerated partial breast irradiation. *Brachytherapy.* 2013;12(4):267–277.
8. Polgar C, Van Limbergen E, Potter R et al. Patient selection for accelerated partial-breast irradiation (APBI) after breast-conserving surgery: Recommendations of the groupe Europeen de curietherapie-European society for therapeutic radiology and oncology (GEC-ESTRO) breast cancer working group based on clinical evidence (2009). *Radiother Oncol.* 2010;94(3):264–273.
9. The American Society of Breast Surgeons. Consensus statement for accelerated partial breast irradiation. https://www.breastsurgeons.org/new_layout/about/statements/PDF_Statements/APBI.pdf.
10. Keisch M, Vicini F, Kuske RR et al. Initial clinical experience with the MammoSite breast brachytherapy applicator in women with early-stage breast cancer treated with breast-conserving therapy. *Int J Radiat Oncol Biol Phys.* 2003;55(2):289–293.
11. Tokita KM, Cuttino LW, Vicini FA et al. Optimal application of the contura multilumen balloon breast brachytherapy catheter vacuum port to deliver accelerated partial breast irradiation. *Brachytherapy.* 2011;10(3):184–189.
12. Yashar CM, Scanderbeg D, Kuske R et al. Initial clinical experience with the strut-adjusted volume implant (SAVI) breast brachytherapy device for accelerated partial-breast irradiation (APBI): First 100 patients with more than 1 year of follow-up. *Int J Radiat Oncol Biol Phys.* 2011;80(3):765–770.
13. Berrang TS, Olivotto I, Kim DH et al. Three-year outcomes of a canadian multicenter study of accelerated partial breast irradiation using conformal radiation therapy. *Int J Radiat Oncol Biol Phys.* 2011;81(5):1220–1227.
14. Hepel JT, Wazer DE. A comparison of brachytherapy techniques for partial breast irradiation. *Brachytherapy.* 2012;11(3):163–175.
15. Lehman M, Hickey BE, Francis DP, See AM. Partial breast irradiation for early breast cancer. *Cochrane Database Syst Rev.* 2014;6:CD007077.

16. Khan AJ, Vicini FA, Brown S et al. Dosimetric feasibility and acute toxicity in a prospective trial of ultrashort-course accelerated partial breast irradiation (APBI) using a multi-lumen balloon brachytherapy device. *Ann Surg Oncol.* 2013;20(4):1295–1301.

17. BrUOG 291: Five fraction partial breast irradiation using non-invasive image-guided breast brachytherapy (NIBB). https://clinicaltrials.gov/ct2/show/NCT01961531.

18. Silverstein MJ, Mai T, Savalia N, Vaince F, Guerra L. Oncoplastic breast conservation surgery: The new paradigm. *J Surg Oncol.* 2014;110(1):82–89.

19. Pezner RD. The oncoplastic breast surgery challenge to the local radiation boost. *Int J Radiat Oncol Biol Phys.* 2011;79(4):963–964.

20. Pezner RD, Tan MC, Clancy SL, Chen YJ, Joseph T, Vora NL. Radiation therapy for breast cancer patients who undergo oncoplastic surgery: Localization of the tumor bed for the local boost. *Am J Clin Oncol.* 2013;36(6):535–539.

21. Kirova YM, Servois V, Reyal F, Peurien D, Fourquet A, Fournier-Bidoz N. Use of deformable image fusion to allow better definition of tumor bed boost volume after oncoplastic breast surgery. *Surg Oncol.* 2011;20(2):e123–e125.

22. Schaverien MV, Stallard S, Dodwell D, Doughty JC. Use of boost radiotherapy in oncoplastic breast-conserving surgery—A systematic review. *Eur J Surg Oncol.* 2013;39(11):1179–1185.

23. Roth AM, Kauer-Dorner D, Resch A et al. Is oncoplastic surgery a contraindication for accelerated partial breast radiation using the interstitial multicatheter brachytherapy method? *Brachytherapy.* 2014;13(4):394–399.

24. Furet E, Peurien D, Fournier-Bidoz N et al. Plastic surgery for breast conservation therapy: How to define the volume of the tumor bed for the boost? *Eur J Surg Oncol.* 2014;40(7):830–834.

29.2.2 Linear accelerator

Icro Meattini

Accelerated partial breast irradiation (APBI) has been introduced as an alternative treatment method for selected patients with early-stage breast cancer. Potential advantages of APBI include shorter treatment time, improved cosmesis secondary to a reduction in volume of breast tissue treated, and cost reduction compared with standard fractionation. The concept of APBI was introduced following published reports from several large-scale prospective randomized trials that questioned the need to irradiate the entire breast tissue after tumor resection. These studies evaluated patients treated with surgery alone or followed by whole breast irradiation. Within these trials, most of recurrences in the residual breast tissue of patients not receiving radiotherapy occurred at or in the region of the lumpectomy cavity.[1-5]

Several techniques have been tested recently in an attempt to administer less adjuvant radiotherapy thereby reducing treatment burden for patients and workload of radiotherapy departments. Thus limited data are emerging to support use of APBI in selected patients. The role of APBI is currently being evaluated in large-scale prospective phase 3 clinical trials (NSABP-B29/ RTOG 0413, IRMA, RAPID, GEC-ESTRO APBI). Furthermore, ongoing research is aimed at exploring other modalities of radiotherapy that will minimize toxicities without reducing effectiveness. Within the various published trials, there were no differences in terms of distant metastases and overall survival for a low-risk, node-negative patient population.[6]

With respect to APBI using linear accelerators, a well-studied modality is intensity-modulated radiotherapy (IMRT). This technique has a theoretical advantage of further increasing dose conformity compared with three-dimensional techniques and permits more normal tissue sparing. To date, only one phase 3 trial from the University of Florence reported outcomes of IMRT compared with whole breast irradiation.[7] In this trial, 520 women aged more than 40 years with early breast cancer ≤25 mm were randomly assigned to receive either whole breast irradiation or APBI using IMRT. Patients in the APBI arm received a total dose of 30 Gy to the tumor bed in five daily fractions. The whole breast irradiation arm received 50 Gy in 25 fractions, followed by a boost to the tumor bed of 10 Gy in five fractions. At a median follow-up of 5 years, the ipsilateral breast tumor recurrence rate was 1.5% in both the partial and whole breast irradiation groups with no significant difference between the two groups (log rank test p = 0.86). The 5-year overall survival was 96.6% for the whole breast irradiation group and 99.4% for the APBI group. The APBI group had significantly better results in terms of acute (p = 0.0001), late (p = 0.004), and cosmetic outcomes (p = 0.045). Results of this trial suggest that APBI using intensity-modulated radiotherapy presents the same efficacy as whole breast irradiation in terms of ipsilateral breast tumor recurrence and overall survival with a favorable toxicity profile. However, there are some limitations of this study such as the small sample series and the low number of ipsilateral breast tumor recurrence events and consequently, longer-term follow-up is needed.

A recently published subgroup analysis on patients aged 70 years or older showed an ipsilateral breast tumor recurrence rate at 5 years of only 1.9% and significantly better results in terms of acute skin toxicity, favoring the APBI arm.[8] Therefore, a significant impact on patient compliance with radiotherapy could translate into a consistent improvement in overall quality of life.

However, mainstream published results on the acute and long-term toxicity profile of APBI are conflicting. Results from the RAPID randomized trial involving over 2000 patients treated with APBI using three-dimensional conformal external beam radiotherapy showed a higher rate of skin adverse events at a median follow-up of 3 years[9] and significantly worse cosmesis at 5 years (33% vs 13%). Reported cosmetic outcomes after external APBI differ widely and range from good/excellent cosmetic results in 89% of the patients,[10] to unacceptable cosmesis in up to 21% at short-term follow-up time.[11,12] However, most published results involve single-center studies, with small numbers of patients and short follow-up. Higher rates of moderate-to-severe late toxicity (as poor cosmesis) are reported in several studies using a breath-holding fashion with 38.5 Gy in 3.85 Gy fractions twice daily.

Possible causes of this unexpectedly poor outcome may be the relatively high volume of breast tissue receiving a significant radiotherapy dose observed in those patients who had fair/poor cosmesis. Another possible explanation is that the twice-daily schedule employed in these studies may have a greater biological effect due to incomplete tissue recovery between doses.[13] Therefore, results from prospective trials such as the combined NSABP-B29/ RTOG 0413 trial are eagerly awaited.[14]

General rules for dose prescription relating to targets and organs at risk represent a major challenge for APBI delivery.

The conventionally fractionated (40 Gy in 15 fractions) partial breast irradiation (PBI) IMPORT LOW trial[15] represents a good example of how appropriate selection of patients for PBI can minimize the risk of local relapse rate for breast cancer patients. Coles and colleagues,[15] demonstrated non-inferiority for local recurrence risk at 5 years for PBI patients compared to standard whole breast irradiation (WBI) [0.5% partial breast irradiation (PBI) vs 1.1% whole breast irradiation (WBI)]. Moreover, PBI significantly reduced the rate and severity of adverse changes in breast appearance using a conventional radiation technique implementable worldwide [moderate or marked changes 15% (PBI) vs 27% (WBI)]. Most patients in this study had node-negative (98%) lower-grade (91%) tumors which were estrogen receptor positive (95%) and human epidermal growth factor receptor 2 negative (94%). These results testify to the effectiveness of PBI and allow integration of new evidence into standard clinical practice. This in turn will promote optimal definition of those patients who are suitable for PBI and clarify for whom these techniques should now be recommended as standard treatment[16] in accordance with guidelines issued by the Groupe Europeen de Curietherapie–European Society for Therapeutic Radiology and Oncology and the updated American Society for Radiation Oncology.[17,18]

REFERENCES

1. Fisher B, Anderson S, Bryant J et al. Twenty-year follow-up of a randomized trial comparing total mastectomy, lumpectomy, and lumpectomy plus irradiation for the treatment of invasive breast cancer. *N Engl J Med* 347:1233–1241, 2002.
2. Holli K, Saaristo R, Isola J et al. Lumpectomy with or without postoperative radiotherapy for breast cancer with favourable prognostic features: Results of a randomized study. *Br J Cancer* 84:164–169, 2001.
3. Veronesi U, Marubini E, Mariani L et al. Radiotherapy after breast-conserving surgery in small breast carcinoma: Long-term results of a randomized trial. *Ann Oncol* 12:997–1003, 2001.
4. Clark RM, Whelan T, Levine M et al. Randomized clinical trial of breast irradiation following lumpectomy and axillary dissection for node-negative breast cancer: An update. ontario clinical oncology group. *J Natl Cancer Inst* 88:1659–1664, 1996.
5. Liljegren G, Holmberg L, Bergh J et al. 10-Year results after sector resection with or without postoperative radiotherapy for stage I breast cancer: A randomized trial. *J Clin Oncol* 7:2326–2333, 1999.
6. Marta GN, Macedo CR, Carvalho Hde A, Hanna SA, da Silva JL, Riera R. Accelerated partial irradiation for breast cancer: Systematic review and meta-analysis of 8653 women in eight randomized trials. *Radiother Oncol.* 2015;114(1):42–49.
7. Livi L, Meattini I, Marrazzo L, Simontacchi G, Pallotta S, Saieva C, Paiar F, Scotti V, De Luca Cardillo C, Bastiani P, Orzalesi L, Casella D, Sanchez L, Nori J, Fambrini M, Bianchi S. Accelerated partial breast irradiation using intensity-modulated radiotherapy versus whole breast irradiation: 5-year survival analysis of a phase 3 randomised controlled trial. *Eur J Cancer.* 2015;51(4):451–463.
8. Meattini I, Saieva C, Marrazzo L, Di Brina L, Pallotta S, Mangoni M, Meacci F et al. Accelerated partial breast irradiation using intensity-modulated radiotherapy technique compared to whole breast irradiation for patients aged 70 years or older: Subgroup analysis from a randomized phase 3 trial. *Breast Cancer Res Treat.* 2015;153(3):539–547.
9. Olivotto IA, Whelan TJ, Parpia S, Kim DH, Berrang T, Truong PT, Kong I et al., Interim cosmetic and toxicity results from RAPID: A randomized trial of accelerated partial breast irradiation using three-dimensional conformal external beam radiation therapy. *J Clin Oncol.* 2013 10;31(32):4038–4045.
10. Formenti SC, Hsu H, Fenton-Kerimian M, Roses D, Guth A, Jozsef G, Goldberg JD, Dewyngaert JK. Prone accelerated partial breast irradiation after breast-conserving surgery: Five-year results of 100 patients. *Int J Radiat Oncol Biol Phys.* 2012 1;84(3):606–611.
11. Jagsi R, Ben-David MA, Moran JM, Marsh RB, Griffith KA, Hayman JA, Pierce LJ. Unacceptable cosmesis in a protocol investigating intensity-modulated radiotherapy with active breathing control for accelerated partial-breast irradiation. *Int J Radiat Oncol Biol Phys.* 2010 1;76(1):71–78.
12. Hepel JT, Tokita M, MacAusland SG, Evans SB, Hiatt JR, Price LL, DiPetrillo T, Wazer DE. Toxicity of three-dimensional conformal radiotherapy for accelerated partial breast irradiation. *Int J Radiat Oncol Biol Phys.* 2009 Dec 1;75(5):1290–1296.
13. Yarnold J, Bentzen SM, Coles C, Haviland J. Hypofractionated whole-breast radiotherapy for women with early breast cancer: Myths and realities. *Int J Radiat Oncol Biol Phys.* 2011 1;79(1):1–9.
14. NSABP B-39, RTOG 0413: A randomized phase III study of conventional whole breast irradiation versus partial breast irradiation for women with stage 0, I, or II breast cancer. *Clin Adv Hematol Oncol.* 2006;4(10):719–721.
15. Coles CE, Griffin CL, Kirby AM, Titley J, Agrawal RK, Alhasso A, Bhattacharya IS et al., Partial-breast radiotherapy after breast conservation surgery for patients with early breast cancer (UK IMPORT LOW trial): 5-year results from a multicentre, randomised, controlled, phase 3, non-inferiority trial. *Lancet.* 2017;390(10099):1048–1060.
16. Meattini I, Livi L, Pallotta S, Marrazzo L. Partial breast irradiation: The time is there! *Breast.* 2018;38:98–100.
17. Polgar C, Van Limbergen E, Potter R et al. Patient selection for accelerated partial-breast irradiation (APBI) after breast-conserving surgery: Recommendations of the groupe Europeen de curietherapie-European society for therapeutic radiology and oncology (GEC-ESTRO) breast cancer working group based on clinical evidence (2009). *Radiother Oncol* 2010;94:264e73.
18. Correa C, Harris EE, Leonardi MC et al. Accelerated partial breast irradiation: Executive summary for the update of an ASTRO evidence-based consensus statement. *Pract Radiat Oncol* 2017;7:73e9.

30

Whole breast radiotherapy (boost) after partial mastectomy

AT A GLANCE

A boost of irradiation to the site of tumor excision has been shown to improve local control at 10 years in both younger and older women, although reduction in rates of local recurrence was <5% for women aged >60 years. Nonetheless, this additional dose of radiation as a component of breast-conservation therapy can exacerbate breast fibrosis and shrinkage and should be used selectively with consideration of skin-sparing mastectomy with whole breast reconstruction as a preferable option to optimize oncologic and cosmetic outcomes. For those patients who require an additional "boost" of radiation treatment to the tumor bed and adjacent tissues, this can be delivered as an intraoperative dose at the time of surgery using either a low energy x-ray source or electron beam therapy. After recovery from the surgical procedure, external beam therapy can be administered with potentially fewer complications. This technique may help destroy microscopic residual tumor cells which might otherwise remain in the surgical field for a period of 4-6 weeks before commencing conventional radiotherapy.

30.1 BOOST OR NO BOOST TO TUMOR BED WITH WHOLE BREAST RADIOTHERAPY AFTER PARTIAL MASTECTOMY

Laura Lozza

Breast conservative surgery followed by whole breast irradiation remains the standard treatment for early breast cancer: randomized trials conducted during the 1970s to the 1990s established the efficacy of breast-conservation therapy as an alternative to mastectomy.[1,2] Satisfactory aesthetic results from breast-conservation therapy have been aided by progress in oncoplastic surgery.[3]

Whole breast radiotherapy is given by conventional (50 Gy/25 fractions) or biologically equivalent hypofractionated regimens, followed by an additional dose of 10–16 Gy to the tumor bed and lowers both the risk of local recurrence[4] and improves overall survival for breast-conserving surgery patients.[5]

Boosting the tumor bed

WHY?

The rationale for boosting the tumor bed is based on several premises: (a) the radiobiological observation of a dose-response relationship for breast cancer, (b) clinical evidence that nearly 70% of the ipsilateral breast recurrences are located in or very close to the primary site,[6] and (c) data supporting the presence of residual microscopic foci around the lumpectomy site.[7]

Randomized phase III trials have confirmed that a boost dose increases rates of local control without modifying either metastasis-free nor overall survival.[8–11]

The 20-year outcomes report from the landmark EORTC 22881–10882 trial which randomized more than 5000 patents to boost versus no boost confirm the impact of a boost on the cumulative incidence of ipsilateral breast tumor recurrence (16.4% in the no boost group versus 12.0% in the boost group). These benefits are greatest in young patients and there is an increased risk of moderate to severe fibrosis when used (1.8% in the no boost group versus 5.2% in the boost group, p < 0.0001).[8]

WHERE?

The optimal delineation of the tumor is usually based on preoperative physical examination, mammograms, ultrasound,[12] or magnetic resonance imaging.[13] Defining the tumor bed can be challenging and the advantages of a multidisciplinary approach for tumor bed localization have been demonstrated in a recent study.[14] Evidence of a postoperative cavity and especially surgical clips placed at the time of lumpectomy[15] will aid interpretation of computed tomography simulation images and aid calculation of tumor bed volume. The precise dosage of a local boost may also depend on the pathologist's assessment of cancer at the inked margin. Nonetheless, all these methods for identification of the tumor bed are limited and the position of the patient for treatment differs between the diagnostic and operating scenarios.[16,17] Furthermore, oncoplastic techniques have engendered new challenges for the radiation oncologist.

Oncoplastic breast surgery has become widespread in recent years,[18] with a variety of plastic surgery techniques employed to provide an aesthetically improved breast shape.

Oncoplastic breast-conserving surgical techniques with parenchymal rearrangement present fresh challenges in terms of localization of the tumor bed and subsequent delivery of a local radiotherapy boost.[19,20] Surgical incisions may have no relationship to the site of the original cancer, and the tumor bed cavity itself may be surgically dissected and separated with different portions ending up in different quadrants of the reconstructed breast.[21]

For the radiation oncologist, localization of the tumor bed can be problematic, if not impossible, and this raises concerns that the risk of local recurrence may be increased if a local boost cannot be delivered. It is therefore important that radiation oncologists and surgeons carefully discuss together these patients undergoing oncoplastic surgery, especially when there has been extensive tissue rearrangement.

HOW?

A boost of between 10 and 16 Gy after whole breast radiotherapy can be applied with several methods including direct electron beams, conformal or reduced tangential photon fields, intensity-modulated radiotherapy, brachytherapy implants, or intraoperative radiotherapy (IORT) techniques. In most studies comparing different boost techniques, no significant differences have emerged for rates of local control and cosmetic outcome.[22,23]

Brachytherapy delivers a high dose over a short time period within a reduced volume and can be adapted for treatment of deeply placed target volumes in large voluminous breasts. This results in a better distribution of dose. In comparison to high energy electrons or photons by reduced tangential fields, this technique allows for reduction of both the skin dose and the volume of tissue receiving a high dose due to improved conformation and underdosing of superficial tissues. Once the energy necessary to cover a deep target volume exceeds 9 MeV, the skin dose increases significantly and the risk of telangiectasia exceeds 10%.[24] On the other hand, if the target volume is superficial or if the volume of boost for brachytherapy is less than 5 mm from the surface, the rate of telangiectasia rises.[25] Intensity-modulated radiotherapy in these circumstances can protect the skin by provision of a more focal and deeply sited irradiation dose.[26]

There is a growing interest in IORT, with much of the evidence for an intraoperative boost preceding whole breast radiotherapy originating from electron treatments with single doses of around 10 Gy. These techniques are associated with exceptionally low local recurrence rates on long-term analysis in selected lower-risk patients. Compared to other boost methods, IORT has the advantage of direct visualization of the tumor bed during surgery which guarantees an accurate dose delivery. This also has relevance in terms of primary reconstruction after lumpectomy and can help optimize cosmetic outcomes. Of particular note, IORT is performed before any mobilization of breast tissue for oncoplastic purposes. As a consequence of direct tissue exposure without distension by hematoma/seroma, IORT permits small treatment volumes and complete sparing of skin which has a positive effect on late tissue tolerance and, hence, cosmetic appearance.[27]

Fibrosis is the most common side effect with IORT and may compromise aesthetic results. In the EORTC trial, the cumulative incidence of severe fibrosis was 1.8% at 20 years in patients without a boost versus 5.2% in the boost group (p < 0.0001).[8]

A randomized trial showed changes in appearance of the breast in more than half (52%) of women at 2 years following two-dimensional conventional breast irradiation. This compared with one-third of patients (36%) when intensity-modulated radiotherapy was employed to maximize homogeneity of breast irradiation.[28]

The criteria for selecting the best technique remain uncertain; decisions may depend on experience of individual units, the preferences of both radiotherapist and patient together with specific parameters of the tumor, costs, and quality of life of patients.

WHEN?

It is a common practice to add a boost dose to the tumor bed after the whole breast radiotherapy schedule, but the optimal timing and scheduling (combination, sequential, or concomitant) has yet to be established.

Incorporation of the boost dose within whole breast irradiation (conventional or hypofractionated) with concurrent delivery, concomitant boost, or simultaneous integrated boost represents an interesting and promising field for clinical research.[29] This strategy has been shown to provide a dosimetric advantage in terms of both organs at risk and target volumes,[7] and its impact on reducing treatment time represents a useful option to optimize treatments both for patients and healthcare providers.

CONCLUSION

The increase of dose to the tumor bed after breast-conserving surgery improves the rate of local control without unduly compromising aesthetic results. Different techniques can be used to deliver this boost and comparison between different techniques has shown no significant differences either for local control or aesthetic results. No randomized trials have been conducted comparing these techniques to draw any definitive conclusions about choice of the optimal technique.

Recent studies on hypofractionated radiotherapy for breast cancer[30] show very low local recurrence rates with whole breast radiotherapy without a local boost. There has been a progressive decline in rates of local recurrence, related to: (a) refinements in selection criteria for breast-conserving surgery, (b) improvements in preoperative breast imaging, (c) achieving negative surgical margins, (d) progress in radiation delivery, and (e) increased use of adjuvant systemic treatment.[23]

It is rational to tailor use of a tumor bed boost according to risk of local recurrence,[31] and some patients undergoing conservation surgery with negative pathologic margins and oncoplastic reconstruction could be adequately treated with whole breast radiotherapy without a boost.[21] Young age is a risk factor for local recurrence in several studies.[32,33] Furthermore, node-positive breast cancer and estrogen receptor negative tumors are associated with a higher risk of local recurrence, although until recently the issue of close margins and local recurrence was controversial.[23]

Application of a boost is recommended for patients under the age of 40 with larger high-grade tumors, close surgical margins, high proliferation indices, negative hormone receptors, and an extensive intraductal component.[26] Additional irradiation dose should be avoided in the majority of patients older than age 60 years.[8,31] We have returned to the need for radiation oncologists to answer the question of the indications to deliver or not a local boost. The more things change, the more they remain the same.[21]

REFERENCES

1. Poortmans P. Evidence based radiation oncology: Breast cancer. *Radiother Oncol* 2007; 84: 84–101.
2. Litiere S, Werutsky G, Fentiman IS et al. Breast-conserving therapy versus mastectomy for stage I–II breast cancer: 20 year follow up of the EORTC 10801 phase 3 randomized trial. *Lancet Oncol* 2012; 13: 412–419.

3. Hennequin C. Late sequelae and cosmetic outcome after radiotherapy in breast conserving therapy. *Cancer Radiother* 2012; 16: 462–469.
4. Clarke M, Collins R, Darby S et al. Effects of radiotherapy and of differences in the extent of surgery for early breast cancer on local recurrence and 15-year survival: An overview of the randomised trials. *Lancet* 2005; 366: 2087–2106.
5. Early Breast Cancer Trialists Collaborative Group (EBCTCG). Effect of radiotherapy after breast-conserving surgery on 10-year recurrence and 15-yer breast cancer death meta-analysis of individual patient data for 10801 women in 17 randomised trials. *Lancet* 2011; 378: 1707–1716.
6. Freedman GM, Anderson PR, Hanlon AI et al. Pattern of local recurrence after conservative surgery and whole breast irradiation. *Int J Radiat Oncol Biol Phys* 2005; 61: 1328–1336.
7. Franco P, Cante D, Sciacero P et al. Tumor bed boost integration during whole breast radiotherapy: A review of the current evidence. *Breast Care* 2015; 10: 44–49.
8. Bartelink H, Maingon P, Poortmans P et al., European organisation for research and treatment of cancer radiation oncology and breast cancer groups. Whole-breast irradiation with or without a boost for patients treated with breast-conserving surgery for early breast cancer: 20-year follow-up of a randomised phase 3 trial. *Lancet Oncol* 2015; 16: 47–56. doi:10.1016/S1470-2045(14)71156-8.
9. Romestaing P, Lehingue Y, Carrie C et al. Role of a 10 Gy boost in the conservative treatment of early breast cancer: Results of a randomized clinical trial in Lyon, France. *J Clin Oncol* 1997; 15: 963–968.
10. Polgar C, Fodor J, Orosz Z et al. Electron and high dose rate brachytherapy boost in the conservative treatment of stage I-II breast cancer. First results of the randomized Budapest Boost trial. *Strahlenther Oncol* 2002; 176: 615–623.
11. Graham P, Browne LH, Capp A et al. The St George Wollongong and Liverpool breast boost trial: 1st planned analysis at 6 year median follow up. *Australas Radiol* 2007; 51: (suppl 3): A85.
12. Coles CE, Cash CJ, Treece GM et al. High definition three-dimensional ultrasound to localise the tumour bed: A breast radiotherapy planning study. *Radiother Oncol* 2007; 84: 233–241.
13. Whipp EC, Halliwell M. Magnetic resonance imaging appearances in the postoperative breast: The clinical target volume-tumor and its relationship to the chest wall. *Int J Radiat Oncol Biol Phys* 2008; 72: 49–57.
14. Kirova YM, Fournier-Bidoz N, Servois V et al. How to boost the tumor bed? A multidisciplinary approach in eight steps. *Int J Radiat Oncol Biol Phys* 2008; 72: 494–500.
15. Weed DW, Yan D, Martinez AA et al. The validity of surgical clips as a radiographic surrogate for the lumpectomy cavity in image-guided accelerated partial breast irradiation. *Int J Radiat Oncol Biol Phys* 2004; 60: 484–492.
16. Oden S, Thureau S, Baron M, Hanzen C. Traitement conservateur du cancer du sein: Optimisation du repérage du lit tumoral. *Cancer/Radiothérapie* 2010; 14: 96–102.

17. Lee PY, Lin CY, Chen SW et al. A topology-based method to mitigate the dosimetric uncertainty caused by the positional variation of boost volume in breast conservative radiotherapy. *Radiat oncol* 2017; 12:55.

18. Rietjens M, Urban CA, Rey PC et al. Long-term oncological results of breast conservative treatment with oncoplastic surgery. *Breast* 2007; 16: 387–395.

19. Schaverien MV, Stallard S, Dodwell D et al. Use of boost radiotherapy in oncoplastic breast-conserving surgery—A systematic review. *Eur J Surg Oncol* 2013; 39: 1179–1185.

20. Furet E, Peurien D, Fournier-Bidoz N et al. Plastic surgery for breast conservation therapy: How to define the volume of the tumor bed for the boost? *Eur J Surg Oncol* 2014; 40: 830–834.

21. Pezner RD. The oncoplastic breast surgery challenge to the local radiation boost. *Int J Radiat Oncol Biol Phys* 2011; 4: 963–964.

22. Hill-Kayser C, Chacko D, Hwang WT et al. Long-term clinical and cosmetic outcomes after breast conservation treatment for women with early-stage breast carcinoma according to the type of breast boost. *Int J Radiat Oncol Biol Phys* 2011; 79: 1048–1054.

23. Verhoeven K, Kindts I, Laenen A et al. A comparison of three different radiotherapy boost techniques after breast conserving therapy for breast cancer. *The Breast* 2015; 24: 391–396.

24. Turesson I, Notter G. The influence of fraction size in radiotherapy on the late normal tissue reaction (I C II). *Int J Radiat Oncol Biol Phys* 1984; 10: 593–606.

25. Van Limbergen E, Pescova-Georg P. The source-skin distance measuring bridge (SSMB) reduces indeed skin telangiectasia after interstitial boost in breast conserving therapy (BCT) for breast cancer: 15 years of clinical experience. *Radiother Oncol* 2000; 55: 32.

26. Graham P, Fourquet A. Placing the boost in breast-conservation radiotherapy: A review of the role, indications and techniques for breast-boost radiotherapy. *Clin Oncol* 2006; 18: 210–219.

27. Sedlmayer F, Reitsamer R, Fussl C et al. Boost IORT in breast cancer: Body of evidence. *Int J Breast Cancer* 2014; 1–6.

28. Donovan E, Bleakley N, Denholm E et al. Randomised trial of standard 2D radiotherapy (RT) versus 3D intensity modulated radiotherapy (IMRT) in patients prescribed breast radiotherapy. *Radiother Oncol* 2002; 64: 15.

29. Souchon R, Sautter-Bihl ML, Sedlmayer F et al. On behalf of the breast cancer expert panel of the German society of radiation oncology (DEGRO): Radiation oncologists view on the Zurich consensus. *Breast Care* 2013; 8: 448–452.

30. Whelan TJ, Pignol JP, Levine MN et al. Long-term results of hyofractionated radiation therapy for breast cancer. *New Engl J Med* 2010; 362: 513–520.

31. Buchholz TA. Use of a tumor bed boost as a part of radiotherapy for breast cancer. *Lancet Oncol* 2015; 16: 5–6.

32. Chen W., Sonke JJ, Stroom J et al. The effect of age in breast conserving therapy: A retrospective analysis on pathology and clinical outcome data. *Radiother Oncol* 2015; 114: 314–321. doi:10.1016/j.radonc.2015.01.010.

33. Kindts I, Laenen A, Depuydt T, et al. Tumour bed boost radiotherapy for women after breast-conserving surgery. Cochrane Database of Systematic Reviews 2017, Issue S1.

30.2 OPTIONS FOR DELIVERY OF RADIOTHERAPY BOOST DOSE AFTER PARTIAL MASTECTOMY

Kathryn Huber and David Wazer

There are several technical options for delivery of a tumor-bed boost as part of adjuvant whole breast external beam radiation. The boost methods allowed as part of the prospective randomized trials that showed improved local control from tumor-bed boost include an *en-face* electron field, multi-catheter interstitial brachytherapy with Ir-192, and mini-tangent photon fields.[1,2] Modern techniques also include simultaneous integrated boost, non-invasive image-guided brachytherapy boost, and intraoperative boost. With so many options, what factors should a radiation oncologist consider when choosing a method of boost delivery? Often selection of method is driven by comfort of the radiation oncologist with a technique and available resources. However, size, shape, and location of the tumor bed in relation to the size and shape of the patient's breast should factor into this decision.

Currently, *en-face* electrons are most commonly utilized for boost delivery given their wide availability and ease of use. One of the challenges of this method is definition of the tumor bed volume. There are several studies that have shown that use of clinical exam and the lumpectomy scar to guide delineation of the tumor bed are inaccurate in the absence of three-dimentional imaging.[3–5] Three-dimensional images may be obtained using computed tomography (CT); however, ultrasound has also been found to be a robust method for identification of the tumor bed. This information, along with operative report and palpation of the breast, is used to define the composite area of the electron field. An additional 2–3 cm of margin is placed around this area to allow for adequate coverage of the target volume. This additional margin is needed to allow for the constriction of the electron beam's dose deposition at depth, as well as to account for uncertainty in the tumor bed location due to set up error and breathing motion. Therefore, one of the shortcomings of this technique is the need for relatively large treatment volumes that often include the nipple-areola complex that can result in increased acute and late toxicity.

In addition, many patients have tumor beds that are located deep along the chest wall with significant overlying breast tissue. Tumor bed coverage of these deep tumors would require use of electron energy over 15 MeV and spillage of the radiation dose beyond the chest wall. This results in excess radiation into the lung and, in some left-sided breast targets, the heart. Prior to the development of technology for electron boost, multi-catheter interstitial brachytherapy was established as a reliable and flexible method for delivering a tumor-bed boost.[6,7] No other method of boost delivery has the same level of conformality, and it is ideal for deep-seated tumor beds. However, there is a significant level of user dependence to ensure tumor bed coverage without areas of dose heterogeneity that result in increased risk of fat necrosis.[8] A more widely utilized method of delivering a boost dose to a deep-seated tumor bed is with mini-tangent photon fields. This utilizes a pair of tangential fields that are similar to whole breast fields; however, gantry angle and the deep border are altered in order to come off the underlying lung and heart and the superior and inferior borders are reduced to 1.5–2 cm from the edge of the tumor bed. Compared to an electron boost, mini-tangents are able to provide the prescribed dose to more of a deep-seated tumor bed with less spillage to the thoracic organs. However, this method tends to treat to an even larger volume of breast tissue, which could result in a greater risk of a poor cosmetic outcome.

Similar to mulit-catheter interstitial brachytherapy, non-invasive image-guided breast brachytherapy (NIBB) is a feasible boost option that eliminates the need for volume expansion to account for breathing motion and set up uncertainties associated with external beam irradiation.[9] With this method, the tumor bed is identified at the time of each treatment through the use of mammography-based radiographs that guide the placement of an 192Ir applicator. As with mammography, compressing the breasts to obtain orthogonal views optimizes visualization of the tumor bed. Due to the decrease in irradiated breast volume and relative skin-sparing of this technique, NIBB may have a favorable toxicity profile compared to electron boost, while providing excellent local control.[10,11] Unfortunately, one limitation of the 192Ir applicator used in NIBB is that treatment of deep-seated tumors is unachievable due to the inability to fully compress tissue immediately abutting the chest wall. In addition, NIBB applicators are not widely available and treatment delivery can be lengthy.

For each of these methods discussed so far, an impediment to delivery is the added time a patient needs to come for daily treatments to an already long course of conventionally fractionated adjuvant breast radiation. One method to decrease this burden is the use of a simultaneous integrated boost.[12–15] The tumor-bed boost is interdigitated within the whole breast treatment by delivering a higher dose per fraction to this region. This method relies on the observation that the majority of in-breast local recurrence occurs near the tumor bed, allowing for a decreased whole breast dose, which provides a favorable toxicity profile despite acceleration.[16] Encouraging results have also been reported for the use of intensity-modulated radiation therapy for the safe delivery simultaneous integrated boost within a hypofractionated course of treatment.[13,15] Currently, there is no one method of tumor-bed boost delivery that is superior in all clinical situations. However, long-term outcomes of integration of tumor-bed boost into a hypofractionated regimen will likely be the focus of future investigation.

REFERENCES

1. Romestaing P et al. Role of a 10-Gy boost in the conservative treatment of early breast cancer: Results of a randomized clinical trial in Lyon, France. *J Clin Oncol* 1997; 15:963–968.

2. Bartelink H et al. Impact of a higher radiation dose on local control and survival in breast-conserving therapy of early breast cancer: 10-year results of the randomized boost versus no boost EORTC 22881-10882 trial. *J Clin Oncol* 2007; 25:3259–3265.

3. Machtay M et al. Inaccuracies in using the lumpectomy scar for planning electron boosts in primary breast carcinoma. *Int J Radiat Oncol Biol Phys* 1994; 30:43–48.

4. Oh KS et al. Planning the breast tumor bed boost: Changes in the excision cavity volume and surgical scar location after breast-conserving surgery and whole-breast irradiation. *Int J Radiat Oncol Biol Phys* 1996; 66:680–686.

5. Solin LJ et al. A practical technique for the localization of the tumor volume in definitive irradiation of the breast. *Int J Radiat Oncol Biol Phys* 1995; 11:1215–1220.

6. Pierquin B et al. The Paris System in interstitial radiation therapy. *Acta Radiol Oncol Radiat Phys Biol* 1978; 17:33–48.

7. Mansfield CM et al. Intraoperative interstitial implantation of Iridium 192 in the breast. *Radiology* 1984; 150:600.

8. Wazer DE et al. Clinically evident fat necrosis in women treated with high-dose-rate brachytherapy alone for early-stage breast cancer. *Int J Radiat Oncol Biol Phys* 2001; 50:107–111.

9. Hamid S et al. A multi-institutional study of feasibility, implementation and early clinical results with noninvasive breast brachytherapy for tumor bed boost. *Int J Radiat Oncol Biol Phys* 2012; 83:1374–1380.

10. Sioshansi S et al. Dose modeling of noninvasive image-guided breast brachytherapy in comparison to electron beam boost and three-dimensional conformal accelerated partial breast irradiation. *Int J Radiat Oncol Biol Phys* 2011; 80:410–416.

11. Leonard KL et al. Breast boost using noninvasive image-guided breast brachytherapy vs. external beam: A 2:1 matched-pair analysis. *Clin Breast Cancer* 2013; 13:455–459.

12. Dellas K et al. Hypofractionation with simultaneous integrated boost for early stage breast cancer. *Strahlenther Onkol* 2014; 7:646–653.

13. Freedman GM et al. Five-year local control in a phase II study of hypofractionated intensity modulated radiation therapy with an incorporated boost for early stage breast cancer. *Int J Radiat Oncol Biol Phys* 2012; 84:888–893.

14. Trombetta M et al. Reduction in radiation-induced morbidity by use of intercurrent boost in the management of early-stage breast cancer. *Int J Radiat Oncol Biol Phys* 2010; 77:1303–1308.

15. Askoxylakis V et al. Simultaneous integrated boost for adjuvant treatment of breast cancer-intensity modulated vs. conventional radiotherapy: The IMRT-MC2 trial. *BMC Cancer* 2011; 11:249–257.

16. Veronesi U et al. Radiotherapy after breast-conserving surgery in small breast carcinoma: Long-term results of a randomized trial. *Ann Oncol* 2001; 12:997–1003.

30.3 INTRAOPERATIVE BRACHYTHERAPY PLUS POSTOPERATIVE LINEAR ACCELERATOR FOR WHOLE BREAST RADIOTHERAPY

Kathryn Huber and David Wazer

To date, there are no randomized trials comparing the efficacy of boost delivery methods as part of breast-conservation therapy; however, non-randomized data support the view that intraoperative brachytherapy may provide a slightly lower rate of in-breast recurrence compared to external beam boost. Reitsamer et al. performed a matched pair retrospective analysis of 188 women who received a 12 Gy fractionated external beam electron boost to compare outcomes to 190 women who received a 9 Gy single fraction intraoperative brachytherapy electron boost at University Hospital Salzburg.[1] Both groups received >50 Gy of postoperative linear accelerator-based whole breast radiation. They report a statistically significant improvement of 5-year in-breast recurrence with intraoperative brachytherapy (0%) compared to external beam therapy (4.3%).[1] An *ad hoc* comparison of the method of boost used in EORTC "boost versus no boost" randomized trial also suggests superior 5-year local recurrence for intraoperative brachytherapy (2.5%) compared to electron (4.8%) or photon (4.0%) external beam therapy.[2] In addition, several single institution reports confirm excellent local control rates achieved using intraoperative brachytherapy.[3–5] However, most impressive are the long-term, pooled results of over 1100 patients treated with intraoperative brachytherapy at seven European centers.[6] This analysis yielded a remarkable 0.8% in-breast recurrence rate for intraoperative brachytherapy (IB) with a median follow-up of over 6 years.

What features of intraoperative brachytherapy might be contributing to such favorable outcomes? Firstly, contrary to external beam therapy where the clinician must reconstruct the location of the tumor bed, the intraoperative brachytherapy operator has direct visualization of the tumor bed, providing a substantial targeting advantage. In addition, there may be a biological advantage to delivering a radiation boost at the time of a partial mastectomy. Conventional external beam radiation cannot begin until 5–6 weeks after the surgery to allow for sufficient healing. However, in patients with subclinical residual disease, cells can theoretically begin to multiply during the postoperative period. With intraoperative brachytherapy, adjuvant radiation is begun at the time of resection, when there is the lowest number of clonogens. Next, the biologically effective dose delivered in intraoperative brachytherapy regimens is approximately double what is delivered with external beam therapy according to the linear-quadratic model with a postulated breast tumor α/β ratio of 4.[6] Finally, in addition to delivery of a higher biological dose in the setting of limited clonogens, the low local recurrence rate following intraoperative brachytherapy may be ascribed to damping of stimulatory growth factors expressed in surgical wound healing, thereby inhibiting residual tumor cell proliferation and invasion.[7]

These advantages could be offset by incomplete pathologic analysis of margin status at the time of surgery. Tumor-bed boost cannot compensate for any added recurrence risk ascribed to positive margins.[8] Therefore, it is vital that the patient be treated with re-excision if there are positive margins, even in the setting of intraoperative brachytherapy. The reported cosmetic outcomes following intraoperative brachytherapy with conventional partial mastectomy are quite varied, with "good-to-excellent" results in 60%–90% cases and up to 50% seroma formation.[9,10] The advent of oncoplastic reconstruction has allowed excellent cosmetic outcomes with larger margins, leading to less chance of margin positivity.[11] A single-institution experience of intraoperative brachytherapy following oncoplastic reconstruction described outstanding outcomes with only 2% seroma formation and "excellent" cosmesis reported by more than 90% of patients.[12] The combination of intraoperative brachytherapy and oncoplastic reconstruction presents an excellent opportunity for maximizing local tumor control and cosmetic outcomes in women with early-stage breast cancer and warrants further investigation.

REFERENCES

1. Reitsamer R et al. The Salzburg concept of intraoperative radiotherapy for breast cancer: Results and considerations. *Int J Cancer* 2006; 118:2882–2887.

2. Poortmans P et al. The influence of the boost technique on local control in breast conserving treatment in the EORTC "boost versus no boost" randomized trial. *Radiother and Oncol* 2004; 72:25–33.

3. Lemanski C et al. Intraoperative radiotherapy given as a boost for early breast cancer: Long-term clinical and cosmetic results. *Int J Radiat Oncol Biol Phys* 2006; 64:1410–1415.

4. Chang DW et al. Prospective study of local control and late radiation toxicity after intraoperative radiation therapy boost for early breast cancer. *Int J Radiat Oncol Biol Phys* 2014; 88:73–79.

5. Wenz F et al. Intraoperative radiotherapy as a boost during breast-conserving surgery using low-kilovoltage X-rays: The first 5 years of experience with a novel approach. *Int J Radiat Oncol Biol Phys* 2010; 77:1309–1314.

6. Fastner G et al. IORT with electrons as boost strategy during breast conserving therapy in limited stage breast cancer: Long term results of an ISIORT pooled analysis. *Radiother Oncol* 2013; 108:279–286.

7. Belletti B et al. Targeted intraoperative radiotherapy impairs the stimulation of breast cancer cell proliferation and invasion caused by surgical wounding. *Clin Ca Res* 2008; 14:1325–1332.

8. Bartelink H et al. Impact of a higher radiation dose on local control and survival in breast-conserving therapy of early breast cancer: 10-year results of the randomized boost versus no boost EORTC 22881-10882 trial. *J Clin Oncol* 2007; 25:3259-3265.

9. Senthi S et al. Cosmetic outcome and seroma formation after breast-conserving surgery with intraoperative radiation therapy boost for early breast cancer. *Int J Rad Onc Biol Phys* 2012; 84:e139-e144.

10. Kraus-Tiefebacher U et al. Long-term toxicity of an intraoperative radiotherapy boost using low energy X-rays during breast-conserving surgery. *Int J Rad Onc Biol Phys* 2006; 66:377-381.

11. Clough K et al. Positive margins after oncoplastic surgery for breast cancer. *Ann Surg Oncol* 2015; 22:4247-4253.

12. Malter W et al. Intraoperative boost radiotherapy during targeted oncoplastic breast surgery: Overview and single center experience. *Int J of Breast Ca* 2014:1-6.

30.4 INTRAOPERATIVE LINEAR ACCELERATOR PLUS POSTOPERATIVE LINEAR ACCELERATOR FOR WHOLE BREAST RADIOTHERAPY

Laura Lozza

The use of intraoperative radiation therapy (IORT) with either linear accelerator-based electron beams (IOERT) or low kilovoltage energy x-rays is increasingly popular for the treatment of early-stage breast cancer and has the advantage of reducing overall treatment time and potentially improving quality of life.[1-3]

In a pooled analysis undertaken by the International Society of Intraoperative Radiation Therapy,[4] IORT was used in 52.2% of cases as a single radiation modality in which it replaced a course of whole breast irradiation (WBRT), while in the remaining cases (47.8%), it was employed as a boost at the time of surgical excision, with the dose ranging from 8 Gy to 12 Gy for electrons and 8 Gy–20 Gy for low energy x-rays.

When used as a boost, IORT delivers a highly effective biological dose in a single fraction which can inhibit the proliferation of tumor cells during the interval between surgery and WBRT and also during fractionated WBRT.[5] Direct visualization of the target volume at the time of IORT ensures appropriate coverage of the breast tissue at risk and to some extent overcomes the limits of conventional postoperative methods in identifying the tumor bed on CT images and reducing the risk of geographic miss. Moreover, the intraoperative technique avoids excessive irradiation of skin and normal tissues such as heart, lung, and ribs.

A particular difficulty with IORT when used as a boost is that tumor pathology is not available at the time of surgery, those patients with positive margins will require re-excision and it may be ineffective or make further surgery more prone to complications. Interpretation of pathological specimens after re-excision of margins may be more difficult and examination of re-excision margins more complex.[6]

The first clinical study of IOERT as a boost dose (10 Gy followed by 50 Gy WBRT) was by Lemanski and colleagues,[7] who reported a 10-year disease-free survival of 83% and good to excellent cosmesis. Fastner and colleagues[8] undertook a pooled analysis of 1110 patients treated with IOERT boost: a median dose of 10 Gy was applied before administering 50–54 Gy WBRT. The 7-year local control rate was 99.2%. For all risk subgroups, rates of local control compared favorably to data reported from other trials with similar length of follow-up, irrespective of which boost method was used.[9,10]

In a retrospective matched-pair analysis, 188 patients with an external boost were compared to the first 190 patients in a pooled analysis of IOERT[11]: at 10-year follow-up, local recurrence rates in the external boost and IOERT groups were 7.2% and 1.6%, respectively. In a series of 211 patients, the role of an IOERT boost (12 Gy) before hypofractionated WBRT (37.05 Gy in 13 daily fractions of 2.85 Gy) has been explored.[12] At a relatively short median follow-up of 9 months, a single case each of grade 3 and grade 4 skin toxicities were found among 108 patients evaluated for late toxicity.

In January 2011, a multicenter trial investigating hypofractionated WBRT (2.7 Gy × 15 fractions) following a 10 Gy IOERT boost was initiated. It is essential that both tumor control and cosmesis (even if tolerance seems excellent) are fully evaluated with long-term follow-up.[13]

Compared to IOERT, clinical experience following IORT boost using low kilovoltage x-rays[14,15] is limited: despite similar criteria for patient selection, sample sizes were significantly smaller and results appear somewhat inferior. One possible explanation for worse local control might relate to superior coverage of breast tissue obtained with electrons, where the tumor bed is treated with uniformly high doses.[16]

Moreover, clinical volumes often appear asymmetric, and this is better compensated by IOERT in terms of spatial direction of dose deposition (margin-directed applicator guidance).[17]

IORT can also be delivered pre-lumpectomy: Yu and colleagues[5] demonstrated the feasibility and safety of 8 Gy IOERT delivered prior to surgery and followed by conventional WBRT in patients with sentinel lymph node metastases or aged younger than 40 years. At a follow-up of 3 years, there was acceptable cosmesis and short-term efficacy in terms of local control.

Large fraction sizes have historically been associated with increased late toxicity, and there is much interest and potential concern about late effects following a single high breast dose of IORT.

First analysis by Sperk and colleagues[18] of long-term toxicity among women who participated in the TARGIT-A trial reported very low rates of chronic skin toxicity and acceptable long-term results in patients treated with a 50 kilovoltage x-ray boost.

No difference was described in cosmetic outcomes after IORT boost patients in comparison to conventional groups in two trials:[19,20] results were rated as good or excellent in 86%–91% of cases for IORT boost and 81%–96% for the control groups.

Excellent tolerance for an IORT boost in conjunction with WBRT was confirmed by Forouzannia and colleagues:[21] none of their 50 patients treated experienced grade 3 or greater toxicity. Although two patients had delayed wound healing, there were no wound infections.

The longest duration of follow-up is provided by Lemanski and colleagues,[7] who reported grade 2 late subcutaneous fibrosis within the boost area in 14% of 42 recurrence-free patients after a median follow-up of 9 years. Overall cosmesis was scored to be good to excellent.

Based on their experience with 48 patients, Wenz and colleagues[22] found inferior cosmetic results when the time interval between orthovoltage IORT and onset of WBRT was less than 30 days.

Even though these various studies used different cosmetic scoring systems, there is no evidence for any consistent negative impact on cosmesis from use of IRT as a boost compared to conventional techniques.[15]

By contrast, an IORT boost may lead to more frequent fat necrosis and localized parenchymal scarring with the need for careful interpretation of mammographic and/or magnetic resonance images by experienced radiologists in uncertain cases.[23,24]

REFERENCES

1. Veronesi U, Orecchia R, Maisonneuve P *et al.* Intraoperative radiotherapy versus external radiotherapy for early breast cancer (ELIOT) a randomized controlled equivalent trial. *Lancet Oncol* 2013; 14:1269–1277.
2. Williams NR, Pigott KH, Keshtgar MRS. Intraoperative radiotherapy in the treatment of breast cancer: A review of the evidence. *Int J Breast Cancer* 2011; 2011:375170. doi:10.4061/2011/375170.
3. Welzel G, Boch A, Sperk E *et al.* Radiation-related quality of life parameters after targeted intraoperative radiotherapy versus whole breast radiotherapy in patients with breast cancer: Results from the randomized phase III trial TARGIT-A. *Radiat Oncol* 2013; 8:9. doi:10.1186/1748-717X-8-9.
4. Krengli M, Sedimayer F, Calvo FA, *et al.* ISIORT pooled analysis 2013 update: Clinical and technical characteristics of intra-operative radiotherapy. *Transl Cancer Res* 2014; doi:10.3978/j.issn.2218-676X.2014.01.02.
5. Yu W, Lin Z, Ju ZJ *et al.* Intraoperative radiation therapy delivered prior to lumpectomy for early-stage breast cancer: A single institution study. *Am J Cancer Res* 2015; 5:2249–2257.
6. Hanna GG, Kirby AM. Intraoperative radiotherapy in early stage breast cancer: Potential indications and evidence to date. *Br J Radiol* 2015; 8 (1049):20140686. doi:10.1259/bjr.20140686.
7. Lemanski C, Azria D, Thezenas S *et al.* Intraoperative radiotherapy given as a boost for early breast cancer: Long term clinical and cosmetic results. *Int J Radiat Oncol Biol Phys* 2006; 64: 1410–1415.
8. Fastner G, Sedimayer F, Merz F *et al.* IORT with electrons as boost strategy during breast conserving therapy in limited stage breast cancer: Long term results of an ISIORT pooled analysis. *Radiother Oncol* 2013; 108: 279–286.
9. Poortmans PM, Collette L, Bartelink H *et al.* EORTC radiation oncology and breast cancer groups The addition of a boost dose on the primary tumour bed after lumpectomy in breast conserving treatment for breast cancer. A summary of the results of EORTC 22881–10882 "boost versus no boost" trial. *Cancer Radiother.* 2008;12 (6–7): 565–570. doi:10.1016/j.canrad.2008.07.014.
10. Clark M, Collins R, Darby S *et al.* Effects of radiotherapy and of differences in the extent of surgery for early breast cancer on local recurrence and 15 year survival: An overview of randomised trials. Early Breast Cancer Trialists'Collaborative Group (EBCTCG). *Lancet* 2005; 366: 2087–2106.

11. Fastner G, Reitsamer M, Kopp M *et al.* Intraoperative (IOERT) versus external electron boost in breast conserving operated breast cancer patients. 10-year results of a matched-pair analysis. *Strahlentherapie und Onkologie* 2011; 187: 73–74.
12. Ivaldi GB, Leonardi MC, Orecchia R *et al.* Preliminary results of electron intraoperative therapy boost and hypofractionated external beam radiotherapy after breast-conserving surgery in premenopausal women. *Int J Radiat Oncol Biol Phys* 2008; 72: 485–493.
13. Fastner G, Reitsamer M, Kopp M *et al.* Hypofractionated WBI plus IOERT boost in early stage breast cancer (HIOB); updated results of a prospective trial. *Radiother Oncol* 2014; 111: 201–202.
14. Valdya JS, Baum M, Tobias JS *et al.* Long term results of TARGeted intraoperative radiotherapy (Targit) boost during breast conserving surgery. *Int J Radiat Oncol Biol Phys* 2011; 81: 1091–1097.
15. Blank F, Kraus-Tiefenbacher U, Welzel G *et al.* Single-center long-term follow up after intraoperative radiotherapy as a boost during breast-conserving surgery using low-kilovoltage x-rays. *Ann Surg Oncol* 2010; 17: S352–S358.
16. Sedlmayer F, Reitsamer R, Fussl C *et al.* Boost IORT in breast cancer: Body of evidence. *Int J of Breast Cancer* 2014; 2014: 1–6.
17. Nairz O, Deutschmann H, Kopp M *et al.* A dosimetric comparison of IORT techniques in limited stage breast cancer. *Strahlentherapie und Onkologie* 2006; 182: 342–348.
18. Sperk E, Welzel G, Keller A *et al.* Late radiation toxicity after intraoperative radiotherapy (IORT) for breast cancer: Results from the randomized phase IIII trial TARGIT A. *Breast Cancer Res Treat.* 2012; 135: 253–260.
19. Ciabattoni A, Fortuna G, Ciccone V *et al.* IORT in breast cancer as a boost: Preliminary results pf a pilot randomized study on use of IORT for Stage I and II breast cancer. (abstract). *Radiother Oncol* 2004; 73 supplement: 35–36.
20. Forouzannia A, Harness JK, Carpenter MM *et al.* Intra-operative electron radiotherapy (IOERT) boost as a component of adjuvant radiation for breast cancer in the community setting. *Am Surg* 2012; 78: 1071–1074.
21. Reitsamer R, Peintiger F, Seldmayer F *et al.* Intraoperative radiotherapy given as a boost after breast conserving surgery in breast cancer patients. *Eur J Cancer* 2002; 38: 1607–1610.
22. Wenz F, Weizel G, Keller A. Early initiation of external beam radiotherapy (EBRT) may increase the risk of long-term toxicity in patients undergoing intraoperative radiotherapy (IORT) as a boost for breast cancer. *Breast* 2008; 17: 617–622.
23. Piroth MD, Fischedick K, Wein B *et al.* Fat necrosis and parenchymal scarring after breast-conserving surgery and radiotherapy with an intraoperative electron or fractionated, percutaneous boost: A retrospective comparison. *Breast Cancer* 2014; 21: 409–414.
24. Wasser K, Schnitzer A, Engel D *et al.* First description of MR mammographic findings in the tumor bed after intraoperative radiotherapy (IORT) of breast cancer. *Clin Imaging* 2012; 36: 176–184.

EDITORIAL COMMENTARY

This collection of chapters on techniques for delivery of radiotherapy underlines dramatic changes in approach to both irradiation of the chest wall after mastectomy and breast after conservation surgery. In terms of the latter, there have been two important developments reflecting improved understanding of radiobiological phenomena and the nature of ipsilateral breast tumor recurrence. Firstly, accelerated hypofractionated whole breast irradiation is now considered an acceptable alternative to conventional whole breast irradiation in which a dose of 40–50 Gy is delivered in 25 fractions over a 5–6 week period. Accelerated schedules for whole breast irradiation are well established in Canada, the United Kingdom, and continental Europe while being increasingly utilized in the United States. Recent studies have confirmed negligible long-term cardiac toxicity for left-sided tumors from higher fraction size (up to 2.7 Gy); concerns about potential cardiotoxicity have hitherto limited uptake of accelerated whole breast irradiation which is typically administered at a dosage of 40–42.5 Gy in 15 or 16 fractions over 22 days (compared with 35 days overall for a conventional schedule of 50 Gy in 25 fractions). Shorter courses of radiotherapy do not compromise local control with recurrence risk at 12 years of 6.7% and 6.2% for conventional and accelerated schedules respectively (Whelan T, et al. *NEJM* 2010; 312: 513–520). Thus breast cancer patients can safely be treated to a lower dose of 40 Gy in 15 fractions with no disadvantage in terms of local recurrence and greater patient convenience—especially in geographically more remote areas. Interestingly, the limits of hypofractionation are being explored in the FAST FORWARD trial that is currently recruiting its target of 4000 patients in the United Kingdom. Fractionation sensitivity is inversely associated with proliferation in normal tissues, and DNA repair processes provide a mechanistic link with relapsing tumors more likely to have high proliferation indices such as Ki-67. Nonetheless, there is currently no clear evidence for any differences in median Ki-67 values between recurrent and non-recurrent tumors (inconsistent cutoff values). At the extreme, some older patients with smaller, non-high-grade, node-negative tumors will derive minimal absolute benefits from any form of whole breast irradiation, and trials are in progress to determine whether breast radiotherapy can be omitted in a selected group of patients with hormone receptor-positive tumors and low Ki-67 who would receive endocrine treatment only (e.g., PRIMETIME study).

Instead of a reduction in total dosage of radiotherapy to the whole breast with hypofractionation, radiotherapy can be delivered to part of the breast only. This approach of partial breast irradiation is discussed in Chapter 26 and is based on the premise that most cases of local recurrence occur in and around the tumor bed. Hence partial breast radiotherapy targets those areas of the breast at greatest risk of local recurrence and should be associated with comparable rates of ipsilateral breast tumor recurrence. A particular advantage of partial breast irradiation is a reduction in late tissue effects leading to breast shrinkage and impaired cosmetic outcomes (along with quality of life). Although earlier trials of partial breast irradiation reported higher rates of recurrence and fibrosis, these failed to apply strict selection criteria and used a variety of modalities for delivery of radiotherapy. More recent trials of partial breast irradiation show promising results that are likely to lead to changes in practice.

Dr. Mukesh and Dr. Coles provide a useful summary of the various techniques for partial breast irradiation—including brachytherapy, intraoperative radiotherapy, 3-D conformal and intensity-modulated radiotherapy. Interstitial brachytherapy techniques have historically been considered rather cumbersome and involve placement of between 10 and 20 catheters within the tumor bed. Intracavitary methods using single or multilumen catheters with remote after-loading have been investigated but published data is limited to date. Intraoperative radiotherapy is a revolutionary method for delivery of partial breast irradiation using a single intraoperative radiotherapy dose of 20 Gy (TARGIT) or 21 G (ELIOT) administered to the tumor bed over 20–25 minutes. These techniques of intraoperative radiotherapy have generated some controversy, especially regarding methodology and analysis of the TARGIT trial. For unselected patients in the TARGIT trial, there was an overall difference in ipsilateral breast tumor recurrence of 2.01% in favor of external beam radiotherapy. The median follow-up was only 2.4 years and although this difference in rate of ipsilateral breast tumor recurrence was statistically significant, it fell within the predetermined non-inferiority margin (2.5%). Longer-term follow-up will indicate whether further divergence of curves for local recurrence will declare non-inferiority. It seems likely that rates of local recurrence will be higher for intraoperative radiotherapy than conventional external beam radiotherapy, but absolute rates will be low for selected node-negative patients at lower risk for relapse. These patients may have a net benefit from partial breast irradiation.

Dr. Meattini further discusses accelerated partial breast irradiation with a linear accelerator and emphasizes benefits of a reduced workload for radiotherapy departments. It should be noted that intraoperative radiotherapy lengthens overall operating time and restricts the number of cases that can be scheduled on a routine operating list. Intensity-modulated radiotherapy offers the opportunity to employ a linear accelerator to deliver external beam radiotherapy with a high level of dose conformity (greater than 3-D conformal) while sparing normal tissues. Dr. Meattini cites an Italian trial randomizing women aged >40 years with node-negative tumors (≤25 mm) to whole breast irradiation (50 Gy in 25 fractions) or intensity-modulated radiotherapy (30 Gy in 5 fractions). This reported similar rates of ipsilateral breast tumor recurrence (1.5%) at 5 years. There is also evidence from another trial involving older women (>70 years) of reduced acute skin toxicity that may be relevant to compliance issues in the older age group. Moreover, the accelerated partial breast irradiation group had fewer late side effects of radiotherapy (p = 0.004) and improved cosmetic outcomes (p = 0.045). It would be interesting to compare a hypofractionated whole breast regimen (e.g., 40 Gy) with intensity-modulated radiotherapy and determine whether a twice-daily schedule increases side effects due to incomplete tissue recovery. The clinical indications for accelerated partial breast irradiation remain unclear at the present time, and results of several ongoing trials are awaited to ascertain rates of local control, acute/late toxicities, and overall survival compared to conventional/hypofractionated whole breast irradiation. The impact of radiotherapy on complications and patient-reported outcomes after breast reconstruction is currently being intensively investigated. The benefits of postmastectomy radiotherapy are apparent from meta-analyses by the Early Breast Cancer Trialists Collaborative Group for selected patients with 1–3 and ≥4 positive axillary nodes. Furthermore, the benefits of breast reconstruction in terms of psychological and other quality-of-life parameters have been established from observational studies. However, integration of postmastectomy radiotherapy with breast reconstruction has proven challenging to clinicians with limited evidence to guide treatment decisions and much variation in practice (based on historical tradition and institutional culture). Indeed, in general, current practice does not reflect shared decision-making informed by good quality data. Multicenter studies to date have involved small numbers of irradiated patients with failure of comparison between different types of reconstruction. The impact of postmastectomy radiotherapy on reconstruction is widely feared but poorly understood. Postmastectomy radiotherapy induces a variety of skin changes, vascular compromise, and eventually fibrosis. These changes can threaten both the viability of reconstruction as well as cosmetic outcomes and necessitate multiple corrective surgeries.

In the opinion of Dr. McCormick, the presence of a reconstructed breast does not greatly interfere with delivery of postmastectomy irradiation. She emphasizes the concept of tissue equivalence and how materials used for breast reconstruction generally have similar density to breast tissue for the purposes of radiotherapy planning. The use of dedicated computed tomography simulators has enabled more accurate treatment planning for breast cancer patients that limit radiation dosage to organs at risk (OARS) such as the heart and lungs. Much more information is now available to radiation oncologists to assist with volume contouring for the breast, chest wall, and regional nodes. A publication from Memorial Sloan Kettering Cancer Center in New York concluded that postmastectomy radiotherapy following immediate reconstruction with a tissue expander or permanent expander implant "is a safe and reasonable" option for patients. Nonetheless, although treatment planning using proton, photon, and electron sources may be satisfactory with optimal coverage of chest wall and regional nodes (acceptable dosage to OARS), there is a high risk of capsular contracture for implant-based immediate breast reconstruction. Furthermore, it is unknown whether use of acellular dermal matrix to improve implant coverage can reduce rates of capsular contracture. Despite concerns over cosmetic outcomes after postmastectomy radiotherapy, there is no evidence for impaired local or distant disease control when postmastectomy radiotherapy is administered to reconstructed compared to nonreconstructed patients with stage I–III breast cancer.

Dr. Strom and Dr. Woodward argue that whole breast reconstruction can interfere with delivery of radiation treatment. They emphasize the importance of optimal coverage of target tissues including chest wall and regional nodes. A meta-analysis of three major trials evaluating regional nodal irradiation (French, MA-20 and EORTC) reveals a benefit for overall and metastases-free survival (HR 0.88; 95% CI 0.8–0.97; p = 0.012). Internal mammary nodal irradiation is associated with low lung toxicity, and a slight excess of cardiac deaths was noted in the French study. However, number of cases was small and it is important to balance cardiac versus breast cancer deaths, particularly for right-sided tumors. Patient selection is a major challenge and only a minority of stage II patients will have malignant involvement of internal mammary nodes. Predictors of positive internal mammary nodes include tumor size, axillary nodal metastases, and vascular invasion. The implications of these findings and sentinel lymph node biopsy positive patients should be treated in the meantime remain unclear.

These authors cite a study analyzing postmastectomy radiotherapy plans for patients undergoing mastectomy with immediate breast reconstruction; strict criteria for chest wall and internal mammary node coverage were applied to define what was termed "optimal uncompromised" radiotherapy plans. A score was derived which also took account of the proportion of lung tissue included in the fields and whether the heart and epicardial vessels were completely excluded. Of note, less than one-quarter of plans were considered to be optimal with issues of inadequate coverage of the chest wall medially and laterally while coverage of the internal mammary chain in the territory of the first three intercostal spaces was absent in half of cases. Another study reported compromised chest wall coverage in one-fifth of patients and similarly found inadequate internal mammary chain irradiation in 55% of cases. It is argued that a reconstructed breast changes the target geometry and adversely influences irradiation of specific chest wall structures—skin, subcutaneous tissue, and chest wall musculature. In particular, a reconstruction lies anterior to chest wall structures (except for a subpectoral implant), and a photon radiation beam is needed which can penetrate to a much greater depth than for chest wall irradiation without reconstruction. There is a trade-off between increasing the photon field to enhance penetration and risk of damage to normal adjacent tissues. It is easier to apply tangential multibeam techniques to the chest wall with a more favorable risk–benefit ratio than for immediate breast reconstruction. Dr. Strom and Dr. Woodford point out that intensity-modulated radiotherapy can be associated with spread of low-dose irradiation to the lungs and opposite breast with risk of inducing carcinogenesis.

There is persistent controversy over use of a boost dose after whole breast irradiation as part of breast-conservation therapy. This was traditionally delivered at a dose of 10–16 Gy to the tumor bed, and results of a large European trial (>5000 patients) have confirmed lower rates of ipsilateral breast tumor recurrence (16.4% vs 12%) especially in younger patients. However, a boost dose is associated with increased breast fibrosis (5.2% vs 1.8%). It is essential that surgeons discuss oncoplastic cases with their radiation oncology colleagues. Extensive rearrangement of glandular tissue can present challenges in terms of localization of the tumor bed. Placement of clips before any tissue displacement will aid interpretation of three-dimensional computed tomography images and the precise boost dose may be modified according to margin status. Several different methods can be used for boost delivery but cosmetic outcomes are similar for each. The method of boost delivery is nuanced to some extent but depends on

the size, shape, and location of the tumor bed relative to breast shape and dimensions. Dr. Lozza outlines the relative advantages of these various methods with much interest currently in intraoperative radiotherapy that has recently been approved as an alternative to whole breast irradiation in selected patients by the National Institute for Health and Clinical Excellence (United Kingdom). In terms of a boost dose, intraoperative radiotherapy is particularly attractive and would necessarily precede whole breast irradiation using external beams. Intraoperative radiotherapy permits accurate and direct visualization of the tumor bed compared with an en-face electron field which has constriction of dose deposition at depth. Irradiation can be done prior to any breast mobilization and glandular rearrangement that ensures accurate delivery of the boost dose to the target volume. Dr. Lozza points out that intraoperative radiotherapy is applied directly to breast tissue without any intervening seroma or hematoma and avoids skin exposure. Minitangent photon fields can be used to boost deeply placed tumor beds with minimal exposure of thoracic structures to stray radiation. In theory, a boost dose can be administered at the same as whole breast irradiation and much research is focused on a simultaneous integrated boost that reduces total treatment time. As described in Section 29.2, the boost dose is "interdigitated" with whole breast irradiation with delivery of a higher fractional dose to the region of the tumor bed. Dr. Huber and Dr. Wazer further discuss the benefits of intraoperative brachytherapy in terms of improved local control compared to an external beam boost. A matched-pair analysis found no cases of local recurrence at 5 years for interstitial brachytherapy compared with 4.3% for an external boost. Moreover, data from the aforementioned EORTC trial supports superior control for intraoperative brachytherapy versus other boost methods. In addition to more accurate targeting, intraoperative radiotherapy treats the tumor bed immediately and may prevent proliferation of residual cancer cells. Moreover, the biologically effective dose may be higher with an intraoperative approach that acts upon a lower tumor burden immediately postexcision and may suppress mitogenic growth factors in wound tissue fluid.

The precise indications for a tumor bed boost vary from one multidisciplinary team to another but include young age, large high-grade tumors with high proliferation indices, and negative hormone receptor status.

Techniques for lymph node transfer

Chapter 31. Transfer of vascularized lymph node tissue 433

31

Transfer of vascularized lymph node tissue

AT A GLANCE

In contrast to more conventional treatments such as extensive skin resection and liposuction, recent focus has been on techniques for lymphatic bypass, transfer of lymphatic groin tissue attached to abdominal free flaps used for breast reconstruction, or transfer of vascularized lymph nodes. The techniques vary and practice differs from one surgeon to another. However, this evolving field has great promise for improving the devastating impact of lymphedema after breast cancer surgery and continues to develop. Recent mention of direct immediate lymphatic channel repair at the time of tumor resection and lymph node(s) removal may significantly decrease the incidence of lymphedema and the need for extensive delayed surgical repair.

31.1 OUR APPROACH (TAIWAN)

Chieh-Han John Tzou and Ming-Huei Cheng

Background of vascularized lymph node flap transfer

Vascularized lymph node flap transfer is a surgical therapy for lymphedema, which can be applied after conservative therapies have been attempted.[1–3] The principle of vascularized lymph node flap transfer is to create a shunting of lymphatic fluid to the venous system and subsequently reduce lymph accumulation in the affected extremity.[1–6]

Mechanism and placement of vascularized lymph node flap transfer

Histologic findings of progressive reduction of lymphatic function and decrease of distal lymph-collecting ducts following proximal injury[7,8] are due to loss of contractility within the lymphatic vasculature[9] and disruption of valve system function.[10] This results in distal lymphatic pump failure and backflow of lymph into lymphatic capillaries, precollectors, and interstitial tissues. This in turn leads to secondary valve regurgitation and bidirectional lymphatic flow.[11] These changes manifest clinically as pitting edema and are more pronounced in the gravity-dependent (distal) portion of the extremities.[12]

Two mechanisms of vascularized lymph node transfer had been proposed: first, the induction of lymphangiogenesis[13–16] and, second, reconstitution of lymphatic channels.[1,3,17,18] With the loss of lymphatic function to transport lymph proximally, the ideal recipient location for a vascularized lymph node flap in extremities affected by obstructive lymphedema is a distal (non-anatomic) placement. This would be the wrist or ankle for upper or lower extremity, respectively[1,3,17,19,20] (**Figure 31.1.1**). Experimental and clinical studies have confirmed the drainage of lymph from the interstitium of a non-anatomically placed vascularized lymph node flap to the lymph nodes then to the pedicle vein of the flap.[21]

Choice of vascularized lymph node flap

The greater number of lymph nodes in a vascularized lymph node flap results in a more efficient reduction of lympedema.[22,23] Duplex ultrasonography has shown that lymph node quantity and density for the submental flap are comparable to the groin flap. Despite reliability of the groin flap, iatrogenic lower-extremity lymphedema following groin vascularized lymph node flap harvest has been reported in almost 40% of patients.[24] For this reason, the authors prefer the vascularized submental lymph node flap, which is acceptable to most patients[25] and is associated with an inconspicuous scar[1–2] with minimal donor site morbidity (**Figure 31.1.2**).

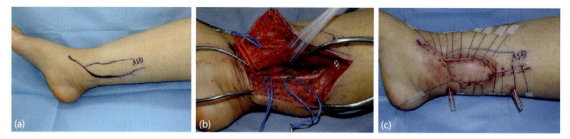

31.1.1 (a) Intraoperative marking of the skin incision and the greater saphenous vein (GSV). (b) Dissection of the posterior tibial vessels: red loop: posterior tibial artery, blue loop: posterior tibial veins, and penrose loop: tibial posterior muscle. (c) Inset of the vascularized submental lymph node flap.

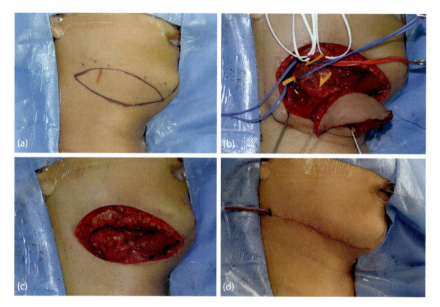

31.1.2 (a) Intraoperative marking of the vascularized submental lymph node flap; dots: mandible and red marking: facial artery. (b) Dissection of the submental flap; white loops: marginal mandibular branches of the facial nerve, blue loop: distal and proximal facial veins, red loop: facial artery, and yellow arrows: sizable lymph nodes. (c and d) Soft tissue defect after flap was raised, which can be closed directly with a hidden scar under the mandible.

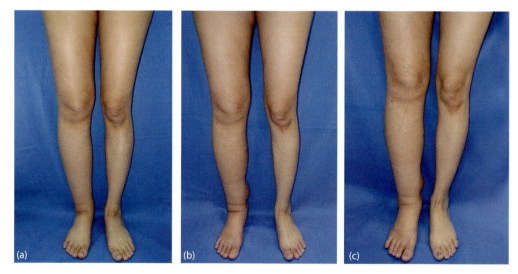

31.1.3 Patient's course with lymphedema of the right lower extremity after liposuction for 10 years ago, with repeating cellulitis five times/year and undergoing complex decompression therapy for the last 5 years, who underwent a vascularized submental lymph node transfer. (a) Preoperative photo. (b) Three months postoperatively, above knee and below knee circumferential reduction rate 5% was 2%. (c) 12 months postoperatively, above knee and below knee circumferential reduction rate was 20% and 12%. No postoperative compression garments were used.

Results of vascularized lymph node transfer

Postoperative follow-up ranging from 9 to 56 months has shown persistent reduction of extremity circumference measurements with reductions of between 35% and 64% for the lower extremities[2,26] and between 24% and 50% for the upper extremities[1,6,26] (**Figure 31.1.3**). Furthermore, the incidence of cellulitis was decreased in more than 80% (11/13) of patients.[6]

CONCLUSION

The transfer of a vascularized groin or submental lymph node flap is an evidence-based approach for the effective treatment of persistent extremity lymphedema which has not responded to conservative therapy. Corresponding reductions in extremity circumference for the upper extremities are between 24% and 50%.

REFERENCES

1. Cheng MH, Chen SC, Henry SL, Tan BK, Chia-Yu Lin M, Huang JJ. Vascularized groin lymph node flap transfer for post-mastectomy upper limb lymphedema: Flap anatomy, recipient sites, and outcomes. *Plastic and Reconstructive Surgery.* 2013;131(6):1286–1298.
2. Cheng MH, Huang JJ, Nguyen DH, Saint-Cyr M, Zenn MR, Tan BK et al. A novel approach to the treatment of lower extremity lymphedema by transferring a vascularized submental lymph node flap to the ankle. *Gynecologic Oncology.* 2012;126(1):93–98.
3. Becker C, Assouad J, Riquet M, Hidden G. Postmastectomy lymphedema: Long-term results following microsurgical lymph node transplantation. *Annals of Surgery.* 2006;243(3):313–315.
4. Campisi C, Davini D, Bellini C, Taddei G, Villa G, Fulcheri E et al. Lymphatic microsurgery for the treatment of lymphedema. *Microsurgery.* 2006;26(1):65–69.
5. Chang DW. Lymphaticovenular bypass for lymphedema management in breast cancer patients: A prospective study. *Plastic and Reconstructive Surgery.* 2010;126(3):752–758.
6. Lin CH, Ali R, Chen SC, Wallace C, Chang YC, Chen HC et al. Vascularized groin lymph node transfer using the wrist as a recipient site for management of postmastectomy upper extremity lymphedema. *Plastic and Reconstructive Surgery.* 2009;123(4):1265–1275.
7. Hara H, Mihara M, Seki Y, Todokoro T, Iida T, Koshima I. Comparison of indocyanine green lymphographic findings with the conditions of collecting lymphatic vessels of limbs in patients with lymphedema. *Plastic and Reconstructive Surgery.* 2013;132(6):1612–1618.

8. Mihara M, Hara H, Hayashi Y. Pathological steps of cancer-related lymphedema: Histological changes in the collecting lymphatic vessels after lymphadenectomy. *PloS One.* 2012;7(7):e41126.
9. Modi S, Stanton AW, Svensson WE, Peters AM, Mortimer PS, Levick JR. Human lymphatic pumping measured in healthy and lymphoedematous arms by lymphatic congestion lymphoscintigraphy. *Journal of Physiology.* 2007;583(Pt 1):271–285.
10. Suami H, Pan WR, Taylor GI. Changes in the lymph structure of the upper limb after axillary dissection: Radiographic and anatomical study in a human cadaver. *Plastic and Reconstructive Surgery.* 2007;120(4):982–991.
11. Mihara M, Hara H, Iida T. Antegrade and retrograde lymphaticovenous anastomosis for cancer-related lymphedema with lymphatic valve dysfuction and lymphatic varix. *Microsurgery.* 2012;32(7):580–584.
12. Patel KM, Lin CY, Cheng MH. From Theory to Evidence: Long-Term Evaluation of the Mechanism of Action and Flap Integration of Distal Vascularized Lymph Node Transfers. *J Reconstr Microsurg.* 2014;31(1):26–30.
13. Can J, Cai R, Li S, Zhang D. Experimental study of lymph node auto-transplantation in rats. *Chinese Medical Journal.* 1998;111(3):239–241.
14. Lähteenvuo M, Honkonen K, Tervala T. Growth factor therapy and autologous lymph node transfer in lymphedema. *Circulation.* 2011;123(6):613–620.
15. Rabson JA, Geyer SJ, Levine G, Swartz WM, Futrell JW. Tumor immunity in rat lymph nodes following transplantation. *Annals of Surgery.* 1982;196(1):92–99.
16. Shesol BF, Nakashima R, Alavi A, Hamilton RW. Successful lymph node transplantation in rats, with restoration of lymphatic function. *Plastic and Reconstructive Surgery.* 1979;63(6):817–823.
17. Saaristo AM, Niemi TS, Viitanen TP, Tervala TV, Hartiala P, Suominen EA. Microvascular breast reconstruction and lymph node transfer for postmastectomy lymphedema patients. *Annals of Surgery.* 2012;255(3):468–473.
18. Sapountzis S, Singhal D, Rashid A, Ciudad P, Meo D, Chen HC. Lymph node flap based on the right transverse cervical artery as a donor site for lymph node transfer. *Annals of Plastic Surgery.* 2014;73(4):398–401.
19. Gharb BB, Rampazzo A, Spanio di Spilimbergo S, Xu ES, Chung KP, Chen HC. Vascularized lymph node transfer based on the hilar perforators improves the outcome in upper limb lymphedema. *Annals of Plastic Surgery.* 2011;67(6):589–593.
20. Althubaiti GA, Crosby MA, Chang DW. Vascularized supraclavicular lymph node transfer for lower extremity lymphedema treatment. *Plastic and Reconstructive Surgery.* 2013;131(1):133e–135e.
21. Cheng MH, Huang JJ, Wu CW, Yang CY, Lin CY, Henry SL et al. The mechanism of vascularized lymph node transfer for lymphedema: Natural lymphaticovenous drainage. *Plastic and Reconstructive Surgery.* 2014;133(2):192e–198e.

22. Nguyen DH, Chou PY, Hsieh YH, Momeni A, Fang YH, Patel KM, Yang CY, Cheng MH. Quantity of lymph nodes correlates with improvement in lymphatic drainage in treatment of hind limb lymphedema with lymph node flap transfer in rats. *Microsurgery*. 2016;36(3):239–245.

23. Gustafsson J, Chu SY, Chan WH, Cheng MH. Correlation between Quantity of Transferred Lymph Nodes and Outcome in Vascularized Submental Lymph Node Flap Transfer for Lower Limb Lymphedema. *Plast Reconstr Surg*. 2018;142(4):1056–1063.

24. Vignes S, Blanchard M, Yannoutsos A, Arrault M. Complications of autologous lymph-node transplantation for limb lymphoedema. *European Journal of Vascular and Endovascular Surgery: The Official Journal of the European Society for Vascular Surgery*. 2013;45(5):516–520.

25. Patel KM, Chu SY, Huang JJ, Wu CW, Lin CY, Cheng MH. Preplanning vascularized lymph node transfer with duplex ultrasonography: An evaluation of 3 donor sites. *Plastic and Reconstructive Surgery Global Open*. 2014;2(8):e193.

26. Patel KM, Lin CY, Cheng MH. A prospective evaluation of lymphedema-specific quality-of-life outcomes following vascularized lymph node transfer. *Annals of Surgical Oncology*. 2014;22(7):2424–2430.

31.2 OUR APPROACH (EUROPE)

Jaume Masià, Gemma Pons, and Elena Rodríguez-Bauzà

Transfer of lymph node tissue in breast cancer related lymphedema is indicated when patients still have functionality of the lymphatic system (active lymphatic channels visualized by indocyanine green (ICG)-lymphangiography) and the axillary area has abundant fibrotic tissue or signs of radiodermitis.[1] The procedure is based on substitution of axillary nodes that have been previously surgically resected or traumatized with a vascularized free tissue transfer flap containing a few lymph nodes (between three and six nodes) from non-risk donor sites. Orthotopically placed lymph nodes may act as a sponge to absorb lymphatic fluid and direct it into the vascular network and/or the transferred nodes may induce lymphangiogenesis.[2]

The procedure aims to replace previously damaged or resected lymph nodes in the axilla with a vascularized free tissue transfer flap containing between three and six lymph nodes from non-risk donor sites. This flap is generally supplied by the superficial inferior epigastric or superficial circumflex iliac vessels. This site is preferred, as morbidity is low and the final cosmetic outcome is satisfactory as the scar is hidden.

These nodes and their vascular pedicle are assessed preoperatively and accurately located according to a set of coordinates using computed tomography angiography (CT-angiography). The number and distribution of the deep nodes are assessed with the aim of ensuring that nodes earmarked for removal are not disturbing normal lymphatic drainage of the lower limb (Figure 31.2.1). Reverse lymphatic mapping techniques are now commonly used to avoid unnecessary harvesting of sentinel nodes from the groin to avoid secondary lymphedema.

Prior to surgery, ICG is injected into the interdigital spaces of the lower limb to locate the lymphatic system that drains the extremity. This maneuver reduces the risk of harvesting a flap containing functionally important lymph nodes whose removal would induce iatrogenic lower limb lymphedema, as has been recently described.[3,4]

Before raising the flap and immediately before the skin incision, 0.1–0.2 mL of ICG and 0.2–0.4 mL of 2.5% patent blue V dye (Guerbet, Roissy-Charles-de-Gaulle, France) is injected intradermally at two or three spots above and below the inguinal fold within the potential drainage area which permits better intraoperative visualization of the lymphatic vessels and nodes draining the lower abdominal wall.

A skin adipose-lymph node flap, with a skin island measuring approximately 8 × 4 cm, is harvested above the inguinal region, and its vascular pedicle is carefully dissected upward to the femoral vessels.

The donor site is closed primarily with a continuous spiral suture, avoiding any dead spaces and spraying the surgical field with a tissue sealant, to reduce the risk of seromas. A closed suction drain is placed in the donor area and left until the drainage is less than 15 cc/day and external compression is applied for 2–3 weeks (Figure 31.2.2).

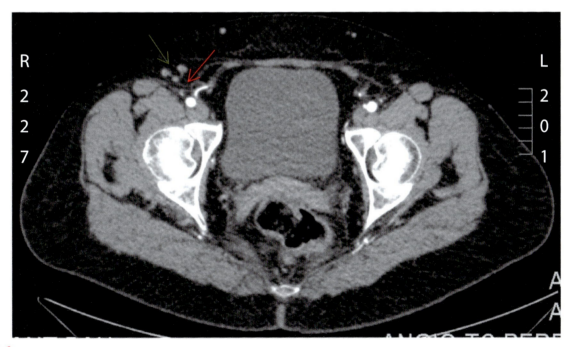

31.2.1 Angio-CT showing right-sided lymph nodes suitable for tranfer as a free tissue flap supplied by the superficial inferior epigastric or superficial circumflex vessels.

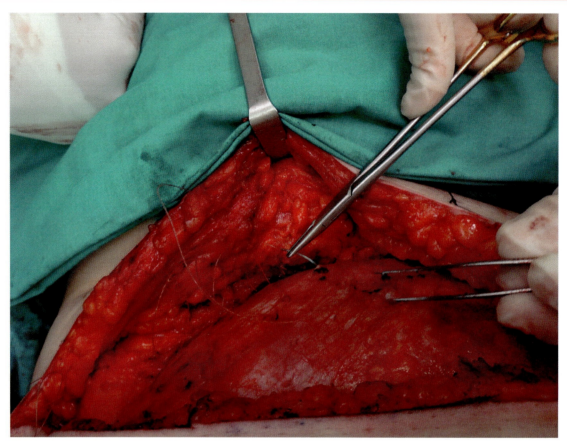

31.2.2 Abdominal donor site closure with continuous spiral suture technique to minimize seroma.

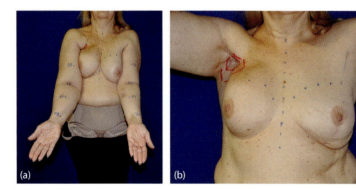 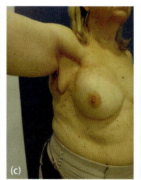 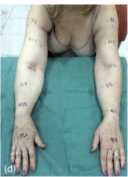

31.2.3 (a–b) Preoperative images of 65-year-old patient affected of GIII secondary lymphedema of upper left extremity with serious retraction of axillary region. (c–d) Postoperative images of recipient axillary area and upper extremity after lymph node transfer procedure.

Anastomosis within the axilla is normally performed between donor vessels of the circumflex scapular system following debridement of fibrotic tissue. It is essential to position the lymph nodes at the apex of the axilla in contact with axillary tissue as this is the site where dominant afferent lymphatic channels arrive from the arm.

The adipose tissue encasing the lymph nodes and the skin island included in the flap are useful to replace the fibrotic tissue in the axillary region and also to facilitate lymph absorption through physiological lymph-venous shunts.[5] Moreover, the skin island makes postoperative monitoring easier (**Figure 31.2.3**).

When simultaneous management of lymphedema and autologous breast reconstruction with an abdominal free flap is proposed, the author's preference is for a compound abdominal deep inferior epigastric artery perforator/ superficial inferior epigastric artery flap containing the lymph nodes with double vascularization and in some cases

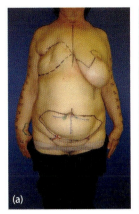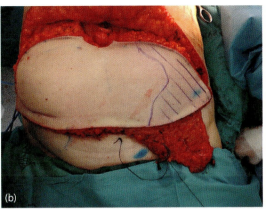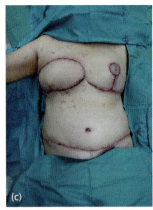

31.2.4 (a) Preoperative image of 56-year-old patient affected of secondary upper limb lymphedema and mastectomy sequelae. (b) DIEP flap including lymph node flap to simultaneously reconstruct the breast and treat upper limb lymphedema. (c) Immediate postoperative image after total breast anatomy restoration procedure.

even with lymph-lymphatic anastomosis. This is a surgical concept that is referred to as total breast anatomy restoration (**Figure 31.2.4**).

REFERENCES

1. Masià J, Pons G, Rodríguez-Bauzà E. Barcelona lymphedema algorithm for surgical treatment in breast cancer-related lymphedema. *J Reconstr Microsurg.* 2016;32(5):329–335.
2. Becker C, Assouad J, Riquet M et al. Postmastectomy lymphedema: Long-term results following microsurgical lymph node transplantation. *Ann Surg.* 2006;243:313–315.
3. Pons G, Masia J, Loschi P, Nardulli ML, Duch J. A case of donor-site lymphoedema after lymph node-superficial circumflex iliac artery perforator flap transfer. *J Plast Reconstr Aesthet Surg.* 2014;67(1):119–123.
4. Viitanen TP. Mäki MT, Seppänen MP et al. Donor site lymphatic function after microvascular lymph node transfer. *Plast Reconstr Surg.* 2012;130(6):1246–1253.
5. Miranda Garcés M, Mirapeix R, Pons G, Sadri A, Masià J. A comprehensive review of the natural lymphaticovenous communications and their role in lymphedema surgery. *J Surg Oncol.* 2016;113(4):374–380.

Nipple-areola complex reconstruction

Chapter 32. Nipple-areola complex reconstruction 443

32

Nipple-areola complex reconstruction

AT A GLANCE

Techniques for nipple and areola reconstruction have focused of late on preventing loss of nipple volume over time that is a frequent recurrence and methods for enhancement of nipple projection. Biologic and synthetics as well as cartilage grafts are being used as adjuvant material to optimize nipple projection over the long term. In addition, a trend toward three-dimensional tattooing has gained traction due to its simplicity and favorable outcomes (an increased range of ink colors are now available).

32.1 NIPPLE-AREOLA COMPLEX RECONSTRUCTION (WITH AND WITHOUT BIOLOGICALS)

Parisa Kamali, Winona Wu, and Samuel J. Lin

Introduction

Nipple-areola complex reconstruction is the final phase of the breast reconstruction process and plays a significant role in patients' overall satisfaction.[1–3] Nipple-areola complex reconstruction techniques have evolved significantly over the years, from simple tattooing to local flaps and grafts.[1,3,4]

The nipple-areola complex is the primary landmark of the breast, as it is located at the prominence of the breast mound. The nipple itself may project as much as 1 cm or more, with a diameter of approximately 4–7 mm.[1] The areola consists of pigmented skin surrounding the nipple proper and is on average approximately 4.2–4.5 cm in diameter, yet wide variability exists as to what constitutes normal dimensions of the complex. The anatomy of a nipple-areola complex is remarkably variable in dimension, texture, and color across ethnic groups and among individuals. Moreover, an appreciable difference often exists between the two nipple-areola complexes in the same patient.[4]

The goal of nipple-areola reconstruction is to replicate the size, shape, texture, projection, and position of the contralateral breast or the preoperative conditions.[4] Timing of reconstruction of the nipple-areola complex is crucial to the final aesthetic result. The ideal timing is approximately 3–5 months after the last revisional reconstructive surgery. This allows for swelling and inflammation to subside, while allowing for settling of the reconstructed breast mound into its final position.[5] Generally, nipple-areola complex reconstruction can be safely performed on an outpatient basis under local anesthesia.

Areola reconstruction

The major challenge for areola reconstruction is to recreate the pigmentation and texture typically associated with the native areola. The most commonly employed techniques involve use of skin grafts, tattooing, and/or a combination of these two techniques. Skin grafting is preferentially performed in the immediate setting or at the time of nipple reconstruction. Currently, tattooing is more popular than traditional grafting and usually occurs at 6–8 weeks after nipple reconstruction.

SKIN GRAFTING OF THE AREOLA

Skin grafting of the areola has the advantages of providing a textured, wrinkled surface and distinct differences in degrees of pigmentation, resembling a normal areola. Dermoepidermal full-thickness grafts can be harvested from the retroauricular area, the vulvar region, revised/excess breast skin, the inguinal region, or other body areas.

TATTOOING

Tattooing is either used by itself or in conjunction with skin grafting and can provide excellent areolar color match with limited morbidity.[4] Tattooing uses intradermal sterile pigments on the needle of the tattoo machine. Rotating the cap of the needle assembly can regulate the depth of pigment placement. Pigment deposited too superficially will result in pigment extrusion and sloughing, while deeper placement leads to macrophage processing and removal, both resulting in early pigment fading. The selected color is typically one or two shades darker than the native areola due to a tendency for color fading over time. The tattooed area will usually undergo sloughing and crusting for 3–5 days. The area should be kept moist with bacitracin or some other type of petroleum jelly. After this period, slight de-pigmentation may occur and many patients will require touch-ups over the next few months.

Nipple reconstruction

While the medical literature contains many technical descriptions regarding nipple reconstruction, there is no consensus to date as to which techniques are superior.[6–14] Despite the multitude of techniques described to preserve nipple shape and projection over time, none have been able to attain consistent results.[15] The most commonly used flaps are associated with loss of nipple projection in up to 70% of cases over the course of the first 3 years postoperatively.[1] This section describes the most commonly used flaps and/or grafts for nipple reconstruction.

SKATE FLAP

The skate flap is a popular type of local flap for nipple reconstruction. The design is based on a central axis. A small circle (the base) measuring the exact size of the proposed new nipple is drawn at the appropriate position. The length of this base tangent should be about three times the diameter of the erect nipple. The line is then split into thirds, the inner and outer thirds will be used as the wings that fold to form the sidewalls of the nipple. After this is established, a semicircular line is drawn from the two edges of the bisected line, which represents the most projected portion of the future nipple. The wings are then elevated full-thickness including underlying deep fat. When the base is reached, the central pedicle is raised, and the wings are rotated into place opposite the base and sutured. The wings depend on their intradermal blood flow and the central pedicle. The donor site is either closed primarily or covered with full-thickness skin graft harvested from the groin or other suitable area (**Figure 32.1.1**).

THE STAR FLAP

The star flap utilizes similar principles in flap design as the skate flap, except skin grafting is not required. When drawing the basic design of the star flap, one has to keep in mind that the central wing base width determines the width of the nipple. The outer wings are elevated in the subdermal fat plane, including subcutaneous fat. The central wing is then elevated from distal to proximal, while including an increasing amount of subcutaneous fat. After flap elevation, one outer wing is rotated along the nipple base and sutured into position, followed by rotation of the second wing around the nipple. The distal end is then sutured anterior to the base of the first outer wing. Finally, the central wing is brought over the top to form the distal tip of the nipple and secured in place. The donor side is closed primarily (**Figure 32.1.2**).

THE S-FLAP (DOUBLE OPPOSING TAB)

The S-flap uses opposing dermal pedicles opposite each other receiving transversely oriented blood supply. The center of the S represents the desired location of the new nipple. Nipple projection is determined by the length of the flaps. Each flap is elevated in the subdermal fat plane to provide bulk and robust vascular supply and sutured loosely to

32.1.1 Skate flap.

32.1.2 Star flap.

each other to allow for swelling. Each flap is de-epithelialized prior to rotation. Finally, circular de-epithelialization and subsequent placement of a skin graft for areolar reconstruction takes place (**Figure 32.1.3**).

THE C-V FLAP

Taking elements of both star and skate flaps, the C-V flap is composed of two V-shaped flaps and a C-shaped flap to create the nipple. The width of the V-flap determines projection, whereas the diameter of the C-flap determines the diameter of the nipple and top of the new nipple. Flap elevation begins at the outer V-segments and proceeds toward the central, C-segment. The V-flaps are thinned to a larger extent toward the periphery. The two flaps are rotated along the base of the nipple and sutured together. The donor side is then closed directly. Finally, the C-flap is raised with a deeper layer of subdermal fat in order to provide bulk to the nipple and used to round the tip of the nipple and sutured in place (**Figure 32.1.4**).

THE BELL FLAP

The design of the bell flap incorporates a purse string areola closure that provides slight areolar projection. The intended nipple is drawn and the bell-shaped flap is raised in the subcutaneous plane. The flap is wrapped upon itself in an inverted box configuration and sutured in place. To produce final projection of the nipple-areola complex, a subdermal nylon suture is placed around the circumference of the circle in a purse string fashion (**Figure 32.1.5**).

Nipple reconstruction with biologics

Due to long-term loss of nipple projection with traditional flaps, several techniques have evolved adding biologics to the existing flaps.[6,16] Previous studies have described auricular cartilage grafting and costal cartilage grafting to "support" the nipple projection (**Figure 32.1.6**), but are infrequently used due to donor side morbidity.[17,18] In the last decades, various nonautologous tissues have emerged for nipple reconstruction to provide stable projection. In 2005, a secondary nipple reconstruction with AlloDerm implantation was presented as an alternative to the existing methods of autologous tissue.[19] Also polyurethane-coated silicone gel implant, hyaluronic acid injection, and calcium

32.1.3 Double opposing tab flap.

32.1.4 C-V flap.

32.1.5 Bell flap.

32.1.6 Nipple creation with acellular dermal matrix.

446 Nipple-areola complex reconstruction

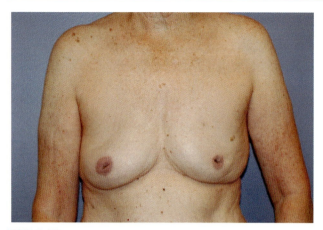

32.1.7 Preoperative view of inverted nipple bilaterally.

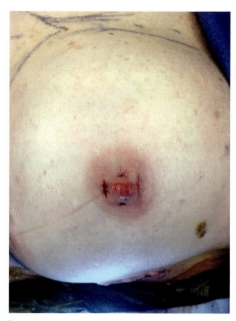

32.1.9 Nipple following placement and prior to closure.

32.1.8 Acellular dermal matrix "rolled" as a central graft.

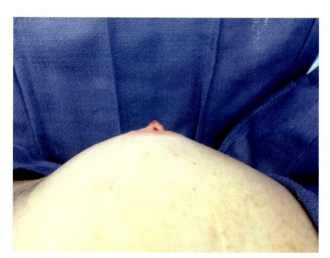

32.1.10 Profile view of nipple inversion correction with acellular dermal matrix.

hydroxyapatite for nipple projection have been used more extensively in the last decades.[16,20–22] The main disadvantage to using nonautologous tissue is the risk of infection and extrusion. **Figures 32.1.7 through 32.1.10** demonstrate the use of acellular matrix for correction of nipple inversion.

REFERENCES

1. Nimboriboonporn, A., Chuthapisith, S. Nipple-areola complex reconstruction. *Gland Surgery* 2014;3:35–42.
2. Momoh, A. O., Colakoglu, S., de Blacam, C. et al. The impact of nipple reconstruction on patient satisfaction in breast reconstruction. *Annals of Plastic Surgery* 2012;69:389–393.
3. Butz, D. R., Kim, E. K., Song, D. H. C-Y trilobed flap for improved nipple-areola complex reconstruction. *Plastic and Reconstructive Surgery* 2015;136:234–237.
4. Farhadi, J., Maksvytyte, G. K., Schaefer, D. J., Pierer, G., Scheufler, O. Reconstruction of the nipple-areola complex: An update. *Journal of Plastic, Reconstructive & Aesthetic Surgery: JPRAS* 2006;59:40–53.
5. Losken, A., Duggal, C. S., Desai, K. A., McCullough, M. C., Gruszynski, M. A., Carlson, G. W. Time to completion of nipple reconstruction: What factors are involved? *Annals of Plastic Surgery* 2013;70:530–532.
6. Tierney, B. P., Hodde, J. P., Changkuon, D. I. Biologic collagen cylinder with skate flap technique for nipple reconstruction. *Plastic Surgery International* 2014;2014:194087.
7. Chang, W. H. Nipple reconstruction with a T flap. *Plastic and Reconstructive Surgery* 1984;73:140–143.

8. Kroll, S. S. Nipple reconstruction with the double-opposing tab flap. *Plastic and Reconstructive Surgery* 1999;104:511–514.

9. Shestak, K. C., Nguyen, T. D. The double opposing periareola flap: A novel concept for nipple-areola reconstruction. *Plastic and Reconstructive Surgery* 2007;119:473–480.

10. Eo, S., Kim, S. S., Da Lio, A. L. Nipple reconstruction with C-V flap using dermofat graft. *Annals of Plastic Surgery* 2007;58:137–140.

11. Gamboa-Bobadilla, G. M. Nipple reconstruction: The top hat technique. *Annals of Plastic Surgery* 2005;54:243–246.

12. Otterburn, D. M., Sikora, K. E., Losken, A. An outcome evaluation following postmastectomy nipple reconstruction using the C-V flap technique. *Annals of Plastic Surgery* 2010;64:574–578.

13. Tyrone, J. W., Losken, A., Hester, T. R. Nipple areola reconstruction. *Breast Disease* 2002;16:117–122.

14. Losken, A., Mackay, G. J., Bostwick, J., 3rd. Nipple reconstruction using the C-V flap technique: A long-term evaluation. *Plastic and Reconstructive Surgery* 2001;108:361–369.

15. Lee, S., Jung, Y., Bae, Y. Immediate nipple reconstruction as oncoplastic breast surgery: The cigar roll flap with inner dermal core technique. *Aesthetic Plastic Surgery* 2015;39:706–712.

16. Seaman, B. J., Akbari, S. R., Davison, S. P. A novel technique for nipple-areola complex reconstruction: The acellular dermal matrix onlay graft. *Plastic and Reconstructive Surgery* 2012;129:580e–581e.

17. Brent, B., Bostwick, J. Nipple-areola reconstruction with auricular tissues. *Plastic and Reconstructive Surgery* 1977;60:353–361.

18. Guerra, A. B., Khoobehi, K., Metzinger, S. E., Allen, R. J. New technique for nipple areola reconstruction: Arrow flap and rib cartilage graft for long-lasting nipple projection. *Annals of Plastic Surgery* 2003;50:31–37.

19. Nahabedian, M. Y. Secondary nipple reconstruction using local flaps and AlloDerm. *Plastic and Reconstructive Surgery* 2005;115:2056–2061.

20. Bernard, R. W., Beran, S. J. Autologous fat graft in nipple reconstruction. *Plastic and Reconstructive Surgery* 2003;112:964–968.

21. Evans, K. K., Rasko, Y., Lenert, J., Olding, M. The use of calcium hydroxylapatite for nipple projection after failed nipple-areolar reconstruction: Early results. *Annals of Plastic Surgery* 2005;55:25–29.

22. Lennox, K., Beer, K. R. Nipple contouring with hyaluronics postmastectomy. *Journal of Drugs in Dermatology: JDD* 2007;6:1030–1033.

32.2 3-D TATTOOING

Vassilis Pitsinis and John R. Benson

Introduction

The final stage of breast reconstruction is formation of a nipple-areola complex and often this involves artificial coloration of a permanent nature. The overall appearance of the nipple area can be greatly enhanced by using safe and reliable tattooing techniques applied at the end of a patient's surgical journey. Techniques for three-dimensional tattooing have gained popularity due to their simplicity and excellent outcomes. Improved body image provides a psychological boost and can help ameliorate problems with sexual relationships and increase self-confidence.[1,2] Nipple-areola tattooing is not a medical treatment, but rather an art form and therefore should be approached from an aesthetic and artistic perspective.[3-5]

Indications for tattooing

The following groups of patients may potentially benefit from tattooing:

- Breast reconstructive surgery
- Breast reductional surgery/mastopexy
- Breast augmentation
- Camouflaging of scars

Nipple-areola tattooing promotes optimal aesthetic outcomes and may permit women to undress in front of partners and show their "new body." Patients may be concerned about pain and should be reassured that the reconstructed breast is insensate. The optimal time for nipple tattooing is 6–8 weeks after nipple-areola reconstruction with a local skin flap which must be fully healed before any attempts at tattooing and non-dissolvable skin sutures removed at this stage.

Contraindications

Patch testing should be routinely undertaken 3–4 weeks prior to the procedure for all patients with a known allergy history. This can be done with a discretely sited needle scratch and examined after a period of 24 hours. Patients with a history of rheumatic fever and mitral valve replacement should receive prophylactic antibiotics and those taking warfarin switched to low molecular weight heparin. Some surgeons are cautious about tattooing in patients prone to keloid formation and in the presence of established keloid tissue as it is more difficult to penetrate with needles.[6,7] Pregnant patients should defer tattooing until after delivery. Those patients with needle phobias will require extra psychological support and local anesthetic cream can be applied before tattooing to partially numb the skin.

Patient consent

Patients should be made aware of the limitations of tattooing and have realistic expectations. Photographic documentation is very important and patients will have consented to photographs being taken before and after each session. Photographic records can aid in the selection of pigment color and can be a useful resource for patient education, training, and information giving. There is a low risk of infection following tattooing and bleeding from rupture of small sub-areolar blood vessels infrequently occurs. Poor pigment uptake may necessitate additional sessions, and a layering strategy is usually employed with two sessions 6 weeks apart rather than a single session which may risk excessive deposition of pigment with migration and spread beyond the point of application.[8]

Equipment

The basic equipment consists of the micro pigmentation device (**Figure 32.2.1**), various types and styles of needle, and a range of flesh-colored pigments. Needles are made of nickel and manufactured in disposable cartridges available in a range of sizes. Tattooing is an aseptic technique and sterile gloves, drapes, and skin-cleansing agents should be available.

Pigments: Colors for medical tattooing are non-synthetic iron containing natural sediments (**Figure 32.2.2**). They come in a huge variety (**Figure 32.2.3**). One should always keep in mind the skin color complexion of the particular patient and choose a lighter color for the nipple and a darker one for the areola—basically another shade of pink to match the nipple. Mixing different flesh-colored pigments is difficult for a beginner, it's a skill that comes with experience and practice, thus, keeping things simple is of paramount importance.[9]

Needles: As for pigments, there are a variety of commercially available needles (**Figure 32.2.4**). They are made of nickel sharp pins (in a range of 3–7 usually) fashioned together in a group in disposable cartridges so to make it feasible to be clipped onto the tip of the

32.2.1 One of the most popular medical micropigmentation devices.

32.2.2 An example of a pigment in the application pot.

32.2.3 Some of the many commercially available pigments.

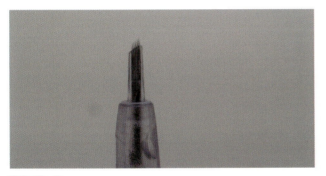

32.2.4 An example of a sloping flat needle.

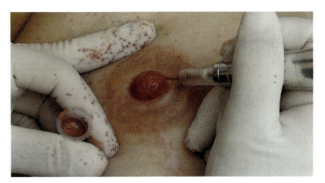

32.2.5 Tattooing an areola.

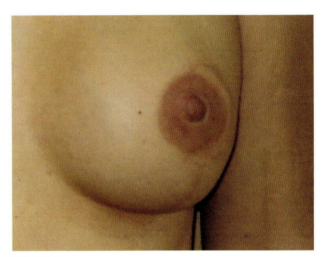

32.2.6 A completed tattoo with the appropriate 3D halo around the nipple.

hand held probe which is part of the micropigmentation device. These needles permit effective penetration of the dermis and deposit pigment at an appropriate depth within the skin.

They are mainly divided into:

- Round needles in which the pins are clustered together (best for use in the nipple)
- Flat needles where the pins are in an array like a paint brush (best for larger flat surfaces like the areola)

Method

The preferred technique for achieving an aesthetically pleasing result is to start at the nipple and work outward toward the areola. Circular movements are most effective, although backward and forward strokes can be used. The velocity of oscillation is set at 130–140 strokes per minute, the color being diluted at 50% from the bottle, and the tattooing pen held at an angle of 45° to minimize migration of the pigment. Small circular movements are employed working from the base of the nipple inward, with a lighter area centrally to create a three-dimensional illusion of height (**Figure 32.2.5**). Similar circular or side-to-side movements are subsequently applied to the areola with feathering around the edge to give a more natural finish (resist hovering on the outer areola border to avoid a hard outline).[3–5,10] A halo around the nipple can create the impression of three-dimensional protrusion (**Figure 32.2.6**).

Minimal dressings only should be applied upon completion, and this will facilitate air dying of the tattooed area. A light piece of dry gauze placed over a thin layer of Vaseline will prevent adherence and can be removed at home as soon as possible leaving the area to air dry especially in the first 24 hours.

CONCLUSION

Three-dimensional nipple-areola tattooing can create an optical effect which greatly enhances the appearance of a reconstructed nipple-areola complex. This contributes to restoring body image, reduces sexual morbidity, and is associated with high levels of patient satisfaction.[9] A degree of fading is inevitable due to pigment change following dermal implantation and anamnestic sessions are usually required every 2–3 years.[11,12] The procedure of nipple tattooing can also be successfully undertaken by clinical nurse practitioners following appropriate training, and these individuals may also be involved with postoperative inflation of implants or aspiration of donor site seromas.[1,13]

REFERENCES

1. Clarkson JH, Tracey A, Eltigani E, Park A. The patient's experience of a nurse-led nipple tattoo service: A successful program in Warwickshire. *J Plast Reconstr Aesthet Surg.* 2006;59:1058–1062.
2. Kesselring UK. The use of intradermal tattoo to enhance the final result of nipple-areola reconstruction [letter]. *Plast Reconstr Surg.* 1987;79(2):303.
3. Becker H. The use of intradermal tattoo to enhance the final result of nipple-areola reconstruction. *Plast Reconstr Surg.* 1986;77:673–676.
4. Drever JM. Tattooing the reconstructed areola without a tattoo machine.[letter]. *Plast Reconstr Surg.* 1988;81(6):995–996.
5. Becker H. Nipple-areola reconstruction using intradermal tattoo. *Plast Reconstr Surg.* 1988;81:450–453.
6. Yactor AR, Michell MN, Koch MS, Leete TG, Shah ZA, Carter BW. Percutaneous tattoo pigment simulating calcific deposits in axillary lymph nodes. *Proc (Bayl Univ Med Cent).* 2013;26:28–29.
7. Honegger MM, Hesseltine SM, Gross JD, Singer C, Cohen JM. Tattoo pigment mimicking axillary lymph node calcifications on mammography. *AJR Am J Roentgenol.* 2004;183:831–832.
8. Spear SL, Convit R, Little JW. Intradermal tattoo as an adjunct to nipple-areola reconstruction. *Plast Reconstr Surg.* 1989;83:907–911.
9. Spear SL, Arias J. Long-term experience with nipple-areola tattooing. *Ann Plast Surg.* 1995;35:232–236.
10. Yoshizawa H. Hepatocellular carcinoma associated with hepatitis C virus infection in Japan: Projection to other countries in the foreseeable future. *Oncology.* 2002;62 Suppl 1:8–17.
11. Levites HA, Fourman MS, Phillips BT et al. Modeling fade patterns of nipple areola complex tattoos following breast reconstruction. *Ann Plast Surg.* 2014;73 Suppl 2:S153–S156.
12. Halvorson EG, Cormican M, West ME, Myers V. Three-dimensional nipple-areola tattooing: A new technique with superior results. *Plast Reconstr Surg.* 2014;133:1073–1075.
13. Potter S, Barker J, Willoughby L, Perrott E, Cawthorn SJ, Sahu AK. Patient satisfaction and time-saving implications of a nurse-led nipple and areola reconstitution service following breast reconstruction. *Breast.* 2007;16:293–296.

EDITORIAL COMMENTARY

The transfer of functional nodal tissue into a previously dissected area represents a promising approach to management of persistent upper limb lymphedema in breast cancer patients. This technique relies on surgical implantation of a vascularized free tissue flap containing a few lymph nodes, which may serve on the one hand to absorb lymphatic fluid and facilitate transfer to the vascular network and on the other induce lymphangiogenesis. The most commonly employed donor site is the groin flap based on the superficial inferior epigastric area or the superficial circumflex iliac artery. Potential problems of donor site morbidity (in up to 40% of cases) have prompted exploration of alternative donor sites; Dr. Tzou and Cheng describe use of a submental lymph node flap which they consider to be acceptable to most patients with an inconspicuous scar and minimal donor site morbidity. Moreover, the quantity and density of lymph nodes is comparable to a groin flap that is important for efficiency of lymph node transfer for reduction of lymphedema.

Whichever donor site is chosen, the vascularized lymph node flap is anastomosed to recipient vessels of the circumflex scapular system. Placement at the apex of the axilla maximizes opportunity for reconstitution of lymphatic channels between the afferent lymphatics of the upper limb and grafted lymph node tissue. A novel method for simultaneously harvesting lymph nodes with an abdominal-based flap for immediate breast reconstruction is mentioned by Dr. Masia and colleagues. This is a compound dual vascularized flap containing lower abdominal pannus and lymph nodes—a concept these authors refer to as T-BAR—total breast anatomy restoration.

Rates of reduction of upper limb lymphedema range from 24% to 50% following lymph node transfer. The latter tends to be utilized after failure of conservative techniques for treatment of upper limb lymphedema. It is possible that success rates might be improved by earlier intervention that can be guided by ICG-lymphography which provides some indication of the functional status of lymphatic vessels.

Although many women decline reconstruction of the nipple-areola complex, for others this represents the "icing on the cake" and psychologically is an important aspect of the reconstructive process. As pointed out by Dr. Lin, it is not so much the detail of the nipple-areola reconstruction that determines patient satisfaction, but rather having something in the center of the reconstructed breast mound which constitutes a primary landmark. Techniques for nipple-areola reconstruction have come full circle with newer methods for three-dimensional tattooing often preferred over local flap methods. Initially simple tattooing was employed, and subsequently, a variety of local flaps and grafts which aimed to achieve durable projection of the nipple and create a distinction between nipple and areola. In recent years, three-dimensional tattooing has become popular and uses a range of "flesh" colors to create the perception of a surgically reconstructed nipple-areola complex. A comprehensive range of pigment colors facilitates creation of a nipple-areola complex, which matches the natural one in terms of size, shape, color, and position (texture cannot be formed although an illusion of this can be obtained with three-dimensional tattooing by darker shading at the base of the nipple).

Some surgeons prefer to fashion a new nipple-areola complex at the time of primary breast reconstruction; however, it is sensible to allow up to 6 months for the breast to settle (especially after radiotherapy). This will permit optimal placement of the nipple-areola complex that may not coincide exactly with the disc of imported skin corresponding to the site of the original nipple-areola complex. A variety of techniques exist for reconstruction of the nipple with no particular advantage of any one method. Surgeon preference will influence choice of method, but loss of projection occurs in more than two-thirds of cases whichever technique is used (all performed under local anaesthesia). The skate flap remains one of the more popular flaps and produces a nicely shaped nipple based on a central axis that helps maintain projection. Areola reconstruction is most commonly done with tattooing about 2 months after nipple reconstruction. If patients wish to recreate the texture of a natural areola, then full-thickness dermoepithelial grafts can be taken from areas such as the retroauricular and vulval areas and applied as an onlay graft. In the past decade, there has been interest in using nonautologous tissue to improve nipple projection in terms of both cosmesis and durability. Materials used for this purpose include Alloderm, polyurethane-coated silicone gel implant, hyaluronic acid, and calcium hydroxyapatite—all of which can be associated with risk of infection and rejection. For these reasons, many patients opt for tattooing either as a definitive alternative to surgical reconstruction or for areola reconstruction alone. The surgically reconstructed nipple (or areola) can be tattooed 6–8 weeks postoperatively to improve color match with the opposite nipple-areola complex. Nonetheless, it is important that patients do not have unrealistic expectations from tattooing although three-dimensional tattooing can yield an optical effect which greatly enhances cosmesis and body image. This can ease any anxiety from appearing naked in front of partners and reduce sexual morbidity.

SECTION XI

Training—breast surgery as a specialty

AT A GLANCE

Oncoplastic surgery embraces both the extirpative and reconstructive aspects of breast cancer surgery, and a modern oncoplastic breast surgeon must combine knowledge of breast oncology with technical competencies enabling remodeling and reconstruction of the breast. Optimal methods for delivering this core repertoire of oncoplastic knowledge and skills continue to evolve and training programs necessarily reflect the position of breast surgery in the wider surgical curriculum; in the United Kingdom, United States, and Australasia, breast surgery is a component of general surgery while in Continental Europe and parts of Asia, it is an adjunct to gynecological surgery. Reconstruction is most commonly undertaken as a joint procedure with plastic surgeons, but there are advantages of a truly "oncoplastic surgeon" who can offer a comprehensive approach with appreciation of both oncologic needs and reconstructive opportunities. Cross-specialty training programs are fostering increasing numbers of oncoplastic breast surgeons. Those individuals without oncoplastic competencies should work in conjunction with plastic surgeons to provide a comprehensive reconstructive service which incorporates all aspects of partial and whole breast reconstruction. Breast surgeons with formal oncoplastic training should adopt a flexible approach to working with plastic surgical colleagues to ensure optimal utilization of skill mix for the benefit of patients

Chapter 33. The modern specialist breast surgeon	455
Chapter 34. Breast surgical training	459

33

The modern specialist breast surgeon

SUE DOWN, ISMAIL JATOI, AND JOHN R. BENSON

INTRODUCTION

Breast surgery requires distinct technical skills and attributes and has emerged over the past 25 years as a subspeciality under the aegis of general surgery. Subspecialization has been driven by a rising incidence of breast cancer, the development of oncoplastic breast surgery techniques, and enhanced patient expectations in terms of treatment and outcomes. The modern specialized breast surgeon must acquire a spectrum of expertise covering oncology, radiology, breast surgery, and an understanding of relevant principles and practice of plastic surgery. In addition, they must also possess excellent team working, communication, and clinical decision-making skills.

Increasing utilization of neoadjuvant therapy to downstage locally advanced disease has permitted more successful rates of breast-conservation therapy (BCS). A progressive decrease in the proportion of patients requiring mastectomy in favor of BCS has coincided with increased demand for either immediate or delayed breast-reconstruction together with evolution of oncoplastic procedures. The latter involves utilization of surgical techniques developed by plastic surgeons for cosmetic reshaping of the breast, subsequently applied by breast surgeons in an oncological context for more extensive resections in BCS.

All newly diagnosed breast cancer cases should be discussed in a multidisciplinary environment with representation from medical oncology, radiology, pathology, plastic surgery, and allied professions to ensure that comprehensive management options are discussed and treatment plans tailored to the specific needs of individual patients. Surgical treatment must maximize the chance of attaining negative resection margins which reduces the risk of local recurrence, but also produce good cosmetic results. There is an innate conflict between the basic aims of oncologic and plastic surgery—eradication of all locoregional disease while preserving breast tissue for optimal cosmesis. Herein lies the challenge of oncoplastic breast surgery, and all surgical personnel must reconcile oncologic and aesthetic aims for optimal patient outcomes. Patients should have clinical access to all appropriate reconstructive techniques, and the choice of surgery should be based on a patient's needs and wishes rather than surgeon preference.

SAFETY OF ONCOPLASTIC BREAST CONSERVATION

Oncoplastic breast surgery aims to retain or enhance the natural appearance of the breast following excision of a cancer. Techniques such as fat transfer can be employed to correct minor defects consequent to surgery and/or radiotherapy at a later stage, but there is growing acceptance that prevention of breast deformity is preferable to treatment thereof.

Initially, concerns were raised that oncologic outcomes might be compromised in attempts to minimize the volume of tissue resected for cosmetic benefit. However, to date, there is no evidence that oncoplastic breast-conservation techniques are less likely to achieve negative resection margins nor are associated with increased rates of re-excision.[1,2] On the contrary, due to the greater volume of tissue removed with oncoplastic procedures, larger tumors can be resected with a high chance of clear resection margins at first surgery. A negative margin does *not* imply absence of residual disease within remaining breast tissue, but implies a residual burden of tumor sufficiently low to be controlled with adjuvant treatments (radiotherapy and chemo/hormonal therapies). Local recurrence is determined by a combination of surgery, tumor biology, radiation, and systemic therapies.[3] An overall reduction in breast volume from "displacement" techniques may also facilitate delivery of radiotherapy by optimizing breast positioning and reducing dose inhomogeneity.

Nonetheless, unresolved controversies remain for oncoplastic breast conservation including: (a) identification of a positive resection margin following glandular mobilization, (b) accurate targeting of the tumor bed for a radiotherapy boost, (c) the upper size limit for safe breast conservation,[4] and (d) sequencing of radiotherapy with two-stage flap-based partial breast reconstruction. Further follow-up studies should help clarify these issues.

SAFETY OF BREAST RECONSTRUCTION

The oncologic safety of retaining the breast skin envelope and any complications attributable to implantable devices are key issues to consider. Skin-sparing techniques have been widely adopted to improve cosmetic outcomes following reconstruction and are now acknowledged to be safe in terms of disease recurrence, provided tumors are non-inflammatory and there is no direct skin infiltration.[5] A further development of the skin-sparing approach is nipple-sparing mastectomy which can further enhance aesthetic outcomes. However, preservation of the nipple-areola complex (NAC) is of unproven safety and only practiced selectively for relatively small tumors located some distance from the NAC or as a prophylactic procedure.[6] Although it is feasible to dissect the skin and subcutaneous tissues from the breast parenchyma without leaving remnant breast tissue, this is not the case for the NAC as the main lactiferous ducts converge upon the nipple. The areola can be readily dissected off the underlying breast tissue, but a thin layer of breast tissue must be retained to ensure viability of the NAC.

OUTCOME DATA

In 2012, the Association of Breast Surgery in the United Kingdom produced oncoplastic breast surgery guidelines for best practice.[7] This document details 25 key quality criteria recommendations covering all aspects of oncoplastic breast surgery including preoperative planning, post operative care, complication rates, training and education, and patient satisfaction outcomes. These guidelines were based on the findings of the UK National Mastectomy and Reconstruction Audit,[8] which identified significant geographical variations in breast surgery practice, unexpectedly high complication rates, and poor postoperative pain control following breast reconstruction.

All specialist breast surgeons should maintain personal records of procedures undertaken, including complication rates, oncological outcome data, and patient satisfaction (using validated tools such as the BREAST-Q,[9] developed at Memorial Sloan Kettering). In addition to quality assurance, this surgeon-specific outcome data inform the consent process and aid patients in making decisions when more than one surgical option is available.

CONTINUING PROFESSIONAL DEVELOPMENT

Breast surgery continues to evolve apace and surgeons must ensure their knowledge and skills base is updated regularly. Several well-established oncoplastic meetings exist which provide information on latest and best practices. Surgeons can further refine their practice by attending a range of masterclasses in oncoplastic breast surgery and visit other institutions for valuable hands-on experience in new techniques (Figure 33.1). Current development of models for surgical simulation will facilitate training in more complex oncoplastic techniques.

Apart from their clinical responsibilities, breast surgeons may choose to maintain or develop an interest in a related domain such as medical education, clinical management, or research. There are numerous opportunities for engagement in cancer networks at regional or national level and membership on boards or committees of professional organizations including designated colleges.

In the United Kingdom, surgeons must demonstrate their commitment to continuing professional development and quality improvement activities as these relate to their individual clinical practices. These are essential requirements for maintaining professional recognition from regulatory medical bodies and are monitored via an annual appraisal process and quinquennial revalidation.

TECHNOLOGY AND THE MEDIA

Breast surgery is a rapidly evolving speciality with frequent exposure to novel devices and techniques. In particular, some of the newer implantable devices for breast reconstruction are released onto the market with limited clinical and scientific evaluation to underpin their usage.

The introduction of acellular dermal matrices and synthetic meshes for implant-based reconstruction has significantly broadened the indications for and uptake of breast reconstruction. However, against this background of surgical enthusiasm, some devices have been officially withdrawn from clinical use due to emergence of safety concerns over relatively short periods of time. Therefore, a judicious approach to adoption of newer technologies outside the setting of clinical trials should be exercised. When trialing new devices, it is imperative to maintain a comprehensive database permitting subsequent analysis of selection criteria, complications, and outcome measures. Local registries can be interlinked and form part of a national or even global registry.

Improvements in technology provide a steady supply of new tools to optimize surgical techniques and planning. Image-guided percutaneous excision of smaller breast

33.1 Oncoplastic clinical skills training.

lesions is now feasible and bio-impedance spectroscopy is being evaluated for intraoperative margin assessment and reduction of re-excision rates.

Patients are increasingly well-informed about treatment options, widespread use of social media and existence of online patient blogs/communities has led to heightened patient expectations regarding outcomes, and the modern breast surgeon must engage more in shared decision-making processes (rather than "paternalism"). They should be aware of unrealistic expectations and direct their patients to authorized websites in order to gain accurate and balanced information. In addition, several tools are now available to aid patient decision-making, including a 3D breast simulation tool to provide a visual approximation of postoperative aesthetic outcomes.

CONCLUSION

Patients are now surviving longer due to advances in breast cancer treatment and expectations have increased accordingly. Improved survivorship has implications for health-related quality of life, and healthcare workers must strive collectively to ensure optimal oncologic, cosmetic, and functional outcomes. Surgeons must balance the oncological and cosmetic needs of patients and be prepared to constantly face new challenges. The number of elderly breast cancer patients is increasing, and oncoplastic surgery should be available to those who are otherwise fit despite their chronological age. Women who have undergone oncoplastic breast conservation or breast reconstruction may require further surgical intervention for late complications or to enhance breast aesthetics. Budgetary restraint can be aided by sensible planning of initial breast cancer treatment which maximizes oncological and cosmetic outcomes and minimizes the need for corrective surgery at a future date.

REFERENCES

1. Chakravorty, A., Shrestha, A. K., Sanmugalingam, N., Rapisarda, F., Roche, N., Querci della Rovere, G., and MacNeill, F.A. How safe is oncoplastic breast conservation? Comparative analysis with standard breast conserving surgery. *European Journal of Surgery Oncology* 2012; 38: 395–398.
2. Down, S. K., Jha, P. K., Burger, A., and Hussien, M. I. Oncological advantages of oncoplastic breast-conserving surgery in treatment of early breast cancer. *The Breast Journal* 2013; 19: 56–63.
3. Morrow, M., Harris, J. R., Schnitt, S. J. Surgical margins in lumpectomy for breast cancer, bigger is not better. *New England Journal of Medicine* 2012; 367: 79–82.
4. Mansell, J., Weiler-Mithoff, E., Martin, J., Khan, A., Stallard, S., Doughty, J.C., and Romics, L. How to compare the oncological safety of oncoplastic breast conservation surgery—To wide local excision or mastectomy? *The Breast* 2015; 24(4): 497–501.

5. Patania, N., Devaliaa, B. H., Andersona, C. A., and Mokbela, K. Oncological safety and patient satisfaction with skin-sparing mastectomy and immediate breast reconstruction. *Surgical Oncology* 2008; 17(2): 97–105.

6. Vase, M. Ø., Friis, S., Bautz, A., Bendix, K., Sørensen, H. T., and d'Amore, F. Breast implants and anaplastic large-cell lymphoma: A Danish population-based cohort study. *Cancer Epidemiology Biomarkers and Prevention* 2013;22(11):2126–2129.

7. Oncoplastic Breast Reconstruction: Guidelines for Best Practice, 2012. ABS/ BAPRAS. https://associationofbreastsurgery.org.uk/media/1424/oncoplastic-breast-reconstruction-guidelines-for-best-practice.pdf (Accessed December 3, 2018).

8. National Mastectomy and Breast Reconstruction Audit, Fourth Annual Report–2011. https://digital.nhs.uk/data-and-information/publications/statistical/national-mastectomy-and-breast-reconstruction-audit-annual-report/national-mastectomy-and-breast-reconstruction-audit-fourth-annual-report-2011 (Accessed December 3, 2018).

9. Breast Q: Breast Cancer, Memorial Sloan Kettering. http://qportfolio.org/breast-q/ (Accessed December 3, 2018).

34

Breast surgical training

34.1 AMERICAN TRAINING SYSTEM

Melissa Anne Mallory and Mehra Golshan

Introduction

Breast surgical training in the United States has undergone considerable changes in the past two decades. Once a field dominated by general surgeons without dedicated advanced training, breast surgery is now a rapidly expanding surgical subspecialty with formal instruction available as part of breast surgical oncology fellowships administered by the Society of Surgical Oncology (SSO). Opinion leaders within the field of breast surgery, many of whom trained before the advent of breast-specific fellowships, have been instrumental in development of the new multidisciplinary training paradigm.

Prior to the recognition of breast surgery as a distinct subspecialty, training in the management of breast disease was provided through general surgical residency programs. Many breast surgeons educated in the United States prior to 2003 followed the same pathway as general surgeons, completing a categorical 5-year general surgical residency program following completion of 4 years of medical school and 4 years of undergraduate coursework. These surgeons primarily gained their specialization in breast procedures through training acquired during residency and "on the job learning" in clinical practice. More recently, advancements in breast cancer care resulting from an improved understanding of the complexities of breast disease have highlighted a role for breast specialists and multidisciplinary care teams. Although existing surgical oncology fellowships offered advanced breast education as part of training, these programs focused broadly on multi-organ oncologic management. With research demonstrating a strong correlation between volume of breast surgical workload and outcomes, the merit of providing breast-specific training to trainees destined to provide specialized breast surgical care

became apparent, and the demand for specialized "breast surgeons" became increasingly prominent.[1,2]

In response to the increasing demand for breast specialist training, the SSO developed an approval process to certify newly formed breast fellowship programs.[3] Interdisciplinary breast surgical fellowship curriculum guidelines were established by three overseeing bodies including the SSO, the American Society of Breast Surgeons, and the American Society of Breast Disease. In 2003, the SSO Training Committee granted 33 Breast Surgical Oncology fellowship programs conditional approval. The computerized matching program subsequently utilized for the surgical oncology fellowship allocation was developed to assist with the first Breast Surgical Oncology fellowship match, which took place in 2004.[3] By 2015, there were 45 approved fellowship programs with an additional one being reviewed each year.

Surgeons today wishing to specialize in breast surgery have more training opportunities than ever before. Although no advanced training is required at this time to perform breast surgical operations in the United States, surgeons may wish to pursue additional advanced training through either a surgical oncology or breast oncology fellowship.

Breast surgery fellowship curriculum

The breast oncology fellowship guidelines are published on the SSO's website (https://www.surgonc.org/wp-content/uploads/2019/06/2019-Breast-Curriculum-and-Training-Requirements-Final.pdf).[4,5] These guidelines, revised most recently in 2014, were jointly established by the SSO, American Society of Breast Surgeons, and the American Society of Breast Disease. The fellowship consists of a minimum of 1 year of multidisciplinary training following successful completion of a general surgery residency program leading to board eligibility. The training is primarily clinical and consists of both surgical and non-surgical rotations, with at least 2 months of breast surgical training. Fellows are required to participate in regular programs including conferences, lectures, journal clubs, and educational courses. Experience is required with interdisciplinary breast specialties including medical oncology, radiation oncology, radiology, plastic and reconstructive surgery, and rehabilitation. This is ideally obtained through rotation on these services and participation in conferences, clinics, and other didactic opportunities. Clinical requirements include active participation in breast surgical procedures, initial outpatient assessment, preoperative decision-making, perioperative management, and patient follow-up, with at least 1 out of every 5 days devoted to preoperative and postoperative ambulatory patient care. The breast surgical oncology fellowship curriculum and minimum training requirements effective as of July 1, 2015 are outlined on the SSO's website under the breast fellowship section (http://www.surgonc.org/docs/default-source/pdf/2014_breast_fellowship_curriculum_training_requirements.pdf?sfvrsn=2).[4]

Oncoplastic surgery within the American model

The majority of breast surgery in the United States is performed by surgeons with general surgery backgrounds, some of whom have undergone the specialized fellowship training in either surgical oncology or breast surgical oncology. At the outset, all breast cancer surgeons balance oncologic with cosmetic outcomes, with the former taking priority. Oncoplastic surgery, first advocated by Dr. Werner Audrescht in 1998, aims to incorporate plastic surgical principles into breast surgical oncology operations, largely through tissue rearrangement techniques.[6] Retrospective and small series research efforts have suggested that oncoplastic approaches may improve aesthetic outcomes without compromising oncological outcomes for patients undergoing breast-conserving surgery and may extend the reach of breast conservation to patients who may have otherwise required mastectomy.[7-12] Although controversy still exists on the benefits of oncoplastic techniques, breast surgeons in the United States are being increasingly exposed to various procedures and their purported benefits. Currently, oncoplastic education is not a formal part of general surgical training programs and even in breast fellowship programs the oncoplastic curriculum is still evolving. Although the most recent breast fellowship guidelines require some oncoplastic training, programs vary widely with respect to the degree of oncoplastic exposure and training they provide. A 2011 study examining experiences for 85 graduates of breast fellowship programs between 2005 and 2009, for example, found that only 53% of graduates felt well-prepared for performing oncoplastic techniques.[13]

While we anticipate a trend toward a more specialist-driven model of breast patient care in the United States, surgical management and comprehensive breast cancer treatment will likely continue to be undertaken by both fellowship and non-fellowship trained surgeons.

Oncoplastic breast surgery is not part of general surgical training, and although the oncoplastic approach is beginning to be incorporated as part of breast surgical oncology fellowships, it has not been fully integrated into these programs. Development of prospective studies with positive outcomes may increase breast surgical oncologists' comfort with the oncoplastic approach and further define oncoplastic surgery's role in the breast surgeon's practice.

REFERENCES

1. Gillis CR, Hole DJ. Survival outcome of care by specialist surgeons in breast cancer: A study of 3786 patients in the west of Scotland. *British Medical Journal*. 1996;312(7024):145–148.

2. Roohan PJ, Bickell NA, Baptiste MS, Therriault GD, Ferrara EP, Siu AL. Hospital volume differences and five-year survival from breast cancer. *American Journal of Public Health*. 1998;88(3):454–457.

3. Berman RS, Weigel RJ. Training and certification of the surgical oncologist. *Chinese Clinical Oncology*. 2014;3(4):45.

4. SSO SoSO. 2014 Breast surigcal oncology fellowship curriculum and minimum training requirements effective July 1st 2015. Accessed October 7, 2015. http://www.surgonc.org/docs/default-source/pdf/2014_breast_fellowship_curriculum_training_requirements.pdf?sfvrsn=2.

5. SSO SoSO. 2015 Training and fellows, breast fellowship program requirements. Accessed October 7, 2015. http://www.surgonc.org/training-fellows/fellows-education/breast-oncology/program-requirements.

6. Audretsch W. Tumor-specific immediate reconstruction in breast cancer patients. *Perspectives in Plastic Surgery*. 1998;11:71–100.

7. Clough KB, Lewis JS, Couturaud B, Fitoussi A, Nos C, Falcou MC. Oncoplastic techniques allow extensive resections for breast-conserving therapy of breast carcinomas. *Annals of Surgery*. 2003;237(1):26–34.

8. Losken A, Dugal CS, Styblo TM, Carlson GW. A meta-analysis comparing breast conservation therapy alone to the oncoplastic technique. *Annals Plastic Surgery*. 2014;72(2):145–149.

9. Losken A, Pinell-White X, Hart AM, Freitas AM, Carlson GW, Styblo TM. The oncoplastic reduction approach to breast conservation therapy: Benefits for margin control. *Aesthetic Surgery Journal*. 2014;34(8):1185–1191.

10. Piper M, Peled AW, Sbitany H. Oncoplastic breast surgery: Current strategies. *Gland Surgery*. 2015;4(2):154–163.

11. Veiga DF, Veiga-Filho J, Ribeiro LM, Archangelo-Junior I, Mendes DA, Andrade VO et al. Evaluations of aesthetic outcomes of oncoplastic surgery by surgeons of different gender and specialty: A prospective controlled study. *Breast*. 2011;20(5):407–412.

12. Crown A, Wechter DG, Grumley JW. Oncoplastic breast-conserving surgery reduces mastectomy and postoperative re-excision rates. *Annals of Surgical Oncology*. 2015;22(10):3363–3368.

13. Sclafani LM, Bleznak A, Kelly T, El-Tamer MB. Training a new generation of breast surgeons: Are we succeeding? *Annals of Surgical Oncology*. 2012;19(6):1856–1861.

34.2 EUROPEAN TRAINING SYSTEM

Fiona MacNeill

The speciality of breast surgery has emerged over the last 20 years. There are multiple drivers for the creation of this new surgical speciality, but one of the most important is the increasing focus on maintenance of the breast aesthetic after breast cancer surgery: now regarded as an important component of a woman's psychosocial/sexual adaptation and pivotal to high-quality survivorship after breast cancer treatment.

For the purposes of this chapter, Europe is defined as the European Union (EU) comprising 28 member states with diverse economies and cultures and a population of over 500 million. Across the EU, there is significant disparity in breast cancer outcomes due to differing demographics, healthcare systems, resources, and provision of breast services. This diversity is also evident in the many different routes to breast surgical training: European breast oncology surgeons are mainly drawn from a general surgery background (with gynecology an alternative route). Moreover, exposure to oncoplastic breast surgery and training is highly variable, and in many countries, ablative breast cancer surgery alone remains the standard of care from a training perspective. Consequently, the challenge is to harmonize training in breast oncology as well as developing oncoplastic surgery with the aim of raising standards in oncological surgery and aesthetic outcomes which will collectively improve patient experience.

The current generation of more senior breast surgeons in the United Kingdom and Europe are mainly trained in general surgery/surgical oncology with a few from gynecology and plastic surgery. However, with an increasing focus on cosmetic outcomes, the next generation of breast surgeons must be fully trained in breast aesthetic surgery regardless of their parent speciality. Furthermore, they must acquire a combination of plastic and oncology surgery skills to equip them to be active members of both oncology and oncoplastic multidisciplinary teams.

Successful breast cancer treatment requires a multimodality approach, and therefore oncology surgeons must have a sound understanding of breast cancer biology and non-surgical treatments to allow them to work in equal partnership with the medical and radiation oncologists. In particular, oncoplastic surgeons must resist becoming oncology technicians: it is vital that as the primary and adjuvant roles of surgery and systemic therapies become more fluid, the breast surgeon understands and engages with the appropriate use and sequencing of all treatment modalities to minimize non-curative radical surgery. Equally, oncoplastic surgeons cannot just focus on aesthetics, nonetheless, any surgeon who operates on the breast must have a deep understanding of breast aesthetics. Whatever their title (be it breast surgeon, oncoplastic surgeon, plastic surgeon), they must work collaboratively with other surgeons, combining individual skills and talents to provide women

access to the full range of surgery techniques now available to promote maintenance of breast cosmesis after conservation or mastectomy.

Oncoplastic breast surgery initially involved only whole breast reconstruction and started due to the serendipitous pairing of like-minded breast and plastic surgeons who could see the benefits to their patients of working across professional boundaries to combine skill sets. This early collaborative ethos remains at the heart of educational and training initiatives which are accessible to both general surgeons and plastic surgeons with the ultimate aim of blurring and shifting traditional boundaries of practice so patients can access the best of both through the oncoplastic multidisciplinary team.[1]

Formal education and training in oncoplastic surgery has been difficult to introduce in Europe. This is largely due to the majority of breast oncology surgeons coming from a general surgery background where the emphasis has been on the delivery of intra-abdominal and emergency general surgery with only basic competencies in ablative breast cancer surgery. In addition, the numbers of plastic surgeons in Europe are relatively few, and their focus has been burns and functional reconstruction. However, both patients and employers increasingly demand oncoplastic trained surgeons, and this is driving specialist oncoplastic breast training for breast and plastic surgeons alike.

In the United Kingdom and Europe, breast and plastic surgery trainees are exposed to oncoplastic breast surgery in the final years of training in local breast centers. This can be supplemented with pre and/or post certification fellowships such as those administered by the European School of Surgical Oncology (ESSO) (http://www.eesoweb.org/). Since 2002, the National Health Service within the United Kingdom has funded ten oncoplastic fellowships which are open to general and plastic surgeons (http://www.icst.org/training:interface-groups/breast-oncoplastic-surgery). This group of about 120 oncoplastic surgeons have since gone on to develop their own oncoplastic teams thus providing wider access to oncoplastic training across the whole of the United Kingdom. This in turn is drawing the speciality of oncoplastic surgery to the attention of increasing numbers of medical students and young aspiring surgeons.

This experiential and skills focused local training is supported by a range of regional, national, and European knowledge and skills based educational courses, the first of which was set up in 1996 by the Royal College of Surgeons (England) (https://www.rcseng.ac.uk/surgeons/courses). The initial emphasis was on cancer management and MDT working for purposes of developing specialist breast skills in general surgeons recruited to support the new NHS breast screening program. The first oncoplastic skills-based courses with cadaveric instruction were set up in 2004, and, more latterly, oncoplastic and reconstructive breast surgery conferences such as ORBS (http://www.orbsmeetings.com/) in Nottingham, Milan, and Barcelona have fulfilled the important role of providing a platform for disseminating and stimulating research and evidence gathering as well as updating knowledge in a rapidly evolving speciality. The Oncoplastic Master's degree was launched by the University of East Anglia in 2011 which provides a mainly online flexible, modular course designed to provide the comprehensive knowledge and skills base required by a modern oncoplastic breast surgeon (https://www.uea.ac.uk/esurgery/ms-oncoplastic-breast-surgery). A similar course solely aimed at plastic surgeons has been launched in Barcelona.

Interest in establishing a specialist breast training program which would ultimately lead to formal certification began in 1996 with recommendations by the Breast Surgeons Group of the British Association of Surgical Oncology for the "Training of a General Surgeon with an Interest in Breast Disease."[2] In 2007, EUSOMA published guidelines on standards for the training of specialized breast surgeons[3] which defined what a specialist breast surgery curriculum should contain including the need for formal assessment. The European Union of Medical Specialties (http://www.uemssurg.org/divisions/breast-surgery) adopted the proposals and in 2010 established the first exam in specialist breast surgery supported by a clearly defined curriculum and exam entry requirements (European Board of Surgery Qualification). Some 20 years after the first publication enunciating the importance of specialist breast training, the European Board of Surgery Qualification is gaining traction and is now recognized by some European nations for certification in breast surgery.

In the United Kingdom, the General Medical Council approved the first oncoplastic curriculum in 2016: the challenge over the next few years will be to incorporate the new curriculum into general and plastic surgery training frameworks without destabilizing provision of cover for emergency surgery. These issues associated with decoupling of breast surgery from general surgery present challenges for training and service delivery worldwide and each nation will have to find the most appropriate solution compatible with their respective healthcare systems.

The richness of educational and training opportunities in oncoplastic breast surgery have spurred a thriving oncoplastic surgery trainees group (the Mammary Fold: http://www.themammaryfold.com/), with oncoplastic breast surgery rapidly becoming one of the most popular choices in surgical training at both undergraduate and postgraduate levels in the United Kingdom.

In summary, much remains to be done to improve access to oncoplastic breast surgery training across Europe, but there has been much progress over the last 20 years and the future of oncoplastic surgery is secure. A future goal will be a European standardized speciality-specific training program that incorporates the best elements from its general oncology and plastic surgery roots such that future oncoplastic breast surgeons can offer the highest quality of care to their patients.

REFERENCES

1. Rusby JE, Gough J, Harris PA, MacNeill FA. Oncoplastic multidisciplinary meetings: A necessity or luxury? *Ann R Coll Surg Engl.* 2011;93(4):273–274.
2. Cataliotti L et al; EUSOMA. Guidelines on the standards for the training of specialised health professionals dealing with breast cancer. *Eur J Cancer.* 2007;43(4):660–675.
3. The Breast Surgeons Group of the British Association of Surgical Oncology. The training of a general surgeon with an interest in breast disease. *Eur J Surg Oncol.* 1996;22 Suppl A:1–4.
4. Benson, JR, Down SK. Coming of age of oncoplastic breast surgery. *Br J Surg.* 2017;104(10):1269–1271.

EDUCATIONAL RESOURCES

- Down SK, Pereira JH, Leinster S, Simpson A. Training the oncoplastic breast surgeon-current and future perspectives. *Gland Surg.* 2013;2(3):126–127. doi:10.3978/j.issn.2227-684X.2013.06.02.
- Miguelena JM, Domínguez CF. Training in breast surgery in Spain. *Cir Esp.* 2016;94(6):323–330. doi:10.1016/j.ciresp.2016.01.007.
- Cardoso MJ, Macmillan RD, Merck B, Munhoz AM, Rainsbury R. Training in oncoplastic surgery: An international consensus. The 7th Portuguese Senology Congress, Vilamoura, 2009. *Breast.* 2010;19(6):538–540. doi:10.1016/j.breast.2010.03.030.
- MacNeill F. Training in breast reconstruction. *Hosp Med.* 2004;65(2):124.
- Baum M. Is it time for a paradigm shift in the training of breast surgeons as a sub-speciality?! *Breast.* 2003;12(3):159–160.

EDITORIAL COMMENTARY

Breast surgery is increasingly recognized as a speciality in many countries across the world although levels of specialization and skills mix vary widely. Notwithstanding the nuances of geographical location, common themes emerge in terms of requirements for specialist breast surgery training, and these are outlined in Sections 34.1 and 34.2. Thus all breast surgeons must acquire expertise not only in breast surgery but also oncology, radiology, and plastic surgery. They are uniquely placed to provide a balanced judgment on oncological and cosmetic aspects of breast surgery in order to maximize clinical outcomes and patient satisfaction. Nowadays, patients have high expectations in terms of the breast aesthetic after ablative surgery and training must adequately equip surgeons to manage these in the context of both treatment and outcomes. With prolonged survivorship, increasing numbers of women are reliant on a favorable cosmetic result to promote psychosocial, sexual, and functional adaptation following a breast cancer diagnosis.

Breast surgeons have traditionally undertaken a general surgical training program with only a minority coming from other disciplines such as gynecology and plastic surgery. An increasing focus on aesthetic outcomes has forced breast surgeons to develop duality of skills in plastic and oncological surgery. Delivery of comprehensive and relevant training programs presents a range of challenges that are both logistical and political. A collaborative ethos was the hallmark of early training programs, and this has been perpetuated into current arrangements that foster a degree of cross-fertilization and blurring of conventional practice boundaries.

The rising incidence of breast cancer coupled with increasing patient expectations is driving demand for specialized oncoplastic breast training. In recent years, training programs in general surgery have progressively incorporated dedicated oncoplastic breast surgery training into the final years with relinquishing of some general surgical on-call commitments. This enables continued provision of emergency general surgery but permits the development of breast surgery skills over and above basic ablative procedures. Both in Europe and the United States, formal instruction in oncoplastic breast surgery and oncology is available from certified fellowship programs administered under the aegis of organizations such as the Training Interface Group (TIG) in the United Kingdom and the Society of Surgical Oncology (SSO) in the United States. These types of fellowships are an important element of breast-specific training and have helped meet the demand for specialized breast surgical care; trainees exposed to a high-volume breast workload which will be echoed in definitive professional appointments. Within the United Kingdom, employees tend to advertise contemporaneously for breast surgeons who can offer a full range of oncoplastic procedures, while in the United States breast surgery can be practiced without any advanced training (often breast surgeons work closely with plastic surgery colleagues who may compensate for lack of oncoplastic competency).

Many European countries and in particular the United Kingdom have well-established oncoplastic surgical training programs with an impressive portfolio of courses, master-classes, and fellowship programs. Oncological and plastic surgery has historically been dichotomized in the United States, but there is increasing experience and awareness of oncoplastic techniques among trainees. These are gradually being assimilated into training programs, whether general surgical or dedicated breast fellowships. Nonetheless, almost half of graduates from American programs sense a lack of confidence in performing oncoplastic procedures independently.

Despite the "coming of age" of oncoplastic breast surgery,[1] several outstanding issues remain pertaining to oncological safety for larger tumors (>5 cm) and the complexity of surgery for some smaller tumors which may involve a contralateral symmetrizing procedure.

It is essential that all specialist breast surgeons maintain personal records of procedures undertaken, including complication rates, oncological outcome data, and patient satisfaction using validated tools. In addition to quality assurance, these surgeon-specific outcome data inform the consent process and aid patients in making decisions when more than one surgical option is available. Surgeons should strive to "get it right first time" and maximize oncological and cosmetic outcomes without the need for corrective surgery and the cost implications of additional operations.

Index

Note: Page numbers in italic and bold refer to figures and tables, respectively.

abdominal flap, 236, 334–335, *335*
abdominal free flaps, 345
abdominoplasty, *367*
accelerated partial breast irradiation (APBI) technique, 405, 411, *412*, 414
acellular dermal matrix (ADM), 13, 30, 56, 226–229, *228*, 241, *247*, *250*, *252*, 277, 384
  -assisted reconstruction, 14, 252, *257*
  biological reactions to, 13–17
  as central graft, *446*
  collagen cross-linking in, 15
  decellularization process, 14–15
  defined, 13
  DTI reconstruction with, *243*
  ECM effects on, 14–15
  Europe, 260–262, 297–298
  impacts on irradiated breast reconstruction, 293–298
  with implants, 257–262
  integration, 15–16, *16*, *293*
  nipple creation with, *445*
  patient and technical factors, 15–16
  USA, 257–258, 293–295
  usage purpose of, 14
ACOSOG Z0011 trial, 72
ACOSOG Z1071 trial, 72
acute inflammation, 14–15
acute skin toxicity, 414
adipocyte, 22–23
adipose-derived MSC, 303
adipose-derived stem cells (ASCs), 26–27
adipose tissue, 22–24, 26, 438
adjuvant radiotherapy, 175, 391
ADM, *see* acellular dermal matrix
adrenaline, 24
AFG, *see* autologous fat grafting
AICAP flap, *see* anterior intercostal artery perforator flap
ALCL, *see* anaplastic large cell lymphoma
ALD, *see* autologous latissimus dorsi flap
AlloDerm, 15, 445
AlloMax, 15
alloplastic techniques, 234–235, 381
ALND, *see* axillary lymph node dissection

American breast surgical training system, 459–460
American College of Surgeons Oncology Group Z0011, 54
American Joint Committee on Cancer staging system, 69
anaplastic large cell lymphoma (ALCL), 13, 19, 30
anastomosis, 365, 438
anterior intercostal artery perforator (AICAP) flap, 131, 134–135, 142, *142*, 179; *see also* breast implant-associated anaplastic large cell lymphoma
APBI, *see* accelerated partial breast irradiation technique
areola reconstruction, 443–444
ASCs, *see* adipose-derived stem cells
atypical cyst liponecrotic cyst, 28
autologous breast augmentation, 133–134
autologous breast reconstruction, 3–4, 179, 214–216, 236, 332, 339, 345, 356
autologous fat grafting (AFG), 22, *167*, 167–168, *168*, 177, 189, 298; *see also* autologous fat transfer method
  ASCs impacts on, 26–27
  breast cancer detection and, 28
  complications, 27–28
  in cosmetic/reconstructive breast surgery, **22**
  graft failure/resorption, 27–28
  liponecrotic cysts, 28
autologous fat transfer method, 23
  cannula/syringe, lipoaspiration, 24–25
  donor site selection, 23–24
  fat injection techniques, 25–26
  graft dimension, 26
  graft placement, 26
  harvested fat processing, 25
  injection cannula, 26
  lipoaspirate, 24
  lipoaspiration, 24–25
  overcorrection, 26
autologous latissimus dorsi (ALD) flap, 312
  advantages, 312
  bilateral metachronous, *313*

complications, 317–318
  disadvantages, 312
  immediate, *312*, *318*
  operative approach, 314–317
  preoperative planning, 313, *313*
  radiotherapy, 318
  recovery, 317–318
  secondary procedures, 318
  shoulder function, 318
autologous nonimplant-based techniques, 185, *186*
autologous tissue flaps
  ALD, 312–318
  boomerang GAP, 351–355
  DIEP, 332–336
  double DIEP, 345–348
  free TRAM, 326–331
  LAP, 362–367
  LD, 309–311, 342–344
  PAP, 349–350
  pedicled TRAM, 320–325
  TAP, 339–341
  TUG, 356–360
autologous transplantation of fat, 22
axillary lymph node dissection (ALND), 38, 54, 72, 96–97

B-06 trial (NSABP protocol), 10
B-18 trial (NSABP protocol), 48
Baker III/IV contracture, 379
banana role, 349
BASO II trial, 406
BCS, *see* breast-conservation/conserving surgery
BCT, *see* breast-conservation therapy
B-cup-sized breasts, 373, *373*
bell flap, 445, *445*
BI-ALCL, *see* breast implant-associated anaplastic large cell lymphoma
bilateral mammoplasty, 176–177, *178*
bilateral metachronous breast reconstruction, *313*
bioengineered breast, 252, *252*, 254, 305
"biological predeterminism" hypothesis, 10
biological reactions
  to ADM, 13–17
  to autologous fat grafting, 22–29

466 Index

biologic scaffolds, 14
biologic tumor markers, 69
biomarkers, 37
BioZorb tissue marker, 411, *412*
blunt-tip cannula, 24–26
boomerang flap, *232, 233,* 338
boomerang GAP flap, 351–355
boost dose, 150, 418, 421, 425, 429
brachytherapy, 165, 392, 394, 411, *412,* 418
   IB, 423, 429
   interstitial, 392, 407, *408,* 421, 427
   intracavity, 392
breast
   augmentation, 13, 19, 28, 133–134
   surgeon, 53–56, 463; *see also* modern
      specialized breast surgeons
   surgery fellowship curriculum, 459–460
   symmetry, 64–65
   tissue coverage, 255, *256,* **256**
breast cancer, 39, 61–62, 69
   multifocal, 43
   national guidelines, 6
   staging with mammography, 71
Breast Cancer Atlas, 400
breast carcinoma
   histologic subtypes, 39–40
   molecular subtypes, 40–44
breast-conservation/conserving surgery
    (BCS), 10–11, 55, 58, 69, 96, 147, 381, 455
   advances, 53
   aesthetic outcome, 58
   disadvantages, 58
   intraoperative assessment, *149*
   mastectomy and, 48–49, 67
   oncoplastic, 163–164
   oncoplastic surgery *versus,* **155**
   patient selection, 10–11, 34
   radiotherapy after, 391
   volumetric symmetry restoration, 176–179
breast-conservation therapy (BCT), 3–4, 33,
    36, 77, 89
breast-conserving therapy
   cosmetic sequelae after, 175
   for DCIS, 36–37
   extensive intraductal component, 42
   goals, 36
   for invasive carcinomas, 40
   PBRT after, 405–415
   radiotherapy and, 405–409
   specimen, *36*
   for triple negative breast cancer, 41
breast implant-associated anaplastic large cell
    lymphoma (BI-ALCL), 19–20
breast ptosis, nipple-sparing mastectomy in,
    208–209
BREAST-Q, 61, 68, 456
breast reconstruction; *see also specific breast*
    reconstruction
   ADM, 14, 252, *257*
   approaches selection, 56, 58–59
   autologous fat grafting in, **22**
   breast surgeon's perspectives, 55–56

Europe, 6–7
   goals, 64–65, 67
   with implants, 284
   mastectomy and, 55–56
   patients' expectations, 64–65
   patients' perspectives, 61–62
   radiotherapy timing and, 50
   surgeon's perspective, 58–59
   with textured silicone implant, *20*
   USA, 3–5
breast revision
   flap based procedures, 385, *385–386*
   implant-based procedures, 384
   partial breast reconstruction, 381
   partial mastectomy, 371–377
   patient evaluation/incision/reconstructive
      procedure selection, 380–381
   patient satisfaction, 379
   whole breast reconstruction, 379–380
BREASTrial, 16
breast surgical training
   American, 459–460
   European, 461–462
breast ultrasound, *see* sonography
brentuximab vedotin, 20
brown fat, 22
"bucket handle" technique, 208

calcifications, 28
CALGB trial, 406
cannula, 24–26
capsular contracture, 380–381
carcinoma
   breast, 39–44
   in situ, 36–39
   invasive, 39–40, 80–81
cartilage grafts, 443, 445
C-cup-sized breasts, *373,* 373–374, *374, 375*
CD30 immunohistochemistry, *20*
cefazolin, 250
cell-assisted lipotransfer, 27
cell survival theory, 23
cellulitis, *434,* 435
central defects, 180
centrifugal force, 25
centrifugation, 25, 27
chronic inflammation, 15, *16*
circular movements, nipple, 449, *449*
COBALT study, 148
Coleman, S., 23
collagen cross-linking, 15
COMET trial, 97
complex reshaping procedures, 176
computed-tomography (CT) angiography,
    327, 437
   abdominal wall perforators, 333–334, *334*
   LAP flap, 363, *363*
concentric mastopexy, 109, *110,* 373, *373*
conformal radiotherapy, 395
constructive remodeling, 13, 15
contralateral breast, 64–65, 165, *166*
   volume augmentation, *168*

contralateral mammoplasty, 110
contralateral mastectomy, 193
contralateral prophylactic mastectomy
    (CPM), 4, 54, 67–68, 77
contralateral symmetrizing surgery, 176
contrast-enhanced MRI, 73–74
contrast-enhanced spectral mammography
    (CESM), 34, 66
cosmetic sequelae, 175
CPM, *see* contralateral prophylactic
    mastectomy
CT, *see* computed-tomography angiography
C-V flap, 445, *445*

Danish Breast Cancer Cooperative
    Group, **394**
DCIS, *see* ductal carcinoma in situ
D-cup-sized breasts, 374, *375, 376, 377*
decellularization process, 14–15
decision-making, 55–56, 61–62, 68
   breast reconstruction approaches
      selection, 56, 58–59
   DCIS, 36
   delayed-immediate oncoplastic repair, 94
   delayed oncoplastic repair, 93
   DTI reconstruction with ADM, *243*
   Europe, 6
   immediate oncoplastic repair, 90
   patient choice, 61–62
   USA, 4
deep inferior epigastric perforator (DIEP)
    flap, *186,* 227, 230–233, 236, 329, 332,
    338, 349, 356–357, 372, 385, 399
   abdominal flaps evolution, 334–335
   advantages, 332
   delayed breast reconstruction, *332*
   drawbacks, 332, *333*
   flap harvest, 334, *335*
   imaging modalities, 333–334
   indications, 333, *334*
   perfusion, abdominal zones, *333*
   reconstruction, 215–216
   versus TRAM flaps, **331,** *336*
   vascular anatomy, 332
de-epithelialization, 208, 230, 233
delayed-after radiotherapy
    reconstruction, 164
delayed-before radiotherapy reconstruction,
    164, *164*
delayed breast reconstruction, *see* delayed
    reconstruction
delayed-delayed breast reconstruction, 221
   with autologous tissue, 222–223
   with implants, 221–222
delayed-immediate breast reconstruction,
    217–218
delayed-immediate oncoplastic repair,
    92–93, **154**
delayed-immediate partial breast
    reconstruction, *164*
delayed-immediate reduction mammoplasty,
    156–157

delayed oncoplastic repair, 93–94, 98, 112, 371
delayed oncoplastic repair, after radiotherapy, 164
  Europe, 175–187
  implications, 165–166
  percutaneous needle scar release and AFG, 167–168
  surgical technique, 171–187
  USA, 171–173
delayed oncoplastic repair, before radiotherapy, 153, 164
  versus immediate repair, 153–154, **154**
  optimal timing for, 158
  pathological margins, issues to, 154–156, *155*, **155**, *156*
  surgical approaches for, 156–158
delayed partial breast reconstruction, 175, *180–181*
delayed reconstruction (DR), 7, 62, 64, 67, 290, *291*, *312*, 323; *see also* immediate reconstruction
  with DIEP flap, *332*
  versus IR, 217, 383
dermis, 13
dermoglandular flap, 124
dermoglandular reduction mammoplasty
  advantage, 109
  Europe, 116–123
  guiding principles, 116
  operation, 116–117
  USA, 109–115
dexamethasone, 305
diagnostic imaging, 33–35, 69
diathermy, 84
DIEP, *see* deep inferior epigastric perforator flap
digital breast tomosynthesis, 69–70
digital *versus* standard mammograms, 255, *255*
direct-to-implant (DTI) reconstruction, 241–242, 245–246
  advantages and disadvantage, 251
  delayed, 248
  immediate two-stages, 247–248
  one-stage implant, 249–250
  patients characteristics for, 251
  surgical technique, 250–251
displacement concentric mastopexy, 373, *373*
distal flaps, 172
dominant vascular pedicle, 356
donor site closure, 328
donor site memory, 24
dorsal lithotomy position, *357*
double-DIEP flap, 230, *231*, 338, 345
  fat graft, 346
  host, 346–347
  vascularized matrix principle, 345–346
double opposing tab flap, 444–445, *445*
doughnut mastopexy, 208

DR, *see* delayed reconstruction
DTI reconstruction, *see* direct-to-implant reconstruction
dual-dermoglandular pedicle technique, *112*
ductal carcinoma, *137–139*
ductal carcinoma, invasive, 39, *39*, *70*, *74*
ductal carcinoma in situ (DCIS), 34, 36, 77–78, 83, 96, 116, *229*
  BCT for, 36–37
  incidence, 86
  local recurrence in, 36–37
  with microinvasion, *37*, 37–38
  treatment, 36
duplex ultrasonography, 433

E-cadherin, 38–39, *40*
electron boost, 421
ELIOT trial, **392**, 395
EORTC trial, 150, 405
estimating the percentage of breast volume excised (EPBVE), 11
estrogen receptor (ER), 40, *41*
Europe
  ADMs in, 260–262, 297–298
  breast reconstruction, 6–7
  delayed oncoplastic repair, after radiotherapy, 175–187
  dermoglandular reduction mammoplasty in, 116–123
  fat grafting, 264–276, 297–298, 301–302
  flap repair before radiotherapy, 131–144
  implant-based whole breast reconstruction, with irradiation, 283–285, 290–292
  lymph node tissue transfer, 437–439
  one-stage implant reconstruction, 245–251
  tissue rearrangement in, 107–108
European Board of Surgery Qualification, 462
European breast surgical training system, 461–462
European School of Surgical Oncology (ESSO), 461
European Union of Medical Specialties, 462
expander insertion technique, *294*
extensive intraductal component, 42
extensive multicentric right breast malignancy, *71*
extensive multifocal breast cancer, 43
external beam radiotherapy, 165
external prosthesis, 64
extracellular matrix (ECM), 13
extreme oncoplasty, 101–105

FAST FORWARD trial, 427
fat
  adipose tissue and adipocyte, 22–23
  autologous transplantation of, 22
  embryology, 22
  function, 22
  harvest, 24–25, 168, 290
  injection techniques, 265–266

lobules, 23
necrosis, 50
transplantation, 269
fat grafting, Europe, 264–267, 297–298
  contour defect and capsular retraction, 270
  contour deformity, 269
  delayed reconstruction, 273–275
  implant malpositioning, 272–273
  on irradiated breast reconstruction, 297–298
  salvage procedure, 275–276
  shape deformity and capsular contracture, 270–271
  surgical technique, 269
  volume defect, 271–272
  for whole breast reconstruction, 301–302
fat grafts/grafting, 22–23, 27–28, 143, 172, 299, 374, 379–380, 385, *385–386*
  autologous, *see* autologous fat grafting
  breast revision after, 385–386
  dimension, 26
  double DIEP flap, 346
  USA, 293–295
  for whole breast reconstruction, 301–305
fat transfer, 167–168, 177, 179, 264, 302, 455
  autologous, *see* autologous fat transfer method
Faxitron, 97, 148, *149*
FFDM, *see* full-field digital mammography
fibroblasts, 385
fibrosis, 418
Fisher, B., 10
flap; *see also* specific flap
  distal, 172
  repair before radiotherapy, *see* intrinsic breast flap oncoplastic reconstruction; pedicled perforator flaps
  vascularity, 16
flap harvest/harvesting, 143
  AICAP, *142*
  ALD, *314*, 314–315
  boomerang, *232*
  boomerang GAP, 351, *352*
  DIEP, 334, *335*
  double-DIEP, *231*
  free TRAM, 327–328
  LD, 309–310
  TDAP, *136–137*
flap inset
  ALD, 316–317
  boomerang GAP, 355
  double-DIEP, 230
  free TRAM, 328
  TAP, 341
  TUG, 357–358, *358*
Florence trial, **393**, 395
formal education and training, 461
Fournier, P., 24
free-flap reconstruction, 206
free nipple grafting method, 209

468 Index

free TRAM flap, 326
advantages, **326**, **329**
classification, **326**
indications and contraindications, **326**,
326–327, **327**
intraoperative surgical technique,
327–328
muscle-sparing, *327*
pedicled TRAM, DIEP flaps *versus*, **331**
perioperative management, 329
preoperative investigations, 327
frozen section examination, 83–84
full-field digital mammography
(FFDM), 96
full-field mammography, 69–70

GAP, *see* gluteal artery perforator flap
GEC-ESTRO trial, 394, **394**, 396, 407, *408*
glandular flaps, 179
gluteal artery perforator (GAP) flap, 338,
351–355
gluteal flap, 351
Gore-Tex suture, *119, 120*
gracilis muscle, 356, *356*
graft, 23
graft survival, 23
gray area, 11
greater saphenous vein (GSV), *434*
growth factor stimulation, 303

Halsted, W.S., 10
Halstedian hypothesis, 10
Halsted mastectomy defect, *265*
hematoma, 418
H&E stain, *39, 43*
Hodgkin's lymphoma, 19
homologous dermis, *251*
human epidermal growth factor receptor 2
(HER2), 40–41, *41*
Hungarian National Institute of Oncology
trial, 392, **392**, 394
hydrodissection, 199
hypofractionated radiotherapy, 419

IB, *see* intraoperative brachytherapy
IBTR, *see* ipsilateral breast tumor recurrence
ICAP, *see* intercostal artery perforator flap
IMAP, *see* internal mammary artery
perforator flap
immediate-before radiotherapy
reconstruction, 163
immediate breast reconstruction, *see*
immediate reconstruction
immediate implant-based reconstruction, 3,
216, 245
immediate oncoplastic repair, 90–91, 97–98
versus delayed repair, 153–154, **154**
partial mastectomy, 371
immediate oncoplastic repair before
radiotherapy
dermoglandular reduction mammoplasty,
109–123

flap-based methods, 124–144
local tissue rearrangement, 101–108
immediate one-stage bilateral reconstruction,
245
immediate one-stage monolateral
reconstruction, *246*
immediate reconstruction (IR), 6, 30, 56,
62, 64, 68, 213, 290–292, *291*; *see also*
delayed reconstruction
with ALD flap, *312, 318*
autologous approach, 214–216
benefits, 68, 213–214
completion mastectomy and, 185–186
versus delayed reconstruction, 217, 383
general considerations, 214
implant-based approach, 3, 216, 245
potential concerns, 214
rates across Europe, 6, **6**
regional and institutional variation, 7
immediate two-stage breast reconstructions,
247–248
implant-based breast reconstruction, 3, 30,
62, 66, 228, 284
breast revision after, 379–381
implant-based whole breast reconstruction,
with irradiation
ADMs and fat grafting, impacts on,
293–298
technique for, 287–292
timing, 279–285
implant-based whole breast reconstruction,
without irradiation
ADM with, 257–262
fat grafting with, 264–276
one-stage, 241–251
two-stage, 252–256
IMPORT LOW trial, **393**, 395, 407–408, *409*
IMRT, *see* intensity-modulated radiotherapy
indocyanine green (ICG)-lymphangiography,
437
inferior partial defects, 180, *185*
inferolateral defects, 172
inflammatory breast cancer, 53
initial breast imaging assessment, 66
in situ carcinoma
DCIS, 34, 36–38, 77–78, 83, 96, 116, *229*
LCIS, *38*, 38–39
in situ disease, 77–78
intensity-modulated radiotherapy (IMRT),
395, 403, 414, 421
intercostal artery perforator (ICAP) flap,
131, *132*
internal breast radiotherapy, 165
internal mammary artery perforator (IMAP)
flap, 131, *132*, 134–135, 143
internal mammary chain (IMC), 402,
402, 405
internal mammary node (IMN), 400
internal mammary vessels, 365
interstitial brachytherapy, 392, 421, 427
GEC-ESTRO trial, 407, *408*
interstitial multi-catheter brachytherapy, 411

interval fat grafting, *295, 385–386*
Intrabeam™, 405
intracavity brachytherapy, 392
intraoperative assessment, 148–150, *149*
margin, 87
of nipple, 195
pathological approach, 83–84, 149
radiological approach, 86–87
intraoperative brachytherapy (IB), 423, 429
intraoperative electron radiotherapy
(IOERT), 425
intraoperative margin assessment, 43
intraoperative radiotherapy (IORT), 395, 405,
427, 429
fat necrosis, 426
fibrosis, 418
low kilovoltage x-rays, 425
parenchymal scarring, 426
tumor bed visualization, 418
WBRT, 425
intraoperative specimen radiography, 148
intraoperative ultrasound, 87, 97
intrinsic breast flap oncoplastic
reconstruction
central defect, 126, *126, 127*
on defect location, 125–130
inferior pole defect, 125, *125*
lateral pole defect, 128, *128, 129*
medial pole defect, 129–130, *130*
postoperative care, 130
preoperative assessment, 124
superior pole defect, 128
surgical techniques, 124–125
invasive breast cancer, 10, 38, 70–71
invasive carcinoma, 39–40, 80–81
ductal, 39, *39, 70, 74*
lobular, 39, *40*, 70
with lymphovascular invasion, *43*, 43–44
IOERT, *see* intraoperative electron
radiotherapy
IORT, *see* intraoperative radiotherapy
ipsilateral breast tumor recurrence (IBTR),
9–10, 55, 147–148
ipsilateral internal mammary chain, 402
ipsilateral LAP flap, 363, *364*
ipsilateral recurrence, 36–38
IR, *see* immediate reconstruction
iridium-192 brachytherapy, 394
IRMA trial, **394**, 395
irradiation breasts defects, 172, *173*
ischemia imbibition, 23

Kaplan-Meier analysis, 222, 281

LAP, *see* lumbar artery perforator flap
lateral decubitus, 363
lateral intercostal artery perforator (LICAP)
flap, 131, 134–135, *140–141*, 140–142
latissimus dorsi (LD) flap, 158, 172, 229–230,
236, 309, 399
to augment volume, 310, *310*
blood supply and innervation, 309

flap harvest, 309–310
inferomedial resection defect, 179, *182–183*
large superior defect, 179, *184*
lateral near-quadrantectomy defect, 179, *181*
muscle-only, 230
role in breast reconstruction, 310–311
secondary procedures, 310
skin paddle, 179, *182*
superior defects, 179, *184*
TE *versus* implant, 310
latissimus dorsi (LD) muscle flap, 342–344
latissimus dorsi myocutaneous flap, 179, 230
LCIS, *see* lobular carcinoma in situ
LD, *see* latissimus dorsi flap
LICAP, *see* lateral intercostal artery perforator flap
lidocaine, 24
linear accelerators, APBI, 414–415
lipoaspiration/lipoaspirate, 24–25
lipofilling, 168, 177, 179, *249*, *250*, 347, 380–381, *381*
lipomodeling technique, 26
liponecrotic cysts, 28
lipostructure, 264–265
liposuction, 22, 433, *434*
lobular carcinoma, invasive, 39, *40*, 70
lobular carcinoma in situ (LCIS), *38*, 38–39
locally advanced breast cancer, 284, *285*
local recurrence, 10–11, 455
DCIS, 36–37
invasive carcinomas, 40
LCIS, 38
local reshaping procedures, 176
local tissue rearrangement, 101–105
locoregional recurrence, 41
LORD trial, 97
LORIS trial, 34, 97
lumbar artery, 362, *362*
lumbar artery perforator (LAP) flap, 362
advantage and disadvantage, 365
anatomy, 362, *362–363*
complications, 367, **367**
imaging, 362, *363*
outcomes, 366–367
postoperative care, 365
preoperative planning, 363, *364*
surgical management, 363–364
techniques, 364–365
lumpectomy, 53, 418, 421
APBI technique, 411, 414
BioZorb tissue marker, 411, *412*
TARGIT-IORT trial, 406, **406**, *407*
lymphangiogenesis, 433, 437
lymphedema, 433, *434*
lymph node tissue transfer
Europe, 437–439
Taiwan, 433–435
lymphoma, 19
lymphovascular invasion, *43*, 43–44, 165

M2 phenotype macrophage, 15
magnetic resonance imaging (MRI), 34, 66
advantages, 73
contrast-enhanced, 73–74
-guided biopsy, 96, 193
preoperative, 66, 73
mammogram images, *71*, *73*, *74*, 255, *255*
mammography, 33, 66, 96, 171, 421
breast cancer staging with, 71
full-field, 69–70
tumor visualization on, 70
mammoplasty, 51, 67, 109; *see also* reduction mammoplasty
bilateral, 176–177, *178*
margin
intraoperative assessment, 87
negative surgical, 9–10, 42, 55, 66–67, 69, 147–148, *148*, **148**
pathological, 154–156
positivity, 155
postoperative margin assessment, 147–151
routine cavity shave, 149
mastectomy, 6, 48–49, 53, 55, 102
BCS and, 48–49, 67
completion, *see* postoperative margin assessment
contralateral, 193
CPM, 4, 54, 67–68, 77
disadvantage, 58
nipple-sparing, *see* nipple-sparing mastectomy
radical, 10
and reconstruction, 55–56, 242
risk-reducing, 7
skin flap vascularity, 16
Mastectomy Reconstruction Outcomes Consortium study, 62
mastopexy, 108, 208, 387
concentric, 109, *110*, 373, *373*
nipple areola complex, 371–372
mature adipocyte, 22
medial defects, 172, *173*
medial supraclavicular areas, 405
medical grade silicone, 13
Memorial Sloan Kettering Cancer Center (MSKCC) algorithms, 279–280, *280*
Memorial Sloan Kettering protocol, *288*
mesenchymal precursor cell, 22
metastatic disease, 72, *72*
microanastomosis, 365
microinvasive carcinoma, *37*, 37–38
micropigmentation device, 448–449, *449*
microvascular anastomoses, 328
mini-DIEP flap, 172
mini-SIEA flap, 172
modern specialized breast surgeons
BCS, 455
breast reconstruction, safety of, 456
oncoplastic breast conservation, 455–456
outcome data, 456
professional development, 456
surgical treatment, 455

technical skills and attributes, 455
technology and media, 456–457
molecular breast imaging, 74
monopedicle TRAM flap, *323*
monotonous tumor cells, *38*
MRI, *see* magnetic resonance imaging
multi-catheter interstitial brachytherapy, 421
multifocal carcinoma, 43
multifocal/multicentric breast cancer, 43, 71–72
murine abdominal wall defect model, 15
muscle-only latissimus dorsi (LD) flap, 230
muscle-sparing free TRAM flap, *327*, *330*
myocutaneous flap, 179, 320

NAC, *see* nipple-areola complex
National Institute for Health and Clinical Excellence (NICE), 6
National Surgical Adjuvant Breast and Bowel Project (NSABP), 10, 48
needles, 448–449, *449*
negative surgical margin, 9–10, 42, 55, 66–67, 69, 147–148, *148*, **148**
neoadjuvant chemotherapy, 34, 48–49, 66, 80, 284
neoadjuvant therapy, 116
neo-nipple-areola complex, 126
nipple, 65
nipple-areola complex (NAC), *126*, 128, *198*, 198–199, 203–204, 229, 372, 374, 421, 451
nipple-areola complex (NAC) reconstruction, 443–444
3-D tattooing, 448–450
nipple necrosis, 200–201
nipple reconstruction
bell flap, 445, *445*
biologics, 445–446
C-V flap, 445, *445*
S-flap (double opposing tab), 444–445, *445*
skate flap, 444, *444*
star flap, 444, *444*
nipple-sparing mastectomy (NSM), 33, 56, 172, 203–204, 227, 229, *229*, 234, 241, *373*, 373–374, 384
adjuvant radiotherapy, 195
areola skin, 194, *194*
bilateral, 200, *200*
in breast ptosis, 208–209
endoscopic approaches to, 206
hydrodissection, 199
incisions for, 205–206
intraoperative assessment, 195
NAC, *198*, 198–199
nipple necrosis, 200–201
predictors, nipple involvement, 194, **195**
reconstruction process, 198, *198*
recurrence risk, 195
skin preservation, 194, 199–200
skin-reduction approach, 200, *201*
surgical planning, 199, **199**

non-Hodgkin's lymphoma (NHL), 19
non-invasive image-guided breast
    brachytherapy (NIBB), 421
non-palpable lesions, 80
NSABP-B39/RTOG 0413 trial, **393**, 395
NSM, *see* nipple-sparing mastectomy

obstructive lymphedema, 433
occult malignancy, 91
omental flap, 381
omitting radiotherapy, 406, **406**
oncologic considerations
    breast surgeon, 53–54
    diagnostic imaging, 33–35
    medical oncologist, 48–49
    pathologist, 36–44
    radiation oncologist, 50–51
oncoplastic breast conservation, 455–456
oncoplastic breast-conserving surgery,
    163–164
oncoplastic breast surgery, 51, 55, 67–68, 455
oncoplastic clinical skills training, *457*
Oncoplastic Master's degree, 462
oncoplastic parenchymal resection
    in situ disease, 77–78
    invasive carcinoma, 80–81
oncoplastic repair, **154**
    delayed, 93–94, 98, 112, 153–158,
        163–187, 371
    delayed-immediate, 92–93
    immediate, 90–91, 101–144
    timing, 89–94, *90*, 124, 158
oncoplastic surgery, 109, 124, 150
    within American model, 460
    versus breast-conservation surgery, **155**
    defined, 9
    negative margin, 9–10
    patients, selection of, 10–11
    purpose, 153
    techniques, 11, 77
Oncotype DX assay, 37
one-stage implant reconstruction, 229, 241
    Europe, 245–251
    USA, 241–244

PAP, *see* profunda artery perforator flap
parascapular adipo-fascial flap, *315*
parascapular flap, *316*
parenchymal flap, 124
partial breast irradiation (PBI), 165–166, 189,
    391, 427
partial breast radiotherapy (PBRT)
    brachytherapy, 392, 394–395, 411, *412*
    conformal/intensity-modulated
        radiotherapy, 395
    intraoperative radiotherapy, 395
    linear accelerator, 414–415
    in low-risk patients, 396
    patient selection, 396
    rationale, 391–392
    targeted radiotherapy, 405–409
    versus WBRT, 392, **392–394**

partial breast reconstruction, 11, 67, 77, 97–98
    breast revision, 381, 383
    delayed, 175, *180–181*
    delayed-immediate, *164*
    technique selection factors for, 176
partial mastectomy
    breast repair after, *114*
    deformity after, *115*
    radiotherapy boost dose delivery after, 421
    tumor bed with WBRT, boosting, 417–419
partial mastectomy, breast revision
    A- and B-cup-sized breasts, 373, *373*
    C-cup-sized breasts, *373*, 373–374, *374*, *375*
    contralateral symmetry procedure, 371–372
    D-cup-sized breasts, 374, *375*, *376*, *377*
    delayed reconstruction, 371
    fibrosis, 372
    irradiated/non-irradiated breast
        reconstruction, 371
    local and distant flaps, 372
    nipple-sparing mastectomy, 373, *373*
    prevention, 371
    stair-step approach, 372, *372*
partial mastectomy defects
    concentric mastopexy technique to, *110*
    dermoglandular pedicle designs to,
        113, *114*
    repair techniques, 153
pathological intraoperative assessment, 83–84
pathological margins, 154–156
pathologic complete response (pCR), 48
patient choice, 61–62
patient-reported outcomes, 61, 68
patient satisfaction
    BreastQ using, **154**, 281
    breast revision, 379
    oncoplastic repair, 91–92, 94, 158
    USA, breast reconstruction, 4
patients' expectations, 64
    accomplishing, 64–65
    cosmetic results, 64
    reasons for choosing breast
        reconstruction, 64
patients selection
    ADMs with implants, 262
    ALD flap, 313
    BCS, 34
    DTI, 251
    intrinsic breast flap oncoplastic
        reconstruction, 124
    oncoplastic surgery, 10–11
    PBRT, 396
PBI, *see* partial breast irradiation
PBRT, *see* partial breast radiotherapy
pectoralis muscle, 379, 381
pedicled perforator flaps, 131
    advantage and disadvantage, 143
    anatomy, 131–133
    complications, 144
    on defect location, *134*
    history, 133
    imaging, 133

outcomes, 143
    patient history and physical findings, 133
    postoperative care, 143
    surgical management approach, 133–135
    surgical technique, 135–143
pedicled TRAM flap, 320
    anatomy, 320, *322*
    complications, 324
    donor site repair and abdominal closure,
        322–323
    flap remodeling, 323–324
    free TRAM, DIEP flaps *versus*, **331**
    patient evaluation, 324–325
    surgical technique, 320–322, *322*
    thoracic defects for, *320*
Peer, L., 23
percutaneous needle scar release, *167*,
    167–168, *168*
perforator flaps, 179, 345–346
pertuzumab, 48, 193
PET, *see* positron emission tomography
PET-CT, 74, 96
photographic documentation, 448
photons, *402*, *403*
pigments, nipple-areola tattooing, 448, *449*
plasma imbibition, 23
pleomorphic lobular carcinoma in situ
    (PLCIS), 38–39, *39*
pluripotent stem cells, 22
PMRT, *see* postmastectomy radiotherapy
Poland's syndrome, *267*
poor ADM integration, 15–16, *16*, 30
portable radiography systems, 87
positron emission tomography (PET), 35, 66
postmastectomy irradiation
    delayed-immediate reconstruction,
        217–218
    immediate reconstruction, 213–217
postmastectomy radiotherapy (PMRT), 54,
    56, 66–67, 210, *215*, 221, 279, *283*, 284,
    284, 297, 399–400, 428
    Breast Cancer Atlas, 400
    chemotherapy, 401
    chest wall and IMN regions, 400
    delayed-delayed reconstruction, 221–223
    electron options, 403, *403*
    intensity-modulated radiation therapy,
        403
    necrosis, *214*
    photon trade-offs, *402*, 402–403
    planning techniques, 400
    standard delayed reconstruction,
        223–224
    survival benefit, 402
    tissue equivalent material, 400
    to TRAM flap, *216*
postmastectomy reconstruction, 133
postoperative margin assessment
    intraoperative assessment, 148–150
    negative margin, 147–148, *148*, **148**
    oncoplastic surgery, 150
    overview, 147

postoperative radiotherapy, 50–51
preadipocyte, 22
preoperative chemotherapy, 48
preoperative MRI, 34, 66, 73
preoperative radiological assessment, 69–74
primary anti-HER2 therapy, 193
PRIME II trial, 406
PROFILE registry, 20
profunda artery perforator (PAP) flap,
    349–350
progesterone receptor (PR), 40, *41*
proliferation, 23
prone decubitus, 363–364
prophylactic antibiotics, 250
prophylactic mastectomy, 7
ptosis, 206

quilting suture technique, 310

radiated mastectomy, *266*
radiation toxicity, 50, 66
radical mastectomy, 10
radiography systems, 87
radiological assessment, 69
radiological intraoperative assessment, 86–87
radiotherapy, 50, 53, 66, 89, 287, 381, 384
    adjuvant, 175, 391
    ALD flap, 318
    BCS after, 391
    breast-conserving therapy and, 405–409
    conformal, 395
    contralateral breast reduction, 165, *166*
    external beam, 165
    hypofractionated, 419
    IMRT, 395, 403, 414, 421
    increasing breast size, 165, *166*
    internal breast, 165
    intraoperative, *see* intraoperative
        radiotherapy
    IOERT, 425
    oedema and hyperpigmentation, 165, *166*
    omitting, 406, **406**
    PBRT, *see* partial breast radiotherapy
    PMRT, *see* postmastectomy radiotherapy
    postoperative, 50–51
    reconstructed breast after, 51
    TE *versus* permanent implant, 287
    timing and breast reconstruction, 50
    wide excision mammoplasty and, *123*
RAPID trial, **393**, 395
reduction mammoplasty
    delayed-immediate, 156–157
    dermoglandular, 109–123
    oncoplastic, 109
    therapeutic, 107–108
re-excision, *see* postoperative margin
    assessment
regional nodal staging, 72–73
RESTORE-2 trial, 167
revascularization, 23, 27
reverse lymphatic mapping techniques, 437
revision surgery, *see* breast revision

risk-reducing mastectomy, 7
robotic LD muscle harvest, 342–344
rotated inset, double-DIEP flap, 230
round needles, 449
routine cavity shave margins, 149
RTOG Cooperative Group, 400
rule out BI-ALCL, 19

SAAP, *see* serratus anterior perforator flap
safety
    of breast reconstruction, 456
    of oncoplastic breast conservation,
        455–456
salvage surgery, *see* breast revision
SEAP, *see* superior epigastric artery
    perforator flap
sentinel lymph node biopsy (SLNB), 38, 54,
    72, 77–78
serratus anterior perforator (SAAP) flap,
    131–132, 135, 140–142
SGAP, *see* superior gluteal artery perforator
    flap
SHARE trial, **394**
sharp-tip cannula, 26
Siamese type flaps, 345, 347
SIEA, *see* superficial inferior epigastric artery
    flap
silicone implant, *20, 380*
simple local reshaping procedures, 176, *177*
single entry intracavitary, 411
skate flap, 444, *444*
skin adipose-lymph node flap, 437
skin grafting, areola, 443
skin-reducing mastectomy, 200, *201*
skin sensation, 65
skin-sparing mastectomy (SSM), 33, 55, 67,
    193–194, 203, *228*, 310, *311*, 417
    evolution, 198
    nipple-areola complex, 199, *200*
    in non-ptotic breast, *316*
    skin flap, 199
    specimen, *36*
    surgical planning, 199, **199**
Society of Surgical Oncology (SSO) website,
    459–460
sonography, 71
    malignant foci assessment using, 72
    regional nodal staging with, 72–73
South America
    two-stage implant reconstruction in,
        255–256
    whole breast reconstruction, 234–236
specimen radiography, 86, *86, 87*
specimen radiology, 97
SSM, *see* skin-sparing mastectomy
stair-step approach, 372, *372*
standard delayed reconstruction, 223–224
standard *versus* digital mammograms,
    255, *255*
star flap, 444, *444*
stem cell expansion, 303
stromal vascular fraction, 23, 26, 303

subcutaneous tissue expander, *223*
superficial epigastric artery perforator
    flap, 179
superficial inferior epigastric artery (SIEA)
    flap, 236, 335, *437*, 437–438
superior epigastric artery perforator (SEAP)
    flap, 131–132, *132*, 134–135, 143
superior gluteal artery perforator (SGAP)
    flap, 351; *see also* boomerang GAP flap
superior partial defects, 179, *184*
superolateral defects, 172
surgical margin, 92; *see also* margin
systemic ALCL, 19–20

Taiwan, lymph node tissue transfer, 433–435
TAP, *see* thoracodorsal artery perforator flap
targeted radiotherapy
    GEC-ESTRO trial, 407, *408*
    IMPORT-LOW trial, 407
    increasing radiation, 405–406
    IORT using NOVAC-7, 406–407
    omitting radiation, 406, **406**
    survival benefit, 407–408, *409*
    TARGIT-IORT trial, 406, *407*
TARGIT-A trial, **393**, 395, 406–407, *408*
TARGIT-B trial, 405
TARGIT-IORT trial, 405–406, *407*
TARGIT trial, 165, 427
tattooing, 444; *see also* three-dimensional
    tattooing
TDAP, *see* thoracodorsal artery perforator
    flap
TE, *see* tissue expander
telangiectasia, 418
textured silicone implant, *20*
therapeutic mammoplasty, 96, 116, *123*,
    176, 180
therapeutic mastopexy, 108
therapeutic reduction mammaplasty,
    107–108
thick-walled liponecrotic cyst, 28
thin-walled liponecrotic cyst, 28
thoracodorsal artery perforator (TAP/
    TDAP) flap, 131, *131*, *132*, 229, 236,
    339–341, *340*
    indications, 339
    muscle-only, 230
    surgical management approach, 135
    surgical technique, 135–139, *136–139*,
        340–341
three-dimensional conformal radiotherapy
    (3-D CRT), 395, 411
three-dimensional (3-D) tattooing, 448–450
TiLOOP Bra, 260, 297
tissue
    assessment, *150*
    equivalent material, 400
    rearrangement, local, 101–105
    response continuum, 14
tissue expander (TE), 227, 234, 280
    versus permanent implant, 287
tomosynthesis, digital breast, 69–70

total breast anatomy restoration, 439, *439*
touch imprint cytology (TIC), 83–84
transverse rectus abdominis myocutaneous (TRAM) flap, 215, *215*, 223, 236, 322, 399, 401
  breast reconstruction and, *216*
  DIEP flap *versus*, **331**, *336*
  free, *see* free TRAM flap
  pedicled, *see* pedicled TRAM flap
  PMRT, *216*
transverse upper gracilis (TUG) flap, 179, 338–339, 349, 356, *359*, *360*
  advantages, 356
  anatomy, 356
  complications and donor site morbidity, 358
  design and dissection, 356–357
  indications for, 356
  PAP flap advantages over, 349
  shaping and inset, 357–358, *358*
trastuzumab, 48, 193
triple-negative breast cancers, 41–42
TUG, *see* transverse upper gracilis flap
tumor bed, 391
tumor-bed boost
  brachytherapy, 418
  en-face electrons, 421
  identification, 418
  intraoperative brachytherapy, 423
  IORT, 418
  irradiation dose, 419
  plastic surgery techniques, 418
  randomized trials, 417–418
  risk of local recurrence, 418–419
  surgical incisions, 418
tumor bed identification, APBI technique, 411, *412*
tumor excision, 405, 417

two-stage breast-conserving surgery procedure, 11
two-stage implant reconstruction, 227–229, 252–256

ultrasound, 33; *see also* sonography
unifocal breast cancer, 72
unilateral breast cancer, 62
United Kingdom (UK)
  breast reconstructive decisions in, 6
  immediate breast reconstruction in, 30
USA
  ADM, 257–258, 293–296
  breast reconstruction in, 3–5
  delayed oncoplastic repair, after radiotherapy, 171–173
  dermoglandular reduction mammoplasty in, 109–115
  fat grafting, 293–296
  flap repair before radiotherapy, 124–130
  implant-based whole breast reconstruction, with irradiation, 279–281, 287–288
  one-stage implant reconstruction, 241–244
  tissue rearrangement in, 101–105
  two-stage implant reconstruction, 252–254
  whole breast reconstruction, optimal method, 227–233

vacuum-assisted closure device, 385
Van Nuys Prognostic Index, 36, 78
vascularized lymph node flap
  duplex ultrasonography, 433
  facial artery, *434*
  ICG-lymphangiography, 437
  mechanism and placement, 433, *434*

  principle of, 433
  results, *434*, 435
vascularized matrix principle, 345–346
vertical folded inset, double-DIEP flap, 230
vertical mastopexy technique, 208
vertical oncoplasty, 109, *111*, 374, *374*, *375*
volume displacement technique, 11, 150
volume rearrangement technique, 171, 179
volume replacement technique, 11, 108, 150, 171–172, 179

white fat, 22
whole breast irradiation (WBI), 165–166, 189, 405, 425
whole breast radiotherapy (WBRT)
  boosting, tumor bed, *see* tumor-bed boost
  intraoperative brachytherapy, 423
  intraoperative/postoperative linear accelerator, 425–426
  versus PBRT, 392–395
  side effects, 391–392
whole breast reconstruction
  autologous tissue flaps for, *see* autologous tissue flaps
  breast revision, 379–380
  fat grafting for, 301–307
  optimal method, 227–236
  PMRT, 399–403
whole breast ultrasound, *see* sonography
wide local excision (WLE), 83–84, 107
Wise pattern mastectomy, *317*
Wise pattern oncoplasty, 109–110, 112, 374, *374*, *375*, *376*, *377*
Wise pattern skin-reducing mastectomy, 200, *201*
Wright Giemsa stain, *20*

z-plasty technique, 128